The **Rough Guide** to

D0187450

San Francisco
& the Bay Area

written and researched by
Nick Edwards and Mark Ellwood

with additional contributions by
Lisa Hix and Charles Hodgkins

ROUGH GUIDES

NEW YORK • LONDON • DELHI
www.roughguides.com

Contents

The hills of San Francisco color section following p.112

Bay Area music color section following p.336

SAN FRANCISCO **Color maps** following p.440

◄◄ Dolores Park ◄ The path down to Fort Funston

San Francisco
& the Bay Area

One of America's most beautiful cities (and one whose locals are not afraid to harp on the claim), San Francisco sits poised on the 47-square-mile fingertip of a peninsula at the western edge of America. Indeed, the city has much to gloat about, not least the breathtaking natural beauty that surrounds it – from rugged coastline and tranquil Bay waters to rambling, fog-capped hills and dense, unspoiled woods. Along the steep streets of the city itself rest a cluster of distinct neighborhoods – by turn quaint or hip, lined by rows of preserved Victorian houses or dotted with chic clubs in converted warehouses. Residents like to think of their home as the cultured Northern counterpart to sunny Los Angeles, mass entertainment capital of Southern California, and to an extent they're right – this was the place that gave birth to the United Nations and is forever associated in the public consciousness with the Beat literary and gay rights movements. Still, San Francisco is undeniably Californian; after all, this is also the city where blue jeans, mountain biking, and topless waitressing first took off.

From its earliest days as a stop on the Spanish chain of missions, through its explosive expansion during the Gold Rush and right up into the Internet boom of the 1990s and less certain first decade of the new millennium, San Francisco's turbulent history is relatively short. Named for St Francis of Assisi, the kindly monk who harbored society's outcasts,

▲ Nightlife in San Francisco

the city sprang up almost overnight in the late 1840s from a sleepy fishing village named **Yerba Buena**. The hilly terrain did not daunt the rough-and-ready prospectors who built on it according to a grid pattern that ignored even the steepest inclines; with its whimsical architecture, its vast irrigated park on the site of a former sand dune, and its cliff-hugging resort buildings, the late nineteenth-century city defied the elements and served as much as a playground as an economic center, luring writers, architects, immigrants, and thousands of transient sailors eager to "make it" in the newest, westernmost metropolis. Though earthquakes, fires, droughts, landslides, and other natural disasters have put the city's very existence to the test, residents have never taken long to rebuild and re-settle, refusing to give in to nature's tantrums. Politically, San Franciscans are known for the same unbreakable character, infusing their city with an activist spirit most evident in the high visibility of once-disenfranchised groups, especially Asian-Americans, gays, and people with AIDS.

Many visitors are drawn as much by the city's nonconformist spirit as its sights – for some, it's a veritable pilgrimage site. But the most common lure of San Francisco is its easy charm – with inescapably quaint pastel street scenes and blossoming parks offset by a sophisticated selection of international cuisine and world-class clubs, making it the ideal American city in which to linger without a serious agenda. Indeed, despite all its activity, San Francisco remains a small town, where having a car is a liability, owing to traffic-jammed streets and a dearth of parking spaces. Provided you don't mind hills, every major sight in town is a short walk, bike, or bus ride away.

Back near Downtown and west of Union Square, the gritty **Tenderloin**, a rundown section of cheap hotels and sleazy porn shops, will snap you back to reality. It rests uneasily next to the **Civic Center**, where the painstakingly restored City Hall is the imposing focus of a concentrated few blocks of public buildings and cultural venues. Cross Market Street and you'll hit SoMa **(South of Market)**, once the city's major industrial enclave and, in the Nineties, home to the offices of a myriad since-defunct Internet start-ups. It has retained

> **The city's hills serve as handy markers between its shifting moods and characters.**

its cultural cachet, too, with the development of the Yerba Buena Gardens and the San Francisco Museum of Modern Art. SoMa's waterfront, long-neglected South Beach, has been rezoned for housing and businesses, anchored by the Giants' baseball stadium.

Inland, the **Mission District** was built around Mission Dolores, the oldest building in San Francisco. The neighborhood's diverse population, which includes a large Hispanic community, is privy to a dense concentration of cafés, restaurants, and entertainment that runs along Valencia Street. Just west is an equally energetic quarter, the **Castro**, the nominal center for San Francisco's gay population and home to most of the best gay bars and clubs. North of the Castro, **Haight-Ashbury** was once San Francisco's Victorian resort quarter before hippies and flower children took over. Today it's a rag-tag collection of used-clothing stores and laid-back cafés, though prices here have kept pace with more chic parts of town. Nearby are a few areas of only marginal interest to visitors: tiny **Japantown**, the slightly tatty **Western Addition**, and the **Lower Haight**, best known for its decent nightlife. Surrounding the central parts of the city, the western and southern sides of San Francisco are where many of the city's locals actually live, in neighborhoods like the **Richmond**, whose two main drags, Clement and

▶ Children enjoying San Francisco's outdoors

Geary streets, are liberally sprinkled with a number of the city's best ethnic restaurants. The Richmond is hugged by the Golden Gate National Recreation Area to the north, along the coast of which you can pick up the four-mile Pacific Coast Trail. Meanwhile, the expansive **Golden Gate Park** borders the south of the district and holds a number of fine museums and gardens in its confines. South of the park, the **Sunset**'s homogenous single-story townhomes stretch on relentlessly;

Liberal San Francisco

From the multiple piercings on view in Haight-Ashbury and openly gay atmosphere of the Castro, to the decidedly leftist politics of City Hall, San Francisco exudes an air of liberalism that leads most middle-American conservatives to view the place as somewhat akin to the fiery pit. If you extend the compass of the city across the Bay to include blue-collar Oakland and intellectual Berkeley, then you have the strongest bastion of progressive thinking and behavior in the country by far.

On a strictly political level, the Bay Area has thrown up some of America's principal activist groups such as Mario Savio's student protesters in Berkeley and the world-renowned Black Panther movement in Oakland, through the resurgent peace movement of recent years. There is also a long list of people who have championed the causes of gay, civil or workers' rights or attempted to stem the prevailing tide of conservatism that has dominated recent decades through elected office, from 1970s gay city supervisor Harvey Milk to current speaker of the House of Representatives, Nancy Pelosi.

Naturally, cultural liberalism has gone hand-in-hand with liberal politics, and not only did San Francisco spawn the Beat Generation and the hippies, but it has remained near the forefront of cutting-edge movements through the punks and beyond.

relief can be found throughout on the western coast, home to the city's best **beaches**. Though San Francisco is undoubtedly the focus of the Bay Area, there's much in the surrounding parts to take in, too. The **East Bay** is centered around the gritty, up-and-coming port city of **Oakland** and the University of California's flagship campus in hipster **Berkeley**, home to the Gourmet Ghetto. To the south, the **Peninsula** contains fast-growing Silicon Valley, with **San Jose** as its hub, still home to many of the computer giants despite the dot-com bust. There are also some surprisingly unspoilt beaches. North of San Francisco, across the Golden Gate Bridge, **Marin County** boasts enormous wealth in spots like the postcard-perfect towns of **Sausalito** and **Tiburon**, plus prime biking and hiking trails in the **Marin Headlands**. Further north, the lush beauty continues in California's famed **Wine Country**, whose principal valleys, **Napa** and **Sonoma**, trace gentle crescents through the myriad vineyards.

9

When to go

San Francisco emphatically does not belong to the California of monotonous blue skies and slothful warmth. Flanked on three sides by water, it is regularly invigorated by the fresh winds that sweep across the Peninsula. The climate is among the most stable in the world, with a daytime temperature that rarely ventures more than 5°F either side of a median 60°F but can drop much lower at night. Summer does offer some sunny days, of course, but it also sees heavy fog roll in through the Golden Gate. This thick mist does much to add romance to the city but it can also dash hopes of tanning at the beach. The western half of the city sees the worst of the fog on summer mornings; later in the year, cooler inland temperatures prevent the fog from taking root. Winters bring most of the city's rainfall, sometimes in torrential storms. Almost everywhere else in the Bay Area is warmer than San Francisco, especially in the summer when the East Bay basks in sunshine and the Wine Country and other inland valleys are baking hot.

If you wish to avoid the crowds, do not come in the summer, although even then most of the tourist congestion is confined to a few of the most popular parts of the city and is rarely too off-putting. The nicest times to visit are late May and June, when the hills are greenest and covered with wildflowers, or in October and November, when you can be fairly sure of good weather and reduced crowds at tourist attractions.

◀ Golden Gate Bridge

San Francisco climate

	Jan	Feb	Mar	Apr	May	Jun	Jul	Aug	Sep	Oct	Nov	Dec
Average temperature												
max (°F)	55	59	61	62	63	66	65	65	69	68	63	57
min (°F)	45	47	48	49	51	52	53	53	55	54	51	47
Average monthly rainfall												
inches	4.7	3.8	3.1	1.5	0.7	0.1	0	0	0.3	1.0	2.5	4.4

17

things not to miss

It's not possible to see everything in and around San Francisco in one trip – and we don't suggest you try. What follows is a selective taste of the city's highlights, in no particular order, which includes everything from major museums to vibrant festivals, arranged in five color-coded categories. All highlights have page references to take you further into the Guide, where you can find out more.

01 Wine Country Page **365** • California's answer to the French countryside, Napa and Sonoma valleys are filled with superlative vineyards and stunning landscapes.

02 **Gay Pride** Page **280** • If you're here in late June, be sure to check out the exuberant Gay Pride parade, which takes over the Castro district.

04 **Musée Méchanique** Page **84** • Relive your misspent youth with this bizarre but entertaining collection of classic arcade games and amusement park slot machines.

03 **Cable cars** Page **55** • Famous for good reason, these glorious old trams furnish irresistible photo opportunities as well as a leisurely way of climbing Downtown's steepest hills.

06 **Taquerias** Page **196** • Nowhere is San Francisco's Mexican heritage more evident than in the taquerias of the Mission District, where you can enjoy tacos, burritos, and enchilladas, among other delights.

05 **Año Nuevo State Reserve** Page **345** • No matter what time of year, you'll see clusters of elephant seals lounging on the beach, but to see hundreds of them at once stop by during December's mating season.

07 **Chinatown** Pages **63** & **168** • Chinatown bustles with sumptuous dim-sum restaurants, traditional herbal stores, and steamy teahouses. Head to local legend the House of Nanking, on the eastern edge of Chinatown, for a superb meal at a bargain price.

08 **Baseball** Pages **107** & **273** • From the upper seats at AT&T Park you can enjoy a fine view of the Bay in between innings when the Giants have a home game. With fun, fact-filled tours of the ground available and even a play area for children, there's something here for everyone.

09 **Painted Ladies** Page **134** • Sooner or later, all visitors to San Francisco come to Alamo Square to view the six colorful Victorians known as the "Painted Ladies."

10 **The San Francisco Museum of Modern Art** Page **106** • The dazzling modern exterior of SFMOMA is as much of a draw as its renowned collection of abstract Expressionist and California School art.

11 The Ferry Building
Page **61** • This newly renovated foodie paradise sells gourmet produce and offers superb views out over the Bay.

12 Legion of Honor Page **139**
• This celebrated museum in Lincoln Park holds an impressive collection, notable for its Rodin sculptures.

13 Coit Tower Page **74** • One of the best views of San Francisco and the Bay can be had from the top of this tower perched on Telegraph Hill.

14 **Nightlife**
Pages **209**
& **241** • Head to
the neighborhoods
for a drink and a
dance. Wild Side
West, a primarily
lesbian version of
an old-style saloon,
is one of the liveliest
nightspots in Bernal
Heights.

16 **Golden Gate Park** Page
142 • It's easy to spend hours
unwinding in the green expanses of Golden
Gate Park, whose Japanese Tea Garden is one
of its main attractions and refreshment stops.

15 **Paramount Theatre** Page
292 • Even if you don't attend a film or
show at the Paramount, it merits a brief visit
just for its eclectic decoration, employing
stained glass, mosaic, and sculpture.

17 **Alcatraz**
Page **85** •
Take a boat ride out
to "The Rock" and
tour the famous
maximum-security
prison, where
Al Capone and
Machine Gun Kelly
did their time.

Basics

Basics

Getting there

Unless you're coming from nearby on the West Coast, the quickest way to San Francisco is via one of its two major airports, San Francisco International Airport or Oakland International Airport (see p.24 for specific details of each). Taking a train comes a slow second, while traveling by bus is the least expensive method, but also the slowest and least comfortable.

Airfares always depend on the **season**, with the highest average prices charged June–August – ironically, when San Francisco's weather is often at its most unpredictable. Fares drop during the "shoulder" seasons – March–May, September–October – conveniently, just as the weather becomes more dependable. You'll get the best prices during the low season, November–February (excluding Christmas and New Year when prices are hiked up and seats are at a premium).

Flights from the US and Canada

Many **domestic flights** into and out of the Bay Area use San Francisco International Airport (SFO); carriers offering the most frequent services here include United (with its West Coast hub at SFO), American, and Delta Airlines. Smaller, more navigable Oakland International Airport (OAK) across the Bay is often a better bet for snagging a bargain fare on airlines such as JetBlue, Southwest, and America West (this last now merged with US Airways). There's also a regular shuttle service from Los Angeles: American, United, and Alaska airlines operate the most frequent services.

The usual price range for nonstop round-trip flights from the Northeast and Mid-Atlantic **New York**, **Boston**, **Washington DC**) to the Bay Area is $350–400, although with a little luck and flexibility, you might be able to find something closer to $300. From south-eastern cities like **Miami** and **Atlanta**, expect fares to hover between $350–500. Round-trip fares from **Chicago** range around $330–450, while shuttle fares from **Los Angeles** run between $150–170.

If traveling from Canada, Air Canada has direct flights to San Francisco from **Vancouver** (around CAN$330 round trip) and **Toronto** (CAN$550).

Flights from the UK and Ireland

There are daily nonstop flights to San Francisco from **London Heathrow** with British Airways and Virgin Atlantic, and regular services by United, Continental, and American Airlines. These flights take about eleven hours, though following winds ensure return flights are always an hour or so shorter. Flights out usually leave Britain mid-morning, while flights back from the US tend to arrive in Britain early in the morning. Most other airlines serving San Francisco, like Air France and KLM, fly from London via their respective European or American hubs. These flights take an extra two to five hours each way, depending on connection times.

Return fares to San Francisco can cost more than £700 between June and August and at Christmas, though £500 is the average range. Prices in winter often fall to under £300. More flexible tickets to San Francisco, requiring less advance booking time or allowing changes or refunds, cost from £125 more whenever and from whomever you buy.

Aer Lingus offers a direct service from **Dublin** to Los Angeles (anywhere from €550–1000, depending on your proposed itinerary), with connecting services to the Bay Area.

From Australia, New Zealand, and South Africa

From **Australia** and **New Zealand**, Los Angeles and San Francisco are the main

Fly less – stay longer! Travel and Climate Change

Climate change is perhaps the single biggest issue facing our planet. It is caused by a build-up in the atmosphere of carbon dioxide and other greenhouse gases, which are emitted by many sources – including planes. Already, **flights** account for three to four percent of human-induced global warming: that figure may sound small, but it is rising year on year and threatens to counteract the progress made by reducing greenhouse emissions in other areas.

Rough Guides regard travel as a **global benefit**, and feel strongly that the advantages to developing economies are important, as are the opportunities for greater contact and awareness among peoples. But we also believe in traveling responsibly, which includes giving thought to how often we fly and what we can do to redress any harm that our trips may create.

We can travel less or simply reduce the amount we travel by air (taking fewer trips and staying longer, or taking the train if there is one); we can avoid night flights (which are more damaging); and we can make the trips we do take "climate neutral" via a carbon offset scheme. **Offset schemes** run by climatecare.org, carbonneutral .com and others allow you to "neutralize" the greenhouse gases that you are responsible for releasing. Their websites have simple calculators that let you work out the impact of any flight – as does our own. Once that's done, you can pay to fund projects that will reduce future emissions by an equivalent amount. Please take the time to visit our website and make your trip climate neutral, or get a copy of the *Rough Guide to Climate Change* for more detail on the subject.

www.roughguides.com/climatechange

points of entry to the US, with Los Angeles better served. Seat availability on these international flights is limited, so it's best to book at least several weeks ahead.

There are daily direct flights to San Francisco with United Airlines from Sydney, and on Air New Zealand from Sydney and Melbourne. Qantas, Japan Airlines, and Korean Air typically fly out of several major Australian cities, with the latter two making en-route stops in Asia. Expect flights to start around A$1500 in low season, adding as much as A$400 if originating from Perth. Tack on an additional A$450–650 at peak times.

Starting from Auckland or Christchurch, Air New Zealand flies via Sydney, Los Angeles, or Honolulu. Off-season fares hover around NZ$2200 – add NZ$300 or so for Wellington.

Travel to San Francisco is not particularly cheap from **South Africa**; prices are about the same out of Cape Town or Johannesburg, but several hundred rand more from Durban and other smaller cities. Fares start at around R10,000 (including all taxes) and rise as high as R14,000 at peak times, which are roughly the same as those from Australia.

Direct flights with US or South African carriers invariably involve a refueling stop (often in Cape Verde), though a more roundabout route on one of the national airlines from further north in Africa can be a less pricey option.

Ticketing alternatives

If San Francisco is only one stop on your longer journey, consider buying a **Round-the-World (RTW) ticket**. Some travel agents can sell you an "off-the-shelf" RTW ticket that will have you touching down in about a half-dozen cities; others will have to assemble one for you, which can be tailored to your needs (but is apt to be more expensive). In recent years, many of the major international airlines have allied themselves with one of two globe-spanning networks: the "Star Alliance" includes Air New Zealand, United, Lufthansa, Thai, SAS, Varig, and Air Canada, while "One World" combines British Airways, Qantas, American Airlines, Aer Lingus, Cathay Pacific, Iberia, and LANChile. Both networks offer RTW deals with three stopovers in each continental sector you visit, with the option of adding additional sectors relatively cheaply.

One-way tickets

A word of warning: it's not a good idea to buy a one-way ticket to the US. Not only are they rarely good value compared to a round-trip ticket, but US immigration officials usually take them as a sign that you aren't planning to return home; as such, they'll probably refuse you entry. And with increased airport security checks, it's unlikely you'll be allowed to board your flight to begin with.

Package deals – such as fly-drive, flight-accommodation, and guided tours – can work out cheaper than arranging the same trip yourself, especially for a short-term stay. The obvious drawbacks are the loss of flexibility and the fact that most schemes use hotels in the midrange bracket, but there are a wide variety of options available.

"Open jaw" tickets can also be a good idea, allowing you to fly into San Francisco and depart from another city for little or no extra charge; fares are calculated by halving the return fares to each destination and adding the two figures together. This makes a convenient option for those who want a fly-drive deal, which gives cut-rate (and sometimes free) car rental when you buy an air ticket. Many airlines also offer **air passes**, which allow foreign travelers to fly between a given number of US cities for one discounted price.

Trains

Amtrak (℡1-800/USA-RAIL, ⓦwww.amtrak .com) services into San Francisco are more picturesque than punctual, best for those looking for a leisurely alternative to flying. There's only one long-distance train per day from the north or east, and only a couple more from the south; all three routes are among the most scenic on the entire Amtrak system.

The most spectacular is the **California Zephyr**, which runs all the way from Chicago via the Rockies, Salt Lake City, and Reno over 4–5 days. There's also the **Coast Starlight**, where San Francisco is the midpoint on a breathtaking, mostly coastal

route between Seattle and Los Angeles. Note that the other LA–SF Amtrak route heads inland by bus to Bakersfield, then by rail north through the comparatively dull San Joaquin Valley.

One-way cross-country coach fares are around $400, though seasonal special offers (for two or more people traveling together, for example) turn up quite often; seniors and students enjoy a fifteen-percent discount on most rail journeys. Check for such offers on the Amtrak website or by phone. If San Francisco is part of a longer journey, Amtrak and VIA (Canada's national rail company) offer a **North America Rail Pass**. It allows thirty days' unlimited travel for $999 or CAN$999 high season (late May to mid-Oct) and $709/CAN$709 low season (rest of year); there's a ten-percent discount for seniors, children, and students.

Note that Amtrak trains don't stop in San Francisco proper, but rather across the Bay in Emeryville – there's a free shuttle bus that runs over the Bay Bridge and drops passengers at San Francisco's Ferry Building.

Buses

Taking a bus is usually the cheapest option for getting into San Francisco, but trips can take seemingly forever. **Greyhound** (℡1-800/231-2222, ⓦwww.greyhound.com) is the sole long-distance operator servicing San Francisco; seven-day advance purchase prices for round-trip tickets should cost around $220 from New York or Boston (3 days), $180 from Chicago (2 days), or $65 from Los Angeles (8–11hr). **Greyhound Discover Passes** buy unlimited travel on the entire Greyhound network, but are only really worthwhile for travelers including San Francisco as part of a longer itinerary, or for those coming from the East Coast. Check Greyhound's website for details.

The other option is to catch one of **Green Tortoise**'s funky buses (℡415/956-7500 or 1-800/867-8647, ⓦwww.greentortoise.com) – they all arrive at the Transbay Terminal in SoMa. These buses come complete with bunks, foam cushions, coolers, and sound systems, and offer a handful of routes to get you to the Bay Area. The company's "Hostel Hopper" links San Francisco with Los Angeles, Las Vegas, and/or selected national parks on one- or two-day adventure trips ($130–350). If you just want to get to San Francisco quickly, overnight express rates are $39 from Los Angeles, $59 from Las Vegas. Additionally, the seven-day "Western Trail" outing ($435) orients you with the California coastline, looping from San Francisco through the Sierra Nevada mountains, Yosemite National Park, and back to San Francisco.

Cars

Driving your own car gives the greatest freedom and flexibility, but if you don't have one (or don't trust the one you do have), one option worth considering is a **driveaway**. Companies operate in most major cities and are paid to find drivers to take a customer's car from one place to another, most commonly between New York and California. The company will normally pay for your insurance and your first tank of fuel – after that, you'll be expected to travel the most direct route and average 400 miles a day. Many driveaway companies aren't keen to use foreign travelers, but if you can convince them you're a safe bet, they'll take something like a $250 deposit, which you'll get back after delivering the car in good condition. It makes obvious sense to get in touch in advance, to spare yourself a week's wait for a car to turn up. Search online by "Automobile transporters and driveaway companies," phone around for the latest offers, or simply try one of the ninety branches of Auto Driveaway, based in Chicago (℡312/341-1900, ⊛www.autodriveaway.com).

If you're looking to **rent a car** to drive to the Bay Area, be sure when booking to get free

unlimited mileage, and be aware that rates can skyrocket if you want to pick up the car in one location and leave it at another. See p.30 for contact details on nationwide rental firms.

Airlines, agents, and operators

Online booking

⊛www.expedia.co.uk (in UK), ⊛www.expedia.com (in US), ⊛www.expedia.ca (in Canada)
⊛www.lastminute.com (in UK)
⊛www.opodo.co.uk (in UK)
⊛www.orbitz.com (in US)
⊛www.travelocity.co.uk (in UK), ⊛www.travelocity.com (in US), ⊛www.travelocity.ca (in Canada)
⊛www.travelonline.co.za (in South Africa)
⊛www.zuji.com.au (in Australia) ⊛www.zuji.co.nz (in New Zealand)

Airlines

Aer Lingus US & Canada ℡1-800/IRISH-AIR, UK ℡0870/876 5000, Republic of Ireland ℡0818/365 000, NZ ℡1649/3083355, SA ℡1-272/2168-32838; ⊛www.aerlingus.com.
Air Canada US & Canada ℡1-888/247-2262, UK ℡0871/220 1111, Republic of Ireland ℡01/679 3958, Australia ℡1300/655 767, NZ ℡0508/747 767; ⊛www.aircanada.com.
Air France US ℡1-800/237-2747, Canada ℡1-800/667-2747, UK ℡0870/142 4343, Australia ℡1300/390 190, SA ℡0861/340 340; ⊛www.airfrance.com.
Air New Zealand NZ ℡0800/737 000, Australia ℡0800/132 476, UK ℡0800/028 4149, US ℡1-800-262/1234, Canada ℡1-800-663/5494; ⊛www.airnz.co.nz, ⊛www.airnz.com.au.
Alaska Airlines US ℡1-800/252-7522, ⊛www.alaska-air.com.
American Airlines US & Canada ℡1-800/433-7300, UK ℡0845/778 9789, Republic of Ireland ℡01/602 0550, Australia ℡1800/673 486, NZ ℡0800/445 442; ⊛www.aa.com.
America West See US Air.
British Airways US & Canada ℡1-800/AIRWAYS, UK ℡0870/850 9850, Republic of Ireland ℡1890/626 747, Australia ℡1300/767 177, NZ ℡09/966 9777, SA ℡114/418 600; ⊛www.ba.com.
Cathay Pacific US ℡1-800/233-2742, Canada ℡1-800/268-6868, UK ℡020/8834 8888, Australia ℡13 17 47, NZ ℡09/379 0861, SA ℡11/700 8900; ⊛www.cathaypacific.com.

Driving miles to San Francisco

Los Angeles 390 miles
Seattle 810 miles
Chicago 2170 miles
Atlanta 2480 miles
Washington DC 2840 miles
New York 2930 miles
Miami 3090 miles
Boston 3130 miles

Continental Airlines US & Canada
☎1-800/523-3273, UK ☎0845/607 6760,
Republic of Ireland ☎1890/925 252, Australia
☎02/9244 2242, NZ ☎09/308 3350, International
☎1-800/231-0856; ⓦwww.continental.com.
Delta Airlines US & Canada ☎1-800/221-1212,
UK ☎0845/600 0950, Republic of Ireland
☎1850/882 031 or 01/407 3165, Australia
☎1300/302 849, NZ ☎09/977 2232; ⓦwww
.delta.com.
Frontier Airlines US ☎1-800/432-1359,
ⓦwww.flyfrontier.com.
Hawaiian Airlines US ☎1-800/367-5320,
ⓦwww.hawaiianair.com.
Iberia US ☎1-800/772-4642, UK ☎0870/609
0500, Republic of Ireland ☎0818/462 000, SA
☎011/884 5909; ⓦwww.iberia.com.
JAL (Japan Airlines) US & Canada ☎1-800/525-
3663, UK ☎0845/774 7700, Republic of Ireland
☎01/408 3757, Australia ☎02/9272 1111, NZ
☎09/379 9906, SA ☎11/214 2560; ⓦwww.jal
.com or ⓦwww.japanair.com.
JetBlue US & Canada ☎1-800/538-2583,
ⓦwww.jetblue.com.
KLM (Royal Dutch Airlines) See Northwest/KLM.
Korean Air US & Canada ☎1-800/438-5000, UK
☎0800/413 000, Republic of Ireland ☎01/799
7990, Australia ☎02/9262 6000, NZ ☎09/914
2000; ⓦwww.koreanair.com.
LanChile US & Canada ☎1-866/435-9526, UK
☎0800/977 6100, Australia ☎1300/361 400 or
02/9244 2333, NZ ☎09/977 2233, SA ☎11/781
2111; ⓦwww.lan.com.
Lufthansa US ☎1-800/399-5838, Canada
☎1-800/563-5954, UK ☎0870/837 7747,
Republic of Ireland ☎01/844 5544, Australia
☎1300/655 727, NZ ☎0800945 220, SA
☎0861/842 538; ⓦwww.lufthansa.com.
Northwest/KLM Airlines US ☎1-800/225-2525,
UK ☎0870/507 4074, Australia ☎1300/767310;
ⓦwww.nwa.com.
Qantas US & Canada ☎1-800/227-4500, UK
☎0845/774 7767, Republic of Ireland ☎01/407
3278, Australia ☎13 13 13, NZ ☎0800/808 767 or
09/357 8900, SA ☎11/441 8550; ⓦwww.qantas
.com.
SAS (Scandinavian Airlines) US & Canada
☎1-800/221-2350, UK ☎00871/521 2772,
Republic of Ireland ☎01/844 5440, Australia
☎1300/727 707; ⓦwww.scandinavian.net.
Southwest Airlines US & Canada ☎1-800/435-
9792, ⓦwww.southwest.com.
Thai Airways US ☎1-212/949-8424, UK
☎0870/606 0911, Australia ☎1300/651 960, NZ
☎09/377 3886, SA ☎11/455 1018; ⓦwww
.thaiair.com.

United Airlines US ☎1-800/UNITED-1, UK
☎0845/844 4777, Australia ☎13 17 77; ⓦwww
.united.com.
US Airways US & Canada ☎1-800/428-4322, UK
☎0845/600 3300, Republic of Ireland ☎1890/925
065; ⓦwww.usair.com.
Varig US & Canada ☎1-800/GO-VARIG, UK
☎0870/120 3020; ⓦwww.varig.com.
Virgin Atlantic US ☎1-800/821-5438, UK
☎0870/380 2007, Australia ☎1300/727 340, SA
☎11/340 3400; ⓦwww.virgin-atlantic.com.

Travel specialists and tour operators

Abercrombie & Kent US & Canada ☎1-800/323-
7308, ⓦwww.abercrombiekent.com. Well-tailored
but rather upmarket tours.
Adventure Center US & Canada ☎1-800/228-
8747, ⓦwww.adventurecenter.com. Hiking and
"soft adventure" specialists.
American Holidays Northern Ireland ☎028/9023
8762, Republic of Ireland ☎01/673 3840; ⓦwww
.american-holidays.com. All sorts of package tours to
the US, including San Francisco, from Ireland.
Backroads US & Canada ☎1-800/462-2848,
ⓦwww.backroads.com. Cycling, hiking, and
multisport tours.
Bon Voyage UK ☎0800/316 3012, ⓦwww
.bon-voyage.co.uk. Flight-plus-accommodation
deals.
Bridge the World UK ☎0870/443 2399, ⓦwww
.bridgetheworld.com. Specializing in RTW tickets,
with good deals aimed at the backpacker market.
Canada & America Travel Specialists Australia
☎02/9922 4600, ⓦwww.canada-americatravel
.com.au. North American specialist offering everything
from flights and hotels to travel passes and adventure
sports.
Contiki Travel UK ☎020/8290 6777, ⓦwww
.contiki.co.uk. West-Coast coach tours aimed at
partiers in the 18-35 age group.
Flight Centre US ☎866/967-5351, UK
☎0870/890 8099, Australia ☎13 31 33, New
Zealand ☎0800/243 544, South Africa ☎0860/400
727, ⓦwww.flightcentre
.com. Near-ubiquitous high-street agency frequently
offering some of the lowest fares around.
Holiday America UK ☎01424/224 400, ⓦwww
.holiday-america.net. Flight-plus-accommodation
and fly-drive combinations.
Journeys Worldwide Australia ☎07/3221 4788,
ⓦwww.journeysworldwide.com.au. All US travel
arrangements available.
Kuoni UK ☎1306/747 002, ⓦwww.kuoni.co.uk.
Flight-plus-accommodation-plus-car deals, often
geared toward families.

Madison Travel UK ☎01273/202-532, ⓦwww
.madisontravel.co.uk. Specializing in gay and lesbian
travel packages, including trips to the Bay Area.
Mountain Travel Sobek US & Canada
☎1-888/687-6235, ⓦwww.mtsobek.com.
Conducts hiking, kayaking, and rafting tours.
North South Travel UK ☎01245/608 291,
ⓦwww.northsouthtravel.co.uk. Nonprofit agency
offering friendly and efficient service.
Peregrine Adventures Australia ☎03/9663 8611,
ⓦwww.peregrine.net.au. Specialists in active small-
group holidays.
REI Adventures US & Canada ☎1-800/622-2236,
ⓦwww.rei.com/travel. Climbing, cycling, hiking,
paddling, and multisport tours.
STA Travel US ☎1-800/781-4040, UK
☎0871/230 0040, Australia ☎134 STA, NZ
☎0800/474 400, SA ☎0861/781 781;
ⓦwww.statravel.com. Worldwide specialists in
independent travel; also student IDs, travel insurance,
car rental, rail passes, and more. Good discounts for
students and under-26s.
Sydney International Travel Centre Australia
☎02/9250 9320, ⓦwww.sydneytravel.com.au.

Individually tailored holidays, flights, bus, and rail
tours.
Trailfinders UK ☎0845/058 5858, Republic of
Ireland ☎01/677 7888, Australia ☎1300/780 212;
ⓦwww.trailfinders.com. One of the best-informed
and most efficient agents for independent travellers.
Travel.com.au Australia ☎02/9249 5444,
ⓦwww.travel.com.au; NZ ☎800/788 336; ⓦwww
.travel.co.nz. Youth-oriented resource offering
reasonable fares.
TrekAmerica UK ☎01295/256 777, ⓦwww
.trekamerica.com. Touring adventure holidays looping
through San Francisco – usually small groups in well-
equipped 4WD vans.
USA Travel Australia ☎02/9250 9320, ⓦwww
.usatravel.au. Good deals on flights, accommodation,
city stays, car rentals, and trip packages.
USIT Northern Ireland ☎028/9032 7111, ⓦwww
.usitnow.com; Republic of Ireland ☎01/602 1906,
ⓦwww.usit.ie. Ireland's premier student travel
center, which can also find good nonstudent deals.
Virgin Holidays UK ☎0870/220 2788, ⓦwww
.virginholidays.co.uk. Flights, fly-drive deals, tailor-
made holidays, and packages.

Arrival

The Bay Area airports are well served by public transport, with a plethora of
transit options to get you quickly into San Francisco. Besides BART (Bay Area
Rapid Transit), there are plenty of buses, minivans, and cabs, all of which will
deliver you into the center of the city in around thirty minutes.

Those arriving by bus in San Francisco pull
into the center of downtown; if you're
coming on Amtrak, you'll need to hop onto a
shuttle bus from Oakland in the East Bay. If
arriving by car, San Francisco is well
signposted, though it's best to stick to the
major routes like I-280 for as long as
possible; the one-way network of roads
Downtown can be devilish to navigate the
first time (see p.28).

By air

There are several ways of getting into town
from the **San Francisco International
Airport** (**SFO**; ☎650/821-8211 or 1-800/
435-9736, ⓦwww.flysfo.com), each of which

is clearly signed from the baggage reclaim
areas. The easiest option is BART: the effort-
less thirty-minute nonstop train journey
whisks you from the airport to the heart of
downtown for only $5.35 (ⓦwww
.bart.gov) and leaves every ten to twenty
minutes. There are signs within the airport
directing you to the station.

A slightly cheaper, yet less convenient
choice is the **San Mateo County Transit**
(SamTrans) buses (☎1-800/660-4287,
ⓦwww.samtrans.org), which leave every half-
hour from the upper level of the airport. The
KX express ($4) takes around thirty minutes
to reach the Transbay Terminal Downtown,
while the slower #292 ($1.50) stops frequently

and takes nearly an hour. On the KX, you're allowed only one carry-on bag; the advantage of the slower #292 is that you can bring as much as you want, provided you can carry it onto the bus yourself. Buses leave from level one (arrivals), terminal two center island, and terminal three curbside; at the international terminal, they stop on level one next to Bus Courtyard G. Due to their door-to-door service, many people opt to take **minibus shuttles** into the city – companies include Supershuttle and American Airporter – which depart every five minutes from the upper level of the circular road and take passengers to any central destination for around $14 a head. Be ruthless – competition for these and the several other companies running shuttle services is fierce and lines nonexistent; follow the signs for "Door to Door Vans" on the lower arrivals level. The **SFO Airporter** bus is slightly cheaper ($10) and makes pickups outside each baggage claim area every fifteen minutes; the snag is that it only serves major hotels Downtown. These services are tagged as "Airporter" on the lower arrivals level.

Taxis from the airport cost $30–35 (plus tip) for any Downtown location, more for East Bay and Marin County – definitely worth it if you're in a group or too tired to care. If you're planning to pick up a rental car, the usual car–rental agencies operate free shuttle buses to their depots, leaving every fifteen minutes from the upper level. Driving from SFO, head north on gritty US-101 or northwest on prettier I-280 for the twenty- to thirty-minute drive Downtown.

Several domestic airlines (including America West, Southwest, and United) fly into **Oakland International Airport** (OAK; ☎510/563-3300, ⓦwww.oaklandairport .com) across the Bay. As close to Downtown San Francisco as SFO, OAK is efficiently connected with the city by the AirBART shuttle bus ($2; exact change only), which drops you at the somewhat seedy Coliseum BART station. Get on BART, and San Francisco's Downtown stops are fifteen minutes away ($3.55) – take the train that terminates at Daly City or SFO. Otherwise, a taxi Downtown should cost $50–55.

The third regional airport, **Norman Y. Mineta San Jose International** (SJC; ☎408/501-7600, ⓦwww.sjc.org), also serves the Bay Area, but should only be considered if you plan to begin your stay in Silicon Valley. Fares in and out of SJC are comparable to the airports north, and public transportation to the city is inconvenient and time-consuming.

By train and bus

At the time of writing, all of San Francisco's **Greyhound** services use the **Transbay Terminal** at 425 Mission St at First, SoMa (☎1-800/231-2222, ⓦwww.greyhound .com). Plans are afoot to redevelop the terminal, so call to confirm first. To connect to the BART network, walk one block north to the Embarcadero station on Market Street; to reach CalTrain, take MUNI bus #10 to the station on Fourth King Street. **Green Tortoise** buses (see p.21) stop behind the Transbay Terminal at the corner of First and Natoma streets, SoMa.

All **Amtrak** trains stop in Oakland at the **Bay Area terminal** (☎1-800/USA-RAIL, ⓦwww.amtrak.com) at Jack London Square. From here, free shuttle buses run across the Bay Bridge to the Transbay Terminal, or you can take BART into town. A more efficient route is to get off Amtrak at Richmond to the north, where you can easily pick up BART nearby. Although it's technically closer to San Francisco, don't get off at Emeryville, the train stop before Oakland, as consistent public transportation to the city doesn't exist, though you can hail a cab there or take an Amtrak bus across the Bay Bridge. An hour late counts as on time for Amtrak, so don't make plans for tight connections.

By car

If you're driving into town from the east, the main route by car is **I-80**, which runs via Sacramento all the way from Chicago. **I-5**, passing fifty miles east of San Francisco, serves as the main north–south route, connecting Los Angeles with Seattle; the **I-580** spur from I-5 takes you to the Bay Area. If you are driving in **from the airport**, head for Hwy-101 North. Stay on this road to reach the city of San Francisco and Marin County; follow signs to I-80 to reach Berkeley, Oakland, and the East Bay. For car-rental information, see p.28.

City transportation

San Francisco is a rare American city where you don't require a car to see everything, and is indeed best viewed on foot. Given the chronic shortage of parking Downtown, horrible traffic, and zealous traffic wardens, it makes more sense to avoid driving altogether. The public transportation system (though unpredictable at times) at least covers every neighborhood inexpensively via a system of trains, cable cars, buses, and trolleys. If you have stout legs to tackle those hills, consider cycling – but, frankly, walking the city is still the best bet. Expect sidewalks to have steps on steeper hills for easier climbing.

If you have questions on any form of public transportation in the Bay Area call ☎511 or check ⓦwww.511.org – there's a point-to-point bus/train route planner online, or live operators to answer any questions on public transportation or even traffic conditions.

MUNI

The city's public transportation is run by the San Francisco Municipal Railway, or **MUNI** (☎415/673-6864, ⓦwww.sfmta.com). A comprehensive network of **buses**, **trolleys**, and **cable cars** runs up and over the city's hills, while the underground **trains** become **streetcars** when they emerge from the Downtown metro system to split off and serve the outer neighborhoods, such as the Sunset, the Richmond, and Noe Valley.

Currently, there are six **tramlines** (J-Church, K-Ingleside, L-Taraval, M-Ocean View, N-Judah, and T-Third), which run underground along Market Street and above ground elsewhere, while the picturesque old-style F-trams shuttle on the surface along Market Street, connecting the Embarcadero and the Castro. Environmentally conscious buses, powered by overhead electric cables rather than gas, cover all the areas not served by streetcars. There are three historic **cable-car lines** (ⓦwww.sfcablecar.com; see p.27 for further details), which are more for

The streets of San Francisco

San Francisco's **street system** can seem maddeningly idiosyncratic at first, since, unlike many American cities, Downtown streets have names rather than numbers (the only grid of numbered streets is that radiating into the dock area south of Market.) Throughout this guide, we've provided the street address, its cross street, and the city neighborhood to make it as easy as possible to locate any listings.

If you need to find another address, there's a basic formula that will help pinpoint your destination. Streets work on blocks of 100 from their Downtown source, which on north–south streets is Market; on east–west streets it's the Embarcadero (or Market in the case of those streets that don't extend all the way east to the Bay). For example, 950 Powell St is on the tenth block of Powell north of Market; 1450 Post St is on the fifteenth block of Post west of Market; 220 Castro St is on the third block of Castro south of Market. Further out from Downtown, in the Richmond and Sunset, the avenues all have their origin at the foot of the Presidio and travel south in increasing blocks of 100.

Handily, block numbers are usually also posted above the street sign, with an arrow indicating if the numbers are increasing or decreasing. When pinpointing an address verbally to a cab driver or when giving directions, San Franciscans always give the crossroad rather than the number, and you'd do well to follow their example.

Main MUNI & cable-car routes

Useful bus routes

#5 From the Transbay Terminal, west alongside Haight-Ashbury and Golden Gate Park to the ocean.

#7 From the Ferry Terminal (Market St) to the end of Haight Street and to Golden Gate Park.

#20 (Golden Gate Transit) From Civic Center to the Golden Gate Bridge.

#22 From the Marina up Pacific Heights and north on Fillmore.

#28 & #29 From the Marina through the Presidio, north through Golden Gate Park, the Richmond, and Sunset.

#30 From the CalTrain depot on Third Street, north to Ghirardelli Square, via Chinatown and North Beach, and out to Chestnut Street in the Marina district.

#38 From Geary Street via Civic Center, west to the ocean along Geary Boulevard through Japantown and the Richmond, ending at Cliff House.

MUNI train lines

MUNI F–Market Line Restored vintage trolleys from around the world run Downtown from the Transbay Terminal up Market Street and into the heart of the Castro. The extension along the refurbished Embarcadero to Fisherman's Wharf is one of MUNI's most popular routes.

MUNI J–Church Line From Downtown to Mission and the edge of the Castro.

MUNI K–Ingleside Line From Downtown through the Castro to Balboa Park.

MUNI L–Taraval Line From Downtown west through the Sunset to the Zoo and Ocean Beach.

MUNI M–Ocean View From Downtown west by the Stonestown Galleria shopping center and San Francisco State University.

MUNI N–Judah Line From the CalTrain station, past Pac Bell stadium, along South Beach to Downtown west through the Inner Sunset to Ocean Beach.

MUNI T-Third Line From the Castro station through Downtown along the Embarcadero and Third Street to the Dogpatch area in the south-east corner of the city.

Cable-car routes

Powell-Hyde From Powell Street/Market along Hyde through Russian Hill to Fisherman's Wharf.

Powell-Mason From Powell Street/Market along Mason via Chinatown and North Beach to Fisherman's Wharf.

California Street From the foot of California Street at Robert Frost Plaza in the Financial District through Nob Hill to Polk Street.

cruising than commuting, but still an unmissable treat.

On buses and trains, the **flat fare** (correct change only) is $1.50; with each ticket you buy, ask for a **free transfer** which is good for another two rides on a train or bus in any direction within ninety minutes to two hours of purchase. Even if you don't plan to transfer, make sure to pick one up, as recent rule changes mean you must be able to produce proof of payment at any time when asked by a MUNI inspector. Note that cable cars cost $5 one-way, and do not accept transfers. The best option if you're planning on using MUNI often is to buy a **MUNI Passport**, available in one-, three-, and seven-day denominations ($11, $18, $24). It's valid for unlimited travel on the MUNI system. A **Fast Pass** costs $45 for a full calendar month and also offers unlimited travel within the city limits on both MUNI and BART.

MUNI trains run throughout the **night** on a limited service, known as the Owl Service, except the streetcars, which stop around 1am when above-ground buses take their place, and the F-Market Street line, which runs 6am–midnight; most buses run all night, but services are greatly reduced after midnight. Note that while MUNI may be cheap, it's not always reliable: the Pac-Man-like train locator maps on the Downtown platforms are charmingly retro, but horribly confusing and often wrong; most bus maps on shelters are years out of date, and bus services on weekends and holidays can be erratic. To counter this, you can buy a handy, up-to-date MUNI map ($3) from the Visitors Information Center at Hallidie Plaza, the cable-car turnaround at Beach and Hyde, or at most bookstores.

BART and CalTrain

Along Market Street Downtown, MUNI shares station concourses with **BART** (Bay Area Rapid Transit; ☎510/465-BART or 415/989-2278, ⊛www.bart.gov), which is the fastest way to get to the East Bay – including downtown Oakland and Berkeley – and south of San Francisco, not to mention the bustling Mission District. **Tickets** aren't cheap ($1.50–6.30 depending on how far you ride), but the service is efficient and very dependable; trains follow four routes on a fixed schedule, usually arriving every ten minutes, although fewer trains run after 8pm, which means transfers and longer waits. Tickets can be purchased on the station concourse; save your ticket after entering the station, as it is also needed when exiting the station via the turnstiles. Free schedules are available at BART stations: trains operate Monday to Friday 4am–midnight, Saturday 6am–midnight, and Sunday 8am–midnight, meaning the last trains leave their departure stations at midnight.

The **CalTrain** commuter railway (depot on Fourth St at Townsend, SoMa) links San Francisco south to San Jose; call ☎650/508-6200 or 1-800/660-4287 or log onto ⊛www.caltrain.com for schedules and fares ($2.25–7.50).

Ferries

A picturesque if not particularly quick or cheap way of touring the Bay is by boat: two companies operate regular services from the city center. The **Blue & Gold Fleet** leaves mainly from Pier 41 at Fisherman's Wharf (☎415/705-8200, ⊛www.blueandgoldfleet.com), along with a few weekday runs from the Ferry Building. It runs boats to Oakland ($6 one-way), Vallejo ($10 one-way), Angel Island ($7.50 one-way), Tiburon, and Sausalito (both $9.50 one-way).

Golden Gate Ferries is based at the Ferry Building on the Embarcadero (☎415/455-2000, ⊛www.goldengate.org): it offers trips to Sausalito and Larkspur (each $7.10 one-way).

For trips to Alcatraz, the newish **Alcatraz Cruises** (☎415/981-7625, ⊛www.alcatrazcruises.com), runs frequently to and from the island during the day from 9am to 1.55pm, departing from Pier 33 just southeast of Fisherman's Wharf. The last day-tour ferry returns at 4.30pm in winter, 6.30pm in summer; the night-tour ferries leave at 6.10pm and 6.50pm and return at 8.40pm and 9.25pm (day tour $24.50, night tour $31.50).

Taxis

Taxis ply the streets, and while you can flag them down (especially Downtown), finding one can be difficult. The granting of more taxi licenses is a contentious issue in San Francisco, many arguing that the streets are clogged enough. Your best bet is to head for one of the larger Downtown hotels, where taxis are mostly likely waiting at a taxi stand, or to call ahead.

Phoning around, try DeSoto (☎415/970-1300), Luxor (☎415/282-4141, ⊛www.luxorcab.com), or Green Cab (☎415/626-4733, ⊛www.sfgreencab.com). Green Cab represents the environmentally friendly mindset of San Francisco, and has the distinction of being the city's only cab company to use all hybrid vehicles. **Fares** (within the city) begin with a fee of $3.10 to start the meter plus 45¢ for each additional 1/5th of a mile or 60 seconds' waiting time. There's a $2 surcharge from SFO airport; expect to add a customary fifteen-percent tip to the final amount.

Driving and car rental

The only reason to **rent a car** in San Francisco is if you want to explore the

The 49-Mile Drive

If you have your own vehicle, you can orient yourself by way of the breathtaking **49-Mile Drive**, a route that takes in the most important scenic and historic points in the city in around half a day. Marked by blue-and-white seagull signs, it circuits Civic Center, Japantown, Union Square, Chinatown, Nob Hill, North Beach, and Telegraph Hill, before skirting Fisherman's Wharf, the Marina, and the Palace of Fine Arts, after which it passes the southern approach of the Golden Gate Bridge and winds through the Presidio. From here it sweeps along the ocean, past the zoo, and doubles back through Golden Gate Park, vaulting over Twin Peaks and dipping down to Mission Dolores, then back to the waterfront for a drive past the Bay Bridge, the Ferry Building, and the Financial District.

Maps of the entire route are available for $1 from the Visitors Information Center at Hallidie Plaza, at the Powell Street cable-car turnaround, or you can download a free copy at ⓦwww.onlyinsanfrancisco.com. Keep in mind that some of the signs are missing along the route, so having a map is essential at times.

greater Bay Area, the Wine Country, or the landscape north or south along the coast. If you're headed out of the city by car, pick up your vehicle at the end of your stay at one of the Downtown desks rather than at the airport on arrival.

When driving in town, pay attention to San Francisco's attempts to control Downtown traffic, all of which effectively make driving diabolical. The posted speed limit is 30mph, speeding through a yellow light is illegal, and pedestrians waiting at crosswalks have the right of way. In addition, it's almost impossible to make a left turn anywhere in Downtown, meaning you'll have to get used to looping the block, making three rights instead of one left. The fact that streets north and south of Market Street don't line up can also be troublesome – if you're headed north out of SoMa, turn right onto Market and then left towards the waterfront whenever you can. Note that California does allow cars to turn right on a red light, if oncoming traffic is clear. Keep in mind also that Downtown traffic during peak rush hours can have you sitting in gridlock for quite a while.

Cheap, available **parking** is even rarer than a left-turn signal, but it's worth playing by the rules: police issue multiple tickets for illegally parked vehicles and won't hesitate to tow your car if it's violating any posted laws. Downtown, plenty of garages exist, most advertised rates beginning at $2.50 per fifteen minutes: note that new public garages – under Union Square Downtown, Portsmouth Square in Chinatown, or Ghirardelli Square near Fisherman's Wharf – are cheaper than the private ones. One of the cheapest is on Broadway east of Stockton, next to the Pacific Motor Inn: it charges a maximum of $15 for a 24-hour period (another $15 bargain is on Pacific Ave in Jackson Square). The smartest overnighting option if you have a rental car to stash is the Sutter Stockton garage above the Stockton Street tunnel: rates are only $7 if you arrive after 6pm and leave by 7am, while the daytime maximum is $26.

Metered spots on the street usually fill up fast, but a good bet is to prowl the residential areas for a spot where you can leave the car for up to two hours. Street parking has its own pitfalls, though: make sure to observe San Francisco's kaleidoscopically confusing **curb colors**. Restricted stoppage for private drivers includes: green (ten-minute limit for all vehicles); white (six-minute limit during adjacent businesses' hours of operation); and blue (vehicles marked with California-issued disabled plates only). Private vehicles cannot stop at red (no stopping or parking anytime); yellow or yellow/black (commercial loading only); or yellow/green/black (cabs only). Also, beware of posted no-parking hours, which could be late-night for street-sweeping or high-traffic commuting hours in the middle of the day.

Take care to observe the San Francisco **law of curbing wheels** – turn wheels into the curb if the car points downhill and away from the curb if it points up. Violators are subject to a $20 ticket. If you're towed, the fee to release your vehicle ranges from $100 to $280: to reclaim your vehicle, call AutoReturn Customer Service Center (☎415/865-8200) or head to its walk-in office at 450 Seventh St, where you can pay your fine and get your car back. For assistance or questions, contact the Department of Parking and Traffic (☎415/553-1235).

Bridge tolls are collected only when entering San Francisco by car; the Golden Gate Bridge toll costs $5, while the Bay Bridge one is $4. There is talk of raising both of these tolls at some point in the next year, so make sure to have extra cash with you just in case.

Car-rental companies

Advantage ☎1-800/777-5500, ⓦwww
.arac.com
Alamo ☎1-800/462-5266, ⓦwww
.alamo.com
Avis ☎1-800/230-4898, ⓦwww.avis.com
Budget ☎1-800/527-0700, ⓦwww.budget.com
Dollar ☎1-800/800-3665, ⓦwww.dollar.com
Enterprise ☎1-800/261-7331, ⓦwww
.enterprise.com
Hertz ☎1-800/654-3131, ⓦwww.hertz.com
National ☎1-800/227-7368, ⓦwww
.nationalcar.com
Payless ☎1-800/729-5377, ⓦwww
.paylesscarrental.com
Rent-a-Wreck ☎1-800/944-7501, ⓦwww
.rentawreck.com
Thrifty ☎1-800/847-4389, ⓦwww.thrifty.com

Bicycles and rollerblades

Cycling is a great way to experience San Francisco. Golden Gate Park, the Marina and Presidio, and Ocean Beach all have great, paved trails and some off-road routes. Tranquil treks through undeveloped nature are available if you head north over the Golden Gate Bridge (the western side is reserved solely for bikes) into the Marin

Headlands for a series of off-road trails along cliffs, ocean, and into valleys. Throughout the city, marked bike routes – with lanes – direct riders to all major points of interest, but note that officials picked the routes for their lack of car traffic, not for the easiest ride. If you get tired, bikes can be carried on most BART trains (during non-rush hours), and newer diesel and trolley MUNI buses have bike racks on the front of the vehicle.

Blazing Saddles, which **rents** bicycles, has several locations (☎415/202-8888, ⓦwww.blazingsaddles.com or ⓦwww .bikethebridge.com); two of the most convenient are 1095 Columbus Ave at Francisco, North Beach, and Pier 41. Rental for bikes is $7/hr, $28/day. Another option, with similar rates, is Bike & Roll, 899 Columbus Ave (☎415/771-0392, ⓦwww.bikeandroll.com). Wheel Fun Rentals, located in Golden Gate Park at 50 Stow Lake Drive (☎415/668-6699, ⓦwww.wheelfunrentals.com), offers bikes, choppers, and surreys at hourly, half-day, and day rates, and is a great way to see the park.

San Francisco's roads and pathways aren't rollerblade-ready, but there are a few good **places to skate** at Marina Green and in Golden Gate Park. On Sunday, most of Golden Gate Park's roads are closed to autos, bringing out hordes of rollerbladers and skaters. Skaters also use the flat sidewalk along Ocean Beach and the good trails around Lake Merced, although both are away from the action of Downtown. San Francisco's many plazas are more welcoming to skateboarding, even if local law conspires to ban them from city limits. You can find skateboarders doing their thing in front of the Ferry Building around the various open plazas. Skates on Haight, 1818 Haight St at Stanyan, Haight-Ashbury (☎415/752-8375, ⓦwww.skatesonhaight.com), rents both rollerskates and rollerblades for $6/hr and $24/overnight.

Tours

As you'd expect from a city as tourist-friendly as San Francisco, there are plenty of tour operators prepared to show you the sights. Frankly, many of the bus trips are overpriced and worth avoiding – we've listed a few exceptions below. If you want to splash out, there are companies offering aerial tours of the breathtaking Bay; otherwise, try a cruise, but bear in mind that the city's iffy weather can mean some trips amount to little more than an hour adrift in the fog. By far the best option is a walking tour: San Francisco is a pedestrian city, and, barring a few hills, the easy pace and knowledgeable guides combine to provide the best value of all.

Aerial tours

San Francisco Helicopters (℡650/635-4500 or 1-800/400-2404, ⓦwww.sfhelicoptertours .com) offers a variety of **spectacular flights** over the Bay Area; prices start at $150 per person for a twenty-minute flight. Trips depart from SFO airport and land at Sausalito; the company will collect you by bus from the city center and take you back at journey's end if you wish. The trips may sound pricey, but the soaring views are a five-star intro to the city. Another high-flying option is San Francisco Seaplane Tours (℡415/332-4843, ⓦwww .seaplane.com), leaving from Pier 39, Fisherman's Wharf, six times daily for tours of the Bay, Golden Gate Bridge, and Downtown. Prices start at $139 per person for a 25-minute flight.

Boat tours

Blue & Gold Fleet (℡415/705-5555, ⓦwww .blueandgoldfleet.com) offers chilly 75-minute **cruises** with breathtaking views of the Bay, leaving from Pier 39 and Pier 41 at Fisherman's Wharf – though be warned that everything may be shrouded in fog, making the price ($22, but check for discount fares online) less than worth it. A similar service is offered by Red & White Fleet from Pier 43 (℡415/673-2900, ⓦwww.redandwhite.com). If you just want to take a loop out under the Golden Gate Bridge and back, several independent boat operators troll for your business along Fisherman's Wharf – expect to pay around $10 per person plus tip.

Bus tours

A number of bus tours afford a variety of sightseeing experiences throughout the Bay Area. **El Camión Mexicano** (℡415/546-3747, ⓦwww.mexicanbus.com; reservations essential) takes evening **bus tours** through the Mission District on a trip that's far more fun than it sounds. For $38, the itinerary takes in local Mexican restaurants and salsa clubs for drinking and dancing. Tours leave 9.15pm sharp every Friday and Saturday from outside *Chevy's* restaurant on Third Street at Howard in SoMa.

The nationwide tour operator **Gray Line Tours** (℡415/434-8687 or 1-800/826-0202, ⓦwww.graylinesanfrancisco.com) trundles round the city for three and a half fairly tedious hours for $41, leaving from Transbay Terminal on First Street at Mission, SoMa. It also offers day-trips to the Monterey Peninsula ($77) and the Napa Wine Country ($140).

Walking tours

A great way to get to know the quieter, historical side of San Francisco is to take a **walking tour**. The better ones keep group size small and are run by natives who truly love their subject matter and jobs. Some, like those sponsored by the library, are free. Reservations are recommended for all walks. The Visitors Information Center can give you a full list of available walks – every neighborhood has at least one – but among those you should consider are these.

Walking-tour companies

Barbary Coast Trail Walking Tour @www
.sfhistory.org. Self-guided, 3.8-mile tour through San
Francisco's oldest and most infamous neighborhoods,
marked by bronze medallions set into the sidewalk.
The tour also includes a brief hop onto a cable-car, to
give yourself a break from climbing the scenic hills.
You can print out a map from the website, but you'll
enjoy the walk far more if you pick up the *Barbary
Coast Trail Official Guide* ($9) available at most local
bookstores.

City Guides T 415/557-4266, @www
.sfcityguides.org. A terrific free series sponsored by
the library and covering every San Francisco
neighborhood, as well as themed walks on topics
ranging from the Gold Rush to the Beat Generation; its
wide-ranging subject matter means you'll often be
trekking alongside locals instead of fellow tourists.
Highly recommended. Schedule varies – call or check
the website for details.

Cruisin' the Castro T 415/255-1821, @www
.cruisinthecastro.com. The Grand Dame of San
Francisco walks, Ms Trevor Hailey, leads you through
her beloved neighborhood and explains how and why
San Francisco became the gay capital of the world.
Tour includes the story of the rise and murder of
Harvey Milk, the city's first openly gay politician – be
aware that Trevor is as much a lecturer as a walker, so
be prepared to sit and listen as often as look at sights.
$35 per person; schedule varies, usually summer only
– call to check.

Haight-Ashbury Flower Power Walking Tour
T 1-800/979-3370, @www.hippiegourmet.com.
Learn about the Human Be-in, Grateful Dead, Summer
of Love, and the Haight's more distant past as a
Victorian resort destination. One of the longest and
most thorough of all the tours. $20 per person; Tues &
Sat 9.30am, Fri 11am.

HobNob Tours T 650/814-6303, @www
.hobnobtours.com. Lively and scurrilous tours around
the Nob Hill homes and haunts of Silver Kings and

Robber Barons. Lead guide Valarie Huff is a fact-
packed delight, and this tour is one of the best in the
city – and since it's often overlooked, groups are
conveniently small. $30; Mon–Fri 10am & 1.30pm.

Mission Mural Walk T 415/285-2287, @www
.precitaeyes.org. Two-hour presentation by mural
artists leads around the Mission District's outdoor
paintings, taking in over 70 murals. Includes a slide
presentation on the history and process of mural art.
Recommended. $12 per person, student/senior
discounts; Sat & Sun 1.30pm.

San Francisco Ghost Tour T 415/922-5590,
@www.sfghosthunt.com. A supernatural tour of
haunted hotspots, led by the eccentric and
entertaining Jim Fassbinder. The first portion of the
night is spent telling San Francisco ghost stories
inside the *Queen Anne Hotel*. $20 per person; nightly
except Tues 7pm.

San Francisco Parks Trust T 415/263-0991,
@www.sfpt.org. Volunteer-led walks round the
various attractions in Golden Gate Park, including the
windmills and the Japanese Tea Garden, as well as
other city greenspaces. Free; call for latest schedules.

Vampire Tour of San Francisco T 650/279-
1840 or T 1-866/424-8836, @www.sfvampiretour
.com. An after-dark stroll through Nob Hill led by
"Vampress" Mina Harker, this two-hour tour is packed
with San Francisco history with a fun gothic twist. $20
per person; Fri & Sat 8pm.

Victorian Home Walk T 415/252-9485, @www
.victorianwalk.com. Leisurely tour through Pacific
Heights and Cow Hollow where you'll learn to tell the
difference between a Queen Anne, Italianate, and
Stick-Style Vic. $20 per person for a two-hour tour;
meets daily at 11am at the corner of Powell and
Post sts.

Wok Wiz Tours T 650/355-9657, @www
.wokwiz.com. A walk through Chinatown run by chef/
writer Shirley Fong-Torres and her twelve-man team.
Fun and fluffy, with plenty of anecdotes but a little thin
on historical information. $30 per person, $40 per
person including lunch; daily 10am.

The media

San Francisco's media are surprisingly parochial: newspaper and TV coverage of all things Californian, especially the Peninsula, may be in-depth but events elsewhere in the country or the world will often receive little attention. It's worth picking up a newspaper, though, to understand the Byzantine bureaucracies that cripple local government and meet the small number of people who seem to have a stranglehold on local politics.

Newspapers and magazines

After almost a century as a two-paper town, today San Francisco's only full-scale daily is the *San Francisco Chronicle* (daily 50¢, Sun $1.50; ⓦwww.sfgate.com). It's most useful for its Sunday edition's *Datebook* (known by most locals simply as the "Pink Section"), which contains previews and reviews for the upcoming week. An often-overlooked alternative is the peppy and well-reported, if tech-heavy, *San Jose Mercury News* (daily 25¢, Sun $1; ⓦwww.mercurynews.com), the thick daily that focuses on the Peninsula but also provides terrific international news. Of course, at a pinch, there's always the *New York Times* (daily $1, Sun $5).

San Francisco is justly proud of its **alternative press**, which picks up the slack from the *Chronicle* and co, and results in two fine free weekly papers: *The San Francisco Bay Guardian* (ⓦwww.sfbg.com) and *SF Weekly* (ⓦwww.sfweekly.com), available from racks around town. Both offer more in-depth features on local life and better music and club listings than the dailies; there's an amusingly fierce, mud-spattered rivalry between the two freesheets that often plays out via their respective editorial and letters pages. Many neighborhoods have their own community newsletters, such as the free *New Mission News* and *Noe Valley Voice* or *Nob Hill Gazette* ($3), which are often available in local cafés or in curbside boxes. The glossy – if rather gummy – *San Francisco Magazine* is often free in hotels; better is its upstart rival, *7x7*, another monthly with a trendier edge and a more in-depth restaurant review section (its name riffs off the idea that the city is just 7 x 7 square miles in size). However,

savvy locals eschew both of these ad-heavy magazines in favour of the more down-to-earth weeklies.

Detailed information on the East Bay can be found in its dailies, the *Oakland Tribune*, the *Berkeley Daily Planet*, or the newbie *Examiner*-style *East Bay Daily News*. There's also an alternative weekly, the *East Bay Express*, as well as UC-Berkeley's two free daily student newspapers.

Television

In San Francisco, you'll have access to all the usual stations: from **major networks** like ABC (channel 7), CBS (channel 5), NBC (channel 3), and Fox (channel 2) to smaller netlets like the WB and UPN. Expect talk shows in the morning, soaps in the afternoon, and marquee-name comedies and dramas in primetime. If that's all too maddeningly commercial-heavy, there's always the rather earnest, ad-free **public broadcasting** station KQED (channel 9), which fills its schedule with news, documentaries, and imported period dramas.

There's a wider choice on **cable**, including CNN for news, and the Food Network for cooking shows or epicurean travelogues; well-regarded premium channels like HBO and Showtime are often available on hotel TV systems, showing original series and blockbuster movies.

Radio

Listening to the radio is often one of the smartest ways to gauge the character of the local area. It's best to skip most specialty stations on the **AM** frequency – although there may be the occasional interesting chat program. An intriguing new addition is 1550

KYOU Radio, which recently dumped its DJs and converted into the world's first podcasting radio station. It offers bite-sized listener-submitted content simultaneously broadcast over the radio and online.

On **FM**, you'll find the usual mix of rock, Latin, and R'n'B – stations are too numerous to list, although the alternative rock KITS (105.3 FM), electronic dance KNGY (92.7 FM), and hip-hop KMEL (106.1 FM) are popular. Expect commercials interrupted by an occasional tune during drive-time (6–9am & 4–7pm). College stations such as UC Berkeley's KALX (90.7 FM) and University of San Francisco's KUSF (90.3 FM) are good picks for finding random local bands and eclectic music. San Francisco airwaves are also home to a number of pirate radio stations. A safe harbor if you're struggling to find satisfying local news is to tune in to **National Public Radio** (NPR), the listener-funded talk station with a refreshingly sober take on news and chat (try KQED 88.5 FM and KALW 91.7 FM). To check for local frequencies for the World Service, log on to the BBC (Ⓦwww.bbc.co.uk/worldservice), Radio Canada (Ⓦwww.rcinet.ca), or Voice of America (Ⓦwww.voa.gov).

Crime and personal safety

San Francisco is largely a safe and easy place for visitors to wander round, whatever the time of day or night; areas like North Beach and the Castro have strong senses of community, which contribute to low crime. However, San Francisco is unusual in that the sketchier parts of town abut the most heavily touristed areas: the Tenderloin, for example, especially along Turk and Eddy streets, is unpleasant day or night. Similarly, take care throughout SoMa, but especially along Sixth Street, where you'll often see drug deals go down in broad daylight. There's still some gang activity in the Mission, often along Mission Street (between 14th and 19th sts) and 24th Street (between Potrero and Mission sts); also, taxis are the best transportation option around Lower Fillmore and the Western Addition after dark.

Security at many public buildings and museums has been significantly increased since the terrorist attacks of September 2001. There are now more visual, physical, and covert checks on anyone entering museums, galleries, and public buildings. You can expect to have to wait in line and have your bags searched before entering, while metal detectors and other security devices are in place at sites throughout the city.

As far as your personal responsibility goes, you should carry ID at all times. Two pieces should suffice, one of which should have a photo – a passport or driver's license and credit card(s) are best. (Incidentally, not having your license with you while driving is an arrestable offense.) A university photo ID might be sufficient, but an International Student Identity Card (ISIC) is often not accepted as valid proof of age, for example in bars or liquor stores. Overseas visitors (often surprised to learn that the legal drinking age is 21) might want to carry their passport, unless they have a photo-style driver's license.

As for **drugs**, keep in mind that possession of under an ounce of marijuana is a noncriminal offense in California, and the worst you'll get is a $200 fine. Being caught with more than an ounce, however, means facing a criminal charge for dealing and a possible prison sentence. Other drugs are completely illegal; it's a much more serious offense if you're caught with any.

If you find yourself in need of **legal advice**, contact the Lawyer Referral Service, 465 California St at Montgomery, Financial District (Mon–Fri 8.30am–5.30pm; ☎415/989-1616).

Mugging and theft

Most visitors will have few (if any) problems – and if things do go wrong, foreign visitors tend to report local **police** are helpful and obliging, although they'll obviously be less sympathetic if they think you brought the trouble on yourself through carelessness.

You shouldn't be complacent. The fact that San Francisco attracts so many tourists means that it has more than its share of **petty crime**, simply because there are plenty of unsuspecting holidaymakers to prey on. Keep your wits about you in crowds, know where your wallet or purse is, and of course, avoid poorly lit parks, parking lots, and streets at night. Be careful when using ATMs in untouristed areas; instead, try to use machines near Downtown hotels, shops, or offices, and during daylight. And if you have to ask directions, choose carefully who you ask (go into a store, if possible).

Should the worst happen, hand over your money and afterwards find a phone and dial ☎**911**, or hail a cab and ask the driver to take you to the nearest police station. Here, report the theft and get a reference number on the report to claim insurance and travelers' check refunds.

Always store valuables in the **hotel safe** when you go out. When inside, keep your door locked and don't open it to anyone you are suspicious of. If they claim to be hotel staff and you don't believe them, call reception to check. In hostels and budget hotels, you may want to keep your valuables on your person, unless you know the security measures to be reliable.

Having bags snatched that contain travel documents can be a big headache, none more so for foreign travelers than **losing your passport**. Make photocopies of everything important before you go (including the business page of your passport) and keep them separate from the originals. If your passport goes missing, visit the nearest consulate and have them issue you a temporary passport (basically a sheet of paper saying you've reported the loss) – this will help get you back home.

Keep a record of the numbers of your travelers' checks separately from the actual checks; if you lose them, call the issuing company on the toll-free number below. They'll ask you for the check numbers, the place you bought them, when and how you lost them, and whether it's been reported to the police. All being well, you should get the missing checks reissued within a couple of days – and perhaps an emergency advance to tide you over.

Finally, it goes without saying that you should *never* **hitchhike** anywhere in or around the Bay Area, or indeed the entire US.

Emergency numbers for lost cards and checks

American Express Cards ☎1-800/992-3404
American Express Checks ☎1-800/221-7282
Citicorp ☎1-800/645-6556
Diners Club ☎1-800/234-6377
Mastercard ☎1-800/826-2181
Thomas Cook/Mastercard ☎1-800/223-9920
Visa Cards ☎1-800/847-2911
Visa Checks ☎1-800/227-6811

Women's safety

In the West Coast's most politically progressive city, women are treated with respect and courtesy almost everywhere and commonly hold positions of power and authority. San Francisco is safer than most American cities, though common sense still applies: look as if you know where you're going and take taxis (or at least make sure you have a companion) after dark, particularly if you find yourself in the Tenderloin, Western Addition, SoMa, or Mission districts. Women traveling alone are not at all unusual, but the successful ones learn to deal with any harassment firmly and loudly. While there is more chance of being mugged in San Francisco than raped – the city has one of the lowest incidences of rape of any metropolitan area in the US – you may feel safer if you carry whistles, and sprays. These items, while probably useless in the event of real trouble, are a confidence booster that can ward off creeps. The SoMa area, where there are lots of clubs, is dark at night, so exercise caution when walking back from living it up.

The National Organization for Women (@www.now.org) is a women's issues group whose lobbying has done much to effect positive social legislation. NOW branches, listed in local phone directories and on the organization's website, can provide referrals for specific concerns, such as rape crisis centers and counseling services, feminist bookstores, and lesbian bars. Specific women's contacts are listed where applicable in the city sections of the guide.

Crisis and support centers

Rape Crisis Center and Hotline 1841 Market St at Octavia, Castro ☏ 415/647-7273 (24hr)
Rape Treatment Center San Francisco General Hospital, 1001 Potrero Ave at 22nd St, Mission ☏ 415/821-3222

Car crime

Crimes committed against tourists driving **rental cars** have garnered headlines around the world in recent years, but there are certain precautions you can take to keep yourself safe. Not driving in San Francisco would be an easy first step – public transportation is good enough that it's not necessary to drive, and the one-way traffic systems Downtown reinforce that you're better off on MUNI or BART. On longer trips, pick up your rental car on the day you leave the city. Any car you do rent should have nothing on it – such as a particular license plate – that makes it easy to identify as a rental car. When driving, under no circumstances should you stop in any unlit or seemingly deserted urban area – and especially not if someone is waving you down and suggesting that there is something wrong with your car. Similarly, if you are "accidentally" rammed by the driver behind, do not stop but drive on to the nearest well-lit, busy area and phone the police on ☏ 911. Keep your doors locked and windows never more than slightly open. Do not open your door or window if someone approaches your car on the pretext of asking directions. Hide any valuables out of sight, preferably locked in the trunk or in the glove compartment (any valuables you don't need for your journey should be left in your hotel safe).

If your vehicle does break down on an interstate or heavily traveled road outside the city, seek out one of the emergency phones often located along highways. One option is to rent a mobile phone with your car, for a small additional charge.

Travel essentials

Children's activities

San Francisco is primarily a place for adults – more so than, say, LA, where Disneyland and Universal Studios are major attractions. Still, kids can take solace in the fine beaches and neighborhood parks; other kid-stops in town lean toward the educational – science museums, zoos, and the like. If you're looking for **amusement parks**, head across the bay to Vallejo or down the coast to Paramount's Great America. There is a useful **babysitting booking service** – call the 24-hour hotline ☏ 415/309-5662 for rates and info.

Attractions

Of San Francisco's few specifically child-oriented **attractions** – all of which are listed in the relevant chapters of this book – the Exploratorium in the Marina District is particularly excellent (the Tactile Dome adventure alone will keep any kid happy for at least half an hour). Otherwise, for natural wonders, head for the Steinhart Aquarium in Golden Gate Park or the newly remodeled San Francisco Zoo with its lush lemur forest and the chance to pet tarantulas (though enclosure security has been an issue here of late). There's also the Aquarium of the Bay at Pier 39 on Fisherman's Wharf, where a moving walkway takes you through the center of a massive, fish-filled glass tank. The only museum in town expressly designed for kids is the Zeum in Yerba Buena Gardens, although its opening hours are patchy; better to head for the enclosed, old-fashioned carousel next door.

Costs

Accommodation will be your biggest single expense: the cheapest reasonable double hotel rooms go for $100 or so a night, although hostels will of course be cheaper. See p.151 for more suggestions. After you've paid for your room, count on spending a minimum of $40 a day for public transportation, three budget meals, and a beer but not much else. Eating fancier meals, taking taxis, and heftier bar tabs will mean allowing for more like $65–75 per day. If you want to go regularly to the theater or major concerts, rent a car, take a tour, or seriously shop, double that figure. As usual, students and people under 26 will receive good **discounts** on museum entrance fees and some other services such as travel costs, if they carry a valid International Student ID Card (ISIC, @www .isiccard.com) or International Youth Travel Card through (IYTC) through STA Travel (see p.24 for details).

Remember that a **sales tax** of 8.5 percent in San Francisco itself and slightly less in the surrounding counties is added to virtually everything you buy except for groceries and prescription drugs; it is seldom included in the quoted price.

Dental treatment

For a free referral to the nearest **dentist**, call the national Dental Society Referral Service (☎415/421-1435 or 1-800/511-8663).

Electricity

Electricity runs on 110V AC and most plugs have two flat pins, although some have a third round one. If coming from outside the USA, make sure you have an adapter that will fit American sockets.

Entry requirements

Although regulations have been continually tightening up since 9/11, citizens of 27 countries, including the UK, Ireland, Australia, New Zealand, and most Western European countries, visiting the United States for a period of less than ninety days can still enter the country on the **Visa Waiver Scheme**. The requisite visa waiver form (I-94W) is provided by the airline during check-in or on the plane, and presented to an immigration official on arrival.

However, all passports accompanying an I-94W must now be **machine readable** and any issued after October 2006 must include a digital **chip** containing biometric data (these are now automatically issued by most countries but check.) Anybody whose passport does not meet these requirements will require some sort of **visa** for even a short stay in America, as will anybody planning to stay over three months: check @www.dhs .gov for updates and the list of Visa Waiver Scheme countries. What's more, even with an I-94W form, each traveler must undergo the US-VISIT process at immigration, where both index fingers are digitally scanned and a digital headshot is also taken for file.

Canadian citizens, used to being able to make an oral declaration, have also had to provide documentation since January 2008, although an enhanced secure driver's license is still an acceptable alternative to a passport. This may change though, so again check for updates.

Prospective visitors from other parts of the world not mentioned above require a valid passport and a non-immigrant **visitor's visa** for a maximum ninety-day stay. How you obtain a visa depends on which country you're in and your status on application, so contact your nearest US embassy or consulate. Whatever your nationality, visas are not issued to convicted felons and anybody who owns up to being a communist, fascist, or drug dealer.

On arrival, the date stamped on your passport is the latest you're legally allowed to stay. The Department of Homeland Security (DHS) has toughened its stance on anyone violating their visa status, so even **overstaying** by a few days can result in a protracted interrogation from officials. Overstaying may also cause you to be turned away next time you try to enter the US.

To get an **extension** before your time is up, apply at the nearest Department of Homeland Security office, whose address will be under the Federal Government Offices listings at the front of the phone book. In San Francisco, the office is at 630 Sansome St at Washington, Jackson Square (☏ 1-800/375-5283; ⊛ www.dhs.gov). INS officials will assume that you're working in the US illegally, and it's up to you to convince them otherwise by providing evidence of ample finances. If you can, bring along an upstanding American citizen to vouch for you. You'll also have to explain why you didn't plan for the extra time initially.

US embassies and consulates abroad

In Australia

Online ⊛ www.usembassy-australia.state.gov
Canberra Moonah Place, Yarralumla, ACT 2600 ☏ 02/6214 5600
Melbourne 553 St Kilda Rd, PO Box 6722, Vic 3004 ☏ 03/9526 5900
Perth 16 St George's Terrace, 13th floor, WA 6000 ☏ 08/9202 1224
Sydney MLC Centre, 59th floor, 19–29 Martin Place, NSW 2000 ☏ 02/9373 9200

In Canada

Online ⊛ www.ottawa.usembassycanada.gov
Calgary 615 Macleod Trail SE, Room 1000, AB T2G 4T8 ☏ 403/266-8962
Halifax Suite 910, Purdy's Wharf Tower II, 1969 Upper Water St, NS B3J 3R7 ☏ 902/429-2480
Montréal 1155 Rue de St Alexandre, Québec, H3B 1Z1 ☏ 514/398-9695
Ottawa 490 Sussex Drive, ON K1N 1G8 ☏ 613/238-5335
Québec City 2 Rue de la Terrasse-Dufferin, Québec, G1R 4T9 ☏ 418/692-2095
Toronto 360 University Ave, ON M5G 1S4 ☏ 416/595-1700
Vancouver 1075 W Pender St, BC V6E 2M6 ☏ 604/685-4311
Winnipeg 201 Portage Ave, Manitoba, R3B 3K6 ☏ 204/940-1800

In Ireland

Dublin 42 Elgin Rd, Ballsbridge ☏ 01/668 8777, ⊛ www.dublin.usembassy.gov

In New Zealand

Online ⊛ www.newzealand.usembassy.gov
Auckland Citibank Building, 3rd floor, 23 Customs St ☏ 09/303 2724
Wellington 29 Fitzherbert Terrace, Thorndon ☏ 04/462 6112

In South Africa

Online ⊛ www.southafrica.usembassy.gov
Cape Town 2 Reddam Ave, Westlake 7945 ☏ 021/421 4280
Durban Old Mutual Building, 31st floor, 303 West St 4001 ☏ 031/305 7600
Johannesburg 1 River St, Killarney 2041 ☏ 011/644 8000
Pretoria 877 Pretorius St, Arcadia 0083 ☏ 012/431 4000

In the UK

Online ⊛ www.usembassy.org.uk
London 24 Grosvenor Square, W1A 1AE ☏ 020/7499 9000; visa hotline (£1.50/min) ☏ 09061/500590
Belfast Danesfort House, 223 Stranmillis Rd, Belfast BT9 5GR ☏ 028/9038 6100
Edinburgh 3 Regent Terrace, EH7 5BW ☏ 0131/556 8315

Foreign consulates in San Francisco

Australia 625 Market St, Financial District (Mon–Fri 8.45am–1pm & 2–4.45pm; ☏ 415/536-1970)
Ireland 100 Pine St, Financial District (Mon–Fri 10am–noon & 2–3.30pm; ☏ 415/392-4214)
New Zealand Suite 400, One Maritime Plaza, Embarcadero (appointment only; ☏ 415/399-1255)
UK 1 Sansome St, Financial District (Mon–Fri 8.30am–5pm; ☏ 415/617-1300)

Gay and lesbian travelers

San Francisco is one of the most **gay-friendly** cities in the world, with around ten percent of its population openly "out." Consequently, it is extremely rare to encounter prejudice in the Bay Area when displaying affection for a member of the same sex. Specifically gay areas such as the Castro (see p.124) are covered in the text and there is a whole chapter of gay listings (see p.235). The issue of active gay politics is also covered in Contexts (see p.402).

Health

Foreign travelers should be comforted to learn that if you have a serious accident while in San Francisco, emergency services will get to you sooner and charge you later. For emergencies, dial toll-free ☎911 on any phone. If you have medical or dental problems that don't require an ambulance, most hospitals have a walk-in emergency room: for your nearest hospital, check with your hotel or dial information at ☎411. Some of the main hospitals are listed below.

Should you need to see a doctor, lists can be found in the *Yellow Pages* under "Clinics" or "Physicians and Surgeons." Be aware that even consultations are costly, usually around $75–100 each visit, which is payable in advance. Keep receipts for any part of your medical treatment, including prescriptions, so that you can claim against your insurance once you're home.

For minor ailments, stop by a **pharmacy**: we've listed some that are open 24 hours below. Foreign visitors should note that many medicines available over the counter at home – codeine-based painkillers, for one – are prescription only in the US. Bring additional supplies if you're particularly brand loyal.

Travelers do not require **inoculations** to enter the US, though you may need certificates of vaccination if you're en route from cholera- or typhoid-infected areas in Asia or Africa – check with your doctor before you leave.

Hospitals

The San Francisco General Hospital, 1001 Potrero Ave at 23rd, Potrero Hill (☎415/206-8000 or 206-8111 emergency), has a 24-hour emergency walk-in service. Castro-Mission Health Center, 3850 17th St at Prosper, Mission (☎415/487-7500), offers a drop-in medical service with charges on a sliding scale depending on income, plus free contraception and pregnancy testing. California Pacific (formerly Davies) Medical Center, Castro and Duboce streets, Lower Haight (☎415/565-6060), has 24-hour emergency care and a doctors' referral service. Haight-Ashbury Free Clinic, 558 Clayton St at Haight, Haight-Ashbury, provides a general health-care service with special services for women and detoxification, by appointment only (☎415/487-5632, phones answered Mon–Wed 9am–9pm, Thurs 1–9pm, Fri 1–5pm except from 12.30–1pm & 5.30–6pm).

Pharmacies

Walgreens 24-hour pharmacies 498 Castro St at 18th, Castro (☎415/861-6276); 3201 Divisadero St at Lombard, Marina (☎415/931-6415).

Insurance

Although not compulsory, international travelers should have some form of **travel insurance**. The US has no national health-care system, and prices for even minor medical treatment can be shocking. It's wise to verify if benefits will be paid during treatment or only after your return home, and whether there is a 24-hour medical emergency phone number. If you need to make a claim, keep receipts for medicines and medical treatment. Also, if you have anything stolen from you, you must obtain an official statement from the police.

A typical travel insurance policy also provides coverage for the **loss of baggage**, tickets, and a certain amount of cash or traveler's cheques, as well as the cancellation or curtailment of your trip. Most policies exclude so-called **dangerous sports** unless an extra premium is paid; in the Bay Area, this can apply to rock climbing, windsurfing, and even off-road mountain-biking. Therefore, if you're planning to do water sports or similar activities, you'll most likely have to pay extra. Before buying travel insurance, American and Canadian citizens should check that they're not already covered. Credit-card companies, home-insurance policies, and private medical plans sometimes cover you and your belongings when you're traveling.

Most travel agents, tour operators, banks, and insurance brokers will be able to help you, or you could consider the travel insurance offered by Rough Guides (see box p.39).

Internet

There's free **Internet access** at almost all the hostels listed on p.153, and most hotels, but there's often a wait to get on a machine; likewise, the Public Library offers fifteen minutes' free access, but again often with a long wait. You can pick up an exhaustive list of almost every Internet café for free from the information desk or check at ⓦwww.world66 .com/northamerica/unitedstates/california /sanfranciscobayarea/sanfrancisco/cyber cafes. Most cafés in the city are tech-savvy enough to offer **wireless access** for laptop-toters, albeit often at a fee – check ⓦwww .zrnetservice.com for locations; it's also worth checking ⓦwww.metrofreefi.com for sites, from cafes and public parks, which offer free Wi Fi.

Laundry

There's a **laundromat** on nearly every other residential block in town. Two standouts are Brainwash, 1122 Folsom St at Langton, SoMa (☎415/861-3663), a combo bar-and-laundromat, and The Little Hollywood Launderette, 1906 Market St at Guerrero, Mission (☎415/252-9357), which is open until midnight, with last wash at 10.45pm. There's no better **drycleaners** in town than Gary's, 1782 Haight St at Shrader, Haight-Ashbury (☎415/387-2035).

Mail

Ordinary **mail** sent within the US currently costs 42¢ for letters weighing up to an ounce, while standard postcards cost 27¢. Letters that don't carry the zip code are liable to get lost or at least delayed; phone books carry a list for their service area and post offices – even abroad – have directories. There's also a handy zip-code finder at ⓦwww.usps.com. For most destinations outside the US, airmail letters cost 90¢ up to an ounce and 72¢ for postcards and aerogrammes. Airmail between the US and Europe may take a week and 12–14 days to Australasia.

You can collect general delivery mail (post restante) from the main post office, 101 Hyde St at Fulton, Civic Center (Mon–Fri 8.30am–5.30pm, Sat 10am–2pm; ☎1-800/275-8777); tell whoever's sending you something to address it with your name, c/o General Delivery, San Francisco, CA 94142. Make sure you take ID with you to collect it. Letters will be held for only ten days before being returned to sender, so make sure there's a return address on the envelope. If you're receiving mail at someone else's address, it should include "c/o" and the regular occupant's name; otherwise it too is likely to be returned. Two other post offices, with general delivery facilities, are at Sutter Street Station, 150 Sutter St at Montgomery, Financial District (Mon–Fri 8.30am–5pm), and Rincon Finance Station, 180 Steuart St at Mission, SoMa (Mon–Fri 7am–6pm, Sat 9am–2pm).

Maps

The maps in this book, along with the free city plans you can pick up from the SFCVB in its *Visitors Planning Guide*, will be sufficient to help you find your way around. If you want something more comprehensive, the *Rough Guide Map to San Francisco* is unbeatable ($12.99) – the waterproof paper will last through even the worst of the city's unpredictable weather, and the attractions, restaurants, and hotels we've listed in the book are all clearly marked.

The best place in town for any and all things travel-related is Get Lost Travel Books

(☎415/437-0529, ⓦwww.getlostbooks .com), 1825 Market St between Valencia and Guererro, on the eastern outskirts of the Castro. If you'll be traveling around the Bay Area, Rand McNally produces good commercial state maps for around $5 each. The American Automobile Association (☎1-800/222-4357, ⓦwww.aaa.com) provides free maps and assistance to its members, and to British members of the AA and RAC.

For details on how best to orient yourself in the city, see p.26.

Money

US currency comes in bills of $1, $5, $10, $20, $50, and $100. All are the same size, so check bills carefully. The dollar is made up of 100 cents in coins of 1 cent (a penny), 5 cents (a nickel), 10 cents (a dime), and 25 cents (a quarter). Change (quarters are the most useful) is needed for buses, vending machines, and public telephones, though automatic machines are increasingly fitted with slots for dollar bills.

As for **exchange rates**, at the time of writing, one pound sterling will buy $1.95–$2; one euro fetches $1.55–1.60; one Canadian dollar is almost identical in value with the US dollar; one Australian dollar is worth around 95¢; and one New Zealand dollar is worth almost 80¢; one South African rand yields about 13¢.

Banks and ATMs

With an ATM card (and PIN number) you'll have access to cash from machines all over San Francisco, though as anywhere, you will be charged a $1.50–4 fee for using a different bank's ATM network. Foreign cash-dispensing cards linked to international networks such as Cirrus and Plus are accepted at just about any ATM and the respective symbol will be on display at the machine. To find the location of the nearest ATM in the Bay Area, call: Amex ☎1-800/227-4669, Plus ☎1-800/843-7587 or Cirrus ☎1-800/424-7787.

Most **banks** in San Francisco are open Monday to Friday from 9am to 3pm and a few open on Saturday from 9am to noon. For banking services – particularly currency exchange – outside normal business hours and on weekends, try major hotels: the rate won't be as good, but it's the best option in a tight financial corner.

Travelers' checks

Travelers' checks should be bought in US dollars only – they are universally accepted as cash in stores or restaurants, as long as you have a photo ID. It's best to bring them in smaller denominations, as some stores will balk at cashing a $100 check. The usual fee for travelers' check sales is one or two percent, though this fee may be waived if you buy the checks through a bank where you have an account. You can also buy checks by phone or online with Thomas Cook and American Express.

Credit and debit cards

For many services in the US, it's simply taken for granted that you'll be paying with plastic. When renting a car or checking into a hotel, you will be asked to show a **credit card** –

Wiring money

Having money wired from home is never convenient or cheap and should be considered a last resort. The quickest way to do this is to have someone take cash to the office of a money-wiring service and have it wired to the office nearest you: in the US, this process should take less than fifteen minutes. You take along ID and pick up the money in cash. Among reliable companies offering this service are **Moneygram International** (ⓦwww.moneygram.com) and, for rather higher fees, **Western Union** (ⓦwww.westernunion.com). If you have a few days' leeway, sending a postal money order through the mail is cheaper; postal orders are exchangeable at any post office. The equivalent for foreign travelers is the international money order but it may take up to seven days to arrive by mail. An ordinary check sent from overseas takes two to three weeks to clear.

even if you intend to settle the bill in cash. Most major credit cards issued by foreign banks are honored in the US: locally, Visa, MasterCard, American Express, and Discover are the most widely used. If you use your credit card at an ATM, remember that all cash advances are treated as loans with interest accruing daily from the date of withdrawal; there will also be a transaction fee on top of this. Not all foreign **debit cards** are valid for transactions in shops in the US.

Visa TravelMoney is a disposable prepaid debit card with a PIN that works in all ATMs that take Visa cards. When your funds are depleted, you simply throw the card away. Since you can buy up to nine cards to access the same funds – useful for couples or families traveling together – it's a good idea to buy at least one extra as a backup in case of loss or theft. You can call a 24-hour toll-free customer service number in the US (☏1-800/847-2911), or visit the Visa Travel-Money website (🌐usa.visa.com). The card is available in most countries from branches of Thomas Cook and Citicorp.

Phones

Greater San Francisco has a single area code – ☏415, and calls within this code are treated as local. You only need to dial the seven digits of the number (no area code) when calling within ☏415. The rest of the Bay Area has no fewer than five codes: East

Bay (☏510 and ☏925), Wine Country (☏707), Palo Alto (☏650), San Jose (☏408). To phone one area code from another, you'll have to dial a 1 before the number; toll-free calls (prefixed ☏800, ☏866, ☏877, or ☏888) also require a 1, no matter where you're calling from. Detailed information about calls, codes, and rates in the Bay Area can be found at the front of the telephone directory in the *White Pages*.

In general, telephoning direct from your hotel room is considerably more expensive than using a payphone, costing up to $1 for a local call, though some hotels offer free local calls. Don't even think of calling abroad direct from a hotel phone – you'll be charged a small fortune. Without doubt, the cheapest way of making **international calls** is to buy a pre-paid **phonecard** with a scratch-off PIN number, available from newsagents and some groceries. These come in denominations of $5 and $10 and can be used from any touchpad phone – hotels rarely charge for accessing the freephone number (but check), although using them from payphones invariably incurs an extra charge or around 50¢. Rates vary but calls to most developed countries only cost a few cents a minute. Another convenient but pricier way of phoning home from abroad is via a telephone **charge card** from your phone company back home. Using a PIN number, you can make calls from most hotel, public, and

---

Useful telephone numbers

Emergencies ☏911 for fire, police, or ambulance
Directory enquiries for toll-free numbers ☏1-800/555-1212
Local and long-distance directory assistance information ☏411
Operator ☏0

International calls to San Francisco
Your country's international access code + 1 for the US + appropriate area code + phone number.

International calls from San Francisco
Remember to leave out the initial 0 of the local area code whenever calling home.
Australia ☏011 + 61 + phone number
Canada ☏011 + 1 + phone number
New Zealand ☏011 + 64 + phone number
Republic of Ireland ☏011 + 353 + phone number
South Africa ☏011 + 27 + phone number
UK and Northern Ireland ☏011 + 44 + phone number

private phones that will be charged to your account: check with your service provider.

Mobile phones

If you are planning to take a **mobile phone** (universally known as cell phones in America) from outside of the USA, you'll need to check with your service provider whether it will work in the country. Unless you have a **tri-band** or **quad-band** phone, it is unlikely that a mobile bought for use outside the US will work there. If you do have such a phone, you'll have to contact your service provider's customer care department to ensure it is enabled for international calls. Be aware that you will incur hefty roaming charges for making calls and also be charged extra for incoming calls, as the people calling you will be paying the usual rate. If you want to retrieve messages while you're away, ask your provider for a new access code, as your home one is unlikely to work abroad. As the cost of using mobiles abroad is still fairly prohibitive, you may want to rent a phone if you're traveling to the US. For a comprehensive overview of the capabilities of various phones and a useful database of roaming charges, check out Ⓦ www.mediacells.com.

Opening hours and public holidays

The opening hours of specific visitor attractions, monuments, memorials, stores, and offices are given in the relevant accounts throughout the Guide. Telephone numbers are provided so that you can check current information with the places themselves.

Opening hours

San Francisco might not be a 24-hour city quite like New York and many locals finish work and eat early, yet outside of the Financial District you will find many stores open until 9pm and restaurants in areas such as North Beach, Union Square, Chinatown, and the Mission serve food till at least 10–11pm.

Tourist attractions are usually amenable – most museums will be open 10am–6pm and a few art galleries stay open until 9pm or so once a month. Smaller, private museums

close for one day a week, usually Monday or Tuesday.

Public holidays

On the national **public holidays** listed below, banks and government offices are liable to be closed all day, stores less certainly so. The traditional summer **tourism season**, when many attractions have extended opening hours, runs from Memorial Day to Labor Day.

San Francisco has a huge variety of special **festivals**, which can be found in Chapter 15, "Festivals and events." Remember that during some of these events, especially Pride, hotels and hostels will book up quickly so make sure to arrange accommodation well in advance.

National holidays

January 1 New Year's Day;
January 3rd Monday Dr Martin Luther King Jr's Birthday
February 3rd Monday President's Day
May Last Monday Memorial Day
July 4 Independence Day
September 1st Monday Labor Day
October 2nd Monday Columbus Day
November 11 Veterans' Day;
November 4th Thursday Thanksgiving Day
December 25 Christmas Day

Senior travelers

Any US citizen or permanent resident aged **62 or over** is entitled to free admission for life to all national parks, monuments, and historic sites, using a Golden Age Passport, for which a once-only $10 fee is charged; it can be issued at any such site. This free entry also applies to any accompanying car passengers or, for those hiking or cycling, to the passport holder's immediate family. It also gives a fifty-percent reduction on fees for camping, parking, and boat launching. Some of these **discounts** are also extended to seniors of other nationalities. As for travel, Amtrak, Greyhound, and many US airlines offer percentage discounts to anyone who can produce ID that proves they're over 62: don't expect hefty price breaks, but it's always worth checking. Museums and art galleries are better, and most will charge a reduced student/seniors rate, often to those 55 or older.

Contacts and resources

American Association of Retired Persons 601 E St NW, Washington, DC 20049 ☏ 202/434-2277 or 1-888/687-2247, ⊛ www.aarp.org. AARP can provide discounts on accommodation and vehicle rental. Membership open to US and Canadian residents aged 50 or over for an annual fee of US $12.50.
Elderhostel 75 Federal St, Boston, MA 02110 ☏ 1-877/426-8056, ⊛ www.elderhostel.org. Runs an extensive worldwide network of educational and activity programs, cruises, and homestays for people over 60 (companions may be younger). Programs generally last a week or more and costs are in line with those of commercial tours.
Saga Holidays 222 Berkeley St, Boston, MA 02116 ☏ 1-800/343-0723 or 617/262-2262, ⊛ www.sagaholidays.com. Specializes in worldwide group travel for seniors, with a few domestic trips. Saga's Road Scholar coach tours and their Smithsonian Odyssey Tours to US parks have a more educational slant.

Time

San Francisco, like the rest of California, operates on **Pacific Standard Time**, which is eight hours behind GMT and three hours behind the east coast. Note that Daylight Saving Time has recently changed across the US, so that clocks now go forward an hour at 2am on the second Sunday of March and do not go back until 2am on the first Sunday of November.

Tipping

When working out your daily budget, allow for **tipping**, which is universally expected. You really shouldn't depart a bar or restaurant without leaving a tip of at least fifteen percent (unless the service is utterly disgusting); twenty percent is more like it in upmarket places. About the same amount should be added to taxi fares – and round them up to the nearest 50 cents or dollar. A hotel porter should get $1 a bag, $3–5 for lots of baggage; chambermaids $1–2 a day; valet parking attendants $1.

Tourist information

The main source of city information for tourists is the San Francisco Visitors Information Center (see below for details). Contact it or visit its website before your trip for brochures, maps, guides, and event calendars; once in San Francisco, you can visit its walk-in branches. There are also several excellent Bay Area-related websites with current information on tours, museums, and the newest restaurants and clubs.

Before leaving for the Bay Area, consider contacting the organizations listed under "Tourist offices" below to help plan your sightseeing itinerary. Upon arrival, maps and information are available from desks in the airports and at most hotels. Your best first stop, though, is the superb **San Francisco Visitors Information Center**, on the lower level of Hallidie Plaza at the end of the cable-car line on Market Street (Mon–Fri 9am–5pm, Sat–Sun 9am–3pm, closed Sun Nov–April; ☏ 415/283-0177, ⊛ www.onlyinsanfrancisco .com). Its staff are exceptionally knowledgeable, and it has free maps of the city and Bay Area, as well as pamphlets on hotels and restaurants. The center can also help with lodging through its toll-free reservation service (☏ 1-888/782-9673). Pick up a copy of the *San Francisco Visitors Planning Guide* – terrific for museums and attractions, although less comprehensive on lodging and dining (it lists only SFCVB members). You can also purchase the City Pass ($54; ⊛ www.citypass.net) at the center. This bargain ticket is valid for entry to the Exploratorium, the Legion of Honor, Steinhart Aquarium and Academy of Sciences, San Francisco Museum of Modern Art (SFMoMA), and passage on a Blue & Gold Fleet San Francisco Bay cruise – all that, plus a free week's pass on MUNI (see p.26). Another, slightly less handy option are Go Cards (⊛ www.gocardusa.com). These work rather differently: the price is higher because the card doesn't just offer one-time, but rather multiple, admissions to any of over 45 different local sights, including tours outside of the city as well as standards like SFMoMA. It's priced in one-, two-, three-, five- or seven-day bundles, and runs to $50–132 per adult.

Another great source for listings once you're in San Francisco are the weekly freesheets, including *SF Weekly*, *San Francisco Bay Guardian*, and *The Onion*. For

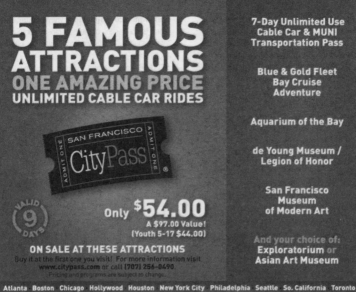

information on these and other publications, see p.33.

State and city tourist offices

Berkeley Convention and Visitors Bureau
2015 Center St, Berkeley ☎510/549-7040,
⊛www.visitberkeley.com
California Travel and Tourism Commission
☎1-800/GO-CALIF, ⊛www.visitcalifornia.com
Marin County Visitors Bureau 1013 Larkspur
Landing Circle, Larkspur ☎415/499-5000, ⊛www
.visitmarin.org
Oakland Convention and Visitors Bureau 463
11th St ☎510/839-9000, ⊛www.oaklandcvb.com
San Francisco Visitors Information Center 900
Market St at Hallidie Plaza, Union Square
☎415/283-0177, ⊛www.onlyinsanfrancisco.com

Travelers with disabilities

San Francisco actively caters to the needs of **disabled travelers**. All public buildings, including hotels and restaurants, are required to have wheelchair-accessible entrances and bathrooms, and the public transit system has kneeling buses to let people aboard – check the comprehensive listings at *Access Northern California* for full details (⊛www.accessnca.com). The one unavoidable disadvantage is steep hills like Nob, Russian, and Potrero: MUNI buses are a solution for any tough gradients.

Resources

There are several excellent resources for **wheelchair-accessible** accommodation in the city: aside from *Access Northern California*, which rates hotels and sights, the San Francisco Convention and Visitors Bureau produces a free 34-page brochure, *Access San Francisco*, aimed at disabled travelers (☎415/283-0177 or 415/227-2619 TDD, ⊛www.onlyinsanfrancisco.com/plan_your _trip/access_guide.asp). It offers detailed access information on more than 150 San Francisco hotels, restaurants, museums, and attractions, also on public transportation; pick it up from the main Visitors Center on Hallidie Plaza, or download from the site directly. The main *Visitors Planning Guide* also includes a special section highlighting hotels that have exceptionally good facilities for disabled visitors. Another terrific resource is the Independent Living Resource Center (☎415/543-6222, ⊛www.freed.org), a longstanding disabled advocacy group that can provide similar information.

Websites

The following is a selective list of San Francisco-related websites to help get you started.

craigslist ⓦ www.craigslist.org. This definitive community website (now operating microsites around the world) began – and is still best – in San Francisco. A terrific resource for everything from jobs to concert tickets.

511.org ⓦ www.511.org. A wealth of up-to-the-minute information on Bay Area transit, traffic, and bicycling. A crucial resource if you plan to venture beyond (or just within) San Francisco.

Mister SF ⓦ www.mistersf.com. An eclectic and well-researched site that's a wonderful repository of San Francisco history.

San Francisco Arts ⓦ www.sfarts.org. Comprehensive arts listings.

San Francisco Magazine ⓦ www.sanfranmag .com. Online version of the local glossy, complete with feature stories. Definitely geared toward the city's "good life."

SFist ⓦ www.sfist.com. Populist, often snarky news and culture site. Writers have a ball covering all things San Francisco, from MUNI meltdowns and City Hall gossip to entertainment picks and slice-of-life essays on local goings-on. Highly recommended.

SF Station ⓦ www.sfstation.com. A top online source for local listings – opinionated, up to date, and easy to use. Especially reliable on nightlife.

The Virtual Museum of the City of San Francisco ⓦ www.sfmuseum.org. An exhaustive source of historical information about the city.

The City

The City

Downtown San Francisco

D ense with history and humanity, **DOWNTOWN SAN FRANCISCO** comprises several vibrantly distinct neighborhoods jammed together between the waterfront and the hills. Most of what the locals call Downtown is clustered within a square mile or two around the northern side of **Market Street** – San Francisco's main commercial and traffic drag, which cuts a diagonal swath across the city's northeastern corner. The area ends abruptly at the edge of San Francisco Bay, where vistas across the water and beyond have come into clear view since the demolition of the Embarcadero Freeway in the early 1990s.

At the heart of it all sits **Union Square**, one of San Francisco's liveliest urban spaces. As the city's main hotel and shopping district, and the junction of its major transportation lines (including cable cars), it makes a logical starting point for wandering Downtown. Immediately west of Union Square, the somewhat quieter **Theater District** is full of old theaters and hotels. Along the waterfront stands the elegant **Embarcadero**, anchored by the Ferry Building and its immensely popular marketplace; the district mostly rests on landfill, partially composed of the remains of ships abandoned by eager forty-niners during the Gold Rush. The Embarcadero rims San Francisco's stalwart **Financial District**, to the northwest of which, **Jackson Square**'s historical district is home to several of the city's original structures dating from the mid-nineteenth century. Slightly further from the water, you'll find **Portsmouth Square**, the site of San Francisco's founding, now all but submerged into frenetic Chinatown, an enclave boasting authentic pockets of Chinese culture, despite rampant tourism.

As with most of central San Francisco, **walking** is the best means of exploration. It's possible, albeit exhausting, to cover the entire Downtown area in a day, but unless you're on the tightest of schedules, you'll get much more out of Downtown (and indeed all of San Francisco) just ambling around.

Union Square and around

A major hub of Downtown San Francisco, the **UNION SQUARE** district is filled with stores, hotels, and flocks of tourists. The plaza itself occupies the entire block north of Geary between Stockton and Powell streets, and was radically

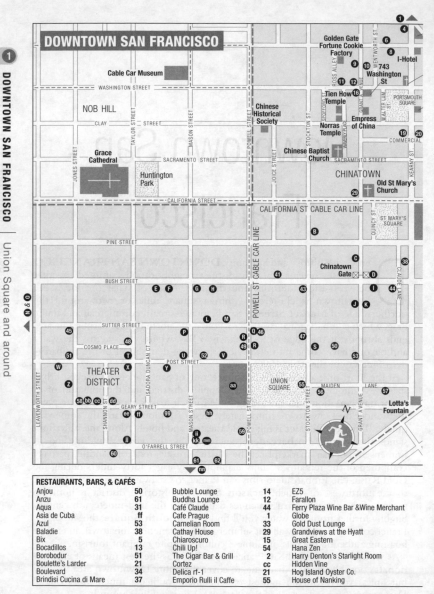

DOWNTOWN SAN FRANCISCO

Cable Car Museum

NOB HILL

CLAY STREET

WASHINGTON STREET

Grace Cathedral

Huntington Park

SACRAMENTO STREET

CALIFORNIA STREET

Golden Gate Fortune Cookie Factory

I-Hotel

743 Washington St

Tien How Temple

PORTSMOUTH SQUARE

Chinese Historical Society

Empress of China

Norras Temple

Chinese Baptist Church

CHINATOWN

Old St Mary's Church

COMMERCIAL

CALIFORNIA ST CABLE CAR LINE

ST MARY'S SQUARE

PINE STREET

Chinatown Gate

BUSH STREET

SUTTER STREET

COSMO PLACE

POST STREET

THEATER DISTRICT

UNION SQUARE

MAIDEN LANE

Lotta's Fountain

GEARY STREET

SHANNON ST

O'FARRELL STREET

POWELL ST CABLE CAR LINE

RESTAURANTS, BARS, & CAFÉS				
Anjou	50	Bubble Lounge	14	EZ5
Anzu	61	Buddha Lounge	12	Farallon
Aqua	31	Café Claude	44	Ferry Plaza Wine Bar &Wine Merchant
Asia de Cuba	ff	Cafe Prague	1	Globe
Azul	53	Carnelian Room	33	Gold Dust Lounge
Baladie	38	Cathay House	29	Grandviews at the Hyatt
Bix	5	Chiaroscuro	15	Great Eastern
Bocadillos	13	Chili Up!	54	Hana Zen
Borobodur	51	The Cigar Bar & Grill	2	Harry Denton's Starlight Room
Boulette's Larder	21	Cortez	cc	Hidden Vine
Boulevard	34	Delica rf-1	21	Hog Island Oyster Co.
Brindisi Cucina di Mare	37	Emporio Rulli il Caffe	55	House of Nanking

transformed with the 2002 unveiling of its new, open layout, which replaced the hedge-divided expanse once popular with homeless sleepers. Today, edged by stout palm trees and sprinkled with potted foliage and plenty of seating, it's an ideal place to take a break from the surrounding bustle, although its reliance on granite appears out of step with San Francisco's typically grassy public spaces.

Union Square takes its name from its role as a gathering place for Unionist supporters on the eve of the Civil War, so it's confusing that the 97-foot column

Columbus Tower		GOLD ST.			Pier One
JACKSON SQUARE				Ferry Building	
Buddha's Universal Church			Maritime Plaza		
Chinese Culture Center			Embarcadero Center	JUSTIN HERMAN PLAZA	
Transamerica Pyramid					
Bank of America Center	FINANCIAL DISTRICT		Embarcadero (MUNI/BART)		

ACCOMMODATION

Adagio	cc	JW Marriot	U
Adelaide Hostel	dd	Kensington Park	V
The Andrews Hotel	T	King George	ii
Baldwin	J	Larkspur Hotel Union Square	M
Beresford	P	Hotel Metropolis	nn
Beresford Arms	W	Monaco	ee
Best Western Hotel California	bb	Orchard Garden Hotel	D
Campton Place	S	Pacific Tradewinds Backpacker Hostel	A
Hotel Carlton	O	Petite Auberge	E
Chancellor Hotel	R	Prescott Hotel	Y
Clift Hotel	ff	Hotel Rex	L
Hotel des Arts	I	Ritz-Carlton	B
Hotel Diva	gg	Serrano Hotel	jj
Hotel Frank	hh	Sir Francis Drake	Q
The Golden Gate Hotel	G	Spaulding Hotel	mm
Grant Hotel	H	Triton	K
Grant Plaza	C	USA Hostel	X
Halcyon Hotel	Z	Westin St Francis	aa
HI-San Francisco Downtown	kk	White Swan Inn	F
		Hotel Vertigo	N

20	Hunan Homes	6	Michael Mina	aa	Sam Wo	16
52	Il Massimo del Panino	17	Millennium	58	Sam's Grill	42
21	Jai Yun	18	Mocca	56	San Francisco Soup Company	40
3	Jeanty at Jack's	24	One Market	26	Schroeder's	28
59	Kokkari	7	Osha Thai	22	Sears Fine Food	49
47	La Salsa	27	Otis	57	Silks	35
8	Le Colonial	48	Perbacco	32	The Slanted Door	21
62	Li Po Cocktail Lounge	10	Plouf	36	Tadich Grill	30
46	The London Wine Bar	23	R&G Lounge	19	Taylor's Automatic Refresher	21
T	Lucky Creation	11	Red Room	45	Ten Ren Tea Company	9
21	Masa's	41	Redwood Room	ff	Tunnel Top	43
4	Mela	60	Rubicon	25	Voda	39

rising from its center should celebrate an 1898 victory in the Spanish–American War. The square was built under the direction of Mayor John White Geary, where a massive sand dune known as O'Farrell's Mountain once stood. The first American leader of San Francisco, Geary bequeathed the land to the city for use as a public plaza in 1850. To level off the dune, all excess sand was shipped over to the seafront and used to fill Yerba Buena Cove, in the process helping create what is now the Financial District.

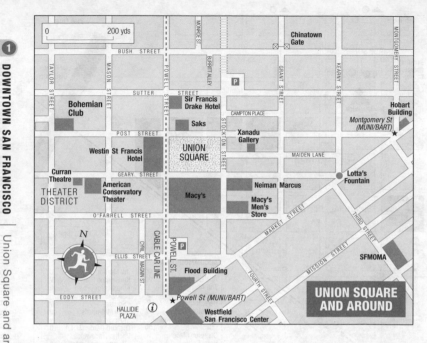

The square is now the nexus of one of the most profitable shopping areas in the country, as well as the home of the city's Christmas tree each holiday season, a tradition started back in the mid-1800s by local kook Joshua Norton (see box, p.53). Below the square sits the world's first underground parking garage, opened in 1942; in its earliest days, it doubled as an air-raid shelter. A large stage sits adjacent to the Post Street side of the plaza, while a roll call of San Francisco leaders – pre-cityhood *alcaldes,* as well as mayors – is etched into a granite slab at the plaza's far northeast corner, although reading the vertical rendering of names and dates may give you neck ache.

On the western face of the square, just across Powell Street, the opulent **Westin St Francis Hotel** is steeped in some of San Francisco's darkest lore. In 1950, Al Jolson died here while playing poker, and just outside, in 1975, President Gerald Ford was nearly assassinated by ex-FBI agent Sara Jane Moore. The hotel still attracts its fair share of visiting bigwigs – whose nations' flags are hoisted out front during their stays – as well as big-spenders with reservations at the hotel's celebrated restaurant, *Michael Mina* (see p.166), just inside the Powell Street entrance. Parts of **Dashiell Hammett**'s detective stories, including *The Maltese Falcon*, were set in the *Westin St Francis*, where the writer had worked as a private investigator in San Francisco during the 1920s. Indeed, he was part of the team that investigated the rape and murder case against silent film star Fatty Arbuckle when a starlet died after a debauched party in the actor's suite at the hotel in 1921. Fans of Hammett will want to step inside *John's Grill*, at 63 Ellis St at Stockton, the favorite dining spot of Hammett's rugged hero Sam Spade, and also frequented by Hammett himself. Up on Burritt Alley, two blocks north of Union Square plaza, a casually surreal plaque marks the spot where Spade's partner, Miles Archer, was shot and killed by *femme fatale* Brigid O'Shaughnessy in the opening moments of *The Maltese Falcon*.

Immediately east of the square and usually closed to vehicles, **Maiden Lane** is dotted with gourmet sidewalk cafés and filled with designer stores – a far cry from the latter half of the 1800s, when it was the vice-ridden heart of the city. Morton Street, as it was then known, was choked with bordellos since, in a pirouette of hypocrisy, local lawmakers decided that rather than eradicating prostitution, they would instead relegate it to side streets where the brothels would be found only by those looking for them. After the 1906 earthquake and fire leveled the street and drove away its shady denizens, it went through several name changes until, without a trace of irony, it was christened Maiden Lane in 1922. Aside from the small jazz ensembles (or odd accordionist) performing for street-table diners, there's one other sight worth noting here: the only **Frank Lloyd Wright**-designed building in San Francisco, at no. 140. Its squat exterior of pale brickwork vaguely resembles an ancient temple and lacks Wright's usual obsession with horizontal lines; the interior, however, is extraordinary, with porthole openings in the walls and a gloriously sweeping ramp that's a clear precursor to Wright's famed Guggenheim Museum in New York. Opened in 1948 to house the V.C. Morris Gift Shop, it's now occupied by Xanadu Gallery (Tues–Sat 10am–6pm; ☎415/392-9999, ⓦ www.folkartintl.com), which specializes in premium Asian art pieces.

Along Market Street

Two blocks east of Union Square amidst the intersection of Market and Kearny Streets sits the caramel-colored – and dry – **Lotta's Fountain**. Reconstructed in 1916 and beautifully restored in 1999, this landmark is named in honor of the actress Lotta Crabtree, who gifted the contraption to her adoptive city in 1875. The fountain was originally intended to provide water to pedestrians and

The Last Emperor

Joshua Norton arrived in San Francisco during the Gold Rush in 1849. Like most other successful entrepreneurs of the time, he didn't mine gold himself, but focused on real estate and commodity speculation through which he amassed an enormous fortune. After failing to corner the rice market in 1854, however, he declared bankruptcy, and vanished.

Five years later, the eccentric and wily Norton reappeared. Gambling on the power of notoriety, he marched into the offices of the *San Francisco Bulletin* dressed in lavish military dress, including a plumed hat, sabre, and epaulettes, and proclaimed himself "Emperor of the United States", a statement the editor printed on the front page. (A month later, Norton added the title Protector of Mexico.) His Imperial Palace was a tiny room in a boarding house at 642 Commercial St, and he lived off the currency of his fame – literally, since a local printer started producing 10-, 25-, and 50-cent bills of Emperor Norton money, which most local businesses accepted. He became a mascot for the city and was allocated official funds to replace his uniform each year; local restaurants eagerly claimed that Emperor Norton ate there.

Master of the publicity stunt and brilliantly balanced on the knife edge between nutty and notorious, Norton began issuing headline-grabbing edicts at regular intervals. Among the countless proclamations were a proposal to President Lincoln suggesting he wed Queen Victoria to cement relations between the US and UK, and a call for the building of a bridge to Oakland (prefiguring a route that was realized 75 years later with the completion of the Bay Bridge). He was also said to be the inspiration for the character of the King in Mark Twain's *The Adventures of Huckleberry Finn*. When he died, suddenly, in 1880, his funeral attracted 30,000 locals who followed the procession of his coffin through the city streets.

▲ Union Square, looking onto the Westin St Francis Hotel

horses (the horse troughs were removed decades ago), but it gained fame for providing a very different form of relief in the wake of the quake and fire of 1906, as families used it as an impromptu message center where they could post news of loved ones lost or missing.

The one place in San Francisco through which almost every visitor will pass is **Hallidie Plaza**, three blocks south of Union Square at the junction of Powell and Market streets. The main **San Francisco Visitors Information Center** (Mon–Fri 9am–5pm, Sat & Sun 9am–3pm, closed Sun Nov–April; ☎415/283-0177, ⓦwww.onlyinsanfrancisco.com) is located on the plaza's lower level, just outside the Powell BART/MUNI station; it's also the terminus for two cable-car lines that run to the northern waterfront. Hallidie Plaza is a terrific spot from which to admire the grand **Flood Building** at 870 Market St. This flatiron structure was constructed in 1904 by the silver-mining Flood family and was one of the few structures in Downtown to withstand the 1906 calamities. Another beguiling antique tower stands several blocks east at 582–592 Market St: the oddly shaped **Hobart Building**. Built in under a year to fit its asymmetrical polygon site in 1914, the narrow, idiosyncratic edifice became the second tallest building in San Francisco, though its speedy construction sparked safety concerns. It stands to this day, and is now more striking than ever, with its north side exposed following the demolition of a neighboring building in 1984.

The Theater District

The area between Union Square and the grubby Tenderloin is known as the **Theater District,** although most of today's playhouses lack the grandeur of some of the old theaters. Despite its proximity to the tourist hub of the city, the neighborhood is a convenient bolthole from shopping crowds and a secluded place to stay Downtown. The district is anchored by the **American**

The cable cars

The brainchild of **Andrew Hallidie**, an enterprising engineer with an eye for the main chance, San Francisco's cable cars first appeared in 1873. Scots-born Hallidie is said to have been inspired to find an alternative to horse-drawn carriages when he saw a team of horses badly injured while trying to pull a dray up a steep hill in the rain. "My attention was called to the great cruelty and hardship to the horses engaged in that work," he wrote. In fact, his attention was also drawn to the enormous volume of manure produced and how vocally locals complained about the problem. More than equine welfare was under threat – his father had patented a strong wire rope that had been extensively used in the mines of eastern California. As the Gold Rush there slowed, Hallidie needed a new application for his family's signature product, and a privately owned transit system like the cable cars offered the ideal solution.

The cable-car pulley system was dubbed "Hallidie's Folly" by doubtful locals. After the first man hired to be a driver backed out just before the inaugural car ride, Hallidie took the reins himself. Soon the cable-car system had revolutionized the city, launching both a transport and a real-estate revolution. San Francisco's most elevated spots (such as Nob Hill) suddenly became accessible, and businesses and homes were constructed along cable-car routes, spreading the urban landscape westward. At their peak, just before the 1906 earthquake, more than 600 cable cars traveled on eight lines and 112 miles of track throughout the city, reaching a maximum 9.5 mph.

With the onset of the automobile, however, the cable system was vulnerable, largely because of its inefficient use of energy and the frequency with which the stressed wire ropes needing replacing. Use of the cable-car system began to decline when the increased popularity of cars was compounded by the devastation wrought by the quake of 1906, which left large chunks of track wrecked.

When it was rumored that the system would be phased out altogether, local activist Frieda Klussman organized a citizens' committee to save them in the late 1940s. She triumphed nearly two decades later, when the cars were put on the National Register of Historic Places and the remaining seventeen miles of track (now down to ten) were saved in 1966. Now there are 44 cars in use – each unique – and around 23 miles of moving cable underground. System-wide shutdowns in 1979 and 1982–84 prompted managing agency MUNI to begin rebuilding all cars by hand, a process that has taken far longer than the ten years originally estimated, requiring as much as 3000 hours and $275,000 per car.

The **Powell-Mason** and the **Powell-Hyde** lines run from Hallidie Plaza off Union Square to Fisherman's Wharf. The Powell-Hyde line is the steepest, reaching a hair-raising 21-degree grade between Lombard and Chestnut streets – that may not sound so frightening, but wait till you're hanging off the side of the cable car as you take the white-knuckle plunge back downhill seemingly right into the Bay itself. The oldest route, the **California** line, climbs Nob Hill along California Street from the Embarca-dero, rattling past some of the fanciest hotels in the city. During their ascent, cars fasten onto a moving two-inch cable, which runs continuously beneath the streets, then release the cable at the top of each hill to glide down the other side. The cars' conductors are typically a cheerful lot and receptive to passengers' questions, and each boasts a signature bell-ringing style shown off during the Cable Car Bell Ringing Contest, held every July in Union Square. For more on the cars' history and background, visit the **Cable Car Museum and Powerhouse** (see p.67).

There are three line-dodging tips for cable-car riders. First, come early in the day as lines are usually shorter before 10am. Second, if you're here during peak hours, head a block or two north along Powell Street to the top of Union Square since drivers usually leave a bit of extra room on board at the start of the journey. Finally, if the Powell Street lines are just too busy, the California Street line (terminus at California and Market streets) crawling up Nob Hill is less popular and normally line-free.

Conservatory Theater's eponymous performance venue at 415 Geary St, and the **Curran Theatre** immediately next door at 445 Geary. Taking design cues from a Napoleonic palace, ACT's grand, colonnaded Neoclassical building opened in 1910 and was originally known as the Geary Theater. It sustained significant structural damage in the 1989 Loma Prieta earthquake and did not reopen until seven years later; it was renamed in 2006. The Curran dates from 1922 and operated as a vaudeville stage in its earliest days; these days, it hosts crowd-pleasing productions such as *A Chorus Line* and *Hairspray*.

The blocks of Post and Sutter streets cutting through the area are home to some of Downtown's least visible landmarks: some fourteen **private clubs** hidden behind discreet facades. Money isn't the only criterion for membership to these highly esteemed institutions – though being *somebody* usually is. The **Bohemian Club**, 624 Taylor St, is best known for its Bohemian Grove retreat on the Russian River, where ex-presidents and corporate giants assemble for Masonic rituals and schoolboy larks; the San Francisco chapter is housed in a Lewis Hobart Moderne-style building.

The Financial District

The boundaries of San Francisco's **FINANCIAL DISTRICT** have increasingly blurred in recent years, particularly with the spate of new office high-rises that continue to go up south of Market Street. Its western edge abuts Chinatown at Kearny Street, while to the north it quietly fades into the residential towers and inviting parks of the Northeast Waterfront beyond Clay Street. As you'd expect, the often gusty canyons that crisscross its blocks of steel, glass, and granite hum most vigorously on weekdays, particularly around lunchtime. Although the Financial District is more relaxed than it used to be – you'll see a higher percentage of dressed-down office workers than you would have in decades past – it's still ground zero for executives whose suits and spirited gaits uphold the district's Wall Street-of-the-West reputation.

At 555 California St at Kearny sits the ominous hulk of the **Bank of America Center**. Though at 779ft not the city's tallest building, this broad-shouldered monolith of dark granite (depending on natural lighting and your vantage point, it can look either brown or vaguely reddish) dominates the San Francisco skyline and has divided the city into fans and those who would like to see it razed to the ground; the latter doubtless cheered when it was used for exterior shots of the burning skyscraper in *The Towering Inferno*. Completed in 1969, it challenged the city not only with its size, but also with the startling contrast of its hue, as San Francisco used to be known as "a city of white." The *Carnelian Room*, an exclusive, jacket-and-tie restaurant, offers a vertigo-inducing promontory from the 52nd floor.

Around the corner is the **Wells Fargo History Museum**, 420 Montgomery St at California (Mon–Fri 9am–5pm; free; Ⓦ www.wellsfargo.com), with an unnatural amount of wall space devoted to the history of bank robberies. The display of old letters upstairs is more intriguing (Wells Fargo ran the postal service between San Francisco and the Sierra Nevada foothill mines for a short time during the 1890s), as is the plush stagecoach you can clamber into on the second floor.

A surprising amount of impressive public art is scattered about the Financial District. One block south of the Wells Fargo Museum, a pair of sculptures flanks

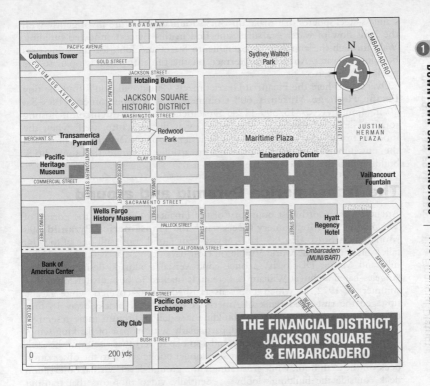

the steps of the imposing **Pacific Coast Stock Exchange** building at 301 Pine St at Sansome. Sculptor Ralph Stockpole designed these giant artworks, jointly entitled *Progress of Man,* on site to complement one another: on the left stands the feminine half of the piece, "Agriculture", while to the far right, its mate "Industry" is represented by masculine figures. The building itself is impressive, its Doric columns beautifully intact, but stick your head inside the hall and you won't see too many frantic neckties, as trading operations were moved entirely to an electronic exchange system in 2002. Following a four-year period of dormancy, the building reopened as a private fitness center that now draws in area workers throughout the day.

Just around the corner, at 155 Sansome St at Pine, take the elevator to the tenth floor of what is now the City Club (a private gathering place for local business bigwigs) for a look at Diego Rivera's early 1930s mural *Riches of California,* his first in the US. Depression-era columnists were bemused at the selection of the decidedly anti-capitalist Rivera to decorate the staircase ceiling of what was then the Pacific Stock Exchange Lunch Club; as with Stockpole's sculptures, themes of agriculture and industry are major elements in the work. The building itself, designed by noted San Franciscan Timothy Pflueger, showcases the finest in Art Deco tendencies, from the indulgent ground-floor lobby to the bronze-framed elevator doors. The security officer in the downstairs lobby may ask as to your business upon entry, but visitors are usually permitted to see the artwork upstairs.

For a more kinetic form of expression, seek out Belgian artist Pol Bury's *L'Octagon* in the lobby of the office tower at 343 Sansome St. The several reflective, stainless-steel spheres that make up Bury's fountain sculpture pivot gently with the light flow of water – a surprising find in this twice-remodeled building. Walk through the entrance on Sacramento Street and look for the shiny orbs bobbing in water. An open-air terrace on the fifteenth floor is open to the public (see box, p.59).

Over near where the Financial District meets Chinatown, you'll find the tiny **Pacific Heritage Museum**, 608 Commercial St at Montgomery (Tues–Sat 10am–4pm; free; ☎415/399-1124, ⓦpacificheritage.citysearch.com), hosting rotating shows of Asian art. The real draw is the structure itself: when the modern, marble-clad office block was built next door, preservationists protected the museum and forced the architect to artfully integrate this squat brick building into the skeleton of the skyscraper.

The Transamerica Pyramid and around

Anchoring the northwest boundary of the Financial District, at the corner of Washington and Montgomery streets, stands the **Transamerica Pyramid**, 600 Montgomery St (☎415/983-4100, ⓦwww.tapyramid.com), still one of the 100 tallest buildings in the world. Visible on clear days from as far as the Napa Valley hills and Mount Diablo, it's a once-controversial landmark designed by Los Angeles-based architect William L. Pereira. It opened to business tenants in the summer of 1972, at which point its crushed quartz-covered white facade upstaged the rust-hued Bank of America Center a few blocks away. Its four triangular sides rise 853ft, and the building is so tall and thin it more resembles a squared-off rocket than a pyramid, particularly with its pair of flanking wings (containing elevator shafts, staircases, and a smoke tower) that rise from the 29th floor. Due to security measures, there's no longer public access to the observation deck on the 27th floor, while frustratingly, the ground-level "virtual observation deck" outside the building's lobby – essentially, video monitors that transmit images from the top of the pyramid's spire – is often in need of repair. Contrary to popular belief, the building is not built on rollers deep beneath the ground; rather, it stands on a steel and concrete foundation designed to move with earthquakes, which helped it remain undamaged in the 1989 temblor.

The Transamerica Pyramid stands on the site of one of San Francisco's greatest lost monuments: the **Montgomery Block**, commemorated by a brass plaque in the lobby. From 1853, when it was built, until 1959, when it was torn down and made into a parking lot, the four-story building was one of the city's important meeting places. Initially built as offices for lawyers, doctors, and businesspeople, it soon evolved into a live-in community of bohemian poets, artists, and political radicals. Rudyard Kipling, Robert Louis Stevenson, Mark Twain, and William Randolph Hearst all rented work space here, and in fact, Twain met a fireman named Tom Sawyer – who later opened a popular San Francisco saloon – in the basement steam baths. Ambrose Bierce, Bret Harte, and Joaquin Miller were frequent visitors to the block's *Bank Exchange* bar and restaurant, while a later habitué was Sun Yat-sen, who ran a local newspaper, *Young China*, from his second-floor office. Rumor has it that Yat-sen wrote the first Chinese constitution here and even orchestrated the successful overthrow of the Manchu (Qing) Dynasty in 1911; a shimmering statue of the man stands three blocks away at St Mary's Square in Chinatown (see p.66).

A block west and north of the Pyramid, you'll find a chapter of more recent history inside the Manilatown Center at the **I-Hotel**, 868 Kearny St at Jackson (Tues–Sat 1–6pm; free; ☎415/399-9580, ⓦwww.manilatown.org). The fourteen-story 2005 incarnation of the International Hotel stands on the site

1

Hidden parks and rooftop gardens

The result of an urban planning policy that requires newly constructed buildings to provide one square foot of open space for every 50ft of commercial space, several semi-obscure public open spaces dot Downtown San Francisco. These humbly sized retreats – far smaller in scale than block-sized parks in the area such as Yerba Buena Gardens, Rincon Park, and Sidney Walton Park – are open to the public during regular business hours (typically Mon–Fri 9am–5pm), although since each is privately owned, accessibility may be subject to the whims of management. Seating is almost always available, and with the exception of 1 Montgomery Roof Garden (which predates the 1985 mandate's signage guidelines), each location described below has a plaque at street level announcing its use as a public open space. In certain cases where access is through a building's lobby, it doesn't hurt to pre-emptively let the security guard know where you're headed, but you shouldn't be hassled too harshly, if at all.

There are over fifteen such spaces around Downtown; these are the most inviting.

Transamerica Redwood Park (Clay St at Sansome). In the immediate shadow of San Francisco's tallest building sits this subtle space flanked by semi-mature redwoods transplanted from the Santa Cruz Mountains south of the city. Two whimsical sculpture pieces – one featuring a small crowd of gravity-defying children jumping through imaginary puddles, the other of frogs leaping about the tiny park's fountain – mingle with workers taking a break in these unlikely woods. It's an utterly unique setting for Northern California's signature tree amidst urban commotion.

343 Sansome Sun Terrace (Sansome St at California). Fleeting views of Treasure Island and Marin County appear through the forest of high-rises that surrounds this promontory. The spacious patio has ample foliage and seating, as well as a colorful obelisk-shaped sculpture by native San Franciscan Joan Brown. Enter through the building's lobby and take the elevator to the fifteenth floor.

1 Montgomery Roof Garden (Montgomery St at Post). Space for this elevated hideaway was created when the top of its building was lopped off in the early 1980s. There's a variety of seasonal plants, a lion-headed fountain, and even a medieval astrolabe at the southeast corner of the plaza, all overlooking the busy confluence of Market, Montgomery, Post, and Second streets. Enter through the lobby of the main building directly below the garden and take the elevator to the top, or via the third floor of Crocker Galleria at 50 Post St (look for the sign on the east side of the center that reads "Roof Garden").

560 Mission Public Space (Mission St at Second). This South of Market nook is wedged between office buildings, but still gets plenty of sun into early afternoon. A number of tables and chairs are available during the day; after hours, you can still have a seat on one of the low stone ledges near the bamboo that rustles in the breeze. Sit and admire the silently mesmerizing sculpture of two round pieces of steel that move with the wind amid the small pool.

1 Sansome Plaza (Sansome St at Sutter). Set in the shell of the circa-1910 Crocker Bank, this glass-canopied atrium boasts stately palms, lots of marble, and plenty of seating. It's an ideal spot if you're looking to relax in the sunlight's warmth, but out of its direct rays.

Empire Park (Commercial St at Montgomery). Near the eastern edge of Chinatown, this slender mini-park slices away from Commercial Street under a latticework flanked by hedges and benches. It abuts an older residential building at its north end, so don't be surprised to see someone's laundry drying on a clothesline a few stories above your head.

of its squat predecessor, which played a pivotal role in this formerly Filipino-dominated stretch of Kearny. The original I-Hotel housed low-income Manong (elderly Filipino males) and Chinese for over fifty years until the building's tenants were forcibly evicted one night in August 1977 following a bitter, protracted battle between tenant-activists and city officials. The old building was eventually razed in 1981; however, plans for additional Financial District office space became mired in red tape and were never realized, and an updated version of the original I-Hotel was finally built as a home for low-income seniors. Today, the ground floor houses a public gallery devoted to community art and the history of Kearny's former identity as the center of Filipino culture in San Francisco.

Finally, where Kearny meets Columbus, look for the distinctive green-copper siding of the **Columbus Tower**, 916 Kearny St, owned by director and San Francisco native Francis Ford Coppola. The building hosts *Cafe Zoetrope* (named for Coppola's production company, American Zoetrope) on its ground floor, decorated with mementos from Coppola's extensive career and Italian paraphernalia.

The Embarcadero

At the northeastern edge of the Financial District, the long stretch of water-front known as **THE EMBARCADERO** has undergone a remarkable transformation in recent years, largely powered by the renovation of the **Ferry Building** at the end of Market Street. The district has become a coveted location, especially for hotels, restaurants, and attractions wishing to take advantage of the spectacular views across San Francisco Bay. It wasn't always this way. Until the 1989 earthquake fatally wounded the double-decker Embarcadero Freeway that blighted the waterfront for over three decades, the area was nothing more than a transport hub; in fact, before the construction of the bridges that connect San Francisco to Oakland and Marin County in the 1930s, the Embarcadero was the main point of arrival for tens of thousands of daily cross-Bay commuters, as well as a teeming port for cargo ships. Once the freeway's demolition was completed, improvements were slowly made to the area: MUNI extended its streetcar lines, Harry Bridges Plaza opened between separated lanes of Embarcadero traffic in front of the Ferry Building, and walkers, runners, and bikers took to the waterfront paths. Several public piers to the north now provide scenic rest stops en route to Fisherman's Wharf (see p.81), while in the other direction lie the South Beach and Mission Bay districts, as well as the San Francisco Giants' AT&T Park (see p.107).

A staple of the new Embarcadero is MUNI's **F-Market line**, which exclusively runs restored streetcars originally from such far-flung cities as Milan, Frankfurt, Philadelphia, and Louisville; often, a car will display a sign giving the year and city in which it made its debut. The vintage streetcars cater mainly to city visitors along the Embarcadero section of the line, which rattles between Fisherman's Wharf and the Castro; disembark at the Steuart stop just south of the Ferry Building to visit the **San Francisco Railway Museum**, 77 Steuart St at Mission (Wed–Sun 10am–6pm; free; ☎415/974-1948, ⊛www.streetcar .org). The small museum, worth a brief visit, opened in 2007 and offers illuminating artifacts of the city's rail history, including such ephemera as bygone fare boxes and traffic signals.

Inland from the waterfront, the area's skyline is dominated by four wispy skyscrapers that compose most of the **Embarcadero Center**, its promenade, lobby, and street levels filled with stores, restaurants, and interestingly, over two dozen dental surgeries. An entertaining side trip is into the towering, triangular atrium of the adjacent **Hyatt Regency**, where the inverted shape of the terraces above gives the feeling that it could cave in at any moment. Mel Brooks fans will recognize this as the spot where the comic lost his marbles in 1977's *High Anxiety*.

Outside, it's perhaps fitting that **Justin Herman Plaza** – named in honor of San Francisco's father of urban renewal who, in the name of progress, bulldozed acres of historic buildings in the Western Addition after World War II – should be home to San Francisco's least revered modernist work of art. French-Canadian artist Armand Vaillancourt's 1971 *Quebec Libre!*, known locally as simply the **Vaillancourt Fountain**, is a tangled mass of square concrete tubing that looks as if it were inspired by air conditioning ducts. (One particularly sour local columnist lambasted it as the product of a giant dog with square bowels.) In fact, the visually jumbled statement on provincial sovereignty attempted to echo the Embarcadero Skyway freeway that rimmed its plaza back when the fountain was built; today, with the freeway gone, there's a movement to have the fountain done away with as well. The structure's most notorious moment came one afternoon in November 1987, near the end of an impromptu set by U2 in Justin Herman Plaza, when vocalist **Bono** – having not yet morphed from rock star to international diplomat – left his artistic mark on it by spray-painting "Rock and roll stops the traffic," as captured in the band's film *Rattle and Hum*. Bono's graffiti stunt drew the ire of then-mayor Dianne Feinstein, who was in the midst of sponsoring an anti-graffiti campaign across the city; the "act of violence" (as it was called by San Francisco police who subsequently confronted Bono) nearly earned the Irishman jail time before cooler heads prevailed. When word reached Vaillancourt in eastern Canada, the feisty Quebecois hopped on a plane to the Bay Area, where he backed Bono by appearing on U2's stage three nights later in Oakland, spray-painting "Stop the Madness" on the stage and lauding graffiti as a relevant means of artistic expression.

These days, skateboarders and trick-bike riders share the open concrete square with gulls and lunching office workers, as well as an unremarkable arts and crafts bazaar on Saturday afternoons. Other events and activities take place here throughout the year, from Korean dance shows to an outdoor ice skating oval that appears each winter holiday season. Across the plaza from the Vaillancourt Fountain, under the *Hyatt Regency* tower, stands the whirling sculpture *La Chiffonière (Rag Lady)*, by Jean Dubuffet. Dubuffet intended for the dark mass of stainless steel, jigsaw-puzzle-like pieces to form the abstract impression of a tattered homeless person – a nod to San Francisco's highest-profile social problem.

The Ferry Building

Now one of San Francisco's true gems, the **Ferry Building** makeover is arguably the most impressive of all the recent public space renovations in the city. Until the freeway flyover that rimmed the Embarcadero was demolished in 1992, however, few paid it any attention. Once the obstruction was removed, locals and visitors were able to appreciate the beauty of this Beaux Arts building's extended nave, Corinthian columns, and Roman curved windows, as well as its 245-foot tall Moorish clock tower modeled after that of the Giralda in Seville, Spain.

When it was built in 1898, the Ferry Building boasted the largest foundation for a building over water anywhere, and was the first structure to use reinforced concrete; this sort of stout construction enabled it to withstand San Francisco's pair of cataclysmic twentieth-century earthquakes with minimal damage (mainly to the tower in 1906). At its peak in the mid 1930s, the building saw 50,000 daily ferry commuters pass through its corridors. But once the Bay and Golden Gate Bridges opened in 1936–37, ferry traffic dried up and the waterfront's longtime linchpin entered an era of sharp decline, its grand, airy nave cordoned off into utilitarian office space in 1955. Two years later, the Ferry Building suffered the ultimate indignation when double-decker slabs of freeway above the Embarcadero severed its physical connection to Market Street and the rest of the city.

Once the freeway was demolished in the early 1990s, the stage was set for the Ferry Building's return to splendor, and after a lengthy period of neglect and misguided modification it emerged, immaculately restored in 2003, following a four-year renovation. It now boasts deluxe offices and, once again, a working ferry terminus for an increasingly revitalized commuter service. Now a National Historic Landmark, it has become one of the city's most visited attractions. The nave is now a **gourmet marketplace** – even those who shudder at the concept should check it out, as the range of merchants here means that almost anyone can find a treat to buy, much of it organic and produced locally (see Ⓦ www.ferrybuildingmarketplace.com for a full list of merchants, restaurants, and services).

The best time to stop by is during the **Ferry Plaza Farmers Market** (year-round Sat 8am–2pm, Tues 10am–2pm; ☏ 415/291-3276, Ⓦ www.ferry plazafarmersmarket.com), with local produce sold from numerous stalls set up in a skirt around the building. Thousands of local foodies flock here to sample snacks from the city's pricey restaurants, which often set up temporary shacks among the fruit and vegetables; there are also regular recipe demonstrations from local namebrand chefs. Many farmers only sell on one of the days, so it's well worth checking back more than once.

Jackson Square and around

The eastern flank of what's now the Financial District wasn't known as **JACKSON SQUARE** until the 1960s, when interior designers who'd recently opened showrooms here decided on a suitably artsy yet old-fashioned name to replace the notorious **Barbary Coast** tag. Through the late 1800s, the area was full of abandoned ships that had become floating hotels, bars, stores, and brothels; as the boats fell into disuse, they were turned into mulched landfill, on which the neighborhood stands today. The constant stream of sailors provided an endless supply of customers looking for illicit entertainment, and earned the district the nickname "Baghdad by the Bay"; the area was also a nexus for shanghaiing, which saw hapless young males given Mickey Finns and, once unconscious, taken aboard sailing ships into involuntary servitude.

The city's 1906 disaster, coupled with dwindling numbers of sailors, sent the area into a decline; the brothel owners responded by sprucing up the streets and turning the dingy dance halls into the early twentieth century's answer to *Studio 54*. The Barbary Coast remained raunchy enough to attract the attention of state lawmakers – courtesy of some shrill lobbying from William Randolph Hearst's *San Francisco Examiner* newspaper – and in 1915, they passed an anti-vice act designed to stifle further shady activity in the neighborhood. Certain locals protested unsuccessfully for two years, but the morning after they lost the final legal battle, the police barricaded the area and shut down almost every establishment on the spot.

Visiting the **Jackson Square Historical District** (bordered by Washington, Columbus, Sansome, and Pacific streets) is one way you can hope to imagine what nineteenth-century San Francisco looked like. Here you'll find the sole cluster of Downtown buildings that escaped the great fire of 1906 unharmed, and it's jarring to realize how different the city might have looked without that three-day orgy of destruction. Note the difference between the buildings on either side of the street: the low-slung, red-brick structures on the northern side date from the 1850s and are relatively simple, while the southern strip, constructed just a decade or so later, shows clear signs of Victorian ornamental excess, its appliqué stonework looking like cubic frosting over the brick base.

At 451–455 Jackson St stands a cheeky landmark: the **Hotaling** (pronounced hote-UH-ling) **Building**. During the conflagration that followed the 1906 earthquake, when the orders came to dynamite this block as a firebreak, the manager of the wholesale whiskey operation housed here protested that the five thousand barrels inside were highly flammable. He saved the building, and thus made sure there was plenty of booze to go around once the fires were finally extinguished. When newspapers across the country sermonized that San Francisco's disaster was God's retribution for the city's hedonistic vices, local wag Charles K. Field responded with doggerel that's still repeated with a smirk: "If as they say God spanked the town for being so over frisky, why did he burn the churches down and spare Hotaling's whiskey?"

A block north of Jackson Street, leafy **Pacific Avenue** was the heart of the post-1906 Barbary Coast, nicknamed Terrific Street and filled with dance halls, cabarets, and upscale bordellos. It was also the home of San Francisco's first jazz clubs, staffed by refugee musicians who brought their music with them from Storyville, New Orleans' answer to the Barbary Coast. Now the street is home to advertising agencies, interior and graphic design studios, and law offices, with the only hint of its raucous past being the ornate light fixtures outside the old *Hippodrome* nightclub at no. 555.

Chinatown

Bustling, noisy **CHINATOWN** is shoehorned into several densely populated blocks between North Beach, the Financial District, and Nob Hill. Home to one of the largest Chinese communities outside Asia, and the oldest such enclave in the US, Chinatown's huge number of residents means that the banks of its river of people are bursting, pouring businesses and residents into surrounding neighborhoods, especially North Beach. As it grows, its diversity increases, adding Taiwanese, Vietnamese, Korean, Thai, and Laotian families, with the cultural fusion most evident in its grocery markets, where alongside traditional Chinese produce, you'll find Italian basil, Mexican kohlrabi bulbs, and uniquely Southeast Asian fruits like the pungent durian.

The neighborhood has its roots in the mostly Cantonese laborers who migrated to the area after the completion of the transcontinental railroad, as well as the arrival of Chinese sailors keen to benefit from the Gold Rush. The city didn't extend much of a welcome to Chinese immigrants, however, and they were met by a tide of vicious racial attacks. Shockingly, such attacks were officially ratified under the unapologetically racist **1882 Chinese Exclusion Act**, the only law ever in America aimed at a single ethnic group. It prevented Chinese naturalization; barred immigration to any Chinese national other than teachers, students, and merchants; and forbade thousands of single Chinese men from dating local women or bringing wives from China, although children could accompany their parents. (Such laws encouraged creative problem-solving – passing off young wives as daughters, for instance.) A rip-roaring prostitution and gambling quarter soon developed in Chinatown, controlled by gangland associations, or *tongs,* of which there were six vying for supremacy at its height. Conditions improved a great deal once immigration laws were loosened and finally repealed after World War II, no doubt due to the US and China becoming allies during wartime. As a result, the population began to swell again, while much of the burgh's seediness receded.

Today Chinatown bristles with activity in spite of its increasingly elderly population base and, in sharp contrast to the districts that surround it, a clear lack of wealth. Many of its restaurants and tourist-geared retailers are clustered in its eastern half, while the western and northern sides are much more residential. Due to the crush of commercial and pedestrian traffic, narrow streets, and paucity of parking, **driving** in Chinatown is only for the foolhardy.

Portsmouth Square and around

Between Washington, Clay, and Kearny streets stands **Portsmouth Square**, San Francisco's first real city center, born in the mid 1800s and now, to all intents and purposes, Chinatown's living room. When John Montgomery came ashore in 1846 to claim the land for the United States, he raised his flag here and named the square after his ship; the spot where he first planted the Stars and Stripes is marked by the one often flying in the square today. Two years later, Sam Brannan's cry of "Gold! Gold at the American River!" here sent property prices and development skyrocketing as hungry prospectors poured in.

There are a few points of interest in Portsmouth Square, although nothing especially outstanding – the plaza is primarily worth visiting to simply absorb everyday life, with spirited games of cards and Chinese chess played atop cardboard boxes and other makeshift tables, and neighborhood children letting off steam in the playground. Near Montgomery's flagpole is a replica of the galleon *Hispaniola* from the novel *Treasure Island,* a monument to writer **Robert Louis Stevenson** who spent much time observing the locals in Portsmouth Square during his brief sojourn in San Francisco and the Monterey Peninsula in the late 1870s. Across the square, a plaque honors **California's first public school**, built here in the late 1840s. The most recent addition to the square is the already weathered bronze *Goddess of Democracy* statue near the playground, a replica of a sculpture in Beijing's Tiananmen Square. In most years, a Hong Kong night market animates the square on Saturday evenings between late July and late October (6–11pm; free; ⓦ www.sanfranciscochinatown.com), with stalls selling everything from fresh honey to leather jackets and performances of classical opera and traditional music.

Just outside Portsmouth Square, at **743 Washington St**, stands a small red pagoda-like structure built in 1909 for the Chinese American Telephone Exchange – it's set on the original site of the office of Sam Brannan's *California Star* newspaper, which carried the news of the earliest ore discoveries back to the East Coast in 1848, and thus played a major role in the Gold Rush. A team of telephone operators worked here throughout the first half of the 1900s, routing calls solely by memory since no Chinatown phone listings existed; it

▲ Chinese chess being played in Portsmouth Square

was restored in 1960 by a bank and remains a financial institution today. Visitors interested in Buddhism should head for **Buddha's Universal Church**, 720 Washington St (☎415/982-6116), where America's largest Zen sect congregates. The five-story building was constructed in the early 1960s by the sect's members from an exotic collection of polished woods, but suffers from the uninviting boxiness strangely popular in architectural circles at the time. Call for tour information, as otherwise it's not open to the public.

Best accessed by a direct walkway from Portsmouth Square over Kearny Street is the **Chinese Culture Center**, long sequestered on the third floor inside the *Hilton's* unappealing poured concrete tower at 750 Kearny St (Tues–Sun 10am–4pm; free; ☎415/986-1822, ⓦ www.c-c-c.org). The exhibition space was granted an overhaul and reopened in 2006, and continues to feature contemporary art and performances; there's also a gift shop in its newly expanded quarters.

Along Grant Avenue

The residential overcrowding that has long characterized Chinatown has for decades been compounded by a brisk tourist trade, most of which is centered along **Grant Avenue**, the neighborhood's main north–south visitor artery. Lined with gold-ornamented portals, brightly painted balconies, and some of the tackiest stores and facades around, Grant is one of the oldest thoroughfares in the city. It was originally known as Dupont Street, a wicked ensemble of opium dens, bordellos, and gambling huts policed – if not terrorized – by *tong* hatchet men. After the 1906 fire, the city decided to rename it in honor of president and Civil War hero Ulysses S. Grant, and in the process excise the seedy excesses for which it had grown infamous.

A popular way to approach Chinatown is through the dramatic **Chinatown Gate**, which frames Grant Avenue where it meets Bush Street at the northern edge of the Union Square shopping district. Facing south, per feng shui precepts, it's a large dragon-clad arch, with a four-character inscription that reads, *Xia tian wei gong*, or "The reason to exist is to serve the public good"; it was presented as a gift to the city from the People's Republic of China in 1969. It's hard to see how that idea is carried out in the blocks ahead; Grant's sidewalks are paved with plastic Buddhas, cloisonné "health balls," noisemakers, and mechanical crickets that chirp above several shop entrances. Two blocks past Chinatown Gate is the red-brick and granite **Old St Mary's Church**, 660 California St at Grant (T 415/288-3800, W www.oldstmarys.org), which predates nearly everything around it and abuts Grant's crass commercial corridor. Designed as a replica of a Gothic church in Vich, Spain (where the first bishop overseeing the diocese was born), it became *Old* St Mary's when the new cathedral of St Mary of the Assumption was dedicated in 1891. In the years that followed, the older church struggled on and was one of the few buildings to weather the 1906 calamities – it survived the earthquake, but the subsequent fire left it as little more than a shell. The church was rebuilt and began ministering to the local Chinese population, as it still does today. Just inside the main doorway behind the banks of pews, there's a fine photo display detailing the 1906 damage to the city and the church. Across California Street in surprisingly quiet **St Mary's Square** shines a twelve-foot statue of **Dr Sun Yat-sen**, founder of the Chinese Republic in 1911, created by noted sculptor Benjamin Bufano. The small park affords fine views of the Financial District.

Back on Grant Avenue, it's entertaining to step inside the lobby of the **Empress of China** restaurant at no. 838 to glance through all the faded photos of celebrities and politicos from the 1970s and 1980s (Erik Estrada, George H.W. Bush, you get the drift) who once visited this old Chinatown haunt. Despite the upstairs restaurant's fabulous views, however, the paucity of recent celebrity photos implies it's no longer a stellar destination.

Waverly Place and around

One half-block west of Grant Avenue runs parallel **Waverly Place**, once the heart of Chinatown's extensive network of brothels and now home to two opulent but skillfully hidden **temples**: Norras on the third floor of no. 109, and Tien Hou on the fourth floor of no. 125. The namesake deity of Norras was the first lama from Tibet to teach Buddhism in China, and the temple itself is a calm refuge from the clatter and clang of the streets below. Taoist Tien Hou, a few doors up the street, bills itself as the oldest temple in San Francisco and is dedicated to the Goddess of Heaven; it's more incense-drenched and formally decorated than Norras, but less contemplative when staff members are conducting business at the desk. Still, it's worth the stair climb to see the interior daubed in gold and vermilion and the hundreds of lanterns and tassels suspended from the ceiling. Both Norras and Tien How are active temples, but are open to visitors (daily 10am–5pm). Note the pyramids of oranges, considered lucky as the Cantonese pronunciation of "orange" sounds similar to the word for wealth. Although the temples don't charge admission, it's respectful to leave a small donation and to refrain from using cameras inside.

South a block, at the **Chinese Baptist Church** (1 Waverly Place at Sacramento St), look for certain bricks that droop from the building and are worn smooth – these survivors of the 1906 fire offer tactile evidence of the scorching temperatures that melted everything in their path. (You'll find similar "clinker bricks" outside the Donaldina Cameron House at 920 Sacramento, one block up the steep hill.) Directly across Sacramento, look for a number of tiny octagonal mirrors – intended to ward off evil spirits – on the building opposite the Clarion Music Center, a shop and resource center dedicated to international musical cultures. Also in this area, and lodged halfway up the east slope of Nob Hill, the **Chinese Historical Society of America Museum and Learning Center** at 965 Clay St (Tues–Fri noon–5pm, Sat 11am–4pm; $3; ☎415/391-1188, ⓦ www.chsa.org), traces the beginnings of the Chinese community in the US with a small but worthy collection of photographs, paintings, and artifacts from the pioneering days of the nineteenth century.

Stockton Street and around

With public housing tenements looming overhead and sidewalks full to bursting with locals on the hunt for that day's meat, fish, and produce, **Stockton Street** is the commercial artery for Chinatown locals. Wander into one of the lively markets, where prices range from $1 for a 16-ounce pack of strawberries to shark fin (a much-sought soup delicacy) that can fetch over $350 a pound. **Ellison Enterprises**, 805 Stockton St at Sacramento, is known as Chinatown's best-stocked herbal pharmacy. Here, you'll find clerks filling orders the ancient Chinese way – with hand-held scales and *abaci* – from drug cases filled with dried bark, roots, cicadas, ginseng, and other staples. On that same block, be sure to take in the striking mural at the **Chinese Cultural Services Center**, 832 Stockton St, commemorating the day in 1869 when a team of 848 Chinese workers laid ten miles of track for the Central Pacific Railway (the usual daily output at the time was about *one* mile.) The heads of certain men in the fresco are wildly disproportional, a design device that makes the piece disarming from any angle.

Anyone with even a moderate sweet tooth will want to duck down Ross Alley and into the fragrant **Golden Gate Fortune Cookie Factory** (daily 7am–8.30pm; free; ☎415/781-3956) at no. 56. True to its name, the cramped plant has been churning out 20,000 fresh fortune cookies a day since 1962 – by hand. A bag of forty cookies is no more than a few dollars, but it costs 50¢ to snap a photo.

Just west of Chinatown in a saddle between Russian and Nob Hills, the **Cable Car Museum and Powerhouse**, 1201 Mason St at Washington (daily: April–Sept 10am–6pm; Oct–March 10am–5pm; free; ☎415/474-1887, ⓦ www.cablecarmuseum.com), transports the visitor back to the world of late nineteenth century industry. Informative placards along the raised viewing platforms help even the least mechanically minded visitor understand how San Francisco's cable-car system operates, while downstairs you can catch a glimpse of the whirring sheaves (giant horizontal gears) working beneath the intersection of Washington and Mason immediately outside. There's also a gift shop, as well as plenty of displays on the cars' history in the city.

2

North Beach and the hills

nland **North Beach** was named when the area sat along San Francisco's original northern waterfront, before the city's landfill expansion above Francisco Street. The neighborhood is best known as home to the city's Italian community, and you'll certainly hear Italian spoken by some of the older residents and restauranteurs – even if it can sometimes seem like the grander linguistic flourishes are put on solely for the benefit of visitors. North Beach was the breeding ground for a number of big-league baseball players (most notably Joe DiMaggio) in the first half of the 1900s; by the 1950s, it had become the home of several Beat poets, thanks to its then-cheap housing and plentiful manual labor on the waterfront. In recent years, North Beach's original blue-collar character has been largely eroded by gentrification; even so, it retains an easy, worn-in feeling, and its sloping residential streets and vibrant main drags are ideal for routeless wandering.

No longer coastal, the sunny neighborhood would be better known as North Valley, sitting as it does in the cleft between two of San Francisco's most prominent hills, **Telegraph** and **Russian.** These primarily residential neighborhoods boast many beautiful old homes, as well as hidden gardens tucked away down pathways off steep hillside streets. **Coit Tower** crowns Telegraph Hill, boasting a spectacular panorama of the city, while a few small, lesser-known parks offer promontories from Russian Hill to the west. At the foot of Telegraph Hill's sharp eastern escarpment, reached via the **Greenwich and Filbert steps**, sits the **Northeast Waterfront**, a brick-clad, erstwhile industrial district along the upper Embarcadero reinvented in recent decades as a home to offices, modern condominium towers, and a handful of fountain-strewn parks.

South of Russian Hill, you'll find pristine, yet historically snooty **Nob Hill.** Wealthy locals first settled this high mount of cathedrals and opulent hotels after the invention of the cable car, and it clings to its sense of separation as it hovers over the less ritzy neighborhoods around it, with its post-1906 mansions just as grandly imposing as the few original buildings that remain. And of course, even if you've seen it in a thousand pictures, a **cable-car ride** up and down Nob and Russian Hills' steep inclines is still an exhilarating, singular experience.

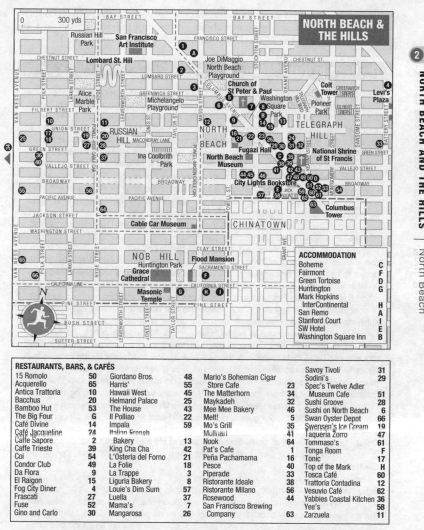

NORTH BEACH & THE HILLS

0 ——— 300 yds

ACCOMMODATION

Boheme	C
Fairmont	F
Green Tortoise	D
Huntington	G
Mark Hopkins	
InterContinental	H
San Remo	A
Stanford Court	I
SW Hotel	E
Washington Square Inn	B

RESTAURANTS, BARS, & CAFÉS

15 Romolo	50	Giordano Bros.	48	Mario's Bohemian Cigar		Savoy Tivoli	31
Acquerello	65	Harris'	55	Store Cafe	23	Sodini's	29
Antica Trattoria	10	Hawaii West	45	The Matterhorn	34	Spec's Twelve Adler	
Bacchus	20	Helmand Palace	25	Maykadeh	32	Museum Cafe	51
Bamboo Hut	53	The House	43	Mee Mee Bakery	46	Sushi Groove	28
The Big Four	G	Il Polliao	22	Melt!	5	Sushi on North Beach	6
Café Divine	14	Impala	59	Mo's Grill	35	Swan Oyster Depot	66
Café Jacqueline	24	Italian French		Mulhall	41	Swensen's Ice Cream	19
Caffe Sapore	2	Bakery	13	Nook	64	Taqueria Zorro	47
Caffe Trieste	39	King Cha Kha	42	Pat's Cafe	1	Tommaso's	61
Coi	54	L'Osteria del Forno	21	Peña Pachamama	16	Tonga Room	F
Condor Club	49	La Folie	18	Pesce	40	Tonic	17
Da Flora	9	La Trappe	3	Piperade	33	Top of the Mark	H
El Raigon	15	Liguria Bakery	8	Ristorante Ideale	38	Tosca Café	60
Fog City Diner	4	Louie's Dim Sum	57	Ristorante Milano	56	Trattoria Contadina	12
Frascati	27	Luella	37	Rosewood	44	Vesuvio Café	62
Fuse	52	Mama's	7	San Francisco Brewing		Yabbies Coastal Kitchen	36
Gino and Carlo	30	Mangarosa	26	Company	63	Yee's	58
						Zarzuela	11

North Beach

Sandwiched by Chinatown to the south and Fisherman's Wharf to the north, **NORTH BEACH** has always been a gateway for immigrants. Italian immigration to San Francisco was ignited by the Gold Rush, although it gained momentum at the end of the nineteenth century when this area began to develop the characteristics – delicatessens, focaccia bakeries, family restaurants – of a true *Piccola Italia*. Much like Chinatown, San Francisco's Little Italy was populated by expats from one main area of the old country – in this instance, fishermen from Liguria, the region around Genoa, as well as a small contingent from Lucca in nearby Tuscany. The freewheeling European flavor here, coupled with robust nightlife and wide availability of housing thanks to an exodus by wealthier Italians to the Marina district, attracted rebel writers like Lawrence

The Beats in North Beach

North Beach has always been something of a literary hangout, serving as temporary home to Mark Twain, Robert Louis Stevenson, and Jack London, among other boomtown writers. Despite its later association with the **Beat literature movement**, however, the San Francisco neighborhood isn't where the movement emerged – credit for that goes to New York in the 1940s, where bohemian Jack Kerouac joined with Allen Ginsberg and others to bemoan the conservative political climate there.

Though the term **"Beat Generation"** was coined by **Kerouac** in conversation with poet John Clellon Holmes in 1948, its meaning is rather muddled. Kerouac wanted to convey that his generation, which had come of age during World War II and was ill suited to civilian life once the war ended, was akin to that of Hemingway and his contemporaries, who had reached majority during World War I: spent and ruined, yet still young, Kerouac and company felt they represented a Beat Generation much as Hemingway's had been a Lost Generation.

In any event, Kerouac, Ginsberg, and friends quickly grew frustrated with New York and moved west, most of them settling in North Beach and securing jobs at the docks to help longshoremen unload fishing boats (the low rent and cheap red wine on offer from Italian-run boardinghouses and restaurants didn't hurt either).

The first rumblings of interest in the movement were felt with the opening, in 1953, of poet Lawrence Ferlinghetti's **City Lights**, the first bookstore in America dedicated solely to paperbacks. However, it wasn't until the publication four years later of Ginsberg's epic, pornographic poem *Howl* – originally written simply for his own pleasure rather than for printing – that mainstream America took notice. Police moved in on City Lights to prevent the sale of the book, inadvertently catapulting the Beats to national notoriety. This attention was only furthered by press hysteria, as much over the Beats' hedonistic antics – including heavy drinking and an immense fondness for pot – as over the merits of the literary work then emerging from San Francisco. Ginsberg's case went all the way to the US Supreme Court, which eventually ruled in 1957 that so long as a work has "redeeming social value," it could not be considered pornographic. Within six months of the ruling, Jack Kerouac's *On the Road*, inspired by several cross-country trips and his friend Neal Cassady's benzedrine-enhanced monologues, had shot to the top of the bestseller lists, cementing the Beats' fame.

The Beats didn't only want to break literary rules to create a more personal style of fiction and poetry – Kerouac, a former speed-typing champion, wrote in a nonstop, freeform style, hammering out his works in emulation of the solos of jazz musicians – but also to challenge the overriding social conventions of the day. Soon, North Beach was synonymous across America with a wild, subversive lifestyle, an image that soon drove away the original intelligentsia, many of whom ended up in Haight-Ashbury (see box, p.133). Instead, heat-seeking libertines swamped the neighborhood, accompanied by tourists on "Beatnik Tours" that promised sidewalks clogged with goateed, black-bereted trendsetters slapping bongos. (The more enterprising fringes of bohemia responded in kind with a "Squaresville Tour" of the adjacent Financial District, for which guides would dress in Bermuda shorts and carry placards that read, "Hi, Squares.") This double blow destroyed much of the neighborhood's Beat sensibility, allowing it to bounce back being a heartily Italian quarter.

The legend of the Beats, though, has yet to die. It's been significantly aided by Ferlinghetti's successful campaign to rename certain smaller streets after local literary figures – the alley next to his bookstore, for example, is now known as Jack Kerouac Alley.

Ferlinghetti, Allen Ginsberg, and Jack Kerouac. They made North Beach the nexus of the Beat Generation in the 1950s, which in turn helped make San Francisco a beacon for counterculturalists in the ensuing decades, from flower children in Haight-Ashbury in the late 1960s, to gays in the Castro in the 1970s and warehouse-dwelling ravers in SoMa in the 1990s.

Columbus Avenue and Broadway

North Beach's lifeline has always been vibrant **Columbus Avenue**, which cuts diagonally through the neighborhood's east-west street grid. Originally the route of the Old Presidio Trail, which connected the commercial settlements downtown with the Spanish fort to the northwest, the road later served as a throughway to the dairy farms of Cow Hollow. Since the early 1900s, however, it's been proudly tagged as San Francisco's Little Italy by the flags painted on each lamppost.

Near its southern end stands **City Lights**, 261 Columbus Ave at Broadway (daily 10am–midnight; ☎415/362-8193, ⓦwww.citylights.com), the independent bookstore and publishing house that was once the heart of North Beach's Beat scene. Opened in 1953 by Lawrence Ferlinghetti, and still owned by him today, it soldiers on despite the encroachment of big-name chains; the best reason to drop in is the upstairs poetry room, where you'll find everything from $1 mini-books and poster-size poems from Beatnik legends to various collections and anthologies, including titles from the City Lights' in-house imprint. Across Jack Kerouac Alley from the bookstore is **Vesuvio**, an old North Beach watering hole once patronized by the likes of Kerouac and Dylan Thomas that's now simply a popular bar with a colourful past. If you're desperate for Beat-inspired souvenirs, head to the huge gift shop at the **Beat Museum** across Columbus from City Lights at 540 Broadway; otherwise, it's an unapologetically commercial tourist trap full of Jerry Garcia T-shirts and assorted disposable knick-knacks that's best avoided.

At Columbus's intersection with **Broadway**, you'll find, among the many strip joints, the sites of many bars and comedy clubs from the 1950s – among them the *Hungry I* and the *Purple Onion*, where many of the era's politically conscious comedians, from Mort Sahl and Dick Gregory to Lenny Bruce, once performed. The strip clubs and porno stores that dominate this part of town first arrived with the Beats' exodus, and gained considerable steam with the topless waitress phenomenon kick-started by Carol Doda (see box, p.72) at the **Condor Club** (300 Columbus St at Broadway) in 1964. For years, a notorious pair of neon nipples were set on the wall outside, but the iconic items were eventually auctioned off to a nostalgic bidder. A few pieces of memorabilia from the club's topless heyday remain intact inside the building, including its piano suspended from the ceiling. It commemorates one of the club's choicest legends, the sad tale of a randy bouncer and dancer who climbed on top of that piano together after hours one night in 1983. In the throes of passion, the hydraulic system that raises and lowers the piano was somehow activated, sending the piano up to the ceiling. The man was crushed to death, but he cushioned the woman beneath him, and she survived.

In the late 1970s, the seedy stretch of Broadway between Columbus and Montgomery was home to San Francisco's nascent **punk rock scene**, although no relic remains today. The **Mabuhay Gardens** at 443 Broadway (now a dance club with a different name, currently Velvet, though that may have changed by the time you read this) led the charge, cut from the same grimy cloth as New York's *CBGB* and Los Angeles's *Whisky A Go Go*. Local heroes such as the Dead

Carol Doda and topless waitressing

Carol Doda is an unsung pioneer of the Sexual Revolution. Like the feminists that followed her, she proudly burned her bra, albeit for very different reasons. Knowing that she'd make bigger tips by baring her best assets, the North Beach cocktail waitress kick-started **topless waitressing** on June 19, 1964, creating a trend that at one point led to almost thirty different topless bars clustered together around the intersection of Columbus and Broadway.

Doda's bra-doffing was much less impromptu than legend has it. The original idea didn't come from Doda, but rather, a bouncer at the *Condor Club*. Davey Rosenberg and the club's owner, Gino del Prete, were brainstorming on how to improve business at their lackluster jazz club. They saw the "monokini" in a newspaper, the scandalous new swimsuit recently unveiled by Rudi Gernreich; Rosenberg smartly reasoned that waitresses in monokinis would instantly turn his go-go bar into the go-to choice for local guys. Doda, with her blonde ringlets, saucy manner, and particularly curvaceous profile, was selected as the nipple-baring pioneer. It didn't hurt that the Republican Convention was in town (which both increased business and fueled the controversy), or that Doda had a plastic surgeon friend keen for her to showcase his handiwork, which over time boosted her natural bust by 10 inches to 44D.

Five years later, on September 3, 1969, Doda broke the final taboo when she started serving stark naked. Her breasts became icons (set in concrete in front of the club), and Doda was awarded Business Person of the Year by a smitten crew from Harvard University. She finally retired from the *Condor* in 1986, turning to TV hosting and rock gigs, singing in a band called Carol Doda and Her Lucky Stiffs. Though the concrete breast impressions are long gone, Carol is commemorated with a bronze plaque on the exterior wall of her one-time workplace – cleverly, the marker is made to resemble an official State of California plaque. These days, Doda owns a lingerie boutique down a quiet courtyard off Cow Hollow's Union Street (see p.248).

Kennedys, Flipper, and the Avengers emerged from the "Fab Mab," which also saw seminal touring acts like the Minutemen and Ramones on its stage.

Further east is San Francisco's oldest bar, **The Saloon**, at 1232 Grant Ave at Broadway. The grungy tavern was first built in the 1860s and survived the 1906 fire; over 100 years on, it persists as a lively, low-brow hardcore blues venue, wonderfully anachronistic among the encroaching boutiques along upper Grant's shopping and dining strip.

The area gets more Italian as you head north from Broadway – expect plenty of cafés, delis, and restaurants selling cured meats, strong coffee, and plates of tagliatelle. One eccentric, minor landmark is **Caffe Trieste**, 609 Vallejo St at Kearny (☎415/982-2605, ⓦwww.caffetrieste.com), where the jukebox plays opera classics and, on certain Saturdays, there's live music: jangling mandolin and Italian folk in the morning, and operatic vocalists in the afternoon (check the café's website for exact dates and times). Photos of star patrons line *Caffe Trieste*'s walls, and legend has it that Francis Ford Coppola wrote most of the screenplay for *The Godfather* at the table beneath where his portrait now hangs.

Looping back toward Columbus, you'll find the **National Shrine of St Francis of Assisi**, 610 Vallejo St at Columbus (☎415/983-0405, ⓦwww.shrinesf.org), a neo-Gothic church built on the site of California's first parish. The current building, which dates from 1860, was the Barbary Coast's neighborhood place of worship (it's rumored there was once a bullfighting ring handily attached) and the structure is one of the area's few survivors of the 1906 fire: though the interior was gutted, the walls held firm, and it was fully restored within twelve years. Behind the rows of pews are a number of interesting

▲ Café life on Columbus Avenue

archival photographs, and the church itself is a brighter, humbler, and more contemplative place than the Church of Saints Peter & Paul, a few blocks to the north (see below).

There's more neighborhood memorabilia at the intimate **North Beach Museum** (Mon–Thurs 9am–4pm, Fri 9am–6pm; free; ☎415/391-6210), located a bit awkwardly on the mezzanine level of a bank at 1435 Stockton St at Columbus. Its heirlooms and photographs offer a fine look at the district's unique Marco Polo mix of Italian- and Chinese-Americans, although it focuses almost exclusively on the period 1850–1950. Not far away, **Fugazi Hall**, 678 Green St at Powell, was donated to the community in 1912 by local banker John Fugazi. Once the site of Beat readings, this elaborate, terracotta-ornamented building has hosted San Francisco's longest-running stage show, *Beach Blanket Babylon* (see p.230), for several years; there's a remarkably lifelike bust of the show's late creator, Steve Silver, just to the right of the main entrance.

Washington Square and around

The soul of North Beach is **Washington Square**, a grassy gathering spot and public back yard that plays host to dozens of older, local Chinese each morning practicing tai chi on and around its expansive lawn. Every year in mid June, the North Beach Festival takes over Washington Square for a weekend with performance stages, food and drink booths, and assorted lollygaggery. Local legend Lillie Hitchcock Coit's (see box, p.75) none-too-subtle fascination with firefighters can be seen on the Columbus Avenue side of the park in the form of the bronze **statue** she commissioned honoring local volunteer firemen. Near the center of the green plaza, look for the statue of Benjamin Franklin donated by local dentist/prohibitionist H.D. Cogswell, who plowed a fortune into this monument by installing taps at the base in the vain hope that people would swill water rather than bootleg liquor.

On the north side of the park, the lacy, cream-colored spires of the **Church of Saints Peter & Paul**, 666 Filbert St at Powell (☎415/421-0809,

Ⓦ www.stspeterpaul.san-francisco.ca.us/church), look like a pair of fairy-tale castles rising from the North Beach flats. Although it's seen as the spiritual home of the local Italian community, the church also offers masses in Cantonese, as well as English and Italian. The interior is a vast nineteenth-century confection, underlit even on sunny days. In 1954, native son Joe DiMaggio and new wife Marilyn Monroe had their wedding pictures taken here, although the actual marriage took place earlier at City Hall since both had been previously divorced. DiMaggio's legacy lives on a few blocks to the north at his namesake **playground**, which occupies most of the city block surrounded by Greenwich, Powell, Lombard, and Mason. The Yankee Clipper played baseball here as a kid in the 1920s, as did other Italian-Americans from the neighborhood like Frank Crosetti and Tony Lazzeri (as well as DiMaggio's own brothers, Vince and Dominic); each went on to star professionally. Today, the space is mostly paved and given over to basketball and tennis courts, as well as a pair of recently renovated indoor community swimming pools.

Telegraph Hill and around

Due east of North Beach and named for a semaphore station that once stood atop its 288-foot peak, **TELEGRAPH HILL**'s steep slopes, hidden walkways, and lush foliage are capped by one of the city's greatest attractions, Coit Tower. Save for the odd corner market, the hill is entirely residential, but it's well worth exploring for its fantastic views – though you'll need comfortable footwear as it's an unforgiving climb to the top. The most direct path up from North Beach is via Filbert Street; though steep, the short walk up the terraced sidewalk, past clapboard houses and an elementary school, is enjoyable. (Non-walkers are best off holding out for the #39 Coit MUNI bus, as there are precious few parking spots at the top of the hill.) Once you reach the summit, it's easy to see why the peak was used as a signal tower for ships entering the Golden Gate. Standing where the statue of Christopher Columbus is today, a watchman on the hill would identify the boat's origin and name by the flags flying on the mast, and relay the information via telegraph to the docks along Fisherman's Wharf.

The Columbus statue stands in **Pioneer Park**, which was donated to the city by private citizens in 1875 and has a lovely green space on its south side ideal for sitting and picking out the sights below. Directly above looms the Moderne-inspired **Coit Tower** (daily 10am–5pm; lobby free, $3.75 for the elevator to the top; ☎ 415/362-0808, Ⓦ www.coittower.org), a 210-foot pillar built in 1933 with a chunk of Lillie Hitchcock Coit's money (see box, p.75) after her death. Provided there isn't too long a line for the cramped elevator, the trip to the open-air viewing platform is well worth the few dollars – it's a stunning, eight-way panorama with unimpeded vistas in every direction.

Coit Tower's ground-floor lobby is notable for more than its handy restrooms: the **frescoes** wrapped around the interior's base were part of a project overseen by the Public Works of Art Project (a forerunner to the better-known Works Progress Administration), which employed artists to decorate public and government buildings during the Depression. Over two dozen painters were chosen for this project – entitled *Aspects of Life in California* – all of them students of the famous Mexican Communist artist, Diego Rivera. As with much of Rivera's work, the figures here are muscular and somber, emphasizing the

Loopy Lillie, the fireman's mascot

Lillie Hitchcock Coit (1844–1929) first became the patron saint of San Francisco firefighters the day she helped the understaffed Knickerbocker Engine Company (No. 5 of the Volunteer Fire Department) tow its truck up Telegraph Hill. The grateful firefighters of the first engine ever to make it up the steep grade made the cheerfully nutty Coit their mascot, nicknaming her Firebelle; in return, she sported a diamond-studded fireman's badge reading "No. 5" all her life and even started signing her name with a five after it. Despite marrying wealthy easterner Howard Coit in 1868, the lifelong tomboy continued attending firemen's balls and playing poker with "her" men of Company No. 5. Coit smoked cigars, gambled avidly, and shaved her head so that her wigs would fit better, and stories were even told of her dashing away from society balls to chase after clanging fire engines. Oddly, she wasn't ostracized by polite society, but indulged as an amusing eccentric.

Coit's enduring legacy, though, stands on Telegraph Hill in the form of the concrete tower that was constructed after her death with the $100,000 she'd left "to be expended in an appropriate manner for the purpose of adding to the beauty of the city which I have always loved." The result, designed by Arthur Brown Jr (architect of City Hall) and Henry Howard, bears an unmistakable (if unintentional) resemblance to a firehose nozzle. Coit's rumored liaisons with firemen add fuel to the speculation that the tower was actually her parting memorial to another part of a fireman's equipment.

glory of labor, although there's a wide variation in style and quality between panels despite their thematic cohesion. Of particular note is Raymond Bertrand's *Meat Industry*, in which the artist cleverly adapts the building's windows to his scene as sausage smokers; also have a good look at *City Life* by Victor Amantoff, who depicts himself in a fur collar and hat next to a rack full of left-wing newspapers. In 1934, when rumors of "subversive" frescoes like these reached the authorities, the commission in charge of maintaining Coit Tower ordered that a hammer and sickle be removed from one of the pieces; it even tried closing the tower until tempers cooled. It didn't help that, at the same time, there was a contentious dispute between local longshoremen and port management, which escalated dangerously after police killed two demonstrators. A picket of the tower was mounted by local unions, keeping it in the headlines until authorities caved in and allowed the exhibit to open several months later. The San Francisco City Guides organization (☎415/557-4266, Ⓦwww.sfcityguides.org) leads a free **tour** of the murals every Saturday at 11am – meet at the tower's main entrance.

The Greenwich and Filbert steps

Coit Tower may be Telegraph Hill's most visible (and visited) attraction, but it's along the pair of canopied **pedestrian paths** clinging to its eastern flank that the true identity of this urban peak comes into focus. These steep walkways pass between oversized bungalows, gardens wild and manicured, and an unlikely pair of restaurant sites. The brick **Greenwich steps** drop from the east side of the small Pioneer Park parking lot (look for the street sign) down to a hillside block of Montgomery Street, at the end of which lurks *Julius' Castle*, a view restaurant dating from 1922 that seems to open and close every few years. Up Montgomery a block at no. 1349, Italian restaurant *Dalla Torre* closed its doors for good in the mid 2000s and, at the time of writing, was being converted into a private residence. Despite their lofted inaccessibility, both restaurants were prime see-and-be-seen hotspots in their mid-twentieth-century heydays – Lauren Bacall and Humphrey Bogart were regulars at *The Shadows* (*Dalla Torre*'s predecessor) during filming of their 1947 noir thriller *Dark Passage*. Conveniently, Bacall's character Irene Jansen lived in the fine Art Deco apartment building at 1360 Montgomery, directly across from the old restaurant. The real-life former home of writer **Armistead Maupin** is nearby at 60–62 Alta St: he penned many of his gloriously romping *San Francisco Chronicle* columns here, later published in book form as *Tales of the City*.

Near 1440 Montgomery St, the Greenwich steps continue down the sharp slope to Sansome Street; while descending to the east, look for the cleared area to the left of the paved path with a newly placed bench and, for comic measure, an uprooted parking meter replanted next to it. Also look and listen for the famed flock of parrots – 200 strong, and counting – that now calls this side of Telegraph Hill home. The birds' green plumage sometimes makes them difficult to spot in the tall trees, but you can't miss their squawking. For more on this quirky phenomenon, seek out the 2005 documentary film *The Wild Parrots of Telegraph Hill*.

A block south of Greenwich, the **Filbert steps** trace an even steeper path up and down Telegraph Hill, with the lengthy stretch of the footpath between Sansome and Montgomery still laid with original wooden planks. There's also boardwalk on the route's most florid offshoot, Napier Lane, which overflows with foliage and is exhilaratingly fragrant with honeysuckle and roses in spring. The cottage at no. 224 Filbert dates from the 1860s and was thoroughly restored in 1978, while many of the other small homes in the immediate area are equally charming. The path continues up to Montgomery, past the old *Dalla Torre* site, and crests adjacent to Pioneer Park.

The Northeast Waterfront

Back on level ground at the foot of both paths, the **Northeast Waterfront** is an attractive, if mostly workaday precinct that extends all the way south to the Financial District. Home to a surprising number of parks and squares – from Sidney Walton Park in the south to Levi's Plaza in the north – this Embarcadero-adjacent area is light on actual sights, but nevertheless worth a stroll for its fleet of restored brick offices made over from industrial warehouses of yesteryear.

Flanking Battery Street between Filbert and Union, below the exposed bedrock of Telegraph Hill, is pleasant **Levi's Plaza**. Completed in 1982, the west half of the square features an ambitious, walk-through fountain and plenty of bench seating; its grassy counterpart across Battery has a number of squat, rolling knolls ideal for lounging on sunny afternoons. The main building on the south side of the plaza serves as headquarters for blue jeans progenitor Levi Strauss & Co, one of San Francisco's original businesses (hence the "SF" on the pocket rivets). If you step inside the airy lobby you'll be subjected to toothless corporate shill on the company's denim products throughout the decades. A room off the lobby called "The Vault" is briefly interesting for its displays of vintage pants, and one of the pavilions in the main area features a number of glib advertisements from bygone eras. However, if you're looking for the company's original factory, it's a few miles away on Valencia Street in the Mission and not open to the public at this time.

Long before the days of 60-inch flat screens and remote controls, science prodigy Philo Taylor Farnsworth worked in his laboratory in this neighborhood, where he concocted a video camera tube – a device that dovetailed directly into his creation of the **world's first television system** here in 1927. Today, there's a plaque on the northwest corner of Green and Sansome that commemorates Farnsworth's watershed invention, from which he never became wealthy.

Russian Hill

Bordering North Beach to the west, elegant **RUSSIAN HILL** is perhaps San Francisco's quintessential romantic neighborhood. The area was so named for six unknown Russian sailors who died on an undocumented expedition here in the early 1800s, and were buried near its southeastern tip. Its luxuriant, tree-lined streets, intimate bistros, and endless vistas invite wandering and lingering, although like its Telegraph Hill counterpart across the flats below, several of its vertigo-inducing inclines are not for the faint of heart.

Russian Hill's most familiar sight, by far, is the one-way block of **Lombard Street** that winds its way between Hyde above and Leavenworth below. It's hardly the white-knuckle drive many make it out to be, however, as the 5mph speed limit prevents any sort of Steve McQueen-like tomfoolery – not that you'll be able to drive much faster even if you tried, given the radius of the street's curves and the hedges that block any potential short-cutting. The best time to enjoy a trip down without having to queue west of Hyde is early morning or, better still, late at night when the city lights twinkle below. (See the box on p.78 for several local streets even steeper than Lombard.)

A few blocks north, the low-rise, Mission-style building of the **San Francisco Art Institute**, 800 Chestnut St between Jones and Leavenworth (daily 9am–8pm; free; ☎415/771-7020, ⓦwww.sfai.edu), clings to the side of a steep street. It's easy to miss the place – although certainly not its students, whose appearance provides sharp contrast to many of this neighborhood's tucked-in residents. It's

▲ Cars negotiating Lombard Street

the oldest art school in the West; Jerry Garcia and Lawrence Ferlinghetti passed through the school's open studios, and Ansel Adams started its photography department. Pause in the peaceful central courtyard with its small pool of fish, and look over the outdoor exhibition of current students' work usually shown along the surrounding walkways. Aside from the multi-level annex in the rear of the school offering terrific rooftop views of northeast San Francisco, the one unmissable sight here is the Diego Rivera Gallery and its outstanding mural, *The Making of a Fresco Showing the Building of a City*. Executed by the painter at the height of his fame in 1931, the fresco cleverly includes Rivera himself sitting with his back to the viewer in the center of the painting – find the chubby figure looking on as others construct a giant human being in front of him.

Russian Hill also boasts a pair of literary points of interest. Along Taylor Street up the hill from Union, the lush, lower, pedestrian-only section of two-block **Macondray Lane** is widely believed to be the inspiration for Barbary Lane, home to Mrs Madigral and her oddball brood in Armistead Maupin's *Tales of the City* saga. Up and over Russian Hill's crest, branching off from Hyde's busy cable-car line, is Russell Street: Jack Kerouac lived at no. 29 in 1952 where, inspired by the tape-recorded sessions with Neal Cassady for *Visions of Cody*, he produced some of his finest works, including *Doctor Sax* and a revision of *On the Road*.

If you're more interested in greenspaces than ghosts, Russian Hill contains some of the loveliest **neighborhood parks** in the entire city. For picnics, a board game on a wooden tabletop, or a few shots on a basketball hoop, Michelangelo Playground on Greenwich Street at Jones can't be beat. There's also immaculate Alice Marble Park (at Larkin and Greenwich), good for tennis or taking a breather on a bench, as well as the tiny patch of space where the Vallejo Street pavement ends far above Taylor, for exceptional views of Downtown and the Bay at night. Finally, Ina Coolbrith Park is a pleasant

San Francisco's steepest (and twistiest) streets

Though no San Francisco street can match Lombard for its fabled curves, there's another, lesser-known auto twistathon in town, adjacent to the US 101 freeway in the Potrero Hill neighborhood: Vermont Street between 20th and 22nd. Its scenery may not be as picturesque as its Russian Hill counterpart, but it's virtually guaranteed that you won't have to wait in a queue to trundle down its one-way turns.

Another uniquely San Francisco thrill – provided your car's brakes and clutch are up to snuff – is to plummet down (or in certain cases when the streets aren't one-way, slog up) any of the city's **steepest streets**. Much pride among locals hinges on a driver's ability to negotiate San Francisco's most precipitous climbs and drops, particularly with a manual transmission vehicle. Here's a quick rundown of the sharpest drivable grades in town, complete with its degree of steepness. We've included the hill's neighborhood to help find it on a map.
• Filbert Street between Leavenworth and Hyde, Russian Hill (31.5°)
• 22nd Street between Church and Vicksburg, Noe Valley (31.5°)
• Jones between Filbert and Union, Russian Hill (29.0°)
• Duboce between Alpine and Buena Vista Avenue East, Roosevelt Terrace (27.9°)
• Jones between Union and Green, Russian Hill (26.0°)
• Webster between Vallejo and Broadway, Pacific Heights (26.0°)
• Duboce between Divisadero and Alpine, Lower Haight (25.0°)
• Jones between California and Pine, Nob Hill (24.8°)
• Fillmore between Vallejo and Broadway, Pacific Heights (24.0°)
• Third Avenue between Irving and Parnassus, Inner Sunset (23.5°)

outpost of green, named for California's first poet laureate. It's directly below the aforementioned lookout, although views are marred to a degree by the 1950s high-rise apartment tower in its midst.

Nob Hill

The posh hotels, stodgy institutions, and multimillion-dollar residences of **NOB HILL**, south of Russian Hill and west of Chinatown, exemplify old San Francisco money in spades. Short on visitor sights but still meriting a quick visit, it's a subdued neighborhood with oddly deserted streets and a suffocating sense of privacy found in few other parts of the city. Originally called California Street Hill, the 376-foot mound was once scrubland occupied by sheep. The invention of the cable car made it accessible to Gold Rush millionaires soon after San Francisco's settlement, and the area garnered its current name which stemmed from any of three sources: "nabob," a Moghul prince; "knob," as in rounded hill; or simply, "snob." Its status as a stronghold of power and wealth was cemented once Leland Stanford, Collis P. Huntington, Mark Hopkins, and Charles Crocker (also known as the "Big Four" – see box, p.80) built their homes here; in fact, Stanford built the California Street cable line expressly to connect his own and his partners' mansions with Downtown below. Ostentatious showplaces built from Marin redwood were the favored design among the railroad barons, but none of the young hilltop palaces escaped the 1906 fire. The sole surviving home on Nob Hill belonged to James C. Flood, who bucked his neighbors' trends in 1886 and poured $1 million into his 42-room, fire-resistant brownstone – a nod to his native New York. Today, the silver millionaire's manor is known as the **Flood Mansion**, 1000 California St at Mason, and houses the Pacific-Union Club, an exclusive fraternal organization.

The other significant fire survivor was the burnt-out shell of the as-yet-uncompleted **Fairmont Hotel**, 950 Mason St at Sacramento. Its owners tapped the architect Julia Morgan for the rebuilding, and the design genius raced to complete the task in exactly one year. Note the flags flying above the *Fairmont*'s loggia: they represent nations attending the 1945 meetings here that led to the formation of the United Nations later that same year. The hotel has a lovely rooftop garden that provides a nice spot to watch the cable cars clank up and down Powell Street far below – to reach it, walk through the plush lobby and down the long, wide corridor to the right of the main desk.

Around the west side of the Flood Mansion are the primly manicured grounds of **Huntington Park**, designed and laid out after the 1906 fire on the site of Collis P. Huntington's house. It's a tame plaza popular with contemplative readers and precious toy dogs prancing around its brick and grass surfaces, although its tortoise-covered fountain – a replica of a Renaissance original in Rome – is an enjoyably quirky installation. Overlooking the park is **Grace Cathedral**, 1100 California St at Taylor (Sun–Fri 7am–6pm, Sat 8am–6pm; ☎415/749-6300, ⓦwww.gracecathedral.org), one of the biggest hunks of neo-Gothic architecture in the US. Construction on the poured concrete monolith began in 1928, but it wasn't completed until the 1960s as one funding delay after another routinely halted construction. The church's lengthy gestation period explains certain hodgepodge aspects of its Notre Dame-reminiscent design – look no further than the faithful replicas of Ghiberti's doors from the Florence Baptistry adorning the main entrance, which look utterly out of place.

The Big Four and California's early railroad

The "nabobs" who gave Nob Hill both notoriety and name were the so-called Big Four. **Leland Stanford, Collis P. Huntington, Mark Hopkins**, and **Charles Crocker** – the foursome met at a Republican Party political rally – made millions from the Central and Southern Pacific Railroads, a transport monopoly that both fed and strangled the development of California's early economy. In return for an initial investment of $15,000, the four financiers received staggeringly generous federal subsidies of $50,000 per mile of track laid – twice what it actually cost. On top of this, they were granted half the land in a forty-mile strip bordering the railroad; as the network expanded, the Southern Pacific became the largest landowner in California, owning over twenty percent of state lands. An unregulated monopoly, usually caricatured in the liberal press as a grasping octopus, the railroad had the power to make or break farmers and manufacturers dependent upon it for the transportation of goods. In the cities, it was able to demand massive concessions from local government as an inducement for rail connections, and by the end of the nineteenth century, the Big Four had extracted and extorted a fortune worth over $200 million each. Naturally, the men preferred to be known more harmlessly as "The Associates" in their own time.

Although they're often lumped together, the four men were vastly different in character. The mastermind was Huntington, a ruthless entrepreneur whose only morals were said to be his scrupulous dishonesty. Vain, self-important Stanford was the makeweight figurehead who had chanced on his wealth when a customer at the grocery store he owned paid off a tab with shares in a mine that soon struck silver. Tiny, penny-pinching Hopkins used to sell vegetables from his cottage garden to neighbors on Nob Hill to make extra money. Crocker was undoubtedly the most appealing of the bunch: a party animal with a popular wife, Mary Ann Deming Crocker, he was known for hands-on supervision of workers, even joining them in ditch-digging. Each man is commemorated with landmarks in the neighborhood, although poor Crocker's the posthumous also-ran – while his cohorts had hotels named in their honor, he's instead immortalized with a concrete parking structure.

Still, the interior feels remarkably European, with a floor labyrinth near the entrance that exactly duplicates the design at Chartres in France (there's another walkable labyrinth to the right of the main entrance) and natural light shining in through the grand, east-facing rose window. Elsewhere inside, the AIDS Interfaith Chapel to the right of the main entrance features a cast-bronze altar as centerpiece, picked out in gold and silver leaf and designed by the late pop artist Keith Haring; its walls are covered with commemorative patches destined to be sewn into the AIDS quilt.

Another sight worth a visit on the hilltop is the modernist **Nob Hill Masonic Center**, across the street from Grace Cathedral at 1111 California St (call for hours; ☎415/776-4702, ⓦwww.sfmasoniccenter.com). Though the venue's used for concerts and various Mason-approved paid exhibits, it's free to wander into the main hall to admire the astonishing window. The graphic design is 1950s naive: symbolically complex, it depicts a group of six men who represent the Masonic settlers who arrived in California by land, overlooked by an all-seeing Masonic eye. Though it resembles stained glass, the window is in fact an extremely rare endomosaic, an obscure art that involves sandwiching colored materials like twigs and sand between two sheets of clear glass. Sadly, the endomosaic is showing its age, and it's so far been impossible to find anyone with skill enough to repair it.

The northern waterfront and Pacific Heights

rom east to west, San Francisco's **northern waterfront** begins with crass commercialism, passes through areas of vast wealth and lands cast off by the military, and ends at the city's most famous landmark. Taken as a whole, it's a section of town almost every visitor at least drops into, if not becomes immersed in – its stunning vistas, opulent (if homogenous) neighborhoods, and even the tourist schlock seem to hold something for everyone.

Each year, millions of visitors plow through the overpriced gimmickry of **Fisherman's Wharf** for a glimpse of what remains of a nearly obsolete fishing industry; a few piers down the waterfront is the only point of access to America's most infamous island jail, **Alcatraz**. Immediately west of the Wharf, the area around and including **Aquatic Park** also pays homage to various forms of seafaring (albeit with more dignity), while around and atop the neighboring bluff sits **Fort Mason**, rescued from the clutches of development and devoted to greenspace, non-profit organizations, and even a hostel.

Things take a turn for the affluent in the **Marina** and **Cow Hollow** neighborhoods, where yacht clubs, boutiques, and all things upmarket dominate the scene. Perched on the tall hill above these tony districts stands stately, exclusive **Pacific Heights**, home to much of San Francisco's oldest money, and some of its new wealth as well. **The Presidio**'s real estate is equally valuable, but as a former military base that's now a national park, it's never been up for private grabs; in fact, its current restoration as a public space (with a few high-profile private lessees) is in full swing. Finally, the **Golden Gate Bridge** lives up to its considerable hype as civic icon *par excellence*.

Fisherman's Wharf

If the districts of San Francisco are a family, then **FISHERMAN'S WHARF** is the boisterous uncle who showed up at the reunion in a ghastly shirt, put

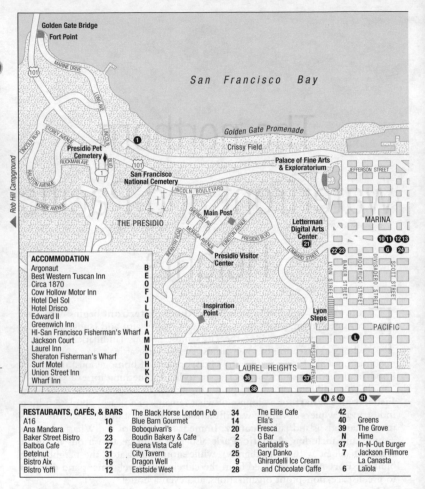

Golden Gate Bridge
Fort Point

San Francisco Bay

Golden Gate Promenade

Crissy Field

Rob Hill Campground

Presidio Pet Cemetery

San Francisco National Cemetery

Palace of Fine Arts & Exploratorium

JEFFERSON STREET

THE PRESIDIO

Main Post

Letterman Digital Arts Center 21

MARINA

10 11 12 13
G 24
22 23

Presidio Visitor Center

Inspiration Point

Lyon Steps

PACIFIC

L

LAUREL HEIGHTS

36   37
38

N & 40   41

ACCOMMODATION

Argonaut	B
Best Western Tuscan Inn	E
Circa 1870	O
Cow Hollow Motor Inn	F
Hotel Del Sol	J
Hotel Drisco	L
Edward II	G
Greenwich Inn	I
HI-San Francisco Fisherman's Wharf	A
Jackson Court	M
Laurel Inn	N
Sheraton Fisherman's Wharf	D
Surf Motel	H
Union Street Inn	K
Wharf Inn	C

RESTAURANTS, CAFÉS, & BARS					
A16	10	The Black Horse London Pub	34	The Elite Cafe	42
Ana Mandara	6	Blue Barn Gourmet	14	Ella's	40	Greens
Baker Street Bistro	23	Boboquivari's	20	Fresca	39	The Grove
Balboa Cafe	27	Boudin Bakery & Cafe	2	G Bar	N	Hime
Betelnut	31	Buena Vista Café	8	Garibaldi's	37	In-N-Out Burger
Bistro Aix	16	City Tavern	25	Gary Danko	7	Jackson Fillmore
Bistro Yoffi	12	Dragon Well	9	Ghirardelli Ice Cream		La Canasta
		Eastside West	28	and Chocolate Caffe	6	Laïola

a lampshade on his head, and never left. It's the one part of town guaranteed to induce shudders of embarrassment from locals, although many of those same San Franciscans may be quietly thankful for a zone specifically designed to entertain and sequester visitors looking for an amusement park-like setting. San Francisco doesn't go dramatically out of its way to court and fleece tourists, but the scores of tacky souvenir shops and overpriced restaurants that crowd the Wharf expose this area's mission of raking in disposable tourist dollars.

Despite its reputation, Fisherman's Wharf remains a massively popular destination, particularly with visiting families. Naturally, it's at its most crowded in summer and on weekends, but if you're willing to arrive a little earlier in the day than most, it's possible to enjoy its sights and views without having to jostle for position. Be sure to steer clear of unofficial "information centers" along its sidewalks, which claim to give visitor advice but are really just fronts for shilling overpriced bus tours.

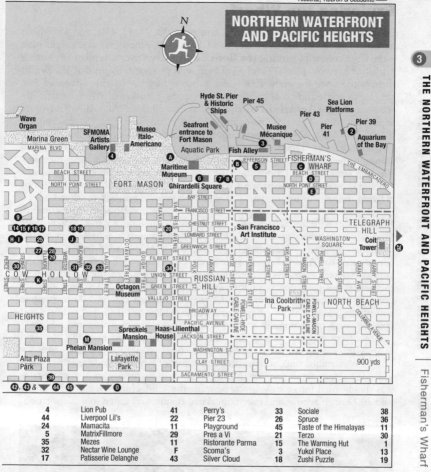

NORTHERN WATERFRONT
AND PACIFIC HEIGHTS

N

Wave Organ
Marina Green
MARINA BLVD
SFMOMA Artists Gallery
Museo Italo-Americano
Hyde St. Pier & Historic Ships
Pier 45
Seafront entrance to Fort Mason
Aquatic Park
Fish Alley
Musee Mécanique
Pier 43
Pier 41
Sea Lion Platforms
Pier 39
Aquarium of the Bay

Maritime Museum
FORT MASON
Ghirardelli Square
JEFFERSON STREET
FISHERMAN'S WHARF
THE EMBARCADERO

BEACH STREET
NORTH POINT STREET
BAY STREET
FRANCISCO STREET
BEACH STREET
NORTH POINT STREET

CHESTNUT STREET
San Francisco Art Institute
TELEGRAPH HILL

LOMBARD STREET
WASHINGTON SQUARE
Coit Tower

GREENWICH STREET
FILBERT STREET
UNION STREET
GREEN STREET
VALLEJO STREET

COW HOLLOW
Octagon Museum
RUSSIAN HILL
NORTH BEACH
Ina Coolbrith Park

BROADWAY
PACIFIC AVENUE

HEIGHTS
Spreckels Mansion
Haas-Lilienthal House
JACKSON STREET
Phelan Mansion
WASHINGTON ST
Lafayette Park
CLAY STREET
SACRAMENTO STREET
Alta Plaza Park

0   900 yds

MARINA BLVD
FRANKLIN STREET
VAN NESS AVENUE
OCTAVIA STREET
GOUGH STREET
POLK ST
LARKIN
HYDE ST
LEAVENWORTH STREET
JONES STREET
TAYLOR STREET
MASON STREET
POWELL STREET
STOCKTON STREET
POWELL-MASON CABLE CAR LINE
POWELL-HYDE CABLE CAR LINE
GRANT AVE
KEARNY STREET
COLUMBUS AVENUE

STEINER STREET
PIERCE STREET
FILLMORE STREET
WEBSTER STREET
BUCHANAN
LAGUNA STREET

4	Lion Pub	41	Perry's	33	Sociale	38
44	Liverpool Lil's	22	Pier 23	26	Spruce	36
24	Mamacita	11	Playground	45	Taste of the Himalayas	11
5	MatrixFillmore	29	Pres a Vi	21	Terzo	30
35	Mezes	11	Ristorante Parma	15	The Warming Hut	1
32	Nectar Wine Lounge	F	Scoma's	3	Yukol Place	13
17	Patisserie Delanghe	43	Silver Cloud	18	Zushi Puzzle	19

    Long before Hooters and the Wax Museum set up shop near the waterfront,
Fisherman's Wharf flourished as a serious fishing port – well into the twentieth
century, in fact. These days, the few fishermen that can afford the exorbitant
mooring charges have usually finished their trawling by early morning and are
gone by the time most visitors arrive. You can still find decent seafood here at
a few of the better restaurants, but worthwhile sights or remnants of the fishing
trade are few and far between. Should you want to head out onto the water,
Bay cruises depart from piers 39, 41, and 43½ several times a day (see p.31).
In addition, a number of independent boaters along Jefferson Street between
Taylor and Jones offer charter tours for small groups; check around, as prices
and restrictions may vary. Provided fog isn't too heavy (which can be the case
any time of year), any of these excursions will boast excellent views and often
pass under the Golden Gate Bridge – an unforgettable experience. Keep in
mind that San Francisco Bay can be very cold and choppy, so dress accordingly
and expect to get at least a little splashed.

Exploring the Wharf

Fisherman's Wharf officially includes five piers: 39, 41, 43, 43½, and 45, whose numbers increase as you head westward. Perhaps the most endearing sight here is the large colony of barking **sea lions** that has taken over a number of floating platforms between piers 39 and 41. These wild pinnipeds have made the Wharf their home since the early 1990s and, protected by the Marine Mammal Act, are free to come and go as they please; no feeding is allowed. More aquatic life is on view at the **Aquarium of the Bay** at Pier 39 (June–Aug daily 9am–8pm; Sept–May Mon–Thurs 10am–6pm, Fri–Sun 10am–7pm; $14.95, children $8; ☎888/732-3483, ⓦ www.aquariumofthebay.com), conveniently located but, alas, not the finest of its kind. Exhibits here are standard fare for sealife museums, although the petting pool with leopard sharks and bat rays is a nice diversion. The top attraction is "Under the Bay," where you get spectacular close-ups of fish and crustaceans that surround you as you trundle slowly through a 300-foot viewing tunnel – assuming you can ignore the cloying muzak overhead.

Carbohydrate-averse visitors will want to avoid the **Boudin Museum & Bakery**, 160 Jefferson St at Mason (Wed–Sun noon–5pm; $3; ☎415/928-1849, ⓦ www.boudinbakery.com) – in fact, it's indeterminate whether even the staunchest supporter of sourdough will find this bubble-headed "museum" truly educational. Bay Area bakery Boudin is famed because its bakers have used the same starter yeast since 1849, when the company was founded; for reasons unclear to science, this particular yeast mix can't survive outside the Bay Area, so it's a uniquely local product. Cheery guides riff on Boudin's extensive history while you watch bakers at work (they churn out 2000 loaves a day), and at tour's end you can gorge on sourdough with various toppings like chocolate and raisin.

A more entertaining pick is the **Musée Mécanique** on Pier 45 (Mon–Fri 10am–7pm, Sat & Sun 10am–8pm; free; ☎415/346-2000, ⓦ www .museemechanique.org), an amusing collection of vintage arcade machines. For years, this paean to all sorts of gaming – from 1920s analog to 1980s digital – was shoehorned into a tiny space beneath the Cliff House (see p.141); in the mid 2000s, its machines and mechanical mannequins relocated to this enormous

▲ Sea lions at Fisherman's Wharf

Bushwhacking at the Wharf

Amidst the glut of benign, unoriginal street performers lining the sidewalks of Fisherman's Wharf lurks the **World Famous Bushman**, née David Johnson. The onetime Market Street shoeshiner moved up to the northern waterfront in 1980, where his act has become one of the city's longest-running hits. From his usual spot on the Jefferson Street sidewalk between Taylor and Jones, Johnson's shtick begins with him sitting on a crate behind a pair of eucalyptus branches; when the right pedestrian approaches, he startles them by popping out from behind the hand-held foliage, usually earning a small wage and, almost invariably, a relieved, if embarrassed chuckle from his victim.

Despite possessing an entertainment permit from the city and having achieved local – if not international, judging by his character's inflated nickname – notoriety over the decades, certain businesspeople, police officers, and port officials have remained unamused. At one point, the San Francisco District Attorney's office had amassed a stack of complaints against the Bushman, including some from commercial boat operators who believed Johnson had been robbing them of business by clogging foot traffic on the sidewalk. However, the DA's office tossed out the nuisance complaints in 2004 once Johnson was acquitted by jury decision of four misdemeanor charges for minor injuries people had sustained in reaction to Johnson's antics. "They'll have to go the Supreme Court to make a whole new law to stop me," the Bushman remarked afterward.

shed. Many of its antique, hand-operated games are relics from Playland-at-the-Beach, the Ocean Beach amusement park that closed in 1972. If you dare, follow the booming cackling you hear to the giant fiberglass case that houses Laughing Sal, a freakish, gap-toothed veteran of Playland who'll howl forever for a mere quarter.

Walk through the identikit crab and chowder stalls at the foot of Taylor Street and head west on Jefferson for a look at the business that gave this area its name. **Alioto-Lazio**, 440 Jefferson St at Leavenworth (call for hours; free; ℡888/673-5868, Ⓦwww.crabonline.com), is a working fish company that's part retailer, part living museum – drop in and someone at the counter will happily explain the finer points (and strict laws) of local fishing and Dungeness crabbing. Finally, around the corner and down at the very end of Leavenworth Street, follow your nose to **Fish Alley**, where the boats and storage sheds offer a backstage look at a seriously ramshackle world few people care to get more than a quick whiff of: the remaining few working boats of the Wharf's namesake anglers.

Back on the Embarcadero around Pier 43, the glut of souvenir stands, hot dog carts, and general tourist tackiness becomes heavier, not to mention the dozens of unoriginal street performers – the one exception being the bizarre Bushman (see box above).

Alcatraz

Visible from the waterfront, **ALCATRAZ** Island – colloquially known as "the Rock" – is evocative even from a distance, keenly conjuring up images of bleak isolation. The islet became a military fortress in the late nineteenth century, and by 1912 the army had built a jail there. Twenty-two years later, it was turned over to civilian authorities and converted into America's most dreaded **high-security**

prison. Surrounded by freezing, impassable water, Alcatraz was an ideal place for a jail – this is where many of America's brand-name criminals (such as Al Capone and George "Machine Gun" Kelly) were held, as well as other dangerous oddballs like the fabled "Birdman of Alcatraz," Robert Stroud.

Although conditions softened as time passed – look for the radio jacks installed in each cell in the 1950s – a stay in one of the tiny, lonely rooms must have been psychologically grueling, especially given the islet's proximity to the glittering lights of San Francisco. The prison's initial policy of silence among inmates also underscored the strict regime, although that law was repealed three years after Alcatraz became a federal prison. Thanks to the violent currents that churn constantly in the chilly Bay waters, escape was virtually unthinkable – in all, nine men managed to get off the island, but none is known to have gained his freedom. One of the more successful attempts was in 1962, when three inmates used a magazine article they'd read (prophetically titled "Escape from Alcatraz") to build a raft out of inflated raincoats powered by a vacuum cleaner engine. None of the men was ever found, and they are presumed dead. Two other men, who stuffed inflated surgical gloves into waxed jackets as makeshift rubber rings, actually made it to land, although they were soon apprehended.

For all its usefulness as a stockade, the island prison turned out to be a fiscal disaster, so US Attorney General Robert Kennedy closed it in 1963; many of its prisoners were transferred to a new, maximum-security facility in Marion, Illinois. Alcatraz remained abandoned until 1969, when a group of American Indians – citing treaties that designated all federal land not in use as automatically reverting to their ownership – staged an occupation as part of a peaceful attempt to claim the island for their people. US government officials, using all the bureaucratic trickery they could muster, finally ousted the movement in 1971 by claiming the operative lighthouse on the island qualified it as active.

Interestingly, Alcatraz got its name as a result of poor map-reading and questionable diction. An early Spanish explorer christened one island in San Francisco Bay *Isla de Alcatraces* (Island of Pelicans) in honor of the hundreds of birds living on it; however, the island he was referring to is not the one known today as Alcatraz. The pelicans' old home is now called Yerba Buena Island because a clumsy English sea captain became confused when mapping the Bay in 1826. He wrongly assumed that the tiny, rocky islet – set between the mainland and Angel Island, and pelted with guano – must be the birds' home, so he marked it down in mangled Spanglish as "Alcatraz," then assigned the name Yerba Buena to the other island that is today's halfway point of the Bay Bridge.

Touring Alcatraz

These days, Alcatraz Island functions as a **museum** operated by the National Park Service (☎415/561-4900, ⓦwww.nps.gov/alcatraz), and at least 750,000 visitors each year take the excellent hour-long audio tour of the abandoned prison. This self-guided tour includes sharp anecdotal commentary, as well as re-enactments of prison life (featuring improvised voices of characters like Capone and Kelly); the real-life stories, such as the man who stayed sane in solitary confinement by endlessly pushing, then searching for, a single button in the darkness, are chilling. Skip the dull twelve-minute introductory film at the dock – you're far better off joining one of the free ranger talks on a variety of themes that run five times daily.

Alcatraz Cruises (frequent departures: mid-May to late Oct 9am–3.55pm, last ferry returns at 6.15pm; late Oct to mid-May 9am–1.55pm, last ferry returns at 4.15pm; day tour $24.50, night tour departing 6.10pm & 6.50pm $31.50;

☎415/981-7625, ⓦwww.alcatrazcruises.com) operates transport **ferries** to and from the island. The port of embarkation is **Pier 33**, just southeast of Fisherman's Wharf (public transportation is highly recommended). Advance reservations are essential – by spring, it's virtually impossible to turn up and travel on the same day, and you can expect at least a one-week wait in peak season. The best ferry to catch is the day's first, since the jail's not packed with other visitors when you arrive and will be evocatively empty; for particularly unflappable souls, night ferries to and from the island are available for a few dollars more. You'd be hard-pressed to spend an entire day on Alcatraz – in fact, two hours or so should be plenty, depending on your appetite for convict ephemera. There's no food service on the island, but packed lunches are allowed in the designated picnic areas, although the island's scrubby plant life and generally grim mood aren't conducive to a lingering lunch. In summer, Alcatraz Cruises also runs a trip that combines a visit to Alcatraz with a stop at nearby Angel Island for $56.50.

Aquatic Park and around

West of the Wharf, the pandering tourist trade recedes, although pockets persist next to **AQUATIC PARK** in the form of caricature portrait artists and dull, occasionally nettlesome street musicians. This area's best asset by far is **San Francisco Maritime National Historic Park**, a low-key complex that includes restored sailing vessels, a superb visitor center, curving jetties, impressive nautical architecture, and a sandy spit. Drop into the fine Visitor Center, 499 Jefferson St at Hyde (late May to late Sept 9.30am–7pm; rest of year 9.30am–5pm; ☎415/447-5000, ⓦwww.nps.gov/safr), which shares its huge brick building – formerly a cannery and factory – with the *Argonaut Hotel* (see p.159). Aside from selling tickets for touring the park's docked ships, this space offers an extensive display of local maritime history. Most interesting are the hand-rotated maps that detail changes in the area's shoreline since the nineteenth century, as well as the displays pinpointing shipwreck locations in and around the Bay.

Aquatic Park itself lies at the end of Jefferson Street, established in the 1930s by the Dolphin Club and the South End Club, longstanding private swimming and rowing organizations still based on Jefferson today. Part of this bayside park's sand was originally excavated from Union Square during excavations for the underground parking garage there; a few decades prior, this had been the dumping ground for much of the rubble from the 1906 earthquake and fire. You're likely to spot hardy men and women dipping in and out of the bracing water here – this cove is a favored practice and workout spot for local swimmers. Note the stone bleachers near the water's edge and the white loudspeaker towers scattered around the park: the former were built for public events that rarely happened, while the latter were never put to use at all. Plenty of benches and grass here make this a pleasant spot for a picnic if the weather's agreeable, while the park's southeast corner is the terminus for the Powell-Hyde cable-car line, the city's steepest.

Closed for an extensive refit at the time of writing, the Nautical Deco structure of the **Maritime Museum**, 900 Beach St at Polk (☎415/561-7100), commands attention directly behind Aquatic Park. It was originally opened as a bathhouse in 1939, and its gently sloping corners emulate the sleek ocean liners of the era. The building is scheduled to reopen sometime in 2009, at which point its extensive interior murals portraying real and mythical sea creatures will again be accessible to the public.

The final notable attraction around San Francisco Maritime NHP is the **Hyde Street Pier** and its painstakingly preserved ships. In its working heyday, the pier itself served numerous ferries that shuttled passengers (and in later years, their cars) between San Francisco and Sausalito, Tiburon, and Berkeley, but the 1937 opening of the Golden Gate Bridge quickly rendered these services useless. Today, there's no charge to wander down the wooden slats perched over the Bay and peruse the exhibits, and free ranger tours meet regularly throughout the day at the foot of the pier. However, to board one of the ships, you'll need to pick up a ticket ($5) at the Maritime Visitor Center (see p.87). Among the half-dozen or so vessels permanently docked here, the Scottish-built *Balclutha* (1886), with its spindly rigging, is the most inviting. Made of solid Douglas fir, this sole survivor of the great sailing ships that journeyed around Cape Horn in the 1800s was put into retirement in 1930, to be dragged out and done up for bit parts in such films as *Mutiny on the Bounty* before settling into its current role as a showboat.

Across the street but outside the national park boundary, looming above the entire scene, is **Ghirardelli Square**, 900 North Point St at Larkin, an erstwhile wool mill and chocolate factory sensitively converted in the 1960s into its current incarnation as an upscale shopping, dining, and soon, residential destination. The complex was among the first in the nation to repurpose disused industrial space as a means for generating new revenue, a trend several US cities have since followed. Its name comes from sweets baron Domenico Ghirardelli, an Italian gold prospector-turned-grocer-turned-chocolatier who arrived in San Francisco via Peru and eventually became patriarch of one of San Francisco's most famous families. When the company moved its manufacturing arm to San Leandro in 1967, the stage was set for the square's conversion; today, its several restaurants and food- and wine-themed shops (including the Ghirardelli Soda Fountain and Chocolate Shop – see p.162) make it a popular gathering spot for city visitors.

Fort Mason

Worth a wander, the rolling lawns, hilltop promontories, and renovated piers of **Fort Mason** are sandwiched between Fisherman's Wharf and the Marina. The expansive space is a dog's breakfast of public uses, and the entire complex is now part of the sprawling Golden Gate National Recreation Area (see box, p.89). The headlands and shore here endured a lengthy period of scattershot duty before finally gaining protected status as part of the GGNRA. Known in its early days as both Sand Dune Point and Black Point, Fort Mason was a defense bulkhead during the early Spanish settlement era. Following the Gold Rush, the first occupant of its then-treeless bluff was Selby Smelting, after which the area became littered with the shanty homes of squatters. Fort Mason became a haven of a different sort after the 1906 earthquake and fire, when it served as a refugee center for the homeless; it was at this point the US military began to actively occupy the site, planting numerous trees and tugging the area under the management auspices of the Presidio about a mile to the west. During World War II, 1.6 million soldiers and 23 million tons of cargo passed through Fort Mason's piers en route to the Pacific Theater, and it served as a logistical support center during the Korean War in the early 1950s. Following the Army's departure in 1970, it was turned over to public use through the efforts of cantankerous US congressman Phillip Burton, who blocked plans to turn the land over to private development. These days, the space is roughly divided into two sections: Upper Fort Mason on the hilltop is parkland, while Lower Fort Mason is home to old warehouses and wharves. **Upper Fort Mason** – best accessed via its main entrance at the northern terminus of Franklin Street where it crosses Bay – includes an enormous meadow, hidden picnic areas, housing, a community garden, and even a hostel housed in a converted Civil War barracks (for lodging details, see p.153). It's rich with the scent of eucalyptus, and although often windswept, there are some lovely picnic areas to be found around the overgrown hilltop batteries behind the hostel. Closely examine the larger-than-life statue of Burton gesturing animatedly across the meadow, and you'll spot a note protruding from his right jacket pocket. It reads, "*The only way to deal with exploiters is to,*" before disappearing into his pocket – a subtle nod to Burton's famously irascible personality, as the late politician always carried a handwritten note reminding him to continually "terrorize" his exploitative opponents.

At the north end of the meadow, steps lead down to **Lower Fort Mason**. This waterfront area, better known as Fort Mason Center (℡415/345-7500, Ⓦwww.fortmason.org), is almost entirely devoted to cultural and educational organizations, as well as celebrated vegetarian restaurant *Greens* (see p.181). About thirty nonprofit groups are headquartered here, including several **theaters** – for which tickets may be purchased at the main box office on the Middle Pier (Tues–Sat 11am–5pm; ℡415/345-7575. Fort Mason Center also houses a handful of galleries and museums. The **SFMOMA Artists Gallery** in Building A (Tues–Sat 11.30am–5.30pm; free; ℡415/441-4777, Ⓦwww .sfmoma.org) presents about eight shows annually, mostly of locally created

The Golden Gate National Recreation Area

Its funding initiative signed into existence in 1972 by the unlikely hand of President Richard Nixon, the **Golden Gate National Recreation Area** was the pet project of US congressional Representative Phillip Burton, who spearheaded its birth in an effort to prevent private development from stripping the San Francisco Bay Area of its signature wildlands and historical sites. The ferocious Burton, a staunch Democrat, had surprisingly few partisan enemies in Washington DC, but nonetheless tended to consider land speculators with contempt.

The GGNRA's first acquisitions in the 1970s were Alcatraz Island and Fort Mason (both purchased from the US Army) and the Marin Headlands (transferred from the Nature Conservancy, which had bought the land from Gulf Oil). Today, the GGNRA's 75,000-plus acres make it one of the largest urban parks anywhere in the world, although its holdings are patchwork and stretch from Tomales Bay in rural west Marin County to the Phleger Estate over thirty miles south of San Francisco. Somewhat confusingly, neither the namesake bridge nor city park is managed by the GGNRA, although much of the land adjacent to each is. GGNRA holdings offer remarkably wide appeal: from Muir Woods and the Presidio, to nude bathing at Golden Gate Beach and kids' educational exhibits and activities at Fort Baker. Visitor centers are located at each of the park's most popular destinations, while the GGNRA's headquarters (℡415/561-4700, Ⓦwww.nps.gov/goga) are inside Building 201 in upper Fort Mason. Alcatraz and Muir Woods are the only units of the park to charge admission fees.

contemporary works. Also worth a visit is the **Museo ItaloAmericano** in Building C (Tues–Sun noon–4pm; free; ☎415/673-2200, ⓦwww.museoitalo americano.org), home to a rotating collection of Italian arts and crafts, as well as a shop selling Italian-made glassware.

The Marina and Cow Hollow

The neighborhood west of Fort Mason, the **MARINA**, enjoys a prime location adjacent to a stretch of waterfront that boasts the Golden Gate Bridge and the Marin Headlands as a backdrop. Today it's one of San Francisco's priciest areas, but its beginnings are far from glamorous, having been created from squelchy land in the Bay in preparation for the Panama–Pacific International Exhibition of 1915. A sea wall was erected parallel to the shoreline north of Cow Hollow, after which the marshland in between was piled high with rubble from the 1906 earthquake and fire, mixed with sand from the ocean floor. Such flimsy foundations ultimately resulted in bitter irony, as the neighborhood originally built to celebrate the rebirth of the city after the 1906 calamities was the worst casualty of the Loma Prieta earthquake in 1989, when tremors sent many structures collapsing into smoldering heaps. Reconstruction was immediate and complete, however, and today among its townhouses, there's barely a speck of evidence of the destruction that ravaged the district.

Short of taking in the Palace of Fine Arts and the Exploratorium, or enjoying a stroll around its dense, beautifully manicured streets, the Marina doesn't offer many compelling reasons for visitors to linger; furthermore, its overwhelmingly young, white, professional, and straight demographic doesn't make for very interesting people-watching. Indeed, spend thirty minutes on main commercial strip Chestnut Street or along the long stretch of turf known as the Marina Green (a fitness mecca), and you're bound to see armies of fit 20- and 30-somethings outfitted in low-slung ballcaps and college sweatshirts – an image much mocked by residents of San Francisco's other neighborhoods.

The Palace of Fine Arts and the Exploratorium

San Francisco's most theatrical piece of architecture lies at the very western edge of the Marina: the **Palace of Fine Arts**, 3301 Lyon St, is not the museum its name suggests, but rather a huge, freely interpreted classical rotunda by **Bernard Maybeck**, the Berkeley-based architect who was also the mastermind of the Christian Science Church across the Bay (see p.309). When first erected for the Panama–Pacific International Exhibition in 1915, the palace was brightly colored with a burnt orange dome, deep red columns, and gold capitals, and widely acknowledged as the most beautiful of all the temporary structures. When the other buildings from the fair, which stretched from here east along the waterfront to Fort Mason, were destroyed to make room for the imminent Marina district, the palace was saved simply because locals thought it too beautiful to lose. Unfortunately, since it was built of wood, plaster, and burlap, it gradually crumbled with dignity until the 1960s, when wealthy local Walter S. Johnson led a fundraising campaign for the structure to be recast in reinforced concrete. (At the time of writing, the palace was swathed in scaffolding amidst a second refit.) To the modern eye, the palace is a mournfully sentimental piece, complete with weeping figures on the colonnade said to represent the melancholy of life without art. Original plans called for the pond in front of the building, which remains popular with swans and ducks, to be filled in. However, Maybeck wisely preserved it, creating an atmosphere of serenity that still fills the park.

Housed in a cramped space behind the Palace of Fine Arts, the **Exploratorium**, 3601 Lyon St (Tues–Sun 10am–5pm; $14, children $9–11, free first Wed of the month; ☎415/397-5673, Tactile Dome reservations ☎415/561-0362, Ⓦwww.exploratorium.edu), has been a prime field-trip destination for Bay Area schoolchildren since it opened in 1969. Rather than obscure the fun of science behind simplistic cartoons, curators wisely allow the magic of the 650-plus hands-on exhibits to keep young visitors enthralled by demonstrating the principles of electricity, sound waves, lasers, and more. The museum's most popular exhibit is the **Tactile Dome**, a total sensory-deprivation environment explored by hands and knees; reservations are essential, and it's definitely not for the claustrophobic.

About a ten-minute walk from the Exploratorium, at the eastern tip of the jetty that forms the yacht harbor next to the Marina Green, look for San Francisco's most subtle environmental art installation, the **Wave Organ**. The site was constructed in the 1980s from reclaimed marble and granite, and includes more than two dozen scattered "organ pipes" made of PVC tubing and concrete that produce sounds from Bay tides. Don't expect theatrical bombast, as the emanated tones generally require sensitive listening. Try visiting at high tide, when the piping produces the most sound.

Cow Hollow

A few blocks inland from the Marina, **Cow Hollow** was originally a small valley of pastures and dairies in the post-Gold Rush years. It takes its name from the days when cows grazed the land between Russian Hill and the Presidio and women brought their loads to one of the only sources of fresh water in town, which came to be known as Washerwoman's Lagoon. Problems with open sewage and complaints from Pacific Heights neighbors about the uninviting odors coming from the cowfields saw the area transformed in the 1950s, when enterprising merchants decided its old clapboard dwellings along **Union Street** had possibilities. The gorgeous old Victorian homes have since been refitted, and the stretch of Union between Steiner and Van Ness is now home to the city's densest concentrations of premium boutiques.

The neighborhood's only real attraction is the oddball **Octagon Museum**, 2645 Gough St at Union (noon–3pm second Sun, second and fourth Thurs of the month, closed Jan; donation suggested; ☎415/441-7512). Eccentric Orson Fowler, a pro-suffrage phrenologist with a passion for Greek mythology, published a book in the 1840s extolling the virtues of eight-sided living. While some called the man a crank, octagonal houses were constructed scattershot across America; 500 of them remain standing today, with this being one of two in San Francisco (the Freusier Octagon House, at 1067 Green St at Jones on Russian Hill, is closed to the public). This house was built in 1861 by local farmer William McElroy, and the time capsule he originally stashed under the stairs offers a captivating glimpse of nineteenth-century local life, including a letter from him, a newspaper, and photographs of his family. Also on display, albeit somewhat out of context, are signatures of 54 of the 56 men who signed the Declaration of Independence.

Pacific Heights

3

Perched on the tall hills that separate Cow Hollow and the Western Addition stands supremely affluent **PACIFIC HEIGHTS**, poised around two lovely parks and home to some of San Francisco's most monumental Victorian residences and stone mansions, as well as much of its social elite. Even when these hills were still bare in the 1860s, their panoramic views earmarked them as potentially fashionable territory once the gradient-conquering cable cars could link them with Downtown. Relatively humble homes covered the neighborhood in its earliest days, but were eventually replaced by the grander chateaus seen today – several of which always seem to be undergoing some sort of construction – after the neighborhood was made transit-accessible.

Pacific Heights is neatly divided by north-south artery **Fillmore Street**: to its west are the gigantic homes that earned the neighborhood its reputation; to its east, classy Moderne apartment buildings that do little to damage it. Upper Fillmore Street north of California is where Pacific Heights locals shop, dine, and otherwise spend piles of disposable cash. It's lively and lined with cafés and boutiques, as well as one of the last remaining single-screen movie houses in town, the Clay Theatre.

Aside from casually strolling Fillmore's sidewalks, Pacific Heights' principal attractions are a few mansions of note and its pair of popular parks, each occupying four square blocks. Across from the cypress-dotted peak of **Lafayette Park**, which begins three blocks east of Fillmore at Laguna and Washington Streets, is a squat brownstone known as the **Phelan Mansion**, 2150 Washington St at Laguna, built by James Phelan, the city's notoriously anti-Asian mayor at the turn of the twentieth century. (Phelan's unsuccessful later senatorial campaign featured posters that included the headline, *Keep California White*; decades later, his namesake beach along the city's northwestern edge saw its name revert back to its original, China Beach.) One block east stands the **Spreckels Mansion** at 2080 Washington St, a gaudily decadent white stone palace constructed for sugar magnate Adolph Spreckels and his wife Alma, a former nude model turned Legion of Honor benefactress. The spread encompasses half a city block and is now owned by bestselling romance pulpist Danielle Steel, who has pumped a tidy fortune into the structure's restoration and upkeep.

Neither of these mansions is open to the public – for that, you'll have to head a few blocks east to the ornate 1886 **Haas-Lilienthal House**, 2007 Franklin St at Jackson (hour-long tours begin every 20–30 minutes Wed & most Sat noon–3pm, Sun 11am–4pm; $8; ☎415/441-3004, ⓦwww .sfheritage.org). This double-size Victorian was built by German-born grocer William Haas (the house's hyphenate combines his surname with that of his son-in-law, who later lived here) and endures as a hushed symbol of old Pacific Heights wealth, although the talky tour is more focused on the day-to-day life of Haas and his family than it is on architecture. The house is significant because, unlike many Victorians which were standard designs overseen by builders, Haas commissioned an architect to custom-design his mansion. The exterior fuses elements of Queen Anne (notably, its circular tower) with holdovers from the San Francisco Stick (see box, p.93) such as large, wooden-carved details. The redwood-faced interior, meanwhile, is largely filled with original furniture, including Tiffany art-glass; also note the uniquely stenciled leather wall paneling. Overall, the mansion has stood the

Victorian architecture

Constructed from redwood culled from Marin County across the Golden Gate, San Francisco's **Victorian houses** enjoyed their greatest popularity in the late 1800s, thanks to an emerging middle class keen to display its modest wealth as showily as possible on a standard 25' by 125' city lot. By 1906, though, the heyday of the Victorians (and Queen Victoria herself) had already passed, and when many of the all-wood houses went up in flames in April of that year, the axe-stripped hillsides of Marin didn't have enough building material left to replace them. This disaster was compounded by the fashion shift away from the Victorians' excessive ornamentation in favor of less embellished stone and stucco homes.

For a good chunk of the twentieth century, local Victorians became an endangered species: many were torn down during Justin Herman's hurricane of urban renewal in the Western Addition (see p.135), while others were maimed simply through their owners' economies. By the 1960s, though, grassroots support swelled for the structures, and the Victorian Alliance was formed to campaign for their preservation. A survey by the National Endowment for the Arts found only 13,487 Victorians remaining in the city (down from a pre-1906 peak of more than 58,000), of which only half had been unaltered. The preservation campaign swiftly succeeded, and Victorian restoration continues to be a lucrative local profession to this day since large swaths of the homes are found in several San Francisco neighborhoods, from Pacific Heights and the Western Addition to Noe Valley, Bernal Heights, and the Haight.

There are three main styles of Victorians to look for in San Francisco. The earliest is the **Italianate** – look for Corinthian columns, a slanted bay window jutting from the front of the house, and heavy brackets at the roofline, as well as false fronts designed to add height and grandeur. Fine Italianates dating to 1874 are found south of Pacific Heights in the Western Addition, along so-called Cottage Row at 2115–2125 Bush St at Webster.

The Italianate was followed in the 1880s by the **San Francisco Stick**. This style is marked by a square bay window, etched or colored glass, porch columns that resemble furniture legs, and decorative vertical "sticks" appliquéd to the facade; in addition, its millwork is more heavily ornate than its predecessor. There's an excellent cluster of 1889 Sticks along the 1800 block of Laguna Street (between Pine and Bush) a few blocks south of Lafayette Park.

The final – and certainly the most flamboyant – style is the Queen Anne, its excesses a rather warped riff on the 1890s vogue. It follows a more diverse architectural template than earlier Victorians, with its steep roof gables and wooden shingles, as well as whimsical touches like plaster garlands and fake stucco swallows' nests fixed to the eaves. Round turrets, the most characteristic feature of this period, were produced thanks to technical leaps that enabled mass production of affordable curved glass. Well-preserved Queen Annes, painted in muted yellows and greens, can be found at 2000–2010 Gough St at Washington, directly across from Lafayette Park's east slope.

Victorians are now often known for their noisy color schemes, but other than a touch of India red or lavender on the larger mansions, most of these rowhouses would have originally been painted pale green or white, with window frames picked out in black. The current penchant for coloration dates to the 1960s, when hippies who had moved into abandoned or unloved Victorians in the Haight were allowed to paint their homes psychedelic colors by grateful, money-saving landlords. Note, too, how most Victorians have twin parlors: nineteenth-century social etiquette held that any guest could be received in the front room, while only intimate friends were invited into the rear parlor.

test of time remarkably well – look for the crack in the stairwell wall, one of the few signs of damage dating back to the 1906 earthquake. For more on local Victorian architecture, see the box on p.93.

West of Fillmore Street, the neighborhood is centered on **Alta Plaza Park** (framed by Jackson, Steiner, Clay, and Scott Streets), where kids frolic on the new playground structures and dog-walkers earn their keep by exercising pampered local pooches. Six blocks northwest at the far west end of Broadway, the **Lyon Steps** lead down a steep incline along the Presidio and into Cow Hollow. The path passes several grandiose homes (including that of former city mayor and current US Senator, Dianne Feinstein) and offers a magnificent view of the Palace of Fine Arts and other points north.

The Presidio

Occupying nearly 1500 hilly, forested acres along the northwest tip of San Francisco, the **PRESIDIO** was a military base for over 200 years before the US Army declared it surplus and handed it over to the National Park Service in the 1990s; like Fort Mason, it's now part of the Golden Gate National Recreation Area (see box, p.89). Along with Mission Dolores across town, it's the site of the earliest European settlement on San Francisco Bay, where Spanish soldiers established a garrison in 1776 to forestall British and Russian claims in the area. It passed through Mexican hands in the early and mid 1800s before becoming American property along with the rest of California in 1848. The Army began developing the site toward the end of the nineteenth century, and it played a significant deployment role in military embroilments from the Spanish American War on through World War II. Its run as the longest continuously operating military base in the US ended quietly with its 1994 transfer to the NPS, although several relics of its military past remain – most visibly at the sobering **San Francisco National Cemetery**, 1 Lincoln Blvd (daily 7am–5pm; free; ⊕650/589-7737, ⊛www.cem.va.gov), the final resting place of over 30,000, and one of San Francisco's only graveyards.

Aside from its stunning setting atop the San Francisco Peninsula, the Presidio is unique as being the only national park in the US with an extensive residential leasing program. The fact that about 2500 people live here further contributes to its hodgepodge of functions and uses, which range from sprawling green-space playground to home of non-profit organizations and bottom line-geared businesses alike (filmmaker George Lucas's Lucasfilm Ltd operates a sparkling new CGI design centre known as Letterman Digital Arts here, and Starbucks Coffee has opened a retail outpost. As you'd expect in an activist center like San Francisco, the Presidio's operational diversity hasn't come without conflict: certain park advocates bemoan the park's operating body, the Presidio Trust, as continually kowtowing to business interests, while those in charge of ensuring the Presidio becomes financially self-sufficient by 2012 – a central tenet of its one-of-a-kind Congressional agreement – point to the park's early (2005) achievement of this goal.

Main Post and around

Traveling its forested roads and strolling its trails are the best ways to begin to get a sense of the Presidio's vastness. A short distance from the Lombard Gate on the park's east side is the **Main Post**, where a number of handsome, red-brick buildings surrounding the former parade ground (now an enormous parking lot) have been recast as private offices and studios. Here you'll find the handy **Presidio Visitor Center**, 50 Moraga Way (daily 9am–5pm; ☎415/561-4323, 🌐www.nps .gov/prsf, also 🌐www.presidio.gov), temporarily located inside the old Officers' Club while its permanent home inside nearby Building 102 is refitted. Just off the Main Post's square across Lincoln Boulevard is the park's **Transit Center**, the hub of the park's free shuttle service, PresidiGo, which runs buses all around the park (weekdays 6.30am–7.30pm, weekends and holidays 11am–6pm). MUNI's #29 Sunset line also runs through here, and its #43 Masonic line stops nearby at the corner of Presidio Boulevard and Letterman Drive.

One of the Presidio's finest lofted vistas is at **Inspiration Point**, just north of the Arguello Gate along Arguello Boulevard, where a newly constructed platform looks out over the mixed forest northeast across the Bay. Other terrific views are scattered around the Presidio, particularly on the park's western reaches where sandy bluffs slope down to meet the waters of the Pacific. San Francisco's only **campground**, Rob Hill, occupies a hilltop adjacent to Washington Boulevard in this area of the park; its sites are earmarked for group use only, and are scheduled to reopen in April 2009 following an extensive expansion and renovation.

Crissy Field and Fort Point

The Presidio's crown jewel – and certainly its most visited – is **Crissy Field**, a bayfront swath of the park that extends west of the Marina. Originally tidal marshland occupied by local Ohlone people, it was landfilled for the 1915 Panama–Pacific International Exhibition; the Army re-appropriated it as an airfield

The rise and fall and rise of the Presidio landscape

Though having already been in the firm grasp of Spanish, Mexican, and American militaries for over 100 years, the Presidio was still a hilly, windswept sandbox in the 1880s when US Army Major W.A. Jones initiated his plan to alter its landscape by planting 100,000 cypress, eucalyptus, and pine trees. Although the extensive plantings certainly had a beautifying effect and provided sharp contrast with the surrounding city, Jones had other ideas: **forestation** of the Presidio would make it difficult for enemy eyes to scope infantry maneuvers from afar. The officer's plan also stated that the influx of foliage would make the base appear "immensely larger than it really is," while also "accentuating the power of the Government." Today, however, many of these trees are nearing the end of their lifespan, and there is talk of returning some of the park's falsely forested areas to its original dune habitat.

Throughout its lengthy military era, the Presidio's landscape enjoyed a rare level of **protection** from the urbanization encroaching outside the fort's borders; furthermore, parts of the base were barely (if at all) developed beyond forestation by military brass. By the same token, certain Presidio lands endured untold **abuse** during the US military's nearly 150-year tenure, as the Army contributed tens of millions of dollars toward the removal of toxic waste material and debris once the land changed hands in the 1990s.

Two newly popular areas of the Presidio that have been returned to their original natural states are former concrete wasteland Crissy Field (see above), and Coyote Gulch, an old seaside dump just west of Lincoln Boulevard newly populated by native wildlife. A few other sites, such as the ghostly, long-shuttered Public Service Health hospital near the 15th Avenue Gate along the park's southern border, still require extensive decontamination.

not long after (look for the old hangars past the west end of the huge expanse of grass). Once it reverted back to the public domain, it became the Presidio's first large-scale reclamation project, with hundreds of volunteers helping restore its lost identity as valuable wetlands in the late 1990s. It's become a wildly popular walking and running destination with striking views all around, and there's even a stretch of sand reserved for dogs (and their guardians). Behind the lagoon, you'll find the nearby Crissy Field Center, Mason and Halleck streets (Wed–Sun 9am–5pm; free; ℡415/561-7761, ⓦwww.parksconservancy.org), which includes a library, bookstore, and café, as well as offering educational programs.

Located near the old stables beneath the Highway 101 flyover, the lovably ramshackle **Presidio Pet Cemetery** is surrounded by a white picket fence amidst a stand of pines. It's a slight side trip inland from Crissy Field to reach the small burial site, which contains the graves of numerous Army pets. Tilted headstones mark the final resting places of Frisky, Smoochy, Skippy, and Moocher, among hundreds of others; as you'd expect, dogs and cats were the pets of choice for many Army families, but you're bound to find the odd iguana or hamster grave site if you hunt thoroughly enough.

Fort Point National Historic Site (Fri–Sun 10am–5pm; free; ℡415/556-1693, ⓦwww.nps.gov/fopo), located at the end of Marine Drive under the southern terminus of the Golden Gate Bridge, was built in the 1850s to guard San Francisco Bay. Spectacularly sited, with the great bridge towering above and the Pacific yawning across the west horizon, its well-preserved casemates make a worthy excursion for military buffs, while Alfred Hitchcock fans will recognize the spot just outside the fort where Jimmy Stewart pulled Kim Novak out of the swirling Bay waters in the 1958 thriller *Vertigo*. Fort Point still stands today thanks to Golden Gate Bridge Chief Engineer Joseph Strauss, who designed the lofted roadway's huge arch to preserve the old brick and

▲ Golden Gate Bridge from Baker Beach

Code 10-31

The Golden Gate is famous for more than just its astonishing span and Art Deco beauty: it's also a leading **suicide** location. On average, someone jumps to their death from one of the bridge's walkways about every two weeks. The first person to leap, World War I veteran Harold Wobber, did so just three months after the bridge opened. Thirty-six years later, in 1973, the number of suicides was set to reach 500; there was a circus-like atmosphere fueled in part by the irresponsible decision of the *Examiner* and *Chronicle* newspapers to chart the countdown publicly. When the number was circling 1000 in the mid-1990s, media reaction was even more callous: one local radio shock jock offered a case of Snapple as a consolation prize to the "winning" victim's family. This time, though, authorities stopped releasing figures so nobody could claim the dubious honor.

It's a four-second, 220-foot freefall from the bridge into the swirling sea below; most people hit the water at more than 75mph, and those not killed by the blunt-force trauma of impact are almost invariably swallowed by the treacherous currents. (Little wonder, then, that only 26 people have ever survived the plunge.) Despite the death toll, there's still no safety barrier – it's easy enough to clamber over the four-foot retaining wall. Since the 1950s, when the idea of a barrier was first broached, efforts to install one have been repeatedly blocked due to a combination of cost and aesthetics. Instead, the city favors constant patrols by policemen to monitor potential jumpers (known in local police parlance as "**code 10-31**"). The idea of a fixed barrier is still pushed from time to time, but there's no official word when, or even if a measure might be passed.

granite encampment, which was otherwise slated for demolition. Candlelight tours are held once monthly during the winter months – call the information line for details.

The Golden Gate Bridge

The focal point of countless photographs since its opening day in May 1937, the orange towers of the **Golden Gate Bridge** (☎415/921-5858, ⓦwww .goldengatebridge.org) remain San Francisco's most iconic image. Built in 52 months – and at the cost of eleven workers killed from falls during construction – the span is as much an architectural feat as an engineering marvel, and it instantly rendered the hitherto essential San Francisco–Marin ferry crossing redundant. Although the project was overseen by Chicago-born Joseph Strauss, the final design was, in fact, the brainchild of a local-born residential architect, Irving Morrow; at 4200ft, it was the world's first massive suspension bridge, designed to withstand gusts up to 100 miles an hour and swing as much as 27ft (and sag as many as ten) in high winds. The bridge has only been closed for weather three times, most recently one day in 1983 when 75-mph gusts blew through the channel.

Handsome on a clear day, the Golden Gate takes on an eerie quality when the area's signature thick white fog pours in and obscures it almost completely. Its color was originally intended as a temporary undercoat before the gray topcoat was applied, but locals liked the primer so much that the bridge has remained orange ever since. Surprisingly, the bridge's famed handle – which comes from the namesake strait it spans – predates the Gold Rush by a few years: explorer

John C. Fremont saw similarities between the San Francisco Bay's entrance and the Golden Horn, the Istanbul strait that connects the Sea of Marmara with the Black Sea. Also, note how the towers aren't the same distance from the center of the span, as the south anchorage was planted far from shore in treacherously deep waters in order to preserve Fort Point below.

Unlike its more heavily trafficked counterpart, the San Francisco–Oakland Bay Bridge, **pedestrians** and **cyclists** are welcome to cross the Golden Gate's Art Deco pathways; in fact, a walk, run, or ride across its 1.7-mile span is the most exhilarating way to experience the bridge's grandeur – and it's free (although unpopular rumblings surface from time to time about charging all comers, rather than just southbound drivers, who currently pay $5). Each end of the bridge features a designated vista-point parking lot, both of which become predictably choked with cars at peak times; clear evenings make for particularly grand viewing of city lights from the Marin shore. MUNI services #28 and #29 stop near the toll plaza on the San Francisco side.

SoMa, the Tenderloin, and Civic Center

The idea of San Francisco as a quaint Victorian-lined utopia on the sea holds fast until you wander into SoMa, the Tenderloin, or Civic Center, to the west and south of Downtown. These areas are thoroughly urban with a conspicuous lack of greenery and plenty of well-worn pavement – places where the flipside of California's prosperity is alive and unwell. After languishing for decades as a blighted warehouse wasteland, **SoMa** took an unimaginable upswing in the mid-1990s, thanks to the district's low rents. Groundbreaking art and music communities were the first to leverage the low prices, but the increased prosperity of the tech industry threatened to drive them out. Since the dot-com crash, though, the techies have cleared out, and the neighborhood has reclaimed its gritty appearance. Parts of the district boom every night with the muffled reverberations of underground dance clubs, but nearer to Downtown, the newly expanded Westfield San Francisco Center mall, the Yerba Buena Center museum and entertainment complex, and several other top-notch museums draw daytime visitors, as does the San Francisco Giants' baseball stadium along the waterfront to the east.

The adjoining **Tenderloin** and **Civic Center** districts reveal harsher realities, with heavy drug traffic and prostitution in evidence, along with a shocking number of homeless people. Their almost constant presence in front of **City Hall** is a stinging reminder of governmental failure to resolve the city's major shortage of affordable housing. While the refurbished City Hall and the adjoining **Opera** and **Symphony** buildings are worthwhile attractions, most visitors will only venture near them when searching for cheap accommodation or hurrying to a performance.

SoMa

SOMA, the distinctly urban district **S**outh of **Ma**rket Street, stretches diagonally from the Mission district in the southwest to the waterfront in the northeast. While the western sections have always been a working-class community (author **Jack London** was born there), the waterfront **Rincon Hill** and the **South Park** district were home to the first of the city's banking

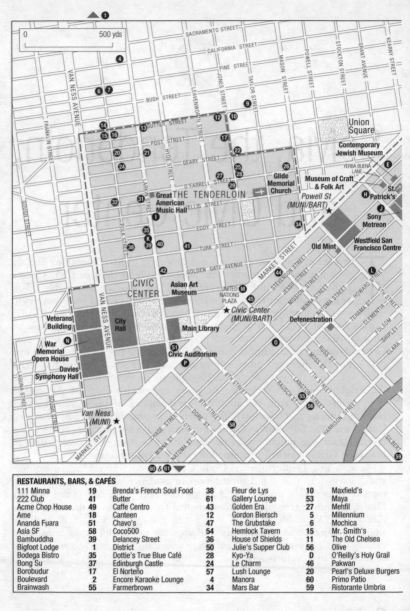

RESTAURANTS, BARS, & CAFÉS

111 Minna	19	Brenda's French Soul Food	38	Fleur de Lys	10	Maxfield's	
222 Club	41	Butter	61	Gallery Lounge	53	Maya	
Acme Chop House	49	Caffe Centro	43	Golden Era	27	Mehfil	
Ame	18	Canteen	12	Gordon Biersch	5	Millennium	
Ananda Fuara	51	Chavo's	47	The Grubstake	6	Mochica	
Asia SF	58	Coco500	54	Hemlock Tavern	15	Mr. Smith's	
Bambuddha	39	Delancey Street	36	House of Shields	11	The Old Chelsea	
Bigfoot Lodge	1	District	50	Julie's Supper Club	56	Olive	
Bodega Bistro	35	Dottie's True Blue Café	28	Kyo-Ya	D	O'Reilly's Holy Grail	
Bong Su	37	Edinburgh Castle	24	Le Charm	46	Pakwan	
Borobudur	17	El Norteño	57	Lush Lounge	20	Pearl's Deluxe Burgers	
Boulevard	2	Encore Karaoke Lounge	4	Manora	60	Primo Patio	
Brainwash	55	Farmerbrown	34	Mars Bar	59	Ristorante Umbria	

elite. By the 1870s, they were drawn away to Nob Hill by the newly invented cable car, and within thirty years, SoMa had been turned over to industrial development and warehouses. The poorer community that remained was largely driven out by fires following the 1906 earthquake, and Rincon Hill was eventually cleared in 1930 to make way for the new **Bay Bridge**. The decades after World War II saw the area converted almost exclusively into an industrial and shipping district, and oversized gray warehouse complexes still

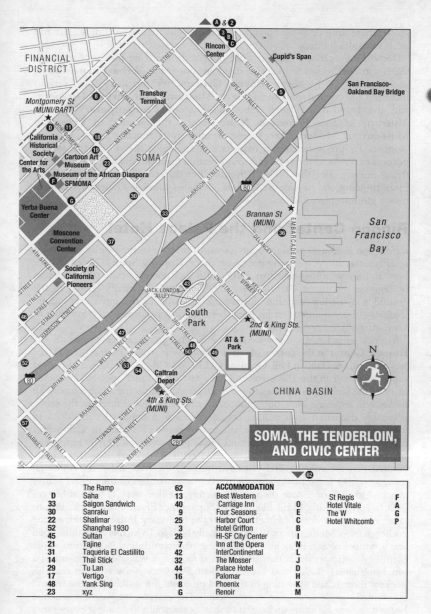

SOMA, THE TENDERLOIN, AND CIVIC CENTER

			ACCOMMODATION			
	The Ramp	62				
D	Saha	13	Best Western		St Regis	F
33	Saigon Sandwich	40	Carriage Inn	O	Hotel Vitale	A
30	Sanraku	9	Four Seasons	E	The W	G
22	Shalimar	25	Harbor Court	C	Hotel Whitcomb	P
52	Shanghai 1930	3	Hotel Griffon	B		
45	Sultan	26	HI-SF City Center	I		
21	Tajine	7	Inn at the Opera	N		
31	Taqueria El Castillito	42	InterContinental	L		
14	Thai Stick	32	The Mosser	J		
29	Tu Lan	44	Palace Hotel	D		
17	Vertigo	16	Palomar	H		
48	Yank Sing	8	Phoenix	K		
23	xyz	G	Renoir	M		

dominate the landscape today. Its loft spaces and low rents made it a prime location during the dot-com mania of the 1990s – factories and warehouses were relentlessly converted to offices for the fledgling Internet industry, drawing young people and creating a more lively neighborhood. However, when the Internet excesses crashed, so did SoMa. Nine years on, there is still plenty of empty office space and areas that are downright dangerous, the most notorious being Sixth Street, which has always been a place where drug deals go down in broad daylight. Stay accordingly alert and keep valuables hidden.

Dot-com disaster and daytime drug deals aside, there are plenty of must-see sights scattered round SoMa. The standout spot is the **Yerba Buena** district, anchored by lovely **Yerba Buena Gardens**; it's surrounded by various museums and cultural spots, including the **Museum of the African Diaspora,** and the brand-new Daniel Libeskind-designed **Contemporary Jewish Museum of San Francisco**. Nearby, too, is the famed **San Francisco Museum of Modern Art**, whose building is as much a must-see as its contents. By the waterfront, it may have taken over a decade for the eastern portion of SoMa to revive after it was liberated from the shadows of the high-flying freeway after the 1989 earthquake, but the stretch between the Ferry Plaza Building and bayside **SBC Park**, home of the San Francisco Giants, is now a glorious place to stroll.

Rincon Center and the Palace Hotel

Before you head into SoMa proper, it's worth nipping to the nearby waterfront to check out an eye-popping public art piece, **Cupid's Span**. This enormous bow-and-arrow was installed in 2003 and is a characteristically playful design by legendary sculptor Claes Oldenburg. The bow is partially buried in the ground and the arrow points downwards as a nod to the city's pop-culture lovability (Tony Bennett left his heart here, and it was home to the Summer of Love, after all).

A block inland from the waterfront at SoMa's northeastern tip stands the **Rincon Center** at the corner of Mission and Spear streets; it's the site of what was once part of Rincon Hill. Originally a US Post Office, it became a yuppified shopping center in the 1980s and still has a few good lunch spots. Constructed in 1939, the building is a fine example of Depression Moderne architecture, with its smooth, imposing lines, outer simplicity, and ornamented interior; the lobby is lavishly decorated with murals, commissioned in a contest by the WPA in 1941. Artist Anton Refregier was selected to paint 27 scenes of Californian history in the largest project of its kind. His angular style was heavily influenced by leftist Diego Rivera, which, combined with Refregier's Russian origins, ensured that the murals barely made it through the McCarthy era. Although some are rather faded now, there are excellent explanations of the subject matter attached to each one; note the scene depicting the discovery of gold at Sutter's Mill, filled with burly, Fagin-like settlers. For another historic landmark, walk or take public transit down Market Street to the legendary **Palace Hotel**, on the corner of New Montgomery. When originally built in 1875, this enormous hotel was a symbol of San Francisco's swaggering new wealth and its position as the premier American city in the West (even if its design was a direct rip-off of a hotel in Vienna). Backer and banker William Ralston's ego was larger than his pockets, though, and drowning in financial problems, he walked into the sea and committed suicide soon after its completion. The extravagant Rococo structure boasted antique furniture and lavish facilities – tragically, like almost every other building Downtown, it was ravaged by the 1906 fire, and subsequent remodelings have dampened its excesses. The one exception is the Garden Court dining room, the only indoor space on the National Register of Historic Places. Here, you can have high tea under the original 1875 Austrian crystal chandeliers suspended from the glass ceiling, which itself dates back to the post-fire refit of 1909. Eighty years later, it cost a staggering $7 million to dismantle, clean, and retouch the 72,000 panes of glass.

The Yerba Buena district and around

Until it was socially fumigated in the mid 1990s, Third Street was a crime-ridden strip, a block from the tourist trail along Market Street. It has since been transformed into the axis of an artsy **Yerba Buena district**. The centerpiece of this new neighborhood is **Yerba Buena Gardens** (daily dawn–10pm; free; ⓦwww.yerbabuenagardens.org). The gardens are an iconic example of urban reclamation, a rare instance of successful greenspace development. They sit on top of the underground Moscone Convention Center, named after the assassinated mayor (see box, p.125). The gardens themselves are a feat of engineering; to reduce the weight on the underground halls of the convention center, the earth here is only a couple of feet deep. As waterfalls drown out much of the street noise, the lawns are a peaceful oasis among the Downtown urban chaos, a place you can have a relaxing picnic lunch, or stretch out for a nap. The smallish, modernist bandshell here hosts more than 200 free concerts every spring and summer – check the website for schedules.

Along the park's southern face is a fifty-foot granite waterfall **memorial to Martin Luther King, Jr**. The water tumbles from a terrace above, while visitors can wander through a cool, mist-spattered stone corridor behind; etched into glass and stone panels are some of his lesser-known quotes – "I believe the day will come when all God's children from bass black to treble white will be significant on the constitution's keyboard" – translated into different languages. Don't miss the **Sister Cities garden** on the upper terrace, either. It's filled with flora from each of the thirteen cities worldwide that are twinned with San Francisco: look for camellias from Shanghai, marguerites from Osaka, and cyclamen from Haifa, among others.

Yerba Buena Center for the Arts, Sony Metreon and the San Francisco Zeum

On the gardens' eastern flank stands the **Yerba Buena Center for the Arts**, 701 Mission St at Third (Tues, Wed, Fri, Sat & Sun noon–5pm, Thurs 11am–8pm; $7, free first Tues of month or with a same-day ticket to an evening performance; ☏415/978-2787, ⓦwww.ybca.org). Initially conceived as a forum for community-art projects, the center has no resident companies; aside from renting out rehearsal/performance space at a pittance to local nonprofit groups, it also brings in international touring exhibitions and performances to the 750-seat theater here. The small second-floor screening room shows works by local experimental filmmakers, as well as themed programs of cult and underground films. There's also an onsite visual arts gallery, with a rotating selection of avant-garde and contemporary works – expect a lot of moody, symbolic installations and plenty of video art from emerging American and international names. For reviews of the various performance venues and ticket information, see p.227.

On the western side of the gardens sits one of the least alluring of the city's sights, the **Sony Metreon**, 101 Fourth St at Mission (daily 10am–10pm). Long a lame-duck mall with stores that were little more than advertisements for the company's high-tech gizmos, it's finally diversifying. There's now a branch of Chronicle Books as well as a large, if bland, food court (with free wi-fi), a hall of arcade claw machines and another arcade featuring a video game called Hyperbowl, that lets players send a giant bowling ball careering through the hills of a virtual San Francisco. The Metreon also holds a bizarre attraction called the Walk of Game – think Hollywood sidewalk stars, only for the pioneers of the videogame industry, ranging from fictitious characters like Sonic the

▲ MLK Memorial at Yerba Buena Gardens

Hedgehog to actual developers. The best reasons to check out the mall are its handy onsite multiplex, complete with IMAX screen, and the unparalleled views of SFMOMA's stunning building from the second floor.

The Yerba Buena complex is split in half by Howard Street; the easiest way to reach its southern chunk is to follow the pedestrian bridge threading south past the Sony Metreon and leading into another range of amenities, most aimed at kids. The banner attraction was supposed to be the **San Francisco Zeum**, 221 Fourth St (mid-June to Aug Tues–Sun 11am–5pm; Sept to mid-June Wed–Fri 1–5pm, Sat & Sun 11am–5pm; $10, children $8; ☏415/820-3320, ⓦwww .zeum.org), a hands-on science center. It's struggling to attract visitors, and only survives now on school groups rather than casual visitors. A free option here is the large, staffed outdoor play area; the separate, glassed-in carousel (daily 11am–6pm, $4) dating back to 1906 and once a part of the Playland-at-the-Beach amusement park is also worth a peek. In the same sprawling complex, you can also go **bowling** or skate on an indoor **ice rink** (hours vary, call for schedule; $8, under-13s $6.25, plus $3 skate rental per person; ☎415/820-3532, ⓦwww.skatebowl.com).

The Society of California Pioneers, Westfield San Francisco Center and around

Along Fourth Street from the Metreon is the **Society of California Pioneers** at no. 300 (Wed–Fri & first Sat of the month 10am–4pm; free; ☎415/957-1849, ⓦwww.californiapioneers.org). This little-known museum is much like a West Coast answer to the Daughters of the Confederacy; the society was founded in 1850 as a club for the city's earliest settlers to reaffirm their Mayflower-style supremacy. Today, exhibitions culled from its own extensive holdings of books, manuscripts, and paintings are mounted in a smallish hall; though many of its precious documents were lost in 1906, all the pioneer diaries were kept in a fire-proof safe, so you can call ahead to see precious items like John Sutter's day book or maps of San Francisco in its first decades.

Spanning Fifth Street, between Mission and Market, is the **Westfield San Francisco Center**, 865 Market St at Fifth (Mon–Sat 9.30am–9pm, Sun 10am–7pm), a mall (holding Nordstrom) that has recently expanded into the vast, long-empty building next door that was once the historic Emporium department store – which opened in 1896 and was rebuilt in 1908, after the earthquake. While the building was gutted to bring it up to seismic standards, the stunning, historic glass dome was restored. The huge new wing of the mall houses a branch of Bloomingdale's, a nine-screen Century Theatres multiplex, and an expanded food court, the highlights of which are a short-order franchise of the locally beloved Vietnamese restaurant *The Slanted Door* and a Bristol Farms grocery store.

Across the street from the Westfield Center, more local history will soon be on display at the magnificent Greek Revival **Old Mint** – nicknamed the Granite Lady – on the corner of Mission and Fifth streets. At the time of writing, the building's reopening was planned for 2012 as the new site of the San Francisco Museum and Historical Society (☎415/537-1105, ⓦwww .sfhistory.org), which, as well as a Bay Area history museum will house booths and tasting bars from prominent local chefs and vintners, similar to what's found at the Ferry Plaza Building. A stretch of the alley nearby, formerly a block of Jessie Street, has already been renovated into a public space called **Mint Plaza**. Designed as a spot for Downtown workers to relax, as well as a place for festivals and live performance, this stone promenade contains gardens, a steel arbor with climbing vines, and plenty of chairs. Behind the Old Mint, the next block of Jessie Street is home to a cavernous nightclub and live-music venue, *Mezzanine*.

Contemporary Jewish Museum and north of Yerba Buena

Immediately north of the gardens, you'll see a striking askew blue cube, which is an atrium gallery attached to the new **Contemporary Jewish Museum of San Francisco**, 736 Mission St (Mon–Wed & Fri–Sun 11am–5.30pm, Thurs 1–8.30pm; $10, under-18s free; ☎415/655-7800, ⓦwww.thecjm.org). Architect Daniel Libeskind was given the job of converting the 1907 Willis Polk-designed former power substation into exhibit space. His design beautifully fuses the turn-of-the-century facade with sleek modernism, smooth blue steel shooting out of the red brick power station like lightning. Libeskind was inspired by the Hebrew phrase "L'Chaim" (to Life) and incorporates two symbolic letters of "chai" (life): "chet," which shows up in the shape of the cube gallery, and "yud," in the wall relief at the museum's entrance. While the museum has no permanent collection, the space hosts cleverly curated exhibitions spanning Jewish history and culture, as well as installations of visual, aural, and multimedia art. The space debuted with a delightful retrospective of the work of *Shrek* creator William Steig, as well as an intriguing pastiche of artists reflecting on Genesis.

The Contemporary Jewish Museum is set back from Mission Street, and most of the old buildings in front of the museum were cleared out, replaced by the museum's open front plaza and fountain. The one still-standing holdover from before the redevelopment is **St Patrick's Catholic Church**, 756 Mission St (daily 6am–6pm; Ⓦwww.stpatricksf.org). Conceived in the afterglow of the Gold Rush by Irish immigrant forty-niners, the building dates back to 1912 and is now the spiritual center for the city's Filipino community; it's best known for free classical music concerts held at midday most Wednesdays.

Around the corner, the more modest **Museum of Craft and Folk Art**, 51 Yerba Buena Lane at Mission (Tues–Fri 11am–6pm, Sat & Sun 11am–5pm; $5, under-18s free; Ⓣ415/227-4888, Ⓦwww.mocfa.org), holds intriguing exhibitions based on various forms of folk art, including fabrics, paper, puppets, ukuleles, and even tattoos.

Museum of the African Diaspora and Cartoon Art Museum

Heading east on Mission from the Yerba Buena Gardens, you'll hit several more standout museums. On the north side of the street is the squat blue-and-white home of the **California Historical Society**, 678 Mission St at Third (Wed–Sat noon–4.30pm; $3; Ⓣ415/357-1848, Ⓦwww.californiahistoricalsociety.org). This tiny, offbeat gem showcases ephemera from the state's history, and is especially strong on the cultural and political fallout from early Spanish settlement. Opposite, the **Museum of the African Diaspora**, 685 Mission St at Third (Wed–Sat 11am–6pm, Sun noon–5pm; $10; Ⓣ415/358-7200, Ⓦwww .moadsf.org), spotlights everything from traditional African art, through work inspired by the horrors of slavery, to modern pieces in a range of media. MOAD puts a particular emphasis on hosting educational events and fostering community discussions about history and racism.

Next door to MOAD stands another overlooked attraction, the **Cartoon Art Museum**, 655 Mission St at New Montgomery (Tues–Sun 11am–5pm; $6, donation only first Tues of month; Ⓣ415/227-8669, Ⓦwww.cartoonart.org). Housed in an enormous concrete gallery space, the museum features rotating exhibits of cells and drawings, usually a sprightly mix of high concept "artoons" by the likes of French illustrator Moebius as well as staples like *Peanuts*.

The San Francisco Museum of Modern Art

Opposite the Yerba Buena Gardens to the east across Third Street is the area's – and perhaps the city's – marquee museum. The **San Francisco Museum of Modern Art**, at 151 Third St (Mon, Tues & Fri–Sun 11am–5.45pm, Thurs 11am–8.45pm, closed Wed; $12.50, $6.25 Thurs 6–8.45pm, free first Tues of month; Ⓣ415/357-4000, Ⓦwww.sfmoma.org), has a striking structure: designed by Swiss architect Mario Botta at a reported cost of $62 million, SFMOMA competes with the Getty and MOCA in Los Angeles to be the West Coast's premier exhibition space. It hosts top-notch touring shows from New York and Europe at the same time as it struggles to assemble a collection worthy of its housing. Head to the upper floors for the standout temporary exhibitions – past shows have included Eva Hesse, Matthew Barney, Alexander Calder, Diane Arbus, Chuck Close, and Keith Haring – and make sure to stop by the fine outdoor sculpture garden on the fourth floor. One level down, you'll find photography amid a reasonable selection of permanent works; look for numerous prints by pioneers like Henri Cartier-Bresson, Ansel Adams, and Alfred Steiglitz, not to mention trippy images by Man Ray. The rest of the permanent collection is curated in rotating displays scattered throughout the building, although the second floor is where most exhibitions take place. Unsurprisingly, the **California school** is well represented, with works by Richard Diebenkorn as well as the Mexican husband-and-wife team of Frida Kahlo and Diego Rivera, who were striking artistic presences in the city during the Depression. There's also a notable collection of **abstract expressionist** works by Mark Rothko, Jackson Pollock, and Robert Rauschenberg; there's a large body of work by Clyfford Still, the cantankerous artist known for once knifing his own painting from its frame in order to reclaim it from an unworthy owner. The museum also possesses part of the world's largest Paul Klee collection, 85 of the 140 works spanning the artist's career, acquired by Dr Carl Djerassi, a Stanford chemistry professor best known for his contribution to the development of the first birth-control pill. Aside from this, there are paintings and sculptures by Matisse, as well as works by Mondrian, Magritte, and Picasso, although little that's especially eye-catching: the museum has tacitly acknowledged that it's unlikely to assemble a world-class collection in this area and has wisely turned funds and attention elsewhere. The **pop art** holdings are snappier and include the famous gilded porcelain statue of Michael Jackson and his pet chimp by Jeff Koons; another well-known piece of whimsy is **Dadaist** Marcel Duchamp's *Fountain*. The building itself is always a treat: a huge central skylight floods the space with light, while the upper galleries are connected by a vertigo-inducing metal catwalk made up of tiny slats that challenge the definition of "adventurous" art.

AT&T Park, China Basin, and Mission Rock

The San Francisco Giants' home turf, **AT&T Park** (formerly SBC Park, and before that, Pac Bell Park), opened in 2000; it's undoubtedly a major improvement over the team's much-denigrated former home at Candlestick Park (see p.127), which was prone to gusts of brutally cold wind. The new stadium, built in one of the sunniest parts of town, has an outfield that opens onto the Bay and includes an extremely short rightfield fence (309ft) that's bested only by the "Green Monster" at Boston's Fenway Park. The official explanation is that the stadium was rotated slightly from its original design to protect players from whipping Bay winds – in the process, the outfield dimensions were truncated by the water. Most people, though, assume it was simply designed to allow star player Barry Bonds to hit home runs more easily; in 2002, Bonds led his team to its first World Series for almost twenty years, though his on-again, off-again career combined with allegations of steroid use have cooled his (and the team's) popularity. Tickets, however, can still be tricky to come by, as is parking: in an effort to get fans to leave their cars at home, the city built an extension to MUNI along the Embarcadero specifically for the stadium, though with only 5000 onsite parking spaces for 50,000 fans, even mass transit can be overwhelmed for big games. Twice-daily **tours** (90min; $10; ☎415/972-2400, ⊛www .sfgiants.com) leave the dugout store on Third Street at 10.30am and 12.30pm on off days, and even non-sports fans should enjoy these brisk, fact-packed jaunts around the building: you'll even stroll out onto the field. At the park, you can't miss the giant bottle of Coca-Cola and enormous mitt looming behind left field. The 80-foot-long soda bottle, which lights up and shoots bubbles every time the Giants hit a home run, contains slides, and is part of the children's area known as the **Coca-Cola Fan Lot** (June–Aug daily 10am–4pm; Sept–May Sat & Sun only). The glove, meanwhile, is a highly detailed 26-foot replica of a 1927 vintage four-fingered baseball mitt. Before leaving, stop to admire the frozen-in-time sculpture of Giants legend Willie Mays in front of the stadium: there are 24 palms ranged around it, a nod to his jersey number.

The spirit of blue-collar, industrial San Francisco perseveres around the abandoned docks and old shipyards known as **China Basin** and **Mission Bay** along the eastern edge of SoMa. This area – completely skippable if you have a short trip –is at the moment only worth visiting if you are particularly enamoured with decaying urban shipyards and boat clubs, and is best seen from a rented bicycle or on inline skates, as it's a long walk. The docks at the **switchyards**, where the drawbridge crosses China Basin Channel, were the site of deadly clashes between striking longshoremen and the city police in the 1930s, one of the country's largest labor uprisings of the twentieth century. To this day, the union maintains a reputation for radicalism. Later, in the 1950s, **Jack Kerouac** worked here as a brakeman while writing the material that was later to appear in *Lonesome Traveler*, detailing scenes of SoMa's skid-row hotels and whores. The site of several distressingly large homeless encampments, the area is generally best avoided after dark. However, 303 acres of Mission Bay are in the process of being redeveloped, as condos, office and retail space, and a new UCSF research campus are under construction. The new development, served by the new Third Street light rail, will also feature plant-filled promenades, a new public school, and new fire and police stations.

Folsom Street

On the western side of SoMa, the strip of **Folsom Street** is rather desolate by day, largely filled with autobody repair shops; but after dark, an eclectic nightlife scene thrives along that same strip between Eighth and 11th streets – its clubs and restaurants catering to every subculture under the stars. Because it's not the sort of club district where partiers pack the sidewalks, except along 11th, it's best to know what spots you're going to hit before you arrive. Most of the action happens behind closed doors, and many of the streets, even those where parties are going on, still give the vibe of an isolated warehouse district with uncomfortably long walks between venues. Folsom Street has been the longtime home to the city's leather community (French postmodernist and renowned S&M fan Michel Foucault claimed to have a near-spiritual relationship with the place), but the leather scene actually maintains a relatively low profile for most of the year, except in September during the **Folsom Street Fair**. This orgy of chaps and public whippings is less raunchy than it once was; hardcore sex fetishists flock instead to the offshoot, Dore Alley, which somewhat incongruously takes place along a side street lined with 1980s-era suburban-style condos (for details, see p.281).

The surrounding blocks hide a variety of art spaces and galleries, though your chances of simply stumbling across them are rather slim. If you happen to be here during daytime hours, wander back east to 214 Sixth St at the corner of Mission to look at **Defenestration**, a Quixotic piece of public art by local artist

Brian Goggin, involving furniture that has been bolted to the outside of an abandoned building. Just don't linger too long – it's one of the nastier corners in town.

The Tenderloin

The **TENDERLOIN**, a small, uninviting area on the north side of Market Street between Civic Center and Union Square, has long been one of the shabbiest sections of town, overrun with tenement houses and mentally unstable homeless people. Local bureaucratic paralysis has continued to aggravate the problem, and, sadly, the area's rougher than ever. The stretch of Taylor Street around Turk and Eddy is especially unpleasant, day or night, although you should be safe as long as you keep your wits about you and don't mind vagrants asking you for money. There are signs, though, that the neighborhood is changing: for one, waves of Pakistani and South Asian immigrants have begun transforming the neighborhood by establishing numerous cheap restaurants. At its upper edge, gentrification has bled down from tony Nob Hill, and realtors have taken to calling the northernmost portion (in a glorious *double entendre*) the Tendernob.

The area's oddball name has never been definitively explained. One tale is that nineteenth-century police were rewarded with choice cuts of steak for serving a particularly perilous tour of duty here. A less flattering version is that, thanks to the constant bribes they collected from the gambling houses and brothels, those same policemen were able to dine in the city's finest restaurants. Still others claim that the name is based on the district's shank shape, or even its notoriety for flesh-flashing brothels. Whatever the answer, it has always been the seediest part of town and the heart of San Francisco's vigorous sex industry (see box, p.110).

One of the brighter places in the area is the **Glide Memorial Methodist Church** at 330 Ellis St at Taylor (☎415/674-6080, ⓦ www.glide.org), providing a wide range of social services for the neighborhood's downtrodden, including a shelter and a soup kitchen for the homeless. Thanks to the forceful personality of Pastor Cecil Williams, a major political figure in the city, the church also conducts a remarkable Sunday service, backed by his rollicking choir. It's a high-octane experience – full of soul, blues, jazz and R&B music, mind-blowing singing soloists, and well-dressed black matrons elbow to elbow with glammed-up drag queens – that's definitely worth the effort to attend. If you want to snag a seat in the main auditorium, you'll need to turn up at least an hour before the service is scheduled; most casual visitors end up in an adjoining room where they can only watch via live television link. If you're not stopping by on a Sunday, step inside to see the AIDS Memorial Chapel – the altarpiece triptych was the last work Keith Haring completed before his death from the disease.

Polk Gulch

At the western limits of the Tenderloin, on Polk Street between O'Farrell and California, lies **Polk Gulch**; this was once a congregating point for the city's transgender community and a hub for the flesh trade, though its sex-soaked past is slipping away. This area inherited many of the displaced residents and merchants who fled Haight-Ashbury in the early 1970s. It's now best known for the several

San Francisco established itself as a center of sin long before the Mitchell brothers (see below) opened shop. During the **Gold Rush era**, thousands of unaccompanied men passed through the city before heading off to the hills, and when they returned to town with a bit of gold in their pocket, they often lost it at one of over one hundred houses of ill repute that had taken root in the city. The twin centers of San Francisco's prostitution industry were in the Tenderloin and the Barbary Coast, near what's now Jackson Square. While the latter is now packed with genteel interior design stores, the former still relies on the sex trade for much of its industry.

Shockingly, some saw the **prostitution** business – which was often run in league with organized gambling halls – as an opportunity for poor women to advance in society; certainly, in the morally liberal atmosphere of nineteenth-century San Francisco successful madams were able to move with the city's elite. Reputed madam **Sarah Althea Hill** even sued her longstanding customer, Senator William Sharon, while former New Orleans courtesan **Belle Cora**, mythologized as the most beautiful woman in the city, hosted salons for society at her brothel – at least until her husband was lynched for defending her honor in a duel. But these women were the exception. For most, notably the many women kept as virtual prisoners in the brothels of Chinatown, it was a miserable existence. However, the industry began to suffocate at the turn of the nineteenth century under the twin engines of women's suffrage and religious fury, notably embodied in one person, Scottish missionary **Donaldina Cameron**. Nicknamed the White Devil, she liberated more than 3000 girls from forcible prostitution. By the beginning of the twentieth century, the brothels were rapidly shutting their doors, while rebellious women such as Oakland-raised Gertrude Stein led a charge into salon society across the country.

Still, San Francisco's reputation as the **sex capital** of America remained ingrained in the popular mythology, and after World War II the city's massage parlors and strip joints thrived again with the sudden presence of numerous GIs who stayed on after being discharged from their service. Ironically, given the city's crushing political correctness, San Francisco must also take responsibility for introducing topless waitressing to the world (see p.72). Later, after AIDS hit in the 1980s, many sex establishments shut down – especially the city's notorious gay bathhouses – only to

historic gay bars that line the street, not to mention the smattering of young hustlers and prostitutes. The intersection of O'Farrell and Polk is home to a neighborhood landmark of sorts, the strip club known as **Mitchell Brothers O'Farrell Theater** (Mon–Thurs 11.30am–1.30am, Fri–Sat 11.30am–2.30am, Sun 5.30pm–1.30am; ☎415/776-6686). The Mitchell boys achieved considerable notoriety in the 1970s when they persuaded young Ivory Soap model Marilyn Chambers to star in their porno film *Behind the Green Door*, which they debuted at the Cannes Film Festival. While the pair slowly slipped back into obscurity over the ensuing decades, they made a tragic return to tabloid fame when Jim Mitchell shot and killed his brother Artie in 1991.

Despite its seedy appearance, Polk Gulch has a thriving nightlife, with its diverse restaurants, stylish lounges, and dive bars like *Hemlock Tavern* and *Edinburgh Castle*, with small, sweaty back rooms where the Bay Area's edgiest bands play. The most esteemed of the Polk Gulch live music venues is also San Francisco's oldest, the **Great American Music Hall**, 859 O'Farrell St at Polk (☎415/885-0750, ⓦwww.gamh.com), right next to the Mitchell Brothers theater. The 5000-square-foot concert hall opened in 1907 as *Blanco's*, a Barbary Coast-era restaurant, bordello, and gambling hall with elaborate Victorian resurface a decade later in different forms. Today, the city retains a laissez-faire attitude toward sex, though a somewhat bizarre zoning law dictates that sex clubs, while legal, may not have private rooms onsite, delighting the city's exhibitionists and voyeurs while frustrating shyer patrons.

Perhaps the best example of how the sex industry has evolved can be found at the **Power Exchange**, 74 Otis St near Mission (☎415/487-9944, ⓦwww.powerexchange .com). Touting itself as the largest sex club in the world, this former power station unblinkingly advertises three floors of playrooms, as well as plenty of equipment for whippings, floggings, fetishes, or more vanilla activities. Safe sex practices are required, and condoms, lubricant, and gloves provided. The Mixed Club is for everyone (hetero-sexuals, lesbians, gays, bisexuals, and transgender), while the smaller Level3 is for couples and single women only.

For more than thirty years, San Francisco has been at the forefront of sex-positive feminism. In 1977, sex educator Joani Blank opened **Good Vibrations** (see p.262), as a "clean, well-lighted" woman-friendly alternative to the usual sex stores. In 1992, the staff of Good Vibrations bought the company from Blank and reorganized as a cooperative; now the store has franchises on Polk Street in San Francisco, in Berkeley, and in Brookline, Mass. Since the 1990s, San Francisco has also been a leader in the movement to **decriminalize prostitution**, unionize sex workers, and protect them from violence, with local women founding groups such as the Exotic Dancers Alliance, the Bay Area Sex Worker Advocacy Network (BAYSWAN), which sponsors the **San Francisco Sex Worker Film and Arts Festival,** a week-long film and art showcase every July featuring work about sex workers and sex industries from around the world, and the United States' version of Australia's Sex Worker Outreach Project. The newest addition to the sex-positive culture here is the **Center for Sex & Culture**, a library and seminar space run by eccentric sexologist Dr Carol Queen (☎415/255-1155, ⓦwww.centerforsexandculture.org). Queen regularly hosts discussion groups and sexual self-help shows at her appointment-only center, 1519 Mission St at 11th, but is best known as ringmistress of the annual Masturbate-a-thon. That's when dozens of the willing gather together one Saturday night in May to lend a hand and raise funds for the center (the current record-holder flunked out just shy of seven hours).

balconies, marble columns, and ornate frescos on the ceiling. Fan dancer Sally Rand, who was adored by locals, bought the place in 1936, dubbed it the *Music Box*, and hosted popular dance parties for a decade. Before it reopened as the *Great American Music Hall* in 1972, the spot had other lives as a jazz club and a Moose Lodge. In 37 years, the hall has continued to draw big-name performers like Duke Ellington and the Grateful Dead and successful local acts, in every genre from punk and indie rock to jazz, blues, and world music.

Civic Center

To the immediate southwest of the grubby Tenderloin stands San Francisco's grandest architectural gesture: the complex of Beaux Arts buildings known as **CIVIC CENTER.** This cluster was the brainchild of brilliant urban planner Daniel Burnham, a follower of the "City Beautiful" movement, whose central tenet was that utopian cities in vaguely classical style would be so beautiful that they'd inspire civic loyalty and upstanding morals in even the most impoverished

San Francisco's homeless

San Francisco's most intractable social problem is **homelessness**, an issue that's clear even to casual tourists. Downtown, much of Market Street west of Hallidie Plaza is filled with vagrants day or night, drawn here by the social service administration buildings that sit on the blocks between Sixth and Eighth streets. In fact, the city has the largest homeless population in the United States, with wanderers attracted to the city for its temperate weather and reputation as a liberal center, with little of the harsh policing tactics used in other big cities to sweep the streets. Laws reforming the mental health-care system signed by Governor Ronald Reagan in the 1970s contributed to the large number of mentally ill living on the streets of San Francisco, and together with those struggling with drug addiction or alcoholism, and the indigent living in decrepit hotels on SoMa's Sixth Street, the sheer volume of people competing both for loose change and for social services has contributed to a culture of desperation and poverty along Sixth Street and the Tenderloin. Governor Gavin Newsom's controversial "Care Not Cash" ballot measure was approved by San Francisco voters in 2002, whereby welfare will not provide string-free support for the homeless; instead of a couple of hundred dollars doled out, no questions asked, each month, shelter and other in-kind support is available – provided one can pass a drug test. Advocates and detractors of the law continue to debate whether it has made an effective impact on the number of homeless on the streets.

resident. Before the devastating earthquake of 1906, he'd already prepared plans with the help of architect Willis Polk to level San Francisco and rebuild it along Parisian lines. These plans featured boulevard-like traffic arteries fanning out like spokes across the city, extensive subways, and a grand civic plaza on the site of a former cemetery at the junction of Van Ness Avenue and Market Street. Unfortunately, after the earthquake, the city was choked by bureaucracy, and his plan was heavily diluted until only the civic plaza was passed. Even then, it wasn't finished until several years after his death.

Despite Burnham's belief that grand architectural answers would silence social questions, Civic Center today is simply the Tenderloin with better buildings. The plaza's crammed with the bulk of the city's homeless, and although police periodically evict them, there are few other places to congregate, and most soon return. The contrast between the finely dressed San Franciscans heading in and out of the opera, ballet, and symphony and the mentally ill or drug-addicted homeless nearby is glaring.

Exploring Civic Center

Most visitors arrive at the Civic Center MUNI and BART station at the corner of Market and Leavenworth streets and are disgorged immediately into the **United Nations Plaza**, built in 1975 to commemorate the founding of the UN here thirty years earlier – look for the UN Charter etched on a black stone shard. The plaza is filled with fountains and homeless people, but on Wednesdays and Sundays the square's transformed into a **Farmers' Market**, a convenient place to pick up a cheap lunch. Thanks to the esteemed Bay Area chef Alice Waters, the Slow Food USA non-profit organization, and more than 100 volunteers, an edible **Victory Garden** has been planted in the lawn in front of City Hall. Inspired by the Victory Gardens of the 1940s, which addressed food shortages during World War II, the garden was initially a part of the 2008 Labor Day festival, Slow Food Nation, celebrating sustainable agriculture and healthy cuisine. The bounty is donated to food banks and meal programs.

The hills of San Francisco

San Francisco would simply not be San Francisco without its signature hills, nor would its treasured cable cars have much reason to exist without the steep inclines adjacent to Downtown. Along with a breezy waterfront setting and persistent fog, the city's fifty-plus high points are its defining natural characteristic, providing heart-thumping exercise, astonishing vistas, and in many cases, behind-the-wheel thrills for locals and visitors alike. Certain heights are thickly settled with residences, but plenty remain entirely in the public domain – so lace up your sturdiest shoes and enjoy an essential city experience.

Signs on Telegraph Hill ▲

Coit Tower on Telegraph Hill ▼

Three to see

A trio of prominent hilltops stands above the crowd, although even these lofty landmarks sometimes can't poke their way out of the city's glurgy fog.

To the east, topped by one of San Francisco's most popular monuments, Coit Tower, **Telegraph Hill** was once a signal tower for ships entering the Golden Gate. Rising above the most densely built section of the city, it's the finest natural vantage point in its area, and its 288-foot rocky mound affords excellent views of Downtown's skyscrapers and the city's central neighborhoods.

Towards the centre of the city, the pair of 900-foot promontories known as **Twin Peaks** was labeled *Los Pechos de la Choca* ("The Breasts of the Indian Maiden") by early Spanish explorers; local geographers eventually settled on the current, less randy handle. The southern hill is 18ft taller than its counterpart, but both provide wide-angle vistas. A number of major points are visible across the Bay on clear days, most notably Mount Diablo, thirty-plus miles to the east. Unlike other San Francisco high points that have been either developed or planted with non-native trees, these peaks maintain a strong resemblance to how they looked during the Gold Rush era.

High atop a bluff along northwest San Francisco's rocky shoreline, **Sutro Heights Park** overlooks the Pacific Ocean 200ft below. A set of benches along the park's westernmost edge offers unlimited views of sandy Ocean Beach, which yawns for several miles toward the city's southern border. The grassy space was donated for public use by original owner (and onetime mayor) Adolph Sutro, whose estate on these grounds was eventually dismantled after his death in the late 1890s.

Other notable hills

Of the city's other hills, the following are particularly worth a climb.

Bernal Heights: With several radio antennae atop its grassy 500-foot summit, Bernal Heights is a popular vantage point for watching fireworks displays around town. Vistas are largely unimpeded, particularly to the north and east.

Mount Davidson: The identifying feature of San Francisco's highest point (927ft) is a 100-foot cross, itself now owned by a local Armenian-American association. Overshadowed by other, more famous promontories in town, Mount Davidson has seen massive overgrowth by non-native eucalyptus trees, but a chaotic, winding network of footpaths persists its way up and around the lush hill's flanks.

Nob Hill: It wasn't until the invention of the cable-car system in the 1870s that this supremely affluent district became easily accessible. Today, it's a quiet repose of luxury hotels and distinguished high-rise residences.

Potrero Hill: Although residentially developed, this surprisingly isolated neighborhood sandwiched between the Mission and San Francisco Bay boasts striking views of Downtown and the SoMa district.

Russian Hill: Full of classic San Francisco residences, vintage apartment towers, and some of the city's most inviting sidewalks, this promontory neighborhood makes for a thoroughly enjoyable afternoon spent rambling up and down its verdant streets.

Strawberry Hill: This island-hill in the middle of Stow Lake provides a noteworthy climb among the otherwise gently rolling slopes of Golden Gate Park.

▲ View from Sutro Heights Park

▼ Mount Diablo seen from Twin Peaks

▼ Cable car on Russian Hill

The Cliff House ▲

Pagoda at the Japanese Tea Garden ▼

The best places to catch your breath

▶▶ **The Cliff House (1900 Point Lobos Ave, Outer Richmond)** Drop into this recently rebuilt seaside fixture directly below Sutro Heights Park and have a seat at the bar at *Sutro's* downstairs, where cocktails and outstanding views of the Pacific have been courting visitors since the city's earliest days. See p.141.

▶▶ **Fairmont Hotel (950 Mason St at California, Nob Hill)** Visit the lovely terrace garden overlooking Powell Street at this opulent hotel; the Tiki-themed *Tonga Room* bar in the basement is also great campy fun, with an indoor rainstorm every fifteen minutes. See p.79 & p.213.

▶▶ **Japanese Tea Garden (Music Concourse, Golden Gate Park)** A short walk from Strawberry Hill and adjacent to the de Young Museum, in San Francisco's gorgeous main public park, you'll find this verdant hideaway with a small café serving tea and Japanese cookies. See p.146.

▶▶ **Mario's Bohemian Cigar Store Cafe (566 Columbus Ave at Union, North Beach)** The portrait of North Beach cool for decades, legendary corner spot *Mario's* is a terrific place for a focaccia sandwich and a glass of wine. See p.178.

▶▶ **Nook (1500 Hyde St at Jackson, Russian Hill)** order a sake or *soju* cocktail at this corner café, grab one of the few outdoor tables, and watch the cable cars pass and turn onto narrow Jackson Street right in front you. See p.178.

▶▶ **Thinkers Cafe (1631 20th St at Connecticut, Potrero Hill)** A main hangout in its tightly knit neighborhood, this mellow café is ideal for reading or quiet conversation. Bring a book or newspaper, order a pastry or salad, and settle in at one of the sidewalk tables. See p.124.

The Public Library and the Asian Art Museum

Immediately to the left of the plaza is the **San Francisco Public Library**, 100 Larkin St at Grove (Mon & Sat 10am–6pm, Tues–Thurs 9am–8pm, Fri noon–6pm, Sun noon–5pm; ☎415/557-4400, ⓦsfpl.lib.ca.us), which moved into its current location in 1996 from its original site, now the Asian Art Museum. This move was controversial since the sleek new library headquarters – which includes a large, light-filled central atrium and plenty of space for lounging readers – didn't incorporate much space for books, and portions of the library's holdings have repeatedly been sold off in order to squeeze everything into the new stacks. At the top floor, the San Francisco History Center, used primarily for research, has a rotating, if ragtag, display of ephemera. Of greater interest, one level below, is the **James C. Hormel Gay and Lesbian Center** (named in honor of the gay activist and meat magnate), the first of its kind in the nation. Topped by a dome with a mural depicting leading figures in gay rights and literary movements, it's a combined reference library, community center, and exhibition space. The library has several computer terminals with Internet access that anyone can use free of charge for fifteen minutes, available on a first-come-first-served basis, and a free wi-fi signal is provided.

Next door stands the **Asian Art Museum**, 200 Larkin St at McAllister (Tues–Wed & Fri–Sun 10am–5pm, Thurs 10am–9pm; $12; ☎415/581-3500, ⓦwww.asianart.org). Originally stuck in cramped quarters in Golden Gate Park, it reopened here in 2003 in what was the city's original Public Library. The Beaux Arts building, put up in 1917 as part of Daniel Burnham's abortive plans, received a stunning makeover from Gae Aulenti, the same architect who turned a derelict train station in Paris into the Musée d'Orsay. She opened up the former library's interior to allow light to reach every corner, while still preserving details like the multicolored, ornamental ceiling decorations visible in the upper galleries. The museum's holdings are vast, and it takes several hours to hit just the highlights: the most famous treasure is probably the oldest known Chinese Buddha image, which dates back to

▲ City Hall

338 AD. Look, too, for the White Tara, a gilded, seated female goddess from Nepal with seven eyes – five extra spread between her palms, feet and forehead – and the wonderful wooden statue of Fudo Myoo, the wrathful Japanese god, with an expression more constipated than thunderous. The best way to tackle the museum is to start on the third floor and work down: the collection's organized by country and loosely arranged so that the upper floor contains religious statuary, while the second holds broader ranges of objects and ephemera. There are free docent talks throughout the day; the introductory **tours**, however, are breathless and hurried – you're better off browsing at leisure with an audioguide.

City Hall

Civic Center Plaza, between the main library and City Hall, is usually filled with a combination of political protestors, the homeless, and misshapen trees. Pause to regard the eighteen flagpoles, each of which displays a flag from Californian history – like the various iterations of Old Glory – with an explanation at its base. Grand **City Hall** on the other side of the park stands on Dr Carlton B. Goodlett Place, an honorary designation to commemorate a local civil rights leader (Mon–Fri 8am–8pm; ☎415/554-4799, ⓦ www.sfgov .org/site/cityhall_index.asp). This is actually the second City Hall – the first, on the site of what's now the public library, was constructed of steel and reinforced concrete. Seven years after its completion in 1899, the earthquake and fire gutted the cheaply constructed building, stripping it down to its skeleton, like a charred birdcage. Nothing could be salvaged, other than the statue from the top of the dome, so the building was pulled down and a contest announced for its replacement. (Ironically, the statue shattered after rolling off the flatbed truck in which it was being transported from the site, so that, ultimately, nothing of the first City Hall survived.) More than seventy local firms submitted designs in hopes of winning the $25,000 prize, and the plan that won out was by Bakewell and Brown, former students at the Ecole des Beaux Arts in Paris, to build a structure inspired by the haughty, gilded dome of Les Invalides there. City Hall cost an astonishing $3.5 million to build, and includes more than ten acres of marble, shipped in from Vermont, New Hampshire, and Italy. In fact, the reason the building didn't open as hoped in time for the Panama–Pacific International Exhibition in 1915 was that marble couldn't be quarried fast enough to finish it. It's conspicuously sumptuous throughout, notably in the priceless carved Manchurian oak walls in the Board of Supervisors Legislative Chamber. Earthquake retrofitting – which involved sliding giant ball bearings under its foundations – allows the entire structure to wobble more than two feet in either direction during a quake, an almost foolproof defense against destruction.

It was here in 1978 that conservative ex-supervisor Dan White climbed in through a window to avoid security guards and assassinated Mayor George Moscone along with openly gay supervisor Harvey Milk (see box, p.125). Later, when White was found guilty of manslaughter (not murder), violent demonstrations took place here as gay protesters set fire to police vehicles and stormed the doors of the building – an event that became known as the "White Night Riot." Although you can wander around the first floor of City Hall on your own, the best way to see the interior of the building is on one of the frequent **free tours** (Mon–Fri 10am, noon, 2pm), which even include a whistle-stop walk through the mayor's private office; sign up at the Docent Tour Kiosk on the Van Ness Avenue side of the main building.

The Opera House, Symphony Hall, and Veterans Building

Directly behind City Hall on Van Ness Avenue are San Francisco's cultural mainstays, most elegant of which is the **War Memorial Opera House**. The United Nations Charter was signed here in 1945; today, it's home to the San Francisco Opera and Ballet. Its understated grandeur is a sharp contrast to the giant modernist fishbowl of the **Louise M. Davies Symphony Hall** one block down, whose curvy lines owe a clear debt to the bridge of the USS *Enterprise*. Built by the well-known modernist firm Skidmore Owings & Merrill in 1980, the hall has some fans in the progressive architecture camp, though the general consensus is that it's an aberration of the otherwise tastefully harmonious scheme of Civic Center. Both buildings enjoy a healthy patronage, and San Francisco's patrician elite gather here regularly: unfortunately, few performances are subsidized, so don't expect budget ticket prices, although symphony tickets can run as low as $20 for the nosebleed section.

The Veterans Building at 401 Van Ness Ave houses two lively museums. The **Museum of Performance and Design** (formerly the San Francisco Performing Arts Library and Museum) is ideal for anyone with love rather than money to lavish on the opera and any other aspect of showbiz (gallery Tues–Sat noon–5pm, library Wed–Sat noon–5pm; free; ☎415/255-4800, ⓦwww.mpdsf .org). It's primarily a research center, boasting the largest collection of performing arts material outside of New York, and the museum has more than two million painstakingly collected programs, photographs, posters, books, videos, and press clippings concentrating on performing arts. Fans could spend hours raking through the memorabilia, a highlight of which is the Isadora Duncan collection, focusing on the influential dancer who was born in the city in 1877. The **San Francisco Arts Commission Gallery** (Wed–Sat noon–5pm; free; ☎415/554-6080, ⓦwww.sfacgallery.org) in the Veterans Building lobby is a terrific place to discover up-and-coming Bay Area artists. The gallery also hosts a satellite space on the lower level of City Hall (Mon–Fri 8am–8pm), and puts on the provocative sidewalk window installations a couple of blocks away at 155 Grove St.

The Mission, the Castro, and south

Together, the **Mission** and the **Castro** make up the beating heart of San
Francisco. Thanks to the hills that shelter them from the chilly coastal
fog, the adjacent low-lying districts are blessed with the best weather in
the city. These residential neighborhoods offer little in the way of
standard tourist traps. Instead, they are filled with galleries, historical murals,
one-of-a-kind local shops, top-notch restaurants, and a thriving nightlife.

While the Mission is the center of San Francisco's largely working-class
Hispanic community, over the last decade, it has experienced an influx of
young Anglo artists, writers, musicians, and computer programmers, all seeking
reasonable rent. The neighborhood draws young cool-hunters from all over the
Bay Area with its sleek nightclubs and dive bars, renowned restaurants and
cheap burritos, and plethora of galleries, performance spaces, and live-music
venues. That said, the neighborhood, which takes its name from **Mission
Dolores**, the oldest building in San Francisco, has not lost its Latin roots –
evident in the hundreds of murals splashed on buildings and a wide array of
Central and South American restaurants, clubs, and stores.

At the foot of **Twin Peaks** to the west, the **Castro** is a mecca of gay culture,
claimed by San Francisco's **gay community** in the mid-1970s, when it
emerged out of the hippie movement as a political force. The rainbow-flag-
decked neighborhood plays host to multiple joyous gay street festivals
throughout the year, bringing out the flashiest drag queens and leather
daddies. But most days, it is a quiet, upscale shopping district, with stores and
bars tailored to the gay community and with its landmarks of gay culture like
Pink Triangle Park, **Harvey Milk Plaza**, and a mural depicting the history
of the Castro. Once a working-class Irish neighborhood, the Castro is now a
place where gay and lesbian couples walk comfortably arm-in-arm as film
buffs flock to the iconic **Castro Theatre** and hipsters pack old speakeasies
and dive bars.

Further south, the **Noe Valley**, **Bernal Heights**, and **Potrero Hill** neighborhoods are even more residential but still possess a distinctly San Franciscan
charm: their main drags (24th St, Cortland Ave, and 18th St respectively) are
dotted with small boutiques, homey bookstores, delightful neighborhood
bars, and terrific restaurants, with opportunities for unusual culinary experiences like Indian pizza or vegan ice cream. Beyond Potrero Hill stands
Candlestick Park, the storied sports arena left to the San Francisco 49ers

when the Giants moved to AT&T Park; it's a pilgrimage best left to hardened sports fans.

The Mission

Gloriously warm and sunny compared to the fog-shrouded districts further west, **THE MISSION** is a lively, colorful neighborhood nestled in the flat stretch between the Castro Valley and craggy Potrero Hill. The district takes its name from nearby **Mission Dolores**, built near a lake (since covered) by Spanish missionaries in 1776. In fact, the city of San Francisco was officially founded here that year, at the first Mass celebrated at Mission Dolores, although the community established on the wet, marshy lands of the Mission District was then known as Yerba Buena.

Ever since the United States wrested California territory from Mexico in 1848, the Mission has drawn immigrants – initially Scandinavians, followed during the Gold Rush by a significant Irish influx that also spilled into the Castro and left a legacy in many of the store and bar names in the area. In the 1960s and 1970s, intense political turmoil in Central and South America brought Latin Americans to the Mission in droves. But now that distinct Hispanic flavor of the neighborhood is fading, as trendy bars, nightclubs, and restaurants jostle for space with old **taquerias** and junk shops. Despite its changes, the Mission remains one of San Francisco's unmissable delights, with its eclectic stores, bright murals, art galleries, and cafés. Note that the area has its sketchy moments, especially at night; though dwindling, there's long been an

▲ Mission Dolores

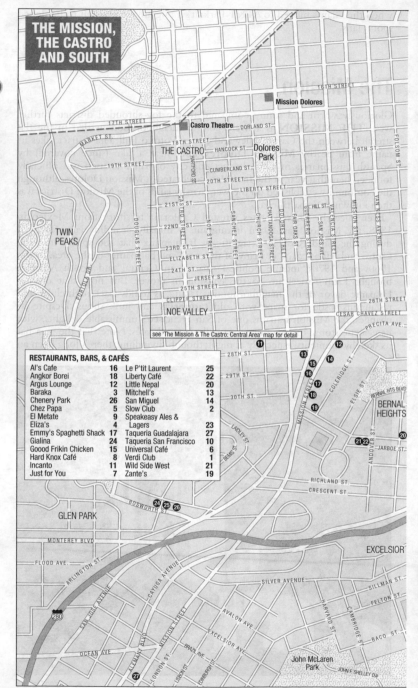

THE MISSION,
THE CASTRO
AND SOUTH

Mission Dolores

Castro Theatre

THE CASTRO

Dolores
Park

TWIN
PEAKS

NOE VALLEY

BERNAL
HEIGHTS

see 'The Mission & The Castro: Central Area' map for detail

GLEN PARK

EXCELSIOR

John McLaren
Park

RESTAURANTS, BARS, & CAFÉS

Al's Cafe	16	Le P'tit Laurent	25
Angkor Borei	18	Liberty Café	22
Argus Lounge	12	Little Nepal	20
Baraka	3	Mitchell's	13
Chenery Park	26	San Miguel	14
Chez Papa	5	Slow Club	2
El Metate	9	Speakeasy Ales &	
Eliza's	4	Lagers	23
Emmy's Spaghetti Shack	17	Taqueria Guadalajara	27
Gialina	24	Taqueria San Francisco	10
Goood Frikin Chicken	15	Universal Café	6
Hard Knox Café	8	Verdi Club	1
Incanto	11	Wild Side West	21
Just for You	7	Zante's	19

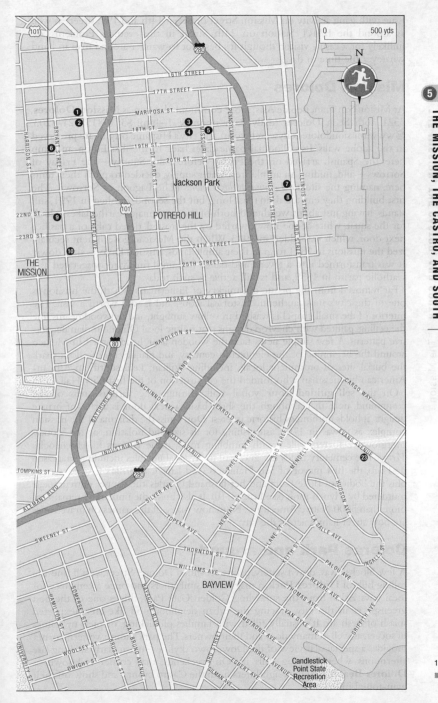

issue with gang activity on Mission Street between 14th and 19th streets as well as around the BART Station on 24th Street in the evening. Problems are unlikely for a casual visitor, though it's best not to wander around map in hand whatever the time of day.

Mission Dolores

At Misión San Francisco de Asis, more commonly known as **Mission Dolores**, 3321 16th St at Dolores (daily 8am–noon & 1–4pm; $3; ℡415/621-8203, Ⓦwww.missiondolores.citysearch.com), the city's Hispanic origins are preserved in the adobe walls. Its colloquial name dates back to the first European camp here: the Spanish arrived on the Friday before Palm Sunday – the Friday of Sorrows – and, finding an ample freshwater supply, decided to pitch their tents here, naming the site *La Laguna de los Dolores* (The Lagoon of Sorrows). The first building they erected didn't last long, but the second, finished in 1791, still stands, having just about weathered both of the city's major earthquakes – look for the squat, white adobe now dwarfed by the frosted, tiered cake of a basilica next door, which was added in 1913. When the Mexican government secularized the missions in 1834 to grab their ample lands, Mission Dolores shut down. It was transformed into a tavern and dance hall until finally reconsecrated as a Catholic parish in 1859, and is still active as such today.

Far removed from the plastic gimmickry of Fisherman's Wharf, the mission is one of the city's most authentic historical icons, and is well worth a visit. The interior of the small chapel is washed in yellow sunlight, and redwood beams line the ceiling, painted with chevron designs that mimic local Ohlone Indian decorative patterns. A few simple pews face the wooden altar, hand-carved in Mexico around the beginning of the eighteenth century, and plaques on the floor mark the burial sites of prominent locals, including William Leidesdorff, an African-American businessman who funded the construction of the first City Hall.

On the **self-guided tour** you'll walk through the various areas of the compound: note that although the shrill basilica next door is a riot of ornate designs, it holds nothing of historic interest. Don't miss the diorama of the mission complex as it was in 1799, astonishing for its size and isolation, or the woody, overgrown cemetery filled with rambling roses, made famous in Hitchcock's *Vertigo*. The cemetery holds the graves of many local notables including Francisco de Haro, the first mayor of San Francisco (and later California's first governor), plus the bodies of Belle Cora and her husband Charles, the dapper entrepreneur murdered by a lynch mob (see box, p.110). It also holds the unmarked remains of more than 5000 Native Americans. Note how many of the names on gravestones are now street names across the city.

Dolores Park and around

A few blocks away, down stately, palm-tree-lined Dolores Street, you'll find the rolling hills of **Dolores Park**, a magnet for sunbathers and once a cemetery for local Jews. Aside from the sprawling Golden Gate Park, this is one of the best greenspaces in the city, gracing the urban neighborhood like an unexpected splash of fresh air. It's usually filled with families picnicking, or pick-up games of soccer, as well as many dogs and their owners. The park's southwestern corner provides a spectacular view of the Downtown skyline – particularly striking late afternoons when the fog rolls in. On weekends, that corner is known as **Dolores Beach**, where weightlifters from the Castro bronze and show off their gym-toned muscles.

THE MISSION & THE CASTRO: CENTRAL AREA

Levi Strauss Building

Mission Dolores

Castro Theatre

THE CASTRO

Dolores Park

Women's Building

THE MISSION

Mission Cultural Center

Balmy Alley Murals

Twin Peaks & Pink Triangle Park

N

0   600 yds

ACCOMMODATION

24 Henry	B
Beck's Motor Lodge	C
Elements Hostel	G
Inn San Francisco	F
Parker Guest House	D
Travelodge Central	A
Village House	E

RESTAURANTS, BARS, & CAFÉS

Ace Cafe	6	Elixir Bar	16	Mecca	4	Spork	51
Anchor Oyster Bar	39	El Trébol	66	Mi Lindo Peru	73	Sumi	34
The Attic	65	Firefly	62	Mission Bar	60	Sushi Zone	1
Barney's	63	Foreign Cinema	49	Mission Pie	71	Tacos El	
The Beauty Bar	37	Homestead Bar	42	Nihon	7	Tonayense	57
Benders	41	Ike's Place	15	Palencia	28	Taqueria Can-cún	36
Bi-Rite Creamery	30	La Copa Loca	56	Panchita's	58	Tartine	33
Bissap Baobab	44	La Mediterranee	13	Papalote	67	Thai House	40
Bollyhood	38	La Taqueria	69	Papa Toby's Revolution Cafe	55	Ti Couz	19
Bombay Ice Creamery	25	La Victoria	68	Pauline's	5	Ti Couz Too	18
Boogaloo's	53	Latin American Club	54	The Phoenix	43	Tokyo Go Go	17
Bruno's	46	Laszlo	49	The Phone Booth	70	Truly Mediterranean	21
Casanova Lounge	24	Lil Baobab	38	Radio Habana Social Club	59	Walzwerk	12
Chez Spencer	8	Lime	14	Ramblas	26	Weird Fish	31
Dalva	20	Limón	23	Range	45	Woodhouse	
Delfina	32	The Lone Palm	52	Ristorante Bacco	61	Fish Company	11
Doc's Clock	50	Lucky 13	10	Samovar Tea Lounge	29	Woodward's Garden	3
Dosa	47	M & L Market	9	Savor	64	Zadin	35
El Rio	72	Mariachi's	22	Serrano's	48	Zeitgeist	2
		Maverick	27				

Sheer jean-ius

Many men struck gold during the Gold Rush without having to mine for it. Instead, they concentrated on supplying hopeful forty-niners with everything they needed to pan for their fortunes. Domenico Ghirardelli (see p.88) was one, and drainage specialist Adolph Sutro (see p.141) another, yet the most famous was **Levi Strauss**. He arrived in San Francisco in 1853 as a dry goods wholesaler, having brought bolts of tan canvas with him from New York which he planned to sell as tents or wagon covers. Through a combination of savvy and serendipity, Strauss noticed that miners needed stout trousers, too, and started producing a few pairs for sale: he was so successful that by 1860 he'd run out of canvas (although it wasn't until 1947 that the company finally gave up on dry goods wholesaling and focused entirely on jeans).

This meant Strauss had to find an alternative, so he turned to *serge de Nîmes*, blue cloth imported from Nîmes, France. The (perhaps fanciful) story goes that the pants he made from this fabric looked like uniforms worn by Italian sailors from Genoa – *Gênes* in French – so his pants were soon colloquially referred to as "jeans." The signature copper rivets were added later, at the suggestion of a tailor who'd noticed that gold nuggets shredded the fabric.

Although no production takes place in San Francisco, Levi's is still headquartered in San Francisco at **Levi's Plaza** (renamed Levi's Plaza, see p.76), home to a disappointing exhibition on the company's history. If you want to buy a souvenir pair, head to massive flagship store in Union Square, at 300 Post St at Stockton (reviewed on p.250), though, sadly, the bathtub where you used to be able to sit as your jeans shrank to fit is long gone.

Continuing south, the hillsides between 19th and 24th streets are quilted with a warren of quiet side streets, and thanks to the firmer ground of the hills, hold many Victorians largely untouched by earthquakes. Most are relatively quaint and modest: for ornate, crow's-nested standouts, head to **Liberty Street** between 20th and 21st streets. Keep your eyes open for ornamental Stars of David, a relic of the area's Jewish past.

Aside from the Mission, history buffs should stop by a twentieth-century landmark, **The Women's Building**, 3543 18th St at Guerrero (☎415/431-1180, ⓦwww.womensbuilding.org). Founded in 1971, the establishment hosts and sponsors a variety of politicized and progressive community groups, workshops, and events, many with a strong feminist or lesbian activism slant – call or check the website for a current calendar. The building is tattooed with an enormous and somewhat awkward mural, known by the horrifically self-conscious name of *Maestrapeace*, designed by seven female designers and executed by a team of one hundred painters. An enormous mother-goddess figure dominates one side, while on the other, there's a gigantic portrait of Rigoberta Menchú, the Guatemalan woman who won the Nobel Peace Prize in 1992.

Valencia Street

Thanks to gentrification, **Valencia Street** holds a dynamic mix of high- and low-end culture: upscale boutiques rub shoulders with thrift stores, chic ethnic restaurants bump up against taquerias and pupuserias, and swanky nightclubs sit beside hole-in-the-wall dive bars. Young artists and innovators, drawn to the area by the cheap rent, cheap tacos, and cheap thrift stores have brought in grungier galleries and creative spaces like **Artists Television Access**, where local directors' projects are screened. Meanwhile quirky stores specializing in taxidermy, vintage furniture, hip records, and old books have popped up alongside Latin apothecaries. Browsing this strip between 16th and 24th streets is one of the delights of San Francisco.

Just north of the heart of the strip, set back from the road at 250 Valencia St near 14th, stands the original **Levi's factory building**, a huge lemon-yellow structure. Though the jeans Levi's makes today bear only a remote resemblance to the original item, invented during the Gold Rush (see box opposite3), their popularity has endured. There are no longer tours of the building's interior, and Levi's has yet to announce what it plans to do with the site.

Mission Street and Balmy Alley

If Valencia Street is the hipster heart of the Mission, then **Mission Street** a couple of blocks east is the commercial hub of the **Latino community**. Between 20th and 25th streets, it's akin to a Spanish Chinatown, lined with five-and-dime shops selling a virtually identical stock of kitschy religious items and blaring Spanish-language music out onto the sidewalk. You'll also spot dozens of taquerias and a clutch of disused Art Deco movie theaters, whose spire-signs are the only high-rise touches hereabouts. For a long time, this strip lay untouched by gentrification, still catering mostly to the needs of local Latin families with everyday essentials like notaries, drugstores, and travel agents; that's finally changing, thanks to a few new hipster-aimed eateries and a specially built hostel that recently opened (for review, see p.153). One of the remaining Latin hubs is the **Mission Cultural Center** at no. 2868 between 24th and 25th streets (Tues–Fri 10am–5.30pm, Sat 10am–6pm; $2; ☎415/821-1155, ⓦwww .missionculturalcenter.org), devoted to making the arts within the local community. The center puts on free workshops for families, plus a couple of galleries devoted to contemporary Latino art. Most of the art is heavily (and heavy-handedly) political, and there's not much to detain a casual visitor.

East of Mission Street, the pace is noticeably slower, especially in the heart of the district along 24th Street, where some two hundred **murals** underscore a strong sense of community pride and Hispanic heritage. The greatest concentration of work can be found on **Balmy Alley**, an unassuming back way between Treat and Harrison streets, where's there barely an inch of wall unadorned. The murals here are painted on wooden fences, rather than stucco walls, and consequently are regularly refreshed and replaced. The project began during a small community-organized event in 1973, but the tiny street has become the spiritual center of a burgeoning Latino arts movement that has grown out of both the US civil rights struggle and the pro-democracy movements of South America. Frankly, many of the murals are more heartfelt than either skilled or beautiful, and while it's worth stopping by for a peek, the political imagery can be wearing. For a tour of the artwork, call the **Precita Eyes Mural Arts Center**, 2981 24th St at Harrison (☎415/285-2287, ⓦwww.precitaeyes.org), which has sponsored most of the paintings since its founding in 1971; the center runs tours every Saturday and Sunday at 1.30pm ($12).

Bernal Heights and Potrero Hill

Directly south and west of the Mission, several residential districts stretch down the Peninsula past the city limits: without a car, transport links to this area are somewhat spotty, but you can take MUNI bus #9 from Downtown to the eastern end of **Bernal Heights**. Note that the neighborhood rivals only Nob Hill for its steep climbs, so it isn't for the easily winded – wear comfortable shoes. Bernal Heights is buzzing with new arrivals, drawn partly by the comparatively low rents in its historic homes, and also by the thriving lesbian (and to a lesser extent, gay) scene, centered on the fantastic beer garden and bar *Wild Side West* on Cortland Avenue. In a city like San Francisco where ethnic groups are so clearly segregated, it's also refreshingly multicultural. Leafy, tree-lined Cortland Avenue's a pleasant place to stroll, with its quiet cafés and independent book or clothing stores; from here, make sure to brave the stiff walk uphill north along Folsom Street. It terminates in **Bernal Park**, from where you'll enjoy a lovely, little-seen view of the whole city.

West of the Mission, expect another hike to reach **Potrero Hill**, boasting similarly glorious views of the city. Dollars were pumped into this quiet residential area during the dot-com boom, and its central artery, 18th Street, boasts the usual cute cafés and gourmet sandwich shops that such gentrification engenders. Now that the Internet boom is over, though, it has regained much of its ambling pace, with an atmosphere more evocative of a country village than a major city – it even has its own weekly newspaper. There's precious little to do, but its leafy streets are perfect for a morning stroll, taking in the panoramic views of Downtown and the docks and pausing for a coffee – the *Thinker* on 20th is a popular spot.

The Castro

A neighborhood bursting with energy, **The CASTRO** is a great spot for window-shopping, people-watching, club-hopping, or just enjoying a leisurely lunch. Sprawling up and down several hillsides between the Lower Haight, the Mission District, and Noe Valley, in the eastern shadows of Twin Peaks, the neighborhood officially called Eureka Valley is a large area, though it's liveliest along Castro Street, between Market and 19th streets. Since its emergence in the 1970s as a hub of global gay culture, the neighborhood has consistently managed to lure gay and lesbian tourists from across the world; these days, it's a blurred fusion of rainbow flags plastered on every retail outlet, shop windows piled high with gay porn, and forests of muscular men toting doll-sized dogs. Much more upscale than the Mission, the Castro is packed with chi-chi boutiques geared toward the well-dressed male couples who stroll the streets arm-in-arm.

The MUNI stops at **Harvey Milk Plaza**, on the corner of Castro and Market (aside from the historic F-tram, which terminates a block east). The Plaza is named in honor of the murdered local politician (see box, p.125), and is where the largest **rainbow flag** in the area flutters proudly. This enormous twenty-by-thirty-foot pennant was recently updated by its designer, Gilbert Baker – dubbed "the gay Betsy Ross" – to include the eight colors he'd originally intended. Back in 1978, tight funds prevented him from including turquoise and fuchsia fabrics along with the more standard shades of red, orange, yellow, green, blue, and purple that have become familiar as the symbol of gay freedom.

North across Market Street, at the junction with 17th, stands the somber **Pink Triangle Park** (Ⓦ www.pinktrianglepark.net). Dedicated in 2002, this monument is the first in the country to be devoted specifically to the gay victims of the Holocaust. There's a pink triangle at its heart, filled with rough rose-quartz shingle; around this, amid spiky agave cacti and pink rose bushes, stand fifteen pink-triangle-topped granite pylons. Each represents 1000 men who were murdered by the Nazis because of their sexuality. Lesbians aren't

The assassination of Harvey Milk

In 1977, eight years after New York's Stonewall riots brought gay political activism into the spotlight, Castro camera-shop owner **Harvey Milk** won election as the city's first openly gay supervisor (or councilor), and quickly became one of the most prominent gay officials in the country. A celebrated figure for the city's gay community, Milk was nicknamed the "Mayor of Castro Street," and it came as a horrifying shock when, in 1978, former supervisor Dan White entered City Hall and shot both Milk and **Mayor George Moscone** dead.

White was angered that the liberal policies of Moscone and Milk clashed with his conservative views. A staunch Catholic, White saw himself as a spokesman for San Francisco's many blue-collar Irish families and, as an ex-policeman, saw himself at the vanguard of the family values he believed gay rights were damaging. At his trial, during which the prosecution never once mentioned the word "assassination" or recognized a political motive for the killings, White claimed that harmful additives in his fast-food-laden diet had driven him temporarily insane. This plea, which came to be known as the "Twinkie defense" after the brand name of the airy cream cakes he liked consuming by the boxful, was shockingly successful: White was sentenced to only five years' imprisonment for manslaughter. The gay community exploded when the news of White's light sentence was handed down, and the "White Night" **riots** that followed were among the most violent San Francisco has ever witnessed, as protesters stormed City Hall, turning over and burning police cars as they went. White was released from prison in 1985 and, unable to find a job, committed suicide shortly afterwards. The anniversary of the murder of Milk and Moscone is marked by a candlelight procession from the Castro to City Hall each November 27. Milk is commemorated by his namesake plaza in the Castro as well as a plaque on 575 Castro St, which was the headquarters for his campaign to be elected supervisor, while the convention center was named in Moscone's honor.

included in this number as they were treated differently by Hitler's regime: since they were able to bear children but chose not to, lesbians wore the black triangle of the Antisocials rather than the pink one of the homosexuals (and so weren't sent to the gas chambers in such significant numbers).

The heart of the Castro is usually packed with people whatever the time of day, and it's especially lively on a Sunday afternoon, crammed with men strolling, cruising, and sipping a coffee on the sidewalk. If you're lucky, you might spot one of the **Sisters of Perpetual Indulgence**, local living landmarks, safe-sex educators, and scourges of the Catholic Church (see box, p.126). If the crowds of people are too much, head for the neighborhood's side streets, scrupulously manicured and lined with neat rows of brightly painted Victorians – a world away from the stores and bars crammed along Castro Street.

The district's one major sight is the **Castro Theater**, 429 Castro St at Market (℡415/621-6120, Ⓦ www.thecastrotheatre.com), flagged by the neon sign that towers above surrounding buildings. Designed by architect Timothy Plueger, the man behind Oakland's landmark Paramount Theatre (see p.292), the Castro Theater is a stunning example of the Mediterranean Revival style, its exterior marked out by lavish stucco decoration and ornate windows. Inside, the decorative riot continues, thanks to foamy balconies, wall-mounted busts of heroic figures, and massive ceiling ornamentation, though you'll have to come for a show to see inside. Be sure to arrive early for pre-screening performances on the "mighty" Wurlitzer organ. The musical medley always draws to a close with Judy Garland's hit *San Francisco*, with the crowd merrily clapping along.

She's gotta habit

One of the Castro's best sights isn't a bar or a building – it's a group of men with some very unusual habits. **The Sisters of Perpetual Indulgence** is an outrageous activist group that dresses up as nuns to promote safe sex and HIV awareness in a gloriously camp pastiche of Catholic pageantry. The Sisters began on Easter Sunday in 1979, when four friends – who'd held onto their habits from a college production of *The Sound of Music* – took to the streets of the Castro in full nun drag, touting water pistols and smoking cigars. Their surreal sense of humor snagged them a spot as cheerleaders at a local gay softball game, and membership soon snowballed. Currently, the group is forty strong. Novices are provided with a single habit, based on an original thirteenth-century design, but must come up with a suitably witty and subversive name for their religious alter ego – past sisters have included Dana Vin Iquity, Quaalewd Conduct, and Missionary Position. Now a registered charity, the group stages monthly Bada-Bingo fundraisers, regularly tours gay bars handing out free condoms, and even guest-teaches courses on human sexuality at SF State University. There are orders across the world, from Berlin to Bogota, as well as satellite convents elsewhere in the United States.

The Sisters have encountered plenty of opposition from Catholic orthodoxy. Having been placed on the official Papal List of Heretics in the mid-1990s, the group made headlines again after the Catholic Church objected to its application for a party permit to close down Castro Street on Easter Sunday 1999 so that a twentieth-birthday fundraiser could be held; these days, the Sisters' alt-Easter bash is held in Dolores Park, and headlined by its Hunky Jesus contest (a recent winner was Viva Las Jesus, a portly man in a late-era-Elvis-inspired gold lamé loincloth). Even so, there's at least one traditional nun who's in sympathy with their habits: Sister Bernie, a local homeless advocate, recently joined her drag counterparts on an AIDS candlelit vigil.

If, like Bernie, you want to hang with the Sisters, you're best off bar crawling through the Castro – favorite hangouts include *Moby Dick's*, *The Edge*, and *440 Castro*. Alternatively, check ⓦ www.thesisters.org for information on upcoming manifestations or one of the gay freesheets like *Frontiers* for Bada-Bingo dates and locations.

Twin Peaks

A quiet neighborhood, safely perched on earthquake-proof granite above the city, **TWIN PEAKS** has one attraction: its **panoramic views** of the city, the Bay, and the Pacific Ocean. The North and South hills here are, respectively, the third highest (904ft) and second highest (910ft) points in the city; they're just pipped by Mount Davidson to the west, which rises to 925 feet. It's well worth the quick ride up here on the curving streets that wind alongside some of the city's priciest, yet remarkably bland, homes. Thanks to television, the Peaks now boast the city's most prominent landmark: a massive **antenna tower** that can be seen from throughout the city and from airplanes on thick San Francisco days, when it pokes up through the highest peaks of downy-white fog.

According to Native American mythology, the Peaks were created when a married couple argued so violently that the Great Spirit separated them with a clap of thunder. Sex-starved Spanish explorers called them "Breasts of an Indian Girl," but Anglo settlers finally agreed on the current, sadly literal name. When architect Daniel Burnham worked on his plans for San Francisco, he imagined two grand centers for the city. One, at what's now Civic Center, would have contained administrative buildings, while the other, on top of Twin Peaks, would have been crowned with an enormous amphitheater; unfortunately, only fragments of his

Civic Center project were ever completed (including City Hall), and nothing appeared on Twin Peaks.

To get to the peaks by car, continue uphill on Market Street from the Castro till it turns into Portola, then turn right on **Twin Peaks Boulevard**. If you're on foot, you can take the #37 bus part of the way, though you're still left with a significant climb. Be warned: the peaks are a major tour-bus destination, and it's not unusual to encounter throngs of photographers lining the pinnacle. A good option for avoiding the rabble lies just downhill, where the small promontory of **Tank Hill**, at the end of Belgrave Avenue just off 17th Street, offers equally impressive views. However, when the weather's bad, you should avoid the area entirely, unless you enjoy playing hide-and-seek in cold, damp fog. Note that it can be rather grim around here after dusk.

Noe Valley and south

Dolores Street marks the boundary between the Mission to the northeast and **NOE VALLEY** to the southwest. A quiet residential community bedded down between steep hills, Noe Valley's heart is **24th Street**, full of restaurants and cafés; it's an affluent place filled with thirty-something professional couples, many pushing baby strollers. Almost every retail outlet seems to have installed an iron bench out front which encourages people to linger and chat along the main drag. The MUNI ride from the Castro along Church Street – crucial, unless you want to tackle the killer hill – is pleasant enough, passing scenic Dolores Park, but once you get here, odds are you'll be hard-pressed to find anything to do besides sip coffee, shop for cardigans or dawdle on one of those benches.

South of Noe Valley, there isn't much more to do. The industrial and shipping industries that were once vital here have fallen by the wayside, while waves of gentrification have pushed poor residents toward the geographic margins. Sitting atop a hill, above the housing projects and tract homes, is **City College** at 50 Phelan Ave near Ocean Avenue (☏415/239-3000, ⓦwww.ccsf.cc.ca.us or ⓦwww.riveramural.org). The institution's theater is its most notable spot, decorated with the *Pan-American Unity* mural of the Mexican socialist painter **Diego Rivera**. Along with the massive artwork at the San Francisco Art Institute (see p.77), this is arguably Rivera's best-known work in the city, and its sweeping, highly colored panels are impressive. Unless you stop in for a performance, actually getting in to see the painting can be tricky; if you want to try, call ☏415/239-3127 to arrange a visit.

The only major attraction in the city's southern half is the chilly promontory of Candlestick Point, home of the **Candlestick Park sports** stadium, now back to its original name after several, corporately influenced changes over the years. Locals call it "the Stick," for short and regard it with equal amounts of nostalgia and disdain. Once the home of baseball's **San Francisco Giants**, the ballpark is notorious for its brutal winds and the otherworldly fog bank that sometimes settles on the field. An even more surreal scene was broadcast live to the nation in October 1989, when a World Series game between the Giants and the Oakland A's was rudely interrupted by the Loma Prieta earthquake. With the Giants having moved, the stadium's sole remaining tenant is the **San Francisco 49ers** football team. For information on catching a game, see p.273.

6

Haight-Ashbury and west of Civic Center

The districts between Civic Center and Golden Gate Park are perhaps the most racially and economically diverse in San Francisco. Once grubby, crime-ridden, and unappealing, they are now an eclectic patchwork of neighborhoods, the best known of which is **Haight-Ashbury**. What began as an upper-class vacation enclave on the city's outskirts became the most famous place in America for a few short summers in the late 1960s, when these few blocks were at the center of the nationwide hippie movement. While most of the remaining hippies have become wily opportunists, parlaying peace-and-love pasts into a full-time-job present hawking the neighborhood's glory days to tourists, the district is worth visiting for its gorgeous Victorian architecture – which rivals many of the buildings in better-known Pacific Heights – as well as the chance to encounter the spectre of the 1960s rebellion. If you're looking to connect with modern-day counterculture, you'll do better to stay in the **Lower Haight** immediately to the east, which is cheaper and edgier. Note that public transport links to the Haight area are patchy: the N-Judah MUNI train stops in Cole Valley at Cole and Carl streets, but the best choice for exploring is to take bus #70 along Haight Street.

The neighborhoods crammed between the Haight and Civic Center have distinctly different personalities. Trendy, friendly **Hayes Valley**, with its tree-lined main street full of upscale boutiques, is a great place to while away an empty afternoon. Immediately to the north of here, a visit to swanky **Alamo Square** will take ten minutes at best, but its six restored Victorian houses provide one of the most popular photo opportunities in the city (and for good reason).

Continuing north, Alamo Square rapidly gives way to chunks of unloved cityscape that make up the sprawling **Western Addition** and the **Fillmore**. Once home to the city's worst housing projects and incidents of violent crime, these heavily African-American areas are still quite economically deprived. Grafted onto the eastern edge of the Fillmore is the artificial development known as **Japantown**. Mostly a Tokyo-style mall of sushi bars, tempura houses, and Japanese book and paper stores, it has become the heart of the city's Japanese community and is a great place to try an authentic Japanese meal.

RESTAURANTS, BARS, & CAFÉS

Abacus	19	Little Star Pizza	14
Absinthe	22	Mad Dog in the	
Alembic	45	Fog	37
Asqew Grill	47	Madrone Lounge	27
Baghdad Nights	41	Magnolia Pub	
Bambino's		& Brewery	40
Ristorante	59	Maki	10
Benkyodo	7	Massawa	39
Blue Jay Café	13	Metro Kathmandu	30
Burgermeister	58	Modern Tea	20
Bushi-tei	9	Molotov's	36
Cheese Steak Shop	18	Momi Tobys	28
Citizen Cake	50	Noc Noc	23
The Citrus Club	38	Nopa	56
Club Deluxe	42	Orbit Room	46
Cuco's	2	Persian Aub	
El Burrito Express	44	Zam Zam	21
Espetus Churrascaria	53	Place Pigalle	8
Estela's	16	Play Ground	49
Fly	1	Pork Store	29
Frankie's Bohemian		Rickshaw Stop	35
Cafe	24	RNM	
Fritz	59	Rosamunde	52
Grandeho's	15	Sausage Grille	25
Kamekyo	26	Sebo	11
Green Chile Kitchen	34	Sophie's Crepes	3
Herbivore	43	SPQR	
Hotel Biron	32	Thai Place II	31
Indian Oven	17	Thep Phanom	55
J's Pots of Soul	12	Toronado	51
Jardiniere	54	Yasukochi's	
Jubili	57	Sweet Stop	5
Kate's Kitchen	6	Zazie	59
Kezar		Zuni	33
Kiss Sushi			

ACCOMMODATION

Best Western		Hotel Kabuki	D
Hotel Tomo	A	Hotel Majestic	C
The Carl	J	Queen Anne	B
Château Tivoli	E	Red Victorian	H
Hayes Valley Inn	F	Stanyan Park	I
Inn 1890	G		

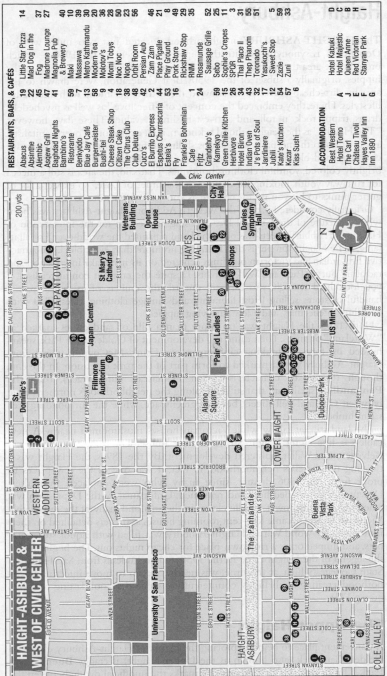

HAIGHT-ASHBURY & WEST OF CIVIC CENTER

▲ Civic Center

▲ Golden Gate Park

Haight-Ashbury

The **HAIGHT-ASHBURY** neighborhood, located just two miles west of Downtown, is synonymous with the hippie movement of the 1960s – which brought the area the notoriety it has capitalized on ever since. At the time, the hippies, originally a subset of the 1950s Beat Generation, were drawn to the area by dirt-cheap rents, which allowed them to experiment with alternative lifestyles. There, they embraced the concept of "free love," as well as psychedelic drugs, trippy rock 'n' roll, and anti-establishment values. These days, however, "The Haight," as the neighborhood is known, is an explosion of overt capitalism, a sort of boho theme-park, with shops shilling hippie memorabilia like tie-dye clothing, hand-blown hookahs, and Grateful Dead Beanie Babies mixed in with brightly colored, youthful clothing boutiques. That said, the area is still a mecca for runaway youth, looking for their own "Summer of Love," so expect a lot of gutter punks to hit you up for change as you walk from store to store.

Originally considered part of the Western Addition, Haight-Ashbury was born when a picture of the Grateful Dead, posing at the sign for the intersection of Haight and Ashbury streets was published and reprinted the world over. For all its fame, "The Haight" proper is tiny, spanning no more than eight blocks of attractive Edwardian and Victorian buildings centered on its namesake intersection and radiating out to Page and Waller streets. Despite the rampant commercialism, if you look hard enough, you can still unearth the embers of its radical past: a handful of stores selling leftist literature and vintage clothing, cafés filled with dawdling intellectuals, and a few surviving hippies.

Until 1865, the Haight was no more than a pile of sand dunes marked as "Wasteland" on maps. Then came the development of Golden Gate Park, spearheaded by forward-thinking city supervisor Frank McCoppin; what's now Haight-Ashbury was earmarked to form part of the park extension. In the end, though (thanks to characteristic San Franciscan bureaucracy), only the **Panhandle**, a small park that still runs along the neighborhood's northern edge between Oak and Fell streets, became greenspace, while the surrounding area sat in limbo.

The land still sat fallow while Victorian houses mushroomed nearby. A new cable-car line along Haight Street and an amusement park, The Chutes, at Belvedere and Waller, bolstered development. By the 1890s, the Haight was a thriving middle-class neighborhood; in fact, it was one of the few places to profit from the 1906 disaster, since many who were displaced from their Downtown homes fled here and remained. Unfortunately, the Depression was a body blow to the lower middle classes in the area, and many of the respectable Victorian homes became low-rent rooming houses as owners defaulted on their mortgages. By World War II, Haight-Ashbury was filled with liquor stores and bars, and limped on as a rundown place for cheap nights out. The beginning of the legend of the Haight came in the 1950s, when students from San Francisco State College (which, at the time, was nearby) began to move into the neighborhood, creating a rebellious, counterculture scene that took lasting root (see box, p.133).

The Upper Haight

A convenient place to begin exploring the chunk of Haight-Ashbury closest to Golden Gate Park (also known as the Upper Haight) is craggy **Buena Vista Park**. This heavily wooded greenspace marks the unofficial divide between the original chunk of hippie-centric Upper Haight and the grungier Lower Haight; the park is where early Spanish soldiers would overnight as they marched from the Mission to the Presidio. On a rare sunny day in the fog-infested Haight, you might spot a few sunbathers, but otherwise the park's best known as a gay cruising spot since dense trees block any chance of views from its summit.

Heading west, you'll find a riot of quirky boutiques, thrift stores, souvenir shops, restaurants and cafés – the most striking storefront, Piedmont Boutique, is marked by a giant pair of fishnet-and-heels-wearing legs hanging out of a second-floor window. Aside from shopping and people-watching, the Upper Haight is a great place to snap pictures of former homes of local rock legends. The first of these, at 112 Lyon St just across from the park, is one of the many places that doomed rock diva **Janis Joplin** lived; constantly shuttling from place to place, she was evicted from this impressive Victorian for owning a dog. A few blocks west, at 710 Ashbury St at Waller, stands hippiedom's answer to Graceland: the **Grateful Dead** house. The band's home from 1965 to 1969, it was here that they were photographed around the time of their notorious 1967 drug bust. It's now a private home, so stay on the sidewalk. Across the street, the highly ornate, turreted Queen Anne Victorian at 715 Ashbury St was the **Hells Angels'** local HQ; hippies and bikers shared the concept of living outside the law, despite their opposing ideals.

On the corner of Haight and Clayton streets stands one of the undisputed treasures of the 1960s: **Haight-Ashbury Free Clinic**. Providing free, no-questions-asked healthcare since drug-related illnesses surfaced in the area almost forty years ago, it has been used as a model for free clinics across the country. The clinic still survives – barely – on contributions, treating anyone in need of help, whether local or not, and a new branch has opened in the Mission (1735 Mission St). Though now a clothing store, the squat building a block further west at 1660 Haight St was the brightly colored **Nickelodeon** from the Chutes amusement park that once stood here and is the only holdover from those days; notice the ornately carved wooden arch above the entrance, topped with a roaring bear. Across the street, no. 1775 was once home to the **Diggers**,

▲ Mural in Haight-Ashbury

a short-lived anarchist art group with an anonymous leadership that took a break from writing Dadaist manifestos to give free food and shelter to the increasing numbers of homeless filling the neighborhood. To this day, the sidewalk in front of the building is a popular gathering spot for local wanderers.

Close by, at 636 Cole St immediately south of Haight Street, is the former home of **Charles Manson**. This nondescript blue building is where Manson lived while recruiting members of his murderous cult; it was torched in a suspicious fire a few years ago, and still sits boarded up and burnt, forlornly awaiting renovation. Further south, 130 Delmar St at Frederick is the site of the **Jefferson Airplane** house. Grace Slick and her band enjoyed psychedelic superstardom in the late 1960s, thanks to anthems *White Rabbit* and *Somebody to Love*, but there's little to see in this oddly modest house.

Right before Haight Street comes to a halt at Golden Gate Park, you'll find **Amoeba Music**, a place of pilgrimage for musicians and music lovers the world over. Opened in 1997 in a former bowling alley as a sister to the independent Berkeley store, the 24,000-square-foot space holds more than 100,000 new and used CDs, records, and tapes, as well as movies and music memorabilia. The staff is made up of musicians and music experts who are more than happy to share their encyclopedic knowledge, and the store often hosts free concerts by up-and-coming acts.

North of Haight Street, you find the **Panhandle**, the finger-slim strip of greenery that eventually leads to Golden Gate Park. The Panhandle was landscaped before the rest of the park back in the 1870s, and for a while was the focus of high-society carriage rides. That changed when, after the 1906 earthquake, it became a refuge for fleeing families, with some thirty thousand living here in tents. During the 1960s, it was the scene for outdoor rock concerts by the likes of Jimi Hendrix that caused considerable wear and tear on the delicate landscape. Today it's rather seedy, though its bike paths and playgrounds also ensure steady use by neighborhood residents.

The Lower Haight

East of Buena Vista Park, the strip of Haight Street between Divisadero and Fillmore is known as **Lower Haight**. It's a more intriguing place than its over-touristed older brother and still has a few blocks of undeveloped buildings – look for the occasional derelict Stick Victorian even on Haight Street itself. You can escape the hippie-seeking hordes in the hilltop Haight by coming here; a strip packed with restaurants, bars and galleries, it's mellow by day – a center for electronic music devotees and the underground DJ scene, where you can dig for rare vinyl, flip through zines, or buy MIDI sequencers – but comes alive at night.

As for historic sites, Proto-Beatnik **Kenneth Rexroth**, best known among literary scholars as an important translator of Chinese poetry, lived at 250 Scott St at Oak. That's where Kerouac and some of his compadres crashed when they first arrived in San Francisco, so gaining a quick initiation into the local creative community.

At the corner of Scott Street and Duboce Avenue, two blocks south, lies **Duboce Park**, a pleasant patch of green hugely popular with dog lovers since pets can run around leash-free. Close by, at the corner of Duboce Avenue and Webster Street, stands the massive new **US Mint** (the Old Mint is in SoMa), one of four currency-producing factories in the country, which rises somewhat menacingly on a granite escarpment.

The **first hippies** were an offshoot of the **Beats**, many of whom had moved out of their increasingly expensive North Beach homes in the early 1960s to take advantage of the low rents and large spaces in the rundown Victorian houses of the Haight. Older Beats were contemptuous of the newbies who weren't cool enough to be true hipsters. The Beats belittled them as junior-grade "hippies," and the name stuck.

The post-Beat bohemia that began to develop in Haight-Ashbury was a small affair at first. Certainly drugs played a role, but the embracing of Eastern religion and philosophy, together with a marked anti-establishment political stance, were also important aspects. Many Beats like Jack Kerouac – who abhorred the hippies – weren't pacifists, and the growing anti-Vietnam War movement, spearheaded by early Flower Children, helped demarcate the line between the two groups. Where the Beats had been a small, cliquish group that stressed self-indulgence as an escape from social oppression, the hippies, on the face of it at least, attempted to be more embracing by emphasizing such concepts as "universal truth" and "cosmic awareness."

Even if experimentation with **narcotics** was not initially the central tenet of hippie life, it grew in importance as the movement matured, notably the use of LSD or acid. The pivotal event that crystallized many of the traits popularly associated with the hippies came in January 1966, when early LSD guinea pig and Stanford drop-out **Ken Kesey** and his **Merry Pranksters** hosted a "Trips Festival" in the Longshore-men's Hall at Fisherman's Wharf. The Pranksters handed out flyers asking "Can you pass the acid test?" and the festival was attended by thousands, most on acid. Along with a "Be-In" at Golden Gate Park later the same year, the festival set a precedent for wild living, challenging authority, and dropping out of the social and political establishment. At the time, LSD was not illegal and was being hyped as an avant-garde art form, consciousness-raising in its effects. Pumped out in private laborato-ries and promoted by the likes of Timothy Leary with the prescription "Turn on, tune in, drop out," LSD galvanized a generation into believing that it could be used to raise the creativity of one and all. The Haight Street scene quickly began to attract national attention, as local bands the **Grateful Dead**, **Jefferson Airplane**, and **Big Brother and the Holding Company** began to make names for themselves, and, backed by the business weight of **Bill Graham**, the psychedelic music scene became a genuine force nationwide.

It wasn't long before large numbers of kids from all over America started turning up in the Haight for the free food, free drugs, and free love. Money became a dirty word, the hip became "heads," the others "straights," and by 1967's **Summer of Love**, this busy little intersection had attracted no fewer than 75,000 transitory residents in its short life as the focus of alternative culture.

The mood in Haight-Ashbury quickly curdled, however. Some soldiers returning from **Vietnam** brought with them newly acquired heroin habits and introduced the drug into local hippie culture. In October 1967, hippies disappointed with the hedon-istic, self-centered direction the movement had taken hosted the three-day Death of the Hippie event in San Francisco, even though the influx was far from over. Slowly, the outcasts, crazies, and villains – who until then had been outnumbered by the nice middle-class kids who simply wanted to get stoned – started to gain power. The most infamous of these was **Charles Manson**, who recruited much of his "family" in the Haight. The darkening clouds continued to gather in 1969, when the Rolling Stones organized their notorious concert in **Altamont**, California (see p.321). The concert was a tragic failure, and the terrifying image of the brutal stabbing of one fan in the midst of the drugged-out crowd marked the end of a cultural movement. Many of the hippies escaped to the countryside as part of a fledgling "Back to the Land" movement, while a splinter group of gay men – including hardcore hippie Harvey Milk – emerged, moved to the Castro, and founded the gay liberation movement.

Cole Valley

Just south of the commercialized strip of Haight-Ashbury's main drag is **Cole Valley**, a tiny but welcome residential refuge, sandwiched between Haight-Ashbury to the northeast and the Sunset to the west. It's home to young professionals and a few families although, like Cow Hollow, the area was originally full of dairy farms. There's little to see or do here, other than eat, and the valley's commercial center at the junction of Cole and Carl streets is crammed with laid-back cafés and a couple of outstanding restaurants. *Crepes on Cole*, 100 Carl St at Cole, was once *The Other Café*, one of the city's premier comedy venues, which hosted early-career gigs by the likes of Robin Williams and Dana Carvey – the original sign's been preserved. A few blocks south at the end of Shrader Street, 600-foot-high Tank Hill provides terrific views over the city. It's named after the enormous 500,000-gallon water tank that used to sit on its peak: note the grove of eucalyptus trees, planted after Pearl Harbor to conceal the tank from potential enemy bombing raids.

Hayes Valley and Alamo Square

Just as San Francisco generally received a full-scale facelift after the destruction caused by the great 1906 earthquake, the seeds of **HAYES VALLEY**'s extraordinary reinvention were sown in the wake of a natural disaster. Prior to the cataclysmic Loma Prieta earthquake of 1989, the neighborhood was a kind of nowhere-land – home to crumbling buildings and crime, the area awkwardly bisected by a looming freeway overpass. After that section of freeway was demolished thanks to extensive structural damage, the district below quickly blossomed into a bustling causeway of distinctive upscale boutiques, art galleries, cafés, and restaurants.

Despite all the gentrification, the neighborhood's boundaries are still just as ill defined physically as they are socially. To the east, the Hayes Valley spills into the almost cavernous, Neoclassical mammoth that is the Civic Center, while just a few blocks to the west, you can barely detect the transition into public housing. Area denizens run the professional gamut from the recent influx of self-made artists, architects, and designers, to those struggling to make ends meet in the nearby projects. Still, though, the heart of the neighborhood is unquestionably Hayes Street between Franklin and Octavia. Anchored by Patrica's Green – a narrow, unpretentious park – the area is a sublime place to pass through on a sunny day, or for those en route to and from the symphony.

Just to the west of Hayes Valley is wealthy, manicured **ALAMO SQUARE**, a hilltop park overlooked by the cluster of restored Victorians known as the "**Painted Ladies**," on Steiner Street between Hayes and Grove streets. They're a staple stop for every tour-bus company in town; look up at the park's southeast slope from Hayes Valley and you'll see ant-sized swarms of amateur photographers snapping shots. These six colorful Victorian houses vie with the Golden Gate Bridge for the title of most clichéd image of the city. Built in 1894 by a single developer and sold for $3500 each, the houses have been fastidiously restored in modern shades of hunter green, cream, and baby blue. This cluster is unusual in that, although Italianate in style, each has a gable – for more on Victorians' architecture, see the box on p.93. Even if you've forgotten your camera, it's still worth the steep climb up here for the brilliant **views** across the city.

The Western Addition and the Fillmore

North of Alamo Square lie two large but loosely organized districts: the **WESTERN ADDITION** and **FILLMORE**, sprawling across the hundred or so blocks between Gough Street, Masonic Avenue, and Bush and Fulton streets. Historically African-American, these twin districts are also troubled by some of the greatest social problems in the city. Granted, the trickle of bargain-hungry hipsters looking for cheap rentals has leavened the neighborhood slightly (and caused social tensions), but there are still dozens of boarded-up shops, vacant lots, and abandoned housing projects everywhere on Fillmore Street, especially between Fulton and Geary.

It wasn't always like this. Before the devastation of the 1906 earthquake, the Western Addition – notably, Fillmore Street – served as San Francisco's main shopping district. Although its buildings were spared the ravages of the fire, its economy was devastated by the aftermath; the city center was rebuilt and reconfigured, with land downtown that once hosted rowhouses turned over to commercial use. The housing void created here by the exodus of wealthier residents taking the chance to escape its poor, fog-bound weather, allowed the influx of a large **Japanese community**, centered on Geary and Fillmore streets. Japanese immigrants had arrived in the city via Hawaii, where they worked on sugar plantations at the start of twentieth century. The community thrived until World War II, when anti-Japanese hysteria swept California following the bombing of Pearl Harbor. Japanese-Americans were forcibly incarcerated in camps across the state by the federal government and forced to sell off their property at below-market prices. They only returned to the area in significant numbers following the construction of **Japantown**.

Many of the cheap homes were sold to lower-waged **African-Americans**, and soon jazz clubs and black-owned businesses lined the streets. That is, until the area was leveled by the dual forces of 1960s urban renewal and blunderheaded civic planner **Justin Herman**. He demolished dozens of blocks of precious Victorian housing, replacing them with acres of monolithic concrete apartment blocks. Thanks to Herman and his henchmen, there's now little to see in the area other than the famed **Fillmore Auditorium**, 1805 Geary Blvd at Fillmore (℡415/346-6000, ⊛www.thefillmore.com), where promoter Bill Graham put on carnivalesque psychedelic rock shows for thousands of hallucinating hippies in the 1960s. There's no access to the interior now unless you shell out for a show.

However, in recent years, the city of San Francisco dubbed the area the **Fillmore Jazz Preservation District** to draw attention to the neighborhood's history, hosting jazz festivals and the like. The promotion inspired **Yoshi's**, a legendary jazz club in Oakland, to open a sister club here. The new *Yoshi's*, with the Fillmore and John Lee Hooker's *Boom Boom Room*, completes a neighborhood triumvirate of heavyweights in three genres: jazz, rock and blues.

Japantown and around

In 1968, in a conciliatory gesture toward San Francisco's Japanese community, the city built the **Japan Center** as a focal point for the reborn **Japantown**, notched into the northeastern corner of the Fillmore. Stretching three blocks along Post Street between Fillmore and Laguna streets, the building, officially known as the **Japanese Cultural and Trade Center,** gives visitors the delightful feeling they've been transported to modern-day Tokyo – even if they're actually just in a mall. Every aspect of Japanese culture, from old-world kimonos, origami, and taiko drums to current J-pop culture like anime, robots, and colorful Harajuku fashion, can be explored here. Despite its artificial origins, the mall is now at the center of a densely concentrated Japanese community (at around 12,000 people, one of the largest in the Bay Area), which shops at the center's food, record, and book stores. It's also filled with dozens of restaurants – though no chains, thanks to local zoning laws. To see the Japan Center at its best, you should stop by during the annual **Cherry Blossom** festival in April (for details, see p.278).

The only notable sight here is the 100-foot **Peace Pagoda**, standing in the outdoor central plaza that links the main buildings. The pagoda looks like a stack of poured-concrete, space-age mushrooms and is clearly intended to echo an atomic cloud. The adjacent **Kabuki Hot Springs**, 1750 Geary Blvd at Fillmore ($16–20; T1-866/218-8077, Wwww.kabukisprings.com), were once a traditional Japanese bathhouse, but have now been made over as a trendy, but appealing, spa. Thankfully, the huge communal steam room has been preserved (women only Sun, Wed, Fri; men only Mon, Thurs, Sat; co-ed Tues). In the same building, the **Sundance Kabuki Cinemas**, formerly the AMC Kabuki 8, have been completely renovated to make movie-going a posh experience, with gourmet food and cocktails, surrounded by elegant decor.

Otherwise, you can stop by the **Buddhist Church of San Francisco** at 1881 Pine St at Octavia (T415/776-3158, Wwww.bcsfweb.org), which offers services in both Japanese (Sun 1.30pm) and English (Sun 9.30am). The building's plain exterior hides a sumptuous interior filled with relics of the Buddha, donated by the king of Siam in 1935.

The Cathedral of St Mary of the Assumption

South of Japantown in an unloved corner of the Western Addition close to the Geary Expressway soars the city's newest and most conspicuous Catholic church, the **Cathedral of St Mary of the Assumption**, 1111 Gough St at Geary (Mon–Fri 6.45am–4.30pm, Sat 6.45am–7pm, Sun 7.30am–4.45pm; T415/567-2020, Wwww.sfarchdiocese.org/cathedral.html), was built in 1971 to replace a fire-damaged predecessor. The cathedral has been the butt of local humor ever since, due to a modernist design that many have likened to a washing-machine agitator (hence its nickname, "Our Lady of the Maytag"). In fact, with its white travertine marble exterior and swooping curves, it's a stunning addition to the cityscape. Set back from the road on wide, sunbaked plazas, and one story above ground, it's impressive enough to approach; once inside, the space is even more striking. The parabolic curves of the cathedral's vaulted 190-foot interior seem to be in constant movement, in part thanks to sunlight playing off the massive metal chandelier. The huge organ within is a spectacle in itself as well – it looks like a pincushion with a Mohawk; try to stop by for one of the recitals every Sunday at 3.30pm or for the wildly popular Christmas Midnight Mass, even if the iffy acoustics here don't do it justice.

The Richmond, Golden Gate Park, and the Sunset

The fog-choked **Sunset** and **Richmond** districts tend to be overshadowed by their beaches and stunning parks. Downtowners sniff about these areas far to the west by the ocean, which were artificially created from a bank of sand dunes at the turn of the twentieth century, and still unfinished as late as the 1940s. In fact, they're refreshingly real – even ordinary – places that provide relief from the self-consciously visitor-friendly sites Downtown. The Richmond especially is an excellent place to visit, and while its network of residential streets may be uninterrupted by official sights, strolling along Clement Street and enjoying the lively bustle of the local Chinese community is worth an afternoon in itself.

The Richmond-Sunset area isn't all suburbia. the western part of the city alternates between swathes of townhouses and vast open spaces like a double-decker sandwich. North of the Richmond and west of the Presidio, the wild greenspace of **Land's End** offers fantastic views of the Golden Gate Bridge and overlooks **Baker** and **China beaches**, two of the best beaches close to the city. Nearby **Lincoln Park** is the site of the grand **Legion of Honor**, one of San Francisco's undeniable treasures and home to a spectacular collection of Rodin sculptures.

Wedged between the Richmond and Sunset is the sculpted expanse of **Golden Gate Park**. Though the park is home to excellent museums, as well as manicured specialist gardens, none compares to the park itself, an artificial masterpiece laid out in the late nineteenth century. At the park's western edge, the city's **coastline** has a hauntingly desolate beauty. Much of the coastal area hereabouts, especially the forlorn remnants of the **Sutro Baths** and the renovated **Cliff House** north of the park, once constituted San Francisco's Playland-at-the-Beach. In better condition is **Ocean Beach**, a thin strip of sand that seals the Sunset's boundary with the ocean, capped at its southwestern corner by the blustery heights of **Fort Funston**. Also in the area is **San Francisco Zoo**, which might tempt visitors with children in tow, though its security has been called into question of late. Further inland, **Stern Grove** is another lush, green escape from the hustle of the city.

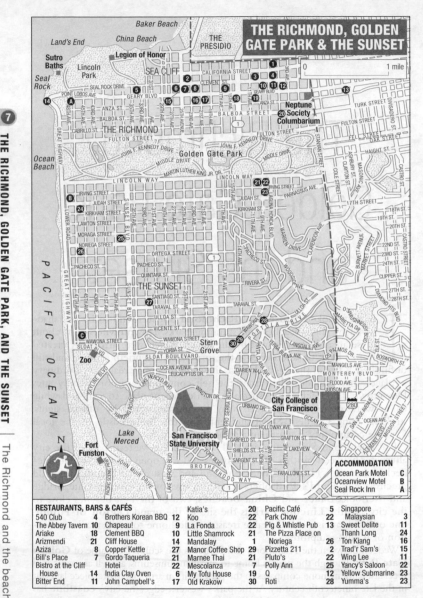

RESTAURANTS, BARS & CAFÉS

540 Club	4	Brothers Korean BBQ	12	Katia's	20	Pacific Café	5	Singapore
The Abbey Tavern	10	Chapeau!	9	Koo	22	Park Chow	22	Malaysian	3
Ariake	18	Clement BBQ	10	La Fonda	22	Pig & Whistle Pub	13	Sweet Delite	11
Arizmendi	21	Cliff House	14	Little Shamrock	21	The Pizza Place on		Thanh Long	24
Aziza	8	Copper Kettle	27	Mandalay	1	Noriega	26	Ton Kiang	16
Bill's Place	7	Gordo Taqueria	21	Manor Coffee Shop	29	Pizzetta 211	2	Trad'r Sam's	15
Bistro at the Cliff		Hotei	22	Marnee Thai	21	Pluto's	22	Wing Lee	11
House	14	India Clay Oven	6	Mescolanza	7	Polly Ann	25	Yancy's Saloon	22
Bitter End	11	John Campbell's	17	My Tofu House	19	Q	12	Yellow Submarine	23
				Old Krakow	30	Roti	28	Yumma's	23

Note: the ACCOMMODATION box reads: Ocean Park Motel C, Oceanview Motel B, Seal Rock Inn A.

The Richmond and the beaches

The **RICHMOND**, often referred to as "new Chinatown," stretches for more than two miles westward from Arguello Boulevard to the beaches, filling the gap between Golden Gate Park and the Presidio. It's without question a melting pot of numerous ethnicities, owing perhaps in part to its tremendous size – there are significant Jewish, Irish, and Russian communities, among others – but it's the local Chinese residents who have given the area its dominant character. Ironically, this buzzing working-class district abuts the swankiest San Francisco neighborhood, **Sea Cliff**, whose residents include local celeb Robin Williams. The entire district is wrapped with sandy **beaches** to the north and south as well as the jagged coastal beauty of **Lincoln Park**.

Clement Street and Geary Boulevard

The Richmond's vibrant Chinese community is most in evidence along **Clement Street** between Park Presidio and Arguello boulevards. On a short stroll, you'll spot dozens of Chinese dim-sum bakeries, grocery stores, and restaurants, not to mention the dense warrens of one of the city's best used-bookstores, **Green Apple Books** (see p.243). At the district's eastern edge – somewhat incongruous now, given the area's strong Asian flavor – stands the airy **Temple Emanu-El**, 2 Lake St at Arguello, a rare public bastion of the city's Jewish population (Ⓦwww.emanuelsf.org).

One block south, the Richmond's main driving thoroughfare, **Geary Boulevard**, showcases the area's European flavor with a myriad of ethnic restaurants; it's fume-choked most of the time, though, and not a pleasant place to dawdle on the sidewalk. The one attraction likely to draw visitors is the **Neptune Society Columbarium**, 1 Lorraine Court near Anza (Mon–Fri 8.30am–5pm, Sat–Sun 10am–3pm; free; Ⓣ415/771-0717, Ⓦwww .neptune-society.com), hidden just off Geary behind the now-shuttered Coronet movie theater. This miniature-scale monument to the city's heady Gold Rush-era high society is home to thousands of urns, which hold the ashes of the fin de siècle rich and famous. When the Columbarium was built in 1898, it stood at the entrance to an exclusive cemetery, and the elaborate decoration – including Tiffany stained-glass windows – is evidence of the money lavished on its construction. The building itself is a natty hybrid of chapel and Roman temple; look for unusual sculptural tributes to the various deceased like a martini shaker and a baseball. The names on the bronze and copper plaques lining the walls mirror the city's social register, from coffee millionaires the Folgers to media magnates the Dimmans and department-store pashas the Magnins.

The Legion of Honor and Land's End

The stately **Legion of Honor** (Tues–Sun 9.30am–5.15pm; $10, free first Tues of month; Ⓣ415/863-3330, Ⓦwww.thinker.org) is one of the best museums in San Francisco. Dramatically situated in **Lincoln Park**, a craggily beautiful greenspace carved into the coast at the easternmost end of Geary Boulevard, at 34th, the museum itself is no less staggering than its setting. It was built in 1920 by Alma de Bretteville Spreckels, with a parade of white columns that replicates the Légion d'Honneur in Paris (a nod to the heavy French emphasis in its holdings). There's a cast of Rodin's *The Thinker*, set dramatically on a pedestal in the center of the museum's front courtyard, which flags Alma's (and the museum's) penchant for the sensual French sculptor.

The museum's **Rodin holdings** are breathtaking in their depth and range, although there are more bronzes than marble sculptures; with over eighty pieces, it's one of the best collections of its kind in the world, and the Rodin rooms alone make this museum unmissable. Notable examples of his work include *The Athlete*, *Fugit Amor*, *The Severed Head of John the Baptist*, *Fallen Angel*, and a small bronze maquette of *The Kiss*, intended for the massive decorative doors he designed based on Dante's *Inferno*. (You can see one version of the *Gates of Hell* south of San Francisco at Stanford University; see p.331.) Don't miss the bust of the sculptor by his lover Camille Claudel, whose own outstanding artistic talent was steamrollered by Rodin's monumental personality.

Sadly, the magnificent museum is somewhat let down by its lackluster collection of **Old Masters**: many of the artworks, including those by Giambologna, Cellini, and Cranach, are "attributed to" or "the workshop of," rather than bona fide masterpieces. A few bright spots include the early gold-ground primitives from Germany, El Greco's chilling *St John the Baptist*, the landscapes and portraits by Gainsborough (including an unkindly telling picture of George IV's mistress Maria Fitzherbert), and an uncharacteristically sketchy portrait by David of his daughter Laure. The Impressionist collection is notable for the lively Degas oil sketches and a tiny view of the Eiffel Tower by Seurat. There's also a wide variety of decorative arts, including period rooms shipped wholesale from France and a dazzling, gilded ceiling brought to America from the Palacio de Altamira in Toledo. Downstairs, you'll find a rotating display of touring shows that vary wildly in quality.

Two sculptures stand in front of the museum. The stark red piece resembling tangled girders is *Pax Jerusalemme* by Mark di Suvero, who was educated locally at UC Berkeley. Hidden behind a wall on the path down to Land's End is George Segal's *The Holocaust*, a somber work (his last) consisting of barbed wire and stark bronze figures washed in white (cast from life using his friends as models), that acts as a raw reminder of wartime atrocities. From here, trails curve along the cliffs beneath the museum, rounding the point of **Land's End**, one of the few true wilderness areas left in the city. Littering the base of the jagged cliffs are the broken hulls of ships that failed to navigate the violent currents; with luck, at low tide you can see chunks of the wooden wreckage. The main trail is a popular jogging path, but the land recedes inland into shady cypress groves that are popular gay cruising spots. Arrive just before dusk for spectacular views of Marin and the Golden Gate Bridge.

Both Land's End and the Legion of Honor can be reached by taking the #38 bus on Geary Boulevard to Lincoln Park Golf Course, from where it's a pleasant – if athletic – walk uphill to the museum. Otherwise, you can wait for bus #18 there, which will take you right to the entrance.

The beaches and around

Rimming the western edge of the Presidio, just north of the Richmond, **Baker** and **China beaches** are popular outdoor destinations for locals who can't face the weekend gridlock on Golden Gate Bridge. Don't expect the usual sun-kissed Californian boardwalk, though: even on the sunniest days (which can be unnervingly unpredictable given the foggy climate, especially in summer), the water here is bone-chillingly cold. Be advised, too, that since both beaches sit at the mouth of the Bay, currents are perilously strong, and swimming is very risky whatever the time of year. That said, either of these beaches is an enjoyable place to while away an afternoon, surrounded by an eccentric mix of nude sunbathers and families on outings.

The strip of sand immediately east of Land's End, China Beach got its name in 1870 when it was home to an encampment of Chinese fishermen. When the government acted on rampant anti-Chinese bigotry and imposed tight restrictions on immigration ten years later or so (see p.397), the beach – supposedly – became a landing place for illegal aliens. These days, it's swankier, more sheltered, and has

To get to the beaches by car, the drive from both the east (the Presidio) and the west (Lincoln Park) along Lincoln Boulevard offers spectacular views of the surrounding landscape as well as the bridge. To get there by MUNI, take bus #29 (daily every 30min 7am–6.30pm), which offers a pleasant tour through the Presidio and deposits you in the main parking lot for Baker Beach. You can also walk, taking one of the public access stairways that drop down to the beach from Lincoln Boulevard.

better facilities than Baker Beach further north, including changing rooms and showers. If you're terrified of tanlines, clamber over the cluster of rocks that divides Baker and China beaches at low tide – the northern end of Baker Beach is mostly nude. Continue past the end of Baker Beach and pick your way down some treacherous trails to reach the isolated **Golden Gate Beach**, arguably the best spit of sand with a stunning view of the bridge. It, too, is a nudist spot, predominantly gay this time, that is often busy at weekends.

Given their position at the edge of the Bay, these beaches have been bulkheads against military aggression from overseas. In 1905, the army placed an enormous 95,000-pound cannon in an underground bunker on the hill above Baker Beach, at the base of cliffs protecting the Presidio's western flank. After a period of heightened militarization on both sides of the Bay during World War II, the cannon was declared obsolete and melted down for scrap, unfired in its forty-year career. A replacement cannon was set up in 1977 for exhibition purposes only, and if you stop by between 10am and 2pm on the first weekend of each month, you might catch the rangers giving a demonstration of how the cumbersome object would have been aimed and fired.

Overlooking China Beach, **Sea Cliff** is the toniest area in the city. It's dotted with ostentatious arches guarding the entrance to each street, and there's little to do other than gawp at the size of the houses and see how many crisply uniformed nannies you can spot on the sidewalks. Unfortunately for residents, the neighborhood's quiet comfort is literally not well founded – during a period of near-biblical rainfall in 1997, massive sinkholes developed in the area, swallowing entire mansions and provoking gleeful bursts of *schadenfreude* from less-well-heeled locals.

Cliff House, Seal Rock, and the Sutro Baths

The western coast of the San Francisco peninsula was a Fisherman's Wharf for the nineteenth century, although it's hard to believe, given how little is left now. The outer districts of San Francisco began as a working-class seaside resort, and a faded brassiness still lingers here, thanks to the ageing amusements, bustling diners, and budget motels. The area was the brainchild of Prussian immigrant **Adolph Sutro**, who managed to sell his mining interests before the deposits were exhausted and invest his subsequent fortune in seaside real estate in San Francisco. In fact, Sutro's former blufftop estate is now picturesque Sutro Heights Park, at the western terminus of Geary Boulevard (The compassionate and civic-minded entrepreneur ended his career as mayor of San Francisco, elected in 1894 on the Populist Party platform.)

Sutro was responsible for almost everything here, including the most prominent holdover from its heyday, **Cliff House**, at 1090 Point Lobos Rd (T 415/386-3300, W www.cliffhouse.com). Cliff House is the last remnant of Sutro's once-impressive amusement park complex named Playland-at-the-Beach; now, though, it's been stripped of any rides and functions as little more than a complex of restaurants. This Cliff House is actually the third house to sit on the site – the first two grand buildings were destroyed by fire, and the current, more modest structure dates back to 1909. The complex underwent a renovation in 2004 to upgrade its rather faded interior, but Cliff House's residual thrill is undoubtedly its natural setting, poised midway between the point of Land's End, to the north, and Ocean Beach, stretching to the south. From here, you can see the windmills that sit oceanside on Golden Gate Park's western edge.

After the delightful coin-operated machine museum, Museé Méchanique, was moved to Pier 45 (see p.84), very few traces of the house's carnival past remain and they've been all but hidden away down an outdoor flight of stairs just to the right of the entrance to the main dining room. From there, a large concrete landing offers views of **Seal Rock**, a popular nesting spot for birds. To the right is a park service station offering maps and information on the Golden Gate National Recreation Area, along with an arresting photographic display of the numerous ships that have run aground on the rocks below. On the landing beneath Cliff House stands a **Camera Obscura** (daily 11am–5pm, weather permitting; $3; ☎415/750-0415, ⊛www.giantcamera.com), one of the few remnants left from the original Playland built around the house. Using a rotating mirror – and a trick of light – the camera allows entrants to see a panoramic view of the surrounding area, including the birds on Seal Rock.

Sutro Baths

Back toward Land's End and down a path from Cliff House are the enormous but sadly unimpressive ruins of the **Sutro Baths**, the rubble blending into the surrounding greenish-brown earth. The abandoned pools are generally filled with brackish seawater now, though photos back at Cliff House ranger station reveal what a splendid spa this used to be. Sutro's baths were a seaside jewel – 100,000ft of stained glass covering more than three acres of sculpted pools filled with fresh - and salt water that could accommodate up to 20,000 people at any one time. Sutro packed his "Tropical Winter Gardens" with fountains, gardens, sculptures, and historical bric-a-brac from around the world, and they opened with great fanfare in 1896. But as public baths grew less popular, the glossy complex frayed, and by 1954, the only remaining open pool was converted to an ice rink, which limped along for another twelve years. Then, just after its closure, when the complex was being readied for demolition, a fire broke out and leveled the place. The lone dramatic remnant of Sutro's grandiose palace is a tunnel through the rocks, on the far end of the pools from Cliff House, which fills with the crashing of waves during high tide. Back at the top of the hill, across Point Lobos Avenue from Cliff House in Sutro Heights Park, only an enormous parapet survives from Sutro's once lavish house, which was demolished in 1939 and its grounds stripped of their ornamental statuary.

Golden Gate Park

Developed in the late nineteenth century, many years before the neighborhoods that surround it, **GOLDEN GATE PARK** (daily dawn–dusk; free; for schedules and tour information call ☎415/263-0991 or 750-5442) manages to be both a pastoral retreat for San Franciscans and a bastion of local culture, with more than a thousand acres of gardens and forest, complemented by some of the city's best museums. Spreading three miles or so west from Haight-Ashbury, it was designed in 1871 by park commissioner **William Hall**, mimicking the style of Frederick Law Olmsted (who created Central Park in New York). It was deliberately planned to be a woodland park, and streets were artfully curved to encourage promenading, rather than ramrod straight for quick cut-throughs. Hall used a dyke to protect the park's western side from the sea, and **John McLaren**, the Scottish park superintendent for 56 years, sculpted numerous miniature environments from what was then an area of wild sand dunes by planting several thousand trees. The resulting living masterpiece is a rugged landscape that undergoes a natural transition as it approaches the ocean, being subject on the park's western half to strong winds and chilly temperatures. Although the original planners intended to keep the park free of buildings, that proved impossible, and its eastern half is now dotted with city sights, such as the California Academy of Sciences. Many of the original buildings date from the 1894 World's Fair, the first held in California, which was designed as a recession-busting sideshow by local newspaperman Michael H. de Young. It was so successful that de Young was honored with a permanent museum here in his name. Now a popular site for everything from hippie drum circles to pick-up soccer games, the park closes its roads to cars on Sundays, making it friendly to bikers and roller-skaters.

The eastern park

If you're entering Golden Gate Park by car or bike, follow Fell Street west until it becomes **John F. Kennedy Drive**, along which most of the major draws are located. The first worthwhile stop is the restored **Conservatory of Flowers** (Tues–Sun 9am–5pm; $5; ☏415/666-7001, ⓦ www.conservatoryofflowers.org). Manufactured in Ireland for a San Jose millionaire who died before he could take possession of it, the building was eventually donated and shipped piecemeal to San Francisco. Local lore is that the redwood and glass structure was modeled after the Palm House at London's Kew Gardens, though it looks nothing like it. Indeed, the building, with its whitewashed wooden frame, resembles the

▲ Bikers in Golden Gate Park

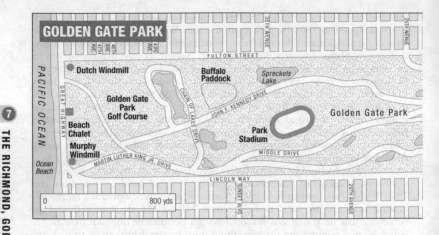

overblown greenhouse of a well-to-do Victorian country home. Its spiffy appearance hides a troubled history: it was closed in 1995 after severe storm damage rocked the building, necessitating the plants being shipped to local nurseries while the ailing conservatory was shored up. After eight years and $25 million worth of renovation, the conservatory is now divided into five sections: a temporary exhibition space, a room filled with Victorian-style potted plants, lowland and highland tropics areas (in the latter, look for the spindly orchids from the Andes), and best of all, a cool, aquatic-plant room boasting tractor-wheel-sized Victoria waterlilies.

Due south of the Conservatory is a **children's play area**, complete with a jungle gym, sand pit, and a classic merry-go-round (25¢ per child), as is the **National AIDS Memorial Grove** (T415/765-0497, W www.aidsmemorial .org) – look for the signs to De La Vega Dell on Middle Drive East. Set up in 1998, this seven-acre memorial garden was the first of its kind in the country, designed to commemorate those who died of AIDS-related illnesses. Rocks with single names dot the edge of the large oval greenspace and though a little rundown these days, it's still peaceful.

The **Music Concourse**, named after the bandshell donated by the sugar magnate Spreckels family at its western end, is wide open, dotted with knobbly trees and flanked by two museums, the de Young Museum and the California Academy of Sciences. The entire area has just been through a decade-long overhaul that hopes to turn it into one of the city's architectural and cultural hotspots. The first phase of the redevelopment is the new **M.H. de Young Museum**, 50 Tea Garden Drive (Tues–Thurs, Sat & Sun 9.30am–5.15pm, Fri 9.30am–8.45pm; $15, free first Tues of each month; T415/750-3600, Wwww .thinker.org), which reopened after several years' reconstruction in late 2005. This art museum has its origin in the California Midwinter International Exposition of 1894, a venture so successful that the Fine Arts Building from the exhibition was turned over to newspaper publisher Michael H. de Young (who'd helped found the *San Francisco Chronicle*) with the purpose of establishing a permanent museum. A hundred years later, the museum had outgrown its home, torn down in favor of a futuristic design from the Swiss architecture firm Herzog & de Meuron, famed for its conversion of a power station into the Tate Modern in London. The twisty, coppery building, made from interlocking boxes, incorporates both a sculpture garden (look for Louise Nevelson's moody

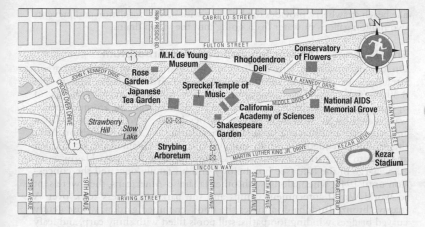

black *Ocean Gate*) and a 144-foot tall tower with impressive views across the park; the entire structure will acquire a greenish patina over the next decade that's intended to blend more harmoniously with the park surroundings. Among its American holdings, standouts include canvases by Impressionist Mary Cassatt – a picture of her mother – as well as John Singleton Copley's *Mrs. Daniel Turner Sargent*; plus a tankard and caster by Paul Revere and furniture by Tiffany and Frank Lloyd Wright. There's also an extensive collection of African, Oceanic, and South American folk art, mostly holdovers from the displays at the 1894 exhibition. Don't miss the four splashy new exhibitions commissioned as site-specific installations from contemporary artists: the most noteworthy is Gerhard Richter's enormous black and white geometric mural which sprawls through the main atrium.

On the southern edge of the plaza here, opposite the brand new De Young, is the site of the **California Academy of Sciences** (Mon–Sat 9.30am–5.15pm, Sun 11am–5pm; $24.95, free third Wed of each month; ☎415/379-8000, ⓦwww.calacademy.org) which reopened to much fanfare in late 2008. After a stint at a temporary site in SoMa, the museum's home quarters have been transformed by eco-friendly architect Renzo Piano (most famous as the designer of Paris's Centre Pompidou). The updated building features restored and expanded versions of the museum's most popular attractions: the Tusher African Center, a detailed diorama of the zoological landscape of Africa, now holds South African penguins in a tank at the end of the hall; the Swamp now boasts a rare white alligator and a lower level where visitors can watch the alligators and turtles swim by; the new-and-improved Planetarium now features a digital projection system with real-time data from NASA. Perhaps the most stunning addition is the Rainforest, located in a glass dome that's 90ft in diameter and recreates the warm, humid rainforest climate. The pathway inside the dome winds up three stories around trees, past live animals native to Borneo, Madagascar, and Costa Rica to the top of the canopy where butterflies and birds fly freely. At the top, visitors take a glass elevator down into the depths of a re-created Amazon River, before walking through an acrylic tunnel into the Steinhart Aquarium, which holds the Academy's popular collection of unique and rare fish and new coral reef. Thanks to Piano's sustainable design, the water is pumped two miles from Ocean Beach to the tanks and used much more efficiently. Meanwhile, the Living Roof, 2.5 acres planted with flowers and plants native to the Bay Area like beach strawberry, provides the building with natural insulation and prevents two million gallons of water from going into the storm drains.

The Japanese Tea Garden and Strybing Arboretum

On the northwestern rim of the Concourse sits one of the best-known attractions in the park, the **Japanese Tea Garden** (daily: March–Oct 8.30am–6pm; Nov–Feb 9am–5pm; $4, free for first and last hours of opening). Ironically, this Asian fantasy of miniature trees and groomed plants was created by an Australian, George Turner Marsh, who had lived in Japan and who operated it as the Japanese Village during the 1894 Exposition. After the exhibition ended, the wildly popular village was renamed the Tea Garden and sold to the park's commissioners. They appointed Makota Hagiwara to take charge of the café (see box below), and his family operated the concession until 1942, when, along with other Japanese-Americans, they were sent to World War II internment camps and the park's gardeners took over. A massive bronze Buddha dominates the nook-crammed garden, whose gently curved bridges, winding footpaths, still pools filled with shiny carp, and leafy bonsai and cherry trees lend the place a peaceful atmosphere despite the busloads of tourists pouring in every day. Make sure to climb the humpback bridge and check out the magnificent, if careworn, pagoda from San Francisco's Pan-Pacific Exhibition in 1915. The best way to enjoy the garden is to get there around 8.30am or 9am when it first opens for a tea and Japanese-cookie breakfast in the teahouse. Incidentally, Marsh was a native of

Good fortune

The history of the **fortune cookie** is as foggy and unreliable as the five-cent predictions each contains. The cookie's certainly a Californian creation, but the arguments over whether it's Japanese or Chinese, San Franciscan or Angeleno, are still raging. The most popular story of its invention involves Makota Hagiwara of the Japanese Tea Garden in Golden Gate Park. In 1907, so the story goes, Hagiwara was ousted from his job there by racist mayor James Phelan. Happily, thanks to heavy pressure from supporters, he was quickly reinstated and invented the cookies as a way of delivering thank-you notes to those friends who'd championed his cause. The rival Father of the Fortune Cookie, David Jung, was a Cantonese immigrant in Los Angeles, who allegedly produced the first cookies after World War I as an uplifting treat for unemployed workers gathered in the streets around his home.

Arguments continued for seventy years before the matter came to court in 1983 – albeit at the tongue-in-cheek Court of Historical Review. This San Francisco tradition is presided over by a real Supreme Court judge, but its past cases have included ruling on the true inventor of the martini and whether the Grinch really stole Christmas (he didn't). Despite Los Angeles' best efforts, the judge ruled in favor of Hagiwara; Jung's supporters still mutter about the ancient Chinese tradition of sending birth announcements wrapped in sweet dough, but for now at least, it looks as if the Japanese tradition has triumphed.

Whatever the fortune cookie's origins, Chinese-restaurant owners quickly recognized that they were a nifty way of attracting white customers who often asked for dessert at the end of a meal, an alien concept in most Chinese provinces. Fortune cookies spread across the country, and the world, although they're still rarely found in China itself. San Francisco's one clear contribution to cookie culture came in 1972, when Edward Louie, a local baker, invented the automatic folding machine and so enabled mass production at a level that hand-wrapping had never allowed.

Richmond in Australia, and when he moved to San Francisco and bought a house in the wild western regions, he named the surrounding area after his hometown – the name it still bears today.

For a less crowded outdoor alternative, wander south to the **Strybing Arboretum** (Mon–Fri 8am–4.30pm, Sat & Sun 10am–5pm; free; T 415/661-1316, W www.sfbotanicalgarden.org), with entrances across from the Tea Garden or at Ninth Avenue and Lincoln Way. The 75-acre botanic garden is home to more than seven thousand varieties of plants, with miniature gardens focusing on plants from regions ranging from desert to tropical; especially appealing is the headily scented garden of fragrance. For a tour, stop by the bookstore inside the Main Gate (weekdays 1.30pm, weekends 10.30am & 1.30pm) or the Ninth Avenue entrance (Wed, Fri, or Sun 2pm). Just outside the Arboretum's north entrance is the **Shakespeare Garden**: this tiny, hedged greenspace, centered on an old-fashioned sundial and dotted with benches, showcases every flower and plant mentioned in Shakespeare's works, whether plays, or poems. There's a metal plaque full of the relevant quotations on a brick wall at the edge of the lawn.

The western park

The center portion and western edges of the park are quieter than the sight-filled eastern plains; head through the many flower gardens and eucalyptus groves that lead toward the ocean to escape the crowds on sunny weekend days. If you want to paddle, **boat rental** is available on marshy **Stow Lake**, near 19th Avenue (daily 10am–4pm; rowboats $19/hr, paddleboats $24/hr, plus $1 deposit; T 415/752-0347) – although it's more fun during the week when it doesn't feel like rush hour on the lake. Sitting at the water's center is Strawberry Hill, a large fake knoll that can also be reached by a footbridge, which takes you to a Chinese Pagoda (a gift from the city of Taipei) at the foot of the hill near a waterfall cascading down the hill. On weekend afternoons the large soccer field nearby is the scene of some very heated games between South and Central American intramural squads.

Inexplicably, there's a small herd of bison roaming around the **Buffalo Paddock** off JFK Drive near 38th Avenue. They've been in the park for decades, artfully contained in a sunken greenspace; you can get closest to these noble giants in their feeding area at the far west end. Continue west along JFK and you'll hit the twin anchors of the park's western edge: enormous windmills. The northwestern corner houses the 1902 **Dutch Windmill**, which was restored to working order in the early 1980s and sits next to a glorious flower patch known as the **Queen Wilhelmina Tulip Garden**. It's a sharp contrast with the once-grand but long-decayed **Murphy Windmill** from 1908 in the southwestern corner. Its 114-foot sails, the largest in the world, have been removed and its main wooden column left to rot; thankfully, preservationists have finally raised enough funds to renovate it, shipping in Dutch engineers to rebuild it using the same kinds of timber and shingles as the original. The Murphy's sails are set to start turning again – oddly, they turn clockwise, the opposite of their Dutch counterparts – in early 2009. Between the two structures, facing the highway, is the **Beach Chalet**, a two-story, white-pillared building designed by Willis Polk; housing a series of 1930s frescoes depicting the growth of San Francisco as a city and the creation of Golden Gate Park, it also holds a small visitors center providing information about the park's numerous guided walking tours. Upstairs there's a lively brewery-restaurant, great for late weekend brunches.

The Sunset and the western coast

Built following World War II to provide cheap housing for returning soldiers, much of the **SUNSET** district is intensely suburban, with around forty blocks of stucco townhouses in pastel colors – originally sold for only $5000 a unit. The main drag, Irving Street between Sixth and 11th – easily reached from Downtown on the N-Judah line – is the place for a subdued night on the town, with British and Irish pubs and critically lauded restaurants. Further down Irving (a block from the N-Judah) around 19th is a third, smaller Chinatown of sorts, where you can sample authentic Chinese cuisine and buy bubble tea, silks, and other gifts.

About forty blocks west of the university, at the end of the N-Judah line, buffeted by sea breezes and fog, the thin barrier of **Ocean Beach** seems to be constantly on the brink of either being washed out to sea or blown into locals' backyards. Aside from a small community of surfers, the windy, debris-strewn beach is the almost exclusive territory of joggers and dogwalkers. During the evenings, bonfires are permitted in the fire pits on the southern portions of the beach near Sloat Boulevard.

Just south of here is the **San Francisco Zoo** (daily 10am–5pm; $11, free first Wed of month; ☎415/753-7080, ⓦwww.sfzoo.org), with a lush Lemur Forest, a three-acre African Savannah, with giraffes, zebras, dik-diks, and kudus, and a Children's Zoo (daily 10am–4pm), complete with a beautifully restored carousel ($2). The zoo's reputation has suffered since a Siberian tiger escaped from her enclosure and killed a visitor in December 2007, and despite upgrades its security has been repeatedly called into question.

In summer, be sure to detour along Ocean Beach's southern run to the small **Stern Grove**. This leafy ravine of eucalyptus, redwood, and fir trees shelters a natural amphitheater where a popular free Sunday concert series is held in the summer months (see p.228 for more info or check ⓦwww.sterngrove.org). The park is tucked at the base of **West Portal**, a pleasant enough row of shops and restaurants near the point where the K, L, and M MUNI lines emerge from the subway tunnel. Further south, a seemingly endless string of malls runs along 19th Avenue, briefly interrupted by the unappealing campus of **San Francisco State University** – long known for its populism and political activism, though now it looks like an unloved 1960s housing complex.

A freshwater pond tucked between the university's campus and the shoreline, undervisited **Lake Merced** provides a quiet getaway, though most of the surrounding greenspace is given over to golf courses. It's hard to believe that this was the site of one of the most notorious events in California history. In 1859, David Broderick, the state's most prominent politician and a US Senator, was challenged to a duel here by David Terry, the Chief Justice of the state's Supreme Court. Terry, a Southern sympathizer who dreamed of bringing California into the Confederacy, shot and killed Broderick, and quickly fled the state. Today, there are two small stone markers showing where each man stood at the time the shot was fired.

Finally, if you've made it this far, soldier on to the city's southernmost corner, where a steep bluff holds scenic **Fort Funston**, a popular dog park. Aside from a few concrete bunkers, there isn't much evidence of a fort here, but the dunes that drop off to the beach below attract hang-gliders – on a gusty day, watching the daredevils swoop and twirl along the cliff face is a true pleasure.

Listings

Listings

Accommodation

esidents of San Francisco complain constantly about skyrocketing rent, and visitors can suffer equally from steep room prices. Expect accommodation to cost around $120 per night in a reasonable hotel or motel, slightly less out of season. We've listed some smart bargains below (some as cheap as $50 a night during offseason), but if you want to snag one of these cheaper rooms, it's essential to call around and book ahead. As always, look for **online specials**: most hotel websites offer discounts or guaranteed lowest rates, while clearing houses like Ⓦwww.hotels.com or Ⓦwww.priceline.com sometimes list luxury rooms for a steal. Wherever you book, though, remember that rates are significantly better in rooms that share baths.

The **Visitor Information Center** (Mon–Fri 9am–5pm, Sat & Sun 9am–3pm; ☏415/283-0177, Ⓦwww.sfvisitor.org) can provide the latest accommodation options, while the local **San Francisco Reservations** (Mon–Fri 6am–11pm, Sat & Sun 8am–11pm; ☏1-800/677-1500, Ⓦwww.hotelres.com) will find you a room from around $120 a double. British visitors can reserve rooms through **Colby International** (Mon–Fri 10am–5pm UK time; ☏0151/220 5848, Ⓦwww.colbyintl.com).

For **B&Bs**, the city's fastest-growing source of accommodation, contact a specialist agency such as Bed and Breakfast California (☏408/867-9662) or Bed and Breakfast San Francisco (☏415/899-0060 or 1-800/452-8249, Ⓦwww.bbsf.com). If funds are tight, look into one of the many excellent **hostels**, where beds start at around $22.

There's nowhere legal to **camp** in San Francisco itself – don't even think about pitching a tent in Golden Gate Park or the Presidio, for example, since it's not only frowned upon but dangerous. If you're determined to sleep underneath the stars, head out across the rest of the area, especially into the East Bay and Marin County.

Hotels and motels

The densest concentration of hotel rooms in San Francisco can be found around **Union Square** (including Chinatown and the Theater District). Thanks to this glut, you should be able to bargain with most of the budget and mid-range hotels in this district during off-peak times – they're all scrabbling to fill rooms, so don't be afraid to haggle. Conversely, on summer weekends, this is a tough place to find any reasonable rooms under $100. Then, it's worth checking out other options like **North Beach** and **Pacific Heights**.

Three local chains run the majority of trendy **boutique hotels** in town: the Kimpton Group (Ⓦwww.kimptonhotels.com), which has more than forty locations across the country, including nine in the city; and Joie de Vivre Hospitality (ⓦ www.jdvhospitality.com), which only has properties in the Bay Area and Los Angeles, and runs sixteen different places in San Francisco proper; Personality Hotels (ⓦ www.personalityhotels.com) runs only eight properties, exclusively on Union Square. They're all funky, fun, and largely good-value alternatives to major names like Hyatt and Hilton.

If you're on a particularly tight budget, the best option is to head to **SoMa**, **the Tenderloin**, and **Civic Center**, where there should be rooms for under $100 at most times of year. Be aware, however, that these neighborhoods can be dodgy, even during the daytime, and there are plenty of seedy hotels. We've listed clean, safe, budget choices below.

There's little difference between motels and budget hotels in San Francisco. The one plus at most motels is that **parking** (often nightmarishly expensive on the street) is included in the overnight rate. If space is tight, the best place to check for availability is along Lombard Street in Cow Hollow, the **main motel drag** in San Francisco.

Bed and breakfasts

The Bay Area is filled with fancy **B&Bs**, most of them housed in historic buildings such as a sumptuously restored Victorian that was once a private mansion or even a school. You may have to sacrifice a private bathroom for the charms of a home-cooked breakfast, but staying at a B&B is almost the only choice if you want a base in the **Castro**, the **Mission**, or **Haight–Ashbury**. Most are communal, chatty experiences so come prepared with conversation and a dressing gown. Expect rates to start around $140, higher in summer.

Hostels

It's in its hostels that the Bay Area truly shines: whether **privately run** or **official HI hostels**, most are spotless, funky, and well equipped, with a liberal, laid-back rulebook and a welcoming staff. In recent years, there's been a spate of new properties opening all over town (including a handy spot in the heart of the Mission district). You can expect terrific, convenient locations across the city and most have a few private rooms available as well as dorms. Either way, they'll provide a bed and a locker for your valuables, though not much else.

To stay at an **HI hostel**, you'll need to be a member: it's $25 per year for US citizens, and $3 per day for international travelers – though after six paid days, the international fee also converts into a year-long membership. Even if you're American, it's worth **bringing your passport** if you plan on staying at a hostel as many places will insist on seeing it before renting you a bed, a measure designed to preserve the place for bona fide travelers. For similar reasons, many hostels also impose a nominal maximum stay of three to five days.

Hostels

Adelaide Hostel 51 Isadora Duncan Lane off Taylor St at Geary, Theater District ☎415/359-1915, ⊛www.adelaidehostel.com. Formerly a hotel, this hostel, hidden away on a tiny lane close to Union Square, features a hundred beds spread across four-, six- and ten-person dorms; some have en-suite bathrooms, others shared bathrooms nearby. Bunks here are built into the wall, much like rail sleeper cars, complete with their own curtains. There are also a handful of two- and three-person private rooms ($60 and up). The unbeatable facilities include a big, peaceful sofa-filled lounge, free wi-fi, backyard deck, clean kitchen where the hefty continental breakfast is served, and a cheap laundry ($1.50/load). Open 24hr. Highly recommended. Dorms $23–26.

Elements Hostel 2524 Mission St at 21st, Mission ☎415/647-4100 or 1-866/327-8407, ⊛www.elementssf.com. Mission St hostel that fills a gaping need for any kind of accommodation, budget or otherwise, in the area. En-suite dorm rooms mostly sleep four people, and there are men-only, women-only, and mixed dorms; couples can opt for one of the few private rooms with twin or double beds ($60). Amenities include 24hr access, wi-fi and Internet access, movie showings, a hearty continental breakfast in *Café Medjool* next door, lockers, linens, and towels. The rooftop terrace view more than compensates for the noise coming from the café. Dorms $25–27.50.

Green Tortoise 494 Broadway at Montgomery, North Beach ☎415/834-1000 or 1-800/867-8647, ⊛www.greentortoise.com. This laid-back hostel has room for 130 people in dorm beds or double rooms (with shared bath; $52, $60 in summer) though it's showing its age, especially given the rash of new budget spaces that have opened. Whether you pay for a dorm or a room, you'll get Internet access, use of the small onsite sauna, foosball and pool tables, and complimentary breakfast; there's even free dinner three nights a week. There's no curfew, and the front desk is staffed 24hr. Dorms $25–29.

HI-San Francisco City Center 685 Ellis St at Larkin, Tenderloin ☎415/474-5721, ⊛www.norcalhostels.org. Converted from the old *Atherton Hotel*, this hostel has two hundred beds divided into four-person dorms, each with en-suite bath; there are also fifteen private rooms, with either double or twin beds. There's no curfew and overall it's friendly and good for meeting other travelers, since there are plenty of activities laid on (such as nightly movies and communal pancake breakfasts) plus a happy hour from 6–7pm every Tues, Thurs, and Fri in the second-floor common room. Its only downside is the location in a sketchier part of the Tenderloin, which means it's not ideal for a solo female coming back late at night. $23 members, $26 others; private rooms $67 members, $70 others.

HI-San Francisco Downtown 312 Mason St at Geary, Union Square ☎415/788-5604, ⊛www.norcalhostels.org. With almost three hundred beds spread between four- and five-bed dorms, this hostel still fills up quickly in peak season, thanks to its central location. The four-person dorms are spotless, sharing bathroom facilities between eight people, while private rooms are pricier and sleep two. Open 24hr, there's a kitchen with microwave and vending machines, a funky little reading room, and Internet access. Dorms $22 members, $25 others; private rooms with shared bath $55 members, $58 others; private en-suite rooms $65 members, $68 others.

HI-San Francisco Fisherman's Wharf Building 240, Fort Mason ☎415/771-7277, ⊛www.norcalhostels.org. Housed in a historic former Civil War barracks on the waterfront between the Golden Gate Bridge and Fisherman's Wharf, this is a choice option for an outdoorsy traveler. There are 180 beds in both mixed and single-sex dorms, with rooms ranging from six to twelve people. Note that the disabled-access extension is available to able-bodied travelers, too, and is the choicest spot – it's effectively a stand-alone apartment with three bedrooms charged at the dorm rate. The hostel is less central than others, but the terrific amenities include a knowledge-able staff, neighborhood info board bursting with leaflets, free breakfast, a huge kitchen, and breathtaking views across the bay. A bus service regularly shuttles Downtown from Fort Mason's main entrance, or it's a short walk to Fisherman's Wharf. Note, too, that this is cheaper than other HI hostels, since its federal locale means no member-ship fee can be charged. All beds $22.50/person.

Pacific Tradewinds Backpacker Hostel 680 Sacramento St at Kearny, Chinatown ☎415/433-7970 or 1-800/486-7975, @www .san-francisco-hostel.com. An appealing budget option in the center of town (no lockout, no curfew), this small hostel offers free high-speed Internet access, tea and coffee, a clean kitchen plus a large, communal dining table that's an easy way to get to know fellow travelers. It's certainly an international hub – house rules are posted in almost forty languages, including Afrikaans and Catalan. There are only 38 beds so

book ahead in high season; check-in available 8am–11.30pm. Dorms $24.

USA Hostel 711 Post St at Jones, Theater District ☎415/440-5600, @www .usahostels.com. A safe, friendly, and fun hostel in the heart of Downtown, with colorful walls, jocular staff, and plenty of opportunities to make new friends. Facilities include a huge common area jammed with bright couches and barstools, plus free billiards and foosball tables; a TV lounge with flat-screen television; high-speed Internet kiosks and free wi-fi; a kitchen with free tea and coffee all day and free all-you-can-make pancakes in the morning; and an onsite laundry with free detergent. Bonding opportunities for travelers include walking tours, pub crawls, and movie nights. All dorm rooms have four beds, and can be all-male, all-female or mixed dorms, with en-suite or shared bathrooms. Private rooms ($83–93) feature one queen bed or two twin beds, again with shared or en-suite bathrooms. Dorm beds $25–28, with a $1 discount for online booking.

Hotels, motels, and B&Bs

Downtown and Chinatown

Adagio 550 Geary St at Jones, Theater District ☎415/775-5000, @www .jdvhospitality.com. The decor at this Joie de Vivre hotel honors its ornate Spanish Revival facade with deep reds and ochers, although the interior is surprisingly modern, and the suite-sized rooms have a calming feng-shui vibe and are well appointed (huge TV, Internet, honor bar). Another plus are the views across Downtown from the upper floors. The *Adagio* also provides free computers with Internet access and free printing facilities. $245.

The Andrews Hotel 624 Post St at Taylor, Union Square ☎415/563-6877or 1-800/9-ANDREWS, @www.andrewshotel.com. This charming little hotel maintains an air of old-fashioned gentility and grace with its small lobby and the elegant, shoebox-sized *Fino Bar & Ristorante*. The room are 1950s retro, with flowered bedspreads, peach walls, green carpeting, avocado-green wooden furniture, and tiled bathrooms. A cute, quiet, and clean bargain for the location. $139.

Baldwin 321 Grant Ave at Bush, Chinatown ☎415/781-2220 or 1-800/6-BALDWIN, @www .baldwinhotel.com. Surprisingly quiet spot, given its location in the heart of Chinatown. The rooms here are outfitted in neutral colors with simple furnishings and ceiling fans, and rates are negotiable offseason. $123.

Beresford 635 Sutter St at Mason, Union Square ☎415/673-9900 or 1-800/533-6533, @www .beresford.com/beresford. With its elaborate Victorian interior – cheerful yellow wallpaper and curved banister – this old-fashioned, family-run hotel, home to the *White Horse Tavern and Restaurant*, seems like it belongs in the English countryside. This hotel has 114 guest rooms with satellite TVs and honor bars, an office space with a telephone modem and DSL Internet console, free continental breakfast, and valet parking. $179.

Beresford Arms 701 Post St at Jones, Theater District ☎415/673-2600 or 1-800/533-6533, @www.beresford.com. An old Theater District hotel, whose sumptuous crushed-velvet lobby belies the rather plain rooms, decorated in dark wood. Each has mirrored wardrobes and window seats – pleasant enough, but oddly suburban. Free continental breakfast is included in the room rate. $189.

Best Western Hotel California 580 Geary St at Jones, Theater District ☏415/441-2700 or 1-800/227-4223, ⓦwww.thesavoyhotel.com. Formerly the *Savoy Hotel*, this Best Western property named after the Eagles song goes above and beyond your standard chain hotel, making it one of the best value in San Francisco. The charming rooms, while small, feature gorgeous antique dark-wood furniture, hardwood floors, and lovely tiled bathroom, individually decorated in a manner that feels homey, vintage-style, and also sophisticated. Guests get a free tequila shot upon check-in. The hotel features extremely comfortable mattresses, high-thread-count linens, free wi-fi and high-speed Internet terminals in the lobby, and valet parking, as well as a free wine and cheese reception from 4–6 pm. There's also a superb vegetarian restaurant, *Millennium*, just off the lobby. $189.

Campton Place 340 Stockton St at Sutter, Union Square ☏415/781-5555 or 1-800/235-4300, ⓦwww.camptonplace.com. Upscale and understated hotel that provides utter seclusion despite being located in the heart of Union Square. Each floor is set around a glassed-in central courtyard, and rooms are decorated in muted russets and greens with Deco-inspired fixtures and deep marble baths. Since Taj Hotels took over in 2007, the decor has been adapted to a more Asian theme, with elegant pearwood panels installed in the closet area. wi-fi and a BoseWave sound system come with the room. $100.

Hotel Carlton 1075 Sutter St at Larkin, Theater District. ☏415/673-0242 or 1-800/922-7586, ⓦwww.hotelcarltonsf.com. One of the Joie de Vivre spots inspired by literature and magazines: in this case, the globetrotting *Carlton* is a guidebook brought to life. The lobby is filled with objects from the Middle East and Africa, the elevator is plastered with world maps, and the rooms have rich ocher bedlinens and inlaid wood tables as well as photographs of Middle Eastern scenes on the walls. $264.

Chancellor Hotel 433 Powell St at Post, Union Square ☏415/362-2004 or 1-800/428-4748, ⓦwww.chancellorhotel.com. Built in 1914, this charming little boutique hotel has

recently renovated its small, cozy rooms. The property offers nice beds, high water-pressure showers, free wi-fi, and cookies and tea in the lobby. The second floor features a lovely little meeting room decked out with murals and a paperback library. $200.

Clift Hotel 495 Geary St at Taylor, Theater District ☏415/775-4700 or 1-800/658-5492, ⓦwww.morganshotelgroup.com. Boutique hotel pioneer Ian Schrager has recovered from his financial problems of the early 2000s, so the *Clift* is still here. It's a good thing, as the vaguely Asian rooms are vintage Starck, with quirky touches like the Louis XIV-style chairs with mirrors on the seat and back, and sleigh beds – pity the bathrooms are so small. Pricey, swish, and ultra-cool: just don't expect smiles from the staff. Note that the walls here are very thin, so bring earplugs. Even if you can't afford a room here, don't miss *The Redwood Room* bar; also here is the *Asia de Cuba* restaurant (see p.211 and p.172 respectively). $455.

Hotel des Arts 447 Bush St at Grant, Theater District ☏415/956-3232 or 1-800/956-4322, ⓦwww.sfhoteldesarts.com. Buzzy spot that's hybrid art gallery and hotel: all but one of the rooms here are custom-decorated by local artists, and there are pictures for sale all over the stark white hall walls. Most of the rooms are en-suite, although the cheaper ones share "European" style baths down the hallway. It's noisy and the space feels, and sometimes smells, like a hostel or college dorm, but it's still a fun, bargain place to stay. Note that check-in is on the second floor – look for the old *Alissa* hotel sign, then take the vintage elevator up from the tiny lobby. $109 shared bath, $149 en suite.

Hotel Diva 440 Geary St at Taylor, Union Square ☏415/885-0200 or 1-800/553-1900, ⓦwww.hoteldiva.com. This boutique hotel taps into sleek 1980s minimalism that's part avant-garde New Wave and part Tom Cruise *Cocktail*-era bachelor pad, with its sleek steel and black leather sofas. As for the rooms, they're large and retro minimalist, recently upgraded with new bedding and lighting and furniture from high-end interiors company Design Within Reach. There are vending machines, including rental DVDs in the corridors, as well as a small onsite gym. $175.

Hotel Frank 386 Geary St at Mason, Theater District ☎415/986-2000 or 1-800/553-1900, ⓦwww.personalityhotels.com. This 1908 hotel, until recently known as the *Maxwell*, has just undergone a $10-million makeover. The rooms are dominated by a large houndstooth pattern on the floor and emerald-green accents, with white couches and elegant hanging lamps, plus 32-inch flat-screen televisions and iPod docking stations. The overall effect is of old-style Hollywood glamour envisioning a sleek Jetsons future. $159.

The Golden Gate Hotel 755 Bush St at Mason, Union Square. ☎415/392-3702 or 1-800/835-1118, ⓦwww.goldengatehotel.com. From its adorable yellow facade to its Edwardian interior, this family-run hotel is a bargain. Rooms are decorated with antiques and wicker furniture, and many of the bathrooms feature claw-foot tubs. The beds have quality mattresses, down pillows and comforters, and there's free wi-fi. $95.

Grant Hotel 753 Bush St at Mason, Chinatown ☎415/421-7540 or 1-800/522-0979, ⓦwww.granthotel.net. Good value for its location close to Union Square (though the strip club next door is a little off-putting), this hotel has small but clean rooms, overpowered somewhat by the relentlessly maroon carpets. There's free continental breakfast (pastries, coffee) included in the room rate, as well as 24hr free Internet access from the terminal in the lobby. Basic but convenient. $75.

Grant Plaza 465 Grant Ave at Pine, Chinatown ☎415/434-3883 or 1-800/472-6899, ⓦwww.grantplaza.com. The terrific location – just one block from the main gateway to Chinatown – isn't the hotel's only advantage. The rooms are brighter than at most budget spots, and look rather like bedrooms from a 1980s sitcom (lots of pink and faux pine) and have hairdryers, TVs, and phones. What's more, the staff are unstintingly helpful. The only downside are that it can be rather noisy, so bring earplugs. $85.

Halcyon Hotel 649 Jones St at Post, Union Square ☎415/929-8033 or 1-800/627-2396, ⓦwww.halcyonsf.com. The rooms and bathroom at this 1912 hotel are extraordinarily small, but serviceable, equipped with wi-fi and with mini-fridge, coffee maker, microwave, toaster and kitchenware crammed in. Everything is clean and infuses with old-world quaintness. $89.

JW Marriott 500 Post St at Mason, Union Square ☎415/771-8600 or 1-800/228-9290, ⓦwww.marriott.com. This luxury hotel, formerly the *Pan Pacific San Francisco*, got an "artsy" redesign when Marriott took over a few years ago. The rooms, featuring big comfy beds, are a tech-lover's dream, each equipped with a 42-inch LCD TV with a plug-in panel, a Bose sound system, an ergonomic office chair, wi-fi and high-speed Internet access, plus a 24hr personal butler button. Chocolates on the pillow only sweeten the deal. $319.

Kensington Park 450 Post St at Powell, Union Square ☎415/788-6400 or 1-800/553-1900, ⓦwww.kensingtonparkhotel.com. Known for its extraordinarily comfortable beds, this boutique hotel envelops you in *Casablanca* ambience the moment you set foot in the lobby with its vaulted ceiling and antique furniture. There's Queen Anne mahogany furniture in the elegant bedrooms, and the hotel offers a complimentary tea and sherry service in the lobby each evening, a 24hr business center, wi-fi and same-day laundry and dry-cleaning services. $189.

King George 334 Mason St at O'Farrell, Union Square ☎415/781-5050 or 1-800/288-6005, ⓦwww.kinggeorge.com. Like a cheaper version of the *Sir Francis Drake* (see p.157), this Brit-themed hotel has heraldic touches in its lobby (think floral carpets and overwrought furniture); other than a dish filled with candy, the rooms are functional and surprisingly spartan (the free high-speed Internet is a plus), but the rates and location more than compensate. $189.

Larkspur Hotel Union Square 524 Sutter St at Powell, Union Square ☎415/421-2865 or 1-800/227-3844, ⓦwww.larkspurhotelunionsquare.com. The airy lobby is like a country-house conservatory, with overstuffed, chintzy armchairs, free newspapers, and a front desk faced with beige marble. The rooms are much plainer – recently updated with modern beige furniture, they're pleasant but nondescript. En-suite bathrooms are fine, but minuscule. $189.

Hotel Metropolis 25 Mason St at Turk, Tenderloin ☎415/775-4600 or 1-800/553-1900, ⓦwww.hotelmetropolis.com. Though in the dodgy Tenderloin district, this hotel, a block from the cable-car turnaround and tourist Downtown, is delightful inside, boasting chic modern decor and a color scheme combining neutral tan with eye-popping comic-book primaries. Amenities include a cozy reading library, a 24hr business center, wi-fi, a cardio center workout room, and a "Holistic/Well-being Room," which may be required after walking down the street. The hotel is pet-friendly, too. $169.

Monaco 501 Geary St at Taylor, Union Square ☏ 415/292-0100 or 1-800/214-4220, ⓦwww .monaco-sf.com. Kimpton Hotels' flagship brand, this quirky boutique hotel is housed in a historical Beaux Arts building. There are canopied beds in each room, and the rest of the decor is equally riotous and colorful; it's a little precious and pricey, but hugely popular. One unusual amenity: the hotel is known for providing complimentary goldfish to keep lonely travelers company in their rooms. $329.

Orchard Garden Hotel 466 Bush St at Grant, Chinatown ☏ 415/399-9807 or 1-888/717-2881, ⓦwww.theorchardgardenhotel.com. Opened a few years ago, this groundbreaking "green" hotel was the third hotel in the United States to receive the Leadership in Energy & Environmental Design certification, thanks to its key-card energy control system, in-room recycling system, chemical-free cleaning products and fluorescent light bulbs. While the decor is rather unexciting, and the "garden" is more of a terrace with a fantastic view, the hotel has much going for it, including high-speed Internet and wi-fi, LCD television, DVD, iPod and CD players, and organic bath products in each room. A sister boutique, the *Orchard Hotel*, is just up the street at 665 Bush St. $349.

Petite Auberge 863 Bush St at Taylor, Theater District ☏ 415/928-6000 or 1-800/365-3004, ⓦwww.petiteaubergesf.com. An opulent B&B-style hotel with 26 rooms decked out in a French country style, full of oak furniture and floral prints, recently bought by the JDV group. There's complimentary afternoon tea, wine, hors d'oeuvres, and of course a sumptuous breakfast. Luxurious and memorable. $199.

Prescott Hotel 545 Post St at Mason, Union Square ☏ 415/563-0303, ⓦwww .prescotthotel.com. Sumptuous and opulent, this small, Kimpton-run four-star hotel has rooms decorated in warm woods and rich colors; service is attentive and polite. The amenities you'll snag by booking one of the concierge-level rooms, like free breakfast and evening drinks, make the splurge

worthwhile. $159 for standard, $259 for club level.

Hotel Rex 562 Sutter St at Powell, Union Square ☏ 415/433-4434 or 1-800/433-4434, ⓦwww .thehotelrex.com. The *Rex* has recently emerged reinvigorated from a massive renovation (as one of Joie de Vivre's earlier hotels, it was looking a little careworn). It's retained the literary theme – allegedly, the *New Yorker* magazine – and its retro, gentleman's club feel, with rich wood paneling and literary quotations decorating the corridors. The lobby bar regularly hosts readings and events. $289.

Serrano Hotel 405 Taylor St at O'Farrell, Theater District ☏ 415/885-2500 or 1-866/289-6561, ⓦwww.serranohotel.com. The sumptuous 17-storey Spanish revival hotel has been painstakingly restored down to the ornate lobby. The rooms, all bold reds and golds with Spanish and Moroccan accents, come with high-speed Internet access and flat-panel TV with on-demand movies and Nintendo games. There are board games in the lobby, and a nightly wine reception with free tarot readings. Challenge the desk person to a round of blackjack when you check in, and win appetizers at the hotel restaurant, *Ponzu*. $183.

Sir Francis Drake 450 Powell St at Sutter, Union Square ☏ 415/392-7755 or 1-800/227-5480, ⓦwww.sirfrancisdrake.com. The lobby here is a hallucinogenic evocation of all things heraldic: it's crammed with faux British memorabilia, chandeliers, and drippingly ornate gold plasterwork. Thankfully, the rooms are subtler, with a gentle apple-green color scheme and full facilities. The lobby and rooms recently received a modern quirky-chic update. The hotel is known for the bar, *Harry Denton's Starlight Room*, on the 21st floor (see p.210). $197 and up.

Spaulding Hotel 240 O'Farrell St at Powell, Union Square ☏ 415/397-4924, ⓦwww .spauldinghotel.com. Don't be fooled by the boutique-style jazzy logo (or put off by the smelly elevators and jail-style hallways) – this is a very basic but reliable hotel. The rooms are clean and nondescript: the bedspreads are dark and floral, and the furniture pale-wood veneers. All rooms have dorm-room-sized mini fridges and private baths. $89.

Triton 342 Grant Ave at Bush, Chinatown ☏ 415/394-0500 or 1-888/364-2622, ⓦwww .hoteltriton.com. An eccentric Kimpton hotel that offers modern amenities, like a 24hr gym, as well as weirder services, including nightly tarot-card readings and an eco-floor of environmentally sensitive rooms. The rooms themselves are stylish but gaudy, painted in rich clashing colors and plenty of gold. A small number of guest rooms have been designed by oddball celebrities like Jerry Garcia and Graham Nash, and the Häagen-Dazs suite comes with a cabinet filled with complimentary ice cream. $195.

Westin St Francis 335 Powell St at Sutter, Union Square ☏ 415/397-7000 or 1-800/WESTIN1, Ⓦ www.westin.com. This completely renovated landmark hotel (see p.52) has an extravagant lobby, four restaurants and lounges, a fitness center, and a spa. Yet aside from the views, the rooms are disappointingly plain. Worth entering the lobby to see the famous clock, ornate ceiling, gaudy painting of Queen Elizabeth amidst American celebs, and the steps where President Gerald Ford almost met his end from a would-be-assassin's bullet. $269.

▲ The lobby at the Westin St Francis

White Swan Inn 845 Bush St at Mason, Union Square ☏ 415/775-1755 or 1-800/999-9570, Ⓦ www.whiteswaninnsf.com. Recently bought by JDV Hospitality, the new owners have retained everything that was most appealing about this top-notch B&B. It follows an English manor theme, with raging fires in the lobby, fireplaces, oak-paneled walls in the rooms, and afternoon tea. $199.

Hotel Vertigo 940 Sutter St at Hyde, Theater District ☏ 415/885-6800 or 1-800/553-1900, Ⓦ www.personalityhotels.com. Formerly known as the *York Hotel* and famous as the place where Alfred Hitchcock filmed the dramatic stairway scenes in *Vertigo* (hence the celebratory new name), this swanky establishment has recently benefited from a $5 million facelift, and boasts a mix of

classic French style and modern urban sophistication. The *Vertigo* swirl motif is prominent in the shockingly modernist orange, white and black rooms, which have flat-screen satellite TVs and iPod docking stations. Bathrooms feature crocodile-patterned tiles, dark walnut vanities, and oversize rain showerheads. Downstairs is celebrity chef Tyler Florence's first restaurant, *Bar Florence*. $169.

North Beach and the hills

Boheme 444 Columbus Ave at Vallejo, North Beach ☏ 415/433-9111, Ⓦ www.hotelboheme .com. Smack in the middle of Beat heartland, this small, fifteen-room hotel has tiny but dramatic rooms, with canopied beds and Art Deco-ish bathrooms, all done in rich, dark colors. Columbus can be noisy, so if you're a light sleeper, ask for a room at the back. All rooms now have wi-fi. $174.

Fairmont 950 Mason St at California, Nob Hill ☏ 415/772-5000 or 1-800/441-1414, Ⓦ www .fairmont.com/sanfrancisco. The most famous of the top-notch hotels, this showy palace has four restaurants and lounges, as well as fantastic views from the rooms – even though it's low rise in comparison with the other hotels round the square. Don't miss the terrace garden, overlooking Powell, and the splendor of the *Tonga Room*, in the basement (see p.213). $299.

Huntington 1075 California St at Taylor, Nob Hill ☏ 415/474-5400, Ⓦ www.huntingtonhotel .com. Originally designed as residential apartments, this landmark hotel was home to Bogart and Bacall for several years. Its common areas are old-money elegant, with chandeliers and vintage prints; the rooms themselves are large, if unexciting, and many have kitchenettes. The onsite spa has spectacular views over the city. $315.

Mark Hopkins InterContinental 1 Nob Hill, 999 California St at Mason, Nob Hill ☏ 415/392-3434, Ⓦ www.interconti.com. Grand, castle-like hotel perched on the southwestern corner of Huntington Park that was once the chic choice of writers and movie stars. It's more corporate these days in both clientele and design, thanks to a beige-heavy renovation. All rooms are identical, but rates rise as the floors do. The *Top of the Mark* rooftop bar is popular with tourists (see p.210). $209.

Ritz-Carlton **600 Stockton St at California, Nob Hill** ☏415/296-7465 or 1-800/241-3333, ⓦwww.ritz-carlton.com. Another luxurious San Francisco hotel, perched on the stylish slope of Nob Hill with gorgeously appointed rooms, a swimming pool, multimillion-dollar art collection, and one of the city's best high teas. Recently, the rooms have been updated with wi-fi access and LCD flat-panel TVs. $429.

San Remo **2237 Mason St at Chestnut, North Beach** ☏415/776-8688 or 1-800/352-7366, ⓦwww.sanremohotel.com. Known for its chatty, helpful staff, this warren-like converted house stands close to Fisherman's Wharf. Rooms are cozy and chintzy – all share spotless bathrooms, and a few have sinks. While there are offbeat additions like massage chairs on each floor, bear in mind that there are no phones or TVs in the bedrooms and no elevator. The *Fior d'Italia* restaurant is onsite. $75 and up.

Stanford Court **905 California St at Powell, Nob Hill** ☏415/989-3500 or 1-800/6-HOTELS-1, ⓦwww.marriott.com. The one-time mansion of railroad magnate and university founder Leland Stanford, this luxury hotel has undergone a $32 million renovation to give it an even smarter Art Deco upgrade, though fortunately its stunning Tiffany glass dome is still intact. $219.

SW Hotel **615 Broadway at Grant, North Beach** ☏415/362-2999, ⓦwww.swhotelsf.com. A well-located bargain on the boundary between Chinatown and North Beach's Little Italy. The decor in the large rooms is modern Asian, with carved armoires and headboards, plus bright yellow bedspreads. Some can be rather dark, but sweet touches like SW-branded mugs, not to mention the sparklingly clean bathrooms and the willing staff, more than make up for it. $149.

Washington Square Inn **1660 Stockton St at Union, North Beach** ☏415/981-4220 or 1-800/388-0220, ⓦwww.wsisf.com. This B&B-style hotel overlooking Washington Square has large, airy rooms, decorated in modern shades of taupe and cream. They vary widely in price and facilities, though all are en suite (albeit mostly shower only) – room no. 1 is the swankiest, with marble bath and views of the park ($259), while the small back room no. 15 is the cheapest ($179). Lavish continental breakfast is included in room rates. $200.

The northern waterfront and Pacific Heights

Argonaut **495 Jefferson St at Hyde** ☏415/397-5572 or 1-800/790-1415, ⓦwww.argonauthotel.com. This new nautical-themed hotel (there's an anchor motif running through much of the decoration) in the Cannery complex has large, lush rooms in brick and timber that feature DVD players, stereos, and impressive views. Surprisingly quiet for its location. $212.

Best Western Tuscan Inn **425 North Point at Mason** ☏415/561-1100 or 1-800/648-4626, ⓦwww.tuscaninn.com. Despite its name, this waterfront hotel is more English country manor than Tuscan farmhouse, with cozy rooms decorated in warm colors. It has attentive touches like an afternoon wine reception and a free limo to Downtown in the mornings. $239.

Circa 1870 **2119 California St at Laguna, Pacific Heights** ☏415/928-3224, ⓦwww.circa1870.com. Plush four-room B&B (three with private baths), whose period rooms are decorated in fancy Victoriana, with rose, oak, and vine motifs everywhere and ornate fireplaces. Even the bathrooms are old-fashioned, complete with claw-footed tubs. $125.

Cow Hollow Motor Inn **2190 Lombard St at Steiner, Cow Hollow** ☏415/921-5800, ⓦwww.cowhollowmotorinn.com. Swiss-chalet–style inn, with plentiful onsite parking and charmingly retro common areas. The rooms, though, are utterly modern, recently refurbished, and enormous. $100.

Hotel del Sol **3100 Webster St at Lombard, Cow Hollow** ☏415/921-5520 or 1-877/433-5765, ⓦwww.thehoteldelsol.com. One of the best places for budget cool in the city, this offbeat, updated motor lodge has a tropical theme, as well as a swimming pool. The color scheme combines zesty walls with chunky mosaics and palm trees wrapped in fairy lights. Amenities include wi-fi, a pillow-lending library, and complimentary handmade aromatherapy soap. $199.

Hotel Drisco **2901 Pacific Ave at Broderick, Pacific Heights** ☏415/346-2880 or 1-800/634-7277, ⓦwww.hoteldrisco.com. The suites in this super-luxurious hotel at the peak of Pacific Heights have spectacular city views, and overall the place feels more like a country-house B&B than a hotel. There are VCRs and free movies to watch in every room, plus complimentary sherry every afternoon and a tasty buffet breakfast each morning. That said, unless you're wedded to staying in the area, there are better hotels for the price Downtown. Rooms from $195, suites from $259.

Edward II 3155 Scott St at Lombard, Cow Hollow ☎415/922-3000 or 1-800/473-2846, ⓦwww.edwardii.com. The rooms at this B&B-style inn are small but pleasant, decorated in a style that would please a wealthy 1980s Californian homemaker: mirrored closets, taupe bedspreads, and plenty of knick-knacks. $85.

Greenwich Inn 3201 Steiner St at Greenwich, Cow Hollow ☎415/921-5162 or 1-800/280-3242, ⓦwww.greenwichinn.com. A sprightly, good-value motel, with friendly owners and decent, if slightly dark, standard rooms. It's one of the cheapest options along the Lombard St motel strip. $89.

Jackson Court 2198 Jackson St at Buchanan, Pacific Heights ☎415/929-7670, ⓦwww.jacksoncourt.com. This B&B-inspired hotel with only ten rooms is housed in a converted 1900s brownstone in the heart of Pacific Heights. It's a romantic bolthole, hidden from the bustle of Downtown, and a great choice for a quiet weekend away – don't miss the fantastic breakfasts. $190.

Laurel Inn 444 Presidio Ave at California, Laurel Heights ☎415/567-8467 or 1-800/552-8735, ⓦwww.thelaurelinn.com. This Laurel Heights motel turned hotel is steps from Sacramento Street's antique shops and near the bustling Fillmore strip of cafés and stores. The decor is a stylish update of 1950s Americana, with muted graphic prints and simple fixtures, and though the rooms are small, each comes with a VCR and CD-player; the hotel also welcomes pets. $199.

Sheraton Fisherman's Wharf 2500 Mason St at North Point, Fisherman's Wharf ☎415/781-2220 or 1-877/271-2018, ⓦwww.sheratonatthewharf.com. Recently renovated to the tune of $33 million, this hotel is stylishly done out in cheerful colors and wired with all mod cons – flat-screen HDTVs, wi-fi and high-speed Internet. The outdoor "living room" with fire pits and the *Spressi* restaurant's community table encourage socializing among visitors. $199.

Surf Motel 2265 Lombard St at Pierce, Cow Hollow ☎415/922-1950. This old-school motel has two tiers of bright, simple rooms that are sparklingly clean. Be sure to ask for

a room at the back, since the busy Lombard St thoroughfare roars past the main entrance. $75.

Union Street Inn 2229 Union St at Fillmore, Cow Hollow ☎415/346-0424, ⓦwww.unionstreetinn.com. Surrounded by a lush, flower-filled garden, this Edwardian B&B offers spacious rooms, gourmet breakfast al fresco (weather permitting), fireplaces, chocolates, fresh flowers, and cookies available all day. $259.

Wharf Inn 2601 Mason St at Jefferson, Fisherman's Wharf ☎415/673-7411, ⓦwww.wharfinn.com. One of the few decent options in the area, with large bland rooms with wi-fi set along motel-style outdoor walkways. The free onsite parking is a major plus. $179.

SoMa, the Tenderloin, and Civic Center

Best Western Carriage Inn 140 Seventh St at Mission, SoMa ☎415/552-8600, ⓦwww.carriageinnsf.com. Joie de Vivre partners with Best Western to offer these enormous, elegant rooms, individually renovated to honor an unconventional San Francisco legend from Lillie Coit to the Mitchell Brothers, with sofas, LCD flat-screen TVs, high-speed Internet access, iPod docking stations, and working fireplaces. There's free room-service breakfast each morning and a shuttle to Union Square, as well as good-value valet parking: the only downside is its location on a slightly sketchy block of SoMa. $169.

Four Seasons 757 Market St at Third, SoMa ☎415/633-3000, ⓦwww.fourseasons.com. The place to stay if you win the lottery or if someone else is paying, this ultra-luxe hotel on Market St affords spectacular views across the city. Its plush rooms are the ultimate indulgence, from the soft, luxurious comforters to the stand-alone two-person shower stocked with Bulgari beauty products. There's an enormous onsite health club with a pool and vast gym that's free to hotel guests. $425.

Hotel Griffon 155 Steuart St at Mission, SoMa ☎415/495-2100 or 1-800/321-2201, ⓦwww.hotelgriffon.com. This secluded hotel close to the waterfront offers elegant and under-stated rooms with exposed brick walls, window seats, CD-player, flat-screen TV, and refrigerator, all wrapped in a vaguely Asian theme. Free wi-fi, newspapers, and continental breakfast included in room rate. $319.

Harbor Court 165 Steuart St at Mission, SoMa ☎ 415/882-1300 or 1-800/346-0555, ⊛ www.harborcourthotel.com. Rooms here are grandly decorated in jewel colors like ruby and deep blue, with canopied beds and velveteen cushions; some have spectacular Bay views. There's free wine and beer every day 5–6pm, wi-fi and high-speed Internet access in the rooms, and free newspapers; no onsite gym, but room rates include a pass to the YMCA next door. $229.

Inn at the Opera 333 Fulton St at Gough, Civic Center ☎ 415/863-8400 or 1-800/325-2708, ⊛ www.innattheopera.com. Small hotel, with a fussy, old-fashioned elegance, located just across the street from the Opera House – hence the lush Symphony and Opera suites. The rooms themselves are well equipped, and all have microwaves and fridges. $169.

InterContinental San Francisco 888 Howard St at Fifth, SoMa ☎ 1-888/811-4273, ⊛ www.baldwinhotel.com. The InterContinental Hotel Group, owners of the *Mark Hopkins* (see p.158), erected this sleek, blue skyscraper hotel for Moscone Center convention goers. It's caused quite a stir with its elegant, minimalist aesthetic rooms featuring floor-to-ceiling windows, Frette linens, mahogany furniture, wi-fi and high-speed Internet, and 42-inch plasma TVs. Downstairs, *Bar 888* specializes in cocktails made from the Italian liquor grappa, and the bright Tuscany-via-Napa restaurant is aptly named *Luce* (Light). If you want to be pampered, head over to the ten-room spa. $188.

The Mosser 54 Fourth St at Market, SoMa ☎ 415/986-4400, ⊛ www.themosser.com. This hotel fuses Victorian touches like ornamental molding with mod leather sofas. The chocolate and olive rooms may be tiny but each is artfully crammed with amenities, including multi-disc CD-players. One of the best values in town, especially for its central location. $129.

Palace Hotel 2 New Montgomery St at Market, SoMa ☎ 415/512-1111, ⊛ www.sfpalace.com. Hushed, opulent landmark building, known for its *Garden Court* tearoom (favored by presidents and heads of state). The grand lobby and corridors are mismatched with rooms that are small for the sky-high prices, decorated in lush golds and greens like an English country house. Stay here for snob value above all. $259.

Palomar 12 Fourth St at Market, SoMa ☎ 415/348-1111 or 1-877/294-9711, ⊛ www.hotelpalomar-sf.com. The location – above a massive Old Navy store – may be unprepossessing, but Kimpton's *Palomar* is a chic, neo-Nouveau bolthole. The decor is dark and smoky, with ebony and leopard print accents; the rooms are pleasantly large with full amenities. Note that there's no access from Market St, despite the signage. $299.

▲ Reception at the Palomar hotel

The Phoenix 601 Eddy St at Larkin, Tenderloin ☎ 415/776-1380 or 1-800/248-9466, ⊛ www.jdvhotels.com/phoenix. This raucous retro motel conversion features a mixed gay-straight clientele and is a favorite with up-and-coming bands when they're in town (the hotel has a hair and make-up artist on call – at a premium – day or night). There's a small pool where breakfast is served each morning, and the 44 rooms are eclectically decorated in tropical colors with changing local artwork on the walls – ask for the "Headliner Suite," which has a separate living room. The adjacent *Bambuddha* lounge keeps the party going into the early hours. $169.

The Renoir 45 McAllister St at Seventh, Civic Center ☎ 415/626-5200 or 1-800/576-3388, ⊛ www.renoirhotel.com. This wedge-shaped building is a historic landmark with 135 rooms that have been florally, if unexcitingly, refurbished. The superior rooms cost $20 more than standard – worth the extra if you can snag one of the oddly shaped large rooms at the building's apex. Especially popular during Gay Pride for its Market St views along the parade route. $159.

St Regis 125 Third St at Mission, SoMa ☏415/781-2220 or 1-800/6-BALDWIN, ⊛www .baldwinhotel.com. Located next door to the San Francisco Museum of Modern Art, naturally, this luxury hotel has visually stunning modern design aesthetics; it's almost like staying inside a work of art. In addition, the rooms come with 32- or 42-inch plasma TVs, 13-inch flat-screen LCD TVs in the bathrooms, a DVD/CD entertainment center, Pratesi bed linens, oversized soaking tubs, and oversized shower heads in the separate shower. Butlers are also at the beck and call of guests. $409.

Hotel Vitale 8 Mission St at the Embarcadero, SoMa ☏415/278-3700. This new, upscale hotel is built on a one-time bus yard – its odd, stepped design is due to local laws preventing new construction from throwing shadows on the small greenspace next door. The modern art-filled rooms are enormous, with comfy beds, flat-screen TVs, and sofas in the window bays so you can make the most of the spectacular setting by the Bay; there are also Bose sounddocks where you can park your iPod. $259.

The W 181 Third St at Mission, SoMa ☏415/777-5300, ⊛www.whotels.com. San Francisco outpost of the hotel that thinks it's a nightclub: loud club muzak, all-black-clad staffers whispering into headsets, and a VIP vibe (it's where you're likeliest to spot a celeb in town for a launch or event). The high-rise, minimalist rooms are large and have stunning views across SoMa; nifty add-on touches like Etch-a-Sketches, free tooth-whitening kits, and Bliss bath products make them extra welcoming. Recently, the hotel went through a full-on redesign based on a furniture-as-art concept, and fashion designer Shanghai Tang was brought in to update the nine suites. $289.

Hotel Whitcomb 1231 Market St at Eighth, SoMa ☏415/626-8000, ⊛www.hotelwhitcomb.com. In the wake of the 1906 earthquake and fire, this 1911 building, affiliated with National Historic Hotels of America, served as City Hall. Formerly the *Ramada Plaza*, the hotel is adorned with Tiffany glass, Italian marble

and Austrian crystal chandeliers and possess one of the city's only parquet dance floors. $189.

The Mission and the Castro

Beck's Motor Lodge 2222 Market St at Sanchez, Castro ☏415/621-8212 or 1-800/227-4360. One of only two accommodation options in the Castro that isn't a B&B, the *Beck's* clientele is more mixed than you'd expect from its location, and the rooms are plusher than the gaudy yellow motel exterior might suggest. If you're a light sleeper, ask for a room well away from the road, as it can be noisy. $93.

Inn San Francisco 943 S Van Ness Ave at 20th, Mission ☏415/641-0188 ⊛www .innsf.com. Superb, sprawling B&B in two adjoining historic Victorians on the Mission's edge. The 1872 mansion is filled with fresh flowers and has onsite wi-fi throughout; its fifteen rooms are dark and stylish, and the views across town from the smokers' terrace on the roof are stunning. The 1904 extension next door holds six more rooms, which are chintzier in decor with frilly valances and tapestries. All rooms have phone, fridge, and TV, and all but two have private baths. The huge breakfast buffet, redwood hot tub in the garden, and onsite parking ($18/night) are also major pluses. Recommended. Private bath from $145, shared bath from $120.

Parker Guest House 520 Church St at 17th, Castro ☏415/621-3222 or 1-800/520-7275 ⊛www.parkerguesthouse.com. This gay-friendly B&B features cozy, old-fashioned rooms decorated in flower prints with down comforters, wi-fi and high-speed Internet, cable TV and chocolates. Also offered for your enjoyment are a wine social, steam room, gardens and sunning areas. $139 shared bath, $179 private bath.

Travelodge Central 1707 Market St at Valencia, Mission ☏415/621-6775 or 1-800/578-7878

Unfortunately, there's little accommodation available in the Mission and the Castro aside from a few B&Bs; most of them, unsurprisingly, are geared toward gay and lesbian travelers. For information on accommodation in these areas, see above and p.237.

Ⓦ www.travelodge.com. Very basic lodging, but it couldn't be more conveniently located – the free onsite parking makes up for the slightly worn, floral motel rooms. Free wi-fi, newspapers and coffee. $129.

Village House 4080 18th St at Castro, Castro ☎ 415/864-0994 or 1-800/900-5686, Ⓦ www.24henry.com. Oddly, given its location, this newish B&B is slightly less gay than its sister hotel, *24 Henry* (see p.238). Popular with visiting parents, its rooms are grander and gaudier, with primary-colored walls and plenty of closet space. For camp Eastern extravagance, ask for room no. 2; or take a trip back to the 1980s in room no. 4. $110.

Haight-Ashbury and west of Civic Center

Best Western Hotel Tomo 1800 Sutter St at Buchanan, Japantown ☎ 415/921-4000 or 1-888/822-8666, Ⓦ www.jdvhotels.com/tomo. Formerly the *Miyako Inn*, and run by Joie de Vivre, *Tomo* is a youthful, anime-themed hotel in neon-bright colors, with action-packed, cartoonish murals on the walls. The gaming suite comes with a PlayStation 3, a Nintendo wi-fi, beanbag chairs and a six-foot LCD projection screen. $139.

The Carl 198 Carl St at Stanyan, Cole Valley ☎ 415/661-5679 or 1-888/661-5679, Ⓦ carlhotel.ypguides.net. Plainer than many of the surrounding B&Bs, this hotel is a bargain for its Golden Gate Park location. Small but pretty rooms, with microwaves and fridges; the six with shared bath are especially well priced. Private bath $145, shared bath $99.

Château Tivoli 1057 Steiner St at Fulton, Fillmore ☎ 415/776-5462 or 1-800/228-1647, Ⓦ www.chateautivoli.com. Rooms in this lavishly furnished Victorian mansion are named after artists like Isadora Duncan and Mark Twain. History is everywhere, whether in the building itself (built for an early lumber baron), or the furniture (one of the beds was owned by Charles de Gaulle). Grand and very serious, but a luxurious alternative to many of the cozy B&Bs elsewhere. Private bath $200, shared bath $100.

Grove Inn 890 Grove St at Fillmore, Fillmore ☎ 415/929-0780 or 1-800/829-0780, Ⓦ www.groveinn.com. Friendly B&B close to Alamo Square, housed in an Italianate mansion from 1885. The *Grove* is chic and

understated, if a little flouncy, and all fifteen rooms have private bath, TV, and phone. The knowledgeable owners – big movers in preservation circles – are a major plus. $120.

Hayes Valley Inn 417 Gough St at Hayes, Hayes Valley ☎ 415/431-9131 or 1-800/930-7999, Ⓦ www.hayesvalleyinn.com. Homely, apple-green rooms in a secluded location. The *Hayes Valley Inn's* furnishings are minimal and baths are shared, but the well-stocked kitchen/breakfast room is a great place to meet people. $84.

Inn 1890 1890 Page St at Shrader, Haight-Ashbury ☎ 415/386-1890 or 1-888/INN-1890, Ⓦ www.inn1890.com. Each of the twelve rooms at this lovely B&B has hardwood floors and a cast-iron bed, as well as a small kitchenette. The house is enormous but delightfully decorated, and well situated close to Golden Gate Park. $99.

Hotel Kabuki 1625 Post St at Laguna, Japantown ☎ 415/922-3220 or 1-800/533-4567, Ⓦ www.jdvhotels.com/kabuki. When Joie de Vivre Hotels took over this place, formerly known as the *Radission Miyako*, the chain brought the Japanese theme into modern times, abandoning the antique style for a more sophisticated, streamlined look. A ritual tea service is offered to each guest upon check-in, and there's a wine reception weekday evenings. Each bathroom features a deep Japanese-style soaking tub, and for a fee, visitors can request any number of bath services. The hotel also offers guests workshops on Japanese traditions such as taiko drumming and origami, as well as passes to the Kabuki spa down the street. $209.

Hotel Majestic 1500 Sutter at Gough, Fillmore ☎ 415/441-1100 or 1-800/869-8966, Ⓦ www .thehotelmajestic.com. A gorgeous 1902 building, with much drapery used to decorate the rooms, the more expensive of which also feature antique furnishings and fireplaces. It is said, like the *Queen Anne* nearby (see below), that a fourth-floor room is haunted; this ghost allegedly likes to fill the claw-footed bathtub up with water. There's a huge butterfly collection on display in the lounge, with rare specimens from New Guinea and Africa $160.

Queen Anne 1590 Sutter St at Octavia, Fillmore ☎ 415/441-2828 or 1-800/227-3970, Ⓦ www.queenanne.com. Gloriously excessive restored Victorian that began as a

There's little reason to stay out at the airport. However, as a last resort or if you're catching an especially early or late flight, the following hotels are your best options:

Best Western Grosvenor 380 S Airport Blvd, South San Francisco ☎650/873-3200 or 1-800/722-7141, ⓦwww.grosvenorsf.com. Large, comfortable hotel with pool and free shuttle service to the airport. $130.

Goose & Turrets Bed and Breakfast 835 George St, Montara ☎650/728-5451, ⓦwww.goose.montara.com. In the seaside hamlet of Montara, a more intimate B&B alternative to other airport accommodation, with five rooms, all en suite. Close to the beaches and hiking trails. $145.

Hyatt Regency San Francisco Airport 1333 Bayshore Hwy, Burlingame ☎650/347-1234 or 1-800/223-1234, ⓦwww.sanfranciscoairport.hyatt.com. Gigantic hotel south of the airport with all the amenities (pool, hot tub, bars) and a free shuttle to the airport. $194.

La Quinta Inn 20 Airport Blvd, South San Francisco ☎650/583-2223, ⓦwww.laquinta.com. Overnight laundry service and a pool make this a comfortable stop over near the airport. Free shuttle service to the airport. $90.

girls' school before becoming a bordello. Each room is stuffed with gold-accented Rococo furniture and bunches of silk flowers. The parlor (where afternoon sherry is served) is overfilled with museum-quality period furniture. Miss Mary Lake, former principal of the school, is said to still make periodic, supernatural appearances in room #410. $95.

The Red Victorian Bed, Breakfast and Art 1665 Haight St at Cole, Haight-Ashbury ☎415/864-1978, ⓦwww.redvic.com. Quirky B&B and Peace Center, owned by Sami Sunchild and decorated with her ethnic arts. Rooms vary from simple to opulent. The best feature is the shared bathrooms, including a goldfish-filled toilet cistern. Breakfast's a lavish but concertedly communal affair, so be prepared to chat with your neighbors while you eat. Private bath $149, shared bath $129.

Stanyan Park Hotel 750 Stanyan St at Waller, Haight-Ashbury ☎415/751-1000, ⓦwww.stanyanpark.com. Overlooking Golden Gate Park, this small hotel has 35 sumptuous rooms that are incongruous in its counter-culture neighborhood, busily decorated in country florals with heavy drapes and junior four-poster beds. Continental breakfast and an ample, cookie-filled afternoon tea are included. $155.

The Richmond and the Sunset

Ocean Park Motel 2690 46th Ave at Wawona, Ocean Beach ☎415/566-7020, ⓦwww.oceanparkmotel.ypguides.net. A fair way from Downtown (25min by MUNI), this is nonetheless a great Art Deco motel (San Francisco's first) and an outstanding example of Streamline Moderne architecture. It's convenient for the beach and the zoo, plus there's a kids' play area and an outdoor hot tub for adults. $100.

Oceanview Motel 4340 Judah St at LaPlaya, Ocean Beach ☎415/661-2300, ⓦwww.oceanviewmotelsf.com. Nondescript lodging out in the Sunset district. The rooms are smallish and simply furnished (though still with wi-fi and flat-screen TVs), but there's free onsite parking and convenient MUNI access. $150.

Seal Rock Inn 545 Point Lobos Ave, Richmond ☎415/752-8000 or 1-800/732-5762, ⓦwww.sealrockinn.com. Well situated for Cliff House and the Sutro baths, this old-fashioned, heavily brown motel is a good option solely for its views – almost every room looks out over the sea. Though the standard boxy bedrooms are fine, a better option is to trade up to one of the suites with a real log fireplace. $139.

Eating

With an abundance of nearby farms showering the city's farmers' markets with fresh produce, a culture that increasingly emphasizes sustainable food practices, and a local population with a sharp proclivity for eating out, it's little wonder that San Francisco is one of the world's leading restaurant cities. Its dining scene may be remarkably convivial, but this is a city where people take few things more seriously than food.

San Francisco has long been known for its four-star **fine-dining restaurant experiences**, and more recently for its wealth of low-end marvels like **taquerias**, **dim-sum eateries**, and **curry houses**. However, the city's eating-out habits are in the midst of a transformation, with a proliferation of excellent, moderately priced **neighborhood restaurants** sending residents on beelines to other areas of town. Whereas a big night out used to exclusively take place at one of the high-end **French** or **seafood** places Downtown, it's just as likely now that the same money will be spent on multiple dinners at less formal, but equally stylish restaurants in neighborhoods away from the city's core (Glen Park, Marina, and Cole Valley, to name a few).

The local slant of cooking, dubbed **California cuisine**, is a development of French *nouvelle cuisine*, preserving the *nouvelle* focus on a wide mix of fresh, locally available foods, but widening the scope of influences considerably. The California style's range of dishes is seemingly endless and could include something as light as a cracker-crusted pizza with shrimp and arugula, or a heavier selection like herb-crusted rack of lamb with root-vegetable hash and watercress; many local California style restaurants also often incorporate a pan-Asian edge to many recipes.

The greatest asset of San Francisco's restaurants is the staggering **variety** – not only in types of cuisine, but in price ranges and overall experiences. Our listings reflect the city's dining diversity, from gourmet **vegetarian** restaurants, **steak-houses**, and **Italian delicatessens**, to **Spanish tapas** joints, **Asian bakeries**, and the city's sole purveyor of **Polish fare**, for everyone from big spenders to budget-minded visitors.

A pair of final notes on San Francisco dining. Firstly, don't plan on enjoying a leisurely cigarette with your aperitif or after-dinner coffee, as California law decrees there's **no smoking** in any public space, including restaurants. **Finally, note that** San Francisco has enacted a new set of mandates providing health care for all restaurant employees; to help defray these costs, many local establishments now add a nominal surcharge (usually 2–4 percent) to diners' tabs.

Downtown and Chinatown

While there are certainly still places in and around the Financial District and Union Square to spend up to (if not beyond) $100 per person on an unforgettable

Top San Francisco restaurants by cuisine

A number of restaurants in this chapter come with a special recommendation, indicated by the ✈ icon (see inside cover for explanation). The following list will also help guide you to some great spots if you're intent on a specific cuisine or particular type of meal.

Asian
Anzu, Theater District p.172
Betelnut, Cow Hollow p.183
Borobudur, Tenderloin p.189
Brothers Korean BBQ, Inner Richmond p.206
Grandeho's Kamekyo, Cole Valley p.202
House of Nanking, Chinatown p.168
Mandalay, Inner Richmond p.208
Marnee Thai, Inner Sunset p.208
The Slanted Door, Embarcadero p.173
Ton Kiang, Outer Richmond p.205

Breakfast/brunch
Dottie's True Blue Cafe, Tenderloin p.185
Just for You, Potrero Hill p.190
Ella's, Presidio Heights p.181
Pat's Cafe, North Beach p.174
Zazie, Cole Valley p.201

Bakeries
Arizmendi, Inner Sunset p.204
Italian French Bakery, North Beach p.175
La Victoria, Mission p.191
Tartine, Mission p.191
Wing Lee Bakery, Inner Richmond p.205

Burgers
Barney's, Noe Valley p.190

Burgermeister, Cole Valley p.199
Mo's Grill, North Beach p.174
Pearl's Deluxe Burgers, Tenderloin p.185
Taylor's Automatic Refresher, Embarcadero p.168

Burritos
El Burrito Express, Western Addition p.203
Gordo Taqueria, Inner Sunset p.207
Papalote, Mission p.195
Taqueria El Castillito, Civic Center p.188
Taqueria San Francisco, Mission p.197

California
Coco500, SoMa p.186
Frascati, Russian Hill p.175
Jardiniere, Hayes Valley p.200
Nopa, Western Addition p.200
Universal Cafe, Mission p.192

Coffee
See box, p.179

Dessert
Bi-Rite Creamery, Mission p.192
Ghirardelli Ice Cream and Chocolate Caffe, Fisherman's Wharf p.162
La Copa Loca, Mission p.192
Mission Pie, Mission p.192
Yasukochi's Sweet Stop, Japantown p.201

meal, Downtown neighborhoods have relinquished a bit of their epicurean dominance to outlying areas of town in recent years. That said, *Michael Mina* and *Masa's* can't be beat for decidedly formal fine dining, while *Bix* and *Aqua* aren't far behind for unapologetic opulence and peerless food. Catering to an enormous daily workforce, this area now features the extraordinary Ferry Building Marketplace, as well as a handful of other handy lunch nooks scattered about. As for Chinatown, the handful of restaurants listed below should steer you clear of the neighborhood's glut of iffy tourist traps.

American

Globe 290 Pacific Ave at Battery, Jackson Square ☎415/391-4132. Look for the wrought-iron globe dangling from the facade of this small, semi-tucked away spot. It's a late-night favorite for local restaurant

industry folks, with a Cal-Ital menu heavy on pizzas (mostly from the onsite wood oven) and fresh fish. Main courses run $18–22.
Michael Mina Westin St Francis, 335 Powell St at Geary, Union Square ☎415/397-9222. Postpone the diet, have your favorite suit dry cleaned, and pack your credit card if

French

Bistro Aix, Marina p.182
Café Jacqueline, North Beach p.175
Chapeau!, Outer Richmond p.206
La Folie, Russian Hill p.175
Le P'tit Laurent, Glen Park p.193

Italian

Acquerello, Russian Hill p.176
Da Flora, North Beach p.176
Delfina, Mission p.193
Sociale, Presidio Heights p.182
Trattoria Contadina, North Beach p.177

Late-night eats

Globe, Jackson Square p.166
Great Eastern, Chinatown p.168
Grubstake, Polk Gulch p.188
Liverpool Lil's, Cow Hollow p.181
Taqueria Can-cún, Mission p.197

Mediterranean/Middle Eastern

Aziza, Outer Richmond p.207
Goood Frikin Chicken, Mission p.195
Helmand Palace, Russian Hill p.177
Kokkari, Financial District p.171
Tajine, Polk Gulch p.187

Neighborhood places

Bambino's Ristorante, Cole Valley p.182
Chenery Park, Glen Park p.190
Laïola, Marina p.184
Le Charm, SoMa p.186
Ristorante Ideale, North Beach p.176

Pizza

Gialina, Glen Park p.193

Little Star Pizza, Western Addition p.202
The Pizza Place on Noriega, Outer Sunset p.206
Serrano's, Mission p.194
Tomasso's, North Beach p.177

Sandwiches

The Cheese Steak Shop, Western Addition p.203
Ike's Place, Castro p.197
M & L Market, Castro p.197
Molinari, North Beach p.179
Saigon Sandwich, Tenderloin p.188

South Asian

Dosa, Mission p.198
India Clay Oven, Outer Richmond p.207
Little Nepal, Bernal Heights p.198
Pakwan, Tenderloin p.189
Shalimar, Tenderloin p.189

Vegetarian

Golden Era, Tenderloin p.188
Greens, Fort Mason Center p.181
Herbivore, Western Addition p.201
Mariachi's, Mission p.195
Millennium, Theater District p.168

When someone else is paying...

Ame, SoMa p.188
Gary Danko, Fisherman's Wharf p.181
Kyo-Ya, SoMa p.187
Masa's, Union Square p.170
Michael Mina, Union Square p.166

you want to enjoy the adventurous menu at this grandly columned, four-star restaurant run by the namesake local chef. Fixed-price selections range from $98–135, with specialties stretching from lobster pot pie to black mussel souffle to Amish chicken – the last of which entails an entire bird being deep-fried in macadamia nut oil, then carved at the table.

One Market 1 Market St at Steuart, Financial District ☎415/777-5577. Chef Mark Dommen's three-course market menu ($48) usually includes both a seafood and a meat dish, while the duck ravioli and pan-seared scallops are menu favorites as well. The space itself is gargantuan, yet vivacious, set

directly across Harry Bridges Plaza from the Ferry Building. Closed Sun.

Sears Fine Food 439 Powell St at Post, Union Square ☎415/986-0700. This civic legend dates back to pre-World War II San Francisco, and local old-timers say its signature breakfast dish – 18 little Swedish pancakes for $8.25, 11,000 of which are made daily – hasn't changed at all over the decades. Throngs of people queue up outside to get in; if this is the case, try sneaking by to find a spot at one of the dining counters. Breakfast is served until 3pm, and come evening, basics like pasta, steak, and fish are a bit pricier ($14–29). Amber chairs and tiled flooring add to the ambience.

Taylor's Automatic Refresher 1 Ferry Building, Embarcadero ☎866/EAT-FOOD. Fancified, yet inexpensive burger stand that expanded operations down from Napa Valley when the Ferry Building reopened in 2003. The immense al fresco dining area off the Embarcadero pedestrian path is a major draw card on sunny afternoons, along with the touted burgers, sweet-potato fries, and super-thick milkshakes, all made with fresh ingredients. Lines form early for lunch, so consider choosing an off-peak time to visit.

Bakeries/tea

Mee Mee Bakery 1328 Stockton St at Broadway, Chinatown ☎415/362-3204. A little-known Chinatown gem with an onsite fortune-cookie bakery that fills the space with a hot, sweet smell. Regular treats are $2.95 for a half pound; specialty (biblical, adult) or flavored (chocolate, strawberry) cookies are $1 more. Closed evenings.

Ten Ren Tea Company 949 Grant Ave at Jackson, Chinatown ☎415/362-0656. Large, inexpensive, and well-stocked tea emporium where you can stop in for tea-by-the-pound or a fresh brew to go. The scented iced teas, thick with gloopy tapioca balls, are delicious.

California

Bix 56 Gold St at Montgomery, Jackson Square ☎415/433-6300. Hidden on a quiet back street lined with 150-year-old brick buildings, this dimly lit bar-restaurant has a touch of Deco-inspired glamor in its amber furnishings. The bar – helmed by avuncular men in white jackets and bow ties – is a popular after-work destination, while diners slip into the bi-level, columned supper club later to enjoy expensive ($32 and up) plates of filet mignon or roast chicken. Live jazz nightly; lunch on Fri only.

Millennium Hotel California, 580 Geary St at Jones, Theater District ☎415/345-3900. Catering to San Francisco's sizable contingent of vegetarians and vegans, this surprisingly pricey standby takes kitchen creativity to meat-free heights by using obscure ingredients such as *sambal, huitlacoche,* and *papazul.* The menu changes frequently – as often as daily – so one night's semolina griddle cake could be maple-glazed smoked tempeh the next.

The dark wood-paneled decor is gauzy and romantic, while the crowd varies from well-dressed opera buffs to young idealists out for a splurge. Dinner only.

Rubicon 558 Sacramento St at Montgomery, Financial District ☎415/434-4100. Having Robin Williams, Francis Ford Coppola, and Robert De Niro as investors will only get a fine-dining restaurant so far in San Francisco. *Rubicon* impresses critics and the local gastro-gentry alike with its design sense – both in its creative entrees (bacon-wrapped hen, syrah-glazed beef shortribs) and its dining room awash in glass sculptures and wood booths. Expect to pay $65 per person. Lunch on Wed only; closed Sun.

Chinese

Great Eastern 649 Jackson St at Kearny, Chinatown ☎415/986-2500. Behind an impressive pagoda facade and a huge chandelier swinging in the picture window, this elegant, traditional, and spendy Chinese restaurant serves braised superior shark's fin soup and geoduck clams, as well as favorites such as sauteed squab with Chinese broccoli. It's also known for its dim sum. Open until 1am daily.

House of Nanking 919 Kearny St at Jackson, Chinatown ☎415/421-1429. With its red-framed windows and clanking metal cafeteria chairs, this snug spot on the easternmost flank of Chinatown has become a local legend. The line is often long but usually moves quickly; once inside, expect a fabulous and underpriced meal, curt service, and a constant clatter of saucepans from the open kitchen.

Jai Yun 680 Clay St at Kearny, Chinatown ☎415/981-7438. If you can plan ahead to feel adventurous, book a table at this hotspot, where Chef Nei' Chia Ji neither offers printed menus nor accepts credit cards, and tends to not let diners know what they'll be eating until countless dishes appear under their noses. Menus start at $45; be aware that the staff doesn't speak much English. Dinner only. Reservations recommended.

Louie's Dim Sum 1236 Stockton St at Pacific, Chinatown ☎415/989-8380. This tiny dim-sum store has glistening, pearly dumplings ranged in vast metal trays before you, and although the variety's limited, they're all

▲ Dim sum in Chinatown

cheap and delicious. There's a small counter for dining in, but most customers take their orders to go.

Lucky Creation 854 Washington St at Stockton, Chinatown ☎415/989-0818. A nice vegetarian option in Chinatown, with a menu full of imaginative, inexpensive faux-meat dishes. Try the assorted glutens, like deep-fried taro with sweet and sour sauce, to see how farfetched things can get.

R&G Lounge 631 Kearny St at Commercial, Chinatown ☎415/982-7877. Behind frosted windows looms this enormous Hong Kong–style restaurant that draws a diverse crowd. The fairly priced dishes (most under $18) are presented family-style, and there's a heavy bias toward seafood. Call a day ahead to order the house special: a whole chicken hollowed out, stuffed with sticky rice, and deep fried.

Sam Wo 813 Washington St at Grant, Chinatown ☎415/982-0596. An ever-popular late-night spot where Kerouac, Ginsberg, and associates used to hold court. Walk through the kitchen and up the slim stairs to reach the dining room, to which cheap plates of greasy food are hoisted via dumbwaiter. The upstairs level is also where Gary Snyder and Kerouac were ejected from due to Snyder's loud and passionate interpretations of Zen poetry. Eat here more for the experience rather than the serviceable (at best) food or famously churlish service.

Yee's 1131 Grant Ave at Pacific, Chinatown ☎415/576-1818. Chinatown's answer to a deli, since the food is priced by weight. The menu scrawled on the wall is only in Chinese, but the staff is usually happy to translate. The inexpensive slabs of suckling pig on the lunch counter are particularly succulent, as is the crunchy sweet-and-sour pork. Eat in or take out.

Eastern European

Cafe Prague 584 Pacific Ave at Kearny, Jackson Square ☎415/433-3811. With goulash, strudel, and close to a dozen soups on offer, this atmospheric bistro on the edge of Jackson Square exudes warmth the moment you walk in the door. The few outdoor raised tables just off the sidewalk are a terrific spot for watching the world go by on adjacent Columbus Ave as you sip a Czech beer. Everything's moderately priced.

Eclectic

Boulette's Larder 1 Ferry Building, Embarcadero ☎415/399-1155. Unique even by Ferry Building standards, this combination shop/restaurant features table service in the morning and afternoon and a private dining room for cooking seminars in the evening – all amidst fragrant, freshly made stocks and herbs available for purchase on your way out. The expensive menu draws from a number of culinary cultures; on a given day, you might choose between Sicilian artichoke soup, poached Alaskan black cod, or beignets.

French

Anjou 44 Campton Place at Grant, Union Square ☎415/392-5373. Serving a reasonably priced prix-fixe lunch menu, cozy *Anjou* draws a steady Downtown clientele in the afternoon – for $16.50, choose between soup or salad, plus entrees like sauteed scallops with baked tomato or mushroom ravioli with peppercorn cognac sauce. The menu becomes somewhat pricier in the evening. Closed Sun & Mon.

Café Claude 7 Claude Lane at Bush, Union Square ☎415/392-3505. Down a tight alley, this impossibly Parisian restaurant features several outdoor tables under umbrellas, heavily accented waiters, and live music Thurs–Sat evenings. Go-to dishes include

If you want to graze on the go, there's nowhere better for a quick bite Downtown than the **Ferry Building Marketplace**. If it's not market day (see box, p.62), there are still plenty of appealing eateries inside selling gourmet treats, including selected favorites listed below. Note that these establishments are all inexpensive and close by early evening; marketplace shop numbers appear in parentheses.

Ciao Bella Gelato (8) ☏415/834-9330. California outpost of the New York gelato and sorbet company, with a selection of about three dozen varieties among more than 200 rotating flavors. Try one of the offbeat gelato concoctions (red bean, rum raisin) or a sorbet like passion fruit. Take-away pints are reasonably priced ($5.25–6.75).

Cowgirl Creamery (17) ☏415/362-9354. Cheese-lovers' heaven, with piles of an astonishingly wide selection of cheese from producers in the US, Canada, and all over Europe. A number of Cowgirl's own creations (made in nearby Point Reyes Station) are also on offer.

Golden Gate Meat Company (13) ☏415/983-7800. Simple, austere pulled pork and barbecue sandwiches ($6–7) are the stars at this butcher shop and charcuterie; for about the same price, you can also get yourself a pot pie or small rotisserie chicken.

Imperial Tea Court (27) ☏415/544-9830. Drop into this hideaway – complete with black granite counter and dragon sofa – to sit and sip a warm cup of tea. There are over 50 different varieties to choose from, including Jade Fire and Dragon Whiskers, alongside more everyday blends like green, black, or herb.

Out the Door (43) ☏415/321-3740. Casual, take-out outpost of adjacent Vietnamese legend, *The Slanted Door* (see p.173). It's a much cheaper and quicker option, with a focus on Vietnamese street food such as sandwiches and steamed buns. Minimal counter seating is available, as are take-away dinner boxes.

Recchiuti Confections (30) ☏415/834-9494. Local artisanal chocolatier, less well known than *Ghirardelli* but of much higher quality. A 16-piece of *fleur de sel* caramels costs $22, while single samples run about $1.65 on average. Handmade marshmallows and brownies are also on hand.

▲ Imperial Tea Court

steak tartare and *porc au miel* (pork filet with honey); most items cost over $20.
Jeanty at Jack's 615 Sacramento St at Montgomery, Financial District ☏415/693-0941. This landmark restaurant, open in one form or another in its tri-level building since 1864, caters to well-dressed, deep-pocketed diners poring over the chunky, rustic menu. The tomato soup served in a puff pastry is justifiably popular; legend has it that Alfred Hitchcock invented the mimosa here.

Masa's 648 Bush St at Stockton, Union Square ☏415/989-7154. An intimate, exclusive restaurant serving four-star meals in a hushed, white-curtained dining room. Food is offered only on a prix fixe basis: $90 (six-course vegetarian), $100 (six courses), and $150 (nine courses). Chef Gregory Short is a veteran of the Napa Valley legend *French Laundry* and has tweaked the menu by pumping up its modern American touches. Dinner only. Jackets required.

Plouf 40 Belden Place at Bush, Financial District ☎ 415/986-6491. Known for mussels served by the bowlful, this expensive bistro is situated on a busy pedestrian alley and features plenty of al fresco seating. It often gets chokingly crowded around the lunch hour, so either plan accordingly or expect to wait. The banana profiteroles served with warm chocolate and caramel sauce are a dessert crowd-pleaser. Closed Sun.

German

Schroeder's 240 Front St at California, Financial District ☎ 415/421-4778. One of San Francisco's oldest restaurants – it's occupied various locations around town since 1893 – *Schroeder's* continues to draw hearty eaters looking to wolf down sausage platters, ham hocks, and of course, schnitzel; particularly brave souls can order a two-litre boot of German pilsner. Dance off all those calories by timing your visit during one of the restaurant's live polka band performances. Most main courses at dinner range from $18–27. Closed Sun.

Italian

Brindisi Cucina di Mare 88 Belden Place at Pine, Financial District ☎ 415/593-8000. Serving everything from margarita pizza to more adventurous choices like oxtail over potato gnocchi, this affordable enclave caters to anyone seeking Pugliese fare. In the unlikely event it's a warm evening, ask for an outdoor table on Belden Place. Closed Sun.

Chiaroscuro 550 Washington St at Montgomery, Financial District ☎ 415/362-6012. This petite eatery sits opposite the Transamerica Pyramid, its industrial-chic interior outfitted with iron arches and pillow-topped concrete seating. Chef Alessandro Campitelli's open kitchen produces some of the city's finest gnocchi. Expect to shell out over $20 per entree. Closed Sun.

Perbacco 230 California St at Front, Financial District ☎ 415/955-0663. Filling a Downtown void, *Perbacco's* northern Italian cooking hasn't taken long to win legions of fans since opening in 2006. The delicate bread-sticks are uncommonly delicious, while main courses such as pork chop with squash/bean stew ($22) are equally loved by patrons lining the lengthy, narrow room. Closed Sun.

Japanese

Delica rf-1 1 Ferry Building, Embarcadero ☎ 415/834-0344. Taking its unusual name from Kozo Iwata's Rock Field Company, which owns and operates this Japanese delicatessen inside the Ferry Building, *Delica rf-1* turns the traditional deli concept on its ear by offering a variety of small dishes designed to be eaten together. Moderately priced staples such as bento boxes and miso soup are available alongside crab-cream croquettes and sushi rolls.

Hana Zen 115 Cyril Magnin St at Ellis, Theater District ☎ 415/421-2101. Set in the shadows of the area's high-rise hotels, this popular, if expensive Japanese grill is best known for its Yakitori skewers – choose from over two dozen, including *sunagimo* (chicken gizzard) and asparagus *maki*. The full bar serves sake and *soju* cocktails, and food is served late (midnight during the week, 1am on weekends).

Mediterranean/Middle Eastern

Baladie 337 Kearny St at Bush, Financial District ☎ 415/989-6629. Small, mostly take-out spot on the western edge of the Financial District that's short on plush decor but dishes out good, cheap Med staples like lentil soup and *shawerma*. The spinach pie is a solid choice.

Cortez Hotel Adagio, 550 Geary St at Jones, Theater District ☎ 415/292-6360. Previously geared toward devotees of small plates, the pricey menu at this long, slender space now includes larger (and creative) entrees like Moscovy duck breast and citrus-baked black cod. Rest assured, however, that soup is still served in tequila shot glasses. Dinner only.

Kokkari 200 Jackson St at Front, Financial District ☎ 415/981-0983. Consistently recognized as the top Greek restaurant in town, *Kokkari* relies on Hellenic staples such as lamb and eggplant, served separately or cooked together as moussaka. Its huge open fireplace heats two bedazzling dining rooms decorated with Oriental rugs and goatskin lampshades, and the whole place retains a cozy feel despite its vast dimensions. Entrees range from $20–30. Closed Sun.

Mexican

La Salsa 280 Battery St at Sacramento, Financial District ☎ 415/391-0604. In a neighborhood rife with poor-value burrito shops,

La Salsa turns out surprisingly strong taqueria fare worth the $9 or so you'll spend. The three-pepper chicken fajitas burrito is a solid bet, and the salsa bar is equally impressive; just don't expect a warm and charming atmosphere. Closed evenings and weekends.

Pan-Asian

Anzu Hotel Nikko, 222 Mason St at Ellis, Theater District ☏ 415/394-1100. Although it's situated off a hotel lobby, *Anzu* manages to pull in locals with a number of smoked, tea-spiced meat and fish entrees, as well as its top-shelf onglet steak ($28). Thrill-seekers will want to try the Rock ($18) – thinly sliced Wagyu beef sirloin cooked tableside on a sizzling Japanese stone. Sushi is available on the lunch menu, and there's a Sun jazz brunch.

Asia de Cuba Clift Hotel, 495 Geary St at Taylor, Theater District ☏ 415/923-2300. Adjacent to the *Redwood Room* bar inside the self-aware *Clift*, *Asia de Cuba* presents thoughtful Asian-Latin hybrid dishes in huge, albeit dizzyingly expensive portions. Certain concoctions, such as rum-glazed pork with sauteed bok choy, or tuna tartare on wonton crisps, work better than others, but you may be too distracted by the towering silk curtains, hand-blown glass lamps, and Venetian mirror-topped communal table to notice.

Silks Mandarin Oriental Hotel, 222 Sansome St at Pine, Financial District ☏ 415/986-2020. Another Downtown hotel restaurant worth a visit, if you've got the cash and don't mind the subdued – if elegant – atmosphere. Unusual for a fine dining restaurant, *Silks* serves breakfast on weekdays (try the chicken sausage hash with poached eggs); come evening, look for cross-cultural favorites like lobster/shellfish tom yum noodles. The Mandarin Lounge menu features more moderately priced options such as sushi and sandwiches.

Sandwiches/soup

Chili Up! Crocker Galleria (Level Three), 50 Post St at Kearny, Financial District ☏ 415/693-0467. Its shopping-center location may be initially off-putting, but this local chainlet is a top Downtown lunch option – the gourmet chili is offered in seven different varieties, from Ballpark (dark beer, beef, and three kinds of beans) to a veggie option called Hoofless. A monthly special such as Colorado (pork and apricot) is also offered. Lunch only. Branch: 4 Embarcadero Center, Financial District.

Emporio Rulli il Caffe Stockton St Pavilion in Union Square Plaza, Union Square ⓦwww.rulli.com. A popular shopping pitstop with mandolin-drenched Italian ballads spilling out of its speakers, this Union Square café serves bracingly strong coffee, as well as breakfast and lunch panini starting around $6. There are tables outside on the square if you want to lounge.

Il Massimo del Panino 441 Washington St at Battery, Financial District ☏ 415/834-0290. This stylish café features an extensive panini sandwich menu, along with beer, wine, and an invitingly cushy couch next to a fireplace. Sandwiches all cost $6.50 (whole) or $3.75 (half). Branch (with outdoor seating): 5 Embarcadero Center at Market, Financial District.

Mocca 175 Maiden Lane at Stockton, Union Square ☏ 415/956-1188. A small café spilling out onto the pedestrianized shopping street, often serenaded by live acoustic jazz. The dapper, mostly Italian staff are decked out in stiff waistcoats and prepare the tangy sandwiches ($8.75 and up) and crispy salads (from $11) to order with a flourish. Cash only.

San Francisco Soup Company 221 Montgomery St at Bush, Financial District ☏ 415/834-0472. Local gourmet chainlet specializing in soups: the menu at this large branch includes a dozen types, from vegetarian-friendly staples like smoky split pea to daily specials such as shrimp bisque. A regular portion is $5; add about $1 more for a large portion, and $1.25 for a fresh-baked bread bowl. Lunch only. Branches: 142 First St at Natoma, SoMa; Crocker Galleria (Level Three), 50 Post St at Kearny, Financial District.

Seafood

Aqua 252 California St at Battery, Financial District ☏ 415/956-9662. Elaborately decorated destination restaurant with oversize flower arrangements and a menu focused on creatively presented seafood. It still pulls in a well-heeled crowd hobnobbing over seared *ahi* tuna and prawns, while the $34 lunchtime prix fixe draws in plenty of suits and Financial District expense accounts; for dinner, expect to put out at least twice that amount.

Farallon 450 Post St at Mason, Union Square ☎415/956-6969. "Coastal cuisine" (aka seafood) is prepared and served with great fanfare at this Union Square notable, although the jellyfish-inspired decor with its dangling luminescent mobiles may not float every visitor's boat. The food is always excellent and surprising, however – champagne-steamed clams are light and tender, while mackerel tartare and tuna carpaccio are oddly delicious, flavor-packed appetizers. Dinner only.

Hog Island Oyster Co. 1 Ferry Building, Embarcadero ☎415/391-7117. This Ferry Building outpost of the Tomales Bay (Marin County) farm hosts mollusc devotees who sit elbow to elbow at the wrap-around granite bar, where the lists of oysters, wines, and beers are equally impressive. It's $9 for three oysters, and about $30 for a dozen. The creamy oyster stew is a perennial hit.

Sam's Grill 374 Bush St at Montgomery, Financial District ☎415/421-0594. The city's oldest fish house (dating back in various incarnations to 1867), this restaurant is known for fresh, moderately priced seafood and cheerfully abrupt service from waiters who look like they helped open the place all those years ago. The onion rings are crunchy and buttery, and there's a mean Hang Town Fry (essentially a bacon/oyster omelette) on the menu. Closed Sun.

Tadich Grill 240 California St at Front, Financial District ☎415/391-1849. A Downtown classic originally opened as a coffee stand by three Croatian brothers during the Gold Rush. Its popularity hasn't waned with the decades, and today it's half-diner/half-gentleman's club, with a seasoned group of waiters nearly as stiff as their white jackets. Eat at the mile-long bar or pull into one of the dark-paneled booths. Most entrees exceed $20. Closed Sun.

South Asian

Mela 417 O'Farrell St at Jones, Theater District ☎415/447-4041. Indian/Pakistani hideaway specializing in family-style tandoori dishes. The menu's extensive and surprisingly affordable, considering the lavish decor like the silken tapestries lining the walls and the lovely fountain in the entryway. After 10pm,

the place becomes a popular hookah lounge, complete with DJs.

Southeast Asian

Le Colonial 20 Cosmo Place at Taylor, Union Square ☎415/931-3600. This Franco-Vietnamese restaurant boasts lush, 1920s-themed dining quarters: the main floor is decked out with tile floors, palm fronds, and ceiling fans, while the upstairs lounge is a salon with rattan couches and faded rugs. Inventive dishes such as *ca hap la chuoi* (steamed sea bass wrapped in banana leaves, $34) arrive in generous portions. Dinner only.

Osha Thai 4 Embarcadero Center, Financial District ☎415/788-6742. This hyper-designed eatery is the *least* stylish among the local chainlet's five restaurants scattered around town. The food's largely terrific and provides an affordable option for Southeast Asian cuisine if you're Downtown; it's also open until midnight.

The Slanted Door 1 Ferry Building, Embarcadero ☎415/861-8329. This one-time Mission landmark swapped its cavernous old digs on Valencia St for an even larger space on the water in the renovated Ferry Building, and the buzz hasn't stopped. Chef Charles Phan's menu is light, French-Vietnamese; there's a raw bar and several deliciously fragrant chicken dishes, and the tea list is impressively diverse. Prix fixes are available at both lunch ($38) and dinner ($48). You'd be well advised to either book in advance or find an off-peak time to drop in.

Spanish

Bocadillos 710 Montgomery St at Jackson, Jackson Square ☎415/982-2622. Basque chef Gerald Hirigoyen of Piperade (see p.179) branched out to Jackson Square in 2004 with this instant hit. The bocadillos themselves – tiny, Spanish-style sandwiches ($7) with serrano ham, chorizo, or catalan sausage between round buns – are outstanding, and the menu gets even more clever with items such as chilled prawns with *huevos diablo* (deviled eggs). Aim for the tables for two wedged by the wall, although the communal table can also be fun if you're feeling extra sociable. Everything on the menu is moderately priced. Breakfast on weekday mornings; closed Sun.

North Beach and the hills

The city's Italian enclave, North Beach, presents the inevitable roster of terrific pasta houses, bakeries, cafés, and delis, while in adjacent Russian Hill, you'll find a notable cache of top French and seafood restaurants, as well as a few Italian spots that rival the more celebrated places in North Beach. This area is also home to a pair of excellent fondue restaurants, *Melt!* and *The Matterhorn*.

American

Fog City Diner 1300 Battery St at Greenwich, Northeast Waterfront ☎415/982-2000. It's no longer the prime destination it portrayed in 1980s credit-card commercials, but this Bay-adjacent eatery still woos customers into its singular, converted railcar setting. The kitchen's leftfield take on global comfort food can hit (beef pot roast with cabernet sauce) or miss (mu shu pork burrito), but at least everything's moderately priced. Brunch on weekends.

Harris' 2100 Van Ness Ave at Pacific, Russian Hill ☎415/673-1888. Proudly old-fashioned, *Harris'* is one of the premier steakhouses in the city. The staff is warm and welcoming (if assiduous at times), as is the decor: padded chairs, comfy leather booths, thick velvet curtains. There's practically every cut of beef imaginable on the menu – from filet mignon to Kobe ribeye – and all are buttery-sweet and tender. Just be sure to pack your credit card. Dinner only.

Luella 1896 Hyde St at Green, Russian Hill ☎415/674-4343. This cozy, family-run restaurant on Russian Hill is decked out in soothing mint green with crisp white tablecloths, while the modern American food is inventive and tasty. The Coca Cola-braised pork shoulder is a hit whenever it appears on the frequently changing menu. Main courses range from $19–27. Dinner only.

Mama's 1701 Stockton St at Filbert, North Beach ☎415/362-6421. Order first, then wait to be seated at this inexpensive, immensely popular diner on a corner across from Washington Square. There's always a wait to get in – bring extra patience if you happen to come on a weekend – but the fine "momelettes" and cheery staff (trained to subtly dissuade solo dining, due to limited table space) are usually worth it. Breakfast and lunch only; closed Mon.

▲ Mama's

Mo's Grill 1322 Grant Ave at Vallejo, North Beach ☎415/788-3779. One of San Francisco's best (and chunkiest) hamburgers. This no-frills shop exclusively cooks Angus beef over a volcanic rock grill; the house fries are also noteworthy, and breakfast is available until mid-afternoon each day. Burgers are under $10.

Pat's Cafe 2330 Taylor St at Chestnut, North Beach ☎415/776-8735. This eminently inviting breakfast/lunch spot moved from a cramped room in Fisherman's Wharf in 2003 to its present location in the upper reaches of North Beach along the Powell-Mason cable car line. It's bright and airy now, with plenty of wall space devoted to local photography and original artwork, but the charming decor doesn't overshadow the delicious, affordable, and occasionally rich food – the peppery home fries and banana granola pancakes are especially recommended. Service is often amiably chatty.

Bakeries

Italian French Bakery 1501 Grant Ave at Union, North Beach ☎415/421-3796. Nestled on a corner along upper Grant's retail drag, this tiny bakery wafts the enticing smell of freshly baked bread up and down the block. Grab a slice of focaccia, a pastry, or a flavored baguette (rosemary, whole wheat), have a seat on one of the stools at the window counter, and while away a few minutes watching folks shuffle by on the sidewalk. **Liguria Bakery 1700 Stockton St at Filbert, North Beach** ☎415/421-3786. Marvelous old-world bakery with vintage scales and cash registers in its front display windows. Fresh focaccia is the smart order here, and there's no shortage of choices: onion, garlic, rosemary, and mushroom, among others. It's best to arrive earlier than later, as it simply closes when the day's goods are sold out. Cash only.

Belgian

La Trappe 800 Greenwich St at Mason, North Beach ☎415/440-8727. Fresh-faced entry on the Italian-dominated North Beach scene, ideal for Euro-beer snobs and large groups. There are about 200 – that's right, 200 – beers available in bottles and on tap, while the expensive plates of massively portioned food hits when it hews the Belgian line (chicken waterzooi-ghent stew, mussels in a white beer sauce) and misses when it veers away from it (mini-burgers, fusilli). Reservations aren't taken. Dinner only; closed Mon.

California

Coi 373 Broadway at Montgomery, North Beach ☎415/393-9000. Pronounced "kwah," this relative newcomer stands apart for its adventurous, eleven-course prix fixe tasting menu that changes daily. It's one of the most expensive restaurants in the city, and that's no small feat; for cut-rate prices, try the à la carte menu in the adjacent lounge. The 32-seat dining room is padded with calm earth tones and couldn't contrast more with the glut of obstreperous strip clubs down the block. Closed Sun & Mon.

🏃 **Frascati 1901 Hyde St at Green, Russian Hill** ☎415/928-1406. Surprisingly intimate considering its prime corner location, this vividly romantic, bi-level bistro has transformed from neighborhood secret

to destination restaurant. It's no wonder, given chef Mike Pawlik's talent for creating uniquely paired dishes that still retain a level of comfort – look no further than the maple-leaf duck breast with herb *spaetzle* and huckleberry sauce ($25). The wine list is always among the most impressive in the area, and a few marriage proposal celebrations are said to have taken place at the few tables for two along the upstairs railing. Dinner only.

Dessert

Swensen's Ice Cream 1999 Hyde St at Union, Russian Hill ☎415/775-6818. *Swensen's* global dessert empire got its humble start here at this corner ice cream shop in 1948, and few things seem to have changed in the decades since – the neon sign, the twinkling lightbulbs, and least of all, the exceptional home-made ice cream. Seating here is non-existent, so arm yourself with napkins and be prepared to enjoy your treats as efficiently and cleanly as possible. Closed Mon.

French

Café Jacqueline 1454 Grant Ave at Union, North Beach ☎415/981-5565. A romantic, candlelit gourmet experience in an airy dining room that feels like a French country cottage. The menu here is entirely made up of chef-owner Jacqueline Margulis' signature soufflés (over $20), both savory and sweet; crab and chocolate are top picks. Since every dish is made to order, plan on making an evening of it. Dinner only; closed Mon–Tues.

🏃 **La Folie 2316 Polk St at Green, Russian Hill** ☎415/776-5577. Magnificent Provençal food served without attitude or pretension. There are five different five-course prix-fixe options to choose from, steeply priced ($75–105) but worth it if you fancy a gourmet treat. Regular dishes include frogs' legs as an appetizer, pot au feu of smoked duck breast or veal sweetbreads as entrees, and a creamy strawberry napoleon for dessert. Dinner only; closed Sun.

Le Petit Robert 2300 Polk St at Green, Russian Hill ☎415/922-8100. Achingly Francophile, this bistro is Nice by way of Russian Hill, from the artfully distressed walls to the wicker furniture and insouciant parents brunching with smartly dressed toddlers. Prices for main courses are moderate (under $20), while the food's sharply prepared in most cases. The corner setting makes for entertaining people-watching when seated outdoors.

Italian

Acquerello 1722 Sacramento St at Polk, Russian Hill ☎415/567-5432. Serving Italian fare unlike anything you'll find over the hill in North Beach, this celebrated, terracotta-toned restaurant welcomes polished crowds into its wood-beamed dining room, which used to serve as a chapel. *Acquerello*'s menu is full of surprises (risotto of sweet prawns, golden trout over wax beans); choose between three prix fixe menus ($60–82). The service, led by co-owner (and Italian wine expert) Giancarlo Paterlini, is peerless. Dinner only; closed Sun & Mon.

Antica Trattoria 2400 Polk St at Union, Russian Hill ☎415/928-5797. Family-friendly corner spot where the entrees are rustic Northern Italian, moderately priced, and hold up well. The desserts are the true stars here, though – save room for the *affogato*, which combines gelato, espresso, amaretto, and hazelnut to delicious effect. Dinner only; closed Mon.

Café Divine 1600 Stockton St at Union, North Beach ☎415/986-3414. Across from Washington Square, this airy, bistro-inspired café (high ceilings, spindly golden chandeliers, tile flooring) does all three meals – a rarity in this neighborhood of delis and swanky eateries. The menu's casual and often light, with the six varieties of pizzetta ($11–14) the most popular items here. Inviting outdoor tables line the sidewalks around the corner space.

Da Flora 701 Columbus Ave at Filbert, North Beach ☎415/981-4664. This hopelessly romantic restaurant on North Beach's main artery has been feted as having the neighborhood's best pasta, and one taste of its trademark sweet potato gnocchi only furthers the notion. Most items on the handwritten menu are distinctly Venetian, and despite all the plaudits, prices remain remarkably reasonable – nothing on the menu exceeds $20. Dinner only; closed Sun.

Il Pollaio 555 Columbus Ave at Union, North Beach ☎415/362-7727. Moderately priced chicken specialist also roasts a few other

meats (beef, pork, rabbit, lamb), but it's the perfect crisped and seasoned poultry that keeps North Beach locals coming back. Don't show up late and expect to be fed, however – it closes at 9pm. Closed Sun.

L'Osteria del Forno 519 Columbus Ave at Green, North Beach ☎415/982-1124. This postage stamp-sized nook is a humble refuge from the gaudy tourist traps right across Columbus Ave. The menu's short and driven by whatever's freshest at the market, although the eight or so *foccacine* sandwiches ($5–7) are a standby. Reservations aren't taken, so a wait may be inevitable even at off-peak times. Cash only; closed Tues.

▲ L'Osteria del Forno

Ristorante Ideale 1309 Grant Ave at Vallejo, North Beach ☎415/391-4129. A plate of ravioli is your wisest choice here, although the thin-crust pizzas (which work well as appetizers) are also a sharp move. It's a festive, distinctly Roman dining experience, all the way down to the occasionally lazy service. Most main courses are under $20. Dinner only.

Ristorante Milano 1448 Pacific Ave at Hyde, Russian Hill ☎415/673-2961. It's worth trundling a few blocks off the beaten path for this restaurant's homey service, excellent gocchi ($16), and delectable tiramisu ($6.50). Italian wines outnumber California varietals by a comfortable margin on the extensive wine list. Dinner only.

Sodini's 510 Green St at Grant, North Beach ☎415/291-0499. Light on pretense and heavy on saucy, homestyle plates of pasta ($11–16), this staple captures the ebullient spirit of North Beach as well as any restaurant in the neighborhood. Depending on your server, you may or may not get called "hon" or "dear," but it's a near-certainty you'll hear something by Louis Prima or Dean Martin at some point during the evening. Reservations not accepted.

Tommaso's 1042 Kearny St at Pacific, North Beach ☎415/398-9696. Claiming to be the West Coast birthplace of the wood-fired pizza oven, this North Beach stalwart – marooned on a semi-seedy block near the edge of the district – hasn't lost a step in popularity since opening in 1935 as *Lupo's*. And for good reason: the thin-crust pizzas ($20–26 for a 15-inch large) are sublime, while the seven-layer lasagne ($15.50) is wonderfully gooey. Expect to wait for a table in the cave-like dining room, as reservations aren't taken.

Trattoria Contadina 1800 Mason St at Union, North Beach ☎415/982-5728. Family-owned, with white cloth-swathed tables and photograph-covered walls, warm and charming *Trattoria Contadina* continues to cater to the local Italian-American community. The rigatoni with eggplant and smoked mozzarella ($15) is a top option, as are old familiars like tortellini with prosciutto in cream sauce ($15). The Powell-Mason cable car will drop you off steps from the front door.

Japanese

Sushi Groove 1916 Hyde St at Green, Russian Hill ☎415/440-1905. Self-consciously stylish restaurant serving inventive and original maki rolls, a sprinkling of Pan-Asian fusion dishes, and furiously strong sake martinis. The two downsides are the sometimes sloppy service and the tiny size of the place, which usually translates into long waits for seating. Expect to spend anywhere from $20–30 for a full meal.

Sushi on North Beach 745 Columbus Ave at Filbert, North Beach ☎415/440-1905. Cozy, moderately priced place on upper Columbus Ave where you might get a spirited greeting from the whole staff when you step in. Elegantly presented varieties of raw fish, with an impressive list of sakes to match. Lunch specials are a particularly good bargain.

Latin American

El Raigon 510 Union St at Stockton, North Beach ☎415/291-0927. This rustically decorated Argentinian steakhouse isn't completely out of place in North Beach, considering Italians' history in the South American country. Cow hides hang on the bare brick walls, and the crowd's often surprisingly dressy. Don't miss the *papas rostisadas* (crisp roast potatoes) with your beef cut, and try the fluffy *dulce de leche* pancakes for dessert. The menu's not prohibitively expensive: main courses are generally under $30. Closed Sun.

Mangarosa 1548 Stockton St at Green, North Beach ☎415/956-3211. Brazilian cuisine with an Italian twist, served in a sleek, dark space full of blue walls, booths, and bent-wood furniture. A young, adventurous crowd chows on expensive combination plates that sound awkward, but usually work – the cambozola cheese with mango lime mint dressing is outstanding, as are the house-made risotto specials. Thurs night is samba night. Dinner only; closed Mon.

Peña Pachamama 1630 Powell St at Green, North Beach ☎415/646-0018. An uncommon find in the city's Italian quarter: organically prepared Bolivian food. Nibble on tapas like *yuca frita* or dive headlong into a full plate of *silpancho* (flattened beef with pico de gallo, fried egg, and rice) while taking in a live music performance in the Carnaval-like atmosphere. Nothing on the menu's over $20. Dinner only; closed Tues.

Mediterranean / Middle Eastern

Helmand Palace 2424 Van Ness Ave at Green, Russian Hill ☎415/345-0072. A 2007 landslide on the south flank of Telegraph Hill prompted a move west for this popular Afghani restaurant, formerly owned by the brother of Premier Hamid Karzai. The menu is filled with tangy and spicy Afghani staples – try the *kaddo* (caramelized pumpkin on a bed of yogurt) or the *chapandaz* (grilled beef tenderloin). Plenty of vegetarian items are also available, and everything's moderately priced. Dinner only.

Maykadeh 470 Green St at Grant, North Beach ☎415/362-8286. A fairly traditional Persian outpost amidst the sea of North Beach trattorias, this is the best place in the area for chicken kebabs and lamb shanks; stunt-eaters will surely want to opt for the boiled brain ($11). Don't miss the *bastani* (Persian ice cream) for dessert.

Mexican

Taqueria Zorro 308 Columbus Ave at Broadway, North Beach ☎415/392-9677. Late-night taqueria with a neon sombrero over its front entrance to match its gaudy strip joint neighbors. The egg-inclusive breakfast burrito here is reason enough to get to bed early the night before; also be sure to slather your tortilla chips with some "Salsa Zorro," a roasted vegetable-laden master-piece. Cash only.

Pan-Asian

The House 1230 Grant Ave at Columbus, North Beach ☎415/986-8612. This tiny nook is popular for its self-dubbed "evolutionary Asian food" – expect the likes of Caesar salad with wok-fried scallops or flatiron steak with *wasabi* noodles, all served amidst charmingly austere decor. Main courses hover around $14–19.

Sandwiches/soup

Caffe Sapore 790 Lombard St at Taylor, North Beach ☎415/474-1222. One block off Columbus, this mellow neighborhood café serves inexpensive baked goods, fresh sandwiches, and all the usual coffee beverages in a sunny room on a corner. Sit and admire the original artwork adorning the walls, or enjoy a glass of wine or beer on one of the outside tables as you watch drivers meticulously navigate Lombard's twisting turns just up Russian Hill.

Giordano Bros. 303 Columbus Ave at Broadway, North Beach ☎415/397-2767. Pittsburgh sports-themed shop serves faithful replicas of the "all-in-one" sandwich popularized in the blue-collar Pennsylvania city – all the way down to the fries stuffed between each sandwich's Italian bread slices. Given all the impossibly masculine decor of the place, the portions are surprisingly downsized. Inexpensive and open late.

Mario's Bohemian Cigar Store Cafe 566 Columbus Ave at Union, North Beach ☎415/362-0536. Stogies haven't been sold on these premises for ages, but the chunky, home-made focaccia sandwiches and corner location make this North Beach insti-tution a terrific place to grab a cheap bite and absorb the neighborhood scene. The pizza and panini aren't bad, either, and the bar's a great spot for an unpretentious nightcap.

Molinari 373 Columbus Ave at Vallejo, North Beach ☎415/421-2337. Classic Italian deli full of locals picking up fresh ravioli and tortellini. It doubles as a hearty sandwich shop, so pick the bread of your choice and order a combo to go – try the North Beach Special, with prosciutto, *provolone*, sun-dried tomato, and sweet peppers. Sandwiches run about $7–8.

Nook 1500 Hyde St at Jackson, Russian Hill ☎415/447-4100. Under the same ownership as *Caffe Sapore* (see above), with sleek cream walls, dark wood tables, and an inexpensive menu chalked on a black-board. There are a few seats outside if you want to watch the cable car turn, while the short list of sake and soju cocktails sets this warm corner spot apart from the usual café fare.

Seafood

Pesce 2227 Polk St at Vallejo, Russian Hill ☎415/928-8025. Featuring Venetian small plates known as *cicchetti*, the menu at this acclaimed seafood bar tempts the adven-turous with brave options such as *polpo* (braised octopus) and spaghetti with "tuna Bolognese" sauce. There are more middle-of-the-road choices like penne pasta with garlic and basil for the less adventurous, while mahogany and teak woodwork add to the room's intimate mood. Expect to spend about $35 per person. Lunch on weekends only.

Yabbies Coastal Kitchen 2237 Polk St at Vallejo, Russian Hill ☎415/474-4088. Shellfish of seemingly every variety served a thousand ways, though oysters chilled on the half shell are the house specialty – there are usually half a dozen or so different varieties at a time, and they're cheapest during the 6–6.30pm happy hour Sun–Thurs. Try the sesame crusted tuna ($22) or linguine with clams ($16). Dinner only.

San Francisco coffee, indie-style

San Francisco has enjoyed a recent proliferation of locally based "microroasters" that offer particularly strong cups of joe. Listed below are a few espresso bars to seek out if you're looking for a robust kickstart any time of day. You won't find any grande eggnog lattes at these places, but you can expect to get a cup of fresh coffee for a mere $1.50–2.25.

Blue Bottle Coffee 315 Linden St at Gough, Hayes Valley ☎415/252-7535. Located down an alley off a main thoroughfare, this quirky spot offers excellent breakfast and dessert items, but it's the own-roasted coffee that has taken San Francisco by storm. Cold-brewed coffee makes a surprising appearance on the menu, as do a few milk-based beverages. Closes at 6pm.

Caffe Trieste 601 Vallejo St at Grant, North Beach ☎415/392-6739. This local institution is where espresso made its West Coast debut in 1956. Today, it's known almost as much for its Saturday mandolin sessions and opera recitals as for its own-roasted, thick-bodied coffee. It operates a shop next to the café where you can purchase a sack of *Caffe Trieste* beans. Open late.

Coffee Bar 1890 Bryant St at Mariposa, Mission ☎415/551-8100. A huge space on an industrial edge of the Mission that serves a consistently bracing cup. One member of the management team is an avowed oenophile, so the place becomes a wine bar of sorts during evening hours; café food (salads, sandwiches, tapas) is served all day long.

Ritual Coffee Roasters 1026 Valencia St at 21st, Mission ☎415/641-1024. The hipster-chic clientele at this vaunted café can't overshadow the outstanding coffee, roasted on the premises using the company's own beans. The intense espresso boasts flavors of hazelnut and caramel.

Trouble Coffee 4033 Judah St at 45th, Outer Sunset ☎415/690-9119. A few blocks in from the coastline sits this pint-sized powerhouse, operated by young eccentrics who are remarkably passionate about their trade. The menu's simple: coffee, coconut, toast. Closed Tuesday.

For a wealth of information on San Francisco coffee purveyors, visit ⓦwww.coffeeratings.com.

Southeast Asian

King Cha Cha 1268 Grant Ave at Vallejo, North Beach ①415/391-8219. A bit more expensive than most Thai places in the city, this roomy place is unique in other ways: it shares space with an English football pub. The menu includes tried-and-true favorites such as pad thai and beef/basil in curry, with a few diversions sprinkled about – oxtails with peanuts and onion, for instance. Most entrees hover around $15.

Spanish

Piperade 1015 Battery St at Green, Northeast Waterfront ☎415/391-2555. Basque restaurant with rustic, wooden tables and much exposed brick. The robust menu includes cod in smoky broth and the namesake, ratatouille-esque stew, while the warm atmosphere and the affable, attentive service are big pluses. Entrees range from $18–30.

Zarzuela 2000 Hyde St at Union, Russian Hill ☎415/346-0800. This perennially popular (and noisy) small-plates specialist occupies a choice location on one of Russian Hill's liveliest corners. The *tortilla espanola* – a Spanish tomato and onion omelette ($4.25), served cold – is a terrific appetizer, and the plate of saucy pork medallions ($19) anchors the list of main courses. Reservations aren't accepted, so plan accordingly. Closed Sun.

Swiss

The Matterhorn 2323 Van Ness Ave at Vallejo, Russian Hill ☎415/885-6116. Lurking in a nondescript apartment building, this Swiss restaurant is known for cheese, beef, and chocolate fondues. The standout choice is the Fondue Ticinese, a thick and spicy blend of cheeses, *peperoncini*, and tomatoes. The restaurant's ski-lodge decor was shipped in pieces from the Swiss motherland and reassembled onsite. Beef fondues for two run $46; cheese fondues for two, $36. **Melt! 700 Columbus Ave at Filbert, North Beach** ☏ 415/392-9290. The calendar here may

read like that of a small college-town café – open mic on Mon and Fri, film noir on Tues, free wireless all week long – but the reasonably priced fondue is what draws in dippers from all over the city. Extra sharp cheddar plays a significant role in many varieties; several kinds of sandwiches (including a croque monsieur) are also on offer.

The northern waterfront and Pacific Heights

San Francisco's sharpest-dressed districts enjoy a plethora of celebrated neighborhood haunts, from new hotspots *Spruce* and *Laïola* to veteran favorites *Ella's* and *Bistro Aix*. This area also includes the kitschy tourist confines of Fisherman's Wharf, where a few true gems (*Gary Danko*, *Ana Mandara*) lurk on the periphery of all the snack kiosks, hot dog carts, and unit-food chain restaurants.

American

Balboa Cafe 3199 Fillmore St at Greenwich, Cow Hollow ☏ 415/921-3944. Reopened by city honcho Gavin Newsom's PlumpJack enterprise in his pre-mayor days, this old-fashioned restaurant was first established in 1913; today's throwback touches include waiters in white aprons and black waistcoats. It's known for its meat entrees, so try the oven-roasted pork chop ($23) or excellent baguette burger ($11.50). There's brunch on weekends, and the bar's open until 2am.

Bistro Yoffi 2231 Chestnut St at Scott, Marina ☏ 415/885-5133. Serving clever modern American dishes like seabass enchiladas and a pancetta-wrapped pork tenderloin (both $15.50), this brightly colored bistro is refreshingly quirky, given its patently tucked-in Marina location. It's packed with potted ferns and mismatched chairs, and there's a lovely courtyard garden, as well as frequent live jazz. You've been warned, however: Wed is open-mic night. Dinner only; closed Mon–Tues.

Boboquivari's 1450 Lombard St at Van Ness, Marina ☏ 415/441-8880. Never mind (if you can) the big top-reminiscent, black-and-red striped awnings, and the creepy clown over the door; "*Bobo's*" serves one of San Francisco's most desired cuts of beef, its bone-in filet mignon ($39). The steakhouse dry-ages its beef off the premises for up to six weeks for its famous taste. If you're thinking of investing, call ahead to ensure the cut will be available. Dinner only.

The Elite Cafe 2049 Fillmore St at Pine, Pacific Heights ☏ 415/346-8668. This expensive Creole and Cajun restaurant-bar can get frighteningly packed with locals – in fact, it's often easier to sit down for dinners of Louisianan staples (buttery blackened catfish, thick gumbo) in one of the welcoming mahogany booths than it is to cozy up to the bar for a drink. Brunch on weekends; otherwise, dinner only.

The Grove 2016 Fillmore St at Pine, Pacific Heights ☏ 415/474-1419. Casual diners drop in for serviceable, fairly priced comfort food morning, noon, and night; it also does double duty as a mellow café in the evenings (wireless is available). There's a couch or two near the hearth, and the whole place maintains a cozy mood, even outside at one of the tables along the Fillmore sidewalk.

In-N-Out Burger 333 Jefferson St at Jones, Fisherman's Wharf ☏ 800/786-1000. Yes, it's fast food, and it couldn't be in a sillier location. Despite all that, this Southern California-based chain churns out first-rate burgers for less than the price of 30min parking at the Wharf. Consult the company website for the "secret menu," which includes a few variants on the iconic restaurant's simple formula. Don't pass over the excellent fries and thick shakes. Open late nightly.

Spruce 3640 Sacramento St at Locust, Presidio Heights ☏ 415/931-5100. Opened in 2007 in a transformed 1930s auto barn, *Spruce*'s gorgeous dining room almost trumps its kitchen's glorious, if quite pricey New American dishes (charred pork tenderloin; harissa chicken with couscous, dates, and almonds). It's been an instant hit with wealthy neighborhood denizens and critics alike. Lunch on weekdays only.

Bakeries

Patisserie Delanghe 1890 Fillmore St at Bush, Pacific Heights ☎415/923-0711. Gourmet French bakery operated by an expat couple. House specials include butter croissants, glistening fruit tarts, and puffy eclairs. There are a few tables near the windows if you wish to linger.

British

Liverpool Lil's 2942 Lyon St at Lombard, Cow Hollow ☎415/921-6664. One of the few restaurants in San Francisco to offer a bracingly British menu (liver and onions, lamb shepherd's pie, fish and chips), this Cow Hollow pub offers a dimly lit alternative to the neighborhood's often trendy dining scene. Dinner entrees range from $12–28.

California

Ella's 500 Presidio Ave at California, Presidio Heights ☎415/441-5669. The wait for weekend brunch at this corner hotspot is among the most notorious in town, so you're better off coming on a weekday when you should be able to sit right down. The chicken hash ($10.75) is *Ella's* star item, a delicious loaf of white meat and potato topped with a hearty flurry of green onions and chives. Other top picks include the meltingly fluffy pancakes (made with sweet potato to keep them moist) and the chunky biscuits. Breakfast and lunch only.

Garibaldi's 347 Presidio Ave at Clay, Presidio Heights ☎415/563-8841. Amidst Presidio Heights' leafy quietude sits this long-popular neighborhood staple, serving hearty portions of Cal-Med staples like artichoke salad and scallop risotto. The menu often features a three-course prix fixe for $30. Lunch only on weekdays.

Gary Danko 800 North Point St at Hyde, Fisherman's Wharf ☎415/749-2060. Don't let the location put you off – this understated oasis regularly vies for the title of best restaurant in food-obsessed San Francisco. Granted, this is performance food served with a

flourish, but it's utterly splurgeworthy. The three- to five-course prix-fixe menus ($65–96) allow diners to choose their own items, so if you're a dessert person, you're allowed to order more than one at the expense of an appetizer. Whatever you do, though, don't miss the impeccable cheese course. Call well ahead for a reservation. Dinner only.

Greens Building A, Fort Mason Center ☎415/771-6222. San Francisco's original vegetarian restaurant remains popular thanks in no small part to a picturesque pier setting featuring massive, gridded windows overlooking the Bay. The airy, pine furniture-filled interior (a converted warehouse) is oddly casual given the quality and price of the food; the twisting tree sculpture-cum-bar in the lounge area is astonishing. A take out-only counter, *Greens To Go* (☎415/771-6330), is available during lunch hours in the restaurant's lobby, and is a terrific choice for picnics at nearby upper Fort Mason.

▲ Greens

Chinese

Dragon Well 2142 Chestnut St at Steiner, Marina ☎415/474-6888. Though the Marina isn't a hotbed for Chinese cuisine, this inviting, moderately priced eatery is the area's best pick for solid, if Americanized versions of dishes like lemongrass chicken and Mongolian beef. Dark wood flooring lends elegance. Dishes are very reasonably priced: $8.50–12.

Dessert

Ghirardelli Ice Cream and Chocolate Caffe 900 North Point St at Larkin, Fisherman's Wharf ☎415/771-4903. Although the chocolate hasn't been made onsite in decades, this perennially popular, old-fashioned ice-cream parlor is the ideal setting to sample a decadent range of Ghirardelli desserts. The sprawling Earthquake Sundae ($19.06, fittingly) is especially gooey – plan to share it with several friends.

Eclectic

Pres a Vi 1 Letterman Drive, Building D, Presidio ☎415/409-3000. The expensive food at this enormous new restaurant in the Letterman Digital Arts Center reflects the ethnic diversity of the Bay Area – even a quick survey of menu items will reveal nods to Filipino, French, Korean, and of course, American cuisines. A meal of duck buns, Hawaiian *mahi-mahi*, and chocolate *dacquoise* may cause taste-bud overexertion, but you'll be well fed in the meantime.

French

Baker Street Bistro 2953 Baker St at Lombard, Cow Hollow ☎415/931-1475. A cramped but charming café with a handful of outdoor tables, where a neighborhood crowd enjoys simple food served by French staff. Wines are reasonably priced, and the $14.50 prix fixe dinner on weeknights is still a remarkable bargain.

Bistro Aix 3340 Steiner St at Lombard, Marina ☎415/202-0100. Cow Hollow's secret about this Gallic bistro is now out all over town – it's been hailed in recent years as one of the top restaurants in town by several influential publications. Fortunately, success hasn't affected its moderate prices, and the heated back patio is as pleasant a place as ever to enjoy a meal. The seared tuna with garlic potatoes ($20) is heavenly. Dinner only; closed Tues.

Italian

A16 2355 Chestnut St at Divisadero, Marina ☎415/771-2216. Named after an Italian highway, this fresh-faced eatery along the Marina's commercial corridor specializes in exceptional, Neapolitan-style pizza, although it's hardly a one-trick pony: house-cured meats, a robust Italian wine list, and a clever Meatball Mondays tradition combine to pack the narrow space nightly. If the wait's too long for a table, remove a layer of clothing, elbow your way to a seat at the long counter, and warm yourself by the heat of the adjacent wood-burning oven. Expect to spend at least $30 per person. Lunch Wed–Fri only.

Jackson Fillmore 2506 Fillmore St at Jackson, Pacific Heights ☎415/346-5288. A casual trattoria serving Romanesque and Southern Italian dishes at surprisingly reasonable prices, considering the upscale neighborhood. Go easy on the complimentary bruschetta and save room for one of the sumptuous desserts like Italian chocolate cake or zabaglione. Dinner only; closed Mon.

Ristorante Parma 3314 Steiner St at Chestnut, Marina ☎415/567-0500. This slice of *paizano* unpretentiousness has been charming diners with its reasonably priced, signature pasta dishes and affordable bottles of chianti for years. Service is suitably welcoming, while the distressed walls provide a bit of Old World ambience. Dinner only; closed Sun.

Sociale 3665 Sacramento St at Spruce, Presidio Heights ☎415/921-3200. Nestled at the end of a verdant pedestrian lane in leafy Presidio Heights, this intimate Italian bistro is worth seeking out for its heated dining courtyard, cozy atmosphere, and fontina-crammed fried olives appetizer ($8). Chef Tia Harrison also operates Avedano's meat market across town, so dishes such as grilled quails ($27) and brick chicken ($24) are assuredly excellent here. The impressive wine list is decidedly Italian-leaning.

Japanese

Hime 2353 Lombard St at Scott, Marina ☎415/931-7900. This super stylish, expensive Japanese spot features strangely glowing bamboo decor and a menu that drifts into Pan-Asian territory on occasion (others in the city do it far better). The excellent, *izakaya*-style sushi rolls, however, anchor the experience. Dinner only; closed Mon.

Zushi Puzzle 1910 Lombard St at Buchanan, Marina ☎415/931-9319. Occasionally slipshod service can't sully an evening at this immensely popular, reasonably priced sushi spot. The sashimi and banjo fish are solid orders, but if you're a sushi novice, the chef will sometimes offer a tutorial. Dinner only; closed Sun.

Latin American

Fresca 2114 Fillmore St at California, Pacific Heights ☎415/447-2668. Peruvian ceviche and tapas presented in vibrant surroundings. Entree-sized courses such as *churrasco* (steak) and salmon are available, but it's in the seafood appetizers where this Upper Fillmore restaurant shines most brightly. Most entrees are less than $20. Lunch on weekdays only.

Mediterranean/Middle Eastern

Mezes 2373 Chestnut St at Divisadero, Marina ☎415/409-7111. Moderately priced Greek restaurant with a strong emphasis on small plates of zucchini cakes, fried cheese, spinach pie, and moussaka. The souvlaki dish (marinated skewers of chicken or pork, with roasted potatoes) is of particular note. The crowd's a good deal more diverse than many other restaurants along Chestnut. Dinner only; closed Mon.
Terzo 3011 Steiner St at Union, Cow Hollow ☎415/441-3200. A few steps off the Union Street promenade, and boasting newly reinvented menu of pan-Med dishes like Pacific cod in *papillote*, this pricey spot's popularity hasn't waned – in fact, it's become even more of a hot ticket. Shelves of wine bottles line the walls of the seductively lit dining room. Dinner only.

Mexican

La Canasta 3006 Buchanan St at Union, Cow Hollow ☎415/474-2627. Slightly larger than a walk-in closet, this take-away-only spot has been the taqueria of choice in Cow Hollow and the Marina since the late 1980s. Quality and value is consistent across the menu board, while the spicy salsas will have you wishing you'd ordered a second beverage. Owner/manager Alberto is one of the friendliest souls along the Union St corridor.
Mamacita 2317 Chestnut St at Scott, Marina ☎415/346-8494. Beautifully presented, reasonably priced dishes with an emphasis on fresh, local ingredients. The ranchero-decorated dining room can get quite loud, but the kitchen's signature *chilaquiles* – refried tortilla chips with shredded chicken, peppers, *queso fresco*, and *chipotle* cream

– might be worth losing a bit of hearing for. Dinner only.

Pan-Asian

Betelnut 2030 Union St at Buchanan, Cow Hollow ☎415/929-8855. Now a jam-packed institution in its Cow Hollow digs, Betelnut was one of the first restaurants in San Francisco to embrace the small-plates concept, as well as offer well-executed tastes from a number of Asian cultures on a single menu. Choose from Malaysian curries, Indonesian chicken, Japanese udon noodles, Singapore prawns, Sri Lankan fish, and more. You should be able to get in and out for less than $30. Open until midnight on weekends.

Sandwiches/soup

Blue Barn Gourmet 2105 Chestnut St at Steiner, Marina ☎415/441-3232. You can't miss this recent addition to the Chestnut promenade – just look for the shopfront with the distressed azure slats. The interior's equally ersatz-rustic, but the highly creative made-to-order salads and sandwiches (all under $10) are the real thing, and there's an entire portion of the menu given over to all sorts of grilled-cheese panini. Plan to take your items away to enjoy elsewhere, as seating is extremely limited.
Boudin Bakery & Cafe Pier 39, Fisherman's Wharf ☎415/421-0185. Not far from the Boudin Museum (see p.84), this offshoot café serves some of the finest sourdough around, made using yeast descended from the first batch in Gold Rush times. A variety of cheap salads, sandwiches, and sourdough pizzas are available, in addition to the inevitable chowder in a bread bowl.
The Warming Hut Building 983, Crissy Field, Presidio ☎415/561-3040. Housed in a welcoming white clapboard building (recently recovered from fire damage) near the Torpedo Wharf pier, this café's humble kitchen churns out inexpensive grilled sandwiches, soups, and snacks. There are a few seats inside, as well as ample picnic tables on the adjacent lawn in the imposing shadow of Golden Gate Bridge. Closed evenings.

Seafood

Scoma's Pier 47, Fisherman's Wharf ☎415/929-1730. If you can't resist the allure of the tourist-targeting seafood palaces that crowd the Wharf, *Scoma's* is likely your safest choice. Just steel yourself for sky-high prices and be sure to make a reservation, as this is reportedly the highest volume restaurant west of the Mississippi.

Swan Oyster Depot 1517 Polk St at California, Russian Hill ☎415/673-1101. Expect no frills at this legendary seafood counter with its huge marble countertop and tiled walls – to find it, follow the smell of fresh fish wafting down the street and duck into the narrow space at the small blue awning. Endure the inevitable wait, grab a stool and hang onto it, and suck down some cheap shellfish or a bowl of chowder. Breakfast and lunch only.

▲ Swan Oyster Depot

South Asian

Taste of the Himalayas 2420 Lombard St at Scott, Marina ☎415/674-9898. Exactly as billed – Nepalese food, served with

congenial warmth among unlikely surroundings in the Marina. The *kukhura chiyau tarkari* (chicken and mushroom curry) defines the subtle differences between Nepalese and North Indian cuisines, while the *momos* (steamed dumplings filled with meat or vegetables) also come highly recommended. Best of all, it won't break the bank, as everything on the menu is moderately priced. Dinner only; open late on weekends.

Southeast Asian

Ana Mandara 891 Beach St at Polk, Fisherman's Wharf ☎415/771-6800. Despite overly busy decor and occasionally sloth-like service, this colonial Vietnamese palace occupying a corner of Ghirardelli Square is a fine choice for painstakingly indulgent Franco-Vietnamese. Provided you can get by the florid names of certain dishes – Enchanting Moments (seared basa), Smoke and Seduction (rack of lamb) – you should be in the clear for a terrific, if pricey meal. There's live jazz in the lounge Thurs–Sat. Lunch on weekdays only.

Yukol Place 2380 Lombard St at Scott, Marina ☎415/922-1599. An unassuming neighborhood place with numbered menu items, glasstop tables, and uncommonly good Thai curries. The serving staff is friendly and happy to make recommendations. Nothing on the menu's over $13, and most entrees are under $10. Lunch on weekdays only.

Spanish

Laïola 2031 Chestnut St at Fillmore, Marina ☎415/346-5641. This compact space draws in loads of neighborhood denizens enjoying Spanish wines (served in 250ml carafinas) and California-influenced, small-plated delicacies such as ham-wrapped figs. For heartier eaters, the menu includes a small number of main courses (all well over $20) incorporating fish, beef, pork, and lamb. Dinner only.

SoMa, the Tenderloin, and Civic Center

SoMa's new-breed restaurant scene is full of vibrant, impeccably stylish (and trendy) restaurant-lounges like *Bong Su* and *Shanghai 1930*, with a smattering of fine-dining entrants (*Boulevard*, *Kyo-Ya*) to remind you that the neighborhood hasn't completed gone to the young and restless. Across Market Street, the gritty Tenderloin and Polk Gulch feature a number of terrific South and Southeast Asian eateries, as well as a diverse clutch of high-end, Indonesian, burger, and sushi spots on the Tenderloin's Nob Hill-adjacent blocks.

American

Acme Chophouse 24 Willie Mays Plaza at AT&T Park (Third St at King), Mission Bay ☎415/644-0240. Despite catering primarily to affluent baseball fans on game days (a side exit leads right onto a ballpark entry ramp), this enormous restaurant is one of San Francisco's finest steakhouses. It's the brainchild of local chef wünderkind Traci Des Jardins (also see *Jardinière*, p.200), where the stars are the grass-fed filet, 22oz ribeye, and sides like the comically buttery mashed potatoes. Closed Sun–Mon.

Boulevard 1 Mission St at Steuart, SoMa ☎415/563-6084. Situated along the Embarcadero and boasting one of the few wood exteriors in the Downtown vicinity to survive the 1906 fire, this impressive space with its Belle-Epoque interior (wrought-iron lamps, brick ceilings) is the setting for Nancy Oakes' classic American cooking, which relies on old-fashioned ingredients such as squash and fennel. Start with an heirloom tomato salad with red onions and mozzarella *di bufala*, and be sure to save room for the terrific desserts. Precious few entrees fall under the $30 mark. Lunch on weekdays only.

Brenda's French Soul Food 652 Polk St at Eddy, Tenderloin ☎415/345-8100. Set on one of the more harmless blocks in its grotty neighborhood, this Creole hideaway dishes out decadent beignets (three for $5), huge biscuits, and fine omelettes and sandwiches, all with New Orleans sass. It's tiny, affordable, and becoming increasingly popular, so consider dropping in on a less busy weekday. Closed Tues.

Canteen Commodore Hotel, 817 Sutter St at Jones, Tenderloin ☎415/928-8870. The hard-edged decor may lack warmth, and the constantly evolving menu may be short on entree choices, but this humbly sized nouveau diner has gathered a fervent local following for its clever (if expensive) take on the New American style (veal tenderloin with artichokes, chicken with bacon and a ragout of lentils). The sole constant on the menu is the vanilla souffle, an unmissable dessert item. Brunch on weekends, lunch Wed–Fri only. Closed Mon.

Delancey Street 600 Embarcadero at Brannan, SoMa ☎415/512-5179. This waterfront restaurant is largely staffed by ex-convicts attempting to get back into life on the right foot, where the unique kitchen dynamic yields an array of tasty comfort food, from burgers to a variety of noodle dishes (all well under $20). The outdoor patio across the Embarcadero from the bay is a particularly delightful spot on sunny days. Closed Mon.

Dottie's True Blue Cafe 522 Jones St at O'Farrell, Tenderloin ☎415/885-2767. An intimate, inexpensive spot that's become immensely popular with locals and visitors – so much so, it draws early birds who wait outside for its 7.30am opening, so you can expect to wait regardless of what time you turn up. The oversize home-made pastries and breads (don't leave without trying the chili cornbread), as well as generous platters of breakfast favorites, make it worth your patience. Check the chalkboard for clever specials like chocolate-chip french toast doused in real maple syrup. Breakfast and lunch only; closed Tues.

Farmerbrown 25 Mason St at Turk, Tenderloin ☎415/409-3276. This excellent eatery uses organic ingredients from local and African-American farmers to deliver on its promise of "farm-fresh soul food." A young and diverse crowd packs the copper-and-brick industrial space nightly, as well as for the all-you-can-eat brunch each Sun (10am–3pm, $25), featuring raucous gospel ensembles and stone ground grits, sweet potato pie, and other Southern staples. Dinner only.

Pearl's Deluxe Burgers 708 Post St at Jones, Tenderloin ☎415/409-6120. An overlooked shoebox that cooks up some of San Francisco's finest budget burgers. You can easily sidestep beef by specifying a buffalo meat patty for a couple dollars extra; chicken, turkey, and veggie options are also scattered about the menu.

Australian/Kiwi

South 330 Townsend St at Fourth, Mission Bay ☎415/974-5599. The menu at San Francisco's only Down Under-inspired restaurant leans heavily on seafood plates such as barramundi fish ($24) and snapper ($23), while touches from other culinary cultures (Persian feta, *wasabi mayo*) provide surprising twists to certain dishes. Brunch is available on weekends, and the comfortable space also serves as a popular wine bar. Lunch Mon–Fri only.

British

The Old Chelsea 932 Larkin St at Geary, Tenderloin ☎415/474-5015. One of the few dedicated chippies in town, the deep fryers at this hole-in-the-wall produce fine chips and capably battered slabs of cod. The oft-surly manager opens the front door in late afternoon, while staff delivers cheap orders wrapped in the previous day's *Chronicle* to the *Edinburgh Castle* pub around the corner on Geary.

California

Coco500 500 Brannan St at Fourth St, SoMa ☎415/543-2222. Chef Loretta Keller delivers deeply flavorful Cal-Med cuisine in a chic setting warmed by caramel and blue walls adorned with local artwork. Don't miss the beef cheeks – whether as a main course with watercress and horseradish cream, or as an appetizer whipped into tasty "tacos" with *molé* – and the signature house cocktail made with Thai basil and kaffir lime vodka. Dinner entrees range $14–23. Lunch Mon–Fri only; closed Sun.

Caribbean

Primo Patio 214 Townsend St at Third, Mission Bay ☎415/957-1129. A terrific choice for a unique, budget lunch, where sandwiches, burgers, and similarly simple dishes are spiced with a subtle Caribbean twist – try the jerk chicken or blackened snapper. The backyard patio offers a pleasant escape from the industrial surroundings. Lunch only; closed Sun.

Chinese

Shanghai 1930 133 Steuart St at Mission, SoMa ☎415/896-5600. This sleek, downstairs destination, designed like a supper club with plenty of sexily decadent decor, has become one of the city's most respected Chinese restaurants. The menu features reasonably priced items, like shrimp and chestnut custard rolls, that reflect the international influences of Shanghai. There's live jazz nightly, and a cigar bar adjacent to the main room. Closed Sun.

Yank Sing 49 Stevenson St at First, SoMa ☎415/541-4949. One of the better (if more expensive) places for dim sum in the city. Though it's routinely packed, the waitstaff can almost always find a spot for you; come early to select from leftfield varieties like snow-pea shoot dumplings that populate the circulating carts. Brunch/lunch only.

Eclectic

Ananda Fuara 1298 Market St at Larkin, Civic Center ☎415/621-1994. Situated on a nondescript corner, this affordable and popular vegetarian restaurant casts a wide net – a group of four could easily sample meatless dishes spanning the culinary styles of Mexico, the Middle East, the American South, and South Asia. The neatloaf sandwich is a sharp choice, as is any one of the host of creative salads on offer. Closed Sun.

French

Crepes A-Go-Go 350 11th St at Folsom, SoMa ☎415/503-1294. Inexpensive, locally beloved crepe joint that got its start in Berkeley before finally opening a few locations in the big city. Several savory and sweet varieties are available, and in the true Parisian tradition, there's plenty of Nutella on hand. Branches: 2165 Union St at Fillmore, Marina; 1220 Polk St at Sutter, Polk Gulch.

Fleur de Lys 777 Sutter at Jones, Tenderloin ☎415/673-7779. An evening inside what is arguably San Francisco's most elegant dining experience will set you back a kingly sum (plan on parting with close to $100 per person), but the superb service, attention to detail, and most importantly, stunning food at this longtime local favorite will help you forget the cost. Four prix-fixe options (including a vegetarian one) are available to enjoy amidst the Moulin Rouge-inspired, tented surroundings. Dinner only; closed Sun.

Le Charm 315 Fifth St at Folsom, SoMa ☎415/546-6128. An unpretentious, mid-priced French place. The light, airy space (with a heated rear patio) is easily matched by southern French bean or fish soups and large, satisfying salads. The evening three-course prix fixe ($30) is a bargain. Lunch on weekdays only; closed Mon.

Irish

O'Reilly's Holy Grail 1233 Polk St at Sutter, Polk Gulch ☎415/928-1233. The Irish-imported stained-glass windows may outshine the food at this bright, curtain-accented destination along Polk St, but that's not to dismiss hearty dishes like the peat-smoked pork shank ($24) or Gaelic steak ($28). A flurry of oyster choices are popular appetizers, and there's a steady stream of live entertainment on the calendar. Dinner only.

Italian

Ristorante Umbria 198 Second St at Howard, SoMa ☎415/546-6985. The food at this corner spot is, unsurprisingly, devoted to the Italian region of Umbria – signature, truffle-inflected appetizers such as bruschetta misto litter the menu. Several outdoor tables line the sidewalks, where patrons enjoy oven-baked eggplant or rigatoni sauteed with pancetta (both $15.75). Lunch on weekdays only; closed Sun.

Japanese

Kyo-Ya Palace Hotel, 2 New Montgomery St at Market, SoMa ☎415/546-5090. Although it may seem as if *Kyo-Ya* caters exclusively to expense account-wielding Japanese businesspeople, it's also popular with well-heeled locals who don't mind venturing into one of San Francisco's most storied hotels. Sushi and sashimi are the menu's stars, while the tranquil setting allows you to hold a conversation without having to raise your voice. Closed Sun.

Sanraku 704 Sutter St at Taylor, Tenderloin ☎415/771-0803. Decorated simply, this sushi purveyor also specializes in favorites like chicken teriyaki, miso soup, and tempura *donburi*. It's one of the more affordable Japanese places in this part of town, and conveniently, one of the best. Branch: the Metreon, 101 Fourth St at Mission, SoMa.

Latin American

Mochica 937 Harrison St at Fifth, SoMa ☎415/278-0480. Diminutive Peruvian hideaway specializing in small plates, ceviche, and punch-packing sangria. Many dishes, from the diced ahi tuna to the *papitas rellenas* (fried potatoes stuffed with chicken, egg, olive, and raisins), benefit from

uncommonly flavorful sauces and marinades. Most entrees are under $18. Closed Tues.

Mediterranean/Middle Eastern

A La Turca 869 Geary St at Larkin, Tenderloin ☎415/345-1011. An inexpensive, yet highly regarded Turkish restaurant on one of the Tenderloin's less slummy blocks, *A La Turca* specializes in *pides* – baked flatbread stuffed with vegetables, meat, and/or cheese. Overlook the minimal decor and linger for the outstanding *kunefe,* a luscious dessert topped with honey and filled with sweet cheese.

Saha Hotel Carlton, 1075 Sutter St at Larkin, Tenderloin ☎415/345-9547. Serving food that combines elements of Yemenese Arabic cooking with the fresh ingredients associated with California cuisine, this classy place has become one of the hottest Middle Eastern restaurants in town. There's a three-course prix fixe for $40; a vegetarian version is only $30. Excellent wine list. Dinner only; closed Sun & Mon.

Tajine 1338 Polk St at Bush, Polk Gulch ☎415/440-1718. Tiny eatery dishing out excellent Moroccan dishes, from kebab plates and pastries to hearty bowls of its namesake stews, all at bargain prices. Friendly owner/chef (and former taxi driver) Mohamed Ghaleb is usually on hand to greet patrons. Cash only.

Mexican

Chavo's 595 Bryant St at Fourth, SoMa ☎415/495-5822. Brave the compound-like entrance, cold industrial surroundings, and adjacent freeway for some of the finest (and cheapest) Mexican dishes in SoMa. This informal eatery specializes in tender, marinated chicken, and anyone unafraid of lard will want to sample the deliciously pasty refried beans. Lunch only.

Maya 303 Second St at Folsom, SoMa ☎415/543-2928. One of the few truly upmarket Mexican restaurants in town, this longtime local favorite proves that, indeed, guacamole can be presented in gourmet fashion. Try the shrimp sauteed with tequila *chipotle* and lime ($21), or the braised pork shoulder with habañero ($19). If you're on a budget, grab a few of the exceptional tacos or a top-rate burrito from the adjacent lunch-only take-out counter.

Taqueria El Castillito 370 Golden Gate St at Larkin, Civic Center ☎415/292-7233. Overshadowed by other higher-profile names in the taqueria-rich Mission, this sparsely decorated bolthole concocts burritos every bit the equal of those made by its more celebrated neighbors a mile or two south. Hearty morning-eaters should visit before lunch for a chance to plow through one of the "Little Castle"'s super breakfast burritos, an early-day gutbomb that replaces rice with scrambled eggs. One of four San Francisco locations; cash only.

Pan-Asian

Ame St Regis Hotel, 689 Mission St at Third, SoMa ☎415/284-4040. Sequestered within the luxurious *St Regis*, this relative newcomer has set the San Francisco dining scene ablaze with its inventive, California-fied take on Far East seafood dishes. The custom-built marble bar is a sight in itself, while the large room is lent intimacy by dark wood paneling and gorgeous curtains. Many main courses soar above $35. Dinner only.

Asia SF 201 Ninth St at Howard, SoMa ☎415/255-2742. Notorious hotspot where gender-illusionist servers perform cheeky dance routines on the bar throughout the evening. The saki martinis are delicious and deadly, while the equally crossbred food (fish burgers, duck quesadillas, truffled *soba* noodles) is surprisingly successful, given the campy surroundings. Prices are surprisingly moderate, and it's popular with large groups (although best avoided by quiet types). Dinner only.

Golden Era 572 O'Farrell St at Leavenworth, Tenderloin ☎415/673-3136. Cheap, clean, and good subterranean restaurant in the heart of the Tenderloin, with all dishes served absent of meat, fish, egg, and MSG. The menu swerves through Thai, Chinese, and Japanese and features many soy-based items set in quotation marks ("beef," "chicken," etc); alternately, a number of entrees are entirely vegetable-based. Closed Tues.

Portuguese

Grubstake 1525 Pine St at Polk, Polk Gulch ☎415/673-8268. Housed in a decommissioned cable car, this old-fashioned diner serves all the American basics; the brave go

for the meat loaf. The real draw, however, are the ten or so Portuguese specialties on offer, including *bacalhau à gomes de sà* (codfish with potato, onion, eggs, parsley, and olives). Open until 4am, it's always a popular late-night destination, so beware of rowdy inebriates once the Polk St bars shut down. Brunch on weekends.

Sandwiches/soup

Caffe Centro 102 South Park St at Jack London, SoMa ☎415/882-1500. A neighborhood favorite serving terrific, affordable sandwiches and salads in comfort. Although there are a few tables inside (as well as out on the leafy South Park sidewalk), the take-out window is a better bargain. Breakfast and lunch only.

🏃 **Crossroads Café 699 Delancey St at Brannan, SoMa** ☎415/836-5624. Waterfront-adjacent offshoot of the Delancey Street restaurant around the corner. The sprawling, inexpensive menu covers all three meals and ranges from fruit smoothies and egg sandwiches to creative salads and tapas dishes, while the relaxed setting encourages lingering – you could easily spend the better part of a morning or afternoon browsing the magazines at the bookshop near the food counter, or enjoying the sunny courtyard along the Embarcadero. Closed Sun evening.

Saigon Sandwich 560 Larkin St at Eddy, Tenderloin ☎415/474-5698. Closet-sized, lunch-only shop selling sizable, made-to-order *bahn mi* (Vietnamese sandwiches) for no more than $2.50: choose between BBQ chicken, BBQ pork, and meatballs, then ask the hardworking ladies behind the counter to add lashings of fresh carrot and bundles of *cilantro*. Expect a line out the door every afternoon. Cash only.

South Asian

Mehfil 600 Folsom St at Second, SoMa ☎415/974-5510. While the table service at the corner Indian restaurant is fine in its own right, it's the take-out lunch specials (available until 3pm) that are the real draw here: choose between four delectable North Indian specialties, all with basmati rice, for no more than $6 each. Dinners are bit more expensive, but still reasonable. Lunch on weekdays only.

Pakwan 501 O'Farrell St at Jones, Tenderloin ☎415/776-0160. Though it's certainly not much to look at on the outside (or the inside, for that matter), the excellent, bargain-priced food at this Tenderloin staple has been drawing in plenty of patrons since it opened in 1999. Vegetarian items like *saag daal* (lentils and spinach) are perennial favorites, as are the various tandoori dishes scattered throughout the menu. Combat all the heady spice with a rich mango lassi.

Shalimar 532 Jones St at O'Farrell, Tenderloin ☎415/928-0333. Another simple South Asian eatery in a neighborhood full of them, *Shalimar* serves delicious, cheap dishes made to order. The chicken tikka masala is the main attraction, while the lamb *saag* is just as exceptional (and generous in its portion). When you finally emerge, expect to smell as if you yourself have been doused in spices and baked in the tandoor oven. Branch:1409 Polk St at Pine, Polk Gulch.

Sultan 340 O'Farrell St at Mason, Tenderloin ☎415/775-1709. More inviting than other South Asian spots in the neighborhood, *Sultan* serves a wide variety of tandoor dishes – prawn, chicken, beef – as well as ample vegetarian options like *malai kofta* (stuffed potato patties). There's a moderately priced, all-you-can-eat lunch buffet on weekdays.

Southeast Asian

Bong Su 311 Third St at Folsom, SoMa ☎415/536-5800. Ultra-stylish restaurant/lounge draws a beautiful crowd sipping hibiscus cocktails before settling in for pricey plates of caramelized black cod and mango tiger prawns. The bamboo-swathed interior helps foster an intimate mood, regardless of how crowded the space gets. Lunch on weekdays only.

Borobudur 700 Post St at Jones, Tenderloin ☎415/775-1512. Start with an order of *roti prata* (grilled, flaky bread) and curry dipping sauce at this Indonesian powerhouse, and you may be hooked for life. The affordable, vegetarian-friendly menu fuses Indian and Thai influences with often extraordinary results – the *kari sayuran* (assorted vegetables in coconut curry sauce) is particularly delicious.

Manora's Thai 1600 Folsom St at 12th, SoMa ☎415/861-6224. Light, flavorful Thai food of the highest order, from papaya salad and more ambitious seafood dishes such as *goong-grobb* (in-shell prawns in garlic sauce). It's no surprise that locals pack the place out night after night – the low entree prices certainly don't hurt. Lunch on weekdays only.

Pagolac 655 Larkin St at Ellis, Tenderloin ☎415/776-3234. The wait to get into this Little Saigon mainstay can require reserves of patience at peak times, but once you're presented with a plate of *Pagolac's* locally revered imperial rolls, you'll understand the draw. The tabletop grill meal is a fun DIY option, while the "seven flavors of beef" tasting menu is fine value at around $15. Lunch only; closed Mon.

Thai Stick 925 O'Farrell St at Polk, Tenderloin ☎415/776-8858. A smart option when other restaurants in the area are too crowded, as the masses seem to continually overlook this quiet, inexpensive winner on an outskirt block of the Tenderloin. *Long song* (sauteed spinach with choice of meat in peanut sauce) is a good choice; if it's a foggy evening, go with a soothing bowl of *tom yum* (hot and sour soup with vegetables and lemongrass).

Tu Lan 8 Sixth St at Market, SoMa ☎415/626-0927. This cramped, dingy space on one of the seediest blocks in town has been a local legend since superstar chef Julia Child first championed its cheap Vietnamese cooking. Should you sit at the sticky counter, you'll be nearly singed by the flames from the stove. Nevertheless, the populist food is consistently fresh and flavorful – just avoid looking up at the grubby ceiling.

The Mission, the Castro, and south

Although the Mission is instantly characterized by many as San Francisco's own Rice and Beans Central, there's much more to the neighborhood than its famous culinary export, the burrito. From the inventive New American menus at *Maverick* and *Spork* to San Francisco's most unique and diet-shattering selection of dessert spots, a visitor could spend a week eating well in the Mission and not set foot in a taqueria. In the neighborhoods around the Mission, you'll find a number of outstanding restaurants slightly off the beaten path, including top-grade thin-crust pizza at Glen Park's *Gialina*, true-to-form French cuisine at Potrero Hill's *Chez Papa*, and Himalayan treats at *Little Nepal* in Bernal Heights.

African

Bissap Baobab 2323 Mission St at 19th, Mission ☎415/826-9287. This bustling West African spot – decked out with bright murals on the walls and a thatched mat ceiling – attracts a diverse crowd of Mission hipsters and African expats. The vegetarian-friendly menu features dishes like vegetable and peanut *mafe* stew ($9.25) from Mali, as well as meatier choices including Senegalese *dibi* (grilled meat with onion sauce, $11.75). The hibiscus margaritas are strong and delicious, and don't pass over the vanilla ice cream-filled crème brulee. Closed Mon.

American

Al's Cafe 3286 Mission St at 29th, Mission ☎415/621-8445. A time machine that also happens to serve supercaloric comfort food, often brought to your table by aged hostesses who call you "sweetie" while refilling your coffee mug for the third time. Maiden Christina's Special ($8) combines nearly every breakfast item under the sun, while the country gravy available on other items is a nice touch. Breakfast and lunch only.

Barney's 4138 24th St at Castro, Noe Valley ☎415/282-7770. Burger standby that's still a great place to dive into a patty of beef (or chicken, turkey, or portobello); menu choices are generally $10. It's tucked away behind a short hedge on the western end of 24th Street's business strip, with a lovely front patio suitable for lingering. Choose from an endless array, from standard cheeseburgers to leftfield varieties like the Milano burger, which adds roasted eggplant, zucchini, and pesto sauce. Salads are generously sized and excellent, while the curly fries are justifiably renowned.

Boogaloos 3296 22nd St at Valencia, Mission ☎415/824-3211. Breakfast is the big draw here: black beans and chorizo feature heavily on the Latinized versions of American diner classics, while the Temple o' Spuds ($6.50) is an orgy of potatoes, melted cheese, sour cream, and green onions. Decor is basic, but perked up with bright orange and yellow tables, mosaics, and rotating art exhibitions on the walls. The crowd, meanwhile, often borders on the comically self-aware, and can make for hefty waits on weekends. Breakfast and lunch only.

Chenery Park 683 Chenery St at Diamond, Glen Park ☎415/337-8537. Comfortable, reasonably priced neighborhood haunt that's easily accessed via BART, where friendly servers present modern American dishes with occasional Cajun flair (*panko*-crusted catfish, spicy seafood gumbo). The wine list leans heavily toward California varietals; Tues is kids' night. Dinner only.

Firefly 4288 24th St at Douglass, Noe Valley ☎415/821-7652. Tucked away in the tree-lined folds of sleepy Noe Valley, this unpretentious spot concocts New American dishes from ingredients both local and farflung. The menu features an unusually abundant array of vegetarian options, and there's a $35 three-course prix-fixe deal Sun–Thurs. Dinner only.

Hard Knox Cafe 2526 Third St at 22nd, Potrero Hill ☎415/648-3770. Honest-to-goodness, moderately priced soul food on the eastern edge of San Francisco – excellent BBQ spare ribs, spicy chicken sandwiches, and robust sides like collard greens and red beans with rice. The interior decor can only be described as "modern Quonset hut," its aluminum walls covered in vintage beverage and traffic signs. Branch: 2448 Clement St at 25th, Outer Richmond.

Just for You 732 22nd St at Third, Potrero Hill ☎415/647-3033. One of San Francisco's true gems, this out-of-the-way destination produces some of the finest, fluffiest (and largest!) beignets outside of New Orleans – take home an extra, all slathered in powdered sugar, for a dollar and change. All breads are home-made (try the raisin cinnamon toast), while the enormous pancakes are the stuff of legend. Service can be as sassy as some of the signs around the place ("We reserve the right to pour coffee on your cell phone; please put it away"). Most everything's under $10. Breakfast and lunch only.

Liberty Café 410 Cortland Ave at Bennington, Bernal Heights ℗415/695-8777. The front of this secluded restaurant/bakery/bar dishes up delicious pies, both savory (chicken pot) and sweet (banana cream). The rear is a café serving full meals like seared day boat scallops and pan-roasted chicken breast for $15 and up, while on the back patio, a delightful wine bar is open Thurs–Sat evenings and also offers a limited menu. Brunch on weekends; closed Mon.

Maverick 3316 17th St at Mission, Mission ℗415/863-3061. The menu at this tiny (ten tables spread about two small dining rooms) and sparsely decorated spot features old favorites like baked mac 'n' cheese alongside plates of *Wagyu* steak atop a bed of seasoned haricot beans. As with many of the newer Mission destination restaurants, the crowd is mostly imported from other neighborhoods, so don't expect much in the way of hipster color. It's impossibly loud at times, although recent soundproofing has lessened the noise issue some. Most entrees exceed $20. Brunch on weekends; otherwise, dinner only.

Range 842 Valencia St at 19th, Mission ℗415/282-8283. One of the most celebrated restaurants to arrive on the local scene in recent years, *Range* attracts food sophisticates from far and wide for its wonderfully idiosyncratic design (look no further than the polished concrete bar) and top-shelf New American cuisine. The menu is in constant flux, but usually riffs on cozy items like white bean soup and fresh halibut ($22). Hope that the lemon pudding cake is on the evening's dessert menu. Dinner only.

Slow Club 2501 Mariposa St at Hampshire, Mission ℗415/241-9390. One of the first restaurants in San Francisco to embrace the sustainable slow-food movement – going so far as to work it into its name – this once-haughty haven has become friendlier and more inviting since its 1991 debut. Its decor remains an artful reflection of its industrial-chic neighborhood, while the menu relies on clever combinations like grilled pork loin with cider-braised cabbage ($15), as well as a good old-fashioned burger ($13). Brunch on weekends; lunch on weekdays only.

Spork 1058 Valencia St at 22nd, Mission ℗415/643-5000. Named in honor of the two-in-one "wonder utensil" foisted upon the world by this building's previous occupant, Kentucky Fried Chicken, this recent entrant packs in scenesters enjoying marvelous, humbly sized burgers, comically salty (but addictive) smashed potato fries, and similar, moderately priced comfort food. Its decor re-imagines items left behind by KFC: a hood that previously cooled deep fryers is now an overhead light.

Woodward's Garden 1700 Mission St at Duboce, Mission ℗415/621-7122. Awkwardly sequestered under the Central Freeway, this intimate spot makes patrons forget their exterior surroundings with gorgeously presented dishes like roast quail with artichoke-thyme stuffing ($20) that rely, in part, on ingredients grown in the restaurant's own garden. The name originates from the Woodward's Gardens amusement park that stood on the site in the nineteenth century. Dinner only; closed Sun & Mon.

Bakeries/tea

La Victoria 2937 24th St at Alabama, Mission ℗415/642-7120. Budget bakery selling various *empanadas* (stuffed pastries) and other Mexican delectables. Everything's made onsite and in large batches, so regardless of what time of day you wander in, they're bound to have just about everything on hand.

Samovar Tea Lounge 498 Sanchez St at 18th, Castro ℗415/626-4700. Earthy, cushion-filled café that serves more than a hundred varieties of tea, as well as tasty Asian snacks like baked tofu with miso chutney; the overstuffed wicker chairs are a great place to curl up with a book for the afternoon. The priciest cup is a $23 brew of 1940 vintage tea. There's a second location at Yerba Buena Gardens, 730 Howard St at Fourth, SoMa.

Tartine 600 Guerrero St at 18th, Mission ℗415/487-2600. Quite possibly San Francisco's most popular bakery, and with good reason: this boulangerie's pies, pastries, hot-pressed sandwiches, and fresh breads are some of the finest around. Consequently, lines often twist out the door.

California

Foreign Cinema 2534 Mission St at 21st, Mission ℗415/648-7600. The "dinner and a movie" concept is redefined at this upscale, expensive restaurant on an otherwise everyday section of Mission St, with films projected onto a large outdoor wall. The

▲ Foreign Cinema restaurant

menu is as noteworthy as the offbeat concept – the house-cured sardines and anchovies ($9) make for a tangy appetizer, while the exhaustive oyster-heavy raw bar ($2–2.50 per oyster) is showy. Main courses run $16–30.

Universal Cafe 2814 19th St at Bryant, Mission ☎415/821-4608. One of the first of the new breed of Mission restaurants to open in this industrial enclave, this sunny, slightly expensive outpost is still one of the best: wooden tables, chatty waitstaff, a clientele aged 25–40, and a weekly-changing menu of Californian staples such as pasta, meat, and fish, all from environmentally sustainable farms and ranches. Brunch on weekends; closed Mon.

Chinese

Eliza's 1457 18th St at Missouri, Potrero Hill ☎415/648-9999. Excellent California-fied Chinese cuisine at one of the few credible Asian eateries in this part of town. Dishes are moderately priced, despite the upmarket, vaguely French surroundings – try the house-special duck, available only Fri–Sat. Reasonable lunch specials. Branch: 2877 California St at Broderick, Western Addition.

Dessert

Bi-Rite Creamery 3692 18th St at Dolores, Mission ☎415/626-5600. A recently opened

offshoot of the fine market across the street, this tiny ice-cream shop hits all the right notes with its artisanal flavors. Usual suspects like mint chip and chocolate share freezer space with unique concoctions such as toasted coconut and honey lavender; there's also sorbet, as well as cakes, pies, and fruity popsicles. Commandeer one of the few benches on the sidewalk and sit with your frozen treat.

Bombay Ice Creamery 552 Valencia St at 17th, Mission ☎415/861-3995. As advertised, an ice-cream counter with an Indian slant. If it seems somewhat out of place in the heart of the Mission, it's nevertheless a popular place with locals and expats looking for a taste of super-sweet flavors like cardamom, masala tea, and cashew raisin.

La Copa Loca 3150 22nd St at Capp, Mission ☎415/401-7424. Remarkably authentic gelateria set amongst all the Latino businesses and eateries here, where three delicious scoops will run you a mere $3.50. A testament to *La Copa Loca*'s allure: several local Italian restaurants serve its gelato.

Mission Pie 2901 Mission St at 25th, Mission ☎415/282-1500. Celebrated pie retailer in a choice corner location. Although open only since 2007, it's already gained a fervent local following for its breadth of pie variations – ginger pear, strawberry rhubarb – and its sustainably minded ethics: the shop is closely affiliated with Pie Ranch, a wheat, honey, and dairy farm along the Santa Cruz coast.

Mitchell's Ice Cream 688 San Jose Ave at 29th, Mission ☎415/648-2300. *Mitchell's* produces its extensive selection of flavors onsite, from the mainstream (French vanilla, strawberry) to the far leftfield (avocado, sweet bean). Despite its somewhat desolate location at the southern end of the neighborhood, there's often a long line out the door, particularly on evenings, weekends, and warm days.

Eclectic

Baraka 288 Connecticut St at 18th, Potrero Hill ☎415/255-0387. Quiet, duskily lit place amidst Potrero Hill's restaurant row, with white flowers on every table and a menu that uses French, Spanish, and Mediterranean influences as springboards. Sides like roasted legumes and grilled flatbread complement seared rare *ahi* ($25) or saffron fettucini ($16). The $25 prix fixe ($35 with wine pairing) is a fine deal.

Savor 3913 24th St at Sanchez, Noe Valley ⊤415/282-0344. Stylish, slightly trendy, yet affordable spot along Noe Valley's most stroller-choked stretch. The shady rear patio's a terrific place to tuck into a hearty omelette, sandwich, or salad (all under $10), while there's a fireplace and plenty of tables inside for when the weather's less cooperative. The diverse menu also features a wide selection of crepes.

Sumi 4243 18th St at Diamond, Castro ⊤415/626-7864. This neighborhood stalwart, in business since the late 1980s, continues to please patrons with its specialty dish of miso roasted chicken, although other entrees (such as pan-roasted duck with port and fig reduction) are worth a look as well. The space itself is a quiet bolthole from the throbbing Castro scene. Most main courses run beyond $20. Dinner only.

French

Chez Papa 1401 18th St at Missouri, Potrero Hill ⊤415/824-8210. Once known only to Potrero Hill residents, this corner bistro has had its veil lifted in recent years. No wonder why: the wine list is extensive, the French fare is hearty and true to form, and the room always seems to be vibrant and buzzing. Signature dishes include the lamb daube ($19) and frites with aioli ($5). Branch: Mint Plaza, 414 Jessie St at Fifth, SoMa.

Chez Spencer 82 14th St at Folsom, Mission ⊤415/864-2191. With a vine-swathed cocktail garden outside and a vaulted loft dining space inside, this slightly off-the-beaten-path Francophile destination draws in a mixed crowd from all around town, despite the high prices ($80 for the tasting menu, $120 with wine pairing). The more budget-conscious may choose items à la carte, from truffle-scented mushroom risotto ($23) to wood-roasted whole squab ($36). Dinner only; closed Sun.

🏃 Le P'tit Laurent 699 Chenery St at Diamond, Glen Park ⊤415/334-3235. New entrant from veteran San Francisco restaurateur Laurent Legendre that's been an instant hit with Glen Park locals and savvy diners from all over. Carnivores won't want to miss the meaty cassoulet ($21,

complete with full leg of duck), while the service and overall vibe are equally warm. Conveniently, it's steps from the Glen Park BART station, making it quickly accessible from Downtown or even the East Bay. Memorable desserts. Dinner only.

Ti Couz 3108 16th St at Valencia, Mission ⊤415/252-7373. This enduringly popular creperie was one of the pioneers of the now-bustling Mission scene on Valencia St. It still holds its place as one of the finer inexpensive restaurants in town, serving savory buckwheat pancakes for under $10, along with flat, plate-served dessert crepes.

German

Walzwerk 381 Van Ness Ave at 15th, Mission ⊤415/551-7181. Cramped German eatery serving hearty comfort food like pork schnitzel with seasonal vegetables ($15) or bratwurst with mashed potatoes and sauerkraut ($16). Framed East German pop records and large portraits of twentieth-century Eastern Bloc industry evoke past eras behind the Iron Curtain. Dinner only.

Italian

Delfina 3621 18th St at Guerrero, Mission ⊤415/552-4055. Great fun, this continually buzzing, dinner-only restaurant attracts nearly every sort of San Franciscan – it's hard to find someone in town who *hasn't* eaten at *Delfina*. The light, Cal-Ital dishes, such as gem lettuce salad with aged gorgonzola ($10) and roasted duck with cherries and polenta ($25), rarely miss. Call well ahead for a reservation if you'd like to get in at prime dining hours; otherwise, just show up and hope for an available spot or two at the eight-seat counter or five-seat bar. Also worth trying is *Pizzeria Delfina* next door, featuring over a half-dozen thin-crust varieties ($10–15) at lunch and dinner.

Emmy's Spaghetti Shack 18 Virginia St at Mission, Mission ⊤415/206-2086. This dark, überfunky nightspot is always filled with local hipsters who give it a laid-back, unpretentious vibe. The simple, tasty food makes it even more appealing: try a hefty plate of spaghetti and house meatballs for under $10. Dinner only.

Gialina 2842 Diamond St at Kern, Glen Park ⊤415/239-8500. Down in up-and-coming Glen Park, this Neapolitan-style outpost has quickly gained a strong foothold in San

Francisco's steadily improving pizzeria scene; the menu changes frequently, but there's always a strong emphasis on fresh, seasonal vegetables. Dining quarters are charming but cramped, but since no reservations are taken, expect to take advantage of the wine list to make your wait a bit more enjoyable. Pies run $11.50–17. Dinner only.

Incanto 1550 Church St at Duncan, Noe Valley ☎415/641-4500. Stately Noe Valley spot specializing in Northern Italian dishes infused with California sensibilities: *pappardelle* with porcini ($17), *salsiccia* (sausage) with braised fennel ($19), and other rustic options abound. The staff's helpful with recommending bottles from the all-Italian wine list. Dinner only; closed Tues.

Pauline's Pizza 260 Valencia St at 14th, Mission ☎415/552-2050. Moderately priced, sit-down pizzeria next door to the former Levi Strauss Co. plant in the northern reaches of the Mission. The pie menu ranges from bold (pesto, $18.75 for large) to out-and-out quirky (Louisiana Andouille, $21.25 for large), with vegan options available. The house wine is Pauline's own Pizza Red ($10 for a 375ml half-bottle), while most ingredients are grown in the restaurant's organic garden. Dinner only; closed Sun & Mon.

Ristorante Bacco 737 Diamond St at Elizabeth, Noe Valley ☎415/282-4969. Dark tiled floors and an airy dining space lend elegance to this restaurant that's worth a diversion from the beaten path. Try the namesake antipasti ($11), which includes *arugula*, radicchio, walnuts, gorgonzola, and balsamic dressing; save room for the exceptional tiramisu ($8). Main courses run $17–27. Dinner only.

Serrano's 3274 21st St at Valencia, Mission ☎415/695-1615. An overwhelming number of potential toppings at this poorly ventilated, no-nonsense pizza joint between the Mission and Valencia corridors. Slices invariably arrive double-sized and slathered in melted mozzarella. Plastic tables flank the door if you'd like some fresh air with your slices.

Japanese

Nihon 1779 Folsom St at 14th, Mission ☎415/552-4400. Several blocks from the Mission's nexus, you'll find this moderately priced, *izakaya*-style hideaway on a warehouse-laden stretch of Folsom St. Excellent sushi and unusual small plates like coke kobe are the main magnets, while the upstairs whiskey lounge could encourage you to stick around after the meal. Dinner only; closed Sun.

Sushi Zone 1815 Market St at Guerrero, Castro ☎415/621-1114. Local sushi enthusiasts brave interminable waits to get into this long-popular spot that seats about two dozen. Plan for an early arrival (the door opens at 5pm) to secure a spot, then choose from an inventive list of rolls incorporating citrus fruits such as mango and papaya. Prices are moderate – under $20. Dinner only; closed Mon.

Tokyo Go Go 3174 16th St at Guerrero, Mission ☎415/864-2288. There's a celebratory atmosphere at this clubby, brightly lit Japanese spot set amidst 16th St's hipster bars and boutiques. Signature dishes include beef tataki and tuna tartare; the sushi menu focuses on seasonal catches, with the roll call of choices ($3.50 each) ranging from *hamachi* to *albacore*. Dinner only.

Latin American

El Trébol 3324 24th St at Mission, Mission ☎415/285-6298. Run by a husband-and-wife team, this café serves excellent versions of Nicaraguan standards like *churrasco* (grilled beef) and *chancho con yucca* (fried pork) in a haphazard atmosphere washed with Latin music. The mouth-puckering *tamarindo* beverage is a singular experience. Most dishes cost well under $10.

Espetus Churrascaria 1686 Market St at Gough, Mission ☎415/552-8792. Extra-pricey Brazilian *rodizio* where the all-you-can-eat menu is a decadently crafted paean to meat on sticks. Skewers are the unquestioned stars of the show – servers roam the large room, offering freshly cooked chicken hearts, filets, lamb, and the like. Each diner receives a two-sided circular chip: Display the green side to let the waitstaff know you're ready to be served, and the red side to indicate it's time for a pillow and nap. Expect to spend at least $45 per person.

Limón 524 Valencia St at 16th, Mission ☎415/252-0918. The highest-profile of a new, stylish breed of South American restaurants around San Francisco, Peruvian entry *Limón* wows patrons with deeply flavorful signature ceviche dishes like *corvina* ($14) and *crema de rocoto* ($13.75). Additionally, the sangria packs a significant wallop. Lunch Tues–Fri only.

Mi Lindo Peru 3226 Mission St at Valencia, Mission ☎415/642-4897. Colorfully decorated, unpretentious, and moderately priced eatery on a lower stretch of Mission St. The emphasis is on the simpler side of Peruvian cooking – expect generous piles of *arroz con pollo*, as well as other dishes built around meat and rice. Make it a destination on a chilly day or night to order one of the huge bowls of seafood soup.

Panchita's 3 3115 22nd St at Capp, Mission ☎415/821-6660. A local chainlet of Salvadorean-Mexican fusion cafés – a bit more upscale than most of the neighborhood's taquerias, with pygmy palm trees and white tablecloths. Try some of the finest Salvadorean *pupusas* in town here: chunky corn tortillas grilled and stuffed with a choice of fillings, all for about the price of a bottle of beer.

Radio Habana Social Club 1109 Valencia St at 22nd, Mission ☎415/824-7659. Patently quirky Cuban hole-in-the-wall, with a few tables jammed together and walls covered with picture frames and knicknacks. The food on the short menu is cheap and tasty, especially the chicken tamal; the crowd's an eclectic mix of old-timers and hipsters, and most everyone in the place drinks sangria. Dinner only; closed Tues.

San Miguel 3263 Mission St at 29th, Mission ☎415/641-5866. The best place in San Francisco for hearty Guatemalan fare: carne asada topped with chirmol sauce ($10), a rotation of dense seafood soups ($12), and simple sandwiches for around $5. It's family-owned and operated, so you can expect to be treated with warmth. Closed Wed.

Mediterranean/Middle Eastern

Goood Frikin Chicken 10 29th St at Mission, Mission ☎415/970-2428. Superbly seasoned poultry that warrants the extra 'o' in this airy restaurant's goofy name. Fluffy pita bread is an ideal accompaniment to the house specialty: a rotisserie half-chicken ($7.95), roasted with an abundance of delectable herbs and spices. Kebab dishes are just as delicious. The recently expanded dining room is cast in various earthtones, with the ceiling and walls covered in soothing landscape murals.

La Méditerranée 288 Noe St at Market, Castro ☎415/431-7210. Neighborhood staple serving delicious, unexpected dishes like chicken pomegranate ($11.75) and Lebanese *kibbeh* ($12.25); the "quiche of the day" option includes three vegetarian slices for $10.75. It's a pleasant place for a relaxed meal, free from the Castro's sceney environs. Branch: 2210 Fillmore St at Sacramento, Pacific Heights.

Truly Mediterranean 3109 16th St at Valencia, Mission ☎415/252-7482. *Truly Med's* inexpensive *shwarmas* are wrapped in thin, crispy lavash bread – though there's barely anywhere to sit and eat them in the tiny windowfront restaurant that's open late most nights. The busy staff's spontaneous singing and dancing is a bonus.

Mexican

El Metate 2406 Bryant St at 22nd, Mission ☎415/285-7117. Although *El Metate's* burritos have improved significantly, its tacos and quesadillas ($5–7) have been drawing people to this outer Mission eatery since it opened in the early 2000s. The atmosphere's as pleasant as any in the neighborhood, with the adjoining dining room washed in vibrant yellow and dotted with foliage; there are also several tables outside.

La Taqueria 2889 Mission St at 25th, Mission ☎415/285-7117. Pass on the often sloppy, poorly constructed burritos at this Mission stalwart and head straight for the menu's true strength: the super taco (under $6, including guacamole). The frantic staff is constantly slicing and chopping sizzling pork and beef behind the counter, so if it's crowded (which it usually is), order from the floating worker in front of the counter, grab a seat at one of the communal benches (or at the outside counter), and enjoy one of the fruitiest *agua fresca* beverages in town.

Mariachi's 508 Valencia St at 17th, Mission ☎415/621-4358. It's ironic that San Francisco's healthiest taqueria menu – well over a dozen vegetarian burrito options are available – serves what may be the most delicious refried beans in the city. The menu indeed sprawls endlessly, so go with the exceptional super *chile relleno* burrito ($6.95), a cheese-laden, meatless confection that's surprisingly light. Other offbeat fillings, including cactus, are also available.

Papalote 3409 24th St at Valencia, Mission ☎415/970-8815. With a particular emphasis

San Francisco's super burrito

Philadelphia has its cheesesteaks, New York its pastrami sandwiches, and Texas its barbecue and 22-oz sides of beef. In San Francisco, the **super burrito** is not only the premier bargain food, but truly a local phenomenon. The city is home to well over 150 **taquerias** – informal Mexican restaurants specializing in tacos, quesadillas, tortas, and of course, burritos – and locals are often heard debating their favorites effusively.

The civic obsession can be traced to September 1961, when El Faro Market's Febronio Ontiveros imaginatively concocted an outsized version of the burrito. Ontiveros' most loyal customers were hungry firemen in his Mission District neighborhood looking for a bulky, handheld lunch alternative to a sandwich. The takeout-friendly slabs of food were an instant hit, and before the end of the decade, a handful of establishments specializing in this new homestyle Mexican-American fast food had popped up around the

▲ A San Francisco taqueria

Mission. By the 1980s the San Francisco super burrito had reached critical mass, and today taquerias extend from one end of the city to the other.

San Francisco's take on the burrito differs from its Southern California cousin not only in its comparatively gargantuan size, but also in its ingredient list. Whereas a San Diego-style burrito can be an austere meal of meat, cheese, and salsa scattered about a standard-size tortilla, the San Francisco version stuffs a jumbo tortilla with any number of grilled or barbecued meats, Spanish rice, beans (choices include whole pinto, black, or refried), melted cheese, *pico de gallo* (a splashy mix of diced tomato, onion, jalapeño, and cilantro), guacamole or slices of avocado, a splatter of salsa, and even sour cream. And with its emphasis on vegetables, grain, and beans, the burrito also easily lends itself to vegetarian and vegan variants.

Most San Francisco taquerias wrap their goods in aluminum foil for easy handling, as the majority of locals eat burritos by hand. Surprisingly to many first-timers, a smartly constructed burrito will create little if any mess, although it's always a good idea to have napkins on hand. Expect to pay anywhere from $5–8 for a super burrito, and to not have much of an appetite for hours afterward. Additionally, certain taquerias offer gratis home-made tortilla chips and salsa as an appetizer. Pass on the utensils, order a Mexican beer or non-alcoholic *agua fresca* (fruit drink) with your foiled meal, and you'll fit right in.

Two locally produced websites, Ⓦwww.burritoeater.com and Ⓦwww.burritophile .com, feature detailed listings and reviews of San Francisco burrito shops.

on fresh ingredients and meatless menu options, Papalote serves peerless Cal-Mex cuisine that's remarkably affordable (everything's well under $10), given the high quality. There's nary a poor choice to be made from the marinated tofu burrito to anything that includes the perfectly grilled carne asada, while the complimentary offering of warm chips and otherworldly chipotle salsa is the real *coup de grace*.

Don't be scared off by the constant crowds – nobody stays long, so you can always find somewhere to sit. Branch: 1777 Fulton St at Masonic, Western Addition.
Tacos El Tonayense Harrison St at 22nd, Mission Ⓣ415/550-9192. Part of a local fleet of "taco trucks," this kitchen on wheels usually sets up its mobile shop at this corner – look for the small crowd of white hipsters and Latinos jostling to order

miniature tacos on morsel-sized tortillas for $1.50 each (on-the-mark super burritos are also available for $6). Seating is minimal at best, so find a nearby bar or park and chow away. Three other *Tonayense* trucks are found around the Mission; check the blocks north from this one along Harrison St.

Taqueria Can-cún 2288 Mission St at 19th, Mission ☎415/252-9560. This standby taqueria features a rose-strewn shrine to the Virgin Mary and some of the finest grilled tortillas in the Mission. The kitchen staff is uncommonly generous with avocado, while the home made *horchata* (an unlikely rice-cinnamon drink) is the ideal foil for one of the terrific, budget-priced super burritos (about $5). For a belt-busting eye-opener, drop in for breakfast. Open late nightly. Branches: 3211 Mission St at Valencia, Mission; 1003 Market St at Sixth, SoMa.

Taqueria Guadalajara 2798 Mission St at Onondaga, Excelsior ☎415/469-5480. Apart from excellent *carnitas* (fried pork) dishes and solid burritos ($6), the chief draw at this corner taqueria in the ungentrified Excelsior is the notorious mango *habañero* salsa – it's likely the spiciest available in San Francisco, so make sure you've got plenty of beverage on hand before unleashing its fury. Branch: 3142 24th St at Shotwell, Mission.

🏃 **Taqueria San Francisco 2794 24th St at York, Mission** ☎415/641-1770. The quintessential San Francisco burrito shop (look no further than its name), regular customers at this corner storefront like to sit at the counter a few feet from the kitchen grills and discuss Mexican *futbol* with the cooks. There's a jar of pickly, peppery *pico de gallo* on each tabletop, and bouncy tuba-pop oozing from the jukebox on the wall. Burritos are characterized by generous heft, flaky tortillas, and rustic meats like *al pastor* (rotisserie-grilled pork) and, for the especially adventurous, *lengua* (tongue) and *sesos* (brain). Cash only.

Sandwiches/soup

Ike's Place 3506 16th St at Sanchez, Castro ☎415/553-6888. Operating a sandwich shop that accepts reservations (it's *that* popular), Ike and his staff take many of their orders ahead on the phone, so even if there isn't a throng milling about, you may have a bit of a wait ahead of you. It's worth it: the sometimes sloppy, always ambrosial creations (all around $8) are available in a number of ways – meat-stuffed, vegan, slathered (or not) in Ike's secret Dirty Sauce. And there's a free lollipop with every order. Lunch only.

M & L Market 691 14th St at Market, Castro ☎415/431-7044. Also known to some as May's Market – and to the overly sensitive as the lair of the "Sandwich Nazi" – this humble grocery includes a deli run by a small crowd of Korean women who've been known to lose their patience with wishy-washy customers. Be sure to have your order straight before stepping to the counter (hint: specify your desired bread first), and prepare to indulge in a hearty, double-decker doorstop of a meal. Lunch only; closed weekends.

Seafood

Anchor Oyster Bar 579 Castro St at 19th, Castro ☎415/431-3990. Small seafooder where the salads and shellfish are best enjoyed with a seafood cocktail. Despite having been at this location on a less rambunctious stretch of Castro St for decades, it remains a surprising secret to many locals. It's on the expensive side (you'll spend around $30 per person), but a fun splurge.

Weird Fish 2193 Mission St at 18th, Mission ☎415/863-4744. Mistruth in advertising: the fish here isn't particularly weird. However, it is delicious, and there aren't many places like this that serve breakfast – create your own scramble for only $6 (a bit more if you want oysters). Later meals see a minor hike in prices, but remain adventurous, and there's no shortage of tofu- and veggie-inclusive choices on the menu. Open late on weekends.

Woodhouse Fish Company 2073 Market St at 14th, Castro ☎415/437-2722. Everything you'd find on the Maine coast or Cape Cod is available here at this New England-style fish house on the edge of the Castro: lobster rolls ($16.50), white clam chowder (cup/$4.50, bowl/$6.50), and steamed PEI mussels with garlic bread ($9.95). There's even Shipyard Ale (a Maine staple) available for about $4 a bottle. The corner location's fun for people-watching.

South Asian

Dosa 995 Valencia St between 20th and 21st, Mission ☎415/642-3672. Casually stylish *Dosa*'s namesake crepe-like item – and its close cousin, the thicker *uttapam* – are the real stars of the menu, while the *channa* (often available as a side dip) is pure heaven in a small bowl. The staff's exceptionally helpful to first-time diners, while the terracotta dining room is welcoming and not too noisy. Most main courses run $12–15, and reservations are only taken for groups of five or more, so arrive early or expect to wait. Brunch on weekends; otherwise, dinner only.

Little Nepal 925 Cortland Ave at Folsom, Bernal Heights ☎415/643-3881. With its pine furniture and crisp white tablecloths, this hospitable neighborhood eatery is a comfortable place to try moderately priced, Indian-inflected dishes like *poleko machha* (tandoori-baked salmon) or *tofu tarkari* (tofu and green bean curry). Dinner only; closed on Mon.

Zante 3489 Mission St at Cortland, Mission ☎415/821-3949. Getting points for uniqueness, if not for ambience and charm, this scruffy spot at the south end of the Mission specializes in curry pizzas, a uniquely flavorful invention. The house special ($23 for a large) tops a thick crust with tandoori chicken, lamb, and a host of vegetables and herbs (spinach, eggplant, ginger). Several meatless options are also available.

Southeast Asian

Angkor Borei 3471 Mission St at Cortland, Mission ☎415/550-8417. One of the few Cambodian restaurants in San Francisco, *Angkor Borei*'s low prices and alluringly aromatic food make it terrific value. Try the *nhoam lahong* (green papaya salad, $6.65) or the slices of beef in a peanut curry sauce ($8.65). Duck in during the afternoon

for the lunch specials, when prices are even lower.

Palencia 3870 17th St at Noe, Castro ☎415/522-1888. Young, Manila-born chef Drey Roxas directs the kitchen at this stylish Filipino spot on the former site of a Hawaiian restaurant. Sharp flavors come through in the *kilawin na isda* ($9), a small plate dish that presents red snapper marinated in sugar-cane vinegar. Staples such as crepe-like *lumpia* ($7.50) are also available. Brunch on Sun; otherwise, dinner only. Closed Mon.

Thai House Express 599 Castro St at 19th, Castro ☎415/864-5000. Street-style Thai food, much like what you'd get in Bangkok. Try the *gui chai* (vegetarian chive cakes, $6) before moving on to a main course of *kao na ped pa-lo* (five-spices duck over rice, $8) or *gang dang* (meat curry over rice, $7.25). Branch: 901 Larkin St at Geary, Tenderloin.

Zadin 4039 18th St at Noe, Castro ☎415/626-2260. The first Vietnamese restaurant to set up shop in the Castro – and as you'd expect in this well-primped neighborhood, it's as chic as can be. The menu incorporates several gluten-free ingredients, but *Zadin*'s pair of chefs (who also happen to be cousins) have ensured authenticity isn't spared: items such as *goi cuon ca* (basa fish rolls, $7.50) and *thit nuong* (lemongrass pork, $13) hit the mark. Dinner only; closed Mon.

Spanish

Ramblas 557 Valencia St at 17th, Mission ☎415/565-0207. Tapas eatery along the heart of Valencia St with artfully mismatched stools and mosaic-topped tables. Small plates like sauteed spinach with garlic and salmon rillets range from $3.75–9.50, while a few full-size paella dishes are available for $16–19. Brunch on Sun; otherwise, dinner only.

Haight-Ashbury and west of Civic Center

With newly opened restaurants *Nopa*, *SPQR*, and *Bushi-tei* quickly joining the ranks of the city's best-loved dining spots, this area has stepped out of the towering culinary shadows cast by its Downtown and Mission neighbors. It's also notable for its dense concentration of top California restaurants (including longtime favorites *Jardinière* and *Zuni*), as well as one of San Francisco's top pizza destinations, the Western Addition's *Little Star Pizza*.

African

🏃 **Massawa 1538 Haight St at Ashbury, Upper Haight** ☎415/621-4129. East African eatery that, despite its sometimes suffocating lack of ventilation, is a terrific spot. Don't expect to keep your hands clean as you stab at deliciously gloopy confections like *kelwa derho* (sauteed chunks of chicken in a thick and spicy sauce) with spongy *injera* bread, presented together family-style on a gigantic platter. Overlook the spare decor – the moderately priced food's excellent and hearty as you'll find anywhere. The traditional honey wine, however, is an acquired taste.

American

Blue Jay Cafe 919 Divisadero St at McAllister, Western Addition ☎415/447-6066. Neighborhood diner serving fairly priced comfort food to a clientele that's a signature Western Addition mix of dapper old black men and slouchy white hipsters. Sit at the U-shaped counter or on the pleasant patio, order a vintage soda to start, and follow with some crispy fried chicken, pork chops with apple chutney, or saucy ribs, and don't forget the extra cheesy mac 'n' cheese. The lunch menu mainly consists of sandwiches; breakfast is also available.

🏃 **Burgermeister 86 Carl St at Cole, Cole Valley** ☎415/566-1274. The original location of this increasingly popular local chainlet broils excellent gourmet burgers (made with Niman Ranch beef); all the usual mainstream choices are available, as well as a handful of unusual options for the adventurous (eg the mango burger). A half-pound slab runs a little under $10. Grab a seat of one of the few outdoor tables in front and watch the MUNI streetcars rattle by as you eat. Branches: 138 Church St at Duboce, Castro; 759 Columbus Ave at Filbert, North Beach.

J's Pots of Soul 203 Octavia St at Page, Hayes Valley ☎415/861-3230. Well-behaved soul food for a newly gentrified Hayes Valley – this dignified eatery feels like more like a comfortable parlor than a dining establishment. The kitchen fare is tidy but tasty (and affordable): a plate of delectable cinnamon French toast, with sprinklings of powdered sugar and a side of bacon, will only set you back $7.50. Breakfast and lunch only; closed Mon.

Kate's Kitchen 471 Haight St at Fillmore, Lower Haight ☎415/626-3984. When you first stare down at the monstrous plates of budget breakfast fare served here, it's a little hard to think about saving room for extras. But treat yourself to some hush puppies to take away – deep-fried lumps of corn meal served with honey-touched "pooh butter." Kate's signature item, however, is the "flanched flarney garney" – essentially a hefty, eggy breakfast sandwich that's more than worth the caloric plunge. The place is massively popular on weekends, so just sign your name on the sheet dangling by the door and wait until you're called.

Momi Tobys Revolution Café 528 Laguna St at Hayes, Hayes Valley ☎415/626-1508. The name may imply Che-level political fury, but the crowd at this hushed, vaguely Parisian café is more likely to be seen reading the arts section of the *New York Times* than *The Communist Manifesto* over their cups of coffee and plates of chicken tortilla casserole ($8.75). Tables under awning heaters stretch along the sidewalk for those seeking an al fresco experience.

Pork Store Cafe 1451 Haight St at Masonic, Upper Haight ☎415/864-6981. Grungy hangout on the neighborhood's main drag that's a good place to spot a mix of locals and weekend visitors. Brave the inevitable lines for burly portions of brunch standbys like eggs and French toast ($7–9); another artery-clogging option's the house special – two pork chops and suitably greasy hash browns ($8). Branch: 3122 16th St at Valencia, Mission. Closed evenings Mon, Tues & Sun.

Rosamunde Sausage Grille 545 Haight St at Fillmore, Lower Haight ☎415/437-6851. Tiny storefront grill with a few stools at the bar, serving inexpensive, top-grade grilled sausages on sesame rolls. Choose from a cherry-laced chicken number to the light flavors of a shrimp, scallop, and snapper sausage; the German potato salad's also a knockout. Savvy customers place their order, head next door to the *Toronado* (see p.219), and await their sausage's delivery over a beer. Also worth knowing: Tues at 11.30am, a limited number of half-pound burgers ($5.50) go on sale to an early-assembled crowd on the sidewalk.

Bakeries/tea

Benkyodo 1747 Buchanan St at Sutter, Japantown ☎415/922-1244. Selling hundreds of confectionary snacks daily – from *mochi* (soft rice cakes with filling) to *manju* (floury treats stuffed with red bean paste) – this popular Japanese bakery is one of San Francisco's oldest businesses. It's been in operation in the neighborhood since 1906, although it was closed through most of the 1940s when its owners, the Okamura family, were interned during World War II. Items are inexpensive, so it's easy to fill up on dessert for a small sum. Closed evenings and Sun.

Modern Tea 602 Hayes St at Laguna, Hayes Valley ☎415/626-5406. Bathed in natural light by day, this lovely corner space plays several roles: tea salon, restaurant, retailer, and art gallery. The tea selection is extensive almost to the point of intimidation, but friendly servers will help you navigate all the hot and iced varieties; the food menu is more compact and includes freshly prepared soups, salads, and on weekends, waffles made with nineteenth-century irons. Closed Sun evening, Mon–Tues.

Belgian

Frjtz 581 Hayes St at Laguna, Hayes Valley ☎415/864-7654. Trendy eatery that recently moved into a space directly next door to its original home, serving cones of thick and crunchy Belgian-style fries ($3.25 for small, $4.75 for large) with dips like creamy wasabi mayo and spicy yogurt-peanut. Sandwiches and crepes are also available under names like "Michelangelo" (roasted red pepper and grilled eggplant sandwich, $9.50) and "Duchamp" (mushroom, chicken, and spinach crepe, $9.75). Pity there's no back patio at the new location, but the nice Belgian-beer selection attempts to compensate. Branch: 590 Valencia St at 17th, Mission.

California

Asqew Grill 1607 Haight St at Clayton, Upper Haight ☎415/701-9301. The Haight outpost of this inexpensive local chain is a refreshing option, specializing in more than a dozen different kinds of grilled skewers – from pork, apple, and pear to shrimp, tomato, and squash. Save room for a delicious brownie. One of four San Francisco locations.

Citizen Cake 399 Grove St at Franklin, Hayes Valley ☎415/861-2228. Stylish, locally famed corner restaurant-bakery specializing in delectable pastries, cookies, and surprisingly strong California dishes like *carnaroli* risotto with peas, nettles, and fava beans ($22). Its signature cake, unsurprisingly also a nod to Orson Welles, is the "Rosebud," a rose-scented crème brûlée tart. Come for weekend brunch, when the menu's most appealing – try the generously portioned brisket hash with an egg for $12. Closed Mon.

Jardinière 300 Grove St at Franklin, Hayes Valley ☎415/861-5555. Run by local big-name chef Traci Des Jardins, this two-story brick space (formerly a jazz club) caters to a pre-opera/ballet crowd with valet parking and plenty of pomp. It's an indulgent splurge, but worth it for every impeccable plate passed your way. The entree menu changes regularly (although thankfully, the aged-cheese platter is a constant), but you can expect innovative dishes like Alaskan halibut with morel mushrooms ($37) or red wine-braised shortribs with horseradish potato purée ($35). Dinner only.

Nopa 560 Divisadero St at Hayes, Western Addition ☎415/864-8643. One of the most heralded newer restaurants in town, *Nopa* (so named for its North of Panhandle home in the Western Addition) features communal dining at long, amber tables in a cavernous space that formerly housed a laundromat. The baked pasta with spicy fennel sausage ($18) is a proven winner, as is the simple but near-perfect grass-fed hamburger ($12, with fries). The decibel-sensitive may blanch at the room's noise – request a table in the newly sound-proofed area beneath the mezzanine. Dinner only; open until 1am nightly.

RNM 598 Haight St at Steiner, Lower Haight ☎415/551-7900. Expensive hotspot that regularly tugs in visitors from less earthy neighborhoods around town. Utterly incongruous to its surroundings and tucked inside a renovated Victorian, *RNM* features a black aluminum awning and an entrance accented with chain-mail curtains. Chef/owner Justine Miner's cooking is graceful and decidedly Californian, from small plates like lobster and mascarpone ravioli or a duck confit pizza (both $14) to a limited menu of full entrees such as pancetta-wrapped pork tenderloin on polenta ($19). The squishy sofas at the mezzanine bar are particularly inviting. Dinner only; closed Sun & Mon.

Zuni 1658 Market St at Gough, Hayes Valley ☎415/552-2522. Once nouveau, now a staple, *Zuni* boasts the most famous Caesar salad in town – made with home-cured anchovies – and an equally legendary focaccia hamburger. The centrally located restaurant's decor is heavy on brick and glass, but the triangular space remains light and airy. If you take a deep breath and go with the custom-roasted chicken ($48), be sure you enjoy the company you're with – you're likely to wait an hour for it to emerge from the kitchen. Closed Mon.

Chinese

Abacus 2078 Hayes St at Cole, Western Addition ☎415/387-2828. Tasty modern Szechuan cuisine in a mellow corner of the Western Addition. Blonde wood paneling lends an air of elegance to lunch or dinner, best started with excellent egg rolls ($5 for four) or mushroom medley soup ($5) before moving on to fresh takes on favorites like *kung pao* chicken ($9), dressed in bell pepper and peanuts. Closed Sun.

Dessert

Yasukochi's Sweet Stop 1790 Sutter St at Buchanan, Japantown ☎415/931-8165. Best known for its heavenly coffee crunch cake ($2.95 for a slice, $25 for a whole cake), this dessert spot inside Japantown's Super Mira Market features other sweet treats in case it's sold out of its star attraction (which it sometimes is) – chocolate cake filled with fresh strawberry whipped cream is a smart backup choice. Closed evenings & Sun.
Jubili 1515 Fillmore St at O'Farrell, Western Addition ☎415/292-9955. Inexpensive frozen yogurt specialist craftily updates the 1980s soft serve frozen-dessert craze with a smattering of flavor choices (original, peach, strawberry sorbet) and a host of nuts, cookie bits, and fresh fruit (including blueberries and kiwi) as toppings. Smoothies and parfaits ($5–6) pad the menu.

Eastern European

Frankie's Bohemian Cafe 1862 Divisadero St at Pine, Western Addition ☎415/921-4725.

Single-room bar-restaurant on a busy street corner that pulls in groups of hearty eaters (and drinkers) to gorge on the house specialty, a burly Czech mess called *brambory* that piles meat and veggies atop a pan-fried bed of potato and zucchini. Like the burgers and salads also on offer, it runs about $10, while a 20-oz beer goes for about $6. Decor is rustic, with walls coated in warm, amber wood.

Eclectic

Herbivore 531 Divisadero St at Fell, Western Addition ☎415/885-7133. There's no meat or dairy in sight at this all-vegan restaurant, boasting popular dishes like lentil loaf with mashed potatoes or giant bowls of coconut noodle soup; everything's under $11. Large front windows look out onto the endlessly interesting Divisadero sidewalk. Breakfast available daily. Branch: 983 Valencia St at 21st, Mission.

French

Absinthe 398 Hayes St at Gough, Hayes Valley ☎415/551-1590. Expensive brasserie-cum-bistro with two separate dining areas, both serving robust French food in an old-world, if trendy, atmosphere. Try the onion soup gratinée ($8.25), pork confit ($24), and coconut *tres leches* cake or assorted cheeses (both $7) for dessert. The bar's a good option for drinks, since it's open until 2am and serves smallish snacks for $4–14 per plate. Avoid the siren call of the sidewalk tables, as area auto traffic is punishingly loud. Brunch on weekends; closed Mon.
Sophie's Crepes 1581 Webster St at Post, Japantown ☎415/929-7732. A solid bet for both *savory* and *sucré* crepes in the central part of the city, *Sophie's* stuffs its hand-held delicacies ($5–7) with an extensive choice of fillings – the banana-chocolate crepe is devilishly good, while the red-bean paste option nods toward this nook's Japantown surroundings.
Zazie 941 Cole St at Carl, Cole Valley ☎415/564-5332. Moderately priced Francophile eatery named after Frederic Malle's 1961 comedy of the same name. It's best known for outstanding breakfasts: light, fluffy pancakes and crumbly coffee cake are the house specialties. The back patio is the best place to sit on a sunny afternoon, while evening visits are rewarded with a terrific $23.50 prix fixe.

Italian

Bambino's Ristorante 945 Cole St at Parnassus, Cole Valley ☏415/731-1343. This inviting spot holds its own on a competitive restaurant block in quiet and reserved Cole Valley. Excellent risotto and pasta dishes ($14–19) are presented with subtle flair by a warm staff of servers, while a limited selection of similarly priced seafood pizzas (shrimp and mushroom; a sauceless salmon variety) offers a rare twist. Brunch on weekends.

🏃 **Little Star Pizza 846 Divisadero St at McAllister, Western Addition** ☏415/441-1118. One of San Francisco's top pizzerias, this dimly lit destination is packed nightly with hipsters enjoying its lively bar and jukebox blasting American and British indie rock. The kitchen bakes deep-dish and thin-crust pizzas with equal aplomb; large (12in) pies run $15–23. Dinner only; closed Mon. Branch: 400 Valencia St at 15th, Mission.

SPQR 1911 Fillmore St at Bush, Western Addition ☏415/771-7779. Affiliated with the Marina's *A16* (see p.182) and borrowing its name from a Latin acronym referring to the government of ancient Rome, this surprisingly moderately priced (entrees $17–19) *osteria* on the cusp of lower Pacific Heights sees a rush of patrons nightly. Reservations aren't accepted, so arrive early to enjoy a glass of wine and a fine plate of pasta; the braised lamb neck is also excellent. Brunch on weekends.

Japanese

Grandeho's Kamekyo 943 Cole St at Parnassus, Cole Valley ☏415/759-8428. Creative, moderately priced items dominate the menu at this family-owned place. The long, wooden sushi bar is popular with Cole Valley and Upper Haight locals, but if you're in the mood for something other than the house specialty, try the *chasoba* noodles. Lunch Tues–Sat only. Branch: 2721 Hyde St at North Point, Fisherman's Wharf.

Kiss Sushi 1700 Laguna St at Sutter, Japantown ☏415/474-2866. With a mere dozen seats available, you'll need to phone ahead for a reservation at this signless, blink-and-you'll-miss-it spot. It's also very expensive, with a full meal often running upwards of $65 per person. All that said, the expert chef and his wife (the establishment's sole two

▲ Sushi in Japantown

employees) go out of their way to make customers feel pampered – expect as many as eight courses if you order the *omakase* course (chef's choice) – although stories exist of particularly slow eaters being shown the door. Dinner only; closed Sun & Mon.

Maki 1825 Post St at Webster, Japantown ☏415/921-5215. One of several humbly sized eateries in the Japan Center to serve delicious, moderately priced fare, *Maki* specializes in both *wappan meshi* (a wood steamer filled with vegetables, meat, and rice) and *chawan mushi* (savory custard). It's also notable for its affable owner and sizable sake selection. Closed Sun & Mon.

Sebo 517 Hayes St at Octavia, Hayes Valley ☏415/864-2122. Despite having two Americans at the helm of the kitchen, this low-key destination serves some of the most authentic sushi in town. Elbow your way to a spot at the six-seat bar and let the chefs lead the way through a multicourse extravaganza: the five-course *omakase* course is about $60, while the seven-course option runs $80 or so. Dinner only; closed Sun & Mon.

Mediterranean/Middle Eastern

Baghdad Nights 682 Haight St at Pierce, Lower Haight ☏415/861-6111. New Iraqi entry on the Lower Haight scene features warm and accommodating staff, a lovely indoor balcony, lots of evocative dark-wood decor, and regular belly dancing. The *hammessa* appetizer is a mushroom lover's delight, while lamb and seafood entree dishes are aromatically enticing. Main courses run $12–16.

Mexican

Cuco's 488 Haight St at Fillmore, Lower Haight ☏415/863-4906. Family-operated Mexican-Salvadorean nook known for super-budget prices, fresh-cut *carnitas* (fried pork) and a smirky proprietress who usually double-checks if you'd like your meal extra-spicy. A clever vegetarian option here is the fried plantains burrito, while the home-made chips are oversize and often served warm. Don't come with a large group if you're looking for somewhere to sit – it's a tiny room. Cash only; closed weekends.

El Burrito Express 1812 Divisadero St at Bush, Western Addition ☎415/776-4246. Now one of the most heralded taquerias in town outside the Mission, this spot boasts an overwhelming burrito menu that holds something for everyone, with most everything costing about $6. The Bronco option passes on the rice, while the Expresso burrito is slathered in cheese and sauce (you'll need a knife and fork). Cash only; closed Sun. Branch (mostly take-out): 1601 Taraval at 26th, Outer Sunset.

Green Chile Kitchen 601 Baker St at Fulton, Western Addition ☎415/614-9411. Deeply flavorful cuisine from the state of New Mexico, further enhanced by robust red and green chilis. A bowl of hearty chicken stew ($7) is the perfect antidote to a chilly San Francisco evening, while a full plate of *tamales* (presented in their husks) with several small side items is only $10; request "Christmas" sauce for a dollar extra, and you'll get red and green chili on (or in) your meal. The handsome corner dining room encourages lingering at the window counter or one of the booths, and includes collections of dried chilis hung from hooks.

Pan-Asian

Bushi-tei 1638 Post St at Laguna, Japantown ☎415/440-4959. Elegant Japanese-inspired cuisine imbued with accents from other continents: lamb chops with port and *wasabi* ($30); roast duck with a mascarpone mustard sauce ($22); seared foie gras over pumpkin pot du creme ($20). The restaurant's gorgeous design includes glass walls that play off wood paneling from nineteenth-century Japan, while certain menu items go so far as to command the use of custom-designed dishware. Brunch on Sun; otherwise, dinner only. Closed Mon.

The Citrus Club 1790 Haight St at Cole, Upper Haight ☎415/387-6366. Vegan-friendly noodle house offering sauteed noodles in a wok or served in a variety of broths. The garlic beef and shiitake mushroom dish is also a good bet. Budget prices (everything on the menu's well under $10) suit the crowd of artfully distressed Haight hipsters well.

Poleng Lounge 1751 Fulton St at Masonic, Western Addition ☎415/441-1751. This restaurant-lounge presents delicious small (but generously portioned) plates of Asian street food, while the clubby aspects of the place (DJs, catwalk-ready servers, an extensive cocktail list) set it apart from other pan-Asian places in the city. *Cebuano* barbecue pork belly ($7), Buddha's Treasures (pan-fried dumplings with minced vegetables, $7.50), and crispy *adobo* wings ($7.50) anchor chef Timothy Luym's strong menu. As you'd expect, the kitchen serves late into the night. Closed Mon.

Sandwiches/soup

The Cheese Steak Shop 1716 Divisadero St at Sutter, Western Addition ☎415/346-3712. Odds are slim you'll bite into a finer cheesesteak sandwich in San Francisco than those you'll get at this immensely popular shop, started by a couple of Philadelphia expats in the early 1980s. The kitchen imports its buns, peppers, and even its Tastykake desserts from Philly; sandwiches come in three lengths (7-, 10-, and 12-in), run the gamut from a bacon cheesesteak to several chicken varieties, and cost between $5-9. Italian hoagies are also available.

Estela's 250 Fillmore St at Haight, Lower Haight ☎415/864-1850. This tiny but industrious shop serves more than thirty sandwich options on a variety of breads. Avocado plays a major role, and the vegetarian choices – including sandwiches built around smoked gouda and brie – are especially creative. There's also a choice of smoothies. Lunch only.

South Asian

Indian Oven 233 Fillmore St at Waller, Lower Haight ☎415/626-1628. Certainly one of the city's leading Indian restaurants, *Indian Oven* is known for its moderately priced baked tandoori items, but the fluffy naan bread is just as memorable; there's also an impressive selection of Indian beers. Despite its local notoriety, it's large enough that you usually won't have to wait long.

Metro Kathmandu 311 Divisadero St at Page, Lower Haight ☎415/552-0903. Nepalese spot with the alluring ambience of a French bistro. Start with a small plate of *momos* (steamed dumplings) before moving on to a dish of succulent, fall-off-the-bone *khasi* (goat) curry; a handful of *kulfi* (ice cream) desserts are worth looking forward to, and the wine list is surprisingly impressive. Entrees are $10–15, with a number of meatless options. Brunch on weekends; otherwise, dinner only.

Southeast Asian

Thai Place II 312 Divisadero St at Page, Lower Haight ☎415/552-6881. Not one of the city's

marquee Thai destinations, but it only means you'll be able to sit down immediately for exceptional plates of sizzling beef ($11) or honey-roasted duck on a bed of spinach ($9).

Thep Phanom 400 Waller St at Fillmore, Lower Haight ☎415/431-2526. This corner Thai spot pulls in diners from all over town – and often, beyond – for its fragrant curries ($9–14). The spinach with peanut sauce is sweet and sharp, while the Three's Company seafood medley in coconut sauce is equally divine. Dinner only.

The Richmond, the Sunset, and around

The **west side** neighborhoods may be short on destination restaurants, but they're full of excellent ethnic eateries (*Brothers Korean BBQ*, Moroccan kingpin *Aziza*) and wonderful niche spots (Irish bakery *John Campbell's*). The area's also home to notables like the groundbreaking *Thanh Long*, flashy-on-a-budget *Spices!*, and the unassailable *Gordo Taqueria*, as well as a pair of bustling Chinatown Wests (and their attendant dining spots) along Clement Street in the Inner Richmond and Irving Street in the Outer Sunset.

American

Bill's Place 2315 Clement St at 24th, Outer Richmond ☎415/221-5262. Classic burger place and soda fountain with back patio and a bit of a timewarp feel. Hamburgers are named after local personalities (Carol Doda, Paul Kantner), and most are well under $10; the milkshakes and ice-cream sundaes are righteously thick.

Bistro at the Cliff House 1900 Point Lobos Ave, Outer Richmond ☎415/386-3330. The less expensive sibling of downstairs fine-dining restaurant *Sutro's*, this seaside destination can still put a dent in your wallet, as the two restaurants share a similar dinner menu. Reliable choices include the clam chowder ($9) and grilled salmon in a light mustard glaze ($25). Views of the Pacific are spectacular anytime of day – all three meals are available, although reservations aren't.

Manor Coffee Shop 321 West Portal Ave at 14th, West Portal ☎415/661-2468. Inexpensive breakfast and lunch spot that's seemingly as old as the hills. Staples like rich omelettes and fluffy pancakes pack customers into cushy booths and a dining counter – it's home to a decidedly local crowd from West Portal and the surrounding neighborhoods. Breakfast is available well into the afternoon hours.

Pluto's 627 Irving St at Seventh, Inner Sunset ☎415/753-8867. Walk in through the dining area, pick up a paper menu as you get in line, and hand it to the servers behind the counter as you order. Custom salads are the big draw here, as they're among the biggest, best, and cheapest ($7 or so) in town. The freshly made sandwiches are tasty, but on the small side, while the turkey and stuffing is a soul-warming option any day of the year. You'll struggle to spend more than $10 on a feast. Branch: 3258 Scott St at Chestnut, Marina.

Q 225 Clement St at Third, Inner Richmond ☎415/752-2298. This lively outpost along Clement St's restaurant row is an over-the-top diner, sporting funky features such as a booth where a tree grows through the table. Portions are generous, and the menu's mostly comfort food like meatloaf on mashed potatoes and beer-battered catfish, although meatless choices are also available. The most expensive entree, a grilled flank steak, is $17. Brunch on weekends.

Bakeries/tea

Arizmendi 1331 9th Ave at Irving, Inner Sunset ☎415/566-3117. The artisanal breads and pastries are reason enough to head to this small, earthy bakery that's an offshoot of Berkeley's famed *Cheeseboard*, but its regular rotation of gourmet pizza is the true surprise treat. Baked goods and pizzas vary daily and everything's inexpensive (pizza slices are $2.25 each), so it's certainly worth visiting more than once. Closed Sun evening & Mon.

John Campbell's 5625 Geary Blvd at 20th, Outer Richmond ☎415/387-1536. Staunchly Irish bakehouse where San Francisco rarities like mince pie, soda bread, and pasties bring back customers again and again. Cardiologists may not necessarily recommend the amazing Belfast Bap breakfast sandwich ($5) – a giant round filled with cheese, egg, sausage, and bacon, so named for proprietor Campbell's former hometown – but you only live once. Closed evenings.

Wing Lee Bakery 503 Clement St at Sixth, Inner Richmond ☎415/668-9481. Cheap, no-nonsense Chinese dim-sum place, one of several on the Clement St strip; there's little English spoken, so it's more of a lucky-dip snack. The fillings are more authentic than at other Chinese bakeries around the city, and you can gorge on pearlescent peanut dumplings for only a few bucks.

California

Pizzetta 211 211 23rd Ave at California, Outer Richmond ☎415/379-9880. Expect inventive and unusual organic thin-crust pizza at this miniscule (only four tables) nook on a residential street in the Richmond. There's a different menu each week, offering whatever's fresh and seasonal – wild *arugula*, *risotto*, and *summer squash* aren't uncommon toppings. Servers are very amiable and have been known to offer wine and even blankets to those waiting outside on chilly evenings. Most pizzas run about $15. Cash only; closed Tues.

Chinese

Clement BBQ 617 Clement St at Seventh, Inner Richmond ☎415/666-3328. The window of this Hong Kong-style café – managed concurrently with the bare-bones *Clement Restaurant*, immediately next door – is filled with glistening ducks and chickens hanging from hooks. There's also other barbecue food sold by the pound for take-out: succulent pork is under $6/lb. Cash only.

Spices! 294 Eighth Ave at Clement, Inner Richmond ☎415/752-8884. This humbly sized

Taiwanese-Szechuan upstart is known for brazen dishes like beef tendon ($4.25) and hot and sour intestine noodle soup ($6.25), although there are plenty of less eyebrow-raising options on the menu. As you'd expect from the name, numbing spice can be added to nearly every dish upon request. Expect crowds of young Asian hipsters, giggly teen servers, and MTV Asia burbling on the overhead television. Cash only. Branch: 291 Sixth Ave at Clement, Outer Richmond.

Ton Kiang 5821 Geary Blvd at 22nd, Outer Richmond ☎415/387-8273. Gigantic, bi-level restaurant whose crowd reflects its diverse neighborhood. A wait is almost inevitable for a table in one of the bustling dining rooms; once inside, try the sliced barbecue pork appetizer ($9) or spicy eggplant dish ($10).

Dessert

Polly Ann 3138 Noriega St at 39th, Outer Sunset ☎415/664-2472. Tidy ice-cream parlor a mile uphill from the coast that produces a staggering 500 flavors, although a rotating selection of a mere 49 is available daily. If you can't decide what to have, ask one of the servers to spin the flavor roulette wheel on the wall behind the counter – you're certain to get something interesting (banana rocky road, sunflower seed, mint marshmallow), and if the spin comes up "lucky," your dessert is on the house. There's only seating for about six.

Sweet Delite 519 Clement St at Sixth, Inner Richmond ☎415/386-8222. Racks and racks of budget-priced Chinese-inflected sandy, including staples like Swedish fish with dried fruits and delicately fragranced Asian sweets. The ice cream bar also serves creamy, scented tea with tapioca balls.

Eastern European

Old Krakow 385 West Portal Ave at 15th, West Portal ☎415/564-4848. Oak chairs and tables, a convivial atmosphere, and delicious, rustic food have made this Polish eatery a popular choice for years. As you'd expect, the menu (written in Polish, but with English translations) is full of hearty meat-and-potatoes favorites, all of which come in under $20. Lunch on weekends only.

Eclectic

Park Chow 1240 Ninth Ave at Lincoln, Inner Sunset ☎415/665-9912. This surprisingly huge space features several fun seating options: a terrific upstairs deck, a small enclosed patio, and a few fireside tables inside. The menu's all over the globe, from salads, American comfort food (try the Burger Royale on a baguette, $9.50), pizzas, and pastas to artisan cheese plates and even a handful of Asian noodle dishes, but everything works, including the dessert pies and cakes. The original, equally busy *Chow* is at 215 Church St at Market, Castro.

French

Chapeau! 1408 Clement St at 15th, Outer Richmond ☎415/750-9787. Provençal-inspired food on a par with several of the big-name French restaurants in the city's central neigh-borhoods. Charming chef Philippe Gardelle's cuisine has gotten a bit more expensive in recent years – you can expect to spend upwards of $45 per person for a complete meal – but there's always the three-course prix fixe for $38, on exclusive offer to early evening patrons and usually consisting of soup or salad, a meat or fish main course, and crème brûlée or profiteroles for dessert. Dinner only; closed Mon–Tues.

Irish

Copper Kettle 2240 Taraval St at 32nd, Outer Sunset ☎415/731-8818. Excellent doughnuts, pastries, and traditional Irish breakfasts (all under $10) at this homey shop set deep in the Sunset street grid. It's right on the L-Taraval MUNI streetcar line if you're coming from another neighborhood. Breakfast and lunch only.

Italian

Mescolanza 2221 Clement St at 23rd, Outer Richmond ☎415/668-2221. Affordable trattoria where no entree is more than $17.50. The unassuming exterior gives way to a softly lit interior where Italian classics like chicken *cacciatore* and *pappardelle* with chicken and mushrooms are done right. Dinner only. **The Pizza Place on Noriega 3901 Noriega St at 46th, Outer Sunset** ☎415/759-5752. New pizzeria a few blocks off Ocean Beach that's become an instant gathering place for the neighborhood surfing community. It's East Coast food served with West Coast flair: Thin-crust pies ($20–26 for a 20-in large) often include numerous fresh vegetables,

while "The Spicoli" is a nod to the double cheese and sausage pizza that Sean Penn had delivered to his classroom in *Fast Times at Ridgemont High*. Grinders (hearty East Coast sandwiches) are also available. Closed Tues.

Japanese

Ariake 5041 Geary Blvd at 15th, Outer Richmond ☎415/221-6210. One of the more moderately priced places you'll find in town for terrific Japanese food, lunch or dinner. Choose from one of four full sushi dinners (none over $19) available at the bar, with names like Faith, Hope, and Love. Other usual suspects such as *gyoza* potstickers ($4.50), tempura plates ($10–12), and steaming bowls of *udon* ($7.50–9) are also available. **Hotei 1290 Ninth Ave at Irving, Inner Sunset** ☎415/753-6045. This smallish, single-room spot steers away from most local Japanese restaurants' obsession with sushi and focuses its attention on *soba* (buckwheat noodles), *ramen*, and titanic bowls of *udon* soup. If you really want sushi, the friendly staff will have it trundled over for you from *Ebisu* across the street. Most dishes are less than $10, while two-piece orders of *nigiri* sushi run about $4 each. The bubbling indoor fountain is a nice touch. Closed Tues. **Koo 408 Irving St at Fifth, Inner Sunset** ☎415/731-7077. Chef Kiyoshi Hayakawa's unique Japanese fusion menu features a combination of cooked plates designed to be shared, as well as plenty of sushi, sashimi, and specialty rolls (try the "Flying Kamikaze" – spicy tuna and asparagus wrapped in *albacore*). The grilled eggplant *dengaku* is a top choice. Plan to spend about $20 per person. Dinner only; closed Mon.

Korean

Brothers Korean BBQ 4128 Geary Blvd at 6th Ave, Inner Richmond ☎415/387-7991. The oldest among a small batch of Korean eateries along Geary, and one of the few with its name emblazoned in English on the front sign. The decor's nothing to look at, but the moderately priced feasts of marinated meats and myriad, pungent side dishes are worth the visit. Certain tables have sunken *hibachis* on which you can cook your own meats, although you may need to towel off the sweat from your brow by meal's end. Open until 2am nightly.

My Tofu House 4627 Geary Blvd at 11th, Inner Richmond ☎415/570-1818. Although its name suggests a meatless kitchen, there's in fact a fair amount of dishes here to sate a carnivore. Go with the *bulgoki* (thin-sliced rib-eye with rice and *kimchi*, $8 for one, $14 for two); alternately, vegetarians will want to try one of the many excellent tofu combination items on the menu.

Mediterranean/Middle Eastern

Aziza 5800 Geary Blvd at 22nd Ave, Outer Richmond ☎415/752-2222. Moroccan fine-dining destination with opulent decor, a superb wine list, and fun touches like a rose water-filled pewter basin presented for premeal handwashing. The menu's packed with California-accented North African specialties: squab with mushroom and thyme ($25) and a couscous plate with turnip, *rutabega*, and onion ($17) top the list. Arrive early and enjoy a drink at the classy, tiled bar. Dinner only; closed Tues.

Yumma's 721 Irving St at 8th, Inner Sunset ☎415/682-0762. Excellent Eastern Mediterranean fare for those on a budget. A host of *shawarma* options ($6–8) anchor the menu, while other Med staples like falafel and tabouleh are equally impressive and affordable. Sunny afternoons are ideal for eating on the cozy back patio; there's also a few seats at the window counter.

Mexican

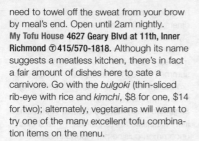 **Gordo laqueria 1233 Ninth Ave at Lincoln, Inner Sunset** ☎415/566-6011. This austere shop lives up to its name (which translates to "fat" in English) by specializing in hefty, stumpy burritos that never miss the mark. The menu's as simple as can be, including only tacos, burritos, and quesadillas, while you'll be hard-pressed to spend more than $7 on your meal. If ordering a burrito, be sure to request a grilled (rather than steamed) tortilla. Cash only. Two branches in the Outer Richmond: 2252 Clement St at 24th, and 5450 Geary Blvd at 19th.

La Fonda 712 Irving St at 8th, Inner Sunset ☎415/681-9205. Inviting taqueria on the neighborhood's main drag known for its extensive menu and comfortable upstairs dining nook. With a host of meatless options

and ten or so various meats to choose from (including the rarely seen *cochinita pibil*, marinated pork with *achiote* sauce and banana leaf), you may need a few minutes to decide, but it's hard to go wrong with anything here. Everything's well under $10, and there are a pair of two-top tables on the sidewalk if the weather's agreeable.

Russian

Katia's 600 Fifth Ave at Balboa, Inner Richmond ☎415/668-9292. Muscovite restaurant with frilly decor, live acoustic music (accordion, guitar), a full slate of Russian tea, and almost every Russian dish you'd hope to find in this part of the world. Choose from a bowl of beet borscht ($5) or a golden-baked *piroshki* ($2.50) as a starter, then move on to a heaping plate of beef stroganoff ($16) or perhaps the poached sturgeon ($19). Lunch Wed–Fri only; closed Mon–Tues.

Sandwiches/soup

Yellow Submarine 503 Irving St at Sixth, Inner Sunset ☎415/681-5652. Premier westside sandwich shop that's light on Beatles memorabilia but heavy on inexpensive, East Coast-style sub sandwiches. Everything's made to order and all meats are freshly grilled, so don't expect to be in and out in a few minutes (although you can phone ahead to speed up your order). The grilled pastrami with hot sauce is second to none in town.

Seafood

Pacific Café 7000 Geary Blvd at 34th, Outer Richmond ☎415/387-7091. The decor of this old-fashioned joint has hardly changed since 1974, when this ever-popular restaurant debuted. There's almost always a wait to sit down, but if the complimentary glass of wine isn't enough of an incentive to invoke reserves of patience, moderately priced dishes like parmesan-crusted halibut or lemon-doused crab cakes with red potatoes should be. Expect a slightly older crowd, and perhaps a family or two. Dinner only; no reservations accepted.

South Asian

India Clay Oven 2436 Clement St at 26th, Outer Richmond ☎415/751-2400. Delightful curry house catering to adventurous Richmond diners unafraid to add "911," the kitchen's highest level of spiciness, to their orders. Medium spice should do the trick for most patrons, however, and there's usually an available table in the large dining room that's set in a lovely, atrium-like space. Most entrees hover around $12.

Roti 53 West Portal Ave at Vicente, West Portal ☏415/665-7684. Highly regarded Indian restaurant in mellow West Portal that's only two streetcar stops away from the bustling Castro. Menu items are smartly prepared (fish enthusiasts may enjoy the tandoori *machchi*, $18), and the "Roti's Feast" is a terrific prix-fixe option for couples ($33 per person, minimum two orders). Lunch Tues–Sat only.

Southeast Asian

Mandalay 4348 California St at Sixth, Inner Richmond ☏415/386-3895. A more accessible choice for Burmese in this area than the overcrowded *Burma Superstar* nearby, *Mandalay*'s go-to appetizer is its *balada*, a crispy pancake tailor-made for dipping in its accompanying curry sauce. There's occasional deviation from Burmese on the menu (chow mein, Singapore-style noodles), but overall the cuisine is a delectable, saucy melange of Thai, Indian, and Chinese. Most entrees are no more than $12.

Marnee Thai 1243 Ninth Ave at Lincoln, Inner Sunset ☏415/731-9999. In a city bursting with neighborhood Thai restaurants, this humming spot still manages to draw in diners from all over. The kitchen's home-style central Thai cooking rolls with the seasons, so winter visitors may see a markedly different menu than those in summer. Prices for most main courses bob around the $10 mark. Branch: 2225 Irving St at 24th, Outer Sunset.

Singapore Malaysian 836 Clement St at Ninth, Inner Richmond ☏415/750-9518. Treading an uncommon cuisine path found in San Francisco, this gem is often overlooked amidst the sea of Chinese and Korean restaurants in its area of the Richmond. It's worth seeking out for tasty, reasonably priced staples of these Asian regions like beef *rendang* and coconut curry soup. Closed Tues.

Thanh Long 4101 Judah St at 46th Ave, Outer Sunset ☏415/665-1146. An unlikely destination restaurant, given its location far from San Francisco's core, *Thanh Long* was San Francisco's first Vietnamese restaurant in the early 1970s, and has become increasingly French-inspired and upscale (even offering valet parking on its ramshackle Outer Sunset corner) in the years since. Specialties include an uncommonly delicious soft-shell crab appetizer ($11.75) and the sizzling claypot main course ($21) – essentially, the day's catch simmered in a medley of vegetables and herbs. The soothing dining room's bedecked in blonde wood paneling and earth tones. Dinner only.

Bars, clubs, and live music

ncreasingly, in party cities like New York or Miami, there's a rather flexible division between **restaurants, bars, and clubs** – and San Francisco is no different. A top-name DJ might stop by for a quiet session at a neighborhood bar instead of one of the warehouse clubs, for example, or a savvy promoter might launch a theme night at a local eatery's bar area instead of a pub. Similarly, most of the popular **live-music** venues are little more than a neighborhood saloon with a stage in the back. Granted, there is a smattering of superclubs and stadium-sized concert halls (including the landmark Fillmore, touchstone for the 1960s psychedelic rock movement), but in general, smaller is better in San Francisco. This also means that even on weekends in the biggest venues, cover charges are usually low, starting around $10 and rarely going above $20.

Remember to bring **ID** to prove you're over 21: most clubs and bars will not admit anyone under that age, since they're serving alcohol. Owing to licensing laws, clubs that stay open after 2am must switch to nonalcoholic beverages – so partying until dawn requires a bit of determination and advance planning. For up-to-date listings on all the venues we've included, either call, check their websites, pick up one of the weekly freesheets like *SF Weekly* or *The Bay Guardian*. Alternatively, there are plenty of **event websites** you can browse, such as SF Station (Ⓦwww.sfstation.com), Upcoming (Ⓦupcoming.yahoo. com), Flavorpill SF (Ⓦwww.flavorpill.com/sanfrancisco), or The Squid List (Ⓦlaughingsquid .com/squidlist/events). Go to Nitevibe (Ⓦwww.nitevibe.com) for DJ music, True Skool (Ⓦwww.true-skool.org) for hip-hop and DJs or Steve Koepke's The List (Ⓦwww.foopee.com/punk/the-list) for rock.

Smoking is banned in virtually all bars and clubs, although we've highlighted a few below that have designated smoking sections. Frankly, you're unlikely to get into trouble for breaking the law, but the glowering glances from other patrons often prove as great a deterrent as the $95 fine.

Bars

Nowhere are the vastly different identities of San Francisco's neighborhoods more evident than in the bar scene. **Downtown** has dozens of bars packed with office workers in the early evening but empty the rest of the time, when most adjourn to the swinging yuppie singles scene in the **Marina** and **Cow Hollow**.

Rooftop bars

There are several rooftop bars across the city, designed to make the most of San Francisco's **spectacular views**. It goes without saying that you'll pay a premium on your drinks for the privilege of looking out over the city.

Carnelian Room 555 California St at Kearny, Financial District ☎415/431-7500. Fifty-two floors up in the Bank of America Building, this elegant spot is the best of the rooftop cocktail lounges. Though often full of boozing Wall Street types, it is worth the hike for the spectacular views.

▲ The Carnelian Room

Grandviews Lounge *Grand Hyatt*, 345 Stockton St at Sutter, Union Square ☎415/403-4847. This bar, 36 stories in the air, has fantastic north-facing views, allowing you to scope out Coit Tower, Alcatraz, and beyond. There's also live jazz most evenings, and as long as you're careful to nurse a single drink, a trip here won't wallop your wallet.

Harry Denton's Starlight Room *Sir Francis Drake Hotel*, 450 Powell St at Sutter, Union Square ☎415/395-8595, ⓦwww.harrydenton.com. Dress up and drink martinis at this famous watering hole. The scene here's sophisticated, and there's live jazz most nights. Note there's a cover charge Wed–Sat ($5–15), and you will be turned away if you're too scruffy (no jeans or sneakers).

Top of the Mark *Mark Hopkins Hotel*, 999 California St at Mason, Nob Hill ☎415/392-3434. The most famous of the rooftop bars, founded in 1939, though now it tends to attract mostly tourists. Expect to pay a cover of $5–10 when there's live jazz – if you get here early, however, you can often avoid shelling out. The martini list runs to more than a hundred different cocktails.

The View *San Francisco Marriott Hotel*, 55 Fourth St at Mission, SoMa ☎415/896-1600. A lovely, romantic modern lounge with a spectacular view of SoMa high-rises, the Bay, and Oakland and Berkeley across the water. Cocktails cost upwards of $15, but they are delicious.

The **Tenderloin** has a few newer, trendy spots amid the grime, while **SoMa** is known more for its clubs than bars, although there are a few places worth the detour. Inevitably, the gay scene dominates almost every bar in the **Castro**, while the nearby **Mission** has arguably the best selection, from grungy pubs to hip lounges. **North Beach**'s bars are primarily Beatnik hangouts a little past their prime, although a few new places, especially wine bars, are opening near Grant Avenue. **Haight–Ashbury** is also rather dated, since the psychedelic groove is long gone; it's better to stick to the pubs and no-nonsense bars of the **Lower Haight**. As for the **Richmond** and the **Sunset**, there are a number of pubs and taverns catering to locals, but nothing worth a special trip.

Downtown and Chinatown

Azul 1 Tillman Place at Grant, Union Square ☎415/362-9750. Tucked away in an alley, this bar is a nice getaway from the hustle and bustle of Union Square with its sleek modern design awash in soothing blue. The sangria is particularly tasty.

The Bubble Lounge 714 Montgomery St at Columbus, Jackson Square ☎415/434-4204. West Coast outpost of the New York City champagne bar that attracts a young, gussied-up crowd to snuggle down in its squishy sofas – there's a vast selection of fizz, divided between light, medium, and full-bodied, as well as classic cocktails like bellinis and chambords.

Buddha Lounge 901 Grant Ave at Washington, Chinatown ☎415/362-1792. This hole-in-the-wall Chinatown bar, with just a few ratty stools and a raucous jukebox, feels far removed from urban America, filled as it is with older locals slapping down mah-jongg tiles. It's a pickup joint, so women alone may feel rather self-conscious. The namesake Buddha is found in a slapdash mural on the rear wall.

The Cigar Bar & Grill 850 Montgomery St at Gold, Financial District ☎415/398-0850. This upscale Spanish-inspired bar and grill feels warm and inviting with its wood-beam ceiling and dark-wood bar. The heated brick courtyard is perfect for relaxing, and as one of San Francisco's few smoking establishments, naturally the bar has a fully stoked humidor. Stop by Thurs through Sat nights for the live salsa and Latin jazz. Also features pool tables, a late-night menu and free wi-fi.

Ferry Plaza Wine Bar & Wine Merchant One Ferry Building #23, Ferry Building Marketplace, Embarcadero ☎415/ 391-9400. Store-cum-wine bar, with a vast selection of Californian that can be sampled either as tastes ($2–7) or by the glass ($4.50–11) alongside snack plates like manchego cheese with organic nuts. Once you've chosen some favorites, get a bottle or two to take home.

Gold Dust Lounge 247 Powell St at Geary, Union Square ☎415/397-1695. Opened in 1933, this is an enjoyably Disney-esque rendition of the city's Barbary Coast days, decked floor-to-ceiling in gold leaf and filled with red-velvet couches and chandeliers. Every night, Johnny Z and the Camaros perform rock, R&B, blues and country favorites, and the band takes requests. No cover.

Hidden Vine 620 Post St at Taylor, Theater District ☎415/674-3567. Intimate and warm, this aptly named wine bar is nestled in the basement of the *Andrews Hotel*. Sneak in here for a glass or two of California wine: sink into one of the comfy armchairs, gaze out of the stained-glass windows and listen to a soundtrack of torch songs.

Li Po Cocktail Lounge 916 Grant Ave at Jackson, Chinatown ☎415/982-0072. Enter through the false cavern front and sit at the very dimly lit bar where Wayne Wang filmed *Chan is Missing*. Named after the Chinese poet, charmingly grotty *Li Po's* is something of a literary hangout among the Chinatown regulars.

The London Wine Bar 415 Sansome St at Sacramento, Financial District ☎415/788-4811. Claiming to be America's first wine bar, this clubby place has a worn mahogany bar and cozy paneled booths. The crowd's older and a little stand-offish, but the enormous wine list more than makes up.

Otis 25 Maiden Lane at Kearny, Union Square ☎415/298-4826. Once a swanky semi-private club, this intimate, elegant bar has opened its doors to the public. The crowd is still mostly Financial District businesspeople and hip, young fashionistas, who sip cocktails in a two-level Art Deco quirky-chic bar decked out in peacock feathers, antlers and snakeskin. A convenient getaway from shopping fatigue.

Red Room *Commodore International*, **827 Sutter St at Jones, Theater District** ☎415/346-7666. Tucked off the lobby of an Art Deco hotel, this sexy bar is – as its name implies – completely red: walls, furniture, glasses, and even many of the drinks. The crowd's young and mixed gay/straight: a friendly place to drink during the week, though the weekend crush is best avoided.

The Redwood Room *Clift Hotel*, **495 Geary St at Taylor, Theater District** ☎415/775-4700. This clubby, landmark bar with its rich wood paneling has received a postmodern makeover by Starck and Schrager, with lightboxes on the wall displaying paintings that shift and fade, and Art Deco-esque fixtures. You can mingle at the bar as well as order snacks from *Asia de Cuba* next door (for review, see p.172). It's a hip enough hangout – just don't choke on the drinks prices.

Rubicon 558 Sacramento St at Montgomery, Financial District ☎415/421-7636. A swanky bar, co-owned by Francis Ford Coppola, Robin Williams, and Robert De Niro (those are his paintings on the walls), *Rubicon* is known for its Blackberry-toting yuppie clientele and a fine cellar that will please even choosy wine snobs. Try the Deux Chapeaux, an in-house wine created by the sommelier.

Tunnel Top 601 Bush St at Stockton, Union Square ☎415/986-8900. On top of the Stockton St Tunnel, this funky dive bar was

While the surrounding countryside may be devoted to winemaking, the city of San Francisco is famous for its beer, specifically its **microbreweries**. The best-known local product is known as "steam" beer, a hybrid lager-bitter. It was invented when early local brewers, finding the ice needed for lager production too expensive, fermented their yeast at room temperature like an ale: the result was a beer with the lower alcohol content of lager but the hearty flavor of bitter. (The origin of the odd name, unfortunately, has never been established.) To find out more, head over to the Anchor Steam Brewery, 1705 Mariposa St at Carolina, Potrero Hill (☎415/863-8350, ⊛www .anchorbrewing.com), for a free 45-minute **tour** (Mon–Fri one tour per afternoon, reservations essential), though the product is universally available at bars and stores. Otherwise, the pick of the local microbrewpubs are:

▲ San Francisco Brewing Company

Beach Chalet, Sunset.

Gordon Biersch, SoMa, see p.215.

Magnolia Gastropub & Brewery, Haight-Ashbury, see p.219.

San Francisco Brewing Company, North Beach, see p.213.

Speakeasy Ales & Lagers, Hunters Point, see p.218.

Thirsty Bear, SoMa.

shuttered for a while – much to many locals' dismay. Its new incarnation is a little swankier than in the past, including cocktails made with fresh juices.

Voda 56 Belden Place at Bush, Financial District ☎415/677-9242. Design-conscious addition to the neighborhood tucked away on Belden Place's restaurant row and owned by the same team as nearby *Plouf* (see p.171). *Voda's* gimmick is a hundred-plus list of vodkas; its appeal is the moody vibe, dressy crowd, and the outdoor banquettes where you can sip a cocktail on a summer evening.

North Beach and the hills

15 Romolo 15 Romolo Place at Broadway, North Beach ☎415/398-1359. This polished, simple and dimly lit bar tucked away on an alley is an elegant refuge from the flashing lights and boisterous strip-club crowd on Broadway. The bar has no sign but boasts a friendly staff and well-stocked jukebox.

Bacchus 1954 Hyde St at Union, Russian Hill ☎415/928-2633. One-time spillover bar for

the nearby *Sushi Groove* eatery (see p.177), this tiny, sleek bar is now a destination in itself (there are only eight stools, so be prepared to stand). It serves saki cocktails as well as fifty different wines, including more than a dozen by the glass (look for exotic touches like a Lebanese variety).

Bamboo Hut 479 Broadway, North Beach ☎415/989-8555. True to its name, this divey Tiki bar is nearly covered in bamboo, and sports a 7-foot-tall 1948 Tiki god as well. With tropical cocktails served in coconut half-shells, it's widely considered the ultimate party destination.

The Big Four Huntington Hotel, 1075 California St at Taylor, Nob Hill ☎415/474-5400. Classy hotel bar, aimed squarely at an older crowd looking for a classic cocktail in equally old-fashioned surroundings.

Condor Club 300 Columbus Ave at Broadway, North Beach ☎415/781-8222. After a stint as a regular sports bar, the birthplace of topless waitressing (see p.72) has brought back the strippers, burlesque and go-go dancers, and the VIP champagne lounges.

Gino and Carlo 548 Green St at Grant, North Beach ☎415/421-0896. The classic drunken pressman's bar, open at 6am for shift-workers on their way home. It's filled with regulars and old-school locals all day, but visitors wanting to stop by to play pinball or pool won't feel unwelcome.

Rosewood 732 Broadway at Powell, North Beach ☎415/951-4886. Deliberately hidden bolthole that doesn't even have a sign outside. The interior's retro groovy, comple-mented by great lounge-core DJs; the downsides are the pricey drinks and the out-of-towners who pour in at weekends.

San Francisco Brewing Company 155 Columbus Ave at Pacific, North Beach ☎415/434-3344. Probably the most touristy of the various microbrewpubs around town, with a bland crowd of non-locals and big shining tanks of beer. Great happy-hour deals 4–6pm.

Savoy Tivoli 1434 Grant Ave at Green, North Beach ☎415/361-7023. Sprawling North Beach institution (dating back to 1907) that recently reopened after a spat with neighbors over noise levels. There's a smoker-friendly open-air patio, a couple of pool tables, a dark-wood bar, and bizarre decorations dotted around the main room – it feels like a boho Beatnik hangout.

Spec's Twelve Adler Museum Café 12 Saroyan Place at Columbus, North Beach ☎415/421-4112. Friendly dive bar in the heart of North Beach, packed with an older, eccentric local crowd and known for its chatty bar staff, who will often serve up cheese and crackers to regulars.

Tonga Room Fairmont Hotel, 950 Mason St at California, Nob Hill ☎415/772-5278. This basement Tiki lounge has grass huts and a floating band at night, not to mention an indoor rainstorm every fifteen minutes. Come for happy hour when there's a terrific all-you-can-eat $7 buffet, as long as you buy one (pricey) drink.

Tonic 2360 Polk St at Green, Russian Hill ☎415/771-5535. A happening little pickup joint, dark and festooned with fresh flowers, serving cheap mixed drinks at a long mahogany bar.

Tosca Café 242 Columbus Ave at Broadway, North Beach ☎415/986-9651. A beautiful old bar with tiles on the floor, bow ties on the bartenders, and opera on the soundtrack; the back room is VIP only, so smile sweetly if you want to wangle a spot in with the

celebs. The jukebox is heavy on opera rather than rock.

Vesuvio Café 255 Columbus Ave at Broadway, North Beach ☎415/362-3370. This famed Beatnik haunt is across the street from City Lights Bookstore. If you're determined to make the pilgrimage, you're now more likely to bump into gawking backpackers than artsy locals.

The northern waterfront and Pacific Heights

A16 2355 Chestnut St at Division, Marina ☎415/771-2216. This southern Italian restaurant (named for the freeway that bisects the region around Naples) serves terrific thin-crust pizzas in the room at the rear; but the real draw's the roomy bar at the front. The dark-wood-paneled spot, with large windows over Chestnut St, offers an extensive wine list, with more than forty different options, mostly southern Italian and Californian, by the glass. Try the Red Flight of five tasting wines for $22.

Ana Mandara Ghirardelli Square, 891 Beach St at Polk, Fisherman's Wharf ☎415/771-6800. The food here (see p.184) is delicious but pricey. As an alternative, check out the beautiful, bamboo-decorated lounge and listen to the fine live jazz.

The Black Horse London Pub 1514 Union St at Franklin, Cow Hollow ☎415/928-2414. This shoebox-sized mock-English pub, if you can squeeze yourself in, seems worlds away from the Marina scene with its old-school San Francisco charm, friendly bar staff and delicious cheese plates.

Buena Vista Café 2765 Hyde St at Beach, Fisherman's Wharf ☎415/474-5044. The walls here are decorated with old newspapers, and the sense of history is reinforced by the bar's claim to have introduced Irish coffee to North America. Given its location, it can get filled with eager tourists wanting to sample the house special.

G Bar Laurel Motor Inn, 444 Presidio Ave at Sacramento, Presidio Heights ☎415/409-4227. Upscale martini bar, with aspirations to the laid-back pretension of LA: there's a vintage Hollywood vibe – at least if Greta Garbo ever slipped into a pair of J Crew slacks. The balcony is a lovely place to slump with a cocktail, though, well away from the pickup scene below.

Lion Pub 2062 Divisadero St at Sacramento, Pacific Heights ☎415/567-6565. Homey neighborhood spot complete with fireplace and lit candles serving a mixed gay/straight crowd of hipsters and young professionals. It's known for fresh-pressed juice cocktails and the free cheese, crackers, and olives set out each night. Note that there's no sign, so just follow the noise on the corner.

Liverpool Lil's 2942 Lyon St at Greenwich, on the edge of the Presidio ☎415/921-6664. This Brit-centric, eccentric old-fashioned pub is refreshingly rough-edged amid the Marina's hordes of wine bars. Come to drink pints of Bass ale and chow down on steak-and-kidney pie until 1am most nights; for some reason, it's popular with local windsurfers at weekends.

Matrix-Fillmore 3138 Fillmore St at Greenwich, Marina ☎415/563-4180. This sleek bar is another project by Mayor Gavin Newsom's restaurant group, Plumpjack, this one inspired by the original *Matrix* that opened on the same spot in 1965 and featured big-name rock acts like Jefferson Airplane. All the two venues share is a name: the current spot is glamorous and a little posey, with a tiny dancefloor, comfortable purple banquettes, and a Marina crowd sipping wine by the glass while they dance to mainstream house and disco.

Nectar Wine Lounge 3330 Steiner St at Chestnut, Marina ☎415/345-1377. Upscale Marina wine haven with a late night, loungey vibe; the crowd's young and pretty, the wine list's eclectic and extensive, and there are tapas-sized California-cuisine snacks.

Perry's 1944 Union St at Buchanan, Cow Hollow ☎415/922-9022. Made legendary by Armistead Maupin's *Tales of the City*, this sprawling, multi-roomed institution is a hugely popular pub. It's still a dark and friendly place to grab a pint with its sports-heavy TVs and blue-and-white-checkered table cloths.

Pier 23 Pier 23, Embarcadero at Greenwich, Telegraph Hill ☎415/362-5125. Sit out on the deck under the heatlamps and enjoy cocktails by the Bay to the sound of a live band, not to mention a gorgeous view of the Bay Bridge. Cover at weekends $8–10.

Playground 1705 Buchanan St at Post, Japantown ☎415/929-1471. This fun Korean-pop-themed bar and restaurant has a distinctly youthful vibe, dark with neon lights and four flatscreen TVs showing Korean music videos. Ask for karaoke, and you'll be led to one of the three private rooms upstairs.

Silver Cloud 1994 Lombard St at Webster, Marina ☎415/922-1977. Brash mainstream bar notable for its raucous karaoke sessions and amusingly abrasive staff; avoid at the weekends when it's clogged with out-of-towners.

SoMa

111 Minna 111 Minna St at Second, SoMa ☎415/974-1719. This loft space is a combination bar, art gallery, and performance venue showcasing the best in local arts, located in an alley not far from SFMOMA. It gets busier, noisier, and more raucous as the evening wears on, so go early if you want to chat. Cover free–$5.

Butter 354 11th St at Folsom, SoMa ☎415/863-5964. Stylized "white trash" bar and diner featuring imitation trailerpark decor, including a bar covered with shingles. The serving window to one side serves only microwave-able junk food like Tater Tots and Beanie Weenies.

District 216 Townsend St at Third, SoMa ☎415/896-2120. This elegant brick and wood-beam bar, not far from the ballpark, features a large, curved bar, a fireplace, art on the walls and chaise longues. With an excellent wine list and a tapas-style menu.

Gallery Lounge 510 Brannan St at Fourth, SoMa ☎415/227-0449. This long, narrow bar is

Gay bars and clubs

The bulk of San Francisco's **gay bars** are situated in the Castro, SoMa, and Polk Gulch, and are listed on pp.234–242 in "Gay and Lesbian San Francisco." At all except the most hardcore places, however, gay-friendly straight people should feel welcome.

Virtually every **nightclub** in town has a "queer" night. Again, we've listed them beginning p.239, but most straight clubbers shouldn't feel out of place if they're drawn to a gay night by a top-name DJ.

chic in its simplicity, the "gallery" a selection of artwork hung on the wall opposite the bar. Draws a hipper, more subdued crowd than your usual baseball fanatics this near to the ballpark.

▲ Gordon Biersch Brewery

Gordon Biersch Brewery 2 Harrison St at Embarcadero, SoMa ☎415/243-8246. Bayfront outpost of the successful Peninsula microbrewery housed in a converted Hills Brothers coffee warehouse with a lovely view of the bridge, good bar food, and some of the best beers in San Francisco (try the Blonde Bock or Hefeweizen). The patio has heatlamps, so it's habitable even on a foggy San Francisco summer evening.

House of Shields 39 New Montgomery St at Mission, SoMa ☎415/495-5436. This is a schizophrenic space: after work, it's an old-school clubby piano bar, opened in 1908, that has preserved its long-term decor (dark wood paneling) and long-term regulars (slightly crumpled businessmen). But late nights, it's been turned over to a promoting team who've brought in avant-garde DJs and a punk crowd.

Julie's Supper Club 1123 Folsom St at Seventh, SoMa ☎415/864-1222. A swinging, delightfully 1920s/30s restaurant and club that features red velvet curtains and a deep-pink Art Deco back bar. The crowd is vintage

chic, and nightly parties range from karaoke to salsa and swing dancing.

Mars Bar 798 Brannan St at Seventh, SoMa ☎415/621-6277. This quirky, out-of-the-way bar, featuring two rooms and a large patio, is done up in charmingly retro 1950s colors with a somewhat incongruous tropical theme, disco ball, Christmas lights, tinsel garland and a red pool table. The Astroturf and plant-filled patio is perfect for lounging on sunny afternoons and fends off the chill with heat lamps at night.

Maxfield's Palace Hotel, 2 New Montgomery St at Market, SoMa ☎415/392-8600. Named after the artist Maxfield Parrish, whose famous mural of the Pied Piper decorates the bar, this mahogany-paneled room is a secluded, elegant place for a martini and a wide range of tasty bar food.

Mr. Smith's 34 Seventh St at Market, SoMa ☎415/355-9991. Although on a grotty block, behind the small door of this "speakeasy" lie chandeliers, exposed brick walls, and dark-wood panels in the main room, a basement where DJs spin house and hip-hop on weekends, and a VIP spot upstairs with its own bar.

The Ramp 855 Terry A. Francois St at Illinois, China Basin ☎415/621-2378. Way out on the old docks, this is well worth the half-mile trek from Downtown to sit out on the patio and sip beers overlooking the abandoned piers and new boatyards.

▲ Maxfield Parrish mural inside Palace Hotel

xyz W Hotel, 181 Third St at Howard, SoMa
☏415/817-7836. Swanky upscale after-work bar on the second floor of the *W Hotel*, popular with the few remaining employed techies in SoMa.

The Tenderloin and Civic Center

222 Club 222 Hyde St at Turk, Tenderloin
☏415/440-0222. Offbeat spot for its location – a former dive bar turned chic hole-in-the-wall, serving cocktails and wine by the glass to a dressy crowd.

Bambuddha Lounge Phoenix Hotel, 601 Eddy St at Larkin, Tenderloin ☏415/885-5088. Low-key lounge, with a New Age-meets-Asia vibe (think swirling, elemental decor and feng shui-favorable fountains). The music's down-tempo dance and world, and there's a small but tasty bar-snacks menu.

Bigfoot Lodge 1750 Polk St at Washington, Polk Gulch ☏415/440-2355. San Francisco outpost of a campy bar from LA, themed as a 1950s ski lodge. Expect plenty of faux wood, hunting trophies, antlers – as well as an enormous papier mâché statue of Bigfoot himself. Try one of the house drinks, all punningly named but strong and delicious.

Edinburgh Castle Pub 950 Geary St at Polk, Tenderloin ☏415/885-4074. Just your average Scottish bar, filled with heraldic Highland memorabilia, although it's actually run by Koreans. The room upstairs regularly hosts comedy and live music; pub food (like an impressive version of fish'n'chips) comes straight from the co-owned restaurant *Old Chelsea* round the corner on Larkin St.

Encore Karaoke Lounge 1550 California St at Polk, Polk Gulch ☏415/775-0442. *Encore* is your quintessential 1980s-style karaoke lounge with big round vinyl booths, a huge stage and a wide array of tunes to choose from.

Hemlock Tavern 1131 Polk St at Post, Polk Gulch ☏415/923-0923. Hipster dive bar hosting regular live gigs from cutting-edge bands, but it is most beloved by smokers for its handy, enclosed patio where you can puff and sip in peace.

Lush Lounge 1092 Post St at Polk, Polk Gulch ☏415/771-2022. With its exotic plants, hanging lamps and snapshots of old Hollywood stars on the wall, this cozy lounge feels like the sort of place you'd find Grace Kelly delicately sipping on a cosmopolitan. The bar is known for its scrumptious sweet cocktails.

Olive 743 Larkin St at O'Farrell, Tenderloin ☏415/776-9814. An elegant, upscale bar in the heart of the seedy Tenderloin. Olives replace the standard peanuts, art hangs on the walls, and everything from the tapas to the watermelon mojitos are delicious.

Vertigo 1160 Polk St at Hemlock, Polk Gulch ☏415/674-1278. This divey space draws a young, jocular crowd that revels in stiff drinks and booty-shaking. Like the *Hemlock* across the street, it's popular with tourists for being one of the few places with a smoking patio.

The Castro

Lime 2247 Market St at Sanchez, Castro ☏415/621-5256. This mod spot is more of a restaurant early in the evening, before morphing into a mixed gay/straight club and bar later on. The music's mostly mainstream house, the crowd young and pretty and the drinks exotic (try a coconut mojito for $8).

Lucky 13 2140 Market St at Church, Castro ☏415/487-1313. A primarily hetero, divey, rocker bar on the border between the Castro and the Lower Haight, filled with people playing pool, chomping on free popcorn, and listening to the Sex Pistols on the jukebox.

Mecca 2029 Market at 14th, Castro ☏415/621-7000. Impressive, if pricey, nightspot serving quirky, fruity cocktails (the vodka mojitos are delicious); try to stop by on Wed when there's live jazz. There's also a restaurant onsite.

The Mission, the Castro and south

Ace Café 1799 Mission St at 14th St, Mission ☏415/861-3002. This motorcycle dive bar is a relatively new kid on the block, taking over an odd little stone-wall spot off 14th. You can nosh on food like fish and chips and hot pastrami sandwiches, while watching the bike races on the TVs. Smoking is allowed, and the pool table is new and not yet scuffed up.

Argus Lounge 3187 Mission St at Valencia, Bernal Heights ☏415/824-1447. Named after the 100-eyed monster whose eyes were preserved on the peacock, this red peacock-themed bar captures the funky Mission aesthetic with fresh-fruit cocktails and hip decor (check out the *Last Supper* paintings).

The Attic 3336 24th St at Mission, Mission ☏415/643-3376. This well-loved dive bar is so dark it takes your eyes some time to adjust to the low red light. Once you can see enough to look around, you can tell the place was inspired by a vintage attic, with oddball antiques in random places. Weekends, it gets so crowded with young hipsters, it's hard to even find a seat.

The Beauty Bar 2299 Mission St at 19th, Mission ☏415/285-0323. Campy and tongue-in-cheek, this San Franciscan import of New York's *Beauty Bar* is decorated with memorabilia from a 1950s hair salon, with plenty of bubblegum pink and rows of retro dryers. On weekends, you can sip on a cocktail while enjoying a manicure, but come during the week if you want to avoid the crowds. Cash only.

Bender's Bar 806 S Van Ness Ave at 19th St, Mission ☏415/824-1800. This rock'n'roll bar was destroyed by a fire in 2006, but has come back fiercer than ever, with pinball machines, pool tables, and thrash metal on the jukebox. It hosts shows like Kiss cover band Destroyer as well as movies and Sun afternoon barbecues.

Casanova Lounge 527 Valencia St at 16th, Mission ☏415/863-9328. Lots of cool lamps and an even niftier selection of music on the jukebox attract the young and stylish to the *Casanova Lounge*. The bartenders are famously chatty and easygoing.

Dalva 3121 16th St at Valencia, Mission ☏415/252-7740. *Dalva* is dark and divey, and though the wafer-thin space is easy to miss, that doesn't stop a diverse, artsy crowd from packing in to lean against one of the narrow tables. Live bands and DJs often squeeze into the slender front room.

Doc's Clock 2575 Mission St at 21st, Mission ☏415/824-3627. Head for the back lounge and its low-lit tables for a quiet drink at this artsy dive. The Deco-style bar is easy to spot, thanks to the hot-pink neon sign blazing out front. If you're feeling energetic, sign up for shuffleboard.

El Rio 3158 Mission St at Fair, Bernal Heights ☏415/282-3325. This neighborhood pub draws a mixed gay and straight crowd, with its multiple rooms, pool table, nice outdoor patio with heat lamps, and live music or DJs nearly every night. Don't miss the über-cheap drink specials.

Elixir Bar 3200 16th St at Guerrero, Mission ☏415/552-1633. Elixir opened in 1858, and is one of the oldest continually running saloons in San Francisco. In 2003, the bar was restored to its wood-paneled Victorian-era glory, when it was rebuilt after the 1906 earthquake. Featuring a do-it-yourself Bloody Mary bar on Sun and original cocktails.

Homestead 2301 Folsom St at 19th, Mission ☏415/282-4663. With its gold pressed-tin ceiling, rococo wallpaper and pot-bellied stove, this saloon feels like it was transported into modern-day San Francisco from the Gold-Rush glory days. For a spot that's so pretty to look at, it's surprisingly mellow, with a good jukebox.

Latin American Club 3286 22nd St at Valencia, Mission ☏415/647-2732. A small, vaguely hip place that still retains a neighborhood feel thanks to its pool table and reasonable prices. The ceiling space above is crammed with piñatas, Mexican streamers and the like.

Lazslo Foreign Cinema, 2532 Mission St at 21st, Mission ☏415/648-7600. This industrial-chic bar, attached to the film-themed restaurant, is unsurprisingly named in homage to the movies – Jean-Paul Belmondo's character's alias in *A Bout de Souffle*. There's a DJ by the door every night except Mon, and it's a fine place for a modern cocktail.

Lil Baobab 3388 19th St at Mission, Mission ☏415/643-3558. Smaller satellite branch of the main eatery (see p.190), this Senegalese café is handier as a homey bar. Instead of eating, order up one of the stiff, exotic $5 cocktails like a ginger or tamarind margarita. Livelier late at night than early in the evening.

The Lone Palm 3394 22nd St at Guerrero, Mission ☏415/648-0109. Like a forgotten Vegas review bar from the 1950s, this dim, candlelit cocktail lounge is a secret gem. The namesake palm is actually metal and there's a TV above the bar playing classic American movies.

Mission Bar 2695 Mission St at 24th, Mission ☏415/647-2300. This basic, unfussy bar has a great rock jukebox, plus a pool table and pinball machine. Determinedly untrendy, and a great break from the gentrification elsewhere in the area.

🏃 **Papa Toby's Revolution Café 3248 22nd St at Mission, Mission** ☏415/642-0474. This hybrid bar and café offers free wi-fi, an upright piano anyone can play, al fresco dining, ginger lattes, and music nightly ranging from jazz and blues to bluegrass and classical. The atmosphere is laid-back, but the place is often packed with hipsters, making tables hard to come by.

The Phoenix 811 Valencia St at 19th, Mission ☎415/695-1811. A welcome break from the über-trendy spots in the Mission, *The Phoenix* is an upscale Irish pub; grab one of the wooden banquettes and sup Guinness and Hefeweizen by the light of the glass chandelier. Happy hour daily 4–7pm with $1 off pints.

The Phone Booth 1398 Van Ness Ave at 25th, Mission ☎415/648-4683. This tiny dive bar, known for its cheap drinks and its naked-Barbie chandelier draws older neighbors, young lesbians and straight hipsters. Smoking is permitted, and a pool table is improbably tucked into the small room.

Speakeasy Ales & Lagers 1195 Evans Ave at Keith, Hunters Point ☎415/642-3371. This spacious warehouse brewery serves great beer and offers a fun Fri happy hour featuring tacos and rock music.

Ti Couz Too 3108 16th St at Valencia, Mission ☎415/252-7373. The bar attached to the well-known local crêperie *Ti Couz* (see p.193) is unfussy and chic, a great place to lounge if you're waiting for a table or before heading out on a Valencia St bar crawl.

Verdi Club 2424 Mariposa St at Potrero, Potrero Hill ☎415/861-9199. The *Verdi Club* was founded in 1916 as an Italian-American social club, and moved to its current location in 1935. It's now only open two nights a week: Tues for Tuesday Night Jump swing dance and Thurs for Mariposa Tango Club, and both nights attract vintage-obsessives in droves.

🏃 **Wild Side West** 424 Cortland Ave at Andover, Bernal Heights ☎415/647-3099. Hands-down the best beer garden in the city, featuring sculpture and lovely greenery, as well as a multi-tiered patio. The interior is done up like an Old West saloon with oddball decor on the wall, sports on the TVs, card tables, and pool tables. While it's known as a lesbian bar, it draws a mixed crowd and everyone is welcomed.

Zeitgeist 199 Valencia St at Duboce, Mission ☎415/255-7505. Once divey "biker bar" (mostly bicycle messengers) that's been given a grungy makeover by its current owners. Now, the large patio (terrific for smokers) is a haven for beer-swilling hipsters here for the cheap drinks, the Bloody Marys and the pinball machines. There's also a short bar-snacks menu, mostly BBQ chicken and burgers. There's an enjoyable film festival held here in the summer (see p.234).

Haight-Ashbury and west of Civic Center

🏃 **The Alembic** 1725 Haight St at Cole, Haight-Ashbury ☎415/666-0822. This classy establishment, with its wooden bar and mustard-yellow walls, has perhaps the best alcohol selection in the city, with a vast range of spirits as well as Magnolia Brewery beer and fancy cocktails.

Club Deluxe 1511 Haight St at Ashbury, Haight-Ashbury ☎415/552-6949. Hangout for the wing-tipped, zoot-suited crowd in a stretch of Upper Haight otherwise dominated by shaggy street punks.

Fly 762 Divisadero St at Grove, Western Addition ☎415/931-4359. This trendy bar-restaurant has no hard-liquor license, so expect creative saki concoctions and a top-notch beer and wine selection. The crowd's mostly young single locals from the artsy Panhandle district nearby.

Hotel Biron 45 Rose St at Gough, Hayes Valley ☎415/703-0403. This wine bar has an easy elegance and a distinctly European atmosphere, with tables and leather couches, and art hanging on the walls. The wine list is impressive, with carefully selected choices from France and California.

Kezar 770 Stanyan St at Waller, Haight Ashbury ☎415/386-9292. If you want to catch a game of soccer on TV, chow down on English pub grub, or chat to an expat or two, come to this Brit-run pub close to Golden Gate Park.

Mad Dog in the Fog 520 Haight St at Steiner, Lower Haight ☎415/626-7279. A British-style pub, with Boddingtons on tap, pool tables and an outdoor patio. It's often packed with jovial sports fans watching everything from rugby and soccer to American football.

Madrone Lounge 500 Divisadero St at Fell, Western Addition ☎415/241-0202. This artsy-hip bar was once a Victorian-era apothecary. Now with its deep-blue walls, vintage couches and art on the walls, it's a mellow place to have a drink, unless a particularly hot DJ spinning hip-hop, funk or electronica brings in the party crowd.

Magnolia Gastropub & Brewery 1398 Haight St at Masonic ☏415/864-7468. Recently remodeled, this pub and restaurant has ditched its hippie-chic atmosphere and psychedelic murals for a sleeker look, but still has terrific microbrewery beers in the tradition of classic English and European ale houses.

Molotov's 582 Haight St at Steiner, Lower Haight ☏415/558-8019. Though clubbers have largely displaced the rocker element elsewhere in the Haight, this is a place where the hardcore still rules – one major plus is plenty of seating.

Noc Noc 557 Haight St at Steiner, Lower Haight ☏415/861-5811. Decor straight out of an Orwellian sci-fi film, with static-filled TV in every corner. The bar doesn't have a license to sell hard alcohol, so all cocktails are made from saki: it's extra dark and worth the trip.

Orbit Room 1900 Market St at Laguna, Castro/ Lower Haight ☏415/252-9525. Smooth, upscale bar-restaurant with tie-clad bartenders serving up specialty cocktails, plus the usual coffees and café food. The enormous bay windows overlooking Market Street are a great place to perch.

Persian Aub Zam Zam 1663 Haight St at Clayton, Haight-Ashbury ☏415/861-2545. The retro jazz jukebox at this Casbah-style cocktail lounge sets the tone. It was famed for its ornery owner, who would arbitrarily kick out customers, usually when they ordered a drink other than his signature gin martini (he was nicknamed the Martini Nazi). When he died a few years ago, the bar was purchased by its regulars to preserve the atmosphere. They've been at least partially successful, and it's still a fun place for a drink or two.

Place Pigalle 520 Hayes St at Gough, Hayes Valley ☏415/552-2671. Decorated in plush, deep reds, this bar displays art on the walls and features live music and readings many nights of the week. It has become a haven for the local creative community, who must be early risers since it shuts at midnight.

Toronado 547 Haight St at Fillmore, SoMa ☏415/863-2276. Known for its vast selection of international ales and lagers, this cash-only dive bar is well loved by beer aficionados.

The Richmond and the Sunset

540 Club 540 Clement St at Sixth, Richmond ☏415/752-7276. This laid-back artsy punk bar, done up in deep reds and black, made a name for itself with regular parties like Catholic School Karaoke. Featuring cheap drinks, trendy music on the jukebox, dartboards and pool tables.

The Abbey Tavern 4100 Geary Blvd at Sixth, Richmond ☏415/221-7767. Quintessentially Irish, this soccer-mad sports bar is friendly and upscale, often hosting live Irish folk music when there aren't any important games on TV. There are free snacks on Friday evenings, and a dozen beers on tap from Boddingtons to Hefeweizen.

Bitter End 441 Clement St at Fifth, Richmond ☏415/221-9538. The youngest, hippest and most brightly lit of the Irish bars on this Richmond drag: there's the usual pool, darts, and wide beer selection. The cozy fireplace is ideal for huddling on a cold San Francisco summer day. The selection of whiskies and single malt scotches is impressively wide.

Little Shamrock 807 Lincoln Way at Ninth, Sunset ☏415/661-0060. The homey, inviting atmosphere at this Irish pub, the second oldest bar in the city, draws many regulars with its fireplace, lived-in couches, board games, free fresh popcorn, and Irish whiskey selection.

Pig & Whistle Pub 2801 Geary Blvd at Wood, Richmond ☏415/885-4779. Thoroughly British pub, serving a good selection of English and Californian microbrews and featuring a pool table, dartboards, and pinball machine, plus a jukebox stacked with English angst-rock classics from The Smiths and the like. Lunches of fish'n'chips or bangers'n'mash hover around $5.

Trad'r Sam's 6150 Geary Blvd at 26th, Richmond ☏415/221-0773. Open since 1939, this is a classic Tiki bar, complete with flaming bowls of exotically named cocktails – try a P38 cocktail, served in a salad bowl with four straws. It's groovier and less student-dominated during the week.

Yancy's Saloon 734 Irving St at Eighth, Sunset ☏415/665-6551. Mellow, plant-festooned collegiate bar on the Sunset's restaurant row. It boasts big couches, free darts, and cheap drinks (the margaritas are lethal).

Live music

San Francisco's **music scene** reflects the character of the city as a whole: progressive and ever evolving, but also a little bit nostalgic. The options for catching live music are wide and the scene is consistently forward-thinking, characterized by the frequent emergence of creative, young underground bands. San Francisco has never recaptured its crucial 1960s role, though in the last twenty years the city has helped launch acid (or beat-heavy) jazz, a classic swing revival, and the East Bay pop-punk sound championed by bands like Rancid and Green Day.

There are a few large venues in the city, but the live rock-music scene relies more on smaller, intimate places, many of which are bars with makeshift stages; we've listed our pick of these below. Most venues won't charge a cover of more than $10, and many events are often free. As for **Latin** music, given the city's thriving Hispanic community, there's surprisingly little chance to catch authentic performers; frankly, you're better off sampling local or touring **jazz** and **blues** bands.

The big venues

The best sources for **buying tickets** to the following venues are Ticketmaster (☏415/421-TIXS, ⓦwww.ticketmaster.com), which has outlets across the city in Rite Aid drugstores and Tower Records, or Tickets.com (☏415/776-1999, ⓦwww.tickets.com). For smaller venues Ticketweb (ⓦwww.ticketweb.com) is often the best option. No matter what, expect to pay a fee in addition to the ticket price.

Bear in mind that some of the Bay Area's best large-scale venues, where the big names tend to play, are actually nearby towns in the South and East Bay: for details, see p.322.

Bimbo's 365 Club 1025 Columbus Ave at Chestnut, North Beach ☏415/474-0365, ⓦwww.bimbos365.com. Don't let the strange name put you off (it's named after the grandfather of the current owner); this traditional 1940s supper club with its plush red decor and tuxedoed bar staff offers more than just Frank Sinatra tribute bands. The savvy booker here schedules underground European acts, kitschy tribute bands, and big-name rock acts in equal proportion. $20 and up.

The Fillmore 1805 Geary St at Fillmore, Japantown ☏415/346-6000, ⓦwww.thefillmore.com. A local landmark, the Fillmore was at the heart of the 1960s counterculture, when it was masterminded by the legendary Bill Graham. It reopened in 1994 after several years' hiatus and is home now to mainly rock acts. Cover varies.

The Great American Music Hall 859 O'Farrell St at Polk, Tenderloin ☏415/885-0750, ⓦwww.musichallsf.com. Starting out as a bordello in the 1900s, the Music Hall's fortunes soon went into decline. It was resuscitated in the 1970s and now the gorgeous venue plays host to a wide variety of rock, country, and world-music acts. $10–20.

▲ The Great American Music Hall

The Warfield 982 Market St at Sixth, SoMa ☏415/567-2060, ⓦwww.bgp.com. In many ways the equal to the more historic Fillmore auditorium, with both a beautiful music-hall setting and top-name touring bands. It's smaller than the Fillmore, with seating, so is better suited to more intimate shows. $25 and up.

Rock, blues, folk, and country

12 Galaxies 2365 Mission St at 21st, Mission ☎ 415/970-9777, ⓦ www .12galaxies.com. Named as a nod to local character Frank Chu, who carries nonsensical protest signs around the streets emblazoned with those two words, this huge, industrial-style club centers on a low-rise stage which holds live performances – whether metal, indie rock, country, comedy or vaudeville – most nights; best views are from the mezzanine. The bar also hosts dance parties, ranging from Grateful Dead and politically themed events to nights celebrating pop, dub or Brazilian grooves. If you don't want to dance, there's a pool table and a small snack menu. $6–16.

Annie's Social Club 917 Folsom St at Fifth, SoMa ☎ 415/974-1585, ⓦ www.anniessocial-club.com. Previously known as the *Covered Wagon Saloon* and then the *Cherry Bar*, this is a serious dive – and determined to stay that way –with a line-up of snarling gutter-punk and metal acts as well as punk-rock karaoke backed by a live band, a stand-up open-mic night, DJ nights and joke-e-oke. Free–$8.

Biscuits and Blues 401 Mason St at Geary, Union Square ☎ 415/292-2583, ⓦ www .biscuitandblue.cityoearch.com. Certainly a tourist trap, but this is still one of the best spots in town to catch classic New Orleans jazz and delta blues, accompanied by delicious, if overpriced, soul food. $12–25.

Boom Boom Room 1601 Fillmore St at Geary, Japantown ☎ 415/673-8000, ⓦ www .boomboomblues.com. Gritty venue in the Fillmore District, close to the Japan Center, that was owned by bluesman John Lee Hooker until he died in 2001. The dark low-rise building plays host to a fine selection of touring blues and funk artists. Closed Mon. Free–$15.

Bottom of the Hill 1233 17th St at Missouri, Potrero Hill ☎ 415/621-4455, ⓦ www .bottomofthehill.com. The best place in town to catch up-and-coming touring indie bands or favorite local rock acts. Frequently packed with college kids and young artists

and scenesters for shows, there's a small patio out back to catch a breath of fresh air. Free–$15.

Brainwash 1122 Folsom St at Seventh, SoMa ☎ 415/861-F00D, ⓦ www.brainwash.com. Café-cum-laundromat by day; every night at 8pm, there's live entertainment – comedy on Thurs, movie classics on Sun and a reliable selection of slam poets, singer-songwriters and punky bands the rest of the week. Stock up on $1 cans of cheap beer during happy hour (daily 4–7pm). Free.

Café du Nord 2170 Market St at Sanchez, Castro ☎ 415/861-5016, ⓦ www .cafedunord.com. One of the most beautiful music venues in the city, this intimate former speakeasy, built in 1907, retains its Victorian faux paneling and wainscoting, as well as the handcarved mahogany bar. The musical line-up includes the hottest indie rock acts, country, cabaret, and hip-hop, and the venue also hosts readings and dance parties on occasion. The upstairs *Swedish American Music Hall* puts on more subdued singer-songwriter shows on occasion. $8–15.

Edinburgh Castle 950 Geary St at Polk, Tenderloin ☎ 415/885-4074, ⓦ www.castlenews.com. This popular Scottish-themed watering hole has a small, dank room upstairs in which you can catch somewhat obscure touring rock bands as well as fiercely independent local acts Thurs through Sun. $5.

El Rio 3158 Mission St at Fair, Bernal Heights ☎ 415/282-3325, ⓦ www.elriosf.com. While it looks like your typical neighborhood dive up front, a somewhat hidden side room plays host to a vastly diverse array of live music and parties, ranging from punk rock, alt-country, and metal to samba, salsa, and reggae, as well as burlesque shows and weekly gay and lesbian parties. Free–$7.

Fat City 314 11th St at Folsom, SoMa ☎ 415/861-2890, ⓦ www.myspace.com /fatcitysf. This spacious, high-ceilinged warehouse-loft-style venue often hosts big-name DJs and industrial acts. Normally, the bands who play here are more obscure, including industrial, goth, metal, punk, electronica, and hip-hop groups. $10–20.

Hemlock Tavern 1131 Polk St at Hemlock, Polk Gulch ☎ 415/923-0923, ⓦ www.hemlocktavern .com. All types of hipster-approved music is performed in the shoebox-sized room at the back of this popular bar, from underground pop to arty noise to electro-punk-disco to ukulele country. Free–$7.

Hotel Utah Saloon 500 Fourth St at Bryant, SoMa ☎415/421-8308 ⓦwww.thehotel utahsaloon.com. Singer-songwriters, country, and rock bands take the stage at this small SoMa bar, which dates back to 1908 and has a vertigo-inducing balcony. There are a dozen different beers on tap, and the Mon open-mic night is particularly popular. $5–12.

House of Shields 39 New Montgomery St at Mission, SoMa ☎415/495-5436. Old-school clubby piano bar after work, this becomes a live-music venue Wed–Sat when there's a mixture of rock, avant-garde DJs, jazz, and reggae/hip-hop performers. Free–$5.

🎿 **The Independent** 628 Divisadero St at Hayes, Western Addition ☎415/771-1421, ⓦwww.theindependentsf.com. Indie venue in the space that once housed the *Justice League* nightclub, with strong sightlines, an impressive sound system, and an eclectic booking policy, bringing in the bigger names in rock to rap. $12–55.

Kimo's 1351 Polk St at Bush, Polk Gulch ☎415/885-4535, ⓦwww.myspace.com /kimosbarsf. The closet-sized music space on the second floor of this dive bar is decidedly cramped, dirty and shabby, and the punk rockers who love *Kimo's* wouldn't have it any other way. But you can hear a wide array of rock and pop music or come out for the jam sessions or 1980s dance parties. $5–10.

The Knockout 3223 Mission St at Valencia ☎415/522-0333, ⓦwww.theknockoutsf.com. Popular with mods and hipsters, this oddly shaped bar brings in garage rockers, honky-tonk bands, retro pop groups, and noise and metal acts. It hosts an equal number of dance parties features oldies, soul, punk, funk, and hip-hop. $2–7.

Lou's Pier 47, 300 Jefferson St at Jones, Fisherman's Wharf ☎415/771-5687. This blues joint by the Bay packs them in nightly. On off-nights and weekend afternoons, things settle down slightly, with local jazz performers. $3–10.

The Make-Out Room 3225 22nd St at Mission, Mission ☎415/647-2888, ⓦwww.makeoutroom .com. This small dark space is primarily a place to drink at the enormous mahogany bar, but there are regular performances by local indie bands and literary events Fri–Sun. $3–8.

🎿 **Mezzanine** 444 Jessie St at Fifth, SoMa ☎415/820-9669, ⓦwww.mezzaninesf .com. Enormous megaclub with mainstream, brand-name hip-hop, electronica, rock, and

DJ acts – make a reservation for the VIP Ultra Lounge if you're feeling flush and flash. The music programming is more eclectic than most; note that it doesn't really get going until well after midnight. $15 and up.

Red Devil Lounge 1695 Polk St at Clay, Polk Gulch ☎415/921-1695, ⓦwww.reddevillounge .com. This neo-goth lounge, kitschly decorated with gargoyles, is *the* place to catch a 1980s band (either a real one making a comeback or a tribute outfit), local indie rock, acid jazz, Mexican pop or a big-name hip-hop act in an intimate space. $5–10.

🎿 **Rickshaw Stop** 155 Fell St at Franklin, Hayes Valley ☎415/861-2011. Cavernous and intriguing neighborhood bar in gentrified Hayes Valley, swathed in red velvet. It's known for its offbeat music programming, artsy, lit-geek crowds and unusual themed parties like "Tots'n'Tonic," a kid-friendly happy hour where parents can tote babies while quaffing cocktails. Open Wed–Sat.

Rockit Room 406 Clement St at Fifth, Richmond ☎415/387-6343, ⓦwww.lastdaysaloon.com. A must-see for live music in the otherwise sleepy Richmond district, popular with nearby students. The line-up varies, with an over-dependence on jangly pop and hippie rock, but it's typically worth checking out. $5–10.

The Saloon 1232 Grant Ave at Vallejo, North Beach ☎415/989-7666. This gritty bar has stood for more than a hundred years (both the building and the bar pre-date the 1906 quake and fire) and in its time has been both a whorehouse and Prohibition speakeasy. Today, the place creaks nightly as blues bands and a youngish crowd shake it up to live funk and R'n'B. Fri–Sat $3–5.

Slim's 333 11th St at Folsom, SoMa ☎415/522-0333, ⓦwww.slims-sf.com. Owned by local Boz Skaggs, what was once a blues bar is now a prime venue to catch an array of punk, indie rock, and world music, played mostly by national touring bands and artists. $12–15.

Thee Parkside 1600 17th St at Wisconsin, Potrero Hill ☎415/252-1330, ⓦwww .theeparkside.com. Roomy and clean for a dive bar, this venue offers everything a greaser or punk would like: garage rock, punk, honky-tonk, and rockabilly, not to mention delicious burgers. The large outdoor patio has ping-pong and sometimes screens vintage soft-core porn. $5–12.

Jazz, Latin, and world music

Amnesia 853 Valencia St at 19th, Mission ☎415/970-8336. Look for the op-artsy mural which covers the entranceway, then duck inside this cozy bar done out speakeasy-style in deep reds. An eclectic crowd of regulars, from Castro refugees to suited 9-to-5ers, pack the place most nights; the best time to stop by is for Tues night's Rock Out Karaoke. Otherwise, there are DJs Fri and Sat, and live bands the rest of the week – ranging from jazz, bluegrass, and cabaret to oddball rock. The best drink option is the house sangria. From $5.

Bruno's 2389 Mission St at 20th, Mission ☎415/648-7701, Ⓦwww.brunoslive.com. Like something from a Scorsese movie, this retro restaurant has an intimate live venue attached, filled with 1960s-style white vinyl furniture surrounding a tiny stage. The music's a mixture of jazz and new-school soul. $5–10; closed Mon.

Clarion Music Center 816 Sacramento St at Grant, Chinatown ☎415/391-1317, Ⓦwww.clarionmusic.com. A cozy little theater located in the back of a music-instrument store, focusing on world-music acts. The schedule of local and touring bands (usually Fri at 8pm) is an equally pleasant surprise. $10–15.

Club Deluxe 1511 Haight St at Ashbury, Haight-Ashbury ☎415/552-6949, Ⓦwww.swedishwrench.com/deluxe/club_deluxe.htm. This 1949 Art Deco nightclub hosts popular jazz jam sessions (Sun & Tues) as well as poetry readings and a standup night. Wed through Sat, you could see anything from swing and country to piano music. No cover.

Dogpatch Saloon 2496 Third St at 22nd, Potrero Hill ☎415/643-8592. This classy retro joint with a checkered floor is the perfect venue for some of the best jazz in the city, performed every Sun (4.30–8.30pm). $5.

Elbo Room 647 Valencia St at 17th, Mission ☎415/552-7788, Ⓦwww.elbo.com. The birthplace of acid jazz, a popular early 1990s local variant that emphasized a danceable groove over complex improvisation. These days, it's better known for its world-music nights from dub and reggae to Afro-Cuban salsa or samba. $6–10.

Enrico's 504 Broadway at Kearny, North Beach ☎415/982-6223, Ⓦwww.enricos.com. A bustling supper club and jazz bar, *Enrico's* offers Italian food and mainstream jazz nightly – grab a drink and settle back on the patio. No cover.

Jazz at Pearl's 256 Columbus Ave at Broadway, North Beach ☎415/291-8255, Ⓦwww.jazzatpearls.com. Jazz vocalist Kim Nalley has revived this once-moribund spot and schedules nightly sets by a rotating cast of regulars, many of whom have gigged with the biggest names around. Nalley herself performs on Tues. For serious jazz lovers, so don't plan to chat through the show. $5–15.

The Plough and Stars 116 Clement St at Second, Richmond ☎415/751-1122. The Irish expat community crams into this terrific pub for hearty pints of Guinness and live folk music six nights a week at 9pm. No cover.

Rassela's 1534 Fillmore St at O'Farrell, Western Addition ☎415/346-8696. Part of former mayor Willie Brown's ambitious but thwarted Jazz Redevelopment District plans for the Western Addition, this somewhat disappointing venue offers a range of local and touring performers, which you can enjoy while eating fine Ethiopian food. Mon are open mic. Free–$5.

Poppy Art House 2698 Folsom St at 23rd, Mission ☎415/826-2402, Ⓦwww.redpoppyarthouse.org. This gallery and performance space, brightly lit and draped with white curtains, presents all varieties of jazz on the weekend – Latin and Indian, Duke Ellington tributes, and chamber jazz. $10–20 suggested donation.

Roccapulco 3140 Mission St at Cesar Chavez, Bernal Heights ☎415/648-6611, Ⓦwww.roccapulco.com. Catering to the Mission's Latino population, this large club books salsa and Tejano music, ranging from performers rarely heard in the US to big names like Celia Cruz. On Wed there are salsa lessons, Thurs are Latino hip-hop nights, while live acts dominate Fri and Sat. Dress up – the no jeans or sneakers rule is rigorously enforced. $8–15.

Savanna Jazz 2937 Mission St at 25th, Mission ☎415/285-3369, Ⓦwww.savannajazz.com. Decked out in vintage records, this elegant, intimate nightclub offers a thriving live jazz scene including regular Latin and Brazilian nights. $5–10.

Yoshi's 1330 Fillmore St at Eddy, Western Addition ☎415/655-5600, Ⓦwww.yoshis.com.

Oakland's fabled jazz club and Japanese restaurant has finally opened a San Francisco venue in the historic Fillmore Jazz Preservation District, with a chic, modern look, a round stage, a balcony, and a wooden dancefloor. Like its East Bay sister venue (p.323), this club draws the biggest names in jazz today. $12–32.

Nightclubs

Still trading on a reputation for hedonism earned decades ago, San Francisco's **nightclubs** trail light years behind those of other large American cities. The upside, of course, is that it's rare to encounter high cover charges, ridiculously priced drinks, feverish posing, or long lines, though a few of the cavernous dance clubs in SoMa do have lines on weekends. Instead, you'll find a diverse range of small to medium-sized, affordable clubs in which leather-clad goths rub shoulders with the bearded and beaded, alongside a number of gay hangouts (listed on p.239) still rocking to the sounds of high-energy funk and Motown. You'll find the occasional DJ hangout that plays house and techno, but what San Francisco does best is all the old favorites – songs you know the words to; clubbing is more of a party than a pose in this city. The greatest concentration of clubs is in SoMa, especially the area around 11th Street and Folsom.

Unlike most other cities, where the action never gets going until after midnight, many San Francisco clubs have a **closing time** of 2am during the week, so you can usually be sure of finding things well under way by 11.30pm. At weekends, most places stay open until 3 or 4am. Very few venues operate any kind of dress code or restrictive admission policy, and only on very busy nights are you likely to have to wait. Unfortunately, most dancing opportunities are restricted to those 21 and over, forcing under-age revellers to be more creative when it comes to late-night entertainment.

In planning your evening, the best places to pick up flyers (or find out through word of mouth what's coming up) are the DJ record stores we've listed on p.259.

Party buses

It all started with *El Volado* (loosely translated as "The Flier"), a brightly painted school bus that looks as though it can barely make it to third gear, let alone take flight. Also known as "The Mexican Bus," it transports Latin-music lovers from party to party while keeping the mood festive en route. Recently, the Mexican Bus people added the equally vivid bio-diesel-fueled eco-bus *Lola* to its fleet as a substitute for the party bus, as well as a vehicle for the company's educational tours around San Francisco. The experience is much less cheesy than it sounds, and worth checking out if you want to sample a variety of the city's venues from *Roccapulco* for salsa to *12 Galaxies* for rock and electronica. The circuit varies nightly, though salsa Thursdays are a particular highlight ($38/person). Check ⓦ www.mexicanbus.com or call ☎ 415/546-3747 for more info.

Meanwhile *Transported SF* has started a new kind of party bus, which keeps the party in the aisles of the bus *DasFrachgut* with a movie screen hanging from the ceiling, a sound system beneath the seats and DJs spinning tunes, while the bus takes a scenic route to places like Treasure Island, Ocean Beach, Twin Peaks or the Marin Headlands. You're encouraged to bring your own booze, and it's around $20 for the trip. Check ⓦ www.transportedsf.com for more info.

330 Ritch St 330 Ritch St at Townsend, SoMa ☎415/541-9574. Formerly a gay bathhouse, the only constants at this small, out-of-the-way club are its location and its high-school-dance atmosphere. Different nights attract wildly varied crowds, but it's best known for the Thurs Popscene party, ground zero for lovers of indie rock and 1980s alternative in San Francisco. $5–15.

1015 Folsom 1015 Folsom St at Sixth, SoMa ☎415/431-1200. Multilevel superclub, popular across the board for late-night dancing: the music's largely house and garage, and expect marquee names like Sasha and Digweed on the main floor. $10–15.

Bollywood Cafe 3372 19th St at Capp, Mission ☎415/970-0362. ⊛www.bollywoodcafe.com. This hip, new restaurant and lounge plays Bollywood movies nonstop and, a few nights a week, hosts global-beat dance parties by the likes of world DJ superstar Cheb i Sabbah that bring out the hard-core bhangra dancers as well as novices.

Cat Club 1190 Folsom at Eighth, SoMa ☎415/703-8965, ⊛www.catclubsf.com. This long, narrow nightclub is best known for its 1980s nights – Hot Pants lesbian night and 1984, which draws glam goths and nostalgic 30-somethings. But the club puts on a wide array of parties from electronica, goth, and industrial to indie rock. $15–20.

The Cellar 685 Sutter St at Taylor, Theater District ☎415/441-5678, ⊛www.cellarsf.com. Brash, kitschy bar-club decorated with dozens of mirrors. There are slouchy booths where you can lounge and enjoy the music if you'd rather not dance. Free–$10.

Club Six 60 Sixth St at Market, SoMa ☎415/863-1221. Mixed gay/straight club, with a program that focuses on hip-hop and hardcore dance music. The narrow beer-spattered space downstairs is usually packed at weekends. On one of the nastier blocks in town, so be careful as you arrive and leave. $5.

DNA Lounge 375 11th St at Harrison, SoMa ☎415/626-1409, ⊛www.dnalounge.com. Changes its music style nightly, but draws the same young hipsters, a mixed gay/straight crowd. Downstairs is a large dance-floor, while the mezzanine is a sofa-packed lounge where you can chill. $15–20.

Element Lounge 1028 Geary St at Polk, Polk Gulch ☎415/440-1125, ⊛www.elementlounge .com. This chic nightclub with its "elemental"

decor and creative cocktails draws a young, energetic crowd with DJs spinning hip-hop, house, 1980s music, and mashups. $10.

Etiquette Lounge 1108 Market St at Seventh, SoMa ☎415/869-8779, ⊛www.etiquettelounge .com. With its red, white, and black Victorian theme, this lounge looks as though it came right out of the mind of Tim Burton. The music is usually old-school hip-hop, R&B, and 1980s pop. Located on a particularly unpleasant strip of Market; women should avoid walking outside alone. No cover.

Glas Kat 520 Fourth St at Bryant, SoMa ☎415/495-6620, ⊛www.glaskat.com. Awash in reds and purples, this expansive lounge is home to both the goth and the mainstream B&D scenes with its two weekly parties, Death Guild on Mon and Bondage-a-Go-Go on Wed. But it's not just a space for the black-eyeliner set, as the club has been known to host salsa, Latin dance, hip-hop, and 1980s and 1990s-themed parties. $3–10.

Il Pirata 2007 16th St at Utah, Potrero Hill ☎415/626-262, ⊛www.ilpirata.com. This small dingy dive bar and Italian restaurant, with its Christmas lights, streamers, a large mural, two rooms, sport on the TVs, and outdoor patio, is the place to go for really down 'n' dirty salsa. No cover.

Jelly's 295 China Basin Way at Pier 50, China Basin ☎415/495-3099, ⊛www.jellsycafe.com. A mix of locals and tourists come to dance by the Bay to live funk and salsa. Not worth making a pilgrimage across town for, but fun for an early evening shimmy if you're in the area (music starts at 4pm). $10.

Mighty 119 Utah St at 15th, Potrero Hill ☎415/626-7001. Massive converted warehouse space huddled close to the freeway in Potrero Hill, it's a combination art gallery, performance venue, club, and lounge – check out the frozen vodka bar. As for the music, it's mostly live funk or DJs spinning old-school house. $10 and up.

Milk 1840 Haight St at Stanyan, Haight Ashbury ☎415/387-6455. DJ bar and lounge in the shadow of Golden Gate Park. There are white booths as well as posh drinks, and one of the best rosters of music in the city – cutting-edge DJs spin hip-hop and house for the dancefloor at the rear most nights. Cover $3–10; free before 9pm.

Mission Rock Cafe 817 Terry Francois Blvd at Mariposa, Potrero Hill ☎415/626-5355, ⊛www .kellysmissionrock.com. This mainstream club and restaurant boasts plenty of dancing space as well as a heated patio right on the Bay. You can get down to hip-hop, Top 40, mashups, R&B, Latin hits, 1980s and 1990s retro, house, techno, breakbeats and hi-tek soul. $15–25.

Nickies 460 Haight St at Fillmore, Lower Haight ☎415/621-6508, ⊛www.nickies.com. Hugely popular, year after year, this old-school, bar-sized club lets you groove to New Orleans funk, Indian techno, and world beat. $5–10.

Pink 2925 16th St at Capp, Mission ☎415/431-8889, ⊛www.pinksf.com. The name's a nod to the candy-colored decor – this place looks like a romance novelist's hideaway, with billowing curtains and candles. Don't let the kitschy design put you off though, as this is a serious place to dance: the DJs are high quality (expect acid jazz and deep house) and the mixed gay/straight crowd friendly. The only downside is the pricey drinks. Tuesday's Taboo night is especially popular. $5–10.

Poleng Lounge 1751 Fulton St at Masonic, Western Addition ☎415/441-1751, ⊛www .polenglounge.com. This cozy, laid-back Southeast Asian-themed restaurant and club has two rooms that often host the best up-and-coming and underground DJs and hip-hop acts $5–10.

Ruby Skye 420 Mason St at Geary, Theater District ☎415/693-0777, ⊛www.rubyskye.com. The hugest mainstream DJs tend to stop through this gorgeous, spacious Victorian dancehall with a high-end sound system that focuses on trance, house, drum 'n' bass, techno, and electronica. Visually, there's never a dull moment, with elaborately costumed go-go dancers, hoop dancers, fire dances or acrobats performing. $15–20.

Shine 1337 Mission St at Ninth, SoMa ☎415/255-1337, ⊛wwwshinesf.com. At this low-ceilinged lounge, it's so dark that everyone looks good, with the hardwood floors and black ceiling covered in disco balls. Local underground DJs spin house, breaks, techno, house, electro, and dubstep. The club also provides a free photo booth, which then posts the pictures on *Shine*'s Flickr page. Free–$5.

Sip Bar & Lounge 787 Broadway at Powell, North Beach ☎415/699-6545, ⊛www .siploungesf.com. This sophisticated lounge,

with its leather couches and curtained walls, features DJs spinning hip-hop, R&B, Top 40, and retro pop and sometimes even features local hip-hop acts. You can reserve a table for four or more and bottle service with a $250 minimum in drink purchases. No dress code, and no cover.

Skylark Bar 3089 16th St at Valencia, Mission ☎415/621-9294. Club-bar hybrid, with low lighting and plenty of booths, marred slightly by its yuppified clientele. During the week, it's more geared to drinking, while at weekends it becomes a full-scale dancehall.

Space 550 550 Barneveld Ave at Oakdale, Hunter's Point ☎415/289-2001. An enormous warehouse club known for its trance and industrial dance programming plus a mixed gay/straight crowd; although it's a long way out, in an iffy part of town, serious clubbers will think its worth the trek. $5–15.

The Stud 399 Folsom St at Ninth, SoMa ☎415/252-7883. This San Francisco legend attracts one of the most mixed crowds in town – gay, lesbian, and straight – with theme nights most evenings. The bar itself has a pool table and several pinball machines, and there's even a model train circling overhead. $3–5.

Temple Nightclub 540 Howard St at First, SoMa ☎415/978-9942, ⊛www.templesf.com. Walk into this opulent, spacious nightclub, with its tall columns and pristine white couches, and you'll feel like you're in a high-end modernist Miami hotel. Descend into the Destiny Lounge and it becomes even more neon-lit and space-agey, and delve even deeper to reach the Catacombs, you'll find yourself in a room resembling a Buddhist-themed cave. This spot is known for its state-of-the-art sound system and rooms featuring house, electro, breaks, hip-hop, funk, and pop. $10–20.

The Transfer 198 Church St at 14th, Castro ☎415/961-7499. This is the ultimate hipster nightclub, drawing a mix of gay and straight clubbers for electro-punk-disco, Top 40, hip-hop, and 1980s retro. Saturday's Frisco Disco party is particularly popular with the skinny-jeans set and other nights feature drag performers and go-go dancers. Free–$5.

Performing arts and film

S
an Francisco rightfully has a reputation for embracing the **performing arts** – there are several major symphony orchestras based in the Bay Area, and the city itself boasts a world-class **ballet troupe** and a highly respected **opera** company. **Theater** is also plentiful, though it's unfortunate that many of the larger venues often fall prey to a schedule of Broadway reruns. The bolder fringe circuit stages new plays with greater frequency, and while quality can be uneven, these smaller concerns tend to offer more interesting options than the crowd-pleasers staged west of Union Square.

Thanks largely to an active club scene, **comedy** in San Francisco is regaining an audience, with local punters turning up in increasing numbers for laugh nights built around stand-up and sketch material.

Film remains nearly as popular an obsession as eating in San Francisco. A surprising range of local cinemas – from old-time, single-screen movie houses to spanking-new multiplexes – show independent and major studio releases alike, while a strong community of underground filmgoers ensures a slate of truly alternative programming at a few leftfield venues around town.

Classical music, ballet, and opera

Major companies

Philharmonia Baroque Orchestra ☎415/252-1288, ⓦ www.philharmonia.org. This much-lauded company performs early music on traditional European instruments in various Bay Area venues during its fall and spring seasons. Over the years, the orchestra's repertoire has expanded beyond its strict chronological boundaries, but its sound remains distinctive. Tickets $30–72.

San Francisco Ballet War Memorial Opera House, 301 Van Ness Ave at Grove, Civic Center ☎415/865-2000, ⓦ www.sfballet.org. The oldest ballet troupe in the US remains in top form. Founded in 1933, it was the first

company to stage full-length productions of *Swan Lake* and *The Nutcracker*, yet despite its illustrious origins, it faced near-bankruptcy by the 1970s and 1980s. Thankfully, the arrival of artistic director Helgi Tomasson (former "premier danseur" of the New York City Ballet) ushered in an era of revived prominence. Since it shares the War Memorial with San Francisco Opera, the Ballet's season runs Jan–May, with *The Nutcracker* showing each holiday season. Tickets begin at $30, while standing-room tickets are sold two hours before each performance for $10–12.

San Francisco Opera War Memorial Opera House, 301 Van Ness Ave at Grove, Civic Center

Ⓣ**415/864-3330,** Ⓦ**www.sfopera.org.** A typical season for this internationally regarded company offers a mixture of avant-garde stagings by composers such as John Adams or André Previn, along with acclaimed productions of perennial favorites by Wagner or Puccini. The War Memorial Opera House provides a suitably opulent setting: opened in 1932, the building's design by Arthur Brown, Jr – also responsible for City Hall and Coit Tower – is a rich gold confection with plush felt seats. The season runs Sept–Dec, with a short summer season in June and July. Tickets are $25–200; same-day rush tickets become available for students, seniors, and military personnel at 11am.

San Francisco Performances Ⓣ**415/398-6449,** Ⓦ**www.performances.org.** Known as the most adventurous large company in town, San Francisco Performances schedules a diverse array of classical recitals, jazz, and contemporary dance programs, often with a European emphasis. Spring and fall programs shuttle between various local theaters, including the Herbst Theatre, Yerba Buena Center for the Arts, and Davies Symphony Hall. Performances vary in both name-recognition and quality. Tickets $15–70.

San Francisco Symphony Louise M. Davies Symphony Hall, 201 Van Ness Ave at Hayes, Civic Center Ⓣ**415/864-6000,** Ⓦ**www .sfsymphony.org.** Since the 1995 arrival of conductor Michael Tilson Thomas, this once-musty institution has catapulted to the first rank of American symphony orchestras. Though Thomas's relentless self-promotion can be off-putting, his emphasis on the works of twentieth-century composers has added considerable vibrancy to the company's programming. The season runs Sept–May, with scattered events at the Legion of Honor as well as the Flint Center in Cupertino, near San Jose. Depending on the performance, tickets generally range from $35–125, with day-of-performance rush tickets available for $20.

Free concerts

A particularly welcome offshoot of San Francisco's thriving performing arts scene is the plenteous free concerts that take place at venues around town, mostly during the summer season.

Golden Gate Park Band Sun 1pm, April through Oct, Spreckels Temple of Music, Golden Gate Park Ⓣ415/831-5500, Ⓦwww.goldengateparkband.org. Since 1882, this populist ensemble has been playing a variety of favorites – Broadway show tunes, marches, folk music – at the bandshell in its namesake park's Music Concourse. Pack a picnic and expect to hum along.

Lindy in the Park Sun 11am–2pm, year-round, John F. Kennedy Drive behind de Young Museum, Golden Gate Park Ⓦwww.lindyinthepark.com. Free swing dance gathering that's fun even for confirmed dual left-footers. There's usually a free lesson at noon.

Noontime Concerts Tues 12.30pm, Old St Mary's Cathedral, 660 California St at Grant, Chinatown Ⓣ415/777-3211, Ⓦwww.noontimeconcerts.org. Impressive lunch-hour classical concerts showcasing mostly well-known works by the likes of Mozart, Beethoven, and Chopin, though there are occasional diversions, such as Baroque chamber works from Italy. A $5 donation is requested.

Stern Grove Festival Sun 2pm, mid-June to mid-Aug, Stern Grove, Sloat Blvd and 19th Ave, Parkside Ⓣ415/252-6252, Ⓦwww.sterngrove.org. An eclectic lineup of performers – from Hawaiian bands, to Latin American rock groups and the San Francisco Opera – entertain the crowds at these hugely popular outdoor shows each summer. Arrive early to secure a spot on the lawn. Public transportation recommended.

Yerba Buena Gardens Festival May–Oct, schedule varies, Yerba Buena Gardens, Mission St at Third, SoMa Ⓣ415/543-1718, Ⓦwww.ybgf.org. More than 200 different daytime concert events – including an occasional outdoor appearance by the San Francisco Symphony – take place here each year.

Smaller ballet companies

Lines Ballet Yerba Buena Center for the Arts, 701 Mission St at Third, SoMa ☎ 415/863-3040, ⓦ www.linesballet.org. A superb contemporary ensemble that started at the San Francisco Dance Center and is now based at the Yerba Buena Center; it also mounts tours around the US. Innovative and avant-garde, Lines is known for its international reach: one well-received production brought African pygmy dancers to perform with the troupe.

Smuin Ballet ☎ 415/495-2234, ⓦ www .smuinballet.org. Founded by former San Francisco Ballet director Michael Smuin, this company spruces up traditional dance with snazzy bits of jazz and pop (everything from Gershwin to k.d. lang). The roving troupe doesn't have a permanent home, but performs in and around San Francisco, venturing as far south as Carmel on occasion. It's perhaps not for ballet purists, but terrific for dance newbies. Tickets $40–55.

Theater

For half-price bargains to shows at major San Francisco houses, try the **Tix Bay Area** booth (Tues–Thurs 11am–6pm, Fri 11am–7pm, Sat 10am–7pm, Sun 10am–3pm; ☎ 415/430-1140, ⓦ www.theatrebayarea.org), located on the west side of Union Square opposite the *Westin St Francis Hotel*. Each day's bargains are listed at noon on the website.

In early September, the **San Francisco Fringe Festival** (☎ 415/931-1094, ⓦ www.sffringe.org) – a marathon of more than 250 experimental performances by some fifty companies – is held at several venues, though the Exit Theater near Union Square is the primary location. Tickets are usually reasonably priced at $8–15.

Stage buffs should also consider a trip across the bay, as the **Berkeley Repertory Theatre** is acknowledged as one of the premier stages in California (see p.324).

Major theaters

American Conservatory Theater (ACT) 415 Geary St at Mason, Theater District ☎ 415/749-2228, ⓦ www.act-sf.org. The Bay Area's leading resident theater group mixes newly commissioned works and innovative renditions of the classics; you can also expect the obligatory holiday season run of *A Christmas Carol*. Particularly noteworthy is the company's inventive set design and staging. Tickets can cost as little as $14 for a preview show, though you'll pay $30–70 most of the time; rush tickets are generally available from noon on performance days.

Curran Theater 445 Geary St at Mason, Theater District ☎ 415/551-2000, ⓦ www.shnsf.com. One of the three San Francisco venues managed by Shorenstein Hays, the Curran is a former vaudeville theater that now presents both hit Broadway plays and musicals. Pre-Broadway tryouts are common here: Tony magnet *Wicked* was workshopped for several weeks at the Curran before hitting New York. Tickets cost $30–90.

Golden Gate Theater 1 Taylor St at Golden Gate Ave, Tenderloin ☎ 415/551-2000, ⓦ www .shnsf.com. Constructed in the 1920s and restored to its original splendor by owners Shorenstein Hays, this auditorium's elegant Rococo decor frequently outclasses its schedule of touring Broadway productions. Cheap seats cost around $30, while most tickets cost upwards of $45.

Marines Memorial Theatre 609 Sutter St at Mason, Union Square ☎ 415/771-6900, ⓦ www .unionsquaretheatres.com. This building was originally designed as a live radio studio in the 1920s; its 650-seat theater now hosts mid-range traveling companies and mainstream crowd-pleasers starring the odd television actor slumming it on the stage. Tickets start around $30.

Orpheum Theater 1192 Market St at Eighth, Tenderloin ☎ 415/551-2000, ⓦ www.shnsf.com. Probably the most spectacular of all the big houses, the third Shorenstein Hays venue is much grander than its lineup of lesser Broadway shows – look for the white gargoyles on the interior molding. Ticket prices typically start around $40 for most performances.

Yerba Buena Center for the Arts 701 Mission St at Third, SoMa ☎415/978-2787, ⒲www.ybca .org. The Center struggled to find an identity for years as it careened between every possible avant-garde performance style in dance, theater, and music. Thanks to artistic director Kenneth Foster, it's finally honing its vision, showcasing local talents in programs like the Hip-Hop Theater Festival as well as touring shows. Tickets $15–50.

Smaller spaces

Actors Theatre 855 Bush St at Mason, Union Square ☎415/345-1287, ⒲www.actors theatresf.org. This company presents high-quality, ensemble-based drama in an intimate space – usually big-name plays (*One Flew Over the Cuckoo's Nest*, *Cat on a Hot Tin Roof*) with an impressive local cast. Ticket prices usually hover around $30.

African American Art & Culture Complex 762 Fulton St at Webster, Western Addition ☎415/922-2049, ⒲www.aaacc.org. Thanks to inspiring executive director London Breed, this fledgling cultural space – home to a cluster of black arts associations – is buzzing. Stage performances are erratically scheduled, but usually take place in the onsite, 210-seat Buriel Clay Memorial Theater. Tickets from $10.

🏃 **BATS Improv Bayfront Theater, Fort Mason Center** ☎415/474-6776, ⒲www .improv.org. Celebrated long-form improv company (its titular acronym stands for Bay Area Theatresports) that hosts classes, guest groups, and an improv competition every Sun night; it also stages its own shows year-round. Tickets $5–20.

🏃 **Beach Blanket Babylon Club Fugazi, 678 Green St at Powell, North Beach** ☎415/421-4222, ⒲www.beachblanketbabylon .com. Founded by the late Steve Silver, a prominent local personality, *Beach Blanket Babylon* has become a San Francisco insti-tution since debuting in the mid 1970s. The revue-style show, which plays about eight shows weekly, is *SNL* meets *The Daily Show*, injected with a liberal dose of Vegas kitsch. It's a constantly rewritten pastiche that lampoons celebrities and current events, using the loose framework of a lovelorn Snow White as its base. The massive wigs worn by the mostly veteran cast – including one depicting the entire city skyline – are the

▲ Beach Blanket Babylon

true showstoppers. Performances are for those 21 and over, except two Sun matinees. Tickets $25–78.

The Dark Room 2263 Mission St at 19th, Mission ☎415/401-7987, ⒲www.darkroomsf .com. This multi-use performance space has a varied programming schedule (usually handwritten on a white board on the door): Fri and Sat typically see troupe comedy or live theater ($10–15), while Sun is Bad Movie Night, for which an unintentionally awful film (*Last Action Hero*, *Waterworld*, etc) is screened for $5.

Exit Theater 156 Eddy St at Taylor, Tenderloin ☎415/673-3847, ⒲www.theexit.org. Its Tenderloin address is dodgy, and its houses are tiny – no more than 90 seats in each of its four spaces – but the Exit is one of the best spots in town for cutting-edge theater. It's known for April's DivaFest, devoted to women-centric plays and performances, as well as producing and being an anchor venue for September's local Fringe Festival. Tickets run $20–25.

Footloose & Shotwell Studios 3252-A 19th St at Shotwell, Mission ☎415/920-2223, ⒲www .ftloose.org. Formerly known as Venue 9, this small company is locally respected for its experimental music and dance shows that often showcase a feminist slant; it also puts on theater, comedy, and multimedia perform-ances. Tickets are usually around $20.

Intersection for the Arts 446 Valencia St at 16th, Mission ☎415/626-3311,

Ⓦ www.theintersection.org. Opened in the 1960s, this is the city's longest-active alternative theater space, still churning out political, community-oriented productions in its tiny venue. Expect low-budget, high-quality performances, with ticket prices around $10 ("pay what you can" nights occur frequently). There's also an onsite visual arts gallery (free; Wed–Sat noon–6pm) with a similarly political bent.

Lorraine Hansberry Theatre Ⓣ 415/474-8800, Ⓦ www.lhtsf.com. This African-American company showcases both new plays and classics like *Porgy and Bess*; however, at the time of writing, it was searching for a new home for the forthcoming season – check the website for updated venue information. Tickets start at $20.

Magic Theatre Fort Mason Center Ⓣ 415/441-8822, Ⓦ www.magictheatre.org. The busiest and largest local company after ACT, the Magic is responsible for some of the top fringe productions in the Bay Area. It specializes in the works of contemporary playwrights, as well as those by emerging new talents. Performances occur at either of two venues at lower Fort Mason: the Northside Theatre or the Sam Shepard Theatre. Tickets are generally $40–45.

The Marsh 1062 Valencia St at 22nd, Mission Ⓣ 800/838-3006, Ⓦ www.themarsh.org. This longstanding alternative space hosts fine solo shows, many with an offbeat bent. Mon nights are test nights for works in progress. Tickets are often made available on a sliding scale between $15–30.

The New Conservatory Theatre Center 25 Van Ness Ave at Fell, Civic Center Ⓣ 415/861-8972 Ⓦ www.nctcsf.org, This mid-size theater is known for its Pride season of gay-themed plays, as well as comedy and cabaret productions. Tickets are $18–40.

Post Street Theatre 450 Post St at Mason, Union Square Ⓣ 415/771-6900,

Ⓦ www.unionsquaretheatres.com. Like its sibling, the Marines Memorial (see p.229), this recently revived 700-seat theater off Union Square usually focuses on smaller commercial hits with a single marquee star; from time to time it also hosts extended runs by a big-name magician. Tickets are around $35, depending on the type of show.

San Francisco Mime Troupe Ⓣ 415/285-1717, Ⓦ www.sfmt.org. Founded in 1959, this group was an early leader in "people's," or radical, theater. The troupe's punchy, not-so-subtle political comedies, performed for free at parks throughout the city, have become a summertime tradition from Independence Day through Labor Day – check its website for a performance schedule.

San Francisco Shakespeare Festival Ⓣ 415/558-0888, Ⓦ www.sfshakes.org. Free Shakespeare performed on weekends around the Bay Area, late June through late Sept. Productions usually hit the Presidio's Main Post Parade Ground Lawn by the last weekend in Aug and are presented through Sept. Arrive early to ensure getting a seat.

Shelton Studios 533 Sutter St at Powell, Union Square Ⓣ 415/433-1227, Ⓦ www.sheltontheater.com. Improv productions and musicals are staged in this tiny showspace; tickets start at $20.

Theater Rhinoceros 2926 16th St at S Van Ness, Mission Ⓣ 415/861-5079, Ⓦ www.therhino.org. The city's prime gay-oriented theater space includes two auditoria, each hosting productions that range from heartfelt political drama to raunchy cabaret acts. Tickets run $15–25.

Thick House 1695 18th St at Carolina, Potrero Hill Ⓣ 415/401-8081, Ⓦ www.thickhouse.org. A small space (85 seats) showcasing new works by Bay Area playwrights, particularly during its PlayGround Festival in May. Tickets around $28.

Comedy

Following an era of glory that saw Robin Williams, Margaret Cho, and Dana Carvey cut their teeth in local clubs before becoming major stars, San Francisco's **comedy** scene endured a fallow period of venue closures and few national breakthoughs. Things are looking up, however, with the recent proliferation of comedy nights staged at bars, music venues, and tiny theaters in the city. Check Ⓦ www.sfstandup.com for an extensive list of comedy shows in and around San Francisco.

Should you find yourself in San Francisco in either January or September and looking for laughs, a pair of annual comedy happenings bear mention. SF Sketchfest (⑩ www.sfsketchfest.com) is an ever-growing event that books big names (The Kids in the Hall, David Cross) and lesser-knowns alike each January at a host of venues around town; it also promotes other local shows throughout the year. Comedy Day (⑩ www.comedyday.com) is held annually at Sharon Meadow in Golden Gate Park, usually on the last Sunday in September (when San Francisco weather is often at its most glorious). The free, afternoon-long festival brings together local comedians and nationally known stars like Paula Poundstone.

Cobb's Comedy Club 915 Columbus Ave at Lombard, North Beach ☎ 415/928-4320, ⑩ www.cobbscomedy.com. A 400-seat room not far from Fisherman's Wharf that consistently hosts mid-profile touring comedians. Tickets can cost $30 for weekend performances, plus a two-drink minimum.

Club Chuckles Hemlock Tavern, 1131 Polk St at Sutter, Polk Gulch ☎ 415/923-0923, ⑩ www.hemlocktavern.com. Monthly $5 side-splitter booked by local empresario Anthony Bedard, who also operates San Francisco comedy record label Talent Moat. Shows are a mixed bag of sketches, musical comedy, stand-up, films, and videos.

Club Deluxe 1511 Haight St at Ashbury, Upper Haight ☎ 415/552-6949, ⑩ www.myspace.com/clubdeluxesf. Mon is comedy night at this Haight St standby, popular with hipsters sporting fedoras and fringe haircuts. Tickets $10.

The Clubhouse 414 Mason St at Post, Union Square ⑩ www.clubhousecomedy.com. This offshoot of San Francisco Comedy College puts on popular weekend shows in a recently enlarged Downtown space; the bring-your-own-alcohol policy ensures a convivial scene. Tickets typically run $5–10.

The Punch Line 444 Battery St at Clay, Financial District ☎ 415/397-7573, ⑩ www.punchlinecomedyclub.com. Frontrunner in name cachet among San Francisco's few full-scale comedy venues, this strangely located cabaret books nightly shows featuring well-known headliners. Tickets usually start at $15, with the obligatory two-drink minimum.

Purple Onion 140 Columbus St at Jackson, North Beach ☎ 415/956-1653, ⑩ www.caffemacaroni.com. Once a stage for Lenny Bruce, Woody Allen, and Phyllis Diller in the 1950s and 1960s, this 80-seat cellar venue has been revived as a comedy venue under the ownership of adjacent restaurant *Caffe Macaroni*. Check the website for upcoming acts, as bookings can be inconsistent. Tickets $8–20.

Film

San Francisco is as much a film town as ever, judging by the fact that five gleaming multiplexes have opened since the mid 1990s. Listed below are many of the city's full-scale cinemas, along with a clutch of alternative venues that show more adventuresome features and shorts. Consult each theater's website for complete listings and showtimes, or simply pick up one of the local dailies or weeklies for a schedule roundup. For **advance online tickets** to certain local cinemas, try Fandango (⑩ www.fandango.com) or Moviefone (⑩ www.moviefone.com).

Multiplexes

Embarcadero Center Cinema 1 Embarcadero Center, Financial District ☎ 415/267-4893, ⑩ www.landmarktheatres.com. Immensely popular new Downtown theater showing both first-run independents and Oscar contenders.

Metreon 15 101 Fourth St at Mission, SoMa ☎ 415/369-6201, ⑩ www.amctheatres.com. This multiplex is the one element of the Metreon that locals have welcomed. There are fifteen screens (plus an IMAX theater) and high-definition sound, plus arena-style seating in every auditorium.

San Francisco Centre 9 845 Market St at Fifth, SoMa ☎415/538-8422, ⓦ www.cinemark.com. Expect Hollywood hits galore (and the occasional arthouse surprise) amidst booming sound systems and imitation leather seats at this state-of-the-art complex. It's on the fifth floor of the Bloomingdales-anchored San Francisco Centre.

🏃 **Sundance Kabuki Cinemas** 1881 Post St at Fillmore, Japantown ☎415/346-3243, ⓦ www.sundancecinemas.com. With advance reserved seating, sustainable-friendly details like "spudware" utensils, and three eating/drinking destinations inside, this recently facelifted facility is like few other cinemas in the US. Programming varies from mainstream fare to eclectic choices. Validated parking is available at the underground parking garage. Expect a $1–3 amenities fee.

Van Ness 14 1000 Van Ness Ave at O'Farrell, Tenderloin ☎415/674-4630, ⓦ www.amctheatres.com. Dating from the 1920s, when it was an auto showroom topped by warehouses, this enormous multiplex in the heart of the city is ornamented in terracotta and painted metal and shows mostly mainstream fare.

Theaters

Balboa Theatre 3630 Balboa St at 37th, Outer Richmond ☎415/221-8184, ⓦ www.balboamovies.com. On a mellow block in the western reaches of the Richmond, the Balboa recently abandoned repertory programming in favor of fresh Hollywood celluloid. It was originally built as a single-screen theater in 1926 before being split into two viewing spaces in the late 1970s.

Bridge Theatre 3010 Geary St at Blake, Laurel Heights ☎415/267-4893, ⓦ www.landmarktheatres.com. There's one large screen in this old Art-Deco cinema, named in 1939 after the then-recently opened Golden Gate. Programming alternates between Hollywood and independent hits.

🏃 **Castro Theatre** 429 Castro St at 17th, Castro ☎415/621-6120, ⓦ www.thecastrotheatre.com. San Francisco's signature movie palace (opened in 1922) offers foreign films, classic revivals, seating for over 1400, and the most enthusiastic audience in town; it also serves as hub for a number of local film festivals. Come early for

▲ Castro Theatre

evening screenings to listen to the Wurlitzer organ and gaze at the spectacular chandelier.

Clay Theatre 2261 Fillmore St at Sacramento, Pacific Heights ☎415/267-4893, ⓦ www.landmarktheatres.com. Circa-1910 single-screen cinema showing arthouse and foreign films in the heart of Pacific Heights.

Lumiere Theatre 1572 California St at Polk, Polk Gulch ☎415/267-4893, ⓦ www.landmark theatres.com. This Nob Hill-adjacent theater, located right on the California cable-car line, offers a mix of short-run rarities and new-release foreign films.

Marina Theatre 2149 Chestnut St at Steiner, Marina ☎415/345-1323, ⓦ www.landmark theatres.com. Completely rebuilt by Lee Neighborhood Theatres (which also operates two other local cinemas), the Marina's two upstairs screens are fine spots to catch mainstream fare like the latest Cameron Diaz vehicle.

Opera Plaza Cinema 601 Van Ness Ave at McAllister, Civic Center ☎415/267-4893, ⓦ www.landmarktheatres.com. Generally the last place in town to catch a movie before it shows up on video. The screens in the two smaller rooms aren't much larger than jumbo televisions.

The Red Vic 1727 Haight St at Cole, Upper Haight ☎415/668-3994, ⓦ www.redvicmovie house.com. Grab a wooden bowl filled with

Bay Area film festivals

February: SF Indie, see p.276.

March: San Francisco International Asian American Film Festival, see p.277.

April: San Francisco International Film Festival, see p.278.

April: San Francisco Women's Film Festival ⓦ www.sfwff.com. Founded by a local film student in 2004, this spring event showcases works by women spanning a number of genres, including documentaries and animation.

May–Ocobert: Film Night in the Park ⓣ 415/453-4333 ⓦ www.filmnight.org. A variety of crowd-pleasers (*Mary Poppins*, *Vertigo*) and cult faves (*Amelie*, *The Breakfast Club*) presented by a local foundation in public parks all around the Bay Area, including Union Square and Dolores Park in San Francisco. Suggested donation.

June: Frameline, see p.279.

June–August: Zeitgeist International Film Festival ⓦ www.overcookedcinema .com. A fusillade of short films screened in "Beer-O-Scope" on a huge patio behind notable Mission bar *Zeitgeist* (see p.218). Marvelously lowbrow.

July: Bicycle Film Festival ⓦ www.bicyclefilmfestival.com. Global event showcasing "velo-cinema" that rolls through San Francisco in summer.

July–August: San Francisco Jewish Film Festival ⓣ 415/621-0556, ⓦ www.sfjff. org. Films from throughout the Jewish diaspora: thought-provoking documentaries to racy Israeli soap operas.

October: Mill Valley Film Festival ⓦ www.mvff.com. This non-competitive festival draws up-and-comers and big names alike to Marin County. Independent and world cinema are heavily emphasized.

November: Film Arts Festival ⓣ 415/552-8760, ⓦ www.filmarts.org. A longstanding festival of Northern California filmmakers, featuring particularly strong programs of documentaries and short films, many of which go on to the Sundance Festival. At the time of writing, its managing organization was in the midst of an emergency fundraising campaign to ensure its future.

popcorn and kick your feet up on the natty chairs and couches at this friendly collective, where the calendar is peppered with cult hits, surf movies, and directors' cuts of past favorites.

The Roxie New College Film Center 3117 16th St at Valencia, Mission ⓣ 415/863-1087, ⓦ www .roxie.com. This venerable and pugnacious indie moviehouse was acquired by the nearby New College in 2006. Thankfully, its adventurous programming hasn't been diluted (although its repertory scheduling has essentially disappeared), as the Roxie has always been willing to take a risk on documentaries and little-known foreign directors.

Other venues

Artists' Television Access 992 Valencia St at 21st, Mission ⓣ 415/824-3890, ⓦ www.atasite.org. A scrappy, non-profit storefront space that shows regular programs of short underground films (often with a political or social theme) about four nights a week for $5.

San Francisco Cinematheque ⓣ 415/552-1990, ⓦ www.sfcinematheque.org. Roving experimental film and video showcase, with screenings at a number of local venues. The organization also sponsors artist residencies.

Yerba Buena Center for the Arts Screening Room 701 Mission St at Third, SoMa ⓣ 415/978-2787, ⓦ www.ybca.org. Screening experimental films, documentaries, and other slipstream works (many from decades past), this intimate, 92-seat space offers bracing alternatives to what you'll find at the adjacent Metreon multiplex.

Gay and lesbian San Francisco

The heart of queer America is, arguably, San Francisco, where it's estimated that up to ten percent of the city's population is **gay**, **lesbian**, **bisexual**, or **transgender**. This concentration has its roots in the permissiveness of the city's Gold Rush era and, more recently, during World War II, when suspected homosexual soldiers, purged by military brass at their point of embarkation, stayed put in town rather than return home to face stigma and shame. These beginnings, along with the advent of gay liberation in the early 1970s, nurtured a community with powerful political and social connections.

Nowadays, most San Franciscans appreciate the positive **cultural and economic impact** gay people have on the city, and a welcoming attitude toward homosexuality predominates. Openly gay politicians or business-people are not the issue to locals they would be in many other areas of the US; this may also have to do with the fact that most of the gay community has effectively moved from the outra-geous to the mainstream, a measure of its political success. Sadly, though (at least to some), the exuberant energy that went into the posturing and parading of the 1970s has taken on a much more sober, down-to-business attitude. Today you'll find more political activists organizing conferences than drag queens throwing parties, but while the city's gay scene has mellowed socially, its parades, parties, and street fairs still swing better than most.

Well-kept and relatively safe, the **Castro** remains one of the world's most prominent gay destinations, but is by no means the sole enclave of queer life in San Francisco. Oft-seedy **Polk Gulch** is the city's center of drag and transgender elements, while leather and fetish scenes continue to flourish in **SoMa**. Although lesbian culture flowered in the city in

▲ Castro Street

235

the 1980s and **Bernal Heights**, **Glen Park**, **Noe Valley**, and parts of the **Mission** each have lesbian communities, many women have migrated across the Bay to Oakland in recent years.

Organizations and resources

A number of community and information centers, as well as health clinics, are available to queer visitors; as you'd expect, most are concentrated in and around the Castro. Also, a few helpful websites have sprouted up, while a limited number of gay and lesbian-focused print publications soldier on.

Walk-in centers

Charles M. Holmes Campus at the Center 1800 Market St at Octavia, Lower Haight ☎415/865-5555, ⊛www.sfcenter.org. Known to most as simply the Center, this is the local gay community's main large-scale gathering and resource venue. Finally opened in 2002 after nearly a decade in the works, it has not only a café and plenty of handy materials at the first-floor information desk, but also regularly hosts workshops as well as performances by comedy and theater groups – everything from stand-up and improve to queer-centric film series. Mon–Fri noon–10pm, Sat 9am–10pm.

Dimensions Clinic Castro-Mission Health Center, 3850 17th St at Noe, Castro ☎415/487-7589, ⊛www.dimensionsclinic.org. Affiliated with Lyric (see below), this low-cost clinic offers health services to queer youth. Thurs 5–8pm, Sat noon–3pm.

GLBT Historical Society Museum 657 Mission St at New Montgomery, Suite 300, SoMa ☎415/777-5455, ⊛www.glbthistory.org. Historical exhibits, programs, and art showings, as well as extensive resource archives and a reading room. Exhibit galleries open Tues–Sat 1–5pm; archives and reading room open to public Sat 1–5pm.

Lyon Martin Women's Health Services 1748 Market St at Gough, Suite 201, Lower Haight ☎415/565-7667, ⊛www.lyon-martin.org. Long-established nonprofit clinic that focuses on helping low-income and uninsured lesbian/bisexual and transgender women. Anonymous HIV testing, gynecological care, pregnancy tests, counseling, and legal help. Mon & Wed 11am–7pm, Tues & Fri 9am–5pm, Thurs noon–5pm.

Lyric 127 Collingwood St at 18th, Castro ☎415/703-6150, ⊛www.lyric.org. Discussion groups, trainings, arts, recreation events, and assistance with women's issues for LGBT (and questioning) youth aged 24 and under. Call for hours.

Magnet 4122 18th St at Castro, Castro ☎415/581-1600, ⊛www.magnetsf.com. Health and wellness center (including rapid HIV testing) combined with a performance space that hosts massage workshops, book readings, social gatherings, and performances. Tues & Sat 11am–6pm, Wed–Fri 2–9pm.

New Leaf: Services For Our Community 103 Hayes St at Polk, Civic Center ☎415/626-7000 ⊛www.newleafservices.org. Outpatient mental health and substance abuse assistance for the LGBT community. Services are provided on a sliding fee scale based on income. Mon–Thurs 9am–8pm, Fri 9am–7pm.

Online/phone services

California AIDS Hotline ☎415/863-2437. 24hr information and counseling.

Castro Online ⊛www.castroonline.com. Robust site featuring travel and calendar listings, original content, and discussion boards. A good first stop for gay travelers planning a visit.

Gay & Lesbian Medical Association ☎415/255-4547, ⊛www.glma.org. Referrals to gay and lesbian physicians.

San Francisco Sex Information ☎415/989-7374, ⊛www.sfsi.org. Providing free, anonymous, and accurate information since 1972. Staffed Mon–Thurs 3–9pm, Fri 3–7pm, Sat 2–6pm, Sun 2–5pm.

The Sisters of Perpetual Indulgence ☎415/820-9697, ⊛www.thesisters.org. Pope-baiting order of outlandish nuns that's been raising hell, safe-sex awareness, and piles of money for charitable organizations as diverse as Friends of the Pink Triangle and the Red Cross since 1979. Naturally, it got its start in San Francisco.

There's barely anywhere in San Francisco that won't welcome handholding gay couples, and hotels or restaurants will comfortably cater to gay travelers. If you're planning a trip to the city and surroundings, we've put together a list of useful resources below.

In the US and Canada

Damron Box 422458, San Francisco, CA 94142 ☎800/462-6654 or 415/255-0404 ⓦwww.damron.com. Publisher of several guides written specifically for gay travelers, all of which feature in-depth sections on San Francisco.

Gayellow Pages Box 533, Village Station, New York, NY 10014 ☎646/213-0263, ⓦwww.gayellowpages.com. Useful directory of businesses in the US and Canada. Order a hard copy via post or download the California chapter as a free PDF from the website.

International Gay & Lesbian Travel Association 915 Middle River Drive, Suite 306, Fort Lauderdale, FL 33304 ☎954/630-1637, ⓦwww.iglta.org. Trade group providing information on gay- and lesbian-owned or -friendly travel agents, accommodations, and other travel businesses.

In the UK

Madison Travel 118 Western Rd, Hove, East Sussex BN3 1DB ☎01273/202 532, ⓦwww.madisontravel.co.uk. Established travel agents specializing in gay and lesbian travel packages, including trips to the Bay Area.

UK Gay Hotel and Travel Guide Box 6991, Leicester LE1 6YS ☎08703/455 600, ⓦwww.gaytravel.co.uk. Operated by the Gay Britain Network.

In Australia and New Zealand

Gay Travel ⓦwww.gaytravel.com. Information source for international holiday excursions, including trip planning and booking.

Parkside Travel 70 Glen Osmond Rd, Parkside, SA 5063 ☎08/8274 1222 or 1800 888 501. Travel agent associated with local branch of Harvey World Travel; all aspects of gay and lesbian travel worldwide, California included.

Silke's Travel 263 Oxford St, Darlinghurst, NSW 2010 ☎02/9380 6244 or 1800/807 860. Long-established specialist with an emphasis on women's travel.

Tearaway Travel 52 Porter St, Prahan, VIC 3181 ☎03/9510 6344 ⓦwww.tearaway .com. Domestic and trans-Pacific travel for gay men and lesbians.

Print

Gloss ⓦwww.sfgloss.com. Free. Lifestyle magazine with interviews, articles, columns, and listings.

San Francisco Spectrum ☎415/255-9760, ⓦwww.sfspectrum.com. Regular freesheet available around the Castro and other gay pockets of San Francisco.

Accommodation

Choose any hotel in San Francisco and a single-sex couple won't raise an eyebrow at check-in. Some inns, like the Queen Anne (see p.163), attract equal numbers of gay and straight visitors. However, here are a few B&Bs and inns that cater especially to queer travelers. For information on prices, see box on p.152.

Elaine's Hidden Haven 4005 Folsom St at Tompkins, Bernal Heights ☎415/647-2726 or 800/446-9050, ⓦwww.sfhiddenhaven.com. Sequestered on a quiet, sloped street with parking, this private, lesbian-operated suite is attached to the owners' home. There's a hammock and burbling fountain in the back garden, and a kitchen if you'd rather cook your own meals. $69 for singles, more expensive for additional guests.

Inn on Castro 321 Castro St at 16th, Castro ☎415/861-0321, ⊛www.innoncastro.com. This luxurious B&B is spread across two nearby houses: it has eight rooms and three apartments available, all of which are brightly decorated in individual styles and have private baths and phones; there's also a funky lounge where you can meet other guests. Two-night minimum on weekends, three-night minimum on holidays. Shared bath from $95, private bath from $115.

🏃 **The Parker House** 520 Church St at 17th, Castro ☎888/520-7275, ⊛www.parker guesthouse.com. This 21-room converted mansion is set in beautiful gardens and features ample common areas, a sunny breakfast room, and even a sauna. Shared bath from $139, private bath from $159.

24 Henry 24 Henry St at Sanchez, Castro ☎415/864-5686 or 800/900-5686, ⊛www.24henry.com. This small blue-and-white home, tucked away on a leafy residential street north of Market, is a predominantly gay male guesthouse with five simple rooms, one with private bath. It makes a friendly bolthole from the cruisey Castro scene nearby. From $85 (check the website for discounted rates).

Willows Inn 710 14th St at Church, Castro ☎415/431-4770 or 800/431-0277, ⊛www .willowssf.com. This Edwardian B&B has a dozen rooms with wicker furniture, armoires, and vanity units. Baths are shared, and it's less than a minute's walk from its front door to Market St bustle. From $95.

Eating

While you're bound to find people of all sexual orientations at the restaurants and bistros listed below, it's a good bet that gays will outnumber straights at many of these.

🏃 **Asia SF** 201 Ninth St at Howard, SoMa ☎415/255-2742. As delicious as the small pan-Asian plates are at this sophisticated SoMa restaurant/club, the food is overshadowed by the "gender illusionist" servers, who periodically hop onto the red runway bar to dance. Popular with bachelorette parties, and moderately priced. Dinner only.

Castro Country Club 4058 18th St at Hartford, Castro ☎415/552-6102. Low-key social and community space housed on the first floor of an old Victorian. Everyone seems to just hang out on the steps out front, but there's also a TV room, pinball, patio, and a coffee-house that serves cheap snacks and non-alcoholic drinks.

Catch 2362 Market St between 16th and 17th, Castro ☎415/431-5000. True to its name, *Catch* specializes in seafood – enjoy wild Alaskan halibut ($22) on the heated patio while listening to live piano jazz. Oysters on the half shell are available for $2 each, and there's pasta and steak dishes ($18–26) for landlubbers. Brunch on weekends.

Firewood Café 4248 18th St at Collingwood, Castro ☎415/243-8908. The thin-crust pizzas and half-chickens here make for one of the most affordable meals in the Castro, while the salads are generously sized. It's a casual, quiet place a few blocks off the rambunctious Castro strip.

Harvey's 500 Castro St at 18th, Castro ☎415/431-4278. A lively, moderately priced restaurant/bar (named in honor of Harvey Milk) that draws a friendly crowd from the neighborhood and beyond. It's a solid all-around option – there's brunch on weekends, as well as live comedy and piano jazz on certain nights. Be sure to check out the cheeky cocktail list, which riffs wildly on the Bloody Mary concept (the Bloody Mary Tyler Moore has more liquor, of course).

Home 2100 Market St at Church, Castro ☎415/503-0333. Located on a prime, triangulated Castro corner, this buzzing bar/eatery serves modern American food that's delicious and reasonably priced; the macaroni and cheese is a popular hit. The crowd is usually a mix of gay men and lesbians, with some straights on hand as well. Weekend brunch features a Build Your Own Bloody Mary bar.

Jumpin' Java 139 Noe St at 14th, Castro ☎415/431-5282. This modest, low-key café is filled with nerdy-cute gay boys and queer grad students, many hovering over their laptops. It's quite a change from the gym bunnies that frequent most spots nearby.

Sparky's 242 Church St at 14th, Castro ☎415/626-8666. Inexpensive, round-the-clock diner serving all the usual alcohol-soaking, 3am specialties; there's also a wide array of ice cream and specialty shakes from the soda fountain. The scene can get colorful on weekends – restaurant-wide singalongs to the jukebox have been documented.

Three Dollar Bill The Center, 1800 Market St at Octavia, Castro ☎415/503-1532, ⓦwww .threedollarbill.com. Airy, quiet café that plays host to book groups and knitting nights. The menu veers toward simple items such as sandwiches and lasagne. Closed Sun. Inexpensive.

Bars

Although there's a wide selection of gay and lesbian bars across the city, the crowd at each place is very defined; as such, listings below indicate what's popular with whom, and when. Nightlife calendars and club programing can change regularly, so it's always worth checking websites and local freesheets *SF Weekly*, *San Francisco Bay Guardian*, or *Gloss* before heading out.

440 Castro 440 Castro St at 17th, Castro ☎415/621-8732, ⓦwww.the440.com. Once the legendary stronghold *Daddy's* known for older, beefy men, this address-eponymous bar now caters to the jeans and leather set – except on Mon, when its underwear party sees bar-goers dressed nearly all the way down.

Aunt Charlie's Lounge 133 Turk St at Taylor, Tenderloin ☎415/441-2922, ⓦwww .auntcharlieslounge.com. A refreshingly divey, diverse bar, attracting a mixed crowd of ageing drag queens, young hipsters, and even a few gym bunnies. Beers are cheap, there are regular drag shows, and it's especially popular on Thurs for its 1970s-themed party, "Tubesteak Connection."

Badlands 4131 18th St at Collingwood, Castro ☎415/626-9320, ⓦwww.sfbadlands.com. A dance/video bar that attracts a pretty, 30-something crowd, usually packed on weekends. There's a wide selection of imported beer, and overall it's one of the less sceney places around the Castro.

Bar on Castro 456 Castro St at 18th, Castro ☎415/626-7220, ⓦwww.thebarsf.com. Swanky bar with a swishy, young crowd that packs its red leather and metal front patio at all hours.

The Café 2369 Market St at 17th, Castro ☎415/861-3846, ⓦwww.cafesf.com. With its mainstream Hi-NRG/house DJs, cheap cover, and nightly happy hour until 9pm, this longtime staple of the Castro club scene remains a crowd-pleaser. It's classic out-and-proud Castro, from the thumping beats

to the rainbow-colored socks strategically placed on male dancers.

Cat Club 1190 Folsom St at Eighth, SoMa ☎415/703-8965, ⓦwww.catclubsf.com. This dark, loud club gets livelier the later you arrive. Thurs here are known for the long-running "1984" party that attracts a mixed crowd, while "Hot Pants" happens every other Fri and attracts lesbians looking to shake it to queer 1980s hip-hop.

The Cinch 1723 Polk St at Washington, Polk Gulch ☎415/776-4162, ⓦwww.thecinch.com. This long, narrow bar along Upper Polk Gulch features video games, free pool on Wed, and a sizable patio for smoking. The upside-down Christmas trees hanging in the main room are a clever design touch.

The Eagle Tavern 398 12th St at Harrison, SoMa ☎415/626-0880, ⓦwww.sfeagle.com. Mostly popular with 30-somethings and older, although its Sun beer bust ($10 until 6pm) brings in a slightly more diverse crowd. Live music on Thurs, and there's even the odd mud-wrestling night.

🏃 **El Rio** 3158 Mission St at Valencia, Mission ☎415/282-3325, ⓦwww.elriosf .com. Unpretentious bar on lower Mission that thinks of itself as a community center almost as much as a party zone. Still, the place jumps on Sun afternoons during its weekly salsa dance, and it's popular with hipsters of all sexual walks every night of the week.

The End Up 401 6th St at Harrison, SoMa ☎415/646-0999, ⓦwww.theendup.com. Best known as the home of Sunday's all-day

"T-Dance" party (6am–8pm), this stalwart club attracts a mixed bag of hardcore clubbers for after-hours dancing on the cramped dancefloor; if you need a break from the beat assault, there's an outdoor patio with plenty of seating. The name's not about end-of-the-night desperation – rather, it was the last gay bar on this drag in the 1970s.

Esta Noche 3079 16th St at Valencia, Mission ℡415/861-5757. A fun, if dingy and smelly Latino drag bar that attracts a youngish, racially mixed clientele. There's a raucous drag revue every Fri and Sat night, and drink specials until 9pm nightly. Expect to hear Ricky Martin.

Ginger's 246 Kearny St at Bush, Financial District ℡415/989-0282, ℗www.gingerstrois .com. A charming, low-rent bar festooned with fairy lights. Expect a group of diehard, slightly older regulars swilling stiff drinks and happily singing along with the showtunes occasionally dialed up on the jukebox by the bartenders.

Hole in the Wall Saloon 289 8th St at Folsom, SoMa ℡415/431-4695, ℗www .holeinthewallsaloon.com. Less outrageous than other places in the neighborhood, although don't be surprised to see an old man in diapers. The 50-cent pool table and cheap, strong drinks are major drawcards. At the time of writing, the owners were attempting a move to nearby Dore Alley.

Lexington Club 3464 19th St at Lexington, Mission ℡415/863-2052, ℗www.lexington club.com. One of the few places in the city where the girls consistently outnumber the boys. It's a bustling lesbian bar which attracts all sorts with its no-nonsense decor and excellent jukebox. Mon features free pool and $1 cans of Pabst Blue Ribbon.

The Lone Star Saloon 1354 Harrison St at 10th, SoMa ℡415/863-9999 , ℗www .lonestarsaloon.com. Large, friendly, and welcoming, much like the local Bears who make this their second home. There's a $9 beer bust every Thurs night from 8pm–midnight.

Marlena's 488 Hayes St at Octavia, Hayes Valley ℡415/864-6672, ℗www.marlenasbarsf.com. An old-school drag bar with high-quality acts, cheap drinks, and a deliciously old-fashioned vibe in the heart of boutiquey Hayes Valley. The regulars are mainly 30- and 40-something guys, plus a few women.

Martuni's 4 Valencia St at Market, Mission ℡415/241-0205. This two-room piano bar on the edge of the Mission, Castro, and Hayes Valley attracts a well-heeled, diverse crowd, with many keen to sing along to classics from Judy, Liza, and Edith. The drink menu's full of kitschy choices, including chocolate martinis.

The Mint 1942 Market St at Buchanan, Hayes Valley ℡415/626-4726, ℗www.straybarsf.com. Not a gay bar per se, but worth noting for its enduring popularity as San Francisco's go-to karaoke venue. The list of available songs goes far beyond the usual Bette and Barbra ballads – expect to hear everything from "Oops! I Did It Again" to "Emotional Rescue" get completely butchered by soused punters.

Mix 4086 18th St at Castro, Castro ℡415/431-8616. One of the few gay sports bars in town. Watch games on TV, play pool, or enjoy a beer on the back patio.

N'Touch 1548 Polk St at California, Polk Gulch ℡415/441-8413, ℗www.ntouchsf.com. San Francisco's sole Asian gay bar comes complete with karaoke, go-go boys, and a daily happy hour until 8.30pm.

Pilsner Inn 225 Church St at 14th, Castro ℡415/621-7058, ℗www.pilsnerinn.com. Mature bar filled with a diverse crowd playing pool and darts. There's a large patio out back, and a generally welcoming, open vibe.

Powerhouse 1347 Folsom St at Ninth, SoMa ℡415/552-8689, ℗www.powerhouse-sf.com. One of the prime pick-up joints in the city, this cruisey bar boasts a patio and plenty of convenient dark corners inside. Every Thurs evening here sees a "wet undie" contest.

Stray Bar 309 Cortland Ave at Bennnington, Bernal Heights ℡415/821-9263, ℗www .straybarsf.com. Miles from the hectic Castro and SoMa corridors, this welcoming neighborhood bar attracts a remarkably mixed crowd, although it's biggest with Bernal Heights lesbians. You may be asked to make room at the stool next to you for a customer's dog.

The Stud 399 Folsom St at 9th, SoMa ℡415/863-6623, ℗www.studsf.com. Legendary club that's been on the scene since the mid-1960s. It's still as popular as ever, attracting a diverse, energetic, and uninhibited crowd. Don't miss the fabulously freaky drag-queen cabaret at

San Francisco's position as America's homo heartland was never clearer than in February 2004, when newly elected mayor Gavin Newsom ordered City Hall to start issuing **same-sex marriage licenses**. The first couple to wed were a pair of long-term lesbian activists, Del Martin and Phyllis Lyon, who finally sealed their 51-year union with a license under Newsom's auspices. For 28 days, there were lines outside City Hall as 4000 gay and lesbian couples waited for their own turn; that's when legal challenges from conservative opponents blocked any further same-sex licenses.

Newsom's official explanation for his promoting gay marriage is anecdotal: on a visit to Washington DC, having heard President Bush refer briefly to the sanctity of marriage in a speech, Newsom was shocked afterwards to overhear derogatory comments about gay marriage from the wife of another prominent Republican. From that point onward, the mayor claims he knew it was a cause he should champion, often likening the civil disobedience of issuing marriage licenses to the bus-based rebellion of Rosa Parks. However, cynics saw Newsom's position as an opportunistic one: gay marriage was a mediagenic, controversial topic that propelled him from regional mayor to national headliner. Other one-time supporters claimed that his aggressive stance on gay marriage was counterproductive, as not only did eleven states pass anti gay-marriage legislation in November 2004 elections, but the controversy buoyed additional support from the evangelical right for George W. Bush's successful presidential run that year.

In late 2004, the California Supreme Court nullified all same-sex marriage licenses issued in San Francisco, ruling that Newsom had stepped beyond his authority the previous winter. Around the same time, State Assemblyman Mark Leno, a former Supervisor in San Francisco, authored the Marriage Equity Bill, which would have legalized same-sex marriage in California. The bill was approved by both the State's Assembly and Senate, but was vetoed by Governor Arnold Schwarzenegger. The two legal sides then slugged it out until spring 2008, when California's Supreme Court overturned a ban on same-sex marriage by ruling that the state's Constitution forbids discrimination based on a person's sexual orientation; this news sent San Francisco's gay and lesbian community into euphoria, and beginning that June, San Francisco's Office of the County Clerk into another flurry of same-sex marriage license-issuing action. At the time of writing, with Schwarzenegger supposedly having since crossed the fence on the issue, it was likely that California's official stance on gay marriage would be thrust before voters in the fall election.

"Trannyshack" every Tues; "Sugar" happens one Sat a month and is one of the best dance nights in town.

Trax 1437 Haight St at Masonic, Upper Haight ☎415/864-4213. The Haight's only gay bar is a dive, though it's been spiffed up slightly from its grungy yesteryear. There's a mix of gays and straights, meaning it's much less cruisey than other bars.

Truck 1900 Folsom St at 15th, Mission ☎415/252-0306, ⊛www.trucksf.com. New spot on the scene that stands out for its everyman quality – fun without the cruisey vibe of certain places in the Castro and along Folsom.

Twin Peaks Tavern 401 Castro St at 17th, Castro ☎415/864-9470, ⊛www.twinpeakstavern.com. Famous as the first gay bar in America to install transparent picture windows, rather than black them out. These days, it's low-key and laid-back, filled with middle-class, older white men.

Wild Side West 424 Cortland Ave at Andover, Bernal Heights ☎415/647-3099. Unpretentious and friendly tavern at the center of the Bernal Heights lesbian scene, with plenty of kitsch Americana to gaze at. There's a lovely garden out back, but without heatlamps, you'd be well advised to stay inside on a cold evening.

Several lesbian- and gay-specific events are held in San Francisco throughout the year. You'll find details of them in Chapter 15, "Festivals and events."

Performing arts and film

Most venues in San Francisco will host occasional lesbian or gay-themed plays and movies, but those listed below are especially noted for their queer-centric programming. For information on the rest of the city's performing arts venues, see p.227.

Brava Theater Center 2781 24th St at York, Mission ☎415/641-7657, ⓦwww.brava.org. San Francisco's premier women's performance space, with a primary focus on presenting new plays by lesbians and women of color.

Castro Theatre 429 Castro St at 17th, Castro ☎415/621-6120, ⓦwww.castrotheatre.com. Gorgeous old movie palace that often hosts revivals of classics, with much audience participation (including hissing at onscreen villains). Come early for evening screenings to listen to the Wurlitzer organ and gaze at the spectacular chandelier.

New Conservatory Theatre Center 25 Van Ness Ave at Oak between Fell and Oak, Civic Center ☎415/861-8972, ⓦwww.nctcsf.org. Hosts a nearly year-round Pride Season, which features theatrical works by local and internationally recognized playwrights.

San Francisco Gay Men's Chorus ⓦwww.sfgmc.org. With over 200 singing members (and three separate ensembles) among its swelling ranks, this nationally respected choral association performs at several celebrated venues around the city, including Davies Symphony Hall and its annual "Home for the Holidays" show at the Castro Theatre.

San Francisco Lesbian/Gay Freedom Band ⓦwww.sflgfb.org. Information on performances – including the group's signature *Dance-Along Nutcracker* – led by artistic director Dr Roberto-Juan Gonzalez.

Theatre Rhinoceros 2926 16th St at S Van Ness, Mission ☎415/861-5079, ⓦwww.therhino.org. Two theaters in one space, each hosting productions that range from heartfelt political drama to raunchy cabaret acts.

Sunbathing and fitness

There are two gay **sunbathing** spots in the city: Dolores Beach is a misnomer, as it's actually a rolling green lawn near the southwest corner of Dolores Park (see p.120). Beyond the Richmond is Golden Gate Beach (see p.141), predominantly nude and popular on sunny weekends with its great view of Golden Gate Bridge. Below are listed a pair of **gyms** with a predominantly gay clientele.

Gold's Gym 2301 Market St at Noe, Castro ☎415/626-4488, ⓦwww.goldsgym.com. Accepts travel cards from other Gold's Gyms. Mon–Thurs 5am–midnight, Fri 5am–11pm, Sat 7am–9pm, Sun 7am–8pm.

The Gym SF 2775 Market St at 17th, Castro ☎415/863-4700, ⓦwww.thegymsf.com.

Cruisey gym for men only. It's on the second floor overlooking Market St, so there's a clear view of – and for – passers-by. Print out a free workout pass from the website. Mon–Fri 5am–11pm, Sat 7am–10pm, Sun 8am–8pm.

Shopping

A side from the retail palaces around **Union Square** (including Macy's, Saks, and practically every major designer label), San Francisco's shopping scene is refreshingly edgy, peppered with one-off boutiques selling locally designed clothes and stylish homeware stores. There's also a brilliantly varied selection of **independent booksellers** as well as terrific **music stores**, some focusing solely on rarities and others jammed with DJs rifling through the latest import 12" records from Europe. We've listed in the box on p.244 the best shopping arteries in the city, as well as their main focus.

Books

Unsurprisingly, for a city with such a rich literary history, San Francisco excels in terrific **specialty bookstores**: from the legendary City Lights in North Beach to the new literary hub in the Mission, home to some of the city's more unique and politically charged bookstores. As for **secondhand booksellers**, the city has a fine selection, but rabid old-book buyers should head across the Bay to Oakland and Berkeley for richer pickings (see p.308). Most bookstores tend to open every day, roughly 10am–8pm, though City Lights is open daily until midnight.

General

The Booksmith 1644 Haight St at Cole, Haight-Ashbury ☎415/863-8688. Good general bookstore stocking mainstream as well as countercultural titles: notable for its high-profile author events. Call the store for the latest or check online at ⓦwww .booksmith.com.

City Lights Bookstore 261 Columbus Ave at Broadway, North Beach ☎415/362-8193. The jewel of North Beach with world renown, City Lights is every bit the excellent bookshop/publisher it was when it first opened its doors in 1953. Founded by Beat poet Lawrence Ferlinghetti (whom you might meet strolling around the neighborhood), the store boasts a redoubtable selection of books, magazines, and chapbooks, as well as an excellent poetry room.

Green Apple Books 506 Clement St at Sixth, Richmond ☎415/387-2272. A wonderfully browsable store with deft, eccentric touches like the regular section of "Books that will never be Oprah's" picks." Not bargain prices, but a pleasure to rummage through the shelves. There's a smaller, less impressive music annex nearby.

Russian Hill Bookstore 2234 Polk St at Vallejo, Russian Hill ☎415/929-0997. Combination card store and secondhand bookshop, selling high-end journals and greetings cards as well as a wide range of books, though it's strongest on fiction.

Solar Light Books 2068 Union St at Buchanan, Cow Hollow ☎415/567-6082. Smallish basement store, with a good remainder selection; its fiction section is dotted with offbeat and interesting staff picks.

Below we've listed San Francisco's prime **shopping strips**, alphabetized according to the neighborhood in which each is situated. It's not an exhaustive list, as there are many other great places to browse, but it should be useful for any shopaholic planning a day of retail therapy.

The Castro Castro Street, between 17th and 19th, and Market Street, between Castro and Church. Gay-oriented boutiques, clubwear, and shoes.

Cow Hollow Union Street, between Fillmore and Gough. Sweet, if rather conservative, boutiques (mostly for women), shoe stores, and cute homeware shops.

The Haight-Ashbury Haight Street, between Stanyan and Masonic. Clothing, especially vintage and secondhand.

Hayes Valley Hayes Street, between Franklin and Laguna. Trendy but upscale, with edgy boutiques for men and women, as well as jewelry galleries and other gorgeous, high-end goodies.

Jackson Square Jackson Street, between Montgomery and Sansome. A cluster of antique-rug, furnishings, and clock shops.

Laurel Heights Sacramento Street, between Arguello and Divisadero. Antiques magnet of San Francisco, with vintage used clothes for women.

The Marina Chestnut Street, between Divisadero and Fillmore. Yuppiefied strip of health-food stores, wine shops, and women's clothing boutiques.

The Mission Valencia Street, between 14th and 21st. The best choice for urban hipsters, with lots of used furniture and clothing stores, bookshops, and avant-garde designer gear.

Noe Valley 24th Street, between Castro and Church. Women's clothing, music, and bookstores.

North Beach Grant Avenue between Filbert and Vallejo. Groovy boutiques, homewares, and divey cafés: one of the top places to find cool clothes.

Pacific Heights Fillmore Street, between Jackson and Geary. Home furnishings, antiques, and designer clothes.

Polk Gulch Polk Street, between Clay and Geary. Used bookstores, shoe stores, and porn outlets.

The Richmond Clement Street, between Second and Tenth. Bustling Chinese groceries and a couple of good used bookstores.

Russian Hill Polk Street between Greenwich and Broadway. Boutiquey cluster of high-end stores and restaurants, including a nascent French Village (see p.77).

The Sunset Irving Street, between Seventh and 23rd. Book, music, and homeware stores.

Rock-bottom bargain books available on the sidewalk, too.

Stacey's Booksellers 581 Market St at Second, Financial District ☎415/421-4687. A larger store for those shoppers who want a broad selection of titles and genres without having to support a national retail giant. The interior is rather sterile, but not unwelcoming.

Secondhand

Aardvark Books 227 Church St at Market, Castro ☎415/552-6733. Particularly strong on mysteries, queer fiction, and lit-crit, this musty neighborhood favorite carries all sorts of titles. As it continually buys and re-sells used books, the stock is always changing.

Abandoned Planet Bookstore 518 Valencia St at 16th, Mission ☎415/861-4695. Encouraging its customers to "Break the TV habit!," this eccentric and utterly San Francisco bookstore crams its black shelves with left-wing and anarchist volumes. A rebellious, oddball holdout against the gentrification evident elsewhere on Valencia St.

Acorn Books 1436 Polk St at Ellis, Polk Gulch ☎415/563-1736. Specializes in first and rare editions. Smells and looks the way an old bookstore should.

Adobe Bookshop 3166 16th St at Valencia, Mission ☎415/ 864-3936. A jumble of Persian rugs and torn Victorian easy chairs offers readers a respite amid the towers of haphazardly stacked books. In back, the shop runs a surprisingly reputable, closet-sized art gallery showcasing local artists.

Black Oak Books 540 Broadway at Columbus, North Beach ☎415/ 986-3872. Both new and used books together in a large, airily shambolic space; there's a particularly good selection of remaindered recent titles. Open until 11pm Sun–Thurs, midnight Fri–Sat.

Chelsea Bookshop 637 Irving Ave at Seventh, Richmond ☎415/566-0507. Next to Green Apple (see opposite) and one of the better used bookstores in town thanks to its well-organized stock. There's also a large children's section.

Chronicle Books Inside the Metreon, 101 Fourth St at Mission, SoMa ☎415/369-6271. Mostly wacky gift books or pop-culture photo specials – expect the likes of an overview of New Wave album covers, Miami Modernist architecture, and Doga (that's yoga for dogs). There's also a small selection of poppy greetings cards and other oddities.

Columbus Books 540 Broadway at Columbus, North Beach ☎415/986-3872. North Beach store with a good selection of new and used books, and a large travel section.

Dog Eared Books 900 Valencia St at 20th, Mission ☎415/282-1901. Smallish corner bookstore with a snappy selection of budget-priced remainders as well as an eclectic range of secondhand titles, all in terrific condition. There's even one rack of low-priced used CDs.

Elsewhere Books 260 Judah St at Seventh Ave, Inner Sunset ☎415/661-2535. Both a bookstore and the proprietor's living room, the space certainly lives up to its name. Its extensive collection of pulp fiction makes this quirky little store a destination for lovers of the genre.

Forest Books 3080 16th St at Valencia, Mission ☎415/863-2755. Slightly musty remainder and secondhand bookstore. Strong on history and anything Zen, whether religious memoirs or New Agey self-help volumes.

Forever After Books 1475 Haight St at Ashbury, Haight-Ashbury ☎415/431-8299. The windows of this store are blocked by the piles of paperbacks that have gradually grown up there for lack of space on the floor. Pick your way through the haphazardly stocked books in this oddball, ramshackle store – it's worth rifling, given the cheap prices, and use the rambling handwritten signs posted everywhere as your guide. The only downside is the crabby, crusty owner.

The Great Overland Bookstore Company 2848 Webster St at Union, Cow Hollow ☎415/351-1538. Cluttered with piles of books, this is a first-rate, old-fashioned store, featuring mint-condition first editions as well as cheap paperbacks – especially strong on pulpy fiction and war.

Phoenix Books and Records 3850 Fourth St at Sanchez, Mission ☎415/821-3477. Wide selection of new and used books at

Shopping categories

Books	
General	p.243
Secondhand	p.244
Specialty	p.246

Fashion	
Accessories, shoes, and jewelry	p.248
Casualwear	p.250
Designer	p.251
Vintage and thrift	p.253

Health & beauty	p.258

Music	
General	p.259
Secondhand and specialty	p.259

Department stores and malls	
Department stores	p.247
Malls	p.247

Food and drink	
Delis and groceries	p.255
Tea, coffee, and spices	p.256
Wines and spirits	p.257

Specialty stores	
Art galleries	p.260
Gifts and oddities	p.261

knockdown prices. Come out with armloads for $20.

Red Hill Books 401 Cortland Ave at Wool, Bernal Heights ☎415/648-5331. Handy, friendly pitstop on the main drag in Bernal Heights: there's a rack full of new magazines, both mainstream and niche, plus plenty of secondhand books – the travel and gender-studies sections are the most impressive.

Specialty

Argonaut Bookshop 786 Sutter St at Jones, Theater District ☎415/474-9067. Best bookstore by far for local history: it specializes in volumes on California and the West, from Gold Rush era to the dot-com bomb. The knowledgeable staff are a major plus.
Borderlands Books 866 Valencia St at 19th, Mission ☎415/824-8203. Sci-fi megastore with classic horror, fantasy, science fiction, TV tie-in books, and graphic novels, plus a few high-end trinkets.
Bound Together Anarchist Collective Bookstore 1369 Haight St at Central Ave, Haight-Ashbury ☎415/431-8355. Store specializing in radical and progressive publications, as well as anarchist posters and everything left of left-wing.
A. Cavalli & Co 1441 Stockton St at Columbus, North Beach ☎415/421-4219. Italian-language bookstore in the heart of Little Italy, carrying magazines, books, and movies from the old country, as well as a few T-shirts.
A Different Light 489 Castro St at 18th, Castro ☎415/431-0891, ⓦwww.adlbooks.com. Open 10am–10pm, this is a well-stocked bookshop featuring gay and lesbian titles, with an especially strong fiction section (and even a kids' lit corner). Readings and events are held here regularly – check the website for up-to-date information.
Fields Bookstore 1419 Polk St at Pine, Theater District ☎415/673-2027. Old-fashioned, old-school bookshop, dedicated to everything New Age, from texts on Sufism to yoga workout books.
Foto-Grafix Books 655 Mission St at Third, SoMa ☎415/495-7242. This photographic store is part of the Cartoon Art Museum simply because the previous tenant in the museum space was a photo gallery. The store survived while the gallery couldn't and sells a smartly edited selection of photography, design, and art books and cards.
Get Lost 1825 Market St at Valencia, Hayes Valley/Mission ☎415/437-0529. Tiny, triangular, travel bookstore, crammed with unusual titles alongside the standard guidebooks; it also stocks a decent assortment of maps and gear for the adventure traveler. The staff are especially helpful.
Kayo 814 Post St at Leavenworth, Theater District ☎415/749-0554. Glorious vintage paperback store, crammed with bargain classics including pulpy mysteries, sci-fi, and campy 1950s sleaze fiction. Closed Mon and Tues.
Kinokuniya 2nd floor, Japan Center, 1581 Webster St, Japantown ☎415/567-7625. Large stock of Japanese and English-language books; where the place really excels, though, is in art books.
McDonald's Bookshop 48 Turk St at Mason, Tenderloin ☎415/673-2235. Massive and messy, this store's the place to come for vintage magazines – it's piled high with ramshackle stacks of any title imaginable. There's little or no filing system, so expect to rummage. There's also a selection of used books and music.
Marcus Bookstore 1712 Fillmore St at Post, Western Addition ☎415/346-4222. Cosy bookstore filled with the smell of incense that focuses on African-American literature and magazines. It also regularly hosts Afrocentric readings and author appearances, both here and in its Oakland store (3900 Martin Luther King Jr Way, ☎510/652-2344).
Modern Times 888 Valencia St at 20th, Mission ☎415/282-9246. Hefty stock of Latin American literature and progressive political publications, as well as a small, but well-chosen, selection of gay and lesbian literature and radical feminist magazines. Stages regular readings of authors' works and offers ten percent off staff's esoteric picks.
San Francisco Mystery Bookstore 4175 24th St at Castro, Noe Valley ☎415/282-7444. Dying for something by Dashiell Hammett? Aching for a little Agatha Christie? Even the most selective noir junkies can satisfy their gumshoe fix here.
Smoke Signals 2223 Polk St at Green, Russian Hill ☎415/292-6025. Enormous newsstand stocking close to any magazine, domestic or foreign, that you can ask for as well as a hefty choice of cigars.
William Stout Architectural Books 804 Montgomery St at Jackson, Jackson Square ☎415/391-6757. One of San Francisco's most esteemed booksellers, with an excellent range of books on architecture, art and design, building, and urban studies.

Department stores and malls

San Francisco has remained more immune to the establishment of large **shopping malls** than most American cities – and those that *have* sprouted up are, by and large, reasonably appealing. Downtown plays host to several **department stores** around Union Square, though these are all branches of upscale national chains that can be found in most major American cities.

Department stores

Barneys New York 77 O'Farrell St at Stockton, Union Square ☎415/268-3500. The famed high-end niche department store finally opened its doors to San Francisco fashionistas in 2007. Die-hards claim this outpost plays second fiddle to the New York locale, but shoppers hungry for that Marc Jacobs sweater won't care.

Bloomingdale's 845 Market St at Powell, Union Square ☎415/856-5300. New to the scene, in the Westfield Centre, this shiny haven boasts a Shiseido cosmetics counter, rows of shoes and handbags, and boutiques from the likes of Louis Vuitton and Dior.

Loehmann's 222 Sutter St at Kearny, Union Square ☎415/982-3215. Root around for terrific designer bargains at this upscale discounter that's often crammed with same-season DKNY and BCBG. Known for "The Back Room," where you can pick up budget-priced ballgowns and high-end designer originals at upwards of 75 percent off. There's a shoe annex nearby at 211 Sutter St ☎415/399-9208.

Macy's Stockton St and O'Farrell St, Union Square ☎415/397-3333. In a gigantic glass-fronted building looming over Union Square, Macy's is the cheapest of the big-name department stores. The larger shop focuses on mainstream women's and children's wear, reliable for basics if a little unexciting; since a major refit in 1999, menswear has been banished to a smaller satellite store on the opposite corner of Stockton St.

Neiman Marcus 150 Stockton St at O'Farrell, Union Square ☎415/362-3900. This branch of the upscale department store is housed in a beautiful building with a glass-domed rotunda capping a top-floor restaurant and bar; from there, you can watch shoppers struggling with packages in Union Square down below. Its merchandise is aimed squarely at a well-to-do, middle-aged crowd.

Nordstrom 865 Market St at Powell, Union Square ☎415/243-8500. Shoppers flock here for the high-quality (and expensive) fashions, as well as a chance to ride on the spiral escalators that climb the four-story atrium from the San Francisco Shopping Center below.

Saks Fifth Avenue 384 Post St at Powell, Union Square ☎415/986-4300. A scaled-down version of its New York sister store, Saks carries a sharper selection of directional fashion than most expect. Great for browsing. The separate men's store, 220 Post St at Grant, Union Square (☎415/986-4300), is especially well stocked.

Malls

Crocker Galleria 50 Post St at Kearny, Financial District ☎415/393-1505, ⊛www.shopatgalleria.com. A modern, Italianate atrium, this Financial District mall features some very pricey showcase boutiques from major names like Versace and Polo Ralph Lauren.

Embarcadero Center Embarcadero BART/MUNI station at the foot of California St ☎415/772-0700, ⊛www.embarcaderocenter.com. Ugly, eight-square-block shopping complex with 125 stores and a few unremarkable restaurants: you won't find any unusual stores here, but it's handy for the local office workers and most crowded at weekday lunches. Oddly, alongside the clothing stores, the center's also home to two dozen dentists.

Ghirardelli Square 900 North Point at Larkin, Fisherman's Wharf ☎415/775-5500, ⊛www.ghirardellisq.com. This place, anchoring the western end of the soul-destroying tourist mile at Fisherman's Wharf, is far better than you might expect. Still, though, the stores are patchy – but many of the restaurants, are worth checking out.

Japan Center Post St at Buchanan, Japantown ☎415/922-6776. Three-building complex of Japanese restaurants and stores: despite its soulless design, it still throbs with Japanese-American shoppers as well as tourists. There's an uncompromising concrete peace pagoda with space-age styling in its central outdoor plaza, plus the Sundance Kabuki Cinema, an elegantly remodelled cineplex, home to the San Francisco International Film Festival, that serves gourmet food as well.

Westfield San Francisco Centre Fifth St and Market, Union Square ☎415/495-5656, ⊛www .sanfranciscocenter.com. Spreading into the former Emporium department store next door, the Westfield Centre – once a good-looking mall with glass, Italian marble, polished green granite, and spiral escalators up its eight stories to Nordstrom – has doubled in size, adding a Bloomingdale's, a Century Theatres multiplex, and an expanded basement-level food court with vast selection of gourmet treats from vendors like a Bristol Farms grocery store, the Slanted Door and Bearded Papa's Cream Puffs. The Emporium's stunning original glass dome is still intact.

Sony Metreon 101 Fourth St at Mission, SoMa ☎415/369-6000 or 1-800/METREON, ⊛www .metreon.com. At one time little more than a 3-D ad for Sony, this mall is slowly changing to incorporate a few attractions for regular shoppers, like a branch of Chronicle Books and a large food court. The handiest feature, though, is the onsite movie multiplex.

Stonestown Galleria Shopping Center 19th Ave and Winston, Sunset ☎415/759-2623, ⊛www .stonestowngalleria.com. Way out in the Sunset, one block from SF State University, this 120-store complex has a Macy's, a Border's Books, a Nordstrom, and upscale clothing and shoe stores along with the usual mall choices.

Fashion

San Francisco may not be on par, fashion–wise, with New York or Los Angeles, but there's still an impressive range of clothing stores in the city. Aside from the upscale international boutiques that sit elbow to elbow in the streets around **Union Square**, there are plenty of local designers who've opened stores in areas like the **Mission**, **Hayes Valley**, and the **Sunset**. But it's in its range, variety, and quality of **secondhand** and **vintage** stores that San Francisco shines: at most of these places, you can enjoy rummaging through top–quality cast–offs and pick most of them up at bargain prices.

Accessories, shoes, and jewelry

Alla Prima 1420 Grant Ave at Green, North Beach ☎415/397-4077. Upscale lingerie outlet with pale-green walls and ornate chandelier: there's a wall of pricey but beautiful frilly bras, fresh flowers everywhere, and high-end sex toys (platinum-plated vibrators and the like) by local faves JimmyJane.

April in Paris 55 Clement St at Arguello, Inner Richmond ☎415/750-9910. French expat Beatrice Ablard was trained by Hermès, and it shows in the superb quality of the bags she now designs and hand-sews at a small Richmond atelier. Staggeringly expensive, but a lifelong treat.

Bulo 3040 Fillmore St at Filbert, Cow Hollow ☎415/614-9959. Quirky European shoes, with an earthy, retro feel: don't come here looking for spike-heeled glamour, but for funky, cool flats that will handle the hills easily and in style. There's a branch for men's shoes at 437-A Hayes St (☎415/864-3244), and one for women's shoes at 418 Hayes St (☎415/255-4939); both are in Hayes Valley.

Camper 39 Grant Ave at Market, Union Square ☎415/296-1005. Devotees of all things Spanish can get their feet kicking in a wide range of retro-inspired and dressy items from the Iberian peninsula.

Carol Doda's Champagne & Lace 1850 Union St #1 at Laguna, Cow Hollow ☎415/279-3666. Small boudoir-like store in a flower-crammed alleyway off the Union St drag, stocking Fredericks of Hollywood-style lacy lingerie personally selected by Queen of Topless Waitressing, Carol Doda (see p.72). Supposedly open daily noon–7pm, though hours are more likely up to Doda's whim.

Cole Haan 324 Stockton St at Post, Union Square ☎415/391-1760. A must for those seeking well-crafted, high-style leather shoes, boots, belts, and sandals.

Daljeets 1793 & 1744 Haight St at Cole, Haight-Ashbury ☎415/668-8500. Haight old-timer that stocks an astonishing selection of shoes from the sensible to the bizarre, plus a nice little sideline in sex toys and fetish wear.

Five and Diamond 510 Valencia St at 16th, Mission ☎415/255-9747. Among the distinctively designed sexy, alt-punk/Victorian-cum-Wild West gear, you can also acquire tattoos and piercings in the onsite parlor.

Ghurka 170 Post St at Montgomery, Union Square ☎415/392-7267. *The* place in San Francisco to buy leather goods like wallets, handbags, and luggage. The products have quite a following due to their durability; scratches wipe off instantly.

Gimme Shoes 50 Grant Ave at Market, Union Square ☎415/434-9242. Local shoe chainlet which has gradually sprung up in most of the major shopping areas; in each branch, you'll find men's and women's shoes from designers like Paul Smith and Helmut Lang, as well as funky bags and unusual accessories. Nothing groundbreaking, but a reliable selection of the season's best. There are branches at 416 Hayes St at Gough, Hayes Valley (☎415/864-0691), and 2358 Fillmore St at Clay, Pacific Heights (☎415/441-3040).

Gucci 200 Stockton St at Geary, Union Square ☎415/392-2808. Sex on a coathanger: Tom Ford may have moved on, but Gucci is still sizzling, with slinky dresses for women and stretchy, often skintight, pants for men. The accessories, though, are the real draw: still handmade and high-quality, as the prices prove.

Hats on Post 2nd floor, 210 Post St at Grant, Union Square ☎415/392-3737. Interesting, odd designs; very contemporary, but only worth shelling out for if you're really into hats.

Hermès 212 Stockton St at Geary, Union Square ☎415/391-7200. Top-notch, if rather stuffy, French luggage and accessories, as well as a capsule clothing range. Aimed squarely at proud traditionalists, although a simple Hermès scarf is an undisputed fashion classic.

Jeanine Payer 762 Market St at Grant, Union Square ☎415/788-2417. Celebrity favorite Payer is known for her poetry-covered jewelry (bracelets, earrings, necklaces) – but these aren't cutesy greeting card ditties, more like love letters on precious metal. Closed Sun & Mon.

John Fluevog 1697 Haight St at Cole, Haight-Ashbury ☎415/436-9784. Clunky, chunky shoes for men and women; many designs are witty, clog-like shapes, which are fun, if a little dated.

Kate Spade 227 Grant Ave at Post, Union Square ☎415/216-0880. The patron saint of girly-girls everywhere showcases her stylish, boxy handbags, classic shoes, and beauty line. Overpriced, but irresistible.

Kenneth Cole 166 Grant Ave at Post, Union Square ☎415/981-2653. The flagship store for this mainstream American designer carries his entire line: although Cole started with shoes, he's branched off into clothes for men and women, too. His shoes are functional and a little funky; the clothes are cooler and pricier.

Laku 1069 Valencia St at 22nd, Mission ☎415/695-1462. Handmade exquisite silk slippers by local designer Yaeko Yamashita. Also sells velvet hair accessories.

Luichiny 1529 Haight St at Clayton, Haight-Ashbury ☎415/252-7065. For those who long for the Spice Girls-driven heyday of cartoonish platforms, this is your store: every shoe is glitzy and utterly over the top.

🏃 **Paolo** 524 Hayes St at Laguna, Hayes Valley ☎415/552-4580. Don't tell anyone but your best friends about this gem: designer Paolo Lantorno produces a limited edition (20–25 pairs) of his own men's and women's shoe designs in Italy, then sells them from his two stores here. Prices hover around $200, and every style is edgy but wearable. Branch: 2000 Fillmore St at Pine, Upper Fillmore ☎415/771-1944.

Paul Frank Store 262 Sutter St at Grant, Union Square ☎415/374-2758. Local outpost for the cutesy accessories designer, known for his wide-mouthed monkey mascot named Julius, applique designs, and 1950s color palette.

Shapur 245 Post St at Union Square, Union Square ☎415/392-1200. Unusual fittings for uniquely cut diamonds and various other gems; each piece is created individually.

Shoe Biz 1422 Haight St at Ashbury, Haight-Ashbury ☎415/861-0313. Three stores in close proximity (nos. 1422, 1446, 1553) selling mainstream shoe labels like Diesel and Camper, for men and women, with most selections priced around $100 per pair. Branch: 3810 24th St at Church, Noe Valley ☎415/821-2528; 877 Valencia St at 19th, Mission ☎415/550-8655.

Shreve & Co 200 Post St at Grant, Union Square ☎415/421-2600. The oldest jeweler in town and quite possibly the best. Known for its fine silverware and flawless diamonds. You can get a replica of the pearl necklace given by the Japanese emperor to Marilyn Monroe on her honeymoon with local hero Joe DiMaggio.

Tiffany 350 Post St at Powell, Union Square ☎415/781-7000. Luxurious two-storied site, where the extraordinarily courteous staff are happy to let you try the stuff on, even if it's obvious that you can't afford it.

Velvet DaVinci 2015 Polk St at Pacific, Russian Hill ☎415/441-0109. Owners Elizabeth Shypertt and Mike Holmes opened this sumptuous jewelry store-cum-gallery more than ten years ago, and it now stocks art pieces by more than fifty designers from ten countries. There's unique work by local names like Julia Turner or Lisa Fidler, whose eye-catching designs look like glittery frogspawn.

Casualwear

American Apparel 2174 Union St at Fillmore, Cow Hollow ☎415/440-3220. Guaranteed sweatshop-free T-shirts from LA worth checking out as much for the endless colors and sharp cut, as for their ethics. Like The Gap, only with better colors and cuts. Branch: 1615 Haight St at Clayton, Haight-Ashbury ☎415/431-4028.

Banana Republic 256 Grant Ave at Sutter, Union Square ☎415/788-3087. Although there are dozens of branches across the city, this enormous outpost of Gap's upscale business casual chain is notable for its location. The White House, a five-story skyscraper built by Albert Pissis, is one of several classic buildings across the country that the chain has adopted and sensitively modernized. The clothes are well priced; the womenswear is far more exciting than the bland men's range.

Brand Fury 780 Sutter St, Theater District ☎415/673-7940. Closet-sized store stocking toys for big hipster boys: obscure logoed tees, Japanese imported action figures, and all things kung fu and cult.

Dharma 1600 Haight St at Clayton, Haight-Ashbury ☎415/621-5597. Cheap, trendy fashions, with an ethnic hippie vibe: girly tops, patterned wraps, and frilly shirts. Branch: 914 Valencia St at 20th, Mission ☎415/920-9855.

Diesel 101 Post St at Kearny, Union Square ☎415/982-7077. Five-story megastore for the witty, wacky Italian casualwear label. Diesel was at the forefront of the denim revolution, and its jeans wall offers trendy styles in a dozen different washes.

Forever 21 7 Powell St at Market, Civic Center ☎415/984-0380. Not recommended for the agoraphobic, Forever 21 is a sea of limbs reaching for the nearest trendy, yet inexpensive halter-top or cardigan. As the name suggests, its fashions are geared towards the young and those aspiring to look young.

The Gap 1485 Haight St at Ashbury, Haight-Ashbury ☎415/431-6336. Yes, the store that defines corporate retailing has an outlet on the very corner of the counterculture world. Locals grumble that The Gap slipped in when it was still selling Levi's (the hippie uniform); whether that's true or not, it fits in perfectly with the rabidly commercial clothing stores and tourists elsewhere on Haight St. The local flagship store is at 890 Market St at Powell, Union Square ☎415/788-5909.

H&M Westfield San Francisco Centre, 845 Market St at Powell, SoMa ☎415/986-0156. Love it or leave it, even its detractors admit that H&M introduced a large population of Americans to affordably priced, sartorially considered clothing. With shoppers literally swarming over discount jackets, jeans, and accessories, the store can be pure chaos. But it's the ideal place to look like a million bucks while having spent very little. There's another branch nearby at 150 Powell St at Ellis, off Union Square ☎415/986-4215.

Huf 808 & 816 Sutter St at Jones, Theater District ☎415/614-9414. Named after its owner, pro-skateboarder Keith Hufnagel, this superb menswear store stocks skate and graffiti footwear and clothing with a fashion edge: think limited-edition Vans and retro decal tees, plus niche magazines, books, and a few skateboards. No. 808 is a vintage sneaker annex (expect 1980s era Nike and Asics).

Levi's 300 Post St at Stockton, Union Square ☎415/501-0100. Four levels of jeans, tops, and jackets set against a thumping backdrop of club music. This flagship offers the Levi's "Original Spin" service, where customers can order customized denim. Since this stocks the entire Levi's line, it carries edgier pieces in the Red line as well as retro-inspired Western wear.

Lululemon 1981 Union St at Buchanan, Cow Hollow ☎415/ 776-5858. Canadian athletic-wear chain that sells trendy, lycra-heavy togs for yoga-loving men and women – a big hit with the Marina's keep-fit crowd.

Nomads 556 Hayes St at Laguna, Hayes Valley ☎415/864-5692. Britpoppy menswear like skinny, slouchy jeans and zipped cardigans from the likes of Ben Sherman, Blue Marlin, Jack Spade, and Fred Perry.

North Beach Leather 224 Grant Ave at Post, Union Square ☎415/362-8300. Leather everything, and in some pretty sickly colors, but for basic black jackets and simple pieces there are some well-made styles. The owner began by clothing the Hell's Angels in 1967 and later outfitted the San Francisco police department, before dressing Elvis Presley in 1969.

The North Face 180 Post St at Grant, Union Square ☎415/433-3223. This store sells rugged outdoor fashions and footwear – its lightweight, tech-fabric jackets are particularly popular.

Patagonia 770 North Point, Fisherman's Wharf ☎415/771-2050. This store could lay claim to being the patron saint of the Bay Area's backpackers: functional performance clothing for hikers, bikers, and other outdoors enthusiasts. Prices are fair, and many products have more of a fashion sensibility than other sportswear stores.

True 1415 Haight St at Ashbury, Haight-Ashbury ☎415/626-2882. Urban clothing from Enyce sits alongside a strong selection of classic sneakers like Nike Dunks, plus watches by Dixon at this store owned by Michael Brown, son of ex-mayor Willie; the womens-wear branch nearby (no. 1427) has a wall filled with vinyl and messenger bags as well as clothing by New York skate label Triple 5 Soul and others.

Urban Outfitters 80 Powell St at Ellis, Union Square ☎415/989-1515. Slackerwear for the college-aged or -minded: great for ironic, irreverent T-shirts and offbeat accessories. Noted, too, for its cheap and kitschy homewares.

Villains 1672 Haight St at Cole, Haight-Ashbury ☎415/626-5939. Youthful, fun clothing from labels like Ben Sherman, Penguin, and Puma: not cheap, but a few bargains across the road in the Vault, at no. 1653 (☎415/864-7727), where sale merchandise is stashed.

Zara 250 Post St at Stockton, Union Square ☎415/399-6930. A well-tailored, continental antidote to Banana Republic's more conservative fashions. Expect snug fits and reasonable prices for runway-inspired clothing for men and women.

Designer

ab fits 1519 Grant Ave at Union, Telegraph Hill ☎415/982-5726. Imaginative men's and women's jeans boutique, starkly decorated in bright red and offering directional clothing at moderate prices. Lines include Band of Outsides and Etro for men, while for women there's fun, girly fashion by Rebecca Taylor and Nanette Lapore, as well as jewelry from local designer Janine Payer. Branch: 40 Grant Ave at O'Farrell, Union Square. ☎415/982-5726.

Agnès b 33 Grant Ave at Market, Union Square ☎415/772-9995. Slinky designs for men and women, primarily in muted navy, black, and grey. Chic and very French, the store also sells quirky pattern shirts and retro shoes.

Anthropologie 880 Market St at Fifth, Union Square ☎415/434-2210. Shoppers here can be overheard simultaneously raving about Anthropologie's punchy styles, embroidery, and big buttons while complaining about the price tag. The store also sells numerous accessories for the body and the home.

Bebe 21 Grant Ave at Market, Union Square ☎415/781-2323. Stretchy, sexy clothes for the superskinny, as well as pertly tailored suits.

Behind the Post Office 1510 Haight St at Ashbury, Haight-Ashbury ☎415/861-2507. Smallish, low-key boutique, stocking designer basics by Seven, Development, and others: there's an especially wide range of cool T-shirts.

Betsey Johnson 160 Geary St at Stockton, Union Square ☎415/398-2516. Kooky, creative clothing in candy colors and floaty fabrics. Surprisingly affordable compared with other nearby designer boutiques. Branch: 2031 Fillmore St at California, Pacific Heights ☎415/567-2726.

Betsy Dee 1322 Haight St at Central Ave, Haight-Ashbury ☎415/861-2527. Smartly edited women's boutique stocking nothing but California-based designers, like Ann Faraday from LA or Erin Mahoney from the Bay Area.

Carrots 843 Montgomery St at Jackson, Financial District ☎415/834-9040. This sleek, jazzy boutique landed in Jackson Square with a great deal of deserved fanfare. It features understated men's and women's fashions by well-established and independent high-end designers, and also sellis extra house-wares to decorate the loft.

Catherine Jane 1234 Ninth Ave at Judah, Sunset ☎415/664-1855. Inner Sunset shop featuring luxurious "fog coats" (shawls made from cashmere and angora) and fashions in silk dupioni, crêpe de Chine, and other cozy fabrics.

Couture SF 185 Clara St at Fifth, SoMa ☎415/896-0116. Christina Hurvis toiled as a Dior peon before setting up her own master tailoring atelier in a loft space on a bleak block South of Market. Gorgeous, made-to-measure gowns from $2500.

Dema 1038 Valencia St at 21st, Mission ☎415/206-0500. Feisty, brightly colored women's clothing with plenty of op-artsy prints and retro detailing, mostly designed by owner Dema Grim. T-shirts start around $30, shirts $90 and up. There's also soft, girly knitwear by the likes of Three Dot and Antoni & Alison.

House of Hengst 924 Valencia St at 20th, Mission ☎415/642-0841. In case the overflow of patterns and fabric swatches in the backroom behind the curtain didn't give it away, all of Hengst's designs are made onsite. Its elegant, daring tailoring comes at a high price, but the no-nonsense designs justify the cost.

Isda & Co. 19 South Park, SoMa ☎415/344-4891. This airy store sells its own label of Gap-style basics, both classic and casual, in lush natural fabrics like wool and cotton for men and women.

Jaxx 1684 Haight St at Clayton, Haight-Ashbury ☎415/431-8393. Once known as Backseat Betty, this store continues to stock a similar range of exquisite, affordable dresses by the likes of Diane von Furstenberg and very feminine separates by lesser-known designers.

Kweejibo Clothing Co. 1580 Haight St at Clayton, Haight-Ashbury ☎415/552-3555. Laconic, ironic retro shirts for men in two fits (boxy or tailored) and dozens of fabrics. Named after an obscure reference to *The Simpsons* cartoon series; it's a pity that the shrug-happy staff lack Bart's sense of humor.

MAC (Modern Appealing Clothing) 387 Grove St at Gough, Hayes Valley ☎415/863-3011. Arguably one of the best boutiques in town, this unisex spot run by brother-and-sister team, Ben and Chris Ospital, stocks

▲ MAC boutique

avant-garde designers like AF Vandervoorst and Martin Margiela as well as local names like Lemon Twist and Dema. It's airy and refreshingly unsnooty for an upscale boutique, thanks to the homey atmosphere and chatty staff.

Manifesto 514 Octavia St at Hayes, Hayes Valley ☎415/431-4778. Local designers Sarah Franko and Suzanne Castillo produce a wacky, retro line of clothing for men and women at this shop-cum-studio. The place to pick up a shirt to make you feel like Sinatra. It's also recently launched a new children's line.

Marc Jacobs 125 Maiden Lane, Union Square ☎415/362 6500. The godfather of grunge – and current darling of fashionistas worldwide – has one of his handful of boutiques in the city down this side street. It sells his vintage, largely 1940s-inspired separates and accessories; expensive but irresistible. There's also a small selection of his men's line.

Martha Egan 1 Columbus Ave at Washington, North Beach ☎415/397-5451. Vintage-inspired clothes made from classic fabrics in eye-popping patterns, fit for an ensemble player in any Doris Day/Rock Hudson comedy: boxy shirts, 1940s-style dresses, and chunky retro bags.

Metier 355 Sutter St at Grant Ave, Union Square ☎415/989-5395. A gallery of up-and-coming designers, with everything from sweaters and scarves to jewelry and handbags.

Miss Sixty 45 Grant Ave at Market, Union Square ☎415/362-9470. Carrying the rough and raw Miss Sixty/Energie brands for men and women, Miss Sixty boasts attractive albeit pricey clothes with the latest trends. The staff border on being clingy, but they're full of great suggestions nonetheless.

R.A.G. 541 Octavia St at Hayes, Hayes Valley ☎415/621-7718. Innovative, mini department store specializing in local designers under 30 – each rents rack space to showcase their ranges. Most are surprisingly afford-able, and the plus is that you'll never bump into anyone else wearing the same outfit. Closed Tues.

Rileyjames 3027 Fillmore St at Greenwich, Pacific Heights ☎415/775-7956. Trendy men's and women's bi-level designer store: the upper section is for girls with the likes of Hollywould, Punk Royal, and Frost French, while the raw concrete basement with DJ deck is devoted to guys with Chip & Pepper, Fake London, and Puma, among others.

Rolo 1235 Howard St at Eighth, SoMa ☎415/355-1122. There are five outposts of this funky retailer across the city. Rolo SoMa is the unisex store, stocking denim and streetwear from the likes of ICR Deth Killers, Robert Graham, and Loomstate. Rolo Market (2351 Market St) is men only: this is the high-end store, stocking designer labels like Generra, Penguin, or Adam+Eve. Best of all is Rolo Garage (1301 Howard St): it's a hospice for designer clothes where previously high-priced gear from G-Star, Ted Baker, and others comes for its final days on sale, marked down by as much as eighty percent.

Saffron Rare Threads 499 Dolores St at 18th, Mission ☎415/626-2533. Plenty of threads to accommodate the hip, office-oriented professional woman as well as the profes-sional cocktail sipper and clubgoer.

The Seventh Heart 1592 Market St at Van Ness, Hayes Valley ☎415/431-1755. Perfect for the hoodie and skinny-jean-wearing set, this shop has all the essentials: Levi's, American Apparel briefs, and a seemingly endless array of screen-printed items by designers of local and wider renown. The delightful staff will help you find what you need.

Smaak 528 Hayes St at Octavia, Hayes Valley ☎415/503-1430. All-Scandinavian clothing boutique, mostly women's with a smattering of men's gear. There's J. Lindeberg and Filippa K among others; most are bright colored and for tall, slim types.

Wilkes Bashford 375 Sutter St at Stockton, Union Square ☎415/986-4380. Four floors of fabulous designer finery for men, and one floor for women. The buyers here sprinkle interesting new names from Italy among the racks of major-label merchandise.

Zeni 567 Hayes St at Laguna, Hayes Valley ☎415/864-0154. Crammed with designer clothes for men and women, this small boutique stocks girly fashions from Anna Sui and Nicole Miller, plus local names like Sharagona, as well as offbeat menswear by Burro, Itsus, and For You. There's also a wide range of natty sunglasses.

Zolita 3335 17th St at Mission, Mission ☎415/551-0900. Featuring an eclectic grouping of fashions perhaps more suited to the Marina yuppy crowd, Zolita has carved a niche for itself in the Mission all the same. With a selection of ruffled, über-girly fashions and equally flashy men's clothes, it's a great place to find Ted Baker-esque clothes by indie designers.

Vintage and thrift

Aardvark's Odd Ark 1501 Haight St at Ashbury, Haight-Ashbury ☎415/621-3141. Haight-Ashbury outpost of this California thrift-store chain: expect plenty of glitz, glam, and dayglo colors, as well as a wide selection of vintage jeans.

American Rag Co 1305 Van Ness Ave at Bush, Tenderloin ☎415/474-5214. As secondhand clothing stores go, this one is expensive, but has a superior collection of stylish clothing.

Buffalo Exchange 1555 Haight St at Clayton, Haight-Ashbury ☎415/431-7733. Cheap and occasionally tatty, but if you've got the patience to search through the piles of clothing, you may turn up some gems. Branch: 210 Valencia St at 22nd, Mission ☎415/647-8332.

Clothes Contact 473 Valencia St at 16th, Mission ☎415/621-3212. Where the rockers come for bomber jackets. Pay by the pound ($8), as weighed at checkout on a vintage scale: be prepared to rummage and rifle through the endless racks, divided solely by type (shirt, coat, dress).

Community Thrift 625 Valencia St at 17th, Mission ☎415/861-4910. Classic thrift store crammed with clothes, furniture, and junk, including old magazines, games, and books in an enormous warehouse space. All proceeds are divided up among local charities.

Cris 2056 Polk St at Broadway, Russian Hill ☎415/474-1191. Sumptuous designer resale store with a hushed atmosphere, proper fitting rooms, and decor like a tasteful millionaire's wife. No wonder, as dozens of them must stop by weekly to drop off barely worn samples by every big name (Prada, Chanel, YSL, and Dior are staples). Everything is current season, in excellent condition (sometimes even with its original price-tag attached), and surprisingly cheap.

Crossroads 2123 Market St at Church, Castro ☎415-552-8740. Californian chainlet selling vintage clothes and remainders from labels like Club Monaco and French Connection. The selection can be a little bland and prices (especially on the new items) are high, but it's great for top-condition basics. Branches: 1901 Fillmore St at Bush, Japantown ☎415/775-8885; 555 Irving St at Seventh, Sunset ☎415/681-0100; and 1519 Haight St at Ashbury, Haight-Ashbury ☎415/355-0555.

Good Byes 3464 Sacramento St at Laurel, Laurel Heights ☎415/346-6388. Stacked with designer labels, this tucked-away boutique is a first-grade consignment store, where you could find last season's Prada or Chanel at vintage prices.

Goodwill 822 Geary St at Hyde, Union Square ☎415/922-0405. There are Goodwill outlets all over the city, stocking everything from lampshades to handbags to three-piece suits. Exhaustive selection of junk and gems. Two more clothing-centric locations are 2279 Mission St at 19th, Mission (☎415/826-5759) and 1580 Mission St at Van Ness Ave, Mission (☎415/575-2240).

Idol Vintage 3162 16th St at Valencia, Mission ☎415/255-9959. Some of the best used boots, Western shirts, wigs, hats, and other retro paraphernalia around. Ideal for costume balls and themed parties.

🏃 **Jeremy's** 2 South Park at Second St, SoMa ☎415/882-4929. Specializing in casual and designer clothes for men and women, seconds, and fashion show outtakes. Jeremy's is a local fashionista favorite, since you can often pick up recent-season

designer-label gems here at rock-bottom prices; expect plenty of Bergdorf Goodman's own label and Ralph Lauren, as well as a superb selection of women's shoes, including plenty of Blahniks and Choos.

My Roommate's Closet 1612 Union St at Franklin, Cow Hollow ☎415/776-7800. This boutique in a converted Victorian is filled with overstocks from designers like Rebecca Taylor, Chaiken, or Alvin Valley, sold for at least fifty percent off the regular price.

Old Vogue 1412 Grant Ave at Green, Telegraph Hill ☎415/392-1522. A pricey vintage store on this trendy shopping strip: the men's selection is especially wide, and there are piles of good-as-new jeans on the upper mezzanine.

Painted Bird 1201A Guerrero St at 24th, Mission ☎415/401-7027. With an attractive but introverted staff, this is a mine of well-selected, affordable items for would-be and established rocker kids. Handbags, vests, jackets, owl pendants, and jeans all converge in a store the size of a postage-stamp.

Repeat Performance San Francisco Symphony Thrift Store 2436 Fillmore St at Washington, Pacific Heights ☎415/563-3123. Casual as well as formal wear and a few vintage items, all selling at top dollar, as the Pacific Heights location would suggest. Also jewelry, kitchenware, and shoes. All proceeds go to the Symphony.

Retro Fit Vintage 910 Valencia St at 20th, Mission ☎415/550-1530. Poppy, kitschy selection of smart vintage clothes: don't expect bargains, but well worth it for a spot-on shirt or just-right jacket. Check out the DIY vintage Ts: pick a style, then flick through an enormous binder filled with retro transfers to customize the shirt, starting at $20. There's also an ample selection of vintage 1960s and 1970s copies of Playboy.

Schauplatz 791 Valencia St at 18th, Mission ☎415/864-5665. With a selection to match the name (which means "happening scene" in German), the racks are bursting with exceptionally well-preserved vintage pieces. And the shopkeepers are just as extraordinary: they'll go out of their way to help you find items that flatter your figure.

Seconds-To-Go Resale Shop 2252 Fillmore St at Clay, Pacific Heights ☎415/563-7806. Nice clothes and housewares sold to benefit the Sacred Heart school. As with other used-clothing stores along Fillmore St, you'll find the prices higher here than elsewhere.

Thrift Town 2101 Mission St at 17th, Mission ☎415/861-1132. Huge and well-displayed selection, with some of San Francisco's better-quality trash, as well as fairly stylish secondhand clothing bargains.

Ver Unica 437b Hayes St at Octavia, Hayes Valley ☎415/431-0688. This vintage store stocks high-grade secondhand clothing alongside a few brand-new retro-inspired pieces, mostly by local designers.

Wasteland 1660 Haight St at Belvedere, Haight-Ashbury ☎415/863-3150. Smart, high-end vintage selection, sorted by style and color. You'll pay for the ease of browsing, but it's one of the best places to find top-condition, fashionable vintage.

▲ Wasteland

Food and drink

Be sure to try such **local specialties** as Boudin's sourdough bread, Gallo salami, and Anchor Steam beer – all of which are gourmet treats. If you're looking for everyday essentials, there are supermarkets across the city, including several branches of Safeway – the large, cruisey outpost on Market Street in the Castro is the most convenient for Downtown. California alcohol laws are liberal: most stores carrying food sell alcohol too, provided you show ID proving you're at least 21 years of age.

Delis and groceries

24th Street Cheese Company 3893 24th St at Sanchez, Noe Valley ☎415/821-6658. Sleepy-looking store hiding behind slatted blinds and heavy awnings; inside, though, the cool space is suffused with delicate aromas from the dozens of cheeses (both domestic and European) sold by the chunk. There's a smallish selection of gourmet dried goods like pasta, too.

Andronico's Market 1200 Irving St at 14th, Sunset ☎415/753-0403. Pricey but gorgeous produce, plus microbrew beers, good wine, craft breads, fancy cheeses, an olive bar, and a pretty good deli. Not the cheapest, but way better quality than your average supermarket.

Artisan Cheese 2413 California St at Steiner, Pacific Heights ☎415/929-8610. Gourmet cheese store that sells locally produced tangy cheeses as well as imported specials from Britain and France.

Casa Lucas 2934 24th St at Guerrero, Mission ☎415/826-4334. Mission store with an astonishing array of exotic fruits and vegetables.

The Cheesery 427 Castro St at 18th, Castro ☎415/552-6676. Reasonably priced coffees (from $5/lb) and cheeses from around the world.

Delessio Market & Bakery 1695 Market St at Gough, Hayes Valley ☎415/552-5559. A beloved local bakery with gourmet pastries, cakes, heavenly salads, and other savory treats. A worthwhile destination in itself.

Good Life Grocery 488 Cortland Ave at Andover, Bernal Heights ☎415/648-3221. There's a vast selection of organic or locally grown produce at this Bernal Heights gourmet grocery, and at the branch located at 1524 20th St at Missouri, Potrero Hill ☎415/282-9204.

Harvest Urban Market 191 Eighth St at Howard, SoMa ☎415/621-1000. Stacked high with largely organic produce from more than two hundred local farmers and bakeries, this sumptuous, healthy supermarket is also known for its gourmet by-the-pound salad bar ($6.59/lb) – expect napa cabbage, rice and beans, or soy protein frittatas, alongside the usual lettuce and tomato. Daily 8.30am–11pm (café opens 7am). Branch: 2285 Market St at Church, Castro ☎415/626 0805.

Kara's Cupcakes 3249 Scott St at Lombard, Cow Hollow ☎415/563-2253. These little desserts aren't for kids: instead, you'll find adults having heated debates over which of the city's bakeries offers the best cupcakes—but surely Kara's is among the top three with delectable, designer goodies.

Lucca Ravioli 1100 Valencia St at 22nd, Mission ☎415/647-5581. A fiercely loyal customer base frequents this scrumptious, old-world market, with a fresh pasta factory that you can spy on through the big picture windows before entering.

Miette Confiserie 449 Octavia at Hayes, Hayes Valley ☎415/626-6221. Impeccably choreographed displays of boutique sweets including, but not limited to, sugar candies, cupcakes, pastries, and chocolates. Even the most jaded sweet-tooth will ache with desire at the wares.

Molinari's 373 Columbus Ave at Vallejo, North Beach ☎415/421-2337. Bustling veteran North Beach deli, jammed to the rafters with Italian goodies both familiar and exotic: there are cheeses, wines, salamis, and olive oils as well as more offbeat Italian items, from AsdoMar tuna to Brioschi-brand antacids.

▲ Molinari Dei sausage

Rainbow Grocery 1745 Folsom St at 13th, SoMa ☎415/863-0620. Progressive politics and organic food rule in this huge employee-owned wholefoods store. Arguably some of the best produce in town.

The Real Food Company 3060 Fillmore St at Filbert, Cow Hollow ☎415/567-6900. Smallish, artsy grocery store selling potions and vitamins alongside health foods. Excellent gourmet meat counter and wholewheat pastries: grab a sandwich and sit outside on the terrace at one of the wrought-iron picnic tables.

San Francisco Herb Company 250 14th St at Mission, SoMa ☎415/861-7174. Large quantities of fresh herbs at wholesale prices.

Sunrise Deli and Café 2115 Irving St at 22nd, Sunset ☎415/664-8210. Specialty Middle Eastern foodstuffs, such as stuffed grape leaves, *bhaba ghanoush*, and hummus.

Yum 1750 Market St at Gough, Hayes Valley ☎415/626-9001. Irresistible and fun hangar-like grocery store, whose slogan is "Have you played with your food today?" Gourmet selections of cookies are especially delicious, and the friendly staff will let you sample most items before you buy. Head to the back of the store for its best feature: refrigerators filled with a vast selection of sodas from around the world (try a bottle of Afri-Cola, oddly from Germany).

Tea, coffee, and spices

Bluebottle Coffee Co. 315 Linden St at Octavia, Hayes Valley ☎415/252-7535. Don't be put off by the fact that they literally operate out of a garage. Locals aren't. You'll wait in a line that often trails around the corner for a smooth, rich brew that will keep you wired for days. These beans are high-octane and fresh-roasted.

Graffeo Coffee 733 Columbus Ave at Filbert, North Beach ☎415/986-2420. Huge sacks of coffee are piled up all around this minimalist, all-granite North Beach store where the Repetto family has been roasting coffee for more than sixty years – you can smell the aroma from half a block away.

Haig's Delicacies 642 Clement St at Eighth Ave, Richmond ☎415/752-6283. Curries, teas, pickles, and spices from around the world.

Spike's 4117 19th St at Castro, Castro ☎415/626-5572. Proffers a vast selection of teas and coffees, sold by the pound, as well

Farmers' markets

Ferry Plaza Farmers' Market Year-round Sat 8am–2pm, Tues 10am–2pm, also April–Nov Thurs 4–8pm, Ferry Building at Market St, Embarcadero ☏415/291-3276, ⓦwww .ferryplazafarmersmarket.com. Higher prices accompany the mostly organic produce in this very popular Downtown market, with beautiful produce and fine foodstuffs. Upscale restaurants often set up makeshift food stalls here, so it's a great place to sample top-notch cuisine at market prices: it's also a foodie star-spotter's heaven, since local names like Alice Waters can often be found browsing the organic produce.

Fillmore Farmers' Market May–Oct Sat 9am–1pm, on O'Farrell Street between Fillmore and Steiner ☏415/ 441-6396, ⓦwww.fillmorejazz.com. There are only a dozen or so stalls at this small market, and it can feel rather forlorn; the produce, though, is top quality.

Heart of the City Farmers' Market Wed & Sun 7am–3pm, at United Nations Plaza at Market Street near the Civic Center. Huge certified farmers' market (which means everything is sold by the growers themselves), distinguished from others by catering to a multi-ethnic inner-city clientele. The produce prices are rock-bottom, but quality can be hit-and-miss, so choose carefully.

San Francisco Farmers' Market Sat dawn–dusk, 100 Alemany Blvd at Crescent Ave ☏415/647-9423. Covered market, established since the 1940s, offering customers the chance to purchase food fresh from the farms at affordable prices. Invaluable if you're cooking for crowds or just love a bargain. Check out the flea market on Sunday, too (6am–3pm).

as rows of old-fashioned candy in huge glass jars.

Teavana 2164 Polk St at Vallejo, Russian Hill, ☏415/931-9301. Growing nationwide chain that combines a lounge-worthy tea room (fireplace, comfy chairs) with a loose leaf by the pound to-go store, plus a vast assortment of teapots, mostly chic and Asian-inspired.

Wines and spirits

California Wine Merchant 2113 Chestnut St at Steiner, Marina ☏415/567-0646. Before you set off for the Wine Country, pick up a sample selection at this Marina wine emporium so you know what to look out for.

Castro Village Wine Co 4121 19th St at Castro, Castro ☏416 /864-4411. Low-key, laid-back neighborhood winery in the heart of the Castro: prices are reasonable and the selection (especially of local wines) is enormous.

Coit Liquor 585 Columbus Ave at Union, North Beach ☏415/986-4036. North Beach specialty wine store, with the accent on rare Italian vintages. Good stock of regular booze, too.

D & M Wine & Liquor Co 2200 Fillmore St at Sacramento, Pacific Heights ☏415/346-1325.

Great selection of Californian wines, but located as they are in Pacific Heights, their specialty is champagne; bargains abound, though.

The Jug Shop 1567 Pacific Ave at Polk, Pacific Heights ☏415/885-2922. The Jug Shop is famous for its cheap Californian wines, but it also has more than two hundred varieties of beer that are similarly well priced.

K & L Wine Merchants 638 4th St at Brannan, SoMa ☏800/437-7421. The well-versed and helpful staff here will guide you through a wide selection of bottles to find a wine that's both unique and in your budget.

PlumpJack Wines 3201 Fillmore St at Greenwich, Cow Hollow ☏415/346-9870. If you're looking for an obscure Californian vintage for an oenophile relative, this is the place to come – it has an enormous, exhaustive selection of wines from across the state. Branch: 4011 24th St at Noe, Noe Valley ☏415/282-3841.

True Sake 560 Hayes St at Laguna, Hayes Valley ☏415/365-9555. An all-sake store that sells more than 100 different varieties. Each bottle is color-coded to show whether it's a light, crisp blend, or a heftier, aged sake much like port.

Urban Cellars 3821 24th St at Church, Noe Valley ☏415/824-2300. The dipsomaniac's dream: hundreds of wines and exotic spirits, taking booze shopping to its zenith. **The Wine Club 953 Harrison St at Sixth, SoMa** ☎415/512-9086. Huge warehouse space where the wine is offered in torn cardboard boxes on the floor: a great place for budget buys as well as fair-priced vintage specials. The selection changes daily.

Health and beauty

Below, we've included a range of beauty and cosmetics stores, from high–profile international brands to funky local stores.

BeneFit 2117 Fillmore St at California, Pacific Heights ☎415/567-0242. This retro, girly store sells a full range of cosmetics for the woman who wants to be part Courtney Love, part Audrey Hepburn. Full salon in back. Branch: 2219 Chestnut St at Divisadero, Marina ☎415/567-1173.

Body Time 1465 Haight St at Ashbury, Haight-Ashbury ☎415/551-1070. Though this Bay Area-born company sold its original name to the UK-based Body Shop, it still puts out a full range of aromatic natural bath oils, shampoos, and skin creams, and will custom-scent anything.

Body Treats 634 Irving Ave at Seventh, Sunset ☎415/661-2284. Soaps, gels, scrubs, and bath oils amidst cozy Irving Ave fun shops.

Common Scents 3920 24th St at Sanchez, Noe Valley ☎415/826-1019. Essential oils and bath salts, as well as hair and skincare products, stocked in bulk and sold by the ounce. It'll refill your empties, as well.

Isa's Salon & Spa 1401 Castro at Jersey, Noe Valley ☎415/641-8948. Combined salon and beauty store that has a great selection of hair and skin-care products, and is ideal for stocking up on quality essentials.

Kiehl's 2319 Market St at Clay, Pacific Heights ☎415/359-9260. Sumptuous, environmentally sustainable skin and hair products for anyone looking for a little spa-class treatment and a smaller carbon footprint.

Nancy Boy 2319 Market St ☎415/626-5021. Idiosyncratic local cosmetics company, best summed up in its slogan "Tested on boyfriends, not on animals"; pick up your brand lotions, moisturizers, and bath products here.

Oui, Three Queens 225 Gough St at Oak, Hayes Valley ☎415/621-6877. This tiny store produces custom-blended cosmetics, including lipsticks, at reasonable prices. The larger-than-life staff will make the process as well as the product utterly memorable, and the baroque, bejeweled space is glorious.

Scarlet Sage Herb Company 1173 Valencia St at 22nd, Mission ☎415/821-0997. Organic herbal apothecary selling tinctures and treatments made from more than three hundred herbs, as well as scented candles and bath oils; you can even arrange a tarot card reading here.

Shu Uemura 1971 Fillmore St at Pine, Pacific Heights ☎415/395-0953. Japanese cosmetics pioneer and makeup artist Shu Uemura got his start in Hollywood, and his new San Francisco shop is the place to go to get transformed into a glamorous starlet.

Skin Zone 575 Castro St at 19th, Castro ☎415/626-7933. Every unguent imaginable at very reasonable prices. Look for Skin Zone's own brand for real bargains.

Music

There are outposts of all the major **record stores** in San Francisco – we've listed them below. But it's with its specialty stores that the city really shines: from old-school soul on vinyl to 12" white-labels for local DJs, there are some superb **independent** and **collectors'** stores. And in **Amoeba Records**, Haight-Ashbury can lay claim to one of the best places to browse and buy music anywhere in the country.

General

🏃 **Amoeba Records** 1855 Haight St at Stanyan, Haight-Ashbury ☎415/831-1200, ⓦ www.amoeba.com. This big sister to Berkeley's renowned emporium (see p.324) is one of the largest used-music retailers in America. Divided between new and used CDs, the massive warehouse space hums with bargain hunters rifling through an encyclopedic selection of modern music. Don't be put off by its rip-off location in the heart of the Haight: this is a treasure trove for any music fan. Be sure to check the calendar to catch one of the in-store buzz-band performances.

Aquarius Records 1055 Valencia St at 21st, Mission ☎415/647-2272. Inviting, ramshackle record store with hip, friendly staff, who clearly devote hours to the detailed labeling for each artist: there's an emphasis on less mainstream music, including experimental, folk, and world, and stock is sixty-percent CDs, forty-percent vinyl. A reliable place to pick up flyers on upcoming concerts.

Rasputin Music 69 Powell St at Ellis, Union Square ☎1-800/350-8700. In Berkeley, the independent local-chain Rasputin is Amoeba's main music-emporium competitor, albeit focused more on CDs. However, this relatively new San Francisco branch doesn't have the same selection, but it is conveniently located on Union Square, with five narrow floors of music, jam-packed with used CDs.

Streetlight Records 3979 24th St at Noe, Noe Valley ☎415/282-3550. A great selection of new and used records, tapes, and CDs. The perfect opportunity to beef up your collection on the cheap. Branch: 2350 Market St at Noe, Castro ☎415/282-8000.

Virgin Megastore 2 Stockton St at Market, Union Square ☎415/397-4525. Three floors packed with music in a wide variety of styles. The third floor has a good stock of current, popular books, and videos, and the *Citizen Cupcake* café with windows overlooking Market St.

Secondhand and specialty

Discolandia 2964 24th St at Harrison, Mission ☎415/826-9446. Join the snake-hipped groovers looking for the latest in salsa and Central American sounds in this Mission outlet.

Groove Merchant Records 687 Haight St at Pierce, Lower Haight ☎415/252-5766. Come here for secondhand soul & funk or jazz: the owner is passionate and knowledgeable about his music, so don't be afraid to ask questions. Stock is split clearly between the two categories, and is largely vintage vinyl.

Grooves Vinyl Attractions 1797 Market St at Octavia, Hayes Valley ☎415/436-9933. This vinyl specialty store adorned with colored albums on the walls is packed to the gills with collector LPs in all imaginable genres – jazz, classical, blues, comedy, lounge, polka. Owned by a husband-and-wife team, this spot also sells books, tapes, and collectables like 1960s rock posters.

Jack's Record Cellar 254 Scott St at Page, Lower Haight ☎415/431-3047. The city's best source for American secondhand records – R'n'B, jazz, country, and rock'n'roll, including 78s. They'll track down rare discs and offer you the chance to listen before you buy. Open by appointment.

The Jazz Quarter 1267 20th Ave at Lincoln Blvd, Sunset ☎415/661-2331. A bit of a trek from Downtown, but if you're a jazz fiend on the lookout for rarities, it's worth the effort.

Medium Rare 2310 Market St at Noe, Castro ☎415/255-7273. Tiny store crammed with CDs, ranging from camp classics like Peggy Lee and other 1950s cocktail lounge singers to throbbing hi-NRG stars like Donna Summer.

Mikado Japan Center 1737 Post St, Japantown ☎415/922-9450. Enormous Japanese record store sprawled across three units of the Japan Center: the staff will let you watch DVDs before you buy. You can pick up import copies of the latest hit CDs and singles from Japan, both Western and local artists.

Open Mind Music 2150 Market St at Church, Castro ☎415/621-2244. Slightly more peaceful alternative to the hordes of bargain hunters who throng to Amoeba: it offers mainly vinyl (both new and used, rock and jazz) but the stock is well chosen and not picked over.

Recycled Records 1377 Haight St at Masonic, Haight-Ashbury ☎415/626-4075. Good all-around record store, with a decent selection of music publications, American and imported.

Ritmo Latino 2401 Mission St at 20th, Mission ☎415/824-8556. This is the place to go for all varieties of Latin music, whether you're

looking for salsa, bolero, mariachi, reggaeton, merengue, or Latin indie rock. **Rooky Ricardo's Records 448 Haight St at Webster, Lower Haight** ☎415/864-7526. This fun, kooky, vinyl-only store is a great place to dig for soul, jazz, funk, blues, and R&B, or just relax and chat about music at the barstools at the counter.
Soundworks 226 Valencia St at Brosnan, Mission ☎415/487-3980. DJ-friendly record store, stocking imports and current club cuts on vinyl plus a small stock of CDs.
Taiyodo Record Shop Japan Center, 1737 Post St, Japantown ☎415/885-2818. One of several record stores in the mall selling the latest

releases by Japanese singers, whether bubblegum pop or Asian alt-rock. Also great for hard-to-find anime DVDs.
Thrillhouse Records 3422 Mission St at Eugenia, Bernal Heights ☎415/826-0233. This not-for-profit all-volunteer-run record store embodies punk DIY spirit, with a selection that centers on punk and hard-core and a label that puts out CDs by local bands. The store even hosts live shows on occasion.
Tweekin Records 593 Haight St at Steiner ☎415/626-6995. A haven for DJs, this spot stocks all the hottest house, downtempo, and techno releases, as well as disco, reggae, funk, and soul.

Specialty stores

Despite the fact that San Francisco's artists must contend with the high-profile giants in NY and LA, anyone gallery-hopping on the first Thursday of the month (when all the galleries in the 49 & 77 Geary buildings stage their openings – see box, p.262) will find confirmation of a thriving **art scene**. Skip the gimmicky tourist traps around Union Square and head into SoMa, the Financial District, and the Mission for an impressive array of contemporary work by artists both local and of renown. Pick up a copy of *SF Weekly* or the *SF Bay Guardian,* which have complete listings and reviews of current exhibitions throughout the city. Alternatively, contact the SF Bay Area Gallery Guide, 1369 Fulton St, San Francisco, CA 94117 (☎415/921-1600), or the SF Art Dealer's Association, 430 Clementina St at Fifth, in SoMa (☎415/278-9818, ⓦwww.sfada.com). For younger, edgier openings, check out Fecal Face for calendar listings (ⓦwww.fecalface.com/calendar). If you're around in October, take advantage of the annual Open Studios event, in which around eight hundred local artists open their creative spaces to the public for free; call ☎415/861-9838 or visit ⓦwww.artspan.org for more details.

Art galleries

Bucheon Gallery 540 Hayes St at Laguna, Hayes Valley ☎415/863-2891, ⓦwww.bucheon.com. Focusing primarily on local, early to mid-career artists, this smallish space stages ten shows each year: though there's nothing too mold-breaking, you can often find a diamond in the rough.
Crown Point Press 20 Hawthorne St at Folsom, SoMa ☎415/974-6273, ⓦwww.crownpoint .com. Two showrooms, with limited editions of prints by internationally recognized artists and a fine bookstore out in front.
Galeria de la Raza 2957 24th St at Bryant, Mission ☎415/826-8009, ⓦwww .galeriadelaraza.org. Hosts community activities, lectures, and socially minded exhibitions by artists largely from the

Mission district, Los Angeles, Central and South America.
Intersection for the Arts 446 Valencia St at 16th, Mission ☎415/626-3311, ⓦwww .theintersection.org. The protest theater venue also hosts a space on the second floor of its Mission home for the visual arts – exhibitions are heavy on Che and Latino politics, and vary wildly in quality. Wed–Sun 12–5pm.
Jack Hanley Gallery 389 & 395 Valencia St at 15th, Mission ☎415/522-1631, ⓦwww .jackhanley.com. The gallery owner also has a well-known outpost in New York's West Side. Featuring an unusual mix of contemporary paintings, photos, installations, and video work by established artists and rising stars.
Mission Cultural Center 2868 Mission St at 25th, Mission ☎415/821-1155. Home to the Galeria

Museo, one of the largest galleries in town, devoted exclusively to Hispanic art. The center offers classes as well as a wide variety of community events, from street fairs to political actions.

Modernism 685 Market St at Third, SoMa ☎415/541-0461, ⊛www.modernisminc.com. Futurism, expressionism, Pop Art, minimalism, and American modern art can all be found at this gallery.

New Langton Arts 1246 Folsom St at Eighth, SoMa ☎415/626-5416, ⊛www .newlangtonarts.org. Noncommercial theater and gallery organization showing experimental works in all media, and hosting new music and jazz concerts, readings, and performances. Closed Mon.

Ping Pong Gallery 1240 22nd St at Mississippi, Potrero Hill ☎415/550-7483, ⊛www .pingponggallery.com. By now, the "Ping Pong Happy Hour" is local legend, featuring the eponymous game for a friendly bout of back-and-forth, as well as an ample supply of Tecate beer. The gallery regularly features alternative conceptual exhibitions of sculpture, paintings, and prints by recent graduates.

Queen's Nails Annex 3191 Mission St at Powers, Bernal Heights ☎415/648-4564, ⊛www .queensnailsannex.com. Punk-/grunge-influenced curators highlight a broad group of artists and media, with challenging and frequently controversial themes.

Ratio 3 Gallery 1447 Stevenson St at 14th, Mission ☎415/821-3371, ⊛www.ratio3.org. Showcases some of the hottest art stars from New York, LA, and Europe. An understated gallery, solidly curated.

Silverman Gallery 804 Sutter St at Jones, Tenderloin ☎415/255-9508, ⊛www .silverman-gallery.com. A relatively new contemporary space mainly focusing on photography, with some installation and film.

Gifts and oddities

826 Valenica Pirate Supply Store 826 Valencia St at 19th, Mission ☎415/642-5905. A front for writer Dave Eggers' nonprofit workshop teaching kids about language, this "pirate store" offers everything a swashbuckler could need, from eyepatches and message bottles to spy glasses and Jolly Rogers, as well as Eggers' publications. The store is an adventure unto itself with treasures in nooks and crannies, and a fish-tank room holding Karl the porcupine pufferfish.

Autumn Express 2071 Mission St at 17th, Mission ☎415/824-2222. Fair-trade stationery store, festooned with brightly colored lanterns and decorations. A lot of the high-grade paper is Nepalese; and aside from stationery by the sheet there are greetings cards and a few paper-related gifts.

Body Manipulations 3234 16th St at Guerrero, Mission ☎415/621-0408. One of the city's most reliable places for piercing, branding, and other body modifications.

Britex Fabrics 146 Geary St at Stockton, Union Square ☎415/392-2910. Crammed with bales of every possible fabric, this local landmark store has supplied San Francisco's local designers for more than fifty years. Great deals on fabric remnants – and the place to stop by if you lose a button when you're in town: it stocks more than 30,000 different styles.

Cardology Crocker Galleria, 50 Post St, Financial District ☎415/391-1966. The best selection of schmaltz-free greeting cards Downtown, along with cheap, throwaway gifts.

🏃 **Cliff's Variety** 479 Castro St at 18th, Castro ☎415/431-5365. Technically a hardware store selling everything useful from toilet paper to gimlets, this is also the Castro's neighborhood kitsch emporium. You can pick up hula hoops and feather boas by the yard as well as power drills here.

Cookin' 339 Divisadero St at Fell, Fillmore ☎415/861-1854. A budget gourmet cook's bargain heaven, selling good-quality secondhand cast-iron pans and various other kitchen oddities.

Crystal Way 2355 Market St at Castro, Castro ☎415/861-6511. New-Age mecca, selling a small range of books and a wide range of crystals, runes, and other ephemera.

Dark Garden 321 Linden St at Gough, Hayes Valley ☎415/431-7684. Fabulous, made-to-measure fetish clothing: campy, vampy lingerie that's half-costume, half-corset.

Diptyque 171 Maiden Lane, Union Square ☎415/402-0600, One of only a handful of boutiques outside France from this deluxe candlemaker – its Tuberose (rose) fragrance is a top seller.

Flicka 1932 Fillmore St at Pine, Upper Fillmore ☎415/292-4928. Scandinavian mini-boutique, stocking homeware, stationery, gifts, and a

49 & 77 Geary Art Galleries

Every first Thursday, the galleries in these two Financial District buildings host openings for top-notch art shows, making them the place to see and be seen in the San Francisco art scene. These vernissages are simply packed to the gills with the city's culturally savvy. Expect to find mostly early 21st century art – that is, contemporary paintings, sculpture, video art, and a whole host of conceptual installations by artists from all around the world. Even if you can't make it for First Thursday, be sure to stop by to check the artwork, so conveniently concentrated in two locales.

49 Geary St

871 Fine Arts Bookstore ☎415/543-5155. Small-scale sculptures and photographs adjacent to an excellent bookshop.

Don Soker Contemporary Art ☎415/291-0966 ⓦwww.donsokergallery.com. Emerging to mid-career artists, specializing in paintings.

Fraenkel Gallery ☎415/981-2661 ⓦwww.fraenkelgallery.com. Late twentieth-century photographers à la Richard Avedon and Diane Arbus.

Gregory Lind Gallery ☎415/296-9661, ⓦwww.gregorylindgallery.com. New York, LA, and local contemporary painting and sculpture.

Mark Wolfe Contemporary Art ☎415/369-9404, ⓦwww.wolfecontemporary.com. Multimedia, site-specific installations in a salon-style setting.

Robert Koch Gallery ☎415/626-5416, ⓦwww.kochgallery.com. Featuring modern and contemporary photography from the 19th century to the present.

Stephen Wirtz Gallery ☎415/433-6879, ⓦwww.wirtzgallery.com. Wide range of internationally recognized experimental and documentary photographers.

Steven Wolf Fine Arts ☎415/263-3677, ⓦwww.stevenwolffinearts.com. Contemporary work in varying media by mid-career to established artists.

77 Geary St

Marx & Zavatero ☎415/627-9111 ⓦwww.marxzav.com. Dedicated West Coast curators, exhibiting group and solo shows of paintings, sculpture, and installations.

Patricia Sweetow Gallery ☎415/788-5126, ⓦwww.patriciasweetowgallery.com. With a floor of its own, the "mezzanine," the raw industrial setting houses rotating shows of contemporary paintings and drawings.

Rena Bransten ☎415/982-3292, ⓦwww.renabranstengallery.com. Impressive range of established national and international artists in varying media.

---

few pieces of clothing, all from Scandinavia – the jazzy Marimekko homeware is especially appealing.

Flight 001 525 Hayes St at Octavia, Hayes Valley ☎415/487-1001, ⓦwww.flight001.com. This sleek, futuristic travel store sells books, funky accessories (including chunky, dayglo luggage tags and all-in-one shaving kits), and dapper carry-on bags. The place to stock up on sundries if you only travel first class – or want to act like it.

Fredericksen Hardware 3029 Fillmore St at Union, Cow Hollow ☎415/292-2950. Since 1896, this store has been selling everything from old clocks to kitchen gadgets – comprehensive, if not cheap.

Good Vibrations 603 Valencia St at 17th, Mission ☎415/522-5460. Gloriously sexy

▲ Good Vibrations

store, run by a co-op of men and women, that's designed to destigmatize sex shops and make browsing fun and comfortable for men, women, and couples. It's packed with every imaginable sex toy, plus racks of erotica and candy-store-style jars of condoms. The co-op recently branched out into producing its own erotic videos in addition to the books it already publishes under the Down There press imprint; all that, plus an onsite vibrator museum. Branch: 1620 Polk St at Sacramento, Polk Gulch ☎415/345-0400.

Happy Trails 2231 Market St at Noe, Castro ☎415/431-7232. Girlier and more inventive than most kitsch emporia, this massive trinket shop sells clothes and gimmickry as well as all the fixings to host your own retro tiki bar.

Just for Fun 3982 24th St at Noe, Noe Valley ☎415/285-2314. Noe Valley neighborhood stationery store with better than average kitschy gifts and wide paper selection; the real reason to stop by, though, is its vast range of current and classic board games.

La Palma Mexicatessan 2884 24th St at Florida, Mission ☎415/647-1500. The place to stock up on authentic Mexican spices, like fresh or dried chilis, as well as equipment, like tortilla presses.

La Place du Soleil 2356 Polk St at Union, Russian Hill ☎415/771-4252. Tiny gifts and houseware gem of a boutique, stocking new and vintage trinkets. But few people come here for that: most are drawn by the mouth-watering selection of imported candy from Europe – sold by the piece or in bulk.

La Sirena Botanica 1509 Church St at 27th, Noe Valley ☎415/285-0612. Featuring a highly unusual selection of new-age books, Santeria items, tarot cards, oils and other potent potions.

Mom's Bodyshop 1408 Haight St at Masonic, Haight-Ashbury ☎415/864-MOMS. Tattoos for those who want to go home with a permanent souvenir. Large selection of Chinese, Celtic, and Tibetan scripts.

Needles and Pens 3253 16th Street at Guerrero, Mission ☎415/255-1534. A compendium of what seems to be every zine and alternative magazine in existence. Locally printed tees, DIY crafts and zines, and a salon-style wall of constantly changing art. For the uninitiated, it's a perfect introduction to San Francisco's underground Mission-school style.

Otsu 3253 16th St at Dolores, Mission ☎415/255-7900. Animal-free boutique (or veganmart, as it calls itself), highlighting alternative materials including recycled tires and oilcloth for bags and belts, as well as a vast, impressive selection of shoes. There are even cruelty-free comics. As for the name, it's an old Japanese word meaning "stylish." Closed Mon & Tues.

Paxton Gate 824 Valencia St at 19th, Mission ☎415/824-1872. Taxidermy central. Mordantly arranged insects, cute (dead) furry fauna, and vintage photos, posters, and succulent plants.

Revival of the Fittest 1701 Haight St at Cole, Haight-Ashbury ☎415/751-8857. A smart selection of retro gifts, including sunglasses and wacky greeting cards.

The Ribbonerie 191 Potrero Ave at Utah, Potrero Hill ☎415/626-6184. Crazy, intriguing little shop stocking nothing but ribbons – all patterns, widths, colors, and materials – as well as a few thimbles and pincushions.

Soko Hardware 1698 Post St at Laguna, Japantown ☎415/931-5510. Soko Hardware is kind of a Cliff's Variety (see p.261) of J-town. Every item known to man is stashed under one roof, and its tools are only a starting point. A no-brainer destination if you're looking for hard-to-find Japanese household goods or a last-minute gift.

Stitch 182 Gough St at Oak, Hayes Valley ☎415/431-3739. Store-cum-studio, devoted entirely to sewing. Come here to stock up on supplies for home clothes-making; or stay for one-on-one lessons, group classes, or the chance to use its professional-grade sewing machines.

Super 7 1628 Post St at Buchanan, Japantown ☎415/409-4700. Adulcts of collectable toys go overboard with the full range of pop-surreal, grotesque, and painfully mawkish wares from Japan. Good for hardcore Godzilla fans, as well as those with a taste for surprisingly affordable art prints.

Under One Roof 549 Castro St at Market, Castro ☎415/252-9430. A unique San Francisco store selling decorative gift items (think West Elm or Williams Sonoma), with all the profits going to 51 AIDS-services organizations. The shop has sold $10 million worth of merchandise in fifteen years of operation.

X21 Modern 890 Valencia St at 20th, Mission ☎415/647-4211. With a highly unusual, and expensive, collection of bizarre decorative items including taxidermied critters, vintage sculptures and signs, and attractive industrial tools – plus a range of modern Danish furniture.

Sports and outdoor activities

W ith its sizable areas of open water and protected parkland, it comes as no surprise that the Bay Area is full of people who enjoy the region's wealth of **outdoor activities**. The fitness exuded by most locals isn't so much the cosmetic "body-beautiful" sort often associated with the California lifestyle, as much as merely a way to get a bit of fresh air, commune with the natural environment, and maybe break a sweat while doing so; that said, a strong percentage of Bay Area residents (particularly in open space-deficient San Francisco) consider gym membership a basic necessity of life.

For more sedentary individuals – or for those simply taking a day off from hiking, cycling, or playing tennis – the region's three major cities are collectively home to teams in all major American **spectator sports**, and taking in a sporting event is a great way to glimpse a different side of the Bay Area, where its signature sophisticated tastes and intellectualism take a back seat to good old-fashioned cheering (and on occasion, booing).

Regardless of how you spend your outdoor time, keep in mind that even when Bay Area skies are gray, the sun's ultraviolet rays still pierce through the clouds and often leave unprepared visitors with a souvenir sunburn.

Participation sports and outdoor activities

Upholding coastal California's reputation as a fitness hub, the Bay Area is home to countless acres devoted to outdoor activities of one sort or another. Few urban areas in the US boast as much open space as this region of over seven million residents: numerous parks lend themselves to hiking and climbing exploration; miles of country roads offer excellent cycling routes; gusty San Francisco Bay itself challenges local riggers; running paths line several of the bay's shores. Tennis and golf are popular pursuits in the mild weather months, while surfers attack the mighty Pacific's swells year-round, although waves reach peak power in December and January.

Walking, running, and climbing

For a relaxed **walk**, simply set out on any of the labyrinthine paths in San Francisco's Golden Gate Park. Crissy Field and Mount Davidson (at 927ft, the city's highest point) are also pleasant spots for off-pavement walks affording expansive vistas. Of course,

The Bay Area's relatively mild year-round weather allows local hikers to set soles to path in any season, although things can sometimes get a bit muddy during the wet months of winter and early spring. With a seemingly limitless network of **trails** accessible in the area – particularly in the Marin Headlands and on Mount Tamalpais in Marin County, along the ridge of the Santa Cruz Mountains in the Peninsula and the South Bay, and on Mount Diablo in Contra Costa County east of San Francisco – the region boasts wild settings often absent in other metropolitan areas with a similar population. A particularly helpful resource for finding and planning Bay Area hikes is Ⓦwww.bahiker.com; also, Tom Stienstra, the highly respected outdoors writer for the *San Francisco Chronicle*, publishes ideas for outings regularly at Ⓦwww.sfgate.com.

San Francisco's northwest corner has a few hikes that don't require much exertion for a payoff of extraordinary views. The **Coastal Trail**, which links Sutro Heights with the Golden Gate Bridge via Baker Beach, follows an old railroad route for part of its length, and a spur trail leads steeply downhill to epic vistas at Land's End on the far northwest tip of the San Francisco Peninsula.

Top trailheads on iconic, 2571-foot **Mount Tamalpais** include Bootjack, Mountain Home, and Rock Spring, all of which are on the southern and western flanks of the mountain and easily reached via the Panoramic Highway. Purchase a trail map at the Mount Tamalpais State Park visitor center (☎415/388-2070, Ⓦwww.parks.ca.gov) at Pantoll Ranger Station and create your own loop hike ranging anywhere from two hours to a full day. Note that trailhead parking lots fill up early, particularly on sunny weekends regardless of season.

A favorite hike among locals, albeit not one for anyone out of shape, is a rigorous seven-mile loop that begins at Stinson Beach and heads up the west side of Mount Tam (as it's colloquially known) before descending back around to the seaside village. Drive to Stinson Beach, park near the fire station at the south end of town, and look for the adjacent **Matt Davis Trailhead**. Climb very steeply (1500ft in a little over two miles) up the Matt Davis Trail, pausing to catch your breath at the ocean vista of Table Rock before continuing to Pantoll through thick forest that eventually opens up into mountainside grassland offering stunning views in three directions. From Pantoll, the approximate halfway point of the hike, drop back down on the aptly named Steep Ravine Trail, a lushly shaded descent featuring ferns, redwoods, a burbling creek, and even a ten-foot step ladder. Return to Stinson Beach on the vista-laden Dipsea Trail and reward your feet with a quick wade in the chilly Pacific across Highway 1.

San Mateo and **Santa Clara Counties** offer similar grassland/forest landscapes amidst a wealth of uncrowded public parks, many managed by the Mid-Peninsula Open Space District (☎650/691-1200, Ⓦwww.openspace.org). **Portola Redwoods State Park** (☎650/948-9098, Ⓦwww.parks.ca.gov), set in a deep and remote canyon on the seaward slope of the Santa Cruz Mountains, requires a slow drive along its curvy entrance road but rewards visitors with excellent hiking and camping in a cool, serene setting.

The **East Bay** counties include a number of trail-rich parks and preserves managed by the East Bay Regional Park District (☎888/327-2757, Ⓦwww.ebparks.org), while **Mount Diablo State Park** (☎925/837-0904, Ⓦwww.parks.ca.gov) features its namesake 3849-foot peak, from which the total visible land area is second only to Africa's Kilimanjaro due to the expansive valley and delta to Diablo's immediate east. An extensive latticework of hiking trails abounds here as well, but be forewarned that temperatures consistently break into the 90s (and sometimes higher) throughout the summer months. Winter and spring are the best time to visit, particularly for the many waterfalls on the mountain's steep northern flank.

(14)

SPORTS AND OUTDOOR ACTIVITIES

provided you watch for oncoming cars at intersections and don't mind a few inclines, San Francisco's sidewalk grid makes for terrific exploration; best of all with urban hiking, you're never far from comfortably seated refreshment. See *The hills of San Francisco* colour section for more on walking San Francisco's famed hills.

The local chunk of the Pacific coastline doesn't offer an abundance of long seafront spits, but there are a handful of lengthy beaches in and near San Francisco. Anyone looking for a sandy stroll would do well to visit Stinson Beach in Marin County, Half Moon Bay State Beach in San Mateo County, or despite its ongoing trash issues, San Francisco's Ocean Beach (free to visit, unlike the first two). Other popular – and paved – paths far inland from the coast's wind and atmospheric fog are Nimitz Way in Berkeley's Tilden Regional Park and the walkways around Oakland's Lake Merritt.

San Francisco remains a big **running** town, although sometimes not the safest one due to clogged streets and distracted drivers. The above-mentioned pedestrianized areas frequented by walkers are popular with runners as well; add to that list the Embarcadero and the Great Highway, which flank the east and west shores of the city. One of the city's zaniest annual events is the **Bay To Breakers**, a 7.5-mile footrace-cum-costume party held each May (see p.278 for further details). Considerably more serious is Marin's cross-country **Dipsea Race** (Ⓦwww.dipsea.org) in June, which sees 1500 runners sprint out of Mill Valley before struggling up and over Windy Gap via 671 discouragingly steep steps. The course then passes through Muir Woods, over Cardiac Hill, and down Steep Ravine before mercifully crossing the finish line in Stinson Beach, 7.1 miles from the starting point. A few weekends later sees the **Double Dipsea** (Ⓦwww.double dipsea.com), which adds to the Dipsea Race's route a run from Stinson Beach to Mill Valley.

Those who wish to put the connection between mind and body through a rigorous test can try **rock climbing** at one of many walls around the bay. Prime outdoor spots include Mickey's Beach a mile south of Stinson Beach (check a tide table before making a trip) and Indian Rock Park in the Berkeley hills. Enthusiasm for the sport has led to a proliferation of local indoor climbing walls, with several owned and operated by Touchstone (Ⓦwww.touchstoneclimbing.com) – daily entrance fees include use of the adjoining gyms (Mon–Fri 6.30am–10pm, Sat & Sun 9am–7pm; $18, $10 before 3pm), while climbing instruction is available for an extra $28.

Cycling and mountain biking

Many visitors best experience San Francisco's parks and natural landscapes by **cycling** through them. Golden Gate Park and the Great Highway Promenade adjacent to Ocean Beach, as well as Crissy Field and the Presidio, all have fine paved trails and some good off-road routes; the bayside Embarcadero is also a popular cycling spot.

The Bay Area's contribution to cycling was the invention of the **mountain bike** in the early 1970s, when a small group of Tamalpais High School students (known as the Canyon Gang) began cruising down the unpaved roads on Mount Tamalpais on one-speed, coaster-brake Schwinn cruisers. These 45-pound bikes with thick balloon tires could handle the roads' rough terrain, and by 1976, the Repack race was begun on Tamalpais-adjacent Pine Mountain; the regular event soon generated major press coverage and led to a national craze, but was discontinued in 1984 due to deteriorating trail conditions and other safety issues. Along with Mount Tam, serious biking aficionados visiting the Bay Area should consider trips to the Marin Headlands, El Corte de Madera

Open Space Preserve in San Mateo County, Mount Diablo State Park in Contra Costa County, and, of course, the Pine Mountain Loop near Fairfax in Marin County. Visit ⓦwww .gatetrails.com for detailed information on Bay Area mountain biking destinations.

For **bicycle rentals and tours**, try Blazing Saddles (☎415/202-8888, ⓦwww.blazingsaddles.com) – two of the most convenient branches are 1095 Columbus Ave at Francisco in North Beach, and Pier 41 in Fisherman's Wharf. Rental rates start at $7/hr, $28/day for adults; a ten-percent discount is offered for reserving online. Another option with similarly priced rentals and tours is Bike and Roll, 899 Columbus Ave at Lombard in North Beach (☎415/229-2000, ⓦwww.bikeandroll.com). On the western side of town, Wheel Fun Rentals (☎415/668-6699, ⓦwww .wheelfunrentals.com) is in the boathouse at Golden Gate Park's Stow Lake and offers all sorts of rolling contraptions for rent, from bikes ($8/hr, $25/day), tandem bikes ($12/hr, $40/day), and scooters ($5/hr) to a cavalcade of fringed surreys ($20–30/hr, depending on size).

Water sports

Swimming is a treacherous activity along much of the Northern California coast, with alarmingly frequent reports of ocean riptides swallowing swimmers. As a result, sea swimming in and around San Francisco can't be recommended, irrespective of your level of expertise. Dipping into the calmer (though hardly calm) waters inside the Golden Gate is a safer move – try Aquatic Park on the city's north shore, where numerous local swimmers train. See the box below for a few other options on Bay Area swimming.

If you'd prefer not to brave the bay's cold estuary waters, San Francisco and its outlying communities maintain a number of **public pools**, some in better condition than others. In the city proper, newly restored North Beach Pool, Lombard Street **at Mason** (☎415/391-0407, ⓦwww.parks .sfgov.org), offers lap swims for a nominal fee; it's in a covered space with lots of roof windows. Temescal Pool at Oakland Technical High School, 371 45th St (☎510/597-5013, ⓦwww.oaklandnet.com), is one of Oakland's top spots for an outdoor pool dip on a warm East Bay day.

Bay Area swimming holes

These Bay Area swim spots offer the best warm-day alternatives to crashing pool parties in suburban back yards or being sucked undersea by swirling ocean currents.

Bass Lake, Point Reyes National Seashore, Marin County ☎415/464-5100, ⓦwww .nps.gov/pore. Reached by a moderate three-mile hike from the Palomarin trailhead near Bolinas. Look for rope swings dangling from trees along its south shore. No lifeguard on duty, no fee.

Crown Memorial State Beach, Eighth Street at Otis, Alameda ☎510/521-7090, ⓦwww.ebparks.org. Relatively warm and shallow bay waters often buffeted by strong breezes. Adjacent bird sanctuary and marine reserve. No lifeguard on duty, picnicking available nearby. $5 parking free, free to swim.

Lake Anza, Tilden Regional Park, Berkeley hills ☎510/843-2137, ⓦwww.ebparks .org. Sheltered from the wind, and there's even a sandy beach. Changing rooms on-site, lifeguard on duty, picnicking available nearby. $3.50 adults, $2.50 kids and seniors.

Lake Temescal, 6502 Broadway Terrace, Oakland hills☎510/652-1155, ⓦwww .ebparks.org. In a less wild setting than Lake Anza, but still a nice spot for a dip. Changing rooms onsite, no lifeguards on duty. $3 adults, $2 kids and seniors.

▲ Windsurfing at Golden Gate Bridge

Local coastal waters tend to be chilly, swirling, and often rife with sharks, so on a mainstream level, **surfing** remains more of a Southern California phenomenon. Nonetheless, tightly knit communities of surfers extend from Santa Cruz to Stinson Beach. Certain Bay Area surf spots can sometimes be territorially guarded by locals, but overall, the scene's fairly welcoming. The San Mateo County coast offers both extremes: Pacifica's Linda Mar Beach is a favorite area for beginners, while down the coast near Princeton-by-the-Sea, the Mavericks break, which hosts a pre-eminent big wave competition most winters, has claimed the lives of some of the world's most accomplished surfers.

If you're up for challenging the Pacific's titanic waves, Aqua Surf Shop, 2830 Sloat Blvd at 46th Ave, in San Francisco's Parkside neighborhood (T 415/242-9283, W www.aquasurf shop.com), rents and sells a variety of gear and also offers instruction referrals. Outside San Francisco, Sonlight Surfshop, 575 Crespi Drive off Highway 1 in Pacifica (T 650/359-0353, W www.sonlightsurfshop), and Live Water Surf Shop, 3448 Highway 1

in Stinson Beach (T 415/868-0333, W www.livewatersurfshop.com) are each located near surf breaks and happy to outfit and train visitors; spend any amount of time in West Marin and you're bound to see the latter shop's iconic "No Sharks" logo stickers on windows, signs, and auto bumpers.

Windsurfers and **kitesurfers** are especially visible in San Francisco around gusty Crissy Field, from where aquatic speed demons race out and around the Golden Gate; other popular windsurfing/kitesurfing areas include the far northern end of Ocean Beach, the Berkeley Marina, and Waddell Beach (16 miles north of Santa Cruz on Highway 1). Visit the San Francisco Boardsailing Association's website at W www.sfba.org for a wealth of information on rental shops and more.

Kayaking and **canoeing** can be done at several Bay Area locations for anywhere from $15 to $100, depending on vessel size and time allotment. In San Francisco, City Kayak (T 415/357-1010; W www.citykayak.com) operates from two bayfront locations: the first, at Pier 40 at South Beach Harbor, offers trips and rentals; the second, at Pier 39 slip A21, only offers trips, no rentals. Calmer bay waters are found near Sausalito, where Sea Trek (☎415/488-1000, ⓦwww.seatrek.com) rents single or double sea kayaks at $20–35 for an hour's worth of paddling. Stinson Beach Surf & Kayak (☎415/868-2739) fits the bill if you prefer to navigate the waters along the Marin coast. Note that there's no experience needed to rent sit-on-top kayaks, but taking a traditional (closed deck) sea kayak out on the open water will require prior training.

Tennis and golf

There are over 150 public **tennis** courts in San Francisco, and while they can't be reserved by individuals, you shouldn't have too much trouble finding a vacant court somewhere in town. Consult ⓦwww.sftenniscourts.com for a complete list, including photos. Pack your own racket in advance, as rental possibilities seem to be virtually non-existent at this time.

San Francisco's cash-strapped municipal **golf** courses are less than the best in terms of maintenance, value, and visitor accessibility, so you're probably better off heading out of town (or cultivating a quick friendship with a member of the exclusive Olympic Club) if you're looking for a quality round on the links. Respected public courses in the area include the par-70 Tilden Park Golf Course in the Berkeley hills ($18–72; ☎510/848-7373, ⓦwww.tildenparkgc.americangolf.com), challengingly windy Metropolitan Golf Links in Oakland ($25–66; ☎510/569-5555, ⓦwww.playmetro.com), and bucolic, gently rolling San Geronimo Golf Course in central Marin County ($28–64; ☎415/488-4030, ⓦwww.sangeronimogc.americangolf.com).

Disc golf has become a popular activity in the Bay Area in recent years, with nearly a dozen courses scattered around the region. One of the best is set amidst stands of eucalyptus in Golden Gate Park, and a second San Francisco course is in the works at McLaren Park; others are located as near as Berkeley and as far as Santa Cruz. It's recommended you invest $35 or so in "driver" and "putter" discs beforehand, or find a well-equipped partner who's happy to share. Some outlying courses require parking fees, and many have donation boxes. Visit ⓦwww.sfdiscgolf.org for more information.

A few San Francisco community centers offer **table tennis**, although unless you're a world-class player, be prepared to suffer ignominious defeat at the hands of any number of impossibly hand-eye-coordinated locals. Try Sunset Recreation Center, 2001 Lawton St at 28th in the Mid Sunset (☎415/753-7098), where merely watching a match can be intimidating; alternately, you're bound to find easier competition and booze-enhanced conviviality (if questionable equipment) at local watering holes *Finnegan's Wake*, 937 Cole St at Carl in Cole Valley (☎415/731-6119), and *Thee Parkside*, 1600 17th St at Wisconsin in Potrero Hill (☎415/252-1330).

Skating

If it seems like San Francisco law has been conspiring to ban **skateboarding** from city limits since the early 1990s – a time when the city's reputation as street skating nirvana reached unassailable levels, with skaters nationwide flocking to the Embarcadero – prospects may start to improve with the recent opening of the Potrero del Sol skate park, on San Bruno Avenue south of 25th Street at the southeast edge of the Mission (no phone; ⓦwww.parks.sfgov.org). Outside of town, a fistful of excellent, purpose-built skate parks have sprung up all around the Bay Area; those in Berkeley, Novato (Marin County), and Sunnyvale (Santa Clara County) command the most respect from area shredders. Check Ⓦwww.sk8parklist .com for an exhaustive list.

Every Sunday (and in summer, every Sat), lengthy stretches of one of Golden Gate Park's main drags, John F. Kennedy Drive, closes to auto traffic, thus providing a prime throughway for **inline skaters**. The number of rollerbladers here has dropped since the pursuit's 1990s heyday, with the old-is-new-again trend of **roller skating** on the rise. Choose your preference at Golden Gate Park Bike & Skate, 3038 Fulton St at Sixth in the Inner Richmond (Ⓣ415/668-1117, Ⓦwww.goldengateparkbikeandskate .com), which rents both skates ($5/hr, $20/day) and inlines ($6/hr, $24/day). Aside from Golden Gate Park, Marina Green along the bay and the paved paths that ring Lake Merced in the southwest corner of town also provide good, flat spots to skate.

Bay Area **ice skaters** are fortunate to have access to a few excellent rinks. In San Francisco, the Embarcadero Center sets up an outdoor oval every holiday season in Justin Herman Plaza (Nov–Jan Mon–Thurs & Sun 10am–10pm, Fri & Sat 10am–11.30pm; $6 adults, $10 with skate rental; $5 children, $8 with skate rental; Ⓣ415/772-0700, Ⓦwww.embarcaderocenter.com). Not far away, indoor Yerba Buena Ice Skating Center, 750 Folsom St at Fourth (hours vary; $8 adults, $11 with skate rental; $6.25 children, $9.25 with skate rental; Ⓣ415/820-3532, Ⓦwww .skatebowl.com), operates year-round in a lovely space bathed in natural light atop Moscone Center.

Beyond the city are two highly touted indoor skating arenas: Olympic-sized Oakland Ice Center, 519 18th St at San Pablo (hours vary; $7.50 adults, $10 with skate rental; Ⓣ510/268-9000, Ⓦwww.oaklandice.com), is available for public skating when it's not training big names in figure skating and ice hockey, while Santa Rosa's Snoopy's Home Ice (Redwood Empire Ice Arena), 1667 West Steele

Lane near Hardies (hours vary; $7–9 adults, $10–12 with skate rental; Ⓣ707/546-7147, Ⓦwww.snoopy shomeice.com), was built by *Peanuts* creator and local hero Charles M. Schulz in the late 1960s. The latter's interior evokes the Swiss countryside and is a cut above most grimly outfitted rinks; there's a Snoopy-themed café next door, and a museum across the street devoted to Schulz's life work (see p.383).

Boating, fishing, and wildlife viewing

While bay **sailing** is largely a pursuit exclusive to the local financial elite, the Cal Sailing Club (Ⓦwww .cal-sailing.org), located at the south side of the Berkeley Marina, is a beginner-friendly co-op with a fleet of about two dozen vessels. Membership is required ($60 for three months, $100 for a year), but includes instruction and sailboat access for anyone keen to learn the ins and outs of boating.

One of the Bay Area's signature outdoor adventures is a **whale-watching** cruise, on which you'll follow pods of mighty California gray whales on their annual migration (generally Jan–May). The best local operator is the nonprofit Oceanic Society (Ⓣ415/441-1106, Ⓦwww .oceanic-society.org), which offers all-day boat trips from San Francisco and half-day excursions from Half Moon Bay and Bodega Bay; consult the organization's website for prices (which vary by point of departure) and booking information. During late spring, summer, and autumn, the Oceanic Society operates tours that ring the nearby Farallon Islands, a seabird rookery over 25 miles offshore where you're bound to see thousands of pelicans, cormorants, and possibly the world's largest mammal, the glorious blue whale. Reservations for whale-watching trips are recommended two weeks in advance, while the more expensive cruises to the

Farallon Islands fill up months beforehand.

Another way to experience the volatile Pacific is by taking a **deep sea fishing** cruise. Huck Finn Sportfishing Center (☎650/726-7133, ⓦ www.huckfinnsportfishing.com) runs a variety of such trips out of Half Moon Bay on its fleet of eight boats, and can also service your rod, reel, tackle, and fishing license needs. For all sea excursions, dress in layers, make appropriate preparations if you're concerned about seasickness, and expect to shell out $50–110 per person, depending on the trip.

Another option for wildlife enthusiasts – especially those hesitant to commit themselves to spending several hours on a floating vessel – is to view **northern elephant seals** from afar during the grotesquely beautiful pinnipeds' mating season. These two-ton creatures spend the winter months at Año Nuevo State Reserve on the coast between Half Moon Bay and Santa Cruz; if you fancy spying on the trunk-nosed males as they battle it out on the sand for the right to procreate, see p.344 for details.

Horseback riding and hang gliding

For **horseback riding**, Miwok Livery Stables, 701 Tennessee Valley Rd in Mill Valley ($75; ☎415/383-8048, ⓦ www.miwokstables.com), offers a one-hour trail ride in the lush Marin County countryside. It's preceded by a thirty-minute lesson and is available at 1.30pm every day except Sunday; reservations are required, and participants must be 12 years or older.

The truly daring (and deep-pocketed) will want to consider **hang gliding** or **paragliding** flights that swoop down 1500ft to Stinson Beach from the west flank of Mount Tamalpais. The instructors at the San Francisco Hang Gliding Center ($295 weekdays, $325 weekends and holidays; ☎510/528-2300, ⓦ www.sfhanggliding.com) will provide a short instructional session before

soaring off the hillside with you on a tandem flight lasting anywhere from ten to thirty minutes, depending on that day's weather. Reservations are suggested, but not imperative.

Fitness centers, pickup basketball, and bowling

A number of San Francisco **fitness centers** feature daily rates for city visitors – it's best to check each individual gym's website before heading out, as hours can vary wildly from place to place. Your best choice in or near Downtown is Gold's Gym, 1001 Brannan St at Ninth in SoMa (day pass $20; ⓦ www.goldsgym.com, ☎415/552-4653); in the Western Addition, try Cathedral Hill Plaza Athletic Club, 1333 Gough St at Geary (day pass $15; ☎415/346-3868, ⓦ www.chpathleticclub.com), which also has swimming and, for an additional fee, tennis. Pacific Heights Health Club, 2356 Pine St at Steiner in its namesake neighborhood (day pass $16; ☎415/563-6694, ⓦ www.phhcsf.com), also offers a robust complement of fitness options. Though off the beaten path for many visitors, Liberty Fitness, 3725 Noriega St at 44th (day pass $12; ☎415/564-4734, ⓦ www.libertyfitness.com), is a popular women-only gym in the Outer Sunset a few blocks from the beach. For fitness centers that cater to a primarily gay crowd, see p.242.

A more bracing alternative to indoor exercise is Boot Camp SF (☎415/921-8537, ⓦ www.bootcampsf.com), an intense **outdoor workout session** held at six locations across the city. Group sessions typically last six weeks, but single class drop-ins ($20) are welcome; there's also weekend trail running in San Francisco and Marin County ($25).

San Francisco's **pickup basketball** scene – informally competitive games of three-on-three (or, less frequently, five-on-five) on public outdoor courts – may not be quite on the same level of those in New York, Chicago, or Los

Angeles, but if you care to brave middling talent and trash-talk galore, head to the courts in the Golden Gate Park Panhandle (between Fell, Oak, Clayton, and Ashbury) on any dry day and you're bound to find a halfcourt game; elsewhere, Julius Kahn Playground on the south edge of the Presidio offers a mellower, friendlier scene. Quieter courts conducive to just shooting around are scattered around town – try Michelangelo Playground (Greenwich St at Jones on Russian Hill) or Noe Valley Courts (Elizabeth St at Douglas in Noe Valley). In the East Bay, a number of Oakland and Berkeley playgrounds feature competitive games.

San Francisco boasts two **bowling** alleys to sate your thirst for kitschy Americana and unfortunate footwear. The twelve-lane Presidio Bowling Center, 93 Montgomery St at Moraga in the Presidio (Mon–Thurs & Sun 9am–midnight Fri & Sat 9–2am $4.25–6.50 per game, $4 shoe rental; ☏415/561-2695, ⊛www.presidio bowl.com), was one of the base's top gathering places in its Army heyday, and has remained just as popular since opening to the public after the military's departure. Over in SoMa, the colorful Yerba Buena Bowling Center, 750 Folsom St at Fourth (Mon–Thurs & Sun 10am–10pm, Fri–Sat 10am–midnight; $4–7 per game, $3 shoe rental; ☏415/820-3532, ⊛www.skatebowl.com), is easier for most visitors to reach than its Presidio counterpart.

Spectator sports

Having been spoiled with several successful **professional teams** during the 1980s and 1990s (chiefly, football's San Francisco 49ers and baseball's Oakland Athletics), the Bay Area has seen something of a downturn in its championship fortunes in recent years. Rivalries still exist between San Francisco and Oakland baseball and football teams, but the existence of "split caps" – on which the Athletics' and San Francisco Giants' logos share equal space – suggest that they're less serious than in other sports-obsessed cities like Chicago and New York.

On the collegiate level, the University of California, Berkeley (invariably known as "**Cal**" in sports circles) and **Stanford** University in Palo Alto dominate local coverage and attention, with a handful of the area's smaller schools occasionally showing up on the front page of local sports pages.

Baseball

Major League Baseball's regular season begins no later than early April and runs until the end of September, with teams playing a staggering 81 home games. October's eight-team playoffs culminate in the sport's final round, the misleadingly titled **World Series**.

Following four decades of wildly inconsistent play at grim, blustery Candlestick Park in the extreme southeast corner of the city, the National League's **San Francisco Giants** (☏415/972-2000, ⊛www .sfgiants.com) moved to a charming waterfront ballyard at the dawn of the new millennium. The red brick ballpark, already on its third name (**AT&T Park**) since opening for the 2000 season, was the first major American sports venue in decades to be built with private funds, and its retro beauty, first-class amenities, and bayside views have made it a hit with all kinds of fans, including casual ones. The team remains popular with locals despite current struggles and never having won a World Series in San Francisco. Ticket prices range from $13 in the center-field bleachers to $75–95 for a seat behind one of the dugouts; an alternate plan is to stop by

▲ Willie Mays statue at AT&T Park

affordable than in San Francisco, however: expect to shell out anywhere from $9–55, depending on the opponent. Conveniently, BART runs directly to the stadium complex.

For those looking for a less **glitzy** ballgame experience, the minor-league **San Jose Giants** (☎408/297-1435, ⓦwww.sjgiants.com) feature young players aspiring to someday reach the majors. The team plays at one of the oldest operating ballparks in the US, **San Jose Municipal Stadium**, an intimate setting where tickets cost a fraction of big-league prices (usually around $10). Kooky promotions, such as two-for-one beers when a certain opposing batter strikes out, occur frequently.

the see-through area on the so-called portwalk beyond the right field fence, where you can watch gratis for up to three innings. MUNI streetcars stop right in front of the Giants' park, which is an easy walk from Downtown.

Across the bay, the once-dominant **Oakland Athletics** (☎510/638-4900, ⓦwww.oaklandathletics.com) play before smaller, but intensely loyal crowds at **McAfee Coliseum**, essentially an old concrete bowl. Known to most as the A's, the team was far and away Baseball's most colorful and successful franchise of the early to mid 1970s, winning three consecutive World Series flags while festooned in garish green-and-gold uniforms and mustaches galore. Glory days returned in the late 1980s and early 1990s, peaking with the team's squashing of the Giants in the 1989 World Series, ingloriously interrupted by the devastating Loma Prieta earthquake. Lacking the financial resources of many other major-league teams, the A's now rely on young talent to keep them in regular contention, though they have not reached a World Series since 1990. Tickets are much more

Football

For five months a year, the **National Football League** rivals organized religion as America's favorite Sunday activity – the regular season runs from early September through late December, plus a month of playoffs. Each team plays a mere eight home contests (not including pre-season exhibitions), thus elevating each game's urgency to remarkable levels of intensity. The season culminates in the **Super Bowl**, generally the year's most-watched television event, held on the first Sunday in February.

The toast of the National Football League – and the entire Bay Area – for most of the 1980s and 1990s, the **San Francisco 49ers** (☎415/656-4900, ⓦwww.sf49ers.com) have fallen on severely hard times, rattling off losing seasons more often than not since last winning the NFL's grand prize after the 1994 season, its record fifth league title. Whereas the waiting list for 49ers tickets was impossibly long during the franchise's glory years, it's now sometimes possible to turn up on game day and spring for a $70-plus seat. Embarrassingly, the number of opposing fans often equals that of the dwindling "49er Faithful" for certain high-profile draws, and the team's decrepit and inaccessible stadium, **Candlestick Park**, doesn't help matters – a major reason why the club is flirting with the idea of a move to the South Bay (see box below).

The antithesis to the 49ers' outdated image as elegant winners, the **Oakland Raiders** (☎510/864-5000, Ⓦwww .raiders.com) revel in their role as the NFL's chief renegades, even if they've been about as awful as their San Francisco counterparts since the early 2000s. In earlier times, the team was one of the league's most successful, propelled to league titles in 1967, 1976, and 1980 by a motley crew of hilarious misfits and dodgy hoodlums; lately, however, the team hasn't much fulfilled its age-old marketing slogan ("Commitment to Excellence"). Sharing **McAfee Coliseum** with the

baseball A's, the Raiders often don't sell out home games, although its fans remain among the most boisterous in American sports. If you fancy sitting among frenzied men and women doused in silver and black face paint and brandishing sword-shaped slabs of aluminum foil, single-game tickets are generally available from around $70.

Basketball, ice hockey, and soccer

Bay Area **basketball** fans pledge undying support for the **National Basketball Association**'s 1975 season champion **Golden State Warriors** (☎888/479-4667, Ⓦwww .nba.com/warriors), who play home games at **Oracle Arena** next door to McAfee Coliseum in Oakland. Consistently one of the league's most woeful franchises since the mid 1990s,

Movement off the field

As with many of the region's residents, nearly every one of the Bay Area's major professional sports franchises came from somewhere else. In fact, the San Francisco 49ers are the only pro team in the area to have always played its home games in one city, a six-decade tenure sure to end if the team follows through on plans to move to Santa Clara, 45 miles southeast of San Francisco.

The **San Francisco Giants** moved west from New York in 1958; feeling underappreciated in later, leaner times, the club twice came within a hair's breadth of slinking away – to Toronto in 1976, then to St Petersburg, Florida in 1992. The **Oakland Athletics** were also imported, arriving from Kansas City in 1968. Despite winning four World Series titles in Oakland between 1972–89, the club has at various times since the late 1970s been rumored to be headed to Denver or Las Vegas; these days, the team is eyeing a move 25 miles down the highway to suburban Fremont.

Jumping the gun a bit, the **San Jose Sharks** played their earliest seasons (1991–93) at Daly City's ancient Cow Palace while the club's gleaming arena was readied in its eventual South Bay hometown. Today's **Golden State Warriors** were known as the San Francisco Warriors upon their arrival from Philadelphia in 1962, although they routinely played home games all around the Bay Area (and even the state!) through the early 1970s. Wisely, the itinerant franchise finally put down full-time roots in Oakland in 1972, but for reasons that remain unexplained to this day, the club continues to shun specific geographic designation by clinging to the awkward Golden State name.

Inarguably, though, the Bay Area's most slippery team has been the **Oakland Raiders**, who spent a strange era in Los Angeles from 1982–94 after a fruitful, two-decade tenure in Oakland. The team even pocketed a Super Bowl victory in its new city following the 1983 season, although even that success couldn't help the franchise ever fully establish itself in Southern California. Its rabid Bay Area fan base finally got its wish when the team returned north, tail between its legs – although other than an embarrassingly botched Super Bowl appearance in 2003, postseason success has eluded the franchise during its second Oakland stint.

the Warriors have enjoyed an upturn of late, even catapulted to national darlings for a short time during an unlikely and entertaining 2007 playoff run. The NBA's regular season is an 82-game death march from late October to mid April, but tickets to Warriors games ($15–140) have always been a hot commodity, even during lean years; the league's equally exhausting, sixteen-team playoff tournament concludes in mid June.

The **National Hockey League**'s **San Jose Sharks** (℡408/287-7070, Ⓦwww.sj-sharks.com) play 41 home games (not including exhibitions and playoffs) at their own arena in central San Jose, **HP Pavilion**. Among all Bay Area pro sports franchises, the Sharks have experienced the most consistent success in recent years, though no Stanley Cups (the NHL's league championship trophy) have yet graced the Sharks' tank. The team's fan base is largely centered in the South Bay, and although ice hockey has yet to capture the imagination of casual sports fans in the traditionally temperate Bay Area, the Sharks draw packed crowds for almost every home contest.

Although **soccer**'s popularity in the US has yet to catch up to international levels, local professional clubs have enjoyed cult followings over the years. The **San Jose Earthquakes** (℡408/985 1625, Ⓦwww.sjearth quakes.mlsnet.com) play in the country's top soccer league, **Major League Soccer**, and host most games at **Buck Shaw Stadium** on the campus of Santa Clara University, with a smattering held at Oakland's multi-purpose McAfee Coliseum. The franchise's predecessor (also known as the Earthquakes before relocating to Houston in 2005) won league MLS titles in 2001 and 2003, and tickets to see the latest incarnation of the club run $20–60, depending on how close to the action you wish to be.

College sports

Both the **California Golden Bears** (℡800/462-3277, Ⓦwww.calbears .com) and the **Stanford Cardinal** (℡800/782-6367, Ⓦwww.gostanford .com) compete in the rugged Pacific-10 athletic conference. Football and men's basketball are traditionally the marquee sports in American intercollegiate athletics, although baseball and women's basketball also maintain increasingly devout national followings; bitter rivals Cal and Stanford regularly field excellent teams in several of these sports, with Cal's football squad and Stanford's baseball and women's basketball teams often among the nation's best. Seasons are considerably shorter than at professional levels.

Auto and horse racing

Infineon Raceway (℡800/870-7223, Ⓦwww.infineonraceway.com), near the junction of Highways 37 and 121 in southern Sonoma County between Novato and Vallejo, hosts a variety of **auto and motorcycle races** between May and October. The venue's big event is NASCAR's Toyota/Save Mart 350 every June, for which thousands of racing fans descend for an entire weekend; other draws throughout the season include the Kawasaki AMA Superbike Showdown in May, Wednesday Night Drags throughout summer and fall, and a regularly scheduled racing drivers' school.

The Bay Area's lone **horse-racing** track, **Golden Gate Fields** (℡510/559-7300, Ⓦwww.goldengate fields.com) next to the shores of San Francisco Bay in Berkeley, soldiers on in the face of declining attendance. Check the racecourse's website for admission details and racing dates, the bulk of which occur between May and July.

Festivals and events

S ince most San Franciscans need little encouragement to slip on a costume and cavort around town, **festivals** here are genuinely fun, filled with locals and offering more than just stalls selling limp French fries. Though there's a wide variety of cultural (and kooky) stuff to do throughout the year, the calendar's busiest in the summer – even if the weather isn't always cooperative: highlights include the Pride parade and the music festival in Stern Grove. At other times, Chinese New Year and Halloween are justly well-known shindigs, though you'll have as much fun at the wild Bay to Breakers race or the lively Cherry Blossom Festival, too.

We've listed contact numbers and websites for all the events; the extremely helpful team at the San Francisco Convention and Visitors Bureau is also a great resource for up-to-date listings (T 415/391-2000, W www.sfvisitor.org).

January

SF Sketchfest (mid-Jan; W www.sfsketchfest .com) This weeklong celebration of sketch comedy, held at venues all over the city, gains a higher profile every year drawing up-and-coming and big-name comedians like Brian Posehn, Eugene Mirman, and Patton Oswalt, as well as esteemed troupes such as The Kids in the Hall. Tickets $10–50.

The Edwardian Ball Weekend (late Jan; T 415/435-7527, W www.edwardianball.com) Inspired by the world of macabre Victorian illustrator and author Edward Gorey, this party at Great American Music Hall has morphed into a three-day festival filled with Tim Burton-esque costumes – lots of corsets, eyeliner, and stripey tights – as well as Edwardian period dress, waltzing, circus performers, burlesque dancers, cabaret

music, Grand Guignol-inspired theater, and myriad odd and slightly creepy artworks. Tickets $18–30.

Chinese New Year (late Jan or early Feb; T 415/986-1370, W www.chineseparade.com) The first big ethnic festival in San Francisco's year, this week of low-key activities in and around Chinatown culminates in the Golden Dragon Parade, the biggest parade of its kind, featuring floats, lion dancers, martial arts, marching bands, and a 75-foot-long dragon.

Vietnamese Tet Festival (late Jan or early Feb; T 415/351-1038, W www.vietccsf.org) The Vietnamese answer to Chinatown's bash takes place along the heart of Little Saigon, Larkin St in the Tenderloin, and is a more authentic event with firecrackers, food, and a festival queen.

February

San Francisco Independent Film Festival (early to mid-Feb; T 415/820-3907, W www.sfindie .com) Sundance without the snow and the

label-toting celebrities, this is the most challenging and intriguing of the city's glut of film festivals. You can catch gritty dramas or lo-fi comedies from new filmmakers based in the Bay and elsewhere at the Roxie, Castro Theatre or Women's Building. The same organization runs a similar festival, focusing on documentaries, in early May, and the Hole in the Head horror, sci-fi, and fantasy festival in June.

San Francisco Bluegrass and Old-Time Festival (early Feb; ⊛ www.sfbluegrass.org) Banjo, ukulele, jug, and washboard players get the spotlight in this festival, held at clubs all over the city, dedicated to the music of times past. Tickets run from free to $30.

St Valentine's Day Pillow Fight (Feb 14; ⊛ www .pillowfight.info) Participation only requires a pillow as San Franciscans let out their romantic frustrations in a huge pillow fight at Justin Herman Plaza.

NoisePop (late Feb; ⊛ www.noisepop.com) This established music festival, which brings well-loved indie-rock bands – think blog buzz bands, college rock, and music critics' favorites – to various venues across the city including *Bimbo's*, *Café du Nord*, and the Castro Theatre. In recent years, the festival has expanded to include film, art, panel discussions, and an exposition. Festival pass is $125 per person, but tickets for individual shows are also available for $10 and up.

WonderCon (late Feb; ☏ 619/491-1022, ⊛ www .comic-con.org/wc) Stormtroopers swarm Downtown San Francisco for this huge, three-day comics convention at the Moscone Center that also brings out characters from anime and every sci-fi and fantasy film imaginable. Intelligent panels address topics such as misogyny in comics, while comic artists and movie stars make appearances, and high-profile films are previewed. Three-day passes are $40, but individual days range $10–15.

March

Other Minds Festival of New Music (early March; ⊛ www.otherminds.org) Top-notch composers in the experimental music field such as Laurie Anderson, John Cage, and Philip Glass debut their latest works at San Francisco Jewish Community Center.

St Patrick's Day (Sun before March 17; ☏ 415/395-8417, ⊛ www.sfstpatricksdayparade .com) The whole city dresses up in green to celebrate St Patrick's Day, which is marked both by excessive consumption of green-tinted beer and a lengthy parade from Second and Market sts along to Civic Center. The parade begins at noon, but for pole position plan on arriving at least three hours before. If you don't want to catch the marchers, head for one of the dozens of Irish pubs (especially the less-touristed spots in the Sunset) for the authentic experience.

San Francisco International Asian-American Film Festival (mid–late March; ☏ 415/863-0814, ⊛ festival.asianamericamedia.org) The nation's premier festival of films both from Asia and by Asian-Americans, with a varied roster ranging from campy kung-fu flicks to intense political dramas. Most films are shown at the Sundance Kabuki Cinema and Castro Theatre, plus a cinema in San Jose and the Pacific Film Archive in Berkeley.

Anarchist Bookfair (late March; ⊛ sfbookfair .wordpress.com) True to San Francisco's dissident spirit, this free book fair at the San Francisco County Fair Building offers radical literature – books, pamphlets and zines – of all stripes, from investigative journalists and queer activists to political dissidents and feminists. Speakers, films, and panels tackle topics such as the occupation of Palestine and the modern anarchist identity.

April

St Stupid Day Parade (April 1; ⊛ www .saintstupid.com) Held on April Fool's Day, this parade starting at Justin Herman Plaza honors all things ridiculous and silly. Expect clownish clothes, circus-sideshow antics, and other displays of nonsensical whimsy.

Sisters of Perpetual Indulgence Easter Celebration (Easter ☏ 415/820-9697, ⊛ www .thesisters.org) This irreverent celebration in Dolores Park is hosted by the Sisters, a group of drag-queen nuns in kabuki makeup who have been at the forefront of

San Francisco gay rights activism for 30 years. Bring a picnic lunch (maybe some deviled eggs) to this cross-dressing celebration with the standard face-painting and egg-hunting for kids and live music, burlesque, and the "Hunky Jesus" contest for adults.

San Francisco International Film Festival (mid-April to early May; ☎415/561-5000, ⓦwww.sffs.org) This two-week-long film fest offers more than two hundred different movies. Inevitably, the selection's eclectic and oddball, though it's a great place to discover lesser-known directors from Africa and Asia. Venues include the Castro Theatre and Sundance Kabuki Cinema.

Cherry Blossom Festival (late April; ☎415/563-2313, ⓦwww.nccbf.org) Superb festival that, for two consecutive weekends, transforms Japantown's artificial concrete jungle into a rowdy celebration of all things Japanese. Highlights include a beauty contest to be queen of the festival and a parade from Civic Center with floats and performers.

May

Maker Faire (early May; ⓦwww.makerfaire.com) All the science geeks and closet inventors get a chance to shine at this two-day festival held by Make Magazine, which celebrates arts and crafts, engineering, and science. Held at the San Mateo County Fairgrounds, the enormous event lets you get your hands dirty with science projects, craft demonstrations, educational workshops, and DIY competitions, and features inventions and oddities such as Life Size Mousetrap, a pedal-powered bus, dueling tesla coils, and a solar-powered chariot pulled by an Arnold Schwarzenegger robot. Tickets $25.

Cinco de Mayo (weekend nearest to May 5; ☎415/647-1533, ⓦwww.sfcincodemayo.com) The Mexican victory at the battle of Puebla is commemorated with a 48-hour party in the Mission. Raucous, booze-filled, and great fun, the festival is in Dolores Park, while the parade runs down Mission St between 24th and 14th sts. If you've a car, it's worth heading out to San Jose, which hosts one of the largest Cinco de Mayo celebrations in the country.

AIDS Candlelight Memorial March & Vigil (third Sun in May; ⓦwww.candlelightmemorial.org) An annual tradition since 1983, this procession leads to Civic Center from the intersection of Castro and Market and commemorates the lives of those who have died from AIDS.

Bay to Breakers Footrace (third Sun in May; ☎415/359-2800, ⓦwww.baytobreakers.com) Founded in 1912 to raise locals' spirits in the wake of the quake six years earlier, this is still one of the best events in the city's calendar. Kooky and campy, Bay to Breakers nominally involves a twelve-kilometre race beginning at 8am at Howard and Spear sts and ending at the ocean. Really, though, it's just another excuse for San Franciscans to go costume-crazy or get naked. Most of the 70,000 runners sport outlandish costumes (look for the group dressed as salmon who run the race in reverse – that's "upstream") or indeed, no costumes at all. There are dozens of side entertainments and stalls along the route, and it's not to be missed if you're in town.

Carnaval (Memorial Day weekend; ☎415/920-0125, ⓦwww.carnavalsf.com) San Francisco's answer to Brazil's Carnaval and New Orleans' Mardi Gras, though without the religious context and held in May, not Feb

▲ Cinco de Mayo celebration

(the better to suit scantly clad samba dancers). Expect huge feathers, dancing ladies, and excellent Brazilian music during the float-packed parade that runs from 24th

and Bryant to Harrison St; the stalls and amusements are set up on Harrison between 16th and 22nd sts.

June

San Francisco Ethnic Dance Festival (throughout June; ☎415/392-4400, ⓦwww .worldartswest.org) After auditioning hundreds of Bay Area dance companies, the festival at the Palace of Fine Arts only showcases the best and brightest, performing every kind of dance under the sun: bharatanatyam to hula, ballet folklorico to flamenco, Chinese-dragon dance to belly dance, odissi to hip-hop. Tickets $22–44.

Haight-Ashbury Street Fair (early June; ☎415/863-3489, ⓦwww.haightashburystreet fair.org) Tackily modern, this weekend-long schlockfest offers yet another chance to pick up a tie-dyed T-shirt or ornamental bong. If you want to check it out, head over early before the crowds are too unbearable.

North Beach Festival (early June; ☎415/989-2220, ⓦwww.sfnorthbeach.org) Centered on Washington Square Park, this is the oldest street fair in the city, and charmingly retro – thanks to its pizza-tossing contests, street art, and dozens of food stalls. Don't forget to bring your dog for one of the pet-blessing ceremonies in the shrine of St Francis of Assisi.

RoboGames (mid-June; ☎415/863-3489, ⓦrobogames.net) The world's largest open robot competition brings the tinkerers and basement inventors to Fort Mason Center for competitions for combat robots, walking humanoids, soccer bots, sumo bots, and kung-fu androids. Tickets $20.

Frameline (mid/late June; ☎415/703-8650, ⓦwww.frameline.org) Expect more than 250 gay- and lesbian-themed films from across the world, including high-brow documentaries and sloppy romances, all centring on LGBT life. The Castro Theatre is the main venue.

San Francisco Lesbian/Gay/Bisexual/ Transgender Pride Celebration Parade (last weekend in June; ☎415/864-0831, ⓦwww .sfpride.org) Crowds of up to half a million pack Market St for this enormous party-cum-parade. Afterwards, City Hall is the scene for a giant block party, with outdoor discos, live bands, and numerous crafts and food stands. Also worth checking out: Pink Night, the evening when the Castro is virtually pedestrianized by thousands of revelers, or the Dyke March that takes place on Fri night.

Stern Grove Midsummer Music Festival (late June to late Aug; ☎415/252-6252, ⓦwww .sterngrove.org) This summer-long program of free Sun concerts is a San Francisco institution. The shows – from jazz to classical to modern dance – all take place in a stunning grove of eucalyptus trees in the Sunset, where you can picnic while you watch. For popular acts, get there early to snag a good seat. There isn't much parking nearby, so make sure to take public transport to 19th Ave and Sloat Blvd.

July

Fourth of July (☎415/705-5500, ⓦwww.pier39 .com) San Francisco's Independence Day shindig takes place in two locales: the stalls and amusements crowd Fisherman's Wharf, while the official fireworks are set off from Crissy Field near the Presidio.

Fillmore Jazz Festival (early July; ☎415/456-6436 or 1-800/310-6563, ⓦwww.fillmorejazz festival.com) Spurred by former mayor Brown's declaration of the Jazz

Redevelopment District in the Fillmore (in other words, optimistic marketing hype hawking its heritage), this festival includes three stages with free, continuous performances from more than three hundred artists. It's centered in Fillmore St between Jackson and Eddy sts.

Fire Arts Festival (early July; ☎415/444-0919, ⓦwww.thecrucible.org/fireartsfestival) Flames shoot every which way and electric sparks light up the night, as The Crucible – an Oakland nonprofit center for industrial arts like welding, blacksmithing, bronze-pouring, jewelry-making, and glass-blowing – hosts this three-day festival featuring a wide array of interactive fire-sculpture installations at the West Oakland BART parking lot. Every year, the mainstage performance brings together ballet, opera, hip-hop, aerial dance, and fire performances.

Mission Creek Music Festival (late July; ☏ 415/920-0125, Ⓦ www.mcmf.org) While NoisePop is the grandfather of San Francisco indie-rock festivals, drawing in marquee-name acts, the edgier Mission Creek Music Festival is now considered the

event for catching the most innovative up-and-coming local and underground national bands.

North Beach Jazz Festival (late July; ☏ 415/252-8773, Ⓦ www.nbjazzfest.com) Sprawled across various venues in the neighborhood, this is a reliable, if rather traditional, showcase for local jazz singers and performers.

Up Your Alley Fair (late July; ☏ 415/777-3247, Ⓦ www.folsomstreetfair.com/alley) Little brother of Folsom Street Fair (see p.281), taking place on nearby Dore Alley. This is much less a goofy gawkfest, and more about raunchy sex and hardcore BDSM – so it's not for the easily shocked.

August

AfroSolo Arts Festival (Aug through Oct; ☏ 415/771-2376, Ⓦ www.afrosolo.org) This annual arts, music, and culture festival, held in various locations, celebrates the works, struggles, and achievements of African-Americans and artists from all over the African Diaspora.

Nihonmachi Street Fair (early Aug; ☏ 415/771-9861, Ⓦ www.nihonmachistreetfair.org) Weekend-long Pan-Asian festival, centered on the Japan Center, with lion dancers, plenty of kids' amusements, and even an Asian-American bike show. The big draw, though, is the delicious food.

Burning Man (last week of Aug & first of Sept; ☏ 415/863-5263, Ⓦ www.burningman.com)

When an artist called Larry was dumped by his girlfriend, he reacted by creating an effigy of her and burning it on Ocean Beach. That single act of romantic defiance has morphed into this surreal event, with very expensive tickets, when locals and visitors now head for a psyche-delic stay in the Black Rock Desert camping in a temporary money-free civili-zation with elaborate art installations, dancing, and generally tripping out, all the activities centered on a fifty-foot sculpture that's ritually burned at the end of the festival. Truly weird, this is for enthusiasts and the adventurous only. Tickets cost $150–200.

September

San Francisco Shakespeare Festival (throughout Sept; ☏ 415/558-0888, Ⓦ www.sfshakes.org) Hosted at the Parade ground in the Presidio, this month-long festival presents Shakespearean classics on outdoor stages every Sat and Sun. Sat performances begin at 7.30pm, while Sun and Labor Day shows are matinees that start at 2.30pm; on either day, be there at least two hours early to be sure of a free ticket. Check the website for an up-to-date schedule of plays.

Ghirardelli Square Chocolate Festival (early Sept; ☏ 415/775-5500, Ⓦ www.ghirardellisq .com) Schlock-choc-fest for fans only – horribly commercial, even if it does all

benefit charity, but a great place to enter a sundae-eating contest.

Madcat Women's International Film Festival (early Sept; ☏ 415/436-9523, Ⓦ www .madcatfestival.org) This acclaimed film festival screens provocative and visionary films from women around the globe, from shorts and documentaries to full-length features.

San Francisco Fringe Festival (early Sept; ☏ 415/931-1094 (info) or 1-800/965-4827 (tickets), Ⓦ www.sffringe.org) This offshoot of the famed Edinburgh Festival was founded when performers were rejected for the Scottish showcase. Don't let the diabolical pretensions of some shows put you off the small gems you'll often uncover in this marathon of more than 250 events over two weeks or so. Tickets cost around $8 or less; the nexus for performances is the Exit Theater Downtown.

Folsom Street Fair (late Sept; ☏415/777-3247, ⓦwww.folsomstreetfair.com) San Francisco's wildest party takes over the SoMa district, along Folsom between Seventh and 12th sts. It's a celebration of all things fetish, with lashings of leather-related events – so don't

forget to wear your harness and skin-tight chaps if you plan on stopping by. Don't be intimidated, though, as the atmosphere's largely friendly and fun.

San Francisco Blues Festival (fourth weekend in Sept; ☏415/979-5588, ⓦwww.sfblues.com) One of the oldest blues festivals in America, this weekend-long event packs the Great Meadow at Fort Mason (make sure to bring a blanket and picnic), thanks to some big-name acts as well as local favorites.

October

The Castro Street Fair (first Sun in Oct; ☏415/841-1824, ⓦwww.castrostreetfair.org) Think arts'n'crafts instead of ass'n'chaps. This fair, the brainchild of legendary late city supervisor Harvey Milk in 1974, offers stalls with food and homemade trinkets.

Fleet Week (early Oct; ☏415/621-2325, ⓦwww .fleetweek.us) The Marina and Embarcadero play host to the visiting US Navy. Servicemen get to drink for free in the city's bars and citizens get to tour the military hardware, as well as enjoy the aerial acrobatics of the Blue Angels precision flying team as they roar their fighter jets over the Bay in stunning maneuvers.

Hardly Strictly Bluegrass (early Oct; ⓦwww .strictlybluegrass.com) This three-day festival is hugely popular with locals, as icons of country, blues, bluegrass, and rock music like Willie Nelson, Dolly Parton, Emmylou Harris, Elvis Costello, T Bone Burnett, and Robert Earl Keen perform for free at Golden Gate Park. Get there early if you want a good spot on the grass.

Litquake (early Oct; ☏415/750-1497, ⓦwww .litquake.org) In a town packed with writers, it makes sense to have a week where literary types can get together and bond. Local literati like Lawrence Ferlinghetti, Daniel Handler, and Gail Tsukiyama read, give talks, or participate in panels in venues all over town, and still others compete in raucous events like Literary Death Match. And for those dreaming of writing the great American novel, there are workshops on how to get your first book published and how to survive the day job.

San Francisco LoveFest (early Oct; ☏415/820-1423, ⓦwww2.sflovefest.org) Something like

a rave held outdoors in the streets of San Francisco, this parade and celebration of dance music revives the old hippie notions that music can make the world a better place, promoting love, tolerance, and communal vibe. The parade begins on Second St at Market.

San Francisco Jazz Festival (late Oct; ☏415/788-7353 or 1-800/850-7353, ⓦwww .sfjazz.org) Technically, this should be called the Bay Area Jazz Festival, as both Oakland and San Francisco host performances during this almost month-long headline grabber. It's pitted against the better-known and snootier Monterey Jazz Fest, and often matches its quality, with local, national, and international performers. Tickets sell out fast, so book well ahead if there's a certain act it's essential you see.

Pumpkin Festival (weekend before Halloween; ☏650/726-9652, ⓦwww.miramarevents.com /pumpkinfest) In nearby Half Moon Bay (the self-proclaimed Pumpkin Capital of the World; see p.343), local farmers open their fields to pumpkin hunters and host a range of pumpkin-based cooking and eating contests. There's carving, a parade, costume contests, and even a giant weigh-off between competing champion pumpkins.

Halloween in the Castro (Oct 31) Once an eagerly awaited celebration each autumn, this event was derailed in 2007 following stabbings and a host of arrests the previous year. Its future remains uncertain at the time of writing, as local politicos and law enforcement continue to wrangle with possible relocation options.

November

Alternative Press Expo (early Nov; ☎ 619/491-1022, ⓦ www.comic-con.org/ape) A huge two-day convention for independent comic artists, DIY crafters, and publishers of zines. Expect booth upon booth of quirky, creative personal projects, many in the spirit of R. Crumb, blunt in matters related to sex and bodily functions, as well as free stickers and candy, and puppy-eyed artists shilling their wares. A few underground stars like Shannon Wheeler and Craig Thompson usually make an appearance. $10 for a two-day pass, $7 per day.

Dia de los Muertos (Nov 2; ☎ 415/595-5558, ⓦ www.dayofthedeadsf.org) Don't expect the riotous fun of Cinco de Mayo at this Day of the Dead, celebrated in the Mission by people dressed as skeletons. The parade starts at 24th and Bryant sts, and there's

celebration and contemplation in the mood of the candlelit procession, that ends at Garfield Park for the Festival of Altars where people pay tribute to their deceased loved ones and ancestors. An even more elaborate celebration happens that weekend across the Bay in Oakland's Fruitvale District, where *pan de muerto* (bread of the dead), sugar and papier-mâché skulls and skeletons are widely available from vendors, and multiple stages host traditional Latin music and dance.

Thanksgiving (last Thurs in Nov; ☎ 415/391-2000, ⓦ www.onlyinsanfrancisco.com) San Francisco's holiday season kicks off with the ceremonial lighting of an enormous Christmas tree in Union Square.

December

Great Dickens Christmas Fair (throughout Dec; ☎ 1-800/510-1558, ⓦ www.dickensfair.com. Something like a Victorian-era version of a Renaissance Fair held at Cow Palace, this event offers unique wares from local artisans, as well as a chance to experience the music and dance of the period and fine foods from the British Empire. Walking around, you're bound to run into characters such as Father Christmas, Ebeneezer Scrooge, and the three Christmas ghosts. Tickets $22.

San Francisco Ballet Nutcracker (throughout Dec; ☎ 415/865-2000, ⓦ www.sfballet.org) The city's ballet company is the oldest in America, and still lavishly praised by critics. This annual production is its best-known and longest tradition: you can snag cheap seats for around $15.

Bazaar Bizarre (mid-Dec; ⓦ www.bazaarbizarre.org/sanfrancisco.html) This craft fair, held at the San Francisco County Fair Building, is a great place to buy last-minute one-of-a-kind Christmas gifts from local artists.

The Bay Area

The Bay Area

The East Bay

T he largest and most-traveled bridge in the US, the **Bay Bridge** – part graceful suspension bridge and part heavy-duty steel truss – connects Downtown San Francisco to the **East Bay**. Built from 1933 to 1936 as an economic booster during the Depression, the structure is made from enough steel cable to wrap around the earth three times. Completed just seven months before the more famous (and better-loved) Golden Gate, it works a lot harder for a lot less respect – local scribe Herb Caen dubbed it "the car-strangled spanner," a reference to its often clogged lanes. A hundred million vehicles cross it each year, though you'd have to search hard to find a postcard with an image of its silvery mass. Indeed, most people worldwide only recall it for the much-broadcast videotape of its partial collapse during the 1989 earthquake. Until the flurry of recent publicity about the ongoing project to replace its eastern half (see box below), its only positive claim to fame was that **Treasure Island**, constructed simultaneously as an adjunct to natural Yerba Buena Island, where the two halves of the bridge meet, hosted the 1939 World's Fair, the memory of which still evokes pride for older locals.

Though commuters returning to San Francisco take the top level of the bridge – with the skyline dramatically before them – those heading away from the city are routed along the lower deck, where dark shadows obstruct any view of hard-working, blue-collar **Oakland**. The city has traditionally earned

The East Span project

Largely as a long-overdue result of the 1989 earthquake damage suffered by a section of the Bay Bridge in West Oakland, a **$7.7 billion project** is afoot to completely replace the eastern half of the bridge between Yerba Buena Island and Oakland. Due to protracted wrangling over finances, however, its grand opening has already been pushed back until at least 2010. Nonetheless the new bridge is gradually taking shape beside the old one, after which the latter section will be carefully dismantled so as to cause minimal ecological damage. Officially titled the San Francisco-Oakland Bay Bridge East Span Seismic Safety Project, but known as the **East Span Project** (or Bay Bridge Project), it actually consists of half a dozen separate stages from the touchdown on the Oakland side, through the skyway and suspension sections, to the Yerba Buena transition. As well as being safer, the new bridge is intended to be more aesthetically pleasing, with a graceful 550-foot tower complementing those of the West Span and Golden Gate Bridges, as well as the natural shape of Yerba Buena Island. Those wishing to find out more will be rewarded by logging onto ⓦ www.newbaybridge.org.

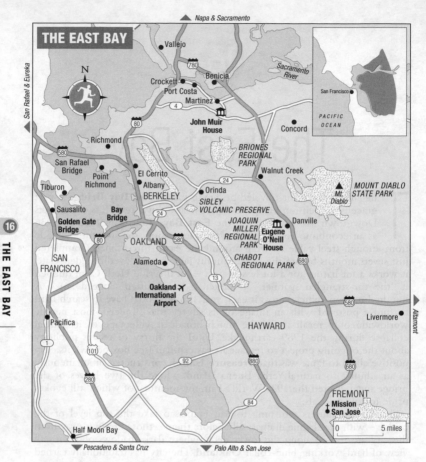

THE EAST BAY

its livelihood from shipping and transportation services, as evidenced by the cranes in the massive Port of Oakland, but Oakland is in the midst of a renaissance as it lobbies to attract businesses and workers from the information technology industry. Oakland spreads north along wooded foothills to **Berkeley**, an image-conscious university town that looks out across to the Golden Gate and collects a mixed bag of international students, heavily pierced dropouts, aging 1960s radicals, and Nobel Prize-winning nuclear physicists in its cafés and bookstores.

Parts of Oakland and Berkeley blend together so much as to make them indistinguishable, and the hills above them are topped by a twenty-mile string of **regional parks**, providing much-needed fresh air and quick relief from the concrete grids below. The rest of the East Bay is filled out by **Contra Costa County**, a huge area that contains some intriguing, historically important waterfront towns – well worth a detour if you're on your way to the Wine Country (see Chapter 19) – as well as some of the Bay Area's most inward-looking suburban sprawl.

North from Berkeley, I-80 curves around the **northern end of the East Bay** from the oil-refinery landscape of Richmond, leading to the towns of Benicia and Port Costa, which face each other across the narrow **Carquinez Strait**.

Strikingly situated, both of these settlements were vitally important during California's first twenty years of existence after the 1849 Gold Rush, but now they are, for all intents and purposes, little-visited ghost towns. In contrast, standing out from the soulless dormitory communities that fill up the often baking-hot **inland valleys**, are the preserved homes of an unlikely pair of influential writers: the naturalist John Muir, who, when not out hiking around Yosemite and the High Sierra, lived most of his life near **Martinez**, and playwright Eugene O'Neill, who wrote many of his angst-ridden works at the foot of **Mount Diablo**, the Bay Area's most impressive peak.

Arrival

You're most likely to be staying in San Francisco when you visit the East Bay, though it is nearly as convenient and sometimes better value to fly direct to **Oakland Airport** (☎510/563-2984, automated flight info ☎1-800/992-7433, ⓦ www.oaklandairport.com), particularly if you're coming from elsewhere in the US. All major domestic airlines serve the facility, which is less crowded and more desirable than its San Francisco counterpart. Plus, it's an easy trip from the airport into San Francisco: the **AirBART** shuttle van (every 15min; $2; ☎510/577-4294) runs to the Coliseum BART station, from where you can hop on **BART** to Berkeley, Oakland, or San Francisco. There are numerous door-to-door **shuttle buses** that run from the airport to East Bay stops, such as A1 American (☎1-877/378-3596, ⓦ www.a1americanshuttle.com); the fare to Downtown Oakland is $18, while into San Francisco will run you around $30–35. Taxis are readily available and cost about $40 into San Francisco, or half that to Oakland itself.

The **Greyhound** station is in a dodgy area just north of Downtown Oakland, alongside the I-980 freeway at 2103 San Pablo Ave (☎510/832-4730). As for trains, **Amtrak** terminates at Second Street near Jack London Square in Downtown Oakland, where a free shuttle bus heads across the Bay Bridge to the Transbay Terminal.

The most enjoyable way to arrive in the East Bay is aboard an Alameda–Oakland **ferry** ($6.50 each way; ☎510/522-3300, ⓦ www.eastbayferry.com), leaving every hour from San Francisco's Ferry Building and Pier 39 to Oakland's Jack London Square. The fleet also runs a service to Angel Island via Pier 41, departing from Oakland (Sat & Sun mid-May to late Oct 9am, returning at 3.10pm; $14 round-trip, including park admission).

Lastly, if you're **driving** into the East Bay from San Francisco, allow yourself plenty of time to get there: the area has some of California's worst traffic, with the Bay Bridge and I-80 in particular jam-packed sixteen hours a day. Having two or more people in the vehicle can save time from 5–9am and 3–7pm, when faster car-pool lanes are in effect. If entering San Francisco via the Bay Bridge on a weekend night, allow an hour for the crossing.

Getting around

The East Bay is linked to San Francisco via the BART **subway** (☎510/465-2278 from the East Bay, ⓦ www.bart.gov; see p.28 for more information). Four lines (one of which starts at Millbrae and stops at San Francisco airport) run from Daly City through San Francisco and on to downtown Oakland, before diverging to service East Oakland out to Fremont or Dublin/Pleasanton, north to Berkeley and Richmond, and northeast into Contra Costa County as far as Concord and Pittsburg/Bay Point. A fifth line operates its entire length in the East Bay between Richmond and Fremont. When getting off at an East Bay BART station, remember to pick up a **transfer**, saving you 25¢ on the $1.75 fares of the revamped AC Transit (℡510/817-1717 ext 1111, ⓦwww.actransit.org), which provides a good **bus service** around the entire East Bay, especially Oakland and Berkeley; bus system maps (and BART maps) are available from any station.

AC Transit also runs buses on a number of routes to Oakland and Berkeley from the Transbay Terminal in San Francisco. These operate all night and are the only way of getting across the Bay by public transit once BART has shut down between midnight and 1am. A smaller-scale bus company, the Contra Costa County Connection (℡925/676-7500, ⓦwww.cccta.org), runs buses to most of the inland areas, including the John Muir and Eugene O'Neill historic houses.

Other than by bus, one of the best ways to get around the East Bay is by **bike**. A fine cycle route follows Skyline and Grizzly Peak boulevards along the wooded crest of the hills between Berkeley and Lake Chabot, while within Berkeley itself, the Ohlone Greenway makes for a pleasant cycling or walking route. Unfortunately, not many places rent bikes in the East Bay, but one exception is Solano Avenue Cyclery, 1554 Solano Ave, Berkeley (℡510/524-1094, ⓦwww.solanoavenuecyclery.com), whose rates are $40 for 24 hours or $140 per week, though that is more than you'd pay for a car.

For those interested in **walking tours**, the City of Oakland sponsors free "discovery tours" (℡510/238-3234) of various neighborhoods; a popular excursion is the Oakland Historical Landmark Tour (Sun 1–3.30pm; free), beginning in front of the Oakland Museum at 10th and Fallon, and covering areas like Chinatown, Lake Merritt, Preservation Park, and Jack London Square.

Information

The **Oakland CVB**, located next to the enormous *Marriot Hotel* at 463 11th St (Mon–Fri 8.30am–5pm; ℡510/839-9000, ⓦwww.oaklandcvb.com), is the best source of maps, brochures, and information on lodging and activities in the metropolitan area. In Berkeley, check in at the **Berkeley CVB**, 2015 Center St (Mon–Fri 9am–noon & 2–5pm; ℡510/549-7040, ⓦwww.visitberkeley.com). The **University of California's Visitor Services**, 101 University Hall (Mon–Fri 8.30am–4.30pm; ℡510/642-5215, ⓦwww.berkeley.edu), at the corner of Oxford and University, has plenty of info on the Berkeley campus, and organizes ninety-minute tours (see p.305).

For information on hiking or riding horses in the many parks that top the Oakland and Berkeley hills, contact the **East Bay Regional Parks District**, 2950 Peralta Oaks Court, Oakland (℡510/562-7275, ⓦwww.ebparks.org). The widely available *East Bay Express* (issued every Wed; free) has the most comprehensive listings of what's on in the vibrant East Bay music and arts scene. The daily *Oakland Tribune* (50¢) is also worth a look for its coverage of local politics and sporting events.

Oakland

...what was the use of me having come from Oakland it was not natural for me to have come from there yes write about it if I like or anything if I like but not there, there is no there there.

Gertrude Stein, *Everybody's Autobiography*

As solidly working class as San Francisco is unconventional, **OAKLAND** is one of the busiest ports on the West Coast and the western terminal of the rail network. Though there are few major sights to lure tourists to "Oaktown," as

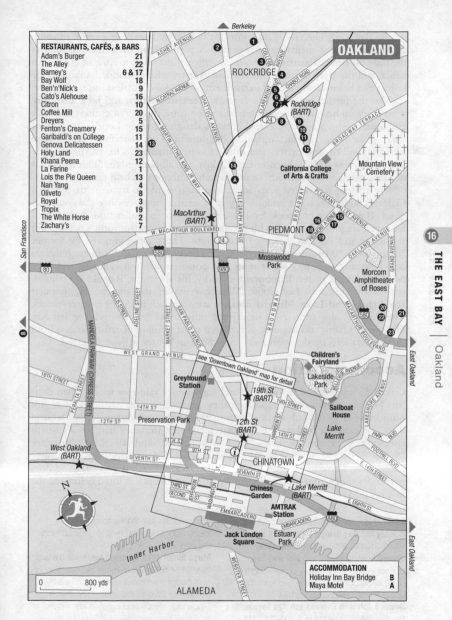

RESTAURANTS, CAFÉS, & BARS	
Adam's Burger	21
The Alley	22
Barney's	6 & 17
Bay Wolf	18
Ben'n'Nick's	9
Cato's Alehouse	16
Citron	10
Coffee Mill	20
Dreyers	5
Fenton's Creamery	15
Garibaldi's on College	11
Genova Delicatessen	14
Holy Land	23
Khana Peena	12
La Farine	1
Lois the Pie Queen	13
Nan Yang	4
Oliveto	8
Royal	3
Tropix	19
The White Horse	2
Zachary's	7

OAKLAND

ACCOMMODATION
Holiday Inn Bay Bridge   **B**
Maya Motel   **A**

snootier San Franciscans sometimes refer to the city, a quick hop over from San Francisco on BART or the Bay Bridge is more than justified by the weather. Considered one of the best in the US, the East Bay's climate is sunny and mild when San Francisco is cold and dreary, making for great hiking around the redwood- and eucalyptus-covered hills above Downtown.

That said, Oakland has more historical and literary associations than important sights, save for the **Oakland Museum**, which ranks as one of the best in the whole Bay Area. The city is infamous for being the spawning ground of some of America's most unabashedly revolutionary **political movements**, such as the militant **Black Panthers**, who drew national attention to African-American issues, and the **Symbionese Liberation Army**, who demanded a ransom for kidnapped heiress Patty Hearst in the form of free food distribution to the poor. It's also the birthplace of literary legends **Gertrude Stein** and **Jack London**, who grew up here at approximately the same time, though in entirely different circumstances – Stein was a stockbroker's daughter, while London, author of *Call of the Wild*, was an orphaned delinquent. The waterfront area where London used to steal oysters and lobsters is now named in his memory, while Stein, who was actually born in East Oakland, is all but ignored. This neglect is not surprising, given her famous proclamation about Oakland cited above.

Nevertheless, for many years locals found it hard to argue with Stein, as Oakland businesses had a long history of deserting the place once the going got good. Residents who stuck by the city through its duller and darker days, however, are pleased overall with recent efforts to revitalize (some say gentrify) the town and slash its infamous crime rate. These were initiated by former Mayor **Jerry "Moonbeam" Brown**, who drew in thousands of new residents by advertising the city's lower rents and consistently sunny climate, and have been continued in less flamboyant style by his successor, Ronald V. Dellums, who took office in late 2006. Already, rents in the increasingly popular **Rockridge** and **Lake Merritt** districts are approaching San Francisco prices. The city has also attracted a significant number of lesbians, who've left San Francisco's Castro and Mission, as well as a great number of artists pushed from their SoMa lofts by sky-high rents into the warehouses of West Oakland.

Accommodation

Oakland's **motels** and **hotels** are barely any better value for money than their San Francisco equivalents. However, they give visitors the chance to stay just outside the city's hubbub while affording easy access to it. As for B&Bs, Oakland does not have the **bed-and-breakfast** scene that Berkeley has, but it's worth checking with the Berkeley & Oakland Bed and Breakfast Network (☏510/547-6380, ⊛www.bbonline.com/ca/berkeley-oakland) for a complete list, anyway. There is no youth hostel in the area, either, but East Oakland does have a decent **campground**. For information on the prices listed below, see the box on p.152.

Hotels, motels, and B&Bs

Holiday Inn Bay Bridge 1800 Powell St, Emeryville ☏510/658-9300 or 1-800/465 4329, ⊛www.holidayinn.com. Modern and functional, but not outrageously pricey considering the great views of the Bay to be had from the upper floors. Free parking. $139.

Howard Johnson Express Inn 423 Seventh St, Oakland ☏510/451-6316 or 1-800/754-1115, ⊛www.oaklandhj.com. Formerly a *Travelodge*, this *HoJo*'s been spruced up, providing one of the best deals Downtown with adequate, compact rooms. $65.

Jack London Inn 444 Embarcadero West, Oakland ☏510/444-2032 or 1-800/549-8780, ⊛www.jacklondoninn.com. Kitschy motorlodge with a 1950s feel thanks to its wooden lobby fittings; located next to Jack London Square. $85.

Maya Motel 4715 Telegraph Ave, North Oakland ☏510/654-5850. Basic motel but tidy enough and better than most of those on nearby Macarthur Blvd to the south. The trendy Rockridge shops and eateries are within walking distance. $49.

Waterfront Plaza Hotel 10 Washington St, Oakland ☏510/836-3800 or 1-888/842-5333, ⊛www.jdvhotels.com. Plush, modern hotel, now run by the Joie de Vivre group, with smart, sizeable rooms located on the best stretch of the Oakland waterfront, right among all the amenities. $149.

Campground

Chabot Family Campground off I-580 in East Oakland ☎ 510/562-2267 or 1-888/327-2757, ⓦ www.ebparks.org. Walk-in, tent-only places, with hot showers and lots of good hiking nearby; reservations wise in summer; sites from $18 for one vehicle and up to ten people.

Downtown Oakland

Coming by BART from San Francisco, get off at the 12th Street–Civic Center station and you're at the open-air shopping and office space of **City Center** in the heart of **DOWNTOWN OAKLAND**. Oddly, the area can seem uncannily deserted outside of rush hours. Downtown's compact district of spruced-up Victorian storefronts overlooked by modern hotels and office buildings is nearing the end of an ambitious redevelopment program that has lasted well over a decade. Fraught with allegations of illegal dealings and incompetent planning, the program has been less than a complete success; for example, to make way for

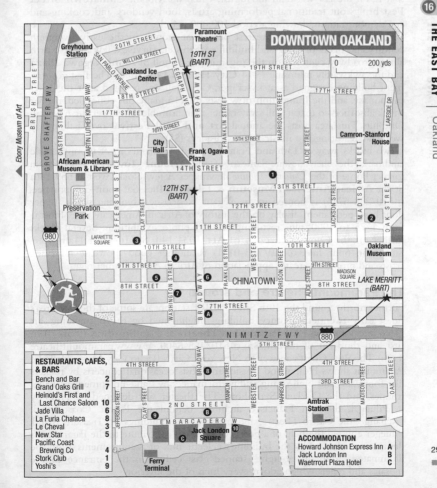

RESTAURANTS, CAFÉS, & BARS

Bench and Bar	2
Grand Oaks Grill	7
Heinold's First and Last Chance Saloon	10
Jade Villa	6
La Furia Chalaca	8
Le Cheval	3
New Star	5
Pacific Coast Brewing Co	4
Stork Club	1
Yoshi's	9

ACCOMMODATION

Howard Johnson Express Inn	A
Jack London Inn	B
Waetrrout Plaza Hotel	C

the moat-like I-980 freeway – the main route through Oakland since the collapse of the Cypress Freeway in the 1989 earthquake – entire blocks were cleared of houses. Yet some efforts were made to maintain the city's architectural heritage, most noticeably in the collection of characterful private properties of **Preservation Park** at 12th Street and Martin Luther King Jr Way.

Similarly, the late nineteenth-century commercial center along Ninth Street west of Broadway, now tagged **Old Oakland**, underwent a major restoration some years ago, and while some of the buildings are still waiting for tenants, others are occupied by architect and design firms, much like San Francisco's Jackson Square. Observing the historic facades, especially between Clay and Washington, provides a glimpse of what Oakland once was. If you are around on a Friday, the section between Broadway and Clay is home to a fine **farmers' market** between 8am and 2pm. Between Seventh and Ninth streets lies Oakland's **Chinatown**, whose bakeries and restaurants are generally not as lively or picturesque as those of its more famous cousin across the Bay. Except, that is, on the last weekend in August, when the vibrant **Chinatown Street Fest** brings out traditional performing artists, food vendors, and cooking and arts demonstrations, drawing a good 100,000 people.

The city experienced its greatest period of growth in the early twentieth century, and many of the grand buildings of this era survive a few blocks north along Broadway, centered on the gigantic grass knoll of **Frank Ogawa Plaza** and the awkwardly imposing 1914 **City Hall** on 14th Street. The first government building designed as a skyscraper, City Hall was restored after the 1989 earthquake, and the foundation now rests on 113 giant, but concealed, rubber shock absorbers so that it will sway rather than crumble whenever the next Big One hits. This area hosts the annual **Art and Soul Festival** over Labor Day weekend, featuring live music and art displays ($5).

Two blocks away, at 13th and Franklin, stands Oakland's most unmistakeable landmark, the chateauesque lantern of the **Tribune Tower**, the 1920s-era former home of the *Oakland Tribune* newspaper. A few blocks west at 659 14th St, the **African American Museum & Library** (Tues–Sat noon–5.30pm; free; ☎510/238-6716) is housed in an elegant Neoclassical building whose upper floor has a permanent display on the history of African-Americans in California from 1775 to 1900, plus revolving art and photo exhibitions. Several blocks further on, the **Ebony Museum of Art**, 1034 14th St (Tues–Sat 11am–6pm, Sun noon–6pm; free; ☎510/763-0141) is another good showcase for black artists and promotes greater appreciation of African American heritage.

The Paramount Theatre and around

Further north, around the 19th Street BART station, are some of the Bay Area's finest early twentieth-century buildings, highlighted by the outstanding Art Deco interior of the 1931 **Paramount Theatre** at 2025 Broadway (tours 10am first and third Sat of month; $5; ☎510/465-6400, @www.paramounttheatre .com). The West Coast's answer to New York City's Radio City Music Hall, the Paramount shows Hollywood classics and hosts occasional concerts by rockers like Tom Waits and Neil Young and performances by stand-up comedians, ballet troupes, and the Oakland Symphony. The theater was designed by Timothy L. Pflueger, the San Francisco architect behind the Pacific Coast Stock Exchange, the Castro Theatre, and many of the buildings on Treasure Island. Pflueger enlisted the help of a group of artists to contribute to the Paramount's design, as evidenced by the building's eclectic mix of accoutrements, from the illuminated "fountain of light" stained-glass ceiling in the entrance to the mosaics and reliefs which adorn every inch of the interior.

Several nearby buildings are equally flamboyant, ranging from the wafer-thin Gothic "flatiron" office tower of the **Cathedral Building** at Broadway and Telegraph, to the Hindu temple-like facade of the magnificent 3500-seat **Fox Oakland** (now closed) on Telegraph at 19th – the largest movie house west of Chicago at the time it was built in 1928. Across the street, the 1931 **Floral Depot**, a group of small, modern storefronts faced in black-and-blue terracotta tiles with shiny silver highlights, is also worth a look. If at any point you tire of walking, you can lace up skates at the nearby **Oakland Ice Center**, 519 18th St (Mon & Wed noon–4pm, Tues, Thurs & Fri noon–5pm, Sat 12.30–5pm, Sun 1.30–5pm, also Tues & Thurs 7–8.30pm, Fri & Sat 7–10pm; $7.50 plus $2.50 skate rental; ⊤510/268-9000, ⓦwww.oaklandice.com). The facility is the finest in the Bay Area and has been used by a number of past Olympians; figure-skating instruction is directed by 1992 World Champion coach Christy Ness.

West of Broadway, the area around the Greyhound bus station on **San Pablo Avenue** is fairly seedy. San Pablo used to be the main route in and out of Oakland before the freeways were built, but many of the roadside businesses are now derelict.

Lake Merritt and the Oakland Museum

Five blocks east of Broadway, the eastern third of Downtown Oakland comprises **LAKE MERRITT**, a three-mile-circumference tidal lagoon that was bridged and dammed in the 1860s to become the centerpiece of Oakland's

▲ Lake Merritt

most desirable neighborhood. Sadly, all that remains of the many fine houses that once circled the lake is the elegant **Camron–Stanford House**, on the southwest shore at 1418 Lakeside Drive, a graceful Italianate mansion whose sumptuous interior is open for visits (Wed 11am–4pm, first & third Sun of month 1–5pm; $5; ☎510/444-1876, ⓦwww.cshouse.org). The lake is also the nation's oldest wildlife refuge, and migrating flocks of ducks, geese, and herons break their journeys here.

The north shore of the lake is lined by **Lakeside Park**, where canoes, rowboats, kayaks, pedal boats, and a range of sailboats ($8–15/hr, $10–20 deposit) can be rented from the **Sailboat House** (March–May Mon–Fri 10.30am–6pm, Sat & Sun 10.30am–5pm; summer Mon–Fri 9am–6pm, Sat & Sun 10am–6pm; ☎510/238-2196, ⓦwww.oaklandnet.com/parks) – provided you can convince the staff you know how to sail. A miniature Mississippi riverboat makes thirty-minute lake **cruises** ($1.50) on weekend afternoons, or you can splash out to be serenaded on the overpriced but romantic Gondola Servizio (from $45 for 30min; ☎510/663-6603, ⓦwww.gondolaservizio .com). As for children, they'll enjoy the puppet shows and pony rides at the **Children's Fairyland** (Wed–Sun 10am–4pm; $6; ☎510/452-2259, ⓦwww .fairyland.org), along Grand Avenue on the northwest edge of the park. Also, the lake is lit up every night by its "Necklace of Lights," a source of local pride, and on the first weekend in June, the park comes to life during the **Festival at the Lake**, when all of Oakland gets together to enjoy non-stop music and performances from local bands and entertainers.

To the north of the water, it's worth strolling under the MacArthur Freeway to soak up the relaxed atmosphere of the cafés and shops along gradually diverging Grand and Lakeshore avenues. Note the huge Art Deco facade of the still-functioning **Grand Lake Movie Theater**, at 3200 Grand Ave, a bastion of subversive political film.

The Oakland Museum

Two blocks south of the lake, or a block up Oak Street from the Lake Merritt BART station, the **Oakland Museum**, 1000 Oak St (Wed–Sat 10am–5pm, Sun noon–5pm; $8, free every second Sun of month; ☎510/238-2200, ⓦwww.museumca.org), is undoubtedly Oakland's prime tourist destination, not only by virtue of the exhibits but also for the superb modern building in which it's housed, topped by a terraced rooftop sculpture garden giving great views out over the water and city. The museum covers three topics on as many floors, the first of which treats California's **ecology** in exhibits simulating a walk from the seaside through various natural habitats and climate zones right up to the 14,000-foot summits of the Sierra Nevada mountains. The second floor deals with California's **history**, from Native American habitats through the Spanish colonial and Gold Rush eras, and up to the present day. Artifacts on display include the guitar that Berkeley-born Country Joe MacDonald played at Woodstock in 1969, while the third floor holds a broad survey of works by Californian artists and craftspeople, some highlights of which are pieces of circa 1900 Arts and Crafts furniture. You'll also see excellent **photography** by Edward Muybridge, Dorothea Lange, Imogen Cunningham, and many others.

Jack London Square

Half a mile south from Downtown Oakland on AC Transit bus #51, at the foot of Broadway on the waterfront, **JACK LONDON SQUARE** is Oakland's main concession to the tourist trade. Accessible by direct ferry from San Francisco (see p.287), this complex of harborfront boutiques and restaurants was named after the self-taught writer who grew up pirating shellfish around here – though it's about as distant from the wandering spirit of the man as could be. Apart from the small cabin from the Alaskan Yukon that London carved his initials into (and which has been reconstructed here), the site most worth stopping at is **Heinold's First and Last Chance Saloon**, a bar, built in 1883 from the hull of a whaling ship, where Jack London actually drank. Be that as it may, real Jack London enthusiasts are better off visiting his ranch in Sonoma County (see p.381). The square is also home to a nine-screen multiplex cinema and **Yoshi's World Class Jazz House**, the Bay Area's, if not the West Coast's, premier jazz club (see p.323).

At the western end of the square, by the foot of Clay Street, are a couple of **historical vessels**; dockside tours are available for both the *Light Ship Relief* (Thurs & Fri 10am–3pm, Sat & Sun 11am–4pm; $3) and the USS *Potomac* (Wed 10.30am–3.30pm, Fri & Sun noon–3.30pm; $7; ⓦwww.usspotomac.org), Franklin D. Roosevelt's famous "floating White House." On Sunday, the square bustles with a weekly **farmers' market**, where you can stock up on food. Otherwise, a few short blocks inland lies a warehouse district with a couple of good places to eat and drink lurking among the train tracks; the area is most lively early in the morning, from about 5am, when a daily **produce market** is held along Third and Fourth streets.

Alameda

Along Broadway in Oakland, the AC Transit bus #51 heads under the inner harbor to **ALAMEDA**, a quiet and conservative island of middle America dominated by a large, empty naval air station, closed in 1995 – although massive nuclear-powered aircraft carriers still dock here occasionally. Alameda, which has been hit very hard by post-Cold War military cutbacks, was severed from the Oakland mainland as part of a harbor improvement program in 1902. The fine houses along the original shoreline on Clinton Street were part of the summer resort colony that flocked here to the *contra costa* or "opposite shore" from San Francisco, near the now-demolished Neptune Beach amusement park. The island has since been much enlarged by dredging and landfill, and 1960s apartment buildings line the long, narrow shore of **Robert Crown Memorial Beach** along the Bay – a quiet, attractive spot.

West Oakland

WEST OAKLAND may be the nearest East Bay BART stop to San Francisco, but it is light years away from that city's prosperity. The increasing gentrification of Emeryville, directly to the north, may well point toward a brighter future for the whole area, but for now there's still little to tempt tourists, as it remains an industrial district of warehouses, housing projects from the 1960s, and decaying Victorian houses.

In the past, the district couldn't have been more colorful. From the end of Prohibition in 1933 right up through the early 1970s (when many buildings were torn down in the name of urban renewal), the heart of the Bay Area's entertainment scene was situated near the West Oakland BART station along **Seventh Street**. The street runs west between the docks and storage yards of the Oakland Army Base and the Naval Supply Depot, ending up at **Port View Park**, a good place to watch the huge container ships that pass by. The small

The Black Panthers

Formed amidst the poverty of West Oakland in 1966 by black-rights activists Huey Newton and Bobby Seale, the **Black Panther Party for Self-Defense** captured the media spotlight with its leather-jacketed, beret-sporting members and their militant rhetoric and occasional gun battles with police.

The party was started as a civil-rights organization influenced by Malcolm X's call to black Americans to rely on themselves for defense and dignity. Mixing socialism with black pride, the Panthers aimed to eradicate poverty and drug use in America's inner cities, arguing that if the government wouldn't do it, they would. They also got involved in other issues of concern to minorities, and one of the first acts of the party was to establish patrols in local communities to monitor police brutality.

The Panthers' membership grew nationally as the group captured the national spotlight over the trial of Newton for the murder of an Oakland police officer in 1969. Released from prison a year later when his conviction was overturned, Newton sought to revamp the Panthers' image – tainted by increasingly negative and sensational press coverage – by developing "survival programs" in black communities, including the establishment of free medical clinics, breakfasts for children, shelter for the homeless, and jobs for the unemployed. But infighting over leadership within the party took a heavy toll, and when Newton fled to Cuba in 1974 to avoid prosecution for drug use, a series of resignations ensued. By the end of the 1970s, stripped of its original leadership and attacked by newspaper accounts of illicit internal activities, the group disbanded.

For more on the Panthers, check out the **Black Panther Legacy Tours** ($20–25; ☎510/986-0660, ⓦwww.blackpanthertours.com), run by the Huey P. Newton Foundation on the last Saturday of each month. Tours depart at noon across from the main Downtown library on West 18th Street.

park stands on the site of the old transbay ferry terminal, used by as many as forty million passengers annually before the Bay Bridge was completed in 1936. The Black Panthers once held court in West Oakland (see box above), and in 1989, Panthers co-founder Huey Newton was gunned down here in a drug-related revenge attack; later the same year, the double-decker I-880 freeway that divided the neighborhood from the rest of the city collapsed in on itself during an earthquake, killing dozens of commuters. Local African-American leaders successfully resisted government plans to rebuild that concrete eyesore; the broad, street-level **Nelson Mandela Parkway** has replaced it, thereby removing the physical justification for the "other side of the freeway" stigma once linked to the place. Now the neighborhood is a magnet for artists and skate punks from across the Bay, who revel in its dirt-cheap rents and open spaces – indicating that the first signs of its surprisingly tardy gentrification are finally afoot.

One area where gentrification has been well under way for years is the district of **Emeryville**, effectively the northern portion of West Oakland. Though still gritty in parts, many of the old warehouses here have been converted into artists' lofts and studios in an ongoing real-life workshop to transform the area into a glitzy design centerpiece. Most intriguing is the new city hall, called **Civic Center**, at Park Avenue and Hollis Street, for which the 1902 town hall has been wrapped in a sheer glass box of 15,000 additional square feet of office space. Nothing indicates the upwardly mobile face of Emeryville better, however, than the fact that the billion-dollar computer animation company **Pixar** is headquartered here at 1200 Park Ave; unfortunately, no tours of the studio are offered.

East Oakland

The bulk of Oakland spreads along foothills and flatlands to the east of Downtown, in neighborhoods obviously stratified along the main thoroughfares of Foothill and MacArthur boulevards. Gertrude Stein grew up here, though when she returned years later in search of her childhood home it had been torn down and replaced by a dozen Craftsman-style bungalows – the simple 1920s wooden houses that cover most of **EAST OAKLAND**, each fronted by a patch of lawn and divided from its neighbor by a narrow concrete driveway.

A quick way out from the gridded streets and sidewalks of the city is to take AC Transit bus #64 from Downtown east up into the hills to **Joaquin Miller Park**, the most easily accessible of Oakland's hilltop parks. It stands on the former grounds of "The Hights," the misspelled home of the "Poet of the Sierras," Joaquin Miller, who made his name playing the eccentric frontier American in the literary salons of 1870s London. His poems weren't exactly acclaimed – even if he did manage to rhyme "teeth" with "Goethe" – but his prose account, *Life Amongst the Modocs*, documenting time spent with the Modoc Indians near Mount Shasta, does stand the test of time. It was more for his outrageous behavior than for his writings that he became famous, wearing bizarre clothes and biting debutantes' ankles. For years, Japanese poet and sculptor Yone Noguchi (father of Isamu Noguchi) lived here; according to one story, he worked the sprinkler while Miller impressed lady visitors with a Native American rain dance.

Perched in the hills at the foot of the park, the pointed towers of the **Mormon Temple**, 4770 Lincoln Ave, look like missile-launchers designed by the Wizard of Oz – unmissable by day or floodlit at night. In December, speakers hidden in the landscaping make it seem as if the plants are singing Christmas carols. Though you can't go inside the temple itself (unless you're a confirmed Mormon), there are great views out over the entire Bay Area from the grounds, and a small adjoining museum explains the tenets of the faith (daily 9am–9pm; free; ☏510/531-1475). If asked, the docent will give a 25-minute tour, after which you can watch any or all of the twelve-part video about the temple. There's also a branch of the Mormons' **genealogical research library** (daily 7am–8pm; ☏510/531-3200), where you can try tracing your family's ancestry, regardless of your faith.

Several miles up in the hills behind the temple stands the **Chabot Space & Science Center**, 10000 Skyline Blvd (Wed & Thurs 10am–5pm, Fri & Sat 10am–10pm, Sun 11am–5pm; $13; ☏510/336-7300, ⓦwww.chabotspace.org). This modern museum features interactive displays and a fine **planetarium** – daytime shows are included in the admission but the evening Sky Tonight costs extra (Fri & Sat 7.30pm; $8), as do screenings at the impressive **Megadome Theater** (various times; $7 with museum entrance, $8 theater only). The museum can be reached on AC Transit bus #53 from the Fruitvale BART station.

Two miles east along Hwy-13 sits the attractive campus of **Mills College**. Founded in 1852 as a women-only seminary, it's still decidedly female (although the graduate class is now open to both sexes). Mills is renowned for its music school, considered one of the best and most innovative in the US, and is worth a visit for its **art gallery** (Sept–June Tues–Sat 11am–4pm, Sun noon–4pm; free), which boasts a fine collection of Chinese, Japanese, and pre-Columbian ceramics. Outside, a broad stream meanders through the lushly landscaped grounds, and many of the buildings, notably the central campanile, were designed in solid California Mission style by Julia Morgan, architect of Hearst Castle as well as nearly five hundred lesser-known Bay Area structures.

Further east, reachable by AC Transit bus #56, is the **Oakland 3** (daily 10am–4pm; $9; T 510/632-9525, W www.oaklandzoo.org) in Knowland Park. Once one of the worst zoos in the country, many of its formerly cramped quarters have now been replaced with large, naturalistic habitats; the most noteworthy of these is the **Malayan sun bear** exhibit, the largest of its kind in the US.

Fremont and the Mission Sán Jose de Guadelupe

Further south, some twenty miles of tract house suburbs stretch along the Bay to San Jose; the only vaguely interesting area is around the end of the BART line in **Fremont**, where the short-lived Essanay movie studios were based. Essanay, the first studios on the West Coast, made more than seven hundred films in three years, including Charlie Chaplin's *The Tramp* in 1914. Not much remains from those pre-Hollywood days, however, and the only real sight is the **Mission San Jose de Guadalupe** on Mission Boulevard, south of the I-680 freeway (daily 10am–5pm; donation). Built in 1797 as the fourteenth mission in the chain of 21 that run along El Camino Real, the structure was completely rebuilt in 1985 to look as it did in the early 1800s. One of the least-visited missions in the chain, it's arguably the most striking of the five in the Bay Area, with crystal chandeliers suspended from its rustic wooden nave and trompe l'oeil balconies painted on its walls. The reconstruction of the church was so faithful to the original that even the gigantic original bells hung in the belfry are now suspended from rawhide straps, just as they were more than two hundred years before.

North Oakland and Rockridge

The horrific October 1991 Oakland **fire**, which destroyed three thousand homes and killed 26 people, did most of its damage in the high-priced hills of **North Oakland**. It took the better part of two years for the now million-dollar houses to be rebuilt, and although the lush vegetation that made the area so attractive will never be allowed to grow back fully in order to prevent any more fires, things are pretty much back to normal. Which is to say that segregation is still in place; these bayview homes, some of the Bay Area's most valuable real estate, look out across some of its poorest – the neglected flatlands below that in the 1960s were the proving grounds of Black Panthers Bobby Seale and Huey Newton.

Broadway is the dividing line between these two halves of North Oakland, and it also gives access (via the handy AC Transit #51 bus) to most of what there is to see and do here. The **Morcom Amphitheater of Roses**, on Oakland Avenue, three blocks east of Broadway (April–Oct daily dawn–dusk; free; T 510/238-3187), has eight acres of pools, trees, and roses, which are best seen from May to September, when they're in full bloom. Nearby **Piedmont Avenue** is lined by a number of small bookstores and cafés, while a mile north along the avenue is the **Mountain View Cemetery**, laid out in 1863 by Frederick Law Olmsted (designer of New York's Central Park and San Francisco's Golden Gate Park), which holds the elaborate dynastic tombs of San Francisco's most powerful families – the Crockers, the Bechtels, and the Ghirardellis. You can jog or ride a bike around the well-tended grounds, or just wonder at the enormous turtles in the pond.

Next door, the columbarium (where they keep the urns), known as **Chapel of the Chimes**, at 4499 Piedmont Ave (daily 9am–5pm; free; T 510/654-0123), was enhanced by Julia Morgan during her decade-long association with the structure, beginning in 1921. The edifice is remarkable for its seemingly endless series of urn-filled rooms, grouped together around sky-lit courtyards, bubbling fountains, and intimate chapels – all furnished with comfortable chairs and connected by ornate staircases of every conceivable length. Morgan wanted the space to sing of life, not death – and she certainly succeeded. Visit the strangely peaceful place during one of the regular concerts held here for a completely unique – and distinctly Californian – experience.

Back on Broadway, just past College Avenue, Broadway Terrace climbs up to small **Lake Temescal** – where you can swim in summer – and continues to the forested ridge at the **Robert Sibley Regional Preserve**, which includes the 1761-foot volcanic cone of Round Top Peak, offering panoramas of the entire Bay Area. The peak has been dubbed the **Volcanic Witch Project** by local media for five strange mazes carved into the dirt in canyons around the crater and lined with stones. No one is sure who began the project, but navigating any of the designs leads to its center, where visitors add to the pile of eclectic offerings ranging from trinkets to cigarettes to poetry. Skyline Boulevard runs through the park and is popular with cyclists, who ride the twelve miles south to Lake Chabot or follow Grizzly Peak Boulevard five miles north to Tilden Park through the Berkeley Hills.

Most of the Broadway traffic, and the AC Transit #51 bus, cuts off onto College Avenue through Oakland's most upscale shopping district, **ROCKRIDGE**. Spreading for half a mile on either side of the Rockridge BART station, the quirky stores and restaurants here, despite their undeniable upwardly mobile overtones, are better than Piedmont's in variety and volume, and make for a pleasant afternoon's wander or night out.

Eating

Oakland is hardly regarded as a gourmet paradise; it does, though, have a tradition of unpretentious all-American diners along with a smattering of good multi-ethnic restaurants. The trendier Rockridge area offers some classier options, especially for Italian food.

Diners and delis

Adam's Burger 3401 Lakeshore Ave, North Oakland ☎510/834-5796. Cheap burgers and fries, and a few dishes like steak teriyaki in a simple down-home setting north of Lake Merritt.

Barney's 4162 Piedmont Ave, North Oakland ☎510/655-7180; 5819 College Ave, Rockridge ☎510/601-0444. The East Bay's most popular burgers, available in a myriad of ways (including veggie).

Genova Delicatessen 5095 Telegraph Ave, North Oakland ☎510/652-7401. Friendly deli complete with hanging sausages that serves up superb sandwiches for around $5.

Holy Land 677 Rand Ave, Oakland ☎510/272-0535. Casual diner-style kosher restaurant just beyond the freeway north of Lake Merritt, serving moderately priced Israeli food, including excellent falafel.

Luis the Pie Queen 851 60th St at Adeline, North Oakland ☎510/658-5616. Famous around the Bay for its Southern-style sweet potato and fresh fruit pies, this cozy diner also serves massive, down-home breakfasts and Sun dinners, all for around $10 or less.

American and California cuisine

Bay Wolf 3853 Piedmont Ave, North Oakland ☎510/655-6004. Chic restaurant whose menu is influenced by the cuisine of Tuscany, Provence, and the Basque country, featuring specials like double mustard-tarragon chicken or grilled Alaskan halibut. Most entrees over $20.

Citron 5484 College Ave, Rockridge ☎510/653-5484. A warm neighborhood gem that rivals San Francisco's best restaurants, featuring unpretentious service and exquisite food such as spicy bayou seafood – expensive, though.

Grand Oaks Grill 736 Washington St, Downtown Oakland ☎510/452-1258. Moderately priced meat and seafood, cooked in a mixture of European and Asian sauces; try the chicken breast marsala or calamari dore.

Asian, African, and Indian

Jade Villa 800 Broadway, Downtown Oakland ☎510/839-1688. For endless dim-sum lunches or traditional Cantonese meals, this is one of the best places in Oakland's Chinatown.

Khana Peena 5316 College Ave, Rockridge ☎510/658-2300. A cut above the average Indian restaurant in terms of both decor and quality of cuisine. A wide range of curries and tandoori dishes is available. There's another branch at 1889 Solano Ave, Berkeley (☎510/528-2519).

🏃 **Le Cheval 1007 Clay St, Downtown Oakland** ☎510/763-8495. Serving exquisite Vietnamese the way it was meant to be, the chic, spacious surroundings and moderate prices here won't let you down.

Nan Yang 6048 College Ave, Rockridge ☎510/655-3298. Burmese food served in large, palate-exciting portions. The political refugee owner/chef is willing to discuss all his esoteric delicacies.

New Star 526 Eighth St, Downtown Oakland ☎510/832-2888. No prizes for decor but this basic Chinese place serves a surprisingly good all-day buffet for $6.

Italian

Garibaldi's on College 5356 College Ave, Rockridge ☎510/595-4000. Quality upmarket Italian with delicious pasta dishes and an emphasis on fine wines. Some of the sauces have a spicy Middle Eastern element.

Oliveto 5655 College Ave, Rockridge ☎510/547-5356. With his back-to-basics recipes and dependence on home-grown ingredients, chef Paul Bertolli creates appetizing gourmet Italian cuisine. The main dining room is very expensive but there's a less pricey basement section with more basic fare on offer.

Zachary's 5801 College Ave, Rockridge ☎510/655-6385. Zealously defended as the best pizzeria in the Bay Area, *Zachary's* is also one of the only places offering rich, deep-dish, Chicago-style pizza.

Mexican, Caribbean, and Latin American

🏃 **La Furia Chalaca 310 Broadway, Downtown Oakland** ☎510/451-4206. Great range of seafood with pasta and various Peruvian sauces, plus some meat dishes like a fine braised pork stew.

Tropix 3814 Piedmont Ave, North Oakland ☎510/653-2444. Large portions of fruity Caribbean delicacies at reasonable prices, with authentic jerk sauce and thirst-quenching mango juice.

Ice cream and desserts

Dreyers 5925 College Ave, Rockridge ☎510/658-0502. Oakland's own rich ice cream, which is distributed throughout California, is served at this small, slightly dull Rockridge café.

Fenton's Creamery 4226 Piedmont Ave, North Oakland ☎510/658-7000. A brightly lit 1950s ice cream and sandwich shop, open until 11pm on weeknights, or midnight on weekends.

La Farine 6323 College Ave, Rockridge ☎510/654-0338. Small but highly rated French-style bakery, with excellent *pain au chocolat*.

Cafés and bars

Oakland does not have the **café** culture of Berkeley to the north, except in snatches at Rockridge. There are a few good down-to-earth **bars**, though. For other nightlife and live music venues, see the listings on pp.322–323.

Cafés and coffeehouses

Coffee Mill 3363 Grand Ave, North Oakland ☎510/465-4224. Spacious room that doubles as an art gallery, and often hosts poetry readings.

Royal 6255 College Ave, Rockridge ☎510/653-5458. Bright, modern, relaxing spot in the Rockridge area, with outdoor seating. Perfect for a leisurely afternoon with the newspaper.

Bars

The Alley 3325 Grand Ave, North Oakland
☎510/444-8505. Ramshackle, black-timber piano bar, decorated with business cards and with live old-time blues merchants on the keyboards.

Ben'n'Nick's 5612 College Ave, Rockridge
☎510/933-0327. Lively and welcoming bar with good taped rock music; tasty food, too, if you're hungry.

Bench and Bar 120 11th St, Downtown Oakland
☎510/444-2266. Primarily African-American and Latino hot spot, with a loyal gay following. Particularly known for its weekend salsa nights, though the crowd and vibe can vary wildly depending on the evening's theme.

Cato's Alehouse 3891 Piedmont Ave, North Oakland ☎510/655-3349. Very local and casual alehouse with a good beer selection. A fine place to kick back with a brew and a pizza or sandwich.

Heinold's First and Last Chance Saloon 56 Jack London Square, Oakland ☎510/839-6761. Authentic waterfront bar that's hardly changed since the turn of the century, when Jack London was a regular. They still haven't bothered to fix the slanted floor caused by the 1906 earthquake.

Pacific Coast Brewing Co 906 Washington St, Downtown Oakland
☎510/836-2739. Oaktown's only real micro-brewery, which conjures up a range of decent brews and offers quite an extensive menu too. Attracts Downtown office workers as well as a younger crowd later on.

The White Horse 6560 Telegraph Ave at 66th St, North Oakland ☎510/652-3820. Oakland's oldest gay bar, *The White Horse* is a smallish, friendly place, with mixed nightly dancing for men and women.

Berkeley

This Berkeley was like no somnolent Siwash out of her own past at all, but more akin to those Far Eastern or Latin American universities you read about, those autonomous culture media where the most beloved of folklores may be brought into doubt, cataclysmic of dissents voiced, suicidal of commitments chosen – the sort that bring governments down.

Thomas Pynchon, *The Crying of Lot 49*

More than any other American city, **BERKELEY** conjures up an image of 1960s student dissent. When college campuses across the nation were protesting against the Vietnam War, it was the students of the University of California, Berkeley, who led the charge gaining a name as the vanguard of what was increasingly seen as a challenge to the authority of the state. Full-scale battles were fought almost daily here at one point, on the campus and on its surrounding streets, and there were times when Berkeley looked almost on the brink of revolution itself: students (and others) throwing stones and gas bombs were met with tear-gas volleys and truncheons by National Guard troops under the nominal command of Governor Ronald Reagan.

Such action was inspired by the mood of the time and continued well into the 1970s, while during the conservative 1980s and Clinton-dominated 1990s, Berkeley politics became far less confrontational. But despite an influx of more conformist students, a surge in the number of exclusive restaurants, and the dismantling of the city's rent-control program, the progressive legacy has remained in the city's independent **bookstores** (see box, p.308) and at sporadic political demonstrations, particularly those inspired by the growing resistance to George W. Bush's warmongering policies. Indeed, Berkeley returned to being a bastion of the **anti-war movement** and streets like Telegraph Avenue became festooned with posters, stickers, and T-shirts questioning the occupation of Iraq and the war against terrorism or lampooning the "dunce-in-chief" during his occupation of the White House.

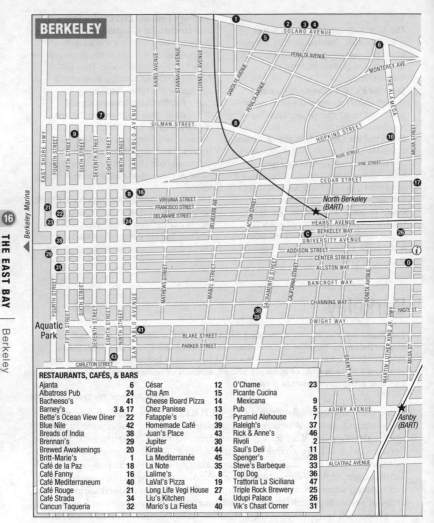

BERKELEY

On top of its ideological rule, the **University of California**, right in the center of town, physically dominates Berkeley and makes a logical starting point for a visit. Its many grand buildings and 30,000 students give off a definite energy that spills down the raucous stretch of **Telegraph Avenue** which runs south from the campus and holds most of the student hangouts, including a dozen or so lively cafés, as well as a number of fine bookstores. Older students, and a good percentage of the faculty, congregate in **North Berkeley**, the section of which immediately north of campus is popularly known as Northside. Residents regularly pop down from their woodsy hillside homes here to partake of goodies from Gourmet Ghetto, a stretch of Shattuck Avenue crammed with restaurants, delis, and bakeries. Of quite distinct character are the flatlands that spread through **West Berkeley** down

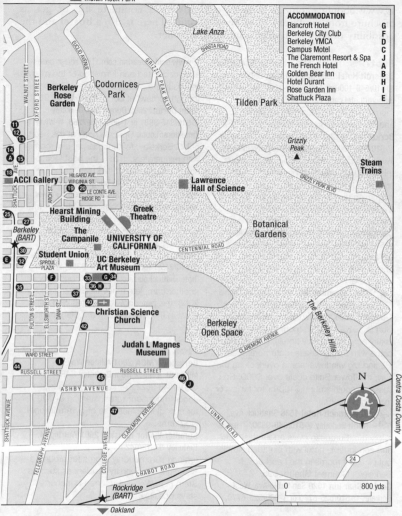

ACCOMMODATION

Bancroft Hotel	G
Berkeley City Club	F
Berkeley YMCA	D
Campus Motel	C
The Claremont Resort & Spa	J
The French Hotel	A
Golden Bear Inn	B
Hotel Durant	H
Rose Garden Inn	I
Shattuck Plaza	E

to the Bay, a poorer (but increasingly gentrified) district that mixes old Victorian houses with builders' yards and light industrial premises, sandwiched around the restaurants and houseware shops of Fourth Street. Along the Bay itself is the **Berkeley Marina**, where you can rent sailboards and sailboats, or just watch the sun set behind the Golden Gate.

Accommodation

Berkeley is without a doubt the most pleasant area to stay in the East Bay. It has a good range of options from cheapish **motels** to some quite classy **hotels**, plus a particularly strong tradition of **bed and breakfasts**; check with the Berkeley & Oakland Bed and Breakfast Network (℡510/547-6380,

Hotels, motels, and B&Bs

Bancroft Hotel 2680 Bancroft Way, Berkeley Ⓣ510/549-1000 or 1-800/549-1002, Ⓦwww .bancrofthotel.com. Small hotel with 22 rooms, a good location right by campus, and fine service. Breakfast included. $129.

Berkeley City Club 2315 Durant Ave, Berkeley Ⓣ510/848-7800, Ⓦwww.berkeleycityclub.com. Two blocks from the UC Berkeley campus, this B&B was designed by Hearst Castle architect Julia Morgan, with indoor swimming pool and exercise room. Each of the spacious rooms has a private bath. $150.

Campus Motel 1619 University Ave, Berkeley Ⓣ510/841-3844, Ⓦwww.campusmotel.com. No-frills motel, but clean and about as cheap as it gets within easy walking distance of downtown. $85.

The Claremont Resort & Spa 41 Tunnel Rd, Berkeley Ⓣ510/843-3000 or 1-800/551-7266, Ⓦwww.claremontresort.com. Built in 1915, the *Claremont* is the lap of luxury among Berkeley hotels. Deluxe rooms come with coffeemakers, data ports, cable TV, and big windows, some overlooking the Bay; the Tower Suite costs over $600. Spa sessions begin around $100/hr for facials or massages. $229.

The French Hotel 1538 Shattuck Ave, North Berkeley Ⓣ510/548-9930. There's a touch of European class about this small and comfortable hotel with eighteen simple but pleasant rooms in the heart of Berkeley's Gourmet Ghetto. $95.

Golden Bear Inn 1620 San Pablo Ave, West Berkeley Ⓣ510/525-6770 or 1-800/525-6770, Ⓦwww.goldenbearinn.com. The most pleasantly decorated and furnished of the many motels in the "flatlands" of West Berkeley, though somewhat out of the way. $79.

Hotel Durant 2600 Durant Ave, Berkeley Ⓣ510/845-8981 or 1-800/238-7268, Ⓦwww .hoteldurant.com. Upscale hotel at the heart of UC Berkeley, featuring large, airy rooms with refrigerators. This is the best location to stay if you can afford it. $169.

Rose Garden Inn 2740 Telegraph Ave, Berkeley Ⓣ510/549-2145 or 1-800/992-9005, Ⓦwww .rosegardeninn.com. Pleasant, if slightly dull, rooms with fireplaces in a pretty mock-Tudor mansion half a mile south of UC Berkeley. $109.

Shattuck Plaza 2086 Allston Way, Berkeley Ⓣ510/845-7300 or 1-800/237-5359, Ⓦwww .hotelshattuckplaza.com. Having undergone another complete renovation by the end of 2008, this hotel now competes with the finest in the area, barring the Claremont. $129.

Hostels

Berkeley YMCA 2001 Allston Way at Milvia St, a block from Berkeley BART Ⓣ510/848-9622. Berkeley's best bargain accommodation; rates, starting at $39 for a single, include use of gym and pool. No dorms.

Summer Visitor Housing 2601 Warring St, Berkeley Ⓣ510/642-4444. Agency that can arrange summer-only rooms for around $50/night in university residences such as Stern Hall. Weekly preferred but shorter stays possible.

The University of California

Caught up in the frantic crush of students who pack the **UNIVERSITY OF CALIFORNIA** campus during the semesters, it's nearly impossible to imagine the bucolic learning environment envisaged by its high-minded founders. When the Reverend Henry Durant and other East Coast academics decided to set up shop here in the 1860s, these rolling foothills were still largely given over to dairy herds and wheat fields, the last remnants of the Peralta family's Spanish land-grant *rancho* which once stretched over most of the East Bay. One day in 1866, while surveying the land, an inspired trustee recited "Westward the course of the empire takes its way," from an eighteenth-century poem by George Berkeley. Moved by the moment, all assembled agreed to name their school after the Irish bishop and philosopher who penned the phrase. Construction

▲ The University of California

work on the two campus buildings – imaginatively named North Hall and South Hall – was still going on when the first two hundred students, including 22 women, moved here from Oakland in 1873.

Since then, an increasing number of buildings have been squeezed into the half-mile-square main campus, and the state-funded university (known to students as merely "Cal" or "UC," but rarely "Berkeley") has become one of America's most prestigious, with so many Nobel laureates on the faculty it's rumored you have to win one just to get a parking permit. UC Berkeley physicists built the first cyclotron, and plutonium was discovered here in 1941 (along with the elements californium and berkelium later in the decade); as such, it was the setting for sketches for the first atomic bomb. Nuclear weaponry connections and overcrowding aside, the beautifully landscaped campus, stepping down from the eucalyptus-covered Berkeley Hills toward the Golden Gate, is eminently strollable. With maps posted everywhere, you'd have to try hard to get lost – though enthusiastic students will show you around on a free ninety-minute **tour** (Mon–Sat 10am, Sun 1pm; ☏510/642-5215), which departs from the University of California's **Visitor Services office**, 101 University Hall, at the corner of Oxford and University.

Sproul Plaza and around

While a number of footpaths climb the hill from the Berkeley BART station on Shattuck Avenue, the best way to get a feel for the place is to follow Strawberry Creek from the top of Center Street across the southeast corner of the campus, emerging from the groves of redwood and eucalyptus trees at **Sproul Plaza**. It's the largest public space on campus, enlivened by street musicians playing for quarters on the steps of the **Student Union** building and conga drummers pounding away in the echoing courtyard below. The Plaza is also lined with tables staffed by student groups advocating one thing or another – from free love to sexual abstinence.

Sather Gate, which bridges Strawberry Creek at the north end of Sproul Plaza, marks the entrance to the older part of the campus. Up the hill, past the imposing facade of Wheeler Hall, the 1914 landmark **Campanile** (Mon–Fri 10am–4pm; $2) is modeled after the one in the Piazza San Marco in Venice; take an elevator to the top for a great view of the campus and the entire Bay Area. At the foot of the tower stands redbrick **South Hall**, the sole survivor of the original pair of buildings.

Inside the plain white building next door, the **Bancroft Library** (Mon–Fri 9am–5pm, Sat 1–5pm; ℡510/642-3781) displays odds and ends from its exhaustive accumulation of artifacts and documents tracing the history of California, including an imitation brass plaque supposedly left by Sir Francis Drake when he claimed all of the West Coast for Queen Elizabeth I. It also contains a collection of manuscripts and rare books, from Mark Twain to James Joyce – though to see any of these you'll have to show some academic credentials. Around the corner and down the hill, just inside the arched main entrance to Doe Library, you'll find the **Morrison Reading Room**, a great place to sit for a while and read foreign magazines and newspapers, listen to a CD, or just ease down into one of the many comfy overstuffed chairs and unwind.

Also worth a quick look is the **Museum of Paleontology** (Mon–Sat 8am–5pm; free; ⓦ www.ucmp.berkeley.edu) in the nearby Valley Life Sciences Building, although only a tyrannosaurus rex skeleton and some other bones and fossils are on general display in the atrium – you need to be on an academic mission to view the wealth of finds within. From here it's a quick walk to the collection of cafés and restaurants lining Euclid and Hearst avenues, and the beginning of North Berkeley.

The Hearst Mining Building, Botanical Garden, and around

The Hearst family name appears with disturbing regularity around the Berkeley campus, though in most instances this is due not to the notorious newspaper baron William Randolph but to his altruistic mother, Phoebe Apperson Hearst. Besides inviting the entire senior class to her home every spring for a giant picnic, she sponsored the architectural competition that came up with the original campus plan and donated a good number of the campus buildings, including many that have since been destroyed. One of the finest survivors, the 1907 **Hearst Mining Building** (daily 8am–5pm; free) on the northeast edge of the campus, conceals a delicate metalwork lobby topped by three glass domes, above aging exhibits on geology and mining – which is how the Hearst family fortune was originally made, long before scion W.R. took up publishing. The building underwent an impressive renovation and seismic retrofit, completed in 2003, during which a suspension system capable of withstanding a metre of lateral movement was installed. Another Hearst legacy is the nearby **Greek Theatre**, which hosts a summer season of rock concerts (see p.322 for details) and is modeled after the amphitheater at Epidauros, Greece.

Higher up in the hills, above the 80,000-seat Memorial Stadium, the lushly landscaped **Botanical Garden** (daily 9am–5pm, closed first Tues of month; $3, free on Thurs; ℡510/643-2755) defeats on-campus claustrophobia with thirty acres of plants and cacti. Near the crest, with great views out over the Bay, a full-size fiberglass sculpture of a whale stretches out in front of the **Lawrence Hall of Science** (daily 10am–5pm; $9.50; ℡510/642-3682, www.lawrencehallofscience.org), an excellent museum and learning center featuring earthquake simulations, model dinosaurs, and a planetarium, plus hands-on exhibits for kids in the Wizard's Lab. Both the gardens and the Lawrence Hall of Science are accessible on weekdays via the free UC Berkeley shuttle bus from the campus or the Berkeley BART station.

The Berkeley Art Museum and around

In the southeast corner of the campus, the brutally modern, angular concrete of the **UC Berkeley Art Museum**, 2626 Bancroft Way (Wed–Sun 11am–5pm; $8, free on first Thurs of month; Ⓦwww.bampfa.berkeley.edu), is in stark contrast to the campus's older buildings. Its skylit, open-plan galleries hold works by Picasso, Cézanne, Rubens, and other notables, but the star of the show is the collection of 1950s American painter Hans Hofmann's energetic and colorful abstract paintings on the top floor. The museum is renowned for its cutting-edge exhibitions: the main space hosts a range of major shows – such as Robert Mapplethorpe's controversial photographs – while the Matrix Gallery focuses on lesser-known, (usually) local artists. The new quarters of the **Pacific Film Archive**, diagonally opposite at 2575 Bancroft Way, feature nightly showings of classic, developing world, and experimental films. The other rep house on campus is **UC Theatre**, 2036 University Ave, featuring funky theme-weeks of noir, melodrama, and other genres. Other artistic fare can be found at **Zellerbach Hall**, which showcases classical music, dance, and performances by modernists like Laurie Anderson and Philip Glass. See listings p.322 for details on all the above.

Across the road from the art museum, the **Phoebe A. Hearst Museum of Anthropology** in Kroeber Hall (Wed–Sat 10am–4.30pm, Sun noon–4pm; $2, free Thurs; ☎510/642-3682 Ⓦwww.hearstmuseum.berkeley.edu) holds a variety of changing exhibits as well as an intriguing display of artifacts made by Ishi, the last surviving Yahi Indian, who was found near Mount Lassen in Northern California in 1911. Anthropologist Alfred Kroeber – father of sci-fi writer Ursula K.Le Guin – brought Ishi to the museum (then located on the UC San Francisco campus), where he lived under the scrutiny of scientists and journalists – in effect, in a state of captivity – until his death from tuberculosis a few years later.

Telegraph Avenue and South Berkeley

Downtown Berkeley lies west of the university campus around the Berkeley BART station on Shattuck Avenue – though most activity is centered on **TELEGRAPH AVENUE**, which runs south of the university from Sproul Plaza. This thoroughfare saw some of the worst of the 1960s riots, and today is still a frenetic bustle, especially for the four short blocks closest to the university, which are packed to the gills with everything from cafés and secondhand bookstores to sidewalk vendors selling handmade jewelry and subversive bumper stickers, and the requisite down-and-outs.

Half a block up from Telegraph between Haste Street and Dwight Way and behind the legendary Amoeba Records (see p.324), **People's Park** has recovered from a fallow period and is once again a reasonably well-kempt place to hang out, at least during daylight hours – at night it tends to become a haven for the homeless and disenfranchised. In the late 1960s the park was a prime political battleground, when organized and spirited resistance to the university's plans to develop the site into dormitories brought out the military, who shot dead an onlooker by mistake. A mural along Haste Street bears the words of

Berkeley's **bookstores** are as exhaustive as they are exhausting – not surprising for a university town – and are perfect for browsing; you won't be made to feel guilty or obliged to buy a book you've been poring over for ages. The CVB has a useful list of over fifty shops, of which the following are a representative selection.

Analog Books 1816 Euclid Ave ☏510/843-1816. A variety of quality books on graphics, art, and music, as well as a good stock of magazines.

Black Oak Books 1491 Shattuck Ave ☏510/486-0698. Huge selection of second-hand and new books for every interest; also holds regular evening readings by internationally acclaimed authors.

Comic Relief 2026 Shattuck Ave ☏510/843-5002. All the mainstream stuff, plus self-published mini-comics by locals.

Easy Going Travel Shop & Bookstore 1385 Shattuck Ave ☏510/843-3533. The essential bookstore for every traveler. Packed with travel paraphernalia, it offers a wide selection of guidebooks and maps for local, countrywide, and international exploration. Talks and slideshows by travel writers are also held on a regular basis.

Lewin's Metaphysical Books 2644 Ashby Ave ☏510/843-4491. The place to come for the best selection on spirituality, religion, astrology, and other arcane subjects.

Moe's Bookstore 2476 Telegraph Ave ☏510/849-2087. An enormous selection of new and used books on four floors, with esoteric surprises in every field of study; perfect for academics, book collectors, and browsers. There's also an excellent art section on the top floor (☏510/849-2133).

Mrs Dalloway's 2904 College Ave ☏510/704-8222. New store specializing in literature and gardening. Hosts regular readings and slideshows.

Revolution Books 2425c Channing Way ☏510/848-1196. Wide range of books on political themes with, as you might expect, an emphasis on leftist and anarchist thought.

Serendipity Books 1201 University Ave ☏510/841-7455. This vast, garage-like bookstore is off the loop of Berkeley bookstores, but is an absolute must for collectors of first-edition or obscure fiction and poetry, as well as Black American writers. The prices are fair, and the owner – incredibly, given the towers of unshelved books – knows exactly where everything is to be found.

Shakespeare and Company 2499 Telegraph Ave ☏510/841-8916. Crammed with quality secondhand books at reasonable prices, Shakespeare and Company is the best place to linger and scour the shelves for finds, especially literature.

student leader Mario Savio: "There's a time when the operation of the machine becomes so odious... that you can't take part." Though the words may serve as inspiration to some of the park's current residents, the university actually owns the land and has repeatedly threatened to develop it, with or without their approval. Efforts to invade the space with volleyball and basketball courts were met with short-lived but violent protests in 1991, when rioters trashed Telegraph Avenue storefronts, and a 19-year-old woman enraged at the university's plans for the park was shot dead by police while trying to assassinate the chancellor. As a compromise, just a couple of courts were built, and they are free to all. In early 2000, community leaders rallied in the park again to show resistance to the university's proposal to develop much-needed student dormitories on the land, but despite some student support owing to the ongoing housing shortage, that project was also shelved and the park remains, for now at least, with the people.

Directly across Bowditch Street from People's Park stands one of the finest buildings in the Bay Area, Bernard Maybeck's **Christian Science Church**. Built in 1910, it's an eclectic but thoroughly modern structure, laid out in a simple Greek-cross floor plan and spanned by a massive redwood truss with carved Gothic tracery and Byzantine painted decoration. The interior is only open on Sundays for worship and for free tours at 11am, but the outside is worth lingering over, its cascade of many gently pitched roofs and porticoes carrying the eye from one handcrafted detail to another. It's a clever building in many ways: while the overall image is one of tradition and craftsmanship, Maybeck also succeeded in inconspicuously incorporating such materials as industrial metal windows, concrete walls, and asbestos tiles into the structure – thereby cutting costs.

Many of the largely residential neighborhoods elsewhere in **South Berkeley** – especially the Elmwood District around College Avenue – are worth a wander, with a couple of specific sights to search out. One of these is the **Judah L. Magnes Museum**, a few blocks south of the campus at 2911 Russell St (Mon–Thurs & Sun 10am–4pm; free). Housed in a rambling old mansion, it has California's largest repository of Judaica, and its exhibits detail the history of Jewish life from ancient times to the present day, along with sacred and ceremonial art.

The other South Berkeley attraction is much harder to miss, towering as it does over the Berkeley–Oakland border. The half-timbered castle style of the **Claremont Hotel** gives a fairly clear hint as to what's inside – it's now one of the Bay Area's plushest resort hotels (see p.304 for details). Built in 1914, just in time for San Francisco's Panama-Pacific International Exhibition, the *Claremont* was designed to encourage day-trippers out across the Bay in the hope that they'd be so taken with the area they'd want to live here. The ploy worked, and the hotel's owners (who incidentally also owned the streetcar system that brought people here, and all the surrounding land) made a fortune.

North Berkeley

NORTH BERKELEY is a subdued neighborhood of professors and postgraduate students, its steep, twisting streets climbing up the lushly overgrown hills north of the campus. At the foot of the hills, some of the Bay Area's finest restaurants and delis – most famously *Chez Panisse*, started and run by Alice Waters, the acclaimed "inventor" of California cuisine – have sprung up along Shattuck Avenue to form the so-called Gourmet Ghetto, a great place to pick up the makings of a tasty al fresco lunch. There are also a few **galleries**, most notably ACCI, 1652 Shattuck Ave (Tues–Thurs 11am–6pm, Fri 11am–7pm, Sat 10am–6pm & Sun noon–5pm; free), an arts-and-crafts co-operative designed to exhibit and sell the work of local artists. Over a mile further northwest, where Berkeley meets Albany, **Solano Avenue** is fast catching up as a trendy shopping and dining area with a dazzling array of outlets, such as Tibetan craft shops, draped along its curved length.

At the far north end of Shattuck Avenue, east of the shops and cafés along Solano, the gray basalt knob of **Indian Rock** stands out from the foot of the hills, challenging rockclimbers who hone their skills on its forty-foot vertical faces; those who just want to appreciate the extraordinary view can take the steps around its back side. Across the street, carved into similarly hard volcanic stone, are the mortar holes used by the Ohlone to grind acorns into flour. In between, and in stark contrast, stands the rusting hulk of a Cold War-era air-raid siren.

Euclid Avenue, off Hearst and next to the north gate of the university, is a sort of antidote to Telegraph Avenue, a quiet grove of coffee joints and pizza parlors frequented by grad students, the focal point of the enclave known as **Northside**. Above Euclid at Bayview Place – if you want to avoid the fairly steep walk, take bus #65 (daily) or the #8 (weekdays only) from Shattuck Avenue – there are few more pleasant places for a picnic than the **Berkeley Rose Garden** (daily dawn–dusk; free), a terraced amphitheater filled with some three thousand varieties of roses and looking out across the Bay to San Francisco. Built as part of a WPA job-creation scheme during the Depression, a wooden pergola rings the top, stepping down to a small spring.

The homes built in an eclectic range of styles on Northside's steep hills are some of the most impressively sited in the Bay Area, designed to meld seamlessly into the wooded landscape. Many were constructed circa 1900 by members of the Hillside Club, a slightly bohemian group of Berkeleyans who also laid out many of the pedestrian paths that climb the hills. Perhaps the single most striking of these hillside homes, the private **Rowell House** – a half-timbered chalet built in 1914 by architect John Hudson Thomas – stands alone at the top of the path up from **Codornices Park**, where it crosses Tamalpais Road. Many of the other houses nearby were designed and built by Bernard Maybeck, architect of the Palace of Fine Arts, First Church of Christ Scientist, and other notable Bay Area buildings; the homes he built for himself and his family still stand around the junction of Buena Vista Way and La Loma Avenue, a hundred yards south.

Tilden Park

Along the crest of the Berkeley hills, a number of enticing parks give great views over the Bay. The largest and highest of them, **Tilden Park** (daily 8am–10pm; free; ☎510/562-7275), encompasses some 2065 acres of near wilderness. Kids can enjoy a ride on the carved wooden horses of the merry-go-round (weekends, daily in summer 8am–10pm; $1) or take the mini-steam train through the grove of redwood trees (weekends, daily in summer 11am–5pm; $2), at the south end of the park. In the warm months, don't miss a dip in clean and soothing Lake Anza (lifeguard on duty May–Oct daily 11am–6pm; $3.50), rare among Bay Area lakes in that swimming is permitted. Another attraction is the beautifully landscaped Botanical Garden (daily 8.30am–5pm; free), which features a number of carefully crafted biospheres from temperate rain forest to high desert. To reach Tilden, head southeast from campus on either Claremont Avenue (passing the *Claremont Hotel*) or Grizzly Peak Boulevard (follow the signs from Euclid Ave). Both routes snake 1600ft to the crest of the Berkeley hills, providing stunning views and myriad hiking trails. It can also be reached on weekends only by AC Transit bus #67.

West Berkeley and the waterfront

From downtown Berkeley and the UC campus, **University Avenue** runs downhill toward the Bay, lined by increasingly shabby motels and massage parlors. The liveliest part of this **WEST BERKELEY** area is around the intersection of University and San Pablo avenues – the pre-freeway main highway north – where a community of recent immigrants from India and Pakistan have set up stores and restaurants that serve some delicious curries, a rarity in the Bay Area.

Between San Pablo Avenue and the Bay, you'll find the oldest part of Berkeley and a handful of hundred-year-old houses and churches, such as the

One place you shouldn't miss in West Berkeley is the **Takara Sake Tasting Room**, just off Fourth Street south of University Avenue at 708 Addison St (daily noon–6pm; free; ☎510/540-8250, ⓦwww.takarasake.com). Owned and operated by one of Japan's largest producers, this plant is responsible for more than a third of all sake drunk in the US. You can sample any of the dozen or so varieties of California-strain sake (brewed from Californian rice), both warm and chilled. Before tasting, you are ushered into the small museum and then sat down to watch a twelve-minute video presentation of the art of sake brewing.

two white-spired Gothic Revival Church structures on Hearst Avenue; these survive from the time when this district was a separate city, known as Ocean View. The neighborhood also holds remnants of Berkeley's industrial past, and many of the old warehouses and factory premises have been converted into living and working spaces for artists, craftspeople, and computer-software companies. The newly polished and gentrified stretch of **Fourth Street** between Gilman and University features upscale furniture outlets and quaint gourmet delis, as well as some outstanding restaurants. An odd toss-in to this area is **Berkeley Steamworks**, 2107 Fourth St (☎510/845-8992), the only Bay Area bathhouse that remained open during the AIDS crisis and still boasting private rooms, unlike San Francisco's sex clubs.

At the western edge of Berkeley, I-80 and the still-used rail tracks that run alongside it pretty well manage to cut the town off from its **waterfront**. If you're determined, the best way to get there is to take AC Transit bus #51, which runs regularly down University Avenue. The main attraction here is the **Berkeley Marina**, once a major hub for the transbay ferry services, and now one of the prime spots on the Bay for leisure activities, especially windsurfing and kayaking. There's a very long pier you can walk out on, where you can chat with the local fishermen and suck in the fresh salty air while getting a great view of San Francisco and its two bridges. People also stretch their own and their dogs' legs in the green confines of **Cesar Chavez Park**, north of the marina.

Eating

With some of the best restaurants in the state, Berkeley is the unofficial home of **California cuisine** and an upmarket diner's paradise. But, it's also a college town, and as such you can eat cheaply and well here, too, especially downtown and around the southern end of the campus, in the environs of Telegraph Avenue.

Diners and delis

Barney's 1591 Solano Ave, North Berkeley ☎510/526-8185. The East Bay's most popular burgers – including meatless ones – smothered in dozens of different toppings.

Bette's Ocean View Diner 1807 Fourth St, West Berkeley ☎510/644-3932. Named after the neighborhood, not the vista, but serving up some of the Bay Area's best breakfasts and lunches. Very popular on weekends, when you may have to wait an hour for a table, so come during the week if possible.

Brennan's 720 University Ave at Fourth St, West Berkeley ☎510/841-0960. Great downhome self-service meals like roast beef and mash. Also a solidly blue-collar hangout that's a great place for drinking inexpensive beers and watching sport TV, including European soccer.

Homemade Café 2454 Sacramento St, Berkeley ☎510/845-1940. Nontraditional, inexpensive

California-style Mexican and Jewish food served for breakfast and lunch, at shared tables when crowded.

Rick & Ann's 2922 Domingo Ave, South Berkeley ☎510/649-8538. Even in Berkeley sometimes folks want meatloaf and mashed potatoes instead of arugula, and as proof, the crowds line up outside this neighborhood diner every weekend.

Saul's Deli 1475 Shattuck Ave, North Berkeley ☎510/848-3354. For pastrami, corned beef, *kreplach*, or *knishes*, this is the place. Great sandwiches and picnic fixings to take away, plus a full range of sit-down evening meals.

Top Dog 2534 Durant Ave, Berkeley ☎510/843-7450. The competition isn't exactly stiff, but when locals and starving college kids get a craving for the all-American treat, this dog always has its day.

American and California cuisine

Café Rouge 1782 Fourth St, West Berkeley ☎510/525-1440. Specializing in delicately prepared organic meats; it has its own butcher shop. Also serves vegetarian pasta dishes for the less carnivorous.

🏃 **Chez Panisse** 1517 Shattuck Ave, North Berkeley ☎510/548-5525. The California restaurant to which all others are compared; chef Alice Waters is widely credited with first inventing California cuisine, with delights like Monterey Bay sardine toast with arugula and fennel, or Sonoma County duck with roasted butternut squash, beets, and *tatsoi*, plus wine. The set menu starts at $50 per head on Mon, rising to $85 at weekends, not including drinks.

Fatapple's 1346 Martin Luther King Jr Way, North Berkeley ☎510/526-2260. Crowded but pleasant family-oriented restaurant with excellent cheap American breakfasts and an assortment of sandwiches and burgers for lunch or dinner.

Lalime's 1329 Gilman St, North Berkeley ☎510/527-9838. A culinary dissertation on irony, as rich leftist Berkeley professors chow down on veal, pâté de foie gras, and other distinctly un-PC fare, in a casual setting. Expect to pay at least $40 per head.

Rivoli 1539 Solano Ave, North Berkeley ☎510/526-2542. Delivering all that is wonderful about Berkeley dining: first-rate fresh food based on Italian and French cuisine, courteous service, and a casual,

friendly atmosphere. All followed by a steepish bill, with entrees around $20.

Spenger's 1919 Fourth St, West Berkeley ☎510/845-7771. With a spacious sit-down restaurant and cheap take-out counter, this is a local institution. As one of the largest chains in the Bay Area, *Spenger's* serves up literally tons of seafood to thousands of customers daily.

Asian, African, and Indian

Ajanta 1888 Solano Ave, North Berkeley ☎510/526-4373. The chef rotates dishes from different regions of India every month, such as duck curry Kerala or Kashmiri *dhanwala murg*. Slightly pricey.

Blue Nile 2525 Telegraph Ave, Berkeley ☎510/540-6777. Filling Ethiopian food, with an adequate range of meat and vegetarian choices all around $10, served with a smile amidst cozy African decor.

Breads of India 2448 Sacramento St, Berkeley ☎510/848-7648. This gourmet curry house turns out delicious fresh daily specials for under $10.

Cha Am 1543 Shattuck Ave, North Berkeley ☎510/848-9664. Climb the stairs up to this small and popular restaurant for deliciously spicy Thai food at moderate prices.

🏃 **Kirala** 2100 Ward St, Berkeley ☎510/549-3486. Many argue that *Kirala* serves the best sushi in the Bay Area. Others claim that it's the best in the world. Moderate pricing, too – expect to pay around $20 to get your fill.

Liu's Kitchen 1593 Solano Ave, North Berkeley ☎510/525-8766. Huge helpings of tasty Chinese fare at very reasonable prices – the pot stickers are a meal in themselves.

Long Life Vegi House 2129 University Ave, Berkeley ☎510/845-6072. Cheap vegetarian cooking (no surprises there) that's perpetually popular with Cal students, although the dishes' good value often exceeds their quality.

🏃 **O'Chame** 1830 Fourth St, West Berkeley ☎510/841-8783. One of the very best Japanese restaurants in the US, with beautifully prepared sushi and sashimi, as well as a full range of authentic Japanese specialties. A treat, in the $15–25 range.

Steve's Barbeque Durant Center, 2521 Durant Ave, Berkeley ☎510/848-6166. Excellent, low-priced Korean food (the *kimchee* is superb); other cafés in the center sell Mexican food, healthy sandwiches, deep-fried doughnuts, and slices of pizza – not to mention bargain pitchers of beer.

Udupi Palace 1901 University Ave, Berkeley ☎510/843-6600. New and very authentic South Indian vegetarian restaurant, which serves ample *thalis*, *dosas*, *iddli*, and *uttapams* in a simple interior.

Vik's Chaat Corner 726 Allston Way at Fourth, West Berkeley ☎510/644-4412. A terrific lunchtime destination offering a wide array of Indian snacks – though you should expect long lines at weekends. The ambience is minimal, leaving nothing to distract you from the delights of *masala dosa* or *bhel puri*. The small portions and low prices only open more possibilities for experimentation.

French and Spanish

Britt-Marie's 1369 Solano Ave, Albany ☎510/527-1314. Along with a fine selection of mostly Californian wines by the glass, *Britt-Marie's* serves well-priced, French home cooking – plus outstanding chocolate cake.

César 1515 Shattuck Ave, North Berkeley ☎510/883-0222. Perpetually crowded tapas bar serving small dishes overflowing with taste. Loosely affiliated with *Chez Panisse*, its combination of quality and a relaxed atmosphere has made this a cultish destination for locals. Can get expensive rather quickly, however.

La Note 2377 Shattuck Ave, Berkeley ☎510/843-1535. The appropriately sunny, light cuisine of Provence such as *bouillabaise Marseillaise* (fish stew) isn't the only flavor you'll find in this petite dining room: students and teachers from the Jazzschool (sic) next door routinely stop in for casual jam sessions.

Italian

Cheese Board Pizza 1512 Shattuck Ave, North Berkeley ☎510/549-3055. Tiny storefront selling top-notch "designer pizza" at very reasonable prices: around $3 a slice, with a different topping every day. Worth searching out, but keeps irregular hours; usually Tues–Sat 11.30am–2pm & 4.30–7pm.

La Mediterranée 2936 College Ave, Berkeley ☎510/540-7773. Good Greek and Middle Eastern dishes, such as Levantine meat tart or various kebabs for $10 or less, served indoors or on the large patio.

LaVal's Pizza 1834 Euclid Ave, North Berkeley ☎510/843-5617. Great graduate student

hangout near the North Gate of campus. Pool table, wide-screen TV broadcasting sports, good selection of beers, and great pizza. Lunch specials a regular feature.

Trattoria La Siciliana 2993 College Ave, Berkeley ☎510/704-1474. Intimate, family-run Italian place with a wide range of antipasti, pastas, risotti, and specialities like stuffed beef roll for under $20.

Latin American and Caribbean

Cafe de la Paz 1600 Shattuck Ave, North Berkeley ☎510/843-0662. This primarily Brazilian eatery (try the *Xim Xim de pollo*) creates inexpensive and authentic enough versions of food from throughout South America, including fried pancakes from both Venezuela and Ecuador.

Cancun Taqueria 2134 Allston Way, Berkeley ☎510/549-0964. Popular, cheap, downtown burrito joint. Self-service but huge portions of tasty food in lively and colorful surroundings.

Juan's Place 941 Carleton St, West Berkeley ☎510/845-6904. The original Berkeley Mexican restaurant, with cheap, great food (in huge portions) and an interesting mix of people.

Mario's La Fiesta 2444 Telegraph Ave, Berkeley ☎510/540-9123. Always crowded with students and other budget-minded souls who flock here for the heaping portions of inexpensive Mexican food.

Picante Cucina Mexicana 1328 Sixth St, West Berkeley ☎510/525-3121. Fine and very reasonably priced tacos, plus live jazz on weekends. Nicely decorated with an outdoor patio for fine weather.

Specialty shops and markets

Acme Bread 1601 San Pablo Ave, West Berkeley ☎510/524-1327. Small bakery that supplies most of Berkeley's better restaurants; the house specialty is delicious sourdough baguettes.

Berkeley Bowl 2777 Shattuck Ave, Berkeley ☎510/841-6346. This converted bowling alley is now an enormous produce, bulk, and health-food market. It's the least expensive grocery in town, with the largest selection of fresh food.

Cheese Board 1504 Shattuck Ave, North Berkeley ☎510/549-3183. Collectively owned and operated since 1967, this was one of

the first outposts in Berkeley's Gourmet
Ghetto and is still going strong, offering over
two hundred varieties of cheese and a
range of delicious breads. Great pizzas a
few doors down, too (see p.313).
Epicurious Garden 1511 Shattuck Ave,
North Berkeley. This new indoor mall of
top-notch produce and takeout snacks
includes half a dozen independent outlets,

such as Alegio Chocolate (T510/548-2466)
and Picoso Mexican (T510/540-4811), as
well as a Japanese tea garden at the back.
**Monterey Foods 1550 Hopkins St, North
Berkeley** T510/526-6042. The main supplier
of exotic produce to Berkeley's gourmet
restaurants, this boisterous market also has
the highest-quality fresh fruit and vegetables
available.

Cafés and bars

One of the great joys in Berkeley is languishing in one of its many student **cafés**
or **coffeehouses**, eavesdropping on earnest political banter. Naturally enough,
the area's many **bars** are also frequented mostly by academics. For more
nightlife and musical venues see p.322.

Cafés and coffeehouses

Bacheeso's 2501 San Pablo Ave, West Berkeley
T510/644-2035. Imaginative breakfasts such
as egg with artichokes and more filling
snacks, as well as a full range of hot
beverages, all served with a smile in brightly
decorated surroundings.
**Brewed Awakenings 1807 Euclid Ave,
North Berkeley** T510/540-8865. Spacious
coffee- and tea-house near the North
Gate of campus frequented by professors
and grad students. Friendly staff,
plenty of seating, and lovely artwork on
the red-brick walls. Annually confirmed
as "Best Café to Study In" by the student
press.
Fanny 1603 San Pablo Ave, West Berkeley
T510/524-5447. Delicious and relatively
cheap breakfasts and lunches in a small and
unlikely space with sparse industrial decor.
Owned by Alice Waters, of *Chez Panisse*
fame.
Café Mediterraneum 2475 Telegraph Ave,
Berkeley T510/841-5634. Berkeley's oldest
café featuring sidewalk seating. Straight out
of the Beat archives: beards and berets
optional, battered paperbacks *de rigueur*.
Café Strada 2300 College Ave, Berkeley
T510/843-5282. Upmarket, open-air café
where art and architecture students cross
paths with would-be lawyers and chess
wizards.

Bars

**Albatross Pub 1822 San Pablo Ave, West
Berkeley** T510/843-2473. Popular student
super-bar, replete with darts, pool, board

games, and fireplace. Serves a large
selection of ales from around the world,
including a pretty good pint of Guinness.
Live jazz, flamenco, and blues music on
weekends. Cover free–$5.
Jupiter 2181 Shattuck Ave, Berkeley T510/843-
8277. Many types of lager, ale, and cider to
select from at this local favorite, which offers
wood-fired pizza and an outdoor beer
garden. There's a real buzz here, especially
for the loud disco nights or live jazz at
weekends.
**Pub (Schmidt's Tobacco & Trading Co)
1492 Solano Ave, North Berkeley**
T510/525-1900. Just past the official
Berkeley limit, this small, relaxed bar lures a
mixture of bookworms and game players
with a good selection of beers. It even gets
away with a semi-open smoking area out
back, perhaps because its other specialty is
selling the evil weed.
Pyramid Alehouse 901 Gilman St, Berkeley
T510/528-9880. Huge post-industrial space
makes a surprisingly casual spot to sip the
suds. Outdoor film screenings on weekend
nights during summer.
Raleigh's 2438 Telegraph Ave, Berkeley
T510/848-4827. Affable pub and grill with
a good range of beers on tap, recorded
indie music, and shuffleboard.
**Triple Rock Brewery 1920 Shattuck Ave,
Berkeley** T510/843-2739. Buzzing, all-
American microbrewery: the decor is
Edward Hopper-era retro, and the beers
(brewed on the premises) a bit fizzy unless
you ask for one of the fine cask-conditioned
ales. Great burgers too.

Beyond the urban East Bay

Compared to the urbanized bayfront cities of Oakland and Berkeley, the rest of the East Bay is sparsely populated, and places of interest are few and far between. The **area** up to the **Carquinez Strait**, which separates the East Bay from the North Bay, is home to some of the Bay Area's heaviest industry – oil refineries and chemical plants dominate the landscape – but there are also a few remarkably unchanged waterfront towns that merit a side-trip if you're passing by. Away from the Bay, the **inland valleys** are a whole other world of dry, rolling hills dominated by the towering peak of **Mount Diablo**. Dozens of tract-house developments have made commuter suburbs out of what were once cattle ranches and farms, but so far the region has been able to absorb the numbers and still feels rural, despite having doubled in population in the past twenty years.

The northern East Bay

North of Berkeley there's not a whole lot to see or do. Off the Eastshore Freeway in mostly mundane **Albany**, Golden Gate Fields has **horse racing** (see p.275) from October through June, and beyond it, the **Albany Mud Flats** are a fascinating place to stroll; impromptu works of art made from discarded materials vie with wild irises to attract the passerby's eye in this reclaimed landfill jutting out into the Bay. Back inland, San Pablo Avenue's strip of bars and clubs, including *Club Mallard* (no. 752, ☎510/524-8450) and *The Hotsy-Totsy* (no. 601, ☎510/524-1661), are some of the best in the East Bay – that is, if you're looking for authentic, gritty saloons featuring live rock'n'roll on weekends, well-stocked jukeboxes, and pool tables reminiscent of San Francisco's Mission district.

Barely a mile further north, the main contribution of **El Cerrito** to world culture was the band Creedence Clearwater Revival, who staged most of their *Born on the Bayou* publicity photographs in the wilds of Tilden Park in the hills above; El Cerrito is still home to one of the best record stores in California: Down Home Music, at 10341 San Pablo Ave (see p.324).

Depressing and rough **Richmond**, at the top of the Bay, was once a boom town, building ships during World War II at the Kaiser Shipyards, which employed 100,000 workers between 1940 and its closure in 1945. Now it's the proud home of the gigantic Standard Oil refinery, the center of which you drive through before crossing the **Richmond–San Rafael Bridge** ($4) to Marin County. About the only reason to stop in Richmond is that it marks the northern end of the BART line, and the adjacent Amtrak station is a better terminal for journeys to and from San Francisco than the end of the line in West Oakland. If you find yourself with time to fill, check out the **Richmond Museum of History** at 400 Nevin Ave (Wed–Sun 1–4pm; free; ☎510/235-7387, ⓦ www.richmondmuseumofhistory.org), which exhibits artifacts, photos, and antique items illustrating the history of Richmond during the first half of the twentieth century. Also worth a visit, **The National Institute of Art and Disabilities** at 551 23rd St (Mon–Fri 8.30am–4pm; free; ☎510/620-0290, ⓦ www.niadart.org) exhibits art created by artists with developmental and physical disabilities; view in an open studio and gallery space where the artists are often at work.

If you're heading from the East Bay to Marin County, **Point Richmond**, a cozy little town tucked away at the foot of the bridge between the refinery and the Bay, is worth a glance for its shoreline and its many Victorian houses – now mostly occupied by upwardly mobile professionals from San Francisco. Brickyard Landing is a redeveloped docklands with modern bayview condos, tennis courts, and a private yacht harbor built around disused brick kilns. The rest of the waterfront is taken up by the broad and usually deserted strand of **Keller Beach**, which stretches for half a mile along the sometimes windy shoreline. There are also a couple of popular weekend retreats, if you want **to stay** in the vicinity: the ⚓ *East Brother Light Station* at 117 Park Place (Thurs–Sun nights only; ☎510/233-2385, ⓦwww.ebls.org; $315) has a handful of rooms in a converted lighthouse, on an island in the straits linking the San Francisco and San Pablo bays, east of the bridge; prices include highly rated gourmet dinners (with wine), as well as breakfast. Alternatively, the recently refurbished 1907 *Hotel Mac*, 10 Cottage Ave (☎510/235-0010, ⓦwww.hotelmac.net; $100), boasts luxurious rooms at not unreasonable prices, given the location in the heart of town.

The Carquinez Strait

At the top of the Bay, some 25 miles north of Oakland, the land along the **CARQUINEZ STRAIT** is a bit off the beaten track, but it's an area of some natural beauty and much historic interest. The still-small towns along the waterfront seem worlds away from the bustle of the rest of the Bay Area, but how long they'll be able to resist the pressure of the expanding commuter belt is anybody's guess. AC Transit #74 runs every hour from Richmond BART north to **Crockett**, at the west end of the narrow straits. This tiny town, cut into the steep hillsides above the water, seems entirely dependent upon the massive C&H Sugar factory at its foot, whose giant neon sign lights up the town and the adjacent Carquinez Bridge ($4), the quickest link to Benicia, Vallejo, and Napa.

From Crockett, the narrow **Carquinez Strait Scenic Drive**, an excellent cycling route, heads east along the Sacramento River. A turn two miles along drops you down to **Port Costa**, a small town that lived off ferry traffic across the straits to Benicia until it lost its livelihood when the bridge was built at Crockett. It's still a nice enough place to watch the huge ships pass by on their way to and from the inland ports of Sacramento and Stockton. If you don't have a bike (or a car) you can enjoy the view from the window of the Amtrak trains running alongside the water from Oakland and Richmond, not stopping until Martinez, at the eastern end of the straits, two miles north of the John Muir house (see p.319).

The North Bay

On the north side of the Strait, I-80 cuts through the rolling hills and most vehicles speed along it en route to Sacramento. Tucked into the coastline to the east and hard to get to without a car, Benicia is well worth a detour if you do have a vehicle. Less appealing but easier to access by public transport, Vallejo lies just west of the freeway and is bisected by Hwy-29 to Napa.

Benicia

BENICIA is the most substantial of the historic waterfront towns, but one that has definitely seen better days. Founded in 1847, it initially rivaled San Francisco as the major Bay Area port and was even the state capital for a time; but despite Benicia's better weather and fine deep-water harbor, San Francisco eventually became the main transportation point for the fortunes of the Gold Rush, and the town very nearly faded away altogether. Examples of Benicia's efforts to become a major city stand poignantly around the very compact downtown area, most conspicuously the 1852 Greek Revival structure that was built as the **first State Capitol** but served this role for just thirteen months. The building has been restored as a museum (daily 10am–5pm; $2), furnished in the legislative style of the time, complete with top hats on the tables and shining spittoons every few feet.

Pick up a walking-tour map of Benicia's many intact Victorian houses and churches from the tourist office (see below) and follow it to the steeply pitched roofs and gingerbread eaves of the **Frisbie-Walsh House** at 235 East L St – a prefabricated Gothic Revival building that was shipped here in pieces from Boston in 1849 (an identical house was put up by General Vallejo as his residence in Sonoma; see p.380). Across City Hall's park, the arched ceiling beams of **St Paul's Episcopal Church** look like an upturned ship's hull; it was built by shipwrights from the Pacific Mail Steamship Company, one of Benicia's many successful nineteenth-century shipyards. Half a dozen former brothels and saloons stand in various stages of decay and restoration along First Street down near the waterfront, from where the world's largest train ferries used to ply the waters between Benicia and Port Costa until 1930. These days the only time this spot draws large crowds is during the annual **Fine Art, Wine, & Jazz Festival** on the last weekend of July, when a host of stalls fill the waterside lot and all sorts of artistic and musical events take place.

For well over a decade now, Benicia has attracted a number of artists and craftspeople; you can watch glass-blowers and furniture-makers at work in the **Benicia Glass Studios** at 675 East H St (Mon–Sat 10am–4pm, Sun in summer noon–5pm; free). Ceramic artist Judy Chicago and sculptor Robert Arneson are among those who have worked in the converted studios and modern light-industrial parks around the sprawling fortifications of the old **Benicia Arsenal** east of the downtown area, whose thickly walled sandstone buildings formed the main army storage facility for weapons and ammunition from 1851 up to and including the Korean War. One of the oddest parts of the complex is the **Camel Barn**, part of the **Benicia Historical Museum** (Wed–Sun 1–4pm; free; ☎707/745-5435, ⓦwww.beniciahistoricalmuseum.org). Occasional concerts are held on the premises these days, but the structure used to house camels that the army imported in 1856 to transport supplies across the deserts of the southwestern US. The experiment failed, and the camels were kept here until they were sold off in 1864.

Practicalities

Benicia's friendly **Chamber of Commerce**, 601 First St (Mon–Fri 8.30am–5pm, Sat & Sun 11am–3pm; ☎707/745-2120 or 1-866/455-2323, ⓦwww.beniciachamber.com), can supply a wealth of information on the area. If you choose **to stay** here, the *Union Hotel and Gardens* at 401 First St (☎707/746-0100, ⓦwww.unionhotelbenicia.com; $109) at one point a bordello, has since been converted into a comfortable bed and breakfast with twelve splendid rooms, all featuring jetted tubs. Among the best **restaurants**, *Captain Blythers*, 123 First St (☎707/745-4082), is a slightly expensive place for seafood with great views of the Bay, while *Sala Thai*, 807 First St (☎707/745-4331), offers moderately priced Thai food, just as delicious here as in any big city.

Vallejo and Six Flags Discovery Kingdom

Across the Carquinez Bridge from Crockett, the biggest and dullest of the North Bay towns, **VALLEJO** was, like Benicia, an early capital of California, though it now lacks any sign of its historical significance. In contrast to most of the other Gold Rush-era towns that line the Straits, Vallejo remained economically vital, largely because of the massive military presence here at the **Mare Island Naval Shipyard**, a sprawling, relentlessly gray complex in the center of town, right on Hwy-29, and covering an area twice the size of Golden Gate Park. Closed in 1997, its less than glamorous history – the yard built and maintained supply ships and submarines, not carriers or battleships – is recounted in the small **Vallejo Naval & Historical Museum** in the old city hall building at 734 Marin St (Tues–Sat 10am–4.30pm; $2; ⓦwww.vallejomuseum.org), where the highlight is a working periscope that looks out across the Bay.

The reason most people come to Vallejo, however, is **Six Flags Discovery Kingdom** (daily June–Aug, also Fri–Sun & school holidays mid–March to May and Sept to early Nov 10am–7pm or later; $39, with better deals online; Ⓣ707/643-6721, ⓦwww.sixflags.com), five miles north of Vallejo off I-80 at the Hwy-37 exit. Billing itself as the nation's only oceanarium, wildlife, and theme park, it offers a well-above-average range of performing sea lions, dolphins, and killer whales in approximations of their natural habitats, as well as land mammals, water-ski stunt shows and a range of rides, including the flying, floorless *Medusa*, on which your legs dangle as you zoom through loops at 65mph. What's more, the shark exhibit lets you walk through a transparent tunnel alongside twenty-foot-long great whites, and the tropical butterfly house is truly amazing. All told, it can be a fun day out, especially for children.

The most enjoyable way to get here from San Francisco is on the Blue & Gold Fleet **ferry** from Fisherman's Wharf, which takes an hour each way ($15 one-way, $27 day pass; Ⓣ415/705-8200, ⓦwww.blueandgoldfleet.com). You can also take BART, getting off at the El Cerrito Del Norte stop to catch the Vallejo BARTLink bus (Ⓣ707/648-4666) to the park.

The inland valleys

Most of the inland East Bay area is made up of rolling hills covered by grass-lands, which are slowly yielding to suburban housing developments and office complexes as more and more businesses abandon the pricey real estate of San Francisco. The great peak of **Mount Diablo** is surrounded by acres of campgrounds and hiking trails; other attractions include two historic homes that serve as memorials to their literate and influential former residents: John Muir and Eugene O'Neill.

BART tunnels from Oakland through the Berkeley Hills to the leafy-green stockbroker settlement of **Orinda**, continuing east through the increasingly hot and dry landscape to the end of the line at **Concord**, site of a controversial nuclear weapons depot. In the mid-1990s a peaceful, civilly disobedient blockade here ended with a protester Brian Wilson (not the Beach Boy) losing his legs under the wheels of a slow-moving munitions train. The event raised public awareness – before it happened few people knew of the depot's existence, and it earned Wilson a place in the Lawrence Ferlinghetti poem *A Buddha in the Woodpile* – but otherwise it's still business as usual.

Martinez and John Muir's house

From the Pleasant Hill BART station, one stop before the end of the line, Contra Costa County Connection buses leave every thirty minutes for **MARTINEZ**, the seat of county government and a major Amtrak depot, passing the **John Muir National Historic Site** at 4202 Alhambra Ave (Wed–Sun 10am–5pm; $3; ☎925/228-8860, ⊛www.nps.gov/jomu), just off Hwy-4 two miles south of Martinez. Muir, an articulate, persuasive Scot whose writings and political activism were of vital importance in the preservation of America's wilderness, spent much of his life exploring and writing about the majestic Sierra Nevada mountains, particularly Yosemite. He was also one of the founders of the **Sierra Club** – a wilderness lobby and education organization still active today. Anyone familiar with the image of this thin, bearded naturalist wandering the mountains with his knapsack and notebook might be surprised to see his very conventional, upper-class Victorian home, now restored to its appearance when Muir died in 1914. Built by Muir's father-in-law, only those parts of the house Muir added himself reflect much of the personality of the man, not least the massive, rustic fireplace he had built in the East Parlor so he could have a "real mountain campfire." The bulk of Muir's personal belongings and artifacts are displayed in his study on the upper floor, and in the adjacent room an exhibition documents the history of the Sierra Club and Muir's battles to protect America's wilderness.

The small cemetery holding **Muir's grave**, a pilgrimage site for conservationists, was acquired in 2000 by the National Park Service, which discourages visitors since the site is bordered by private property. Nonetheless, Muir's plot, tucked back in the pear orchard and not marked with a trail, draws hundreds each year, many led by a rule-bending park ranger. If you want to leave an offering or pay homage to the father of America's national park system, inquire at Muir's home.

Behind the bell-towered main house is a large, still productive orchard where Muir cultivated grapes, pears, and cherries to earn the money to finance his explorations (you can sample the fruits free of charge, pre-picked by staff gardeners). Beyond the orchard is the 1849 **Martinez Adobe**, homestead of the original Spanish land-grant settlers and now a small **museum** (included in entry to Muir House) of Mexican colonial culture. The contrast between Mexican and American cultures in early California is fascinating and, as a bonus, the building's two-foot-thick walls keep it refreshingly cool on a typically hot summer day.

Eugene O'Neill's house and Mount Diablo

At the foot of Mount Diablo, fifteen miles south, playwright **Eugene O'Neill** used the money he got for winning the Nobel Prize for Literature in 1936 to build a home and sanctuary for himself, which he named **Tao House**. It was here, before he was struck down with Parkinson's disease in 1944, that he wrote many of his best-known plays: *The Iceman Cometh*, *A Moon for the Misbegotten*, and *Long Day's Journey into Night*. Readings and performances of his works are sometimes given in the house, which is open to visitors, though you must reserve a place on one of the **tours** (Wed–Sun 10am & 12.30pm; free; ☎925/838-0249, ⊛www.nps.gov/euon). Inside, O'Neill's study is slowly being restored to its original condition; the effort involves a nationwide search for the Chinese furniture he purchased during the home's construction. There's no parking on site, so the tours pick you up in the tiny town of **Danville**, off I-680 south of Walnut Creek and north of Dublin and San Ramon, home of the

▲ Cyclist on Mount Diablo

Blackhawk Automotive Museum, 3700 Blackhawk Plaza Circle (Wed–Sun 10am–5pm; $8; ☎925/736-2277, Ⓦwww.blackhawkmuseum.org), an impressive collection of classic and antique cars from Britain, Germany, Italy, and the US from 1920 to 1960, and artwork inspired by them. The nearby shops of Blackhawk Plaza are frequented by the richest of the East Bay's rich.

Majestic **MOUNT DIABLO** itself rises up from rolling ranchlands to a height of nearly four thousand feet, its summit and flanks preserved within **Mount Diablo State Park** (daily 8am–sunset; parking $6). North Gate Road, the main route through the park, reaches to within three hundred feet of the top, its terminus a popular place to enjoy the marvelous view: on a clear day you can see over two hundred miles in every direction. Three campgrounds with running water and restrooms are open here year-round for RVs and tents (☎510/837-2525; book through ReserveAmerica ☎1-800/444-7275, Ⓦwww.reserveamerica.com; $20). To reach the park, you'll need a car or the ability to cycle a long way uphill, though the Sierra Club sometimes organizes day trips: for details, check with the park's interpretive center at the summit (Wed–Sun, March–Oct 11am–5pm, Nov–Feb 11am–4pm; ☎925/837-2525, Ⓦwww.mdia.org).

Two main entrances lead into the park, both well marked off I-680. The one from the southwest by way of Danville passes by the **ranger station**, where you can pick up a trail map ($5) listing the best **day hikes**. The other runs from the northwest by way of Walnut Creek, and the routes join together five miles from the summit. March and April, when the wildflowers are blooming, are the best months to come, and since mornings are ideal for getting the clearest view, you should drive to the top first and then head back down to a trailhead for a hike, or to one of the many picnic spots for a leisurely lunch. Keep in mind that in summer it can get desperately hot and dry, and parts of the park are closed because of fire danger.

Livermore and Altamont

Fifteen miles southeast of Mount Diablo on I-580 out of the Bay Area, or via WHEELS #12X from the Dublin/Pleasanton BART, the rolling hills around sleepy **LIVERMORE** are covered with thousands of shining, spinning, high-tech **windmills**, placed here by a private power company to take advantage of the nearly constant winds. It's the largest wind farm in the world, and you'll probably have seen it used in a number of TV ads as a space-age backdrop to hype flashy new cars or sexy perfumes. Though the federal government provides no funding for this nonpolluting, renewable source of energy, it does spend billions of dollars every year designing and building nuclear weapons and other, less sinister applications of modern technology at the nearby **Lawrence Livermore Laboratories**, where much of the research and development of the nuclear arsenal takes place. Reassuringly, none of the weapons themselves is actually stored here. The small **Discovery Center** (Tues–Fri 1–4pm, Sat 10am–2pm; free; ☎925/423-3272, ⓦwww.llnl.gov) two miles south of I-580 on Greenville Road holds hands-on exhibits showing off various scientific phenomena and devices.

Up and over the hills to the east near the town of Tracy, before I-580 joins I-5 for the four-hundred-mile route south through the Central Valley to Los Angeles, stands the still-functioning **Altamont Speedway**, officially known as the Altamont Raceway Park, site of the nightmarish Rolling Stones concert in December 1969 (see box below). Needless to say, no historical plaque marks the site, yet if you wish to make the pilgrimage, the easiest way is by taking the Grant Line Road exit from I-580, then turning right after a mile or so onto Midway Road and continuing for a further mile and a half, crossing back over the freeway in the process.

Nemesis at Altamont

Uncannily timed in the dying embers of the 1960s and often referred to as "the nemesis of the Woodstock generation," the concert headlined by the **Rolling Stones** at the **Altamont Speedway** on December 6, 1969 ended in total disaster. The free event had been intended to be a sort of second Woodstock, staged in order to counter allegations that the Stones had ripped off their fans during a long US tour. The band, however, inadvisedly hired a chapter of **Hell's Angels** instead of professional security to maintain order, and the result, predictably enough, was chaos. Three people ended up dead, one kicked and stabbed to death by the Hell's Angels themselves.

The whole sorry tale was remarkably captured on film by brothers David and Albert Maysles (plus co-director Charlotte Zwerin) in their documentary **Gimme Shelter**, released the following year. The footage of the concert clearly shows the deteriorating mood and atmosphere of growing menace in the crowd, exemplified by the scene when **Jefferson Airplane** vocalist Marty Balin jumped down into the crowd to break up a fight, an intervention which earned him a broken jaw. By the time the Stones came on stage matters were blatantly out of hand and after several interruptions and pleas for sanity by Mick Jagger, all hell broke loose during, ironically, *Sympathy for the Devil*. The glint of the knife is plainly seen just before the fatal stabbing, which actually takes place after the following number, *Under My Thumb*. Perhaps even more poignant is the numb look on the faces of Jagger, Richards, and company as they watch the evil deed over and over again in the studio during filming.

East Bay listings

This section summarizes the best the East Bay has to offer in the way of nightlife, musical and theatrical performances, shops, and galleries. Listings for accommodation, eating, and drinking are given in the preceding text separately for Oakland and Berkeley. Details concerning sports and leisure pursuits for the entire Bay Area can be found in Chapter 14.

Nightlife

Nightlife is where the East Bay really comes into its own. Even more than in San Francisco, dancing to canned music and paying high prices for flashy decor is not the thing to do, which means that discos are virtually nonexistent here. Instead there are dozens of **live music** venues, covering a range of musical tastes and styles – from small, unpretentious jazz clubs to buzzing R'n'B venues – in which Oakland's hotspots are unsurpassed. Berkeley's clubs tend more toward folk and world music, with occasional bouts of hardcore thrash, and, in truly democratic fashion, the open-mic scene is thriving. The university itself holds two of the best medium-sized venues in the entire Bay Area, both of which attract touring big-name stars. **Tickets** for most venues are available at their box office or, for a small service charge, through Tickets.com (℡510/762-2277, ⓦwww.tickets.com) or similar agents.

The East Bay **theater** scene isn't exactly thriving, and shows tend to be politically laudable rather than dramatically innovative. By contrast, the range of **films** is first class, with over a dozen movie theaters showing new releases, and Berkeley's revamped Pacific Film Archive, one of the world's finest film libraries, fills its screens with obscure but brilliant art flicks. Check either of the following weekly papers that are issued free every Wednesday for details of who and what's on: the *East Bay Express* (ⓦwww.eastbayexpress.com) or the *SF Weekly* (ⓦwww.sfweekly.com).

Large performance venues

Berkeley Community Theater 1930 Allston Way, Berkeley ℡510/845-2308. Jimi Hendrix played here, and the 3500-seat theater still hosts major rock concerts and community events. Tickets through major agents.

Center for Contemporary Music Mills College, 5000 MacArthur Blvd, North Oakland ℡510/430-2191, ⓦwww.mills.edu. One of the prime centers in the world for experimental music.

Oakland Coliseum Complex at Coliseum BART, near the airport ℡510/639-7700, ⓦwww.coliseum.com. Mostly stadium shows, inside the 18,000-seat arena or outdoors in the adjacent 55,000-seat coliseum. Used to be one of the Grateful Dead's favorite venues.

Paramount Theatre 2025 Broadway, downtown Oakland ℡510/465-6400, ⓦwww.paramount theatre.com. Beautifully restored Art Deco masterpiece, hosting classical concerts, big-name crooners, ballets, operas, and a growing roster of rap and rock shows.

Ticket office Tues–Sat noon–5pm; tickets $20–85. Some nights they play old Hollywood classics for $8.

Zellerbach Hall/Greek Theatre on the UC Berkeley campus ℡510/642-9988, ⓦwww.calperfs.berkeley.edu. Two of the prime spots for catching touring big names in the Bay Area. Zellerbach regularly showcases classical music and dance, while the outdoor Greek welcomes occasional pop and rock acts. Tickets $20–100.

Live music venues

924 Gilman 924 Gilman St, West Berkeley ℡510/525-9926, ⓦwww.924gilman.org. On the outer edge of the hardcore punk scene in a bare, squat-like warehouse. Weekends only; cover $5–10.

Ashkenaz 1317 San Pablo Ave, West Berkeley ℡510/525-5054, ⓦwww.ashkenaz.com. World music and dance café. Acts range from modern Afro-beat to the best of the Balkans. Kids and under-21s welcome. Cover $10–15.

Blakes on Telegraph 2367 Telegraph Ave, Berkeley ☎510/848-0886, ⓦblakeson telegraph.com. Student-patronized saloon with a funky roster of live music most nights of the week and DJs the rest. Latin, funk, soul, hip-hop, roots, rock, reggae, blues, and more. Cover $3–12.

Freight and Salvage 2020 Addison St, West Berkeley ☎510/548-1761, ⓦwww .freightandsalvage.org. Singer-songwriters in a coffeehouse setting. Cover mostly under $20, open-mic nights only $5.

Kimball's Carnival 215 Washington St, Downtown Oakland ☎510/658-2555, ⓦwww .kimballs.com. Black and Latin crossover vibes, either live or with DJs or karaoke. Cover free to $30.

La Peña Cultural Center 3105 Shattuck Ave, Berkeley near Ashby BART ☎510/849-2568, ⓦwww.lapena.org. More folk than rock, along with some Latin music, often politically charged – the website encourages cultural activism for social change. $8–20.

Maiko Dance Club 1629 San Pablo Ave, West Berkeley ☎510/527-8226. Salsa and ballroom dance set to a live band. Very chic. Lessons available for around $20. Performances $10–20.

Mile High Club 3629 Martin Luther King Jr Way, North Oakland ☎510/654-4549, ⓦwww .oaklandmilehigh.com. The best of the Bay Area blues clubs. Waitresses balance pitchers of beer on their heads to facilitate a safer passage through the rocking crowds. Cover $8–20.

Starry Plough 3101 Shattuck Ave, Berkeley near Ashby BART ☎510/841-2082, ⓦwww .starryploughpub.com. Music veers all over the map, from noisy punk to country and traditional Irish folk, and the crowd is just as varied. Open-mic on Wednesdays. Doubles as a friendly saloon and restaurant in the afternoon and early evening. Cover free to $8.

Stork Club 2330 Telegraph Ave, North Oakland ☎510/848-0886, ⓦwww.storkcluboakland.com. Boasting a loud sound system, this place cranks up the volume for its mainly punk, hardcore, and metal bands. Cover usually $5.

Yoshi's World Class Jazz House 510 Embarcadero West, Oakland ☎510/238-9200, ⓦwww.yoshis.com. The West Coast's premier jazz club, located near Jack London Square, attracts a world-class roster of performers nightly. The place is almost always full. Cover $10–50.

Cinemas

Act One and Act Two 2128 Center St, Berkeley ☎510/548-7200. Foreign films and non-mainstream American options are played in these downtown movie halls.

Grand Lake Movie Theater 3200 Grand Ave, Oakland ☎510/452-3556. The grand dame of East Bay picture palaces, right on Lake Merritt, showing the best of the current major releases, with a special emphasis on politically alternative works.

Oaks Theater 1875 Solano Ave, Albany ☎510/526-1836. A mixture of mainstream and political films are shown at this cozy, renovated Art Deco cinema, built in 1925.

Pacific Film Archive 2575 Bancroft at Bowditch, Berkeley ☎510/642-5249, ⓦwww.bampfa .berkeley.edu. The archive's splendid new digs plays the West Coast's best selection of cinema. Classic, third world, and experimental films played nightly, plus revivals of otherwise forgotten favorites. Two films a night; tickets $8, $4 additional feature.

UC Theatre 2036 University Ave, Berkeley ☎510/843-3456. Popular revival house, with a huge auditorium and a daily double feature featuring funky theme-weeks of *noir*, melodrama, and other genres. Tickets $5 matinee, $7 thereafter.

Theater

Berkeley Repertory Theater 2025 Addison St, Berkeley ☎510/845-4700, ⓦwww.berkeleyrep .org. One of the West Coast's most highly respected theater companies, presenting updated classics and contemporary plays in an intimate modern theater. Tickets $40–60; fifty-percent discounts for students and under-30s with advance booking.

Black Repertory Group 3201 Adeline St, Berkeley ☎510/652-2120, ⓦwww. black repertorygroup.com. After initial struggles, this politically conscious company has been encouraging new talent with great success. Tickets $15–30.

California Shakespeare Festival Siesta Valley, Orinda ☎510/548-3422, ⓦwww.calshakes.org. This annual, summer-long festival has a gorgeous open-air home in the wooded East Bay Hills. Tickets $30–60.

Julia Morgan Center for the Arts 2640 College Ave, Berkeley ☎510/845-8542, ⓦwww .juliamorgan.org. A variety of touring shows stop off in this cunningly converted old church. Tickets $10–30.

Shops and galleries

Though it does not offer anything like the variety in **shopping** or chic designer outlets to be found in San Francisco, the East Bay has its fair share of places to indulge your consumer habit. Berkeley is particularly strong on bookshops, eclectic music emporia, and secondhand stores. Likewise, the top **galleries** are located across the Bay, but a handful of notable arthouses are listed here.

Books and comics

For Berkeley bookstores, see box on p.308.

Diesel 5433 College Ave, Rockridge ☎510/653-9965. Dependable selection of both fiction and non-fiction, along with the occasional poetry reading.

Pegasus & Pendragon Books & Music 5560 College Ave, Rockridge ☎510/652-6259. College-oriented new and used books, with an emphasis on the fantastic and mysterious.

Walden Pond Books 3316 Grand Ave, Oakland ☎510/832-4438. Large used and new bookstore carries the best selection of international fiction around at reasonable prices.

Music

Amoeba Records 2455 Telegraph Ave, Berkeley ☎510/549-1125. Berkeley's renowned emporium is one of the largest used-music retailers in America. Stocked to the gills with hard-to-find releases, both new and used, on vinyl and CD.

Disc Kabob 1607 Solano Ave, North Berkeley ☎510/526-6997. Wide selection of bootleg CDs and rare vinyl from the 1960s to the present day – but at a price.

Down Home Music 10341 San Pablo Ave, El Cerrito ☎510/525-2129. As you might guess from the name, Down Home stocks an excellent selection of folk, blues, and bluegrass, making it well worth the trek across to the East Bay. One of the best record stores of its kind in the US.

Hear Music 1809 Fourth St, Berkeley ☎510/204-9595. Like the San Francisco location, Hear boasts an extensive selection of jazz, Celtic, and international artists.

Mod Lang 2136 University Ave, Berkeley ☎510/486-1850; mail order ☎510/486-1880. Knowledgeable staff will inform and sell you a whole range of indie and progressive CDs and vinyl.

Rasputin's 2350 Telegraph Ave, Berkeley ☎510/848-9004. Good for jazz, rock, and ethnic recordings; it's open late – until 11pm – too.

Clothes and accessories

Jil Cappuccio 3026 Ashby Ave, Berkeley near Ashby BART ☎510/549-9316. One-of-a-kind designs, including popular men's shirts patched together from mismatched cloth found at garage sales.

Molly B 2112A Vine St ☎510/843-1586, also at 1811 Fourth St, Berkeley ☎510/548-3103. Eclectic designer frocks for gals with dough.

Nordstrom Rack 1285 Marina Blvd, San Leandro ☎510/614-1742. After merchandise has been in the San Francisco store for three months, it's sold at a fifty percent discount here.

The Walk Shop 2120 Vine St, Berkeley ☎510/849-3628. Down-to-earth but still stylish shoes that feel good to walk in.

Secondhand clothes and thrift stores

Berkeley Flea Market Ashby BART Station, corner of Ashby Ave and Martin Luther King Jr Way, Berkeley ☎510/644-0744. Parking lot is open on weekends for independent vendors to sell secondhand clothes and furniture.

Buffalo Exchange 3333 Lakeshore Ave, Oakland ☎510/452-4464, also at 2512 Telegraph Ave, Berkeley ☎510/644-9202. Part of the second-hand clothing chain, the Oakland branch is the dumping ground for residents of the upscale Piedmont community. High-class treasures aplenty. The Telegraph Ave store has last year's castoffs from the college crowd, current fashions, and classic Levi's.

Carousel Consignment 1955 Shattuck Ave, Berkeley ☎510/845-9044. Classy women's contemporary clothing and accessories.

Crossroads Trading Company 5636 College Ave, Oakland ☎510/420-1952. Secondhand clothing of high quality, but more casual wear than vintage apparel. Styles for men and women.

Jeremy's 2967 College Ave, Berkeley ☎510/849-0701. Casual wear, designer samples, and end-of-the-year castoffs.

Salvation Army Thrift Store 1382 Solano Ave, Albany ☎510/524-5100. Low-priced clothes, shoes, and furnishings from gunk to great.

Sharks 2505 Telegraph Ave, Berkeley ☎510/841-8736. Great prices on retro Americana. Dress up as the young Frank Sinatra or as his date.

Slash Clothing 2840 College Ave, Berkeley ☎510/841-7803. There's barely room to walk in this tiny, non-trendy basement with secondhand Levi's piled from floor to ceiling.

Health and beauty care

Body Time 2911 College Ave, Berkeley ☎510/845-2101. Natural scents, lotions, soaps, and hair-product collection. Other outlets on Shattuck Ave.

Whole Foods Market 3000 Telegraph Ave, Berkeley ☎510/649-1333. For the alternative-remedy addict, an excellent selection of homeopathic herbs and medicinal products in an upscale natural-foods supermarket.

Wines and spirits

Beverages & More 836 San Pablo Ave, Albany ☎510/525-9582, also at Jack London Square, Oakland ☎510/208-5126. Huge selection of wines, craft brews, and spirits; also cigars and party nibbles.

Paul Marcus Wines 5655 College Ave, Oakland ☎510/420-1005. Located in trendy Market Hall, where employees are used to matching patron's gourmet groceries with appropriately sophisticated selections.

Takara Sake USA 708 Addison St, Berkeley ☎510/540-8250. The producers of ShoChiku Bai sake give free tastings in an intimate bar, from noon to 6pm. See box, p.311.

Trader Joe's 5700 Christie Ave in Powell St Plaza, Emeryville ☎510/658-8091. This popular grocery store has the widest range of affordable wines – many of them imports – in the Bay Area.

Vino! 6319 College Ave, Oakland ☎510/652-6317. Small Bay Area chain works at

stocking rare but affordable (under $10) selections. Very knowledgeable, friendly staff.

Vintage Berkeley 2113 Vine St, North Berkeley ☎510/665-8600. Excellent outlet for quality domestic and imported wines, mostly under $20, housed in a cute old pump station. The highly knowledgeable staff will match a wine with any meal.

Specialty stores

The Bone Room 1569 Solano Ave, Berkeley ☎510/526-5252. Animal and human bones, skulls, preserved insects, and what-not, for the natural historian or just the curiosity-seeker.

East Bay Vivarium 1827-C Fifth St, Berkeley ☎510/841-1400. The largest collection of living reptiles for sale under one roof in the region. Even if you're not in the market, there's no harm in looking.

Narain's 1320 San Pablo Ave, Berkeley ☎510/527-2509. Custom sewing and outdoor-gear repair shop, also with a good line in travel pouches.

Art galleries

ACCI 1652 Shattuck Ave, Berkeley ☎530/843-2527. An arts-and-crafts co-operative designed to exhibit and sell the work of local artists.

Arts Benicia Gallery 991 Tyler St, Benicia ☎707/747-0131. A good base for exploring for the Benicia arts scene, the gallery presents workshops, poetry readings, and a changing series of exhibitions Fri–Sun noon–4pm. The first weekend in May, Arts Benicia hosts open studios all over town.

Pro Arts 461 Ninth St, Oakland ☎510/763-4361. Changing exhibitions, concentrating on local artists and community issues, six times a year in this bright, modern space. Worth a look, and a good resource for the East Bay art scene.

The Peninsula

The city of San Francisco sits at the tip of a five-mile-wide neck of land commonly referred to as the **Peninsula**. Home of old money and new technology, the Peninsula stretches for fifty miles of relentless suburbia south from San Francisco along the Bay, past wealthy enclaves such as Hillsborough and Atherton, winding up in the futuristic roadside landscape of the **"Silicon Valley"** near **San Jose**, still the fastest-growing city in California and now the tenth largest in the US.

There was a time when the region was largely agricultural, but the computer boom – spurred by Stanford University in **Palo Alto** – has replaced orange groves and fig trees with office complexes and parking lots. Surprisingly, however, most of the land along the **coast** – separated from the bayfront sprawl by an attractive ridge of redwood-covered peaks – remains rural and undeveloped; it also contains some excellent **beaches** and a couple of affably down-to-earth communities, all well served by public transportation.

Getting around

BART only travels down the Peninsula as far as Daly City, from where you can catch SamTrans **buses** (℡1-800/660-4287, ⒲www.samtrans.com) south to Palo Alto or along the coast to Half Moon Bay. For longer distances, **CalTrain** (℡650/817-1717 or 1-800/660-4287, ⒲www.caltrain.com) offers an hourly rail service from its terminal at Fourth and Townsend streets in Downtown San Francisco, stopping at most bayside towns between the city and Gilroy ($2.25–11) via San Jose ($7.50), and Greyhound runs regular buses along US-101 to and from its San Jose terminal at 70 S Almaden Ave, on the corner of Santa Clara Street. Finally, Santa Clara Valley Transit Authority (VTA) ($1.75, day pass $5.25; ℡408/321-2300, ⒲www.vta.org) runs buses and modern trolleys around metropolitan San Jose.

Most major domestic airlines fly direct into **Norman J. Mineta San Jose International Airport** (℡408/501-7600, ⒲www.sjc.org), close to downtown San Jose; the VTA SJC Airport Flyer bus runs to downtown and Santa Clara for $3.50 and there is the usual choice of taxis, limos, and shuttles for fancier rides.

South along the Bay

US-101 runs south from San Francisco along the Bay, lined by light-industrial estates and shopping malls, to San Jose. The first worthwhile stop, only a couple of miles south of the airport in **Burlingame**, is the **Pez Museum** (Tues–Sat

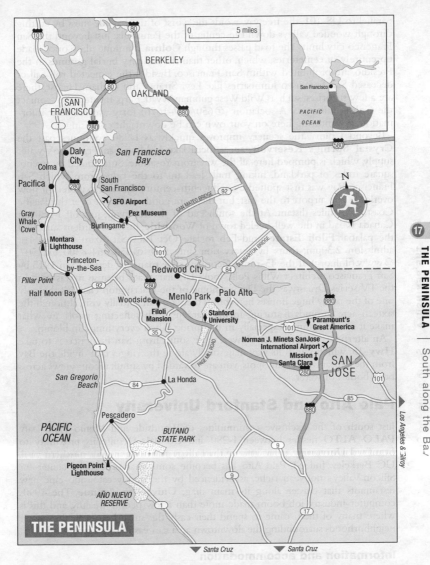

BERKELEY

OAKLAND

SAN FRANCISCO

San Francisco Bay

San Francisco

PACIFIC OCEAN

Daly City

Colma

Pacifica

South San Francisco

SFO Airport

Pez Museum

Burlingame

San Mateo Bridge

Gray Whale Cove

Montara Lighthouse

Princeton-by-the-Sea

Pillar Point

Half Moon Bay

Redwood City

Woodside

Menlo Park

Palo Alto

Filoli Mansion

Stanford University

Dumbarton Bridge

Paramount's Great America

Norman J. Mineta San Jose International Airport

Mission Santa Clara

SAN JOSE

Page Mill Road

San Gregorio Beach

La Honda

PACIFIC OCEAN

Pescadero

Butano State Park

Pigeon Point Lighthouse

AÑO NUEVO RESERVE

THE PENINSULA

▼ Santa Cruz   ▼ Santa Cruz

10am–6pm; $3; ☎650/347-2301, ⓦwww.burlingamepezmuseum.com), 214 California Drive, home to all 600 or so Pez dispensers in existence, as well as other rare toys and games. The educational **Coyote Point Museum** (Tues–Sat 10am–5pm, Sun noon–5pm; $6; ☎650/342-7755, ⓦwww.coyoteptmuseum.org) is located in the large bayside Coyote Point Park ($5 per vehicle) several miles further south, off Poplar Avenue, **San Mateo**. Here examples of the natural life of the San Francisco Bay – from tidal insects to birds of prey – are exhibited in engaging displays, enhanced by interactive computers and documentary films.

Six-lane freeways don't usually qualify as a scenic route, but an exception is **I-280**, one of the newer and more expensive freeways in California. Running parallel to US-101, the freeway avoids the worst of the bayside mess by cutting through wooded valleys down the center of the Peninsula. Just beyond the San Francisco city limits, the road passes through **Colma**, a unique place once made up entirely of cemeteries, which, other than the military burial grounds in the Presidio, are prohibited within San Francisco. Besides the expected roll call of deceased San Francisco luminaries like Levi Strauss and William Hearst, there are a few surprises, such as Wild West gunman Wyatt Earp. If interested, contact the Colma Historical Association (℡650/757-1676) for graveyard tour information, as venturing out on your own can be downright confusing.

Beyond Colma, the scenery improves quickly as I-280 continues past the **Crystal Springs Reservoir**, an artificial lake holding San Francisco's water supply, which is pumped here all the way from Yosemite. Surrounded by twenty square miles of parkland, hiking trails lead up to the ridge from which San Francisco Bay was first spotted by eighteenth-century Spanish explorers; it now overlooks the airport to the east, but there are good views out over the Pacific Coast, two miles distant. At the south end of the reservoir, just off I-280 on Canada Road in the well-heeled town of **Woodside**, luscious gardens surround the palatial **Filoli Estate** (mid-Feb to late Oct Tues–Sat 10am–3.30pm, last admission 2.30pm; tours by reservation only $10; ℡650/364-8300 ext 507, ⓦwww.filoli.org). If the 45-room Georgian-style mansion, designed in 1915 by San Francisco architect Willis Polk, looks familiar, that's because it was used in the TV series *Dynasty* as the Denver home of the Carrington clan. It's the only one of the many huge houses hereabouts that you can actually visit, although the sixteen-acre grounds featuring formal gardens with reflecting pools are what make it worth coming, especially in the spring when everything's in bloom.

An alternative, albeit much slower, route south from San Francisco is to take **Hwy-35**, which winds its way majestically along the ridges that divide the Bay from the Ocean. At certain spots, you are rewarded by simultaneous views across both bodies of water.

Palo Alto and Stanford University

Just south of the exclusive communities of Woodside and Menlo Park, leafy **PALO ALTO** nestles between I-280 and US-101. Despite its proximity to **Stanford University**, it has little of the college-town vigor of its northern rival, UC Berkeley. Indeed, Palo Alto has become somewhat of a social center for Silicon Valley's nouveau riche, as evidenced by the trendy cafés and chic new restaurants that cluster along its main drag, **University Avenue**. The 1990s computer-industry job boom made more than a few people wealthy, and this is where many of them came to spend their cash; the small houses in the quaint neighborhoods surrounding the downtown area can easily cost a million dollars.

Information and accommodation

The Palo Alto **Chamber of Commerce**, 122 Hamilton Ave (Mon–Fri 9am–5pm; ℡650/324-3121, ⓦwww.paloaltochamber.com), is best for information on local restaurants and bike routes. For details on Stanford University, visit the campus visitor center (Mon–Fri 8am–5pm, Sat & Sun 9am–5pm; ℡650/723-2560, ⓦwww.stanford.edu) in the Memorial Auditorium opposite Hoover Tower, or get a copy of the free *Stanford Daily*, published weekdays. To find out what's on in the area, look out for the free *Palo Alto Weekly*, available at most local stores, or log onto the paper's website, ⓦwww .paloaltoonline.com, a well-organized, rich database of everything from local bike shops and restaurants to history and movie times.

The environs of Palo Alto contain a range of **accommodation** to suit most budgets, mainly used by parents and academics visiting Stanford. Some visitors to San Francisco choose to stay further south up the Peninsula rather than in the city, a good way to save money if you have wheels: dozens of $50/night **motels** line Hwy-82 – "El Camino Real," the old main highway. For hotels by the airport, see box, p.164.

Hotel California 2431 Ash St, Palo Alto ☎650/322-7666, ⓦwww.hotelcalifornia.com. Conveniently placed for both Stanford and downtown, and with a free shuttle to campus, this friendly hotel has twenty compact but nicely furnished rooms. And yes, the website opens with "Welcome to...." $96.

Cardinal Hotel 235 Hamilton Ave, Palo Alto ☎650/323-5101, ⓦwww.cardinalhotel.com. European-style hotel in the heart of downtown Palo Alto, featuring a winning combination of affordable rates and comfortable rooms, some with shared bathrooms. $80.

Coronet Motel 2455 El Camino Real, Palo Alto ☎650/326-1081, ⓦwww.coronetmotel.com.

Just around the corner from lively California Ave, this friendly motel has the best prices for en-suite rooms. Very clean and there's a pool. $90

Cowper Inn 705 Cowper St, Palo Alto ☎650/327-4475, ⓦwww.cowperinn.com. Restored Victorian house with attractive rooms close to University Ave. The cheaper rooms have shared bathrooms. $105.

Stanford Park Hotel 100 El Camino Real, Menlo Park ☎650/322-1234 or 1-800/368-2468, ⓦwww.stanfordparkhotel.com. Very pleasant, luxurious first-class hotel in extensive grounds near Stanford University. Offers good packages and online rates. $160.

Palo Alto

Though a great place for a lazy stroll and a gourmet meal, Palo Alto doesn't have a lot to offer in terms of sights other than its older Spanish Colonial homes along **Ramona Street** between Hamilton and University avenues. In particular, look for the 1925 home at 520–526 Ramona, built right around a live oak tree and impressive for its carved wooden doors, wrought-iron balconies, tiled roof, and fountains. If you get tired of house-spotting walks and browsing in the overpriced designer furniture stores dotted around downtown – one of the town's main preoccupations, apparently – try cycling around the many well-marked bike routes; a range of bikes is available for $20–30 a day from Action Sports Limited at 1047 El Camino Real (☎650/328-3180).

Be aware, however, that **East Palo Alto**, on the Bay side of US-101, has a well-deserved reputation for gang- and drug-related violence, with one of the highest per capita murder rates of any US city. Perhaps best known as the childhood home of the Grateful Dead's Jerry Garcia, the area was founded in the 1920s as the utopian Runnymeade Colony, a poultry-raising co-operative, and the local preservation society (☎650/329-0294) can point out the surviving sites should you be interested.

Stanford University

Across the CalTrain tracks from town and spreading out from the west end of University Avenue, **STANFORD UNIVERSITY** is by contrast one of the tamest places you could hope for. The university is among the top – and most expensive – in the United States, though when it opened in 1891, founded by railroad magnate Leland Stanford in memory of his dead son, it offered free tuition. Ridiculed by East Coast academics, who felt that there was little need for a second West Coast university (after UC Berkeley), Stanford was built anyway, a defiant hybrid of Mission and Romanesque buildings on a huge arid campus covering an area larger than the whole of Downtown San Francisco.

The origins of Silicon Valley

Though the name **"Silicon Valley"** is of relatively recent origin, Santa Clara county's history of electronic innovation reaches back to 1909, when **Lee de Forrest** completed work on the vacuum tube – a remarkably simple device that made possible numerous technological achievements from television to radar – at Stanford University. Stanford's entrepreneurial spirit was best embodied by **Frederick Terman**, however, a professor of radio engineering who encouraged students to found their own companies rather than bury themselves within massive corporations. When the school decided to raise some cash for post-World War II expansions, Terman helped convince the university to lease land to two students' fledgling local company, **Hewlett Packard**, and helped found the Stanford Industrial Park, earning himself the nickname "Father of Silicon Valley." The unique public–private partnership between the school and its alumni made the Valley central to development of radar, television, and microwave products, attracting a free-thinking engineering community that thrived in the region's hothouse intellectual environment.

It was from these roots that the modern Silicon Valley bloomed in the late 1970s, when the local folks at Intel invented first the **silicon semiconductor** and then the **microprocessor**, both radically smaller and more efficient than vacuum-tube technology, and initiated the computer revolution. In 1976, the "two Steves," **Wozniak** and **Jobs**, former high-school friends from Los Altos, founded **Apple Computers** in a garage, creating the first hardware for their systems using scavenged parts from calculators and money raised by selling a VW bus; the new computers sold for $666.66 apiece. In 1994, capitalizing on this new market, two young Stanford students named **Steve Yang** and **Jerry Filo** founded Yahoo!, a portal that allowed casual computer users to explore the **Internet**, which had previously been used as a computer network for government officials and academics.

Since then, the Bay Area – and the world – has never been the same, and even with the Internet industry implosion in 2000, the green of Silicon Valley has far from faded. While many small businesses went under during the first two years of the millennium, the Big Players have regrouped successfully, and business is once more brisk if not booming.

The university, whose reputation as an arch-conservative thinktank was enhanced by Ronald Reagan's offer to donate his video library to the school (Stanford politely declined), hasn't always been an entirely boring place, though you wouldn't know it to walk among the preppy future-lawyers-of-America that seem to comprise the majority of the student body. Ken Kesey came here from Oregon in 1958 on a writing fellowship, working nights as an orderly on the psychiatric ward of one local hospital, and getting paid $75 a day to test experimental drugs (LSD among them) in another. Drawing on both experiences, Kesey wrote *One Flew over the Cuckoo's Nest* in 1960 and quickly became a counter-culture hero, a period admirably chronicled by Tom Wolfe in *The Electric Kool-Aid Acid Test*.

Approaching from the Palo Alto CalTrain and SamTrans bus station, which acts as a buffer between the town and the university, the campus is entered via a half-mile-long, palm-tree-lined boulevard that deposits you at its heart, the **Quadrangle**, bordered by the phallic **Hoover Tower**, whose observation platform (daily 10am–4.30pm; $2) is worth ascending to for the view, and the colorful gold-leaf mosaics of the **Memorial Church**. Like the rest of the campus, the church was constructed in memory of Leland Stanford, Jr, and its elaborate, mosaic entrance has a fittingly elegiac feel.

From here, the campus's covered sidewalks and symmetrical red-roofed brownstone buildings – designed by Frederick Law Olmsted – branch out

▲ Hoover Tower, Stanford University

around a central fountain. Free hour-long **walking tours** (☎650/723-2560) conducted by students depart from the Memorial Auditorium just east of Hoover Tower (daily 11am & 3.15pm); if you'd rather not walk across the large campus, driving tours in a golf cart ($5) are offered daily at 1pm during term from the same meeting point.

The highlight of any trip to the campus is the **Iris and B. Gerald Cantor Center for Visual Arts** (Wed & Sun 11am–5pm, Thurs 11am–8pm, free, ☎650/723-4177, Ⓦwww.stanford.edu./dept/ccva), one of the finest museums in the Bay Area, comprising 27 galleries spread over 120,000 square feet, and containing treasures from six continents, some dating back to 500 BC. Housed in the old Stanford Museum of Art at the intersection of Lomita Drive and Museum Way (to the north of Palm Drive as you approach Stanford's "Quad"), the Cantor Center is the result of a decade-long refurbishing effort undertaken to repair the damage done to the museum from 1989's Loma Prieta earthquake. The enchanting result incorporates the former structure with a new wing, including a bookshop and café. Visiting exhibitions have featured such artists as Duchamp, Oldenburg, and Lucien Freud. One of the finest pieces in the permanent collection of photography, painting, sculpture, ceramics, and artifacts from around the globe is the stunning *Plum Garden, Kameido*, by Japanese wood-block print artist Hiroshige. Another reason to visit is to have a look at its distinguished collection of over two hundred **Rodin sculptures**, including a *Gates of Hell* flanked by a shamed *Adam and Eve*, displayed in an attractive outdoor setting on the museum's south side. There's a version of *The Thinker* here, as well, forming a sort of bookend with the rendition that fronts the Palace of the Legion of Honor Museum in San Francisco.

Nearby, history buffs will enjoy the **Herbert Hoover Memorial Exhibit Pavilion** (Tues–Sat 11am–4pm; free), which displays changing exhibits from the vast Hoover collection of posters, photographs, letters, and other documents. If you are more interested in the latest trends in subatomic behavior, you won't want to miss the **Stanford Linear Accelerator** (visitor center Mon–Fri 9am–4pm; tours by appointment only; free; ☎650/926-2204, Ⓦ www.slac .stanford.edu), a mile west of the central campus on Sand Hill Road, where infinitesimally small particles are crashed into one another at very high speeds to see what happens. For a bird's-eye view of the campus (and the rest of the Bay Area), head up one of the **hiking trails** that leads from the gate along Junípero Serra Boulevard at Stanford Avenue to Stanford's giant communications dish atop the foothills to the west of the campus.

Eating

For a college town, most **eateries** in downtown Stanford around University Avenue are on the chic side, though that's not so surprising, given the exclusive nature of the university. Cheaper alternatives tend to cluster around El Camino Real.

Bistro Elan 448 S California Ave, Palo Alto ☎650/327-0284. Spiffy Cal cuisine such as duck confit and pan-seared Maine scallops served to the cyber elite. Dinner prices are rather steep at around $20 per entree, so consider a lunchtime visit.

Bistro Vida 641 Santa Cruz Ave, Menlo Park ☎650/462-1686. Giving Silicon Valley a much-needed style infusion by serving delicious Left Bank Parisian bistro fare, but at rather inflated prices.

Evvia 420 Emerson St, Palo Alto ☎650/326-0983. California/Greek lamb and fish dishes with names like *païdakia arnisia* and *arni kapama*, as well as baked fish and other Hellenic faves, served in a cozy yet elegant dining room. Full bar.

🔥 **Hyderabad House** 448 University Ave, Palo Alto ☎650/327-3455. Inexpensive Indian restaurant combining dishes from both north and south, with touches of ginger and coconut. The lamb *Achari Ghost*, cooked in a spicy pickle sauce, is a Hyderabadi specialty.

Joanie's Cafe 447 California Ave, Palo Alto ☎650/326-6505. Homestyle breakfasts and lunches are the hallmarks of this comfortable neighborhood restaurant.

John's Market Town and Country Village, Embarcadero at El Camino, Palo Alto

☎650/321-8438. Steer past the high-school kids on lunch break to get one of the best (and biggest) deli sandwiches around. Located across the street from Stanford Stadium.

Krung Siam 423 University Ave, Palo Alto ☎650/322-5900. Classy but not too expensive restaurant serving beautifully presented traditional Thai fare, including red, green, and yellow curries.

Le Cheminée 530 Bryant St, Palo Alto ☎650/329-0695. Quality fare such as lavender-encrusted halibut or pork dijon are among the delights at this French bistro. The prices, mostly under $20 per entree, are not too outrageous either.

Mike's Café Etc. 2680 Middlefield Rd, Palo Alto ☎650/473-6453. Unpretentious neighborhood restaurant hidden behind a hardware store. Excellent fresh salads, pastas, and simple meat dishes are sometimes brought to your table by Mike himself.

St Michael's Alley 806 Emerson St, Palo Alto ☎650/326-2530. This former student café hangout has transformed itself into one of Palo Alto's hottest bistros featuring "casual California" cuisine. A fine wine list and weekend brunch ($10–15) keep guests coming back for seconds.

Cafés and bars

For a student town, the **nightlife** in Palo Alto is very low-key, although the Stanfordites make up for the lack of nightclubs by browsing and chatting until late in the many cafés.

Blue Chalk Café 630 Ramona St, Palo Alto
⊤650/326-1020. Young professionals and other Siliconites have been flocking to this wildly successful bar/pool hall/restaurant ever since it opened in 1993.

🏃 **Caffè del Doge 419 University Ave, Palo Alto** ⊤ 650/323-3600. Relaxing, colorful hangout for Palo Alto's intellectual crowd, a branch of the Venetian original.

Caffè Verona 236 Hamilton Ave, Palo Alto ⊤650/326-9942. Relaxing hangout for Palo Alto's intellectual crowd, who read,

converse, or work on their computers over cappuccino.

Gordon Biersch Brewery 640 Emerson St, Palo Alto ⊤650/323-7723. Among the first and still the best of the Bay Area's microbrewery-cum-restaurants. Other branches in San Francisco (see p.215) and in downtown San Jose.

Printer's Cafe 320 California Ave, Palo Alto ⊤650/323-3347. Good food and coffees served adjacent to Palo Alto's best bookstore.

San Jose

Burt Bacharach could hardly miss **SAN JOSE** these days. Sitting at the southern end of the Peninsula, the city – about an hour's drive from San Fran – has emerged as the civic heart of Silicon Valley, spurred by the growth of local behemoths such as Apple, Cisco, Intel, and Hewlett Packard. And though it's seen by some as the city of the future (surrounded as it is by miles of faceless high-tech industrial parks), San Jose's 1777 founding makes it one of the oldest settlements – and the oldest city – in California, and for centuries it was little more than a sleepy agricultural community of prune farms.

Not anymore: San Jose has long held the title of the fastest-growing city in California – and, though it's not strong on sights, in area and population it's already close to twice the size of San Francisco. As befits a constantly expanding city, San Jose's current priority is the development of a culture outside the surrounding computer labs; as such, new museums, shopping centers, restaurants, clubs, and performing-arts companies have mushroomed throughout the compact downtown area. All in all, though the nightlife and cultural scene here can't begin to compete with San Francisco, there are enough attractions around the city's clean and sunny streets to warrant at least a day trip or overnight stay. In addition, the **coast** is just 45 minutes away west on Hwy-17, over the mountains residents call "The Hill." It's a wild drive, and worth it, if only to escape the heat of the valley – where summer temperatures hang around 100°F – for the cool 70°F climate along the coast.

Information and accommodation

The **San Jose CVB** sits beside the Convention Center at 408 S Almaden Blvd (Mon–Fri 8am–5pm; Sat & Sun 11am–5pm; ⊤408/295-9600 or 1-800/726-5673, Ⓦ www.sanjose.org), although it is more geared towards helping visiting businesspeople than the casual traveler. For local news and events, pick up a copy of the excellent *San Jose Mercury* (Ⓦ www.mercurynews.com) or the free weekly *Metro* (Ⓦ www.metroactive.com) – although the latter usually lists as many events for San Francisco as it does for the South Bay. The website Ⓦ www.siliconvalley.citysearch.com also holds a cache of reviews and features on the area.

San Jose's **hotels** are mainly aimed at business travelers and are not particularly charming, but competition keeps a lid on prices and there can be some very good deals at weekends. There are a couple of fine **hostels** tucked in the hills outside the city.

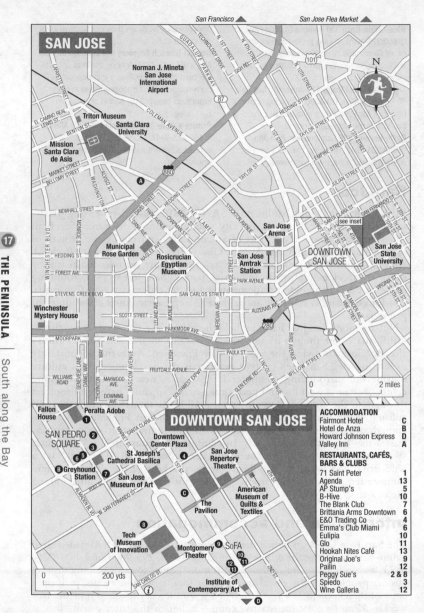

Hotels and motels

Hotel de Anza 233 W Santa Clara St ☎408/286-0500 or 1-800/843-3700, ⓦwww.hoteldeanza.com. Plush business and conference-oriented hotel with full amenities, located in one of the livelier sections of town. Good weekend packages. $120.

Fairmont Hotel 170 S Market St ☎408/998-1900 or 1-800/527-4727, ⓦwww.fairmont.com. San Jose's finest hotel is part of the luxury chain which began in San Francisco. All amenities, such as room service, swimming pool, and lounge, to go with sparkling rooms. $110.

17

THE PENINSULA | South along the Bay

Howard Johnson Express **1215 S First St**
☎ 408/280-5300 or 1-800/509-7666, ⓦ www
.hojo.com. Simple, characterless rooms
downtown, conveniently situated near the
city's main nightlife strip. $55.
Valley Inn 2155 The Alameda
☎ 408/241-8500, ⓦ www.valleyinnsanjose
.com. Above-average motel with compact,
well-kept rooms, not far from the
Rosicrucian Museum. $65.

Hostels
Hidden Villa 26807 Moody Rd, Los Altos Hills
☎ 650/949-8650, ⓦ www.hiddenvilla.org.

Located on an 1800-acre ranch in the
foothills above Silicon Valley, this hostel
has both private rooms and dorms;
members $21, others $24. Private
cabins $35–50.
Sanborn Park Hostel 15808 Sanborn Rd,
Saratoga ☎ 408/741-0166, ⓦ www.sanbornpark
hostel.org. Comfortable rooms in a beautiful
wooded area 15min outside San Jose.
Call from downtown Saratoga and they
will arrange to pick you up. Open 7–9am
& 5–11pm (curfew); members $14, others
$16.

Downtown San Jose

Downtown, the only sign of San Jose's history is the 1797 **Peralta Adobe**, at
184 W St John St (Sat & Sun noon–5pm; $6; tours by appointment only
☎ 408/918-1055, ⓦ www.historysanjose.org), notable more for its having
survived the encroaching suburbia than anything on display in its sparse, white-
washed interior. Admission includes a tour of the Victorian **Fallon House**
across the street, a mansion built in 1855 by the city's seventh mayor, a
frontiersman in the Fremont expedition. The guided tours may not include all
of the fifteen period-furnished rooms, as the house is currently undergoing
extensive renovations, but there is a comprehensive video presentation on the
home and the adobe. The two blocks of San Pedro Street running south of the
adobe form a restaurant row known as **San Pedro Square**, clearly marked by
an iron gate at the intersection with W Santa Clara Street. There's no central
plaza as such, just a collection of some of San Jose's best eateries and a considerable amount of activity on weekend nights.

Plaza de Cesar Chavez

San Jose's most popular downtown attractions are best reached on foot, with the
main places of interest centered around the palm-dotted **Plaza de Cesar
Chavez**, just two blocks south of San Pedro Square. An oval island of green in
the midst of Market Street, clustered around a modern fountain, the Plaza is an
ideal spot to relax on the grass. To the north of the plaza, the **Cathedral
Basilica of St Joseph** stands on the site of the first Catholic parish in
California, which was built in 1803. The present building was dedicated in 1997,
and is worth entering for a glimpse of its painted cupola, stained-glass windows,
and Stations of the Cross. Masses are held daily, often in Spanish.

Next door at 110 S Market St is the fantastic **San Jose Museum of Art**
(Tues–Sun 11am–5pm; $8; ☎ 408/294-2787, ⓦ www.sjmusart.org). Set in an
1892 post office building with a contemporary new wing added in 1991, the
museum contains more than a thousand twentieth-century works, with the
spotlight on post-1980 Bay Area artists. The sweeping, open galleries are flooded
with light, as is the attached café, including an outdoor patio facing the Plaza.
Through a special partnership, the museum regularly features work from the
permanent collection of the Whitney Museum of American Art in New York.

Facing the southwest corner of the plaza, downtown's biggest draw is the
Tech Museum of Innovation, 201 S Market St (daily 10am–5pm; $8;
ⓦ www.thetech.org), with its hands-on displays of high-tech engineering

spread over three floors, plus the inevitable IMAX theater (one show included in entry; extra show $4; feature film $10). Highlights include an opportunity to design your own virtual rollercoaster, regular demonstrations of high-tech surgical instruments, and the chance to communicate with interactive robots. Unfortunately, the lines to access many of the best exhibits can seem endless, and, unless you're a computer nerd yourself, you may still leave the museum feeling like you've just read a particularly impervious software manual.

Just west of the Tech, the **Children's Discovery Museum,** 180 Woz Way (Tues–Sat 10am–5pm, Sun noon–5pm; $8; ℡408/298-5437, Ⓦwww.cdm.org), draws raves from kids and parents alike for its hands-on displays, such as a real fire truck that can be climbed on, a Model A Ford, a Wells Fargo stagecoach, a bubble room, and a play table, where kids can fingerpaint and draw – though it's all aimed at the pre-adolescent set.

SoFA

Aside from the attractions around the Plaza, San Jose's other area worth walking through is the "**SoFA**" (short for South First Street) entertainment district. To get here from the southern tip of the Plaza, turn east on San Carlos Street and walk one block to First Street. SoFA forms the heart of San Jose's nightlife, a dozen or so clubs and discos along with a popular wine bar. There's plenty to see during the day as well, including the **Institute of Contemporary Art**, 451 S First St (Tues–Sat noon–5pm; free; ℡408/283-8155, Ⓦwww.sjica.org), which, in a large, sunny room, exhibits modern art by (mainly) Bay Area artists. On the same street is downtown San Jose's **art cinema** house, the Camera 1, no. 366 (℡408/998-3300, Ⓦwww.cameracinemas.com), and at no. 490, one of its performing-arts companies, **The Stage** (℡408/283-7142, Ⓦwww.sanjosestage .com). Performances of contemporary work, like the critically acclaimed musical *Alter Boyz*, regularly run Wed–Sat, with tickets available for $20–50.

Walking north on First Avenue leads past the **Pavilion** shopping center, which has undergone a major renovation to become the anchor of commercial San Jose. The area needed it, having lain stagnant for decades as locals shopped at suburban malls. To further combat this flight, city planners have zoned all of First and Second streets for a much vaunted multi-billion-dollar redevelopment. Finally, one block over on Second Street, the blue building resembling a giant Lego construction is the home of the **San Jose Repertory Theater** (℡408/367-7255, Ⓦwww.sjrep.com); the resident company has formed a relationship with Dublin's Abbey Theatre, which exports its players and programs during specific engagements.

Outer San Jose

The outskirts of San Jose, especially to the west and north around Santa Clara, hold a number of attractions, most notably the wonderful Rosicrucian Museum and, for cheesy family fun, the Winchester Mystery House. Although the locations below are within reach of public transport, you'd be hard pushed to get to more than a couple in a day without your own vehicle.

West of downtown

West from San Pedro Square, Santa Clara Street becomes Alameda, which leads into the **Alameda Business District**, where, out from under the shadow of downtown's sparkling office buildings, you get something of a feel for the old farm town San Jose once was. Within a cluster of cafés, restaurants, and shops is

Bay Area music

The Bay Area has long been a breeding ground for popular music. San Francisco itself remains synonymous with the Haight-Ashbury-bred bands of the 1960s, but a handful of local jazz, funk, and punk artists have also left their stamp on national scenes over the years. Oakland and Berkeley have, arguably, produced even more hits and household names – particularly in the more streetwise styles of punk and hip-hop, where the East Bay's reputation as the working-class answer to glamorous San Francisco has, ironically, helped lift a few of its homespun musicians to unlikely levels of fame and notoriety.

Jazz

Throughout the 1950s and 1960s, jazz was significant in San Francisco: the *Blackhawk* club in the Tenderloin hosted major touring acts, while smaller North Beach clubs drew sizable crowds for local ensembles. Berkeley's legendary **Fantasy Records** released groundbreaking albums by locals **Dave Brubeck**, **Cal Tjader**, and **Vince Guaraldi**, while the East Bay would eventually produce three big names of the 1990s and 2000s – guitarist **Charlie Hunter**, saxophonist **Joshua Redman**, and pianist **Benny Green**. Sadly, the vibrant jazz, R&B, and blues scene centered along Fillmore Street in San Francisco's Western Addition was curtailed in the name of urban renewal in the decades following World War II; live jazz in North Beach suffered a similar fate, as strip clubs and discotheques supplanted smoky jazz haunts along Broadway by the end of the 1960s.

Performers at the Fillmore Jazz Festival ▲

Sign for the Fillmore Jazz Festival ▼

Early rock

San Francisco was host to the Summer of Love, and Bay Area acts cast tall shadows over the blossoming rock scene of the mid/late 1960s and early 1970s. Proto-jam rockers **The Grateful Dead** led the psychedelic charge on their long, strange trip through the decades, while across the Bay, **Creedence Clearwater Revival** enjoyed a nonstop barrage of swampy hits between 1969 and 1971. **Jefferson Airplane** and **Janis Joplin**'s **Big Brother & the Holding Company** also ranked as first-tier contributors to the era's LSD-soaked Haight-Ashbury scene, while the local mob of funk- and soul-rockers in **Sly & the Family Stone** played a pivotal role in redrawing the race and gender boundaries of rock.

Punk

Early punk's blink-and-miss songs and brusque performances were the antithesis of psychedelia's meandering guitar solos and peace-sign-waving hippies. Bay Area punk stalwarts the **Dead Kennedys** held court, beginning in the late 1970s at the Mabuhay Gardens in North Beach; the **Avengers**, the shambolic **Flipper**, and outrageous **Crime** (who once performed at nearby San Quentin State Prison in police uniforms) were also influential. By the time punk became MTV-friendly in the 1990s, local scrappers **Rancid, AFI, Jawbreaker,** and eventual global superstars **Green Day** – each rising through touchstone Berkeley club *924 Gilman* – had become the face of Bay Area punk.

▲ Janis Joplin

▼ 2Pac

Hip-hop and soul

The Bay Area has been bumping beats since Oakland's Too $hort and Digital Underground became top-sellers in the late 1980s and early 1990s; in fact, **2Pac** (Tupac Shakur), who attended high school in Mill Valley, began his career as a dancer, roadie, and occasional rapper for the latter group before his ascent to superstardom was abruptly halted by his 1996 murder. Others with sizable followings in the Nineties included San Francisco gangstas **RBL Posse** and militant solo rapper **Paris**, as well as Oakland one-hit wonders **Luniz**. Today, the East Bay's **Hieroglyphics** and the **Coup** deliver intelligent lyricism and funk- and jazz-based beats, while **E-40** and the late **Mac Dre** (both from Vallejo) helped establish the "hyphy" style's pounding, up-tempo beats as the Bay's signature sound in the mid-2000s. In modern soul, Oakland has been the region's hotbed of big-name talent, with **En Vogue** and **Tony! Toni! Tone!** top attractions in the 1990s.

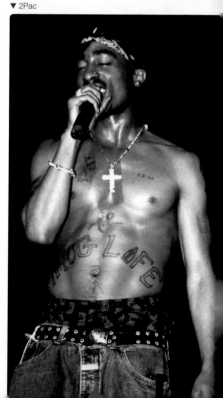

The Fillmore ▲

Amoeba Records, San Francisco ▼

Great American Music Hall ▼

Top Bay Area music venues

From storied, intimate spaces like San Francisco's Fillmore and Great American Music Hall to large theatres such as Oakland's grand old Paramount Theatre, the Bay Area is rich in atmospheric venues that play regular host to a variety of live music performances. And if you're on a budget or can't get tickets to a sold-out show, Amoeba Records on both sides of San Francisco Bay presents several mini-shows each month, gratis.

▶▶ **Amoeba Music, Berkeley and San Francisco** The unquestioned kingpin of the region's record store scene frequently hosts free in-store performances by local and touring artists at both locations. See p.324 & p.260.

▶▶ **The Fillmore, San Francisco** Classic ballroom auditorium from the 1960s that's still a terrific place to catch up-and-comers and longtime favorites alike. See p.220.

▶▶ **Great American Music Hall, San Francisco** Onetime bordello turned ornate performance palace, where the best vantage points are along the edge of the wraparound balcony. See p.220.

▶▶ **Greek Theatre, Berkeley** The finest outdoor venue in the region – small enough to feel intimate, large enough to evoke a sense of grandeur. See p.322.

▶▶ **Paramount Theatre, Oakland** Art Deco showplace that plays host to everything from comedy and ballet to soul revues and rock shows. See p.292.

▶▶ **Yoshi's, Oakland and San Francisco** The area's best bet for big names in jazz; the San Francisco club is brand new, while both rooms boast extraordinary sound. See p.323 & p.224.

the city's only **revival cinema**, The Towne, at 1433 Alameda (☎408/287-1433). Next door, on the corner of Hester and Alameda, is *Uncommon Grounds*, a café housed in the historic 1926 Bank of Italy building – it's worth a peek for the ornate interior alone.

Further northwest on Alameda, over two miles from downtown, some of San Jose's more intriguing sights languish in the suburbs. The **Rosicrucian Museum**, 1342 Naglee Ave (Tues–Fri 10am–5pm, Sat & Sun 11am–6pm; $9; ☎408/947-3636, ⓦwww.egyptianmuseum.org), is situated in an elaborate complex of buildings designed in ancient-Egyptian style. The museum itself holds an astounding collection of Assyrian and Babylonian artifacts, including ancient amulets, jewelry, decorative art, and both animal and human mummies – one of them acquired, as guides will proudly tell you, through an early Neiman Marcus catalog. Though the museum is rather dark and musty, there's an unmissable flash-lit tour through a subterranean **Egyptian tomb** – a composite of three real tombs – re-created in painstaking detail here. When earnest members of the Rosicrucians' mysterious order (learn more at ⓦwww.rosicrucian.org) lead you through the depths of the gloomy space, they seem convinced that the figures illuminated on its walls are alive and well. There is also a **planetarium** (Tues–Sun 2pm, Sat & Sun also 3.30pm; free), with shows covering such esoteric subjects as *The Mithraic Mysteries*. Aside from the exhibits within, another great reason to visit the Rosicrucian is its **garden grounds**, featuring a full replica of the Akhenaten temple from Luxor.

More lovely grounds can be visited two blocks west of the museum at the **Municipal Rose Garden** (daily 8am–sunset; free), a beautiful expanse of green lined with rose bushes and centered on a fountain that's a popular wading pool for local kids. Roll up your pants, soak your feet, and take in a nice view of the Santa Cruz mountains to the west amidst the sweet scents.

A good eight miles out in San Jose's suburbs sits the **Winchester Mystery House**, 525 S Winchester Blvd, just off I-280 near Hwy-17 (daily 9am–5pm, 9am–7pm in summer; Mansion Tour $23.95, Guided Behind-the-Scenes Tour $20.95, combo $28.95; ☎408/247-1313, ⓦwww.winchestermysteryhouse.com). The house belonged to Sarah Winchester, heiress to the Winchester rifle fortune, who was convinced upon her husband's death that he had been taken by the spirits of the men killed with his weapons. The ghosts told her that unless a room was built for each of them, the same fate would befall her. Work on the mansion took place 24 hours a day for the next thirty years, though the house was never finished and is a hodgepodge of extensions and styles: extravagant staircases lead nowhere and windows open onto solid brick walls. Ever since construction on the house stopped, the place ran rampantly commercial; today, visitors are channeled through a gauntlet of ghastly gift stores and soda stands to get in and out.

Southeast of downtown

Nearly three miles southeast of downtown, the **History Park**, at 1650 Senter Rd in spacious Kelley Park (Sat & Sun noon–5pm; $6; grounds only Tues–Fri noon–5pm; free; ☎408/287-2290, ⓦwww.historysanjose.org), is a 25-acre historic town that tries to replicate nineteenth-century San Jose and Santa Clara Valley through a series of restored buildings – among them a vintage ice-cream parlor – and a historic trolley system. Just down the road, peek into the **Japanese Friendship Gardens** (free), at 1300 Senter Rd, modeled after the Korakuen Garden in San Jose's Japanese sister city, Okayama, with ornate footbridges spanning koi-stocked ponds.

North of downtown

About five miles northwest of San Jose, the small community of **Santa Clara** holds a few sights of its own. The late eighteenth-century **Mission Santa Clara de Asis**, just south of Alameda (Route 82), is one of the least impressive structures in the chain of missions that runs along the California coast on the traces of El Camino Real. But while there's little left to see of the original mission-era buildings that formed the original complex (they burned in a 1926 fire), it's interesting to note how what remains has been integrated into the campus of the Jesuit-run University of Santa Clara. The bell in the church's belfry is original, a gift from King Carlos IV of Spain in 1798, and the **de Saisset Museum** (Tues–Sun 11am–4pm; free; ⓦ www.scu.edu/desaisset) in the grounds traces the history of the mission through a permanent display of objects recovered from its ruins, along with changing shows of contemporary art.

At the north end of the grounds, a towering Benjamin Bufano sculpture stands near the entrance to the **Triton Museum of Art**, 1505 Warburton Ave (Tues 10am–9pm, Wed–Sun 10am–5pm; $2; ⓦ www.tritonmuseum.org), which features mainly Californian artists' work. Santa Clara's other notable stop is the **Intel Museum**, 2200 Mission College Blvd (Mon–Fri 9am–6pm, Sat 10am–5pm; free; ⓦ www.intel.com/museum), which showcases the process of making computer chips – actually, more interesting than it sounds – and explains how they and transistors work.

Due north of Santa Clara, **Paramount's Great America** (summer daily 10am–10pm; rest of year Sat & Sun 10am–dusk; $51.99, much better deals in advance online; ⓣ 408/988-1776, ⓦ www.pgathrills.com) is a hundred-acre amusement park on the edge of San Francisco Bay, well signposted just off US-101. It is hardly in the same league as Disneyland, but the range of high-speed thrills and chills available – including the looping Top Gun Jetcoaster and Stealth, which zooms over the rails at 65mph – should satisfy even the most hardcore adrenaline junkies.

A few miles further along US-101 and then east on Hwy-237 take you to the tiny town of **Alviso**, a predominantly Latino community with excellent tacquerias. Follow the railroad tracks two miles north to the ghost town of **Drawbridge**, little more than a few weathered wooden buildings, though nearly a hundred salt-box homes stood here in the 1930s. The town met with a swift demise when a sewage plant was built nearby in the 1960s, and by the 1980s, Drawbridge was added to the San Francisco Bay National Wildlife Refuge (ⓣ 510/792-0222), which has sadly discontinued guided tours.

Around four miles northeast of downtown San Jose, just beyond US-101, are a final assortment of attractions. San Jose's **Flea Market**, 1590 Berryessa Rd (Wed–Sun dawn–dusk; ⓣ 408/453-1110), features more than two thousand vendors plying their wares. For the more culturally inclined, the **Mexican Heritage Plaza**, 1700 Alum Rock Ave near King (Tues–Fri noon–6pm, Sat & Sun 10am–4pm; free; ⓣ 408/928-5500, ⓦ www.mhcviva.org), has two gallery spaces featuring temporary exhibits of work by Mexican and Mexican-American artists; there are also frequent film, theater, and cultural events, highlighting this community that makes up nearly a quarter of San Jose's population. A particularly lively time to visit is during the Day of the Dead festival on November 1–3.

Eating and drinking

As you might expect for a city of its size, San Jose has plenty of **restaurants** to suit all palates and budgets, although it is not renowned for gourmet fare.

For **nightlife**, it can scarcely compete with its northerly neighbor San Francisco or even the East Bay, but the SoFA area, in particular, attracts sizeable crowds of revelers.

Restaurants and cafés

71 Saint Peter 71 N San Pedro St ☎480/971-8523. Patio dining and oyster bar centered on a menu of filet mignon, pork loin, chicken, and salads. A hot spot with the in-crowd. Lunch Mon–Fri only, dinner nightly.

E&O Trading Company 96 S First St ☎480/938-4100. Upscale Southeast Asian grill featuring curried fish and other Vietnamese/Indonesian fare. Entrees approaching $20.

Eulipia 374 S First St ☎480/280-6161. Stylish dinner spot featuring well-prepared versions of California cuisine staples including grilled fish and fresh pastas. Entrees from $14–30. Mouthwatering desserts a specialty. Closed Mon.

Hookah Nites Café 371 S First St ☎480/286-0800. Avant-garde art is showcased in this spacious and trendy venue, which serves fresh coffee and pastries. Main attraction is the cool water pipes, though, which include flavours like mango and blueberry.

La Victoria Taqueria 140 E San Carlos St ☎480/298-5335. Cheap and cheerful Mexican joint, featuring all the favorites and late-night dining. The filling burritos surpass even the fine tacos in tastiness.

Original Joe's 301 S First St ☎480/292-7030. Grab a stool at the counter or settle into one of the comfy vinyl booths and enjoy a burger and fries or a plate of pasta at this San Jose institution, where $10 still goes a long way.

Pailin 325 S First St ☎400/998-3306. Delicious Chinese with authentic dishes from the southern Trieu Chau region and nearby Cambodia. Try the spicy beef. Most dishes well under $10.

Peggy Sue's 29 N San Pedro St ☎480/298-6750. Inexpensive milkshakes, burgers, and fries served in a 1950s setting. Also has a vegetarian and kids' menu. There's another outlet a few blocks away at 183 Park Ave (☎480/294-0252).

Spiedo 151 W Santa Clara St ☎480/971-6096. Handmade pasta, pizza, calamari, salmon, and more delight the tastebuds at lunch and dinner daily. Entrees begin around $15, a little less for pasta dishes.

ThepThai 23 N Market St ☎480/292-7390. Very inexpensive and authentic Thai cuisine, including a wide range of meat and seafood dishes, a couple of which are baked in clay pots.

Bars and clubs

Agenda 399 S First St ☎480/287-3991. A bar/restaurant/lounge in SoFA that heralded the arrival of nightlife in San Jose. DJ dancing and live jazz nightly.

B-Hive 372 S First St ☎480/298-2529. Upstairs dance club spinning hip-hop, R'n'B, and reggae. Rhythm Records, below, keeps them supplied with loops. Over 21s only.

The Blank Club 44 S Almaden Ave ☎408/292-5265. Live shows most nights and the only regular space for indie, punk and alternative sounds.

Britannia Arms Downtown 173 W Santa Clara St ☎480/266-0550. One of the growing chain of British-themed pubs with fish'n'chips, real ale, footie (meaning soccer) on TV, and a trivia quiz night.

Emma's Club Miami 177 W Santa Clara St ☎480/279-3670. Huge San Pedro Square bar/Mexican restaurant with Latin music and dancing on weekends. Great patio.

Glo 394 S First St ☎480/280-1977. Dance music from light hip-hop to heavy disco is featured at this club, which imports top DJs from SF, LA, and Vegas on Sat nights.

Wine Galleria 377 S First St ☎480/298-1386. Large wine bar with plush sofas to relax in. Huge array of vintages for sale by the glass, with specials such as five for $20.

The coast

The **coastline** of the Peninsula south from San Francisco is worlds away from the valley of the inland: mostly undeveloped, a few small towns, and countless beaches trace the 75 miles south to the mellow summer fun of Santa Cruz and Capitola. Along the way, bluffs protect the many nudist beaches from prying eyes and make a popular launching pad for hang-glider pilots. **Skyline Boulevard** follows the coast south from San Francisco, beginning where the San Andreas Fault enters the sea at Fort Funston and passing the repetitious tracts of proverbial ticky-tacky houses that make up Daly City, before heading inland toward Woodside at its intersection with Hwy-1, which continues south along the coast. Driving Hwy-1 can be a relaxing jaunt, providing jaw-dropping views of the ocean – though on summer and weekend afternoons you'll find the route clogged with RVs creeping along at 30mph and few opportunities to pass. Try hitting the road early in the morning; provided the fog isn't obscuring everything, you can expect a magic ride. Apart from the possibility of **camping** in the woods by the ocean, those with time to explore the coast can stay in a couple of unique **hostels** converted from lighthouses and at a number of picturesque restaurants.

Pacifica and around

San Pedro Point, a popular surfing beach fifteen miles south of San Francisco proper, along with the town of **PACIFICA**, marks the southern extent of the city's suburban sprawl. Pacifica is a pleasant stop-off for lunch and wave-gazing around Rockaway Beach; try *Nick's Seashore Restaurant,* 101 Rockaway Beach Ave (☎650/359-3903), an all-purpose joint providing cheap breakfasts, moderate pasta options, and pricier steak/seafood dishes, or the simpler diner *Rock'n'Rob's,* 450 Dundee Way (☎650/359-3663). You might even decide to stay here at either the *Pacifica Motor Inn,* 200 Rockaway Beach Ave (☎650/359-7700 or 1-800/522-3772, ⓦwww.pacificamotorinn.com; $75), whose simple but large motel rooms are just a block inland from the beachfront *Sea Breeze Motel* 100 Rockaway Beach Ave (☎650/359-3903, ⓦwww.nicksrestaurant.net; $80), whose smaller rooms, attached to *Nick's,* have the advantage of ocean views. It's also just a few yards to the small but pretty black-sand beach.

For information, stop in at the ultra-friendly **Chamber of Commerce**, 225 Rockaway Beach Ave (Mon–Fri 9am–5pm, Sat & Sun 10am–4.30pm; ☎650/355-4122, ⓦwww.pacificachamber.com). Look in particular for the free maps of the area, including trail guides for **Sweeney Ridge**, from where Spanish explorer Gaspar de Portola discovered the San Francisco Bay in 1769. Also worth a quick look in town is the **Sanchez Adobe**, 1000 Linda Mar (Tues–Thurs 10am–4pm, Sat & Sun 1–5pm; free; ☎650/359-1462), an 1846 hotel and speakeasy, now a museum with various Native American artifacts on display.

Pacifica's old **Ocean Shore Railroad Depot**, now a private residence, is one of the few surviving remnants of an ill-advised train line between San Francisco and Santa Cruz. Wiped out during the 1906 earthquake, the line was in any case never more than a third complete. Its few patrons had to transfer back and forth by ferry to connect the stretches of track that were built, the traces of which you can still see scarring the face of the bluffs. If you're interested, over one hundred photos of the attempt can be seen at *Ash's Vallemar Station Restaurant* at 2125 Hwy-1 at Reina Del Mar (☎650/359-7411). The continually eroding cliffs make construction along the coast treacherous at best, as evidenced a mile south by the **Devil's Slide**, where a new cement support has been added to lessen the regularity with which the highway is washed away by winter storms. An interesting side note is that the slide area here was a popular dumping spot for corpses of those who fell foul of rum-runners during Prohibition, and is featured under various names in many of Dashiell Hammett's detective stories.

Gray Whale Cove to Venice Beach

Just south of the Devil's Slide, the sands of **Gray Whale Cove State Beach** (daily dawn–dusk; free) are clothing-optional. Despite the name, it's not an especially great place to look for migrating gray whales, but the stairway at the bus stop does lead down to a fine strand of sand. Two miles south, the red-roofed buildings of the 1875 **Montara Lighthouse**, set among the windswept Monterey pine trees at the top of a steep cliff, have been converted into the *HI-Point Montara Lighthouse* youth hostel (☎650/728-7177, Ⓦwww .norcalhostels.org; office hours 7.30–10am & 4.30–9.30pm, 11pm curfew; members $20, non-members $25, private rooms $55–94; reservations essential in summer), where guests can take a dip in a hot tub perched out on the coastal rocks where violent waves come crashing in at high tide. From San Francisco, SamTrans bus #1L or #1C (Mon–Fri until 5.50pm, Sat until 6.15pm) will take you to the lighthouse entrance on Hwy-1.

South of the hostel, on California Street, the **Fitzgerald Marine Reserve** (☎650/728-3584; free) has three miles of diverse oceanic habitat, peaceful trails, and, at low tide, the best tidal pools of the Bay Area. Rangers often give free guided walks through the reserve at low tide, too (call for low-tide times). At the south end of the reserve, **Pillar Point** juts out into the Pacific. Further down, just off Hwy-1 at **Moss Beach**, you can replenish yourself at *Moss Beach Distillery* (☎650/728-0220). If you don't feel like paying $20 per entree at the popular restaurant, snuggle up under a wool blanket, order a drink and an appetizer, and watch the sunset from the patio overlooking the ocean.

Mavericks Beach, south of Pillar Point beyond an enormous communications dish, has what are said to be the largest waves in North America, attracting some of the world's best (and craziest) surfers when conditions are right; just watching them can be an exhilarating way to spend an hour or so. The beach hosts the annual **Mavericks Surf Contest**, an event so secretive and dependent on the right wave-creating conditions that invitations are emailed to participants just two days in advance. There's a long breakwater to walk out on, too, but remember never to turn your back on the ocean; rogue waves have crashed in and swept unsuspecting tourists to their deaths.

A little to the east, almost back on Hwy-1, fishing boats and yachts dock at **Pillar Point Harbor**. The surrounding village of **PRINCETON-BY-THE-SEA** has numerous eating options, but rather than dine in the rather anodyne mall-like strip at the harbour, head a few hundred yards west to the excellent ⅄ *Half Moon Bay Brewing Company*, 390 Capistrano Ave (☎650/728-2739), where you can wash down a full meal or cheaper bar snack with their own finely crafted ales. Oceanfront *Barbara's Fish Trap*, almost opposite at 281 Capistrano Rd (☎650/728-7049), serves good-value fish and seafood dinners with an unbeatable view. If you really like the spot, cosily furnished rooms with harbour-facing bay-window seats are available at *Pillar Point Inn* (☎650/728-7377 or 1-800/400-8281, Ⓦwww .pillarpointinn.com; $225).

Further south, more good surfing is to be had at the long strand of **Miramar Beach**; after dark, head for the beachfront *Douglass Beach House* (☎650/726-4143, Ⓦwww.bachddsoc.org), an informal seaside jazz club and beer bar that attracts surprisingly big names. Slightly further to the south lie **Dunes Beach** and **Venice Beach**, two more beautiful expanses of sand and ocean. You can ride a horse along these beaches from the jointly run **Sea Horse/Friendly Acres Ranches**, at Hwy-1 one mile north of the intersection with Hwy-92 (☎650/726-9903, Ⓦwww.horserentals.com/seahorse.html); activities range from a twenty-minute pony ride ($10), through a one-hour trail ride ($40) or ninety-minute beach ride ($50) to a combined beach and trail ride ($60).

Half Moon Bay

HALF MOON BAY, twenty miles south of the southern reaches of the city, takes its name from the crescent-shaped bay formed by Pillar Point. Lined by miles of sandy beaches, the town is surprisingly rural, considering its proximity to San Francisco and Silicon Valley, and sports a number of ornate Victorians around its center. The oldest of these, built in 1849, is at the north end of Main Street, just across a little stone bridge over Pillarcitos Creek. The **Half Moon Bay Chamber of Commerce**, 520 Kelly Ave (Mon–Fri 9am–4pm; ℡650/726-8380, ⓦwww.halfmoonbaychamber.org), gives out walking-tour maps and information on accommodation; there is also a small kiosk under the clocktower at the corner of Kelly Avenue and Main Street that opens at weekends (10am–3pm). Both locations can also fill you in on the two annual festivals for which the town is best known. These are the **Holy Ghost and Pentecost Festival**, a parade and barbecue held on the sixth Sunday after Easter, and the **Art and Pumpkin Festival** (see box, p.343). Finally, free,

▲ Half Moon Bay

The Art and Pumpkin Festival

Every year in mid-October, Half Moon Bay comes alive for the annual **Pumpkin Festival**, when all manner of competitions are held to find the largest, tastiest, and most perfectly shaped pumpkin. The orange monsters mostly come from the many farms in the immediate vicinity, but such is the prestige of the event that some folk bring the results of their mammoth nurturing efforts from much farther afield. If you ever wanted to see a vegetable the size of a compact car, then this is the place for you.

The fun, which takes place on Main Street, begins with the Safeway World Championship Pumpkin Weigh-off, the winner of which scoops $18,000. This is followed by a variety of pumpkin-themed **events** such as the Great Pumpkin Parade, Pie-Eating Contests, and the Pumpkin Run. The **art** part comes into play with the Pumpkin Carving Competition, as Halloween is only just around the corner. Non-biodegradable arts and crafts are also on display, however, along with a host of other stalls, while there are **live music** and other performances on three stages. Admission is free and the hours are 10am–5pm (call ☎650/72 6-9652 for exact dates).

basic campgrounds line the coast in **Half Moon Bay State Beach** (daily 8am–sunset; $6), under a mile west of the town. Stop here if you're low on gas, as the fifty-mile stretch of Hwy-1 to Santa Cruz doesn't offer many places to fill up.

If you want to use Half Moon Bay as a base for explorations of the coast, there are several lovely **B&Bs** in town. Top of the tree is the intricately designed and luxurious ⚘ *Mill Rose Inn*, 615 Mill St (☎650/726-8750 or 1-800/900-7673, Ⓦwww.millroseinn.com; $225), whose garden gazebo contains a huge hot tub. This is followed by the *Old Thyme Inn*, 779 Main St (☎650/726-1616 or 1-800/720-4277, Ⓦwww.oldthymeinn.com; $155), a Victorian house with cozy and beautifully furnished rooms, while *San Benito House*, down the road at 356 Main St (☎650/726-3425, Ⓦwww.sanbenitohouse.com; $80), offers simpler but restful rooms in another hundred-year-old property. **Camping** is available in the woods behind the sands at Half Moon Bay State Beach (☎650/726-8820; $20). For sustenance, the classiest option is the huge dining room of the award-winning Mediterranean restaurant ⚘ *Cetrella*, 845 Main St (☎650/726-4090), with delights such as braised Australian lamb shank for around $25; the relaxed bar often features live jazz. Other establishments worth a try are *Château des Fleurs*, 523 Church St (☎650/712-8837), a small, reasonably priced French restaurant, and *M Coffee*, 522 Main St (☎650/726-6241), a good spot for hot beverages, sandwiches, and ice cream in homey surroundings. Just to the south of town at 1410 S Cabrillo Hwy (Hwy-1), you can wash down good pub grub with an English pint, watch British football and even smoke on a double-decker bus at *Cameron's Inn* (☎650/726-5705).

From San Fran, SamTrans bus #294 route ends in Half Moon Bay; to continue south, transfer to route #15, which runs every three hours to Waddell Creek, twenty miles away. Along the way, **San Gregorio State Beach** (daily 8am–sunset; $6), ten miles south of Half Moon Bay, is at its best in the spring, when flotsam architects construct a range of driftwood shelters along the wide beach south of the parking area. On hot summer days, the beach is packed with well-oiled bodies, but the sands around the bluffs to the north are quieter. For those so inclined, you can bathe nude at the predominantly gay **San Gregorio Private Beach** ($5); follow Hwy-1 one mile north of San Gregorio Road and watch for the small white gate on the left that subtly marks the entrance to the parking area.

The Butano Redwood Forest and the Año Nuevo State Reserve

If you've got a car and it's not a great beach day, head up into the hills above the coast, where the thousands of acres of the **BUTANO REDWOOD FOREST** feel at their most ancient and primeval in the grayest, gloomiest weather. About half the land between San Jose and the coast is protected from development in a variety of state and county parks, all of which are virtually deserted; any one of a dozen roads heads through endless stands of untouched forest, and even the briefest of walks will take you seemingly miles from any sign of civilization. Hwy-84 climbs up from San Gregorio through the Sam McDonald County Park to the hamlet of **LA HONDA**, where Ken Kesey had his ranch during the Sixties and once notoriously invited the Hell's Angels to a party. From here you can continue on to Palo Alto, or, better still, loop back to the coast via Pescadero Road. A mile before you reach the coast, you pass through the quaint town of **PESCADERO**, which has one of the best places to eat on the Peninsula – ⚶ *Duarte's*, 202 Stage Rd (☎650/879-0464), where you can feast on artichoke soup and huge portions of fish in a downhome atmosphere. Another route via Cloverdale Road heads south to **Butano State Park** (8am–sunset; $6 per vehicle), where you can hike and camp (☎650/879-2040; reserve through ReserveAmerica ☎1-800/444-7275; $25) among the redwoods overlooking the Pacific.

Back on Hwy-1, just north of the turn-off to Pescadero, **Pescadero State Beach** is yet another fine spot for a dip, with no time restrictions or parking fee. *Costanoa Coastal Lodge & Camp*, 2001 Rossi Rd, on the eastern side of Hwy-1, just south of Pescadero (☎650/879-1100 or 1-877/262-7848, Ⓦwww .costanoa.com) offers a pampered night under the stars with accommodation ranging from modest cabins ($95) to luxury suites ($275). Five miles south of Pescadero you can stay the night in the old lighthouse-keeper's quarters and soak your bones in another marvelous hot tub at the ⚶ *HI-Pigeon Point Lighthouse Hostel* (☎650/879-0633, Ⓦwww.norcalhostels.org; 7.30–10am & 5.30–10pm; check-in from 4.30pm, curfew 11pm; members $20, others $25, private rooms $55–63, minimum two people; reservations essential in summer). The grounds of the light station are open to visitors (daily 8am–sunset; free; ☎650/879-2120) and you can call to see if one of the occasional tours is imminent. The calmest, most pleasant beach along this stretch in which to wade is at **Bean Hollow State Beach**, a mile north of the hostel – it's also free but has very limited parking.

Año Nuevo State Reserve

If you're here during December through March, continue south another five miles to the **AÑO NUEVO STATE RESERVE** for a chance to see one of nature's most bizarre spectacles – the mating rituals of the northern elephant seal. These massive, ungainly creatures, fifteen feet long and weighing up to three tons, were once found all along the coast, though they were nearly hunted to extinction by whalers in the nineteenth century. During the mating season the beach is literally a seething mass of blubbery bodies, with the trunk-nosed males fighting it out for the right to sire as many as fifty pups in a season. At any time of the year, though, you're likely to see a half-dozen or so dozing in the sands. The reserve is also good for birdwatching, and in March you might even catch sight of migrating gray whales.

The slowly resurgent Año Nuevo seal population is still carefully protected, and during the breeding season the obligatory **guided tours** – designed to protect spectators as much as to give the seals some privacy – begin booking in September (hourly 8am–4pm; $4 per person, $6 per vehicle; ☎650/879-2025 or 1-800/444-4445). Otherwise, tickets are usually made available to people staying at the *Pigeon Point Hostel*, and SamTrans (☎1-800/660-4287) sometimes runs charter-bus tours from the town of **San Mateo** on the Bay side of the Peninsula. South of Año Nuevo, it's clear sailing down Hwy-1 to Santa Cruz, Monterey, and Southern California.

Marin County

cross the Golden Gate from San Francisco, Marin County (pronounced "Ma-RINN") is an unabashed introduction to Californian self-indulgence. An elitist zone of conspicuous luxury and abundant natural beauty, with sunshine, sandy beaches, high mountains, and thick redwood forests, Marin is reportedly the second-wealthiest county in the US, home to a sizeable contingent of Northern California's richest professionals, many of whom grew up during the Flower Power years of the 1960s and lend the place its New Age feel and reputation. And, even if many of the cocaine-and-hot-tub devotees who populated the swanky waterside towns back in the 1970s have traded in their drug habits for mountain bikes – which were invented on the fire roads of Mount Tamalpais – life in Marin still centers around personal pleasure. The throngs you see hiking and cycling at weekends, not to mention the hundreds of esoteric self-help practitioners – rolfing (deep-tissue massage), rebirthing, and soul-travel therapists fill up the classified ads of the local papers – prove that Marinites work hard to maintain their easy air of physical and mental well-being.

To get to the county, you can of course take the **Golden Gate Bridge**, or you can use the flashy modern ferries, appointed with fully stocked bars, that sail across the Bay from San Francisco and give a marvellous initial view of the area. As you head past desolate Alcatraz Island, curvaceous **Mount Tamalpais** looms larger until you land at its foot in one of the chic bayside settlements of **Sausalito** or **Tiburon**. **Angel Island**, in the middle of the Bay but accessible most easily from Tiburon, provides relief from the excessive style-consciousness of both towns, retaining a wild, untouched feeling among the eerie ruins of derelict military fortifications.

Sausalito and Tiburon (and the lifestyles that go with them) are only a small part of Marin, though. The bulk of the county rests on the slopes of the ridge of peaks that divides the Peninsula down the middle, separating the sophisticated harborside towns in the east from the untrammeled wilderness of the Pacific Coast to the west. The **Marin Headlands** just across the Golden Gate Bridge hold time-warped old battlements and gun emplacements that once protected San Francisco's harbor from would-be invaders, and now overlook hikers and cyclists enjoying the acres of open space and wildlife. Along the coastline that stretches north, the broad shore of **Stinson Beach** is the Bay Area's finest and widest stretch of sand. Beyond Stinson, Hwy-1 clings to the coast as it runs past the rural village of **Bolinas** to the phenomenal valleys, forests, and seascapes around **Point Reyes**, where whale- and seal-watchers congregate year-round for glimpses of migrations and matings.

Inland, the heights of Mount Tamalpais – and specifically its sister park to the east, **Muir Woods** – are a magnet to sightseers and nature-lovers, who come to

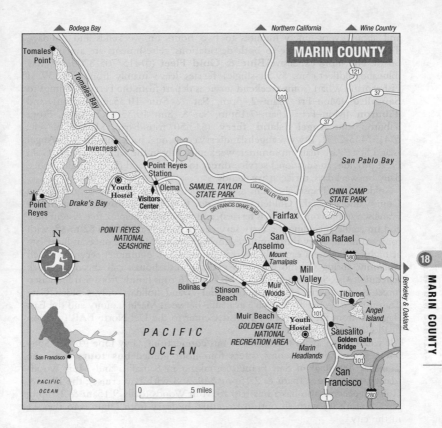

Tomales Point
Tomales Bay
Inverness
Point Reyes Station
Youth Hostel
Olema
Visitors Center
Point Reyes
Drake's Bay
POINT REYES NATIONAL SEASHORE
SAMUEL TAYLOR STATE PARK
LUCAS VALLEY ROAD
SIR FRANCIS DRAKE BLVD
Fairfax
San Anselmo
Mount Tamalpais
Mill Valley
Bolinas
Stinson Beach
Muir Woods
Muir Beach
GOLDEN GATE NATIONAL RECREATION AREA
Youth Hostel
Marin Headlands
San Pablo Bay
CHINA CAMP STATE PARK
San Rafael
Tiburon
Angel Island
Sausalito
Golden Gate Bridge
San Francisco
PACIFIC OCEAN
PACIFIC OCEAN
San Francisco
N
0   5 miles
Berkeley & Oakland

18

MARIN COUNTY

wander through one of the few surviving stands of the native coastal redwood trees. Such trees covered most of Marin before they were chopped down to build and rebuild the dainty wooden houses of San Francisco. The long-vanished lumber mills of the rustic town of **Mill Valley**, overlooking the Bay from the slopes of Mount Tamalpais, bear the guilt for much of this destruction; today, the oldest town in Marin County is home to an eclectic bunch of art galleries and cafés. Further north, Marin's largest town, **San Rafael**, is best bypassed, though the undervisited preserved remnants of an old Chinese fishing village in nearby **China Camp State Park** are worth a stroll. Moving northward, the upper reaches of Marin County border the bountiful wine-growing regions of the Sonoma and Napa valleys, detailed in Chapter 19.

Arrival and getting around

Just getting to Marin County can be a great start to a day out from San Francisco. **Golden Gate Transit** ferries (℡415/923-2000 in San Francisco, ℡415/455-2000 in Marin, ⦿www.goldengate.org) leave from the Ferry Building on the Embarcadero, crossing the Bay past Alcatraz to **Sausalito** (Mon–Fri 7.40am–7.55pm, Sat & Sun 10.40am–6.30pm) and **Larkspur** (Mon–Fri 6.25am–9.35pm, Sat & Sun 12.30–7pm); they run every thirty to forty minutes during the rush hour, roughly hourly during the rest of the day, and about every ninety minutes to two hours on weekends and holidays. Tickets cost $7.10 single to both destinations; refreshments are available on board. The more expensive **Blue & Gold Fleet** (T415/705-8200, Wwww .blueandgoldfleet.com; $9.50 single) ferries leave mainly from Pier 39 at Fisherman's Wharf (some weekend services depart from the Ferry Building) to **Sausalito** (Mon–Fri 11am–2.45pm, Sat & Sun 10.35am–5.05pm) and **Tiburon** (Mon–Fri 7.15am–7.15pm, Sat & Sun 10.35am–5.05pm). From Tiburon, the **Angel Island ferry** ($13.50 round-trip, $1 per bicycle; T415/435-2131, Wwww.angelislandferry.com) nips back and forth to Angel Island State Park (daily in summer, weekends only in the winter). Blue & Gold Fleet provides an additional service direct to Angel Island ($7.50 single), twice daily on weekdays, thrice at weekends.

Golden Gate Transit also runs a comprehensive **bus service** around Marin County and across the Golden Gate Bridge from the Transbay Terminal in San Francisco (same contact info as ferries), and publishes a helpful, free system map and timetable, including the ferry services. Bus fares range from $2 to $8, with routes running every thirty minutes throughout the day, and once an hour late at night. Some areas can only be reached by GGT commuter services, which run only during the morning and evening rush hours (call ahead to check schedule). Also, San Francisco's MUNI bus #76 runs hourly from San Francisco direct to the Marin Headlands on Sundays and holidays only. Golden Gate Transit bus #40, the only service available between Marin County and the East Bay, runs from the San Rafael Transit Center to the Del Norte BART station in El Cerrito via Richmond.

If you'd rather avoid the hassle of bus connections, Gray Line (T415/558-9400, Wwww.grayline.com) offers four-hour guided **bus tours** from the Transbay Terminal in San Francisco, taking in Sausalito and Muir Woods (daily year-round 9.15am & 2.15pm; $49, $68 with Bay cruise); the Blue & Gold Fleet ferry also has a bus trip to Muir Woods (daily 9.15am & 2.15pm; 3hr 30min; $50) with an option to return by ferry from Tiburon to Pier 41 in the city.

Once you're in Marin, one of the best ways to get around is by **bike**, particularly using a mountain bike to cruise the many trails that crisscross the county, especially in the Marin Headlands. If you want to ride on the road, **Sir Francis Drake Highway** – from Larkspur to Point Reyes – makes a good route, though it's best to avoid it on weekends, when the roads can get clogged up with cars. All ferry services (except those to Alcatraz) allow bicycles.

Marin County bus services on Golden Gate Transit

#2: San Francisco–Marin Headlands–Marin City–Sausalito; weekdays.

#4: San Francisco–Mill Valley; weekdays.

#8: San Francisco–Tiburon–Sausalito; weekdays.

#10: San Francisco–Sausalito–Marin City; daily.

#18: San Francisco–Corte Madera–College of Marin–Larkspur; weekdays.

#24: San Francisco–Greenbrea–San Anselmo–Fairfax–Lagunitas; weekdays.

#26/27: San Francisco–San Rafael–San Anselmo–Sleepy Hollow; weekdays.

#29: San Anselmo–Larkspur Ferry–San Rafael; Mon–Sat.

#63: Marin City–Stinson Beach; weekends only.

#70/80: San Francisco–San Rafael–Novato–Petaluma–Santa Rosa; daily.

#93: San Francisco Civic Center–Golden Gate Bridge; weekdays.

Information

Three main on-the-spot sources can provide further **information** on Marin County: the inconveniently located **Marin CVB**, signposted off US-101 at 1 Mitchell Blvd, San Rafael (Mon–Fri 9am–5pm; ☎415/925-2060 or 1-866/925-2060, ⊛www.visitmarin.org); the **Sausalito Chamber of Commerce**, occupying a modest hut at 780 Bridgeway Ave (Tues–Sun 11.30am–4pm; ☎415/332-0505, ⊛www.sausalito.org); and the **Mill Valley Chamber of Commerce**, 85 Throckmorton Ave (Mon–Fri 10am–noon & 1–4pm; ☎415/388-9700, ⊛www.millvalley.org), in the center of the town.

For information on **hiking** and **camping** in the wilderness and beach areas, depending on where you're heading, contact the **Marin Headlands Visitor Center** (daily 9.30am–4.30pm; ☎415/331-1540, ⊛www.nps.gov/goga); other outlets are the **Mount Tamalpais State Park Visitor Center**, 801 Panoramic Hwy, Mill Valley (daily 8am–5.30pm; ☎415/388-2070, ⊛www.mttam.net); or the Point Reyes National Seashore's **Bear Valley Visitors Center**, Point Reyes (Mon–Fri 9am–5pm, Sat & Sun 8am–5pm; ☎415/464-5100, ⊛www.nps.gov/pore). Information on cultural events in Marin can be found in the widely available local freesheets, such as the down-to-earth *Coastal Post* (⊛www.coastalpost.com) or the New-Agey *Pacific Sun* (⊛www.pacificsun.com).

Accommodation

You might prefer simply to dip into Marin County using San Francisco as a base, and, if you've got a car or manage to time the bus connections right, it's certainly possible, at least for the southern half of the county. However, if time is of little concern, consider taking a more leisurely look at Marin, staying over for a couple of nights in some well-chosen spots. Sadly, there are few **hotels**, and most charge well in excess of $100 a night; **motels** tend to be the same as anywhere, though there are a couple of attractively faded ones along the coast. If you want to stay in a B&B, contact the **Bed and Breakfast Exchange**, 45 Entrata Drive, San Anselmo (☎415/485-1971, ⊛www.marinbedandbreakfast.com), which can fix you up with rooms in comfortable private homes all over Marin County from around $70/night for two, ranging from courtyard hideaways on the beach in Tiburon to houseboats in Sausalito. The best bet for budget accommodation is a dorm bed in one of the beautifully situated **hostels** along the western beaches.

Motels and hotels

Acqua Hotel 555 Redwood Hwy, Mill Valley ☎415/380-0400 or 1-888/662-9555, ⊛www.jdvhotels.com. Sumptuous hotel on Richardson Bay with fifty luxurious rooms and oriental touches in its stylish decor, part of the upmarket Joie de Vivre chain. $159.

Casa Madrona 801 Bridgeway Ave, Sausalito ☎415/332-0502 or 1-800/567-9524, ⊛www.casamadrona.com. Deluxe, all mod cons hotel with an extension spreading up the hill above the Bay. Spa facilities available. $219.

Colonial Motel 1735 Lincoln Ave, San Rafael ☎415/453-9188 or 1-800/554-9118, ⊛www.colonialinnmarin.com. Quiet, well-furnished, friendly motel with decent rates in a residential neighborhood. $65.

Grand Hotel 15 Brighton Ave, Bolinas ☎415/868-1757. Just two budget rooms in a funky, run-down old hotel above a secondhand shop. Shared bath. Unbeatable character, including the quirky owner. $50.

Hotel Sausalito 16 El Portal, Sausalito ☎415/332-0700 or 1-888/442-0700, ⊛www.hotelsausalito.com. Sixteen rooms, decorated in French Riviera style, with views across the park and harbor. Owned and run by an entertaining Scot. $155.

The Lodge At Tiburon 1651 Tiburon Blvd, Tiburon ☎415/435-3133, ⊛www.thelodgeattiburon.com. Smart modern hotel with a

rustic feel. Comfortable rooms, all with CD/
DVD players, some with Jacuzzis. Rather
inept staff though. $169.

Mill Valley Inn 165 Throckmorton Ave,
Mill Valley ⊤ 415/389-6608 or 1-800/595-
2100, ⓦ www.millvalleyinn.com. Now also
owned by Joie de Vivre, Mill Valley is a
gorgeous, European-style inn with elegant
rooms, lavishly furnished in period style, and
two private cottages. $189.

Point Reyes Seashore Lodge 10021 Hwy-1,
Olema ⊤ 415/663-9000 or 1-800/404-5694,
ⓦ www.pointreyesseashore.com. Attractive,
largely wooden lodge that's the size of a
hotel but with the personal touch of a B&B.
All rooms overlook the garden and brook.
$135.

Stinson Beach Motel 3416 Shoreline Hwy,
Stinson Beach ⊤ 415/868-1712, ⓦ www
.stinsonbeachmotel.com. Basic roadside motel
right on Hwy-1, with tiny rooms. 5min walk
to the beach. $90.

B&Bs

Blue Heron Inn 11 Wharf Rd, Bolinas
⊤ 415/868-1102, ⓦ www.blueheron-bolinas.com.
Lovely double rooms in an unbeatable
locale close to the waterfront, complete with
its own fully operational restaurant. Friendly
welcome. $125.

Gerstle Park Inn 34 Grove St, San Rafael
⊤ 415/721-7611 or 1-800/726-7611, ⓦ www
.gerstleparkinn.com. Set in the leafy suburbs
towards the hills of central Marin, this
characterful Victorian house has ten
spacious suites with touches from both Asia
and Europe making for a classy ambience.
$189.

Lindisfarne Guest House Green Gulch Zen
Center, Muir Beach ⊤ 415/383-3134, ⓦ www
.sfzc.org. Restful rooms in a meditation
retreat set in a secluded valley above Muir
Beach. Price includes excellent vegetarian
meals. $140.

Mountain Home Inn 810 Panoramic Hwy, Mill
Valley ⊤ 415/381-9000 or 1-877/381-9001,
ⓦ www.mtnhomeinn.com. Romantically
located on the crest of Mount Tamalpais,
this B&B offers great views and endless
hiking. Some rooms with hot tubs. Ample
cooked breakfasts. $195.

Olema Inn 10000 Sir Francis Drake Blvd, Olema
⊤ 415/663-9559 or 1-800/532-9252, ⓦ www
.theolemainn.com. Wonderful little B&B near
the entrance to Point Reyes National
Seashore, on a site that's been a hotel

since 1876. Comfy rooms and absolutely
no nightlife or traffic noise to speak of; has
its own fine dining. Book by phone only.
$150.

Pelican Inn 10 Pacific Way, Muir Beach
⊤ 415/383-6000, ⓦ www.pelicaninn.com.
Very comfortable rooms in a romantic
pseudo-English country inn, with good bar
and restaurant downstairs. Two-min walk
from beautiful Muir Beach. $190.

Ten Inverness Way 10 Inverness Way,
Inverness ⊤ 415/669-1648, ⓦ www
.teninvernessway.com. Quiet and restful, with
a hot tub and complimentary evening wine,
in a small village of good restaurants and
bakeries on the fringes of Point Reyes.
$162.

Hostels

HI-Marin Headlands Building 941, Fort
Barry, Marin Headlands ⊤ 415/331-2777,
ⓦ www.norcalhostels.org. Hard to get to
without a car – it's near Rodeo Lagoon just
off Bunker Rd, five miles west of Sausalito –
but worth the effort for its setting, in cozy
old army barracks near the ocean. On Sun
and hols only, MUNI bus #76 from San
Francisco stops right outside. Closed
10am–3.30pm, except for check-in. Dorm
beds $21 a night, private rooms $55.

HI-Point Reyes in the Point Reyes
National Seashore ⊤ 415/663-8811, ⓦ www
.norcalhostels.org. Also hard to reach without
your own transportation: just off Limantour
Rd six miles west of the visitor center and
two miles from the beach, it's located in an
old ranch house and surrounded by
meadows and forests. Closed 10am–
4.30pm; office hours 7.30–10am & 4.30–
9pm; no check-in after 9.30pm. Dorm
beds from $20 a night; one private room
from $58.

Campgrounds

Angel Island State Park Angel Island
⊤ 415/435-5390, ⓦ www.angelisland.org. Nine
primitive walk-in (and one kayak-in) sites
with great views of San Francisco, which
explains why they cost as much ($20
summer/$15 winter) per night as more
developed sites elsewhere. In summer
it's essential to book through Reserve-
America ⊤ 1-800/444-7275, ⓦ www
.reserveamerica.com.

China Camp State Park off N San Pedro Rd,
north of San Rafael ⊤ 415/456-0766. Walk-in

plots (just 600ft from the parking lot) overlooking a lovely meadow. First-come-first-camping for $25 a night in summer ($20 winter). April–Oct reserve through ReserveAmerica ℡1-800/444-7275, ⓦwww.reserveamerica.com.
Marin Headlands just across the Golden Gate Bridge ℡415/561-4304, ⓦwww.nps.gov/goga. Five campgrounds, the best of which is the very popular *Kirby Cove* (open April–Oct only), at the northern foot of the Golden Gate Bridge (reservations ℡1-877/444-6777, ⓦwww.recreation.gov; $25). Of the remaining sites, one is a group campground ($25), and the other three are free.

Mount Tamalpais State Park above Mill Valley ℡415/388-2070. Two separate campgrounds ($20) for backpackers, one on the slopes of the mountain and the other towards the coast at Steep Ravine, which also has a few rustic cabins ($65). Reserve through ReserveAmerica ℡1-800/444-7275, ⓦwww.reserveamerica.com.
Point Reyes National Seashore 40 miles northwest of San Francisco ℡415/663-1092. A wide range of hike-in sites for backpackers, near the beach or in the forest. Reserve sites up to two months in advance (weekdays 9am–2pm; ℡415/663-8054; $15).

Across the Golden Gate: Marin Headlands and Sausalito

The largely undeveloped **Marin Headlands** of the Golden Gate National Recreation Area (across the Golden Gate Bridge from San Francisco) afford some of the most impressive views of the bridge and the city behind. As the regular fog rolls in, the breathtaking image of the bridge's stanchions tantalizingly drifting in and out of sight and the fleeting glimpses of downtown skyscrapers will abide long in the memory. Take the first turn as you exit the bridge (Alexander Ave) and follow the sign back to San Francisco – the one-way trip back to the bridge heads first to the west along Conzelman Road and up a steep hill. You'll pass through largely undeveloped land, dotted by the concrete remains of old forts and gun emplacements standing guard over the entrance to the Bay, dating from as far back as the Civil War and as recent as World War II. The coastline here is much more rugged than it is on the San Francisco side, making it a great place for an aimless clifftop hike or a stroll along one of the beaches dramatically situated near the crushing waves at the bottom of treacherous footpaths.

The first installation you'll see as you climb the steep hill up the Headlands is **Battery Wallace**, the largest and most impressive of the artillery sites, cut as it is through a hillside above the southwestern tip of the Peninsula. Satisfyingly, the clean-cut military geometry survives today, framing views of the Pacific Ocean and the Golden Gate Bridge. From here, continue along Conzelman until it turns into a one-way road for incredible views of the city from any of the many turn-offs; at the road's end, walkways lead from a parking area to birdwatching trails and vistas of Rodeo Beach and the lighthouse far below.

For birding, walk from the Battery Wallace parking lot through tunnels that lead five hundred yards to the opposite bluff, overlooking **Point Bonita Lighthouse** (tours Sat–Mon, 12.30–3.30pm; free), standing sentry at the very end of the Headlands. You have to walk the last half-mile from an even smaller parking area down to the beckoning structure, a beautiful stroll that takes you through a tunnel cut into the cliff and across a precarious suspension bridge. The lighthouse casts its beam over 25 miles out to sea.

Heading back on Conzelman, fork off to the left, heading northeast onto Bunker Road. To the left lies the **Nike Missile Site**, an abandoned 1950s

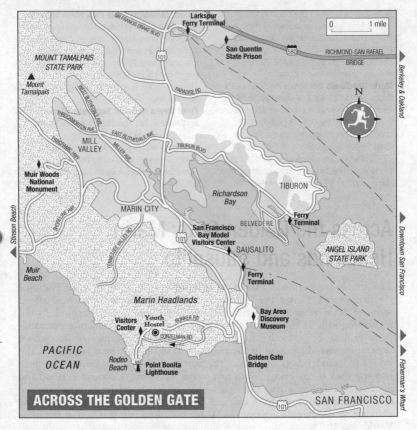

ballistic missile launchpad, complete with disarmed nuclear missiles (first Sun of month 12.30–3.30pm; free; Ⓦ www.atomictourist.com/nike.htm). A bit further on, the **Marin Headlands Information Center**, alongside Rodeo Lagoon (see p.349 for details), has free maps of popular hiking trails in the area and a **historical walk**, which loops 5.5 miles into Gerbode Valley and tells the story of the ruins of **Marincello**, a town begun and abandoned in the late 1960s in the headlands near Tennessee Valley. A bit further along Bunker Road, the largest of **Fort Barry**'s old buildings has been converted into the spacious but homely *HI-Marin Headlands Hostel* (see p.350), an excellent base for more extended explorations of the inland ridges and valleys.

To the west, Bunker Road snakes down to wide, sandy **Rodeo Beach** (#76 MUNI bus from San Francisco: Sun & holidays only), which separates the chilly ocean from the warm marshy water of **Rodeo Lagoon**, where swimming is prohibited to protect nesting seabirds. North of the lagoon, the **Marine Mammal Center** (no fixed hours; ☎415/289-7333, Ⓦ www.tmmc.org) rescues and rehabilitates injured and orphaned sea creatures, such as dolphins and sea otters. The main building is currently closed to the public for renovations but a temporary **visitor center** at Building 1049 (daily 10am–4pm) gives a glimpse into their work and sells T-shirts and posters.

Biking the Coastal Trail

San Franciscans love the Headlands for their many excellent, groomed mountain-bike trails, the best of which is the **Coastal Trail**. Beginning at the northern end of the Golden Gate Bridge, it climbs up the mountain facing back toward the city before plummeting down into Rodeo Valley to the west. At Rodeo Beach, where you can also pick up the trail on foot, it continues past gun embankments along the quiet coast to Tennessee Valley Beach, from where cyclists can loop back to Bunker Road via the marked Miwok Trail. Contact the **Marin Headlands Information Center** (see p.349) to obtain a detailed map on this and other trails in the area. For information on renting bikes in the Bay Area see p.288.

Sausalito

SAUSALITO, along the Bay below US-101, is a pretty, snug little town of exclusive restaurants and pricey boutiques along a picturesque waterfront promenade. Expensive, quirkily designed houses climb the overgrown cliffs above **Bridgeway Avenue**, the main road and bus route through town. Sausalito was once a fairly gritty community of fishermen and sea-traders, full of bars and bordellos. Fifty years ago it even served as one of the settings for Orson Welles's murder mystery, *The Lady from Shanghai*. Despite its present pretensions, Sausalito still makes a fun day out from San Francisco by ferry, with boats arriving next to the Sausalito Yacht Club in the center of town. Hang out in one of the waterfront bars and watch the crowds strolling along the esplanade, or climb the stairways above Bridgeway and amble around the leafy hills.

If you have sailing experience and enough company, split the $172–375 daily rental fee of a four- to ten-person **sailboat** at Cass's Marina, 1702 Bridgeway (☏415/332-6789, ⊛www.cassmarina.com). The other main diversion is **sea kayaking**, and Sea Trek (☏415/488-1000, ⊛www.seatrekkayak.com) rents single or double sea kayaks beginning at $15/25 for an hour's worth of paddling the Bay. It offers sit-on-top kayaks, lessons, and safe routes for first-timers, or closed kayaks and directions around Angel Island for more experienced paddlers.

At the waterfront, the old working wharves and warehouses that made Sausalito a haven for smugglers and Prohibition-era rum-runners are long gone; most have been taken over by dull steakhouses. However, some stretches of it have, for the moment at least, survived the tourist onslaught. A mile north of the town center along Bridgeway Avenue, an ad hoc community of exotic barges and houseboats – some of which have been moored here since the 1950s – is perennially threatened with eviction to make room for yet another luxury marina and Bay-view office development. In the meantime, many of the boats – one looks like a South Pacific island, another like the Taj Mahal – can be viewed at Waldo Point, half a mile beyond the cavernous concrete building that houses the **Bay Model Visitor Center**, 2100 Bridgeway (March to late May Tues–Sat 9am–4pm; late May to early Sept Tues–Fri 9am–4pm, Sat & Sun 10am–5pm; free; ☏415/332-3870, ⊛www.spn.usace.army.mil/bmvc). Here, elevated walkways lead you around a massive working scale model of the Bay, along with its surrounding deltas and aquatic inhabitants, simulating changing tides and powerful currents and offering insight on the vastness and diversity of this confluence of waters.

One of Sausalito's biggest family draws, situated back toward the Golden Gate Bridge at 557 McReynolds Rd, is the constantly expanding **Bay Area**

▲ Houseboats in Sausalito

Discovery Museum (Tues–Fri 9am–4pm, Sat & Sun 10am–5pm; $10, children $8; ☎415/339-3900, ⓦwww.baykidsmuseum.org). Located in the remodeled barracks of **Fort Baker**, it comprises a series of activities and workshops for youngsters from tots to 10 or so, including art and media rooms as well as the outdoor Lookout Cove area, where kids can play in a mini-tidepool, on a shipwreck, or on the model of the Golden Gate Bridge as it was during construction – pretty cool as the real one is visible in the distance if it's clear.

The Marin County coast to Bolinas

The **Shoreline Highway**, Hwy-1, cuts off west from US-101 just north of Sausalito, following the old main highway towards Mill Valley (see p.357). The first turn on the left, Tennessee Valley Road, leads up to the less-visited northern expanses of the Golden Gate National Recreation Area. You can take a beautiful three-mile hike from the parking lot at the end of the road, heading down the secluded and lushly green **Tennessee Valley** to a small beach in a rocky cove, or you can take a guided tour on horseback from Miwok Livery at 701 Tennessee Valley Rd ($65/90min; ☎415/383-8048, ⓦwww.miwokstables.com).

On from the turn-off, Hwy-1 twists up the canyon to a crest, where **Panoramic Highway** spears off to the right, following the ridge north to Muir Woods and Mount Tamalpais; Golden Gate Transit bus #63 to Stinson Beach follows this route every hour on weekends and holidays only. Be warned, however, that the hillsides are more often than not choked with fog until 11am, making the drive both dangerous and visually uninteresting.

Two miles down from the crest, a small unpaved road cuts off to the left, dropping down to the bottom of the broad canyon to the **Green Gulch Farm and Zen Center** (T 415/383-3134, W www.sfzc.org), an organic farm and Buddhist retreat, with an authentic Japanese teahouse and a simple but refined prayer hall. On Sunday mornings the center is open from 8.15am for a public meditation period and an informal lecture on Zen Buddhism at 10.15am, after which you can stroll down to Muir Beach. If you are interested in learning more, inquire about the center's Guest Student Program, which enables initiates to stay from three days to several weeks at a time (it costs about $15 a night). Residents rise well before dawn for meditation and prayer, then work much of the day in the gardens, tending the vegetables that are eventually served in many of the Bay Area's finest restaurants (notably *Green's* in San Francisco). If you just want a weekend's retreat, you can also stay overnight in the attached *Lindisfarne Guest House* (see p.350) and take part as you choose in the communal life.

Beyond the Zen Center, the road down from Muir Woods rejoins Hwy-1 at **Muir Beach**, usually uncrowded and beautifully secluded in a semicircular cove. Three miles north, **Steep Ravine** drops sharply down the cliffs to a small beach, past very rustic cabins and a campground, bookable through Mount Tamalpais State Park (see p.356). A mile on is the small and lovely **Red Rocks** nudist beach, down a steep trail from a parking area along the highway. **Stinson Beach**, whose wide strand is stunning and justifiably the most popular in the county despite the rather cold water, is a mile further. Unfortunately both the beach and the village behind it get packed at weekends in summer, when the traffic can be nightmarish. You can rent kayaks at Off the Beach Boats, 15 Calle del Mar ($25/2hr, $100 all weekend, cheaper in winter; T 415/868-9445).

Bolinas and southern Point Reyes

At the tip of the headland, due west from Stinson Beach, is the village of **BOLINAS**, though you may have a hard time finding it – road signs marking the turn-off from Hwy-1 are removed as soon as they're put up by locals hoping to keep the place to themselves. The campaign may have backfired, though, since press coverage of the "sign war" has done more to publicize the town than any road sign ever did; to get there, take the first left beyond the estuary and follow the road to the end. Bolinas is surrounded by federal property: the Golden Gate National Recreation Area and Point Reyes National Seashore. Even the lagoon was recently declared a National Bird Sanctuary. Known for its leftist hippie culture, the village itself is a small colony of artists, bearded handymen, stray dogs, and writers, who have included the late trout-fishing author Richard Brautigan and basketball diarist Jim Carroll. There's not a lot to see apart from the small **Bolinas Museum**, 48 Wharf Rd (Fri 1–5pm, Sat & Sun noon–5pm; free; T 415/868-0330, W www.bolinasmuseum.org), which has a few historical displays and works by local artists in a set of converted cottages around a courtyard. Mostly, though, it's just a place for people-watching and taking in the laid-back atmosphere.

Beyond Bolinas, the rocky beach at the end of Wharf Road, west of the village is great for calm surf waves. **Duxbury Reef Nature Reserve**, half a mile west at the end of Elm Road, is well worth a look for its tidal pools, full of starfish, crabs, and sea anemones. Otherwise, Mesa Road heads north from Bolinas past the **Point Reyes Bird Observatory** (T 415/868-0655, W www.prbo.org) – open for informal tours all day, though best visited in the morning. The first bird observatory in the US, this is still an important research and study center. If you time it right you may be able to watch, or even help, the staff as they put colored bands on the birds to keep track of them. Beyond here, the unpaved road leads onto the **Palomarin Trailhead**, the southern access into the Point Reyes National Seashore (see p.360). The best of the many beautiful hikes around the area leads past a number of small lakes and meadows for three miles to **Alamere Falls**, which throughout the winter and spring cascade down the cliffs onto **Wildcat Beach**. **Bass Lake**, the first of several lakes along the trail, is a great spot for a swim, best entered by swinging out and dropping from one of the ropes that hang from the trees above its shore.

Back at the turn-off from Hwy-1, the Bolinas–Fairfax Road leads due east through redwoods and grassy hillside – a superb drive as long as the road has not been closed for one of the frequent landslides or washouts that occur here. When you reach the T in the road, turn left to get to Fairfax, or right to scale Mount Tamalpais.

Mount Tamalpais and Muir Woods

MOUNT TAMALPAIS dominates the Marin skyline. Hulking over the cool canyons of the rest of the county in a crisp yet voluptuous silhouette, Mount Tam, as it's locally known, divides the county into two distinct parts: the wild western slopes above the Pacific Coast and the increasingly suburban communities along the calmer Bay frontage. Panoramic Highway branches off from Hwy-1 along the crest through the center of **Mount Tamalpais State Park** (☏415/338-2070, ⊛www.mtia.net), which has some thirty miles of hiking trails and many campgrounds, though most of the redwood trees which once covered its slopes have long since been chopped down to form the posts and beams of San Francisco's Victorian houses. One 560-acre grove of these towering trees does remain, however, protected as the **MUIR WOODS NATIONAL MONUMENT** (daily 8am–sunset; $5; ☏415/388-2595, ⊛www.nps.gov/muwo), a mile down Muir Woods Road from Panoramic Highway. It's a tranquil and majestic spot, with sunlight filtering through the 300-foot trees down to the laurel and fern-covered canyon below. The canyon's steep sides are what saved it from Mill Valley's lumbermen, and today it's one of the few old-growth redwood groves between San Francisco and the fantastic forests of Redwood National Park, up the coast toward the Oregon border.

Its proximity to San Francisco makes Muir Woods a popular target, and the **paved trails** nearest the parking lot are often packed with bus-tour hordes. However, if you visit during the week, or outside midsummer, it's easy enough to leave the crowds behind, especially if you're willing to head off up the steep trails that climb the canyon sides. Winter is a particularly good time to come, as the streams are gurgling – the main creek flows down to Muir Beach, and salmon have been known to spawn in it – and the forest creatures, including the colonies of ladybugs that spend their winter huddling in the rich undergrowth, are more likely to be seen going about their business. Keep an eye out for the various species of salamanders and newts that thrive in this damp environment; be warned, though, that some are poisonous and will bite if harassed. One way to avoid the crowds, and the only way to get here on public transportation, is to enter the woods from the top by way of a two-mile hike from the **Pan Toll Ranger Station** (☏415/388-2070) on Panoramic Highway – which is a stop on the Golden Gate Transit #63 bus route. As the state park headquarters, the station has maps and information on hiking and camping, and rangers can suggest hikes to suit your mood and interests. From here, the **Pan Toll Road** turns off to the right along the ridge to within a hundred yards of the 2571-foot summit of Mount Tamalpais, where there are breathtaking views of the distant Sierra Nevadas, and red-necked turkey vultures listlessly circle. Hike the 0.3-mile wood-planked trail up to Gardner Lookout from the parking lot for an even better view.

Mill Valley

From the east peak of Mount Tamalpais, a quick two-mile hike downhill follows the **Temelpa Trail** through velvety shrubs of chaparral to **MILL VALLEY**, the oldest and most enticing of Marin County's inland towns – also accessible every thirty minutes by Golden Gate Transit bus #10 from San Francisco and Sausalito. Originally a logging center, it was from here that the destruction of the surrounding redwoods was organized. The **Mill Valley and Mount Tamalpais Scenic Railroad** – according to the blurb, "the crookedest railroad in the world" – was cut into the slopes above the town in 1896, twisting up through nearly three hundred tight curves in under eight miles. The trip proved so popular with tourists that the line was extended down into Muir Woods in 1907, though road-building and fire combined to put an end to the railroad by 1930. You can, however, follow its old route from the end of Summit Avenue in Mill Valley, a popular trip with daredevils on all-terrain bikes, which were, incidentally, invented here. The route is also used each June for the **Dipsea**, a tooth-and-nail seven-mile cross-country footrace across the mountains to Stinson Beach.

Upscale Mill Valley now makes a healthy living out of tourism, especially during the **Mill Valley Film Festival** (℡415/383-5346, ⓦwww.mvff.com) in early October, which draws Bay Area stars like Robin Williams and Sharon Stone, and a host of up-and-coming directors. The restored town is centered around the redwood-shaded square of the *Depot Bookstore and Café* (Mon–Sat 7am–10pm, Sun 8am–10pm; ℡415/383-2665), a popular browsing hangout at 87 Throckmorton Ave, next door to the Chamber of Commerce (see p.349), which stocks free maps of Mount Tam and hiking trails. Across the street, at no. 74, the Pleasure Principle (℡415/388-8588) is a reminder of the Northern California eclecticism that lurks beneath Mill Valley's posh facade – this self-declared UFO headquarters also advertises a collection of vintage porn.

Tiburon and Angel Island

TIBURON, five miles southeast of Mill Valley on the other side of US-101, is another ritzy harborside village to which hundreds of people come each weekend, many of them via direct Blue & Gold Fleet **ferries** from San Francisco (see p.348 for details). It's a relaxed place, a bit less touristy than Sausalito, and if you're in the mood to take it easy and watch the boats sail across the Bay, sitting out on the sunny deck of one of the many cafés and bars can be idyllic. There are few specific sights to look out for, but it's pleasant enough to simply wander around, browsing the galleries and antique shops. The best of these are grouped together in **Ark Row**, at the west end of Main Street, where the quirky buildings are actually old houseboats that were beached here early in the twentieth century. Further along, you can get a taste of the Wine Country at the Windsor Vineyards tasting room, 72 Main St (daily 10am–6pm; ℡415/435-3113, ⓦwww.windsorvineyards.com). On a hill above the town stands **Old St Hilary's Church** (April–Oct Wed–Sun 1–4pm; ℡415/789-0066), a Gothic beauty that is best seen in the spring, when the surrounding fields are covered with multicolored buckwheat, flax, and paintbrush.

Tiburon is known for a couple of good bike rides – though you'll have to bring a bike over via the ferry or from Sausalito, as there are no rental shops here. Begin by cruising around the many plush houses of **Belvedere Island**, just across the Beach Road Bridge from the west end of Main Street, enjoying the fine views of the Bay and Golden Gate Bridge. More ambitious bikers can continue along the waterfront bike path, which winds from the bijou shops and galleries three miles west along undeveloped Richardson Bay frontage to a bird sanctuary at **Greenwood Cove**, where a pristine Victorian house is now the western headquarters of the National Audubon Society and open for tours on Sundays (10am–4pm; free; ℡415/388-2524, ⓦwww.audubon.org). A small interpretive center has displays on local and migratory birds and wildlife.

Another fine ride heads east from Tiburon along winding Paradise Road, around the mostly undeveloped headland three and a half miles to **Paradise Beach**, a county park with a fishing pier and close-up views of passing oil tankers heading for the refinery across the Bay in Richmond. If you want to make a full circuit, Trestle Glen Boulevard cuts up and over the Peninsula from near Greenwood Cove, linking with Paradise Road two miles northwest of Paradise Beach.

Angel Island

The pleasures of Tiburon are soon exhausted, and you'd be well advised to take the Angel Island Ferry (see p.348 for details) a mile offshore to the largest island in the San Francisco Bay, ten times the size of Alcatraz. **Angel Island** is now officially a state park, but over the years it's served a variety of purposes, everything from a home for Miwok Native Americans to a World War II prisoner-of-war camp. It's full of ghostly ruins of old military installations but it's the nature that lures visitors to the island, with its oak and eucalyptus trees and sagebrush covering the hills above rocky coves and sandy beaches, giving the island a feel quite apart from the mainland. The island offers some pleasant biking opportunities: a five-mile road rings the island, and an unpaved track (plus a number of hiking trails) leads up to the 800ft hump of **Mount Livermore**, with panoramic views of the Bay Area.

The ferry arrives at **Ayala Cove**, where a small snack bar selling hot dogs and cold drinks provides the only sustenance available on the island – better to bring a picnic if you plan to spend the day here. The nearby **visitor center** (daily 9am–4pm; ℡415/435-1915, ⓦwww.angelisland.org), in an old building that was built as a quarantine facility for soldiers returning from the Philippines after the Spanish–American War, has displays on the island's history. Around the point on the northwest corner of the island, the **North Garrison**, built in 1905, was the site of a prisoner-of-war camp during World War II, while the larger **East Garrison**, on the Bay half a mile beyond, was the major transfer point for soldiers bound for the South Pacific. Around the point, **Quarry Beach** is the best on the island, a clean sandy shore that's protected from the winds blowing in through the Golden Gate; it's also a popular landing spot for kayakers and canoeists who paddle across the Bay from Berkeley. **Camping** on Angel Island (see p.351 for details) affords glittering views of San Francisco and the East Bay by night. The campground's nine sites fill up fast, so reserve well in advance. For **tours** of Angel Island, contact Angel Island TramTours (☏415/897-0715, ⓦwww.angelisland.com), which gives one-hour tours ($13.50) and rents mountain bikes ($10/hr, $35/day).

Sir Francis Drake Boulevard and central Marin County

The quickest route to the wilds of the Point Reyes National Seashore, and the only way to get there on public transportation, is by way of **Sir Francis Drake Boulevard**, which cuts across central Marin County through the inland towns of **San Anselmo** and **Fairfax**, reaching the coast thirty miles west at a crescent-shaped bay where, in 1579, Drake supposedly landed and claimed all of what he called Nova Albion for England. The route makes an excellent day-long cycling tour, with the reward of good beaches, a youth hostel, and some tasty restaurants at the end of the road.

The Larkspur Golden Gate Transit **ferry**, which leaves from the Ferry Building in San Francisco, is the longest of the Bay crossings. Primarily a commuter route, it docks at the modern space-frame terminal at Larkspur Landing. The monolithic, red-tile-roofed complex you see on the bayfront a mile east is the maximum-security **San Quentin State Prison**, which houses the state's most violent and notorious criminals, and of which Johnny Cash sang, "I hate every inch of you." If you arrive by car over the Richmond-San Rafael Bridge, you can follow road signs off Hwy-101 to the **San Quentin Prison Museum**, Building 106, Dolores Way (Mon–Fri 10am–4pm, Sat 11.45am–3.15pm; $2; ☏415/454-8808). The tour takes about an hour, during which you'll see a prison cell, a replica of the gas chamber, the original gallows, and the solitary confinement pen known as "The Dungeon." At the end of the tour, you can buy prisoner-made artwork and even a collection of the inmates' favorite recipes, collected in the book, *Cooking with Conviction*.

San Anselmo, Fairfax, and Point Reyes Station

SAN ANSELMO, set in a broad valley two miles north of Mount Tam, calls itself "the antiques capital of Northern California" and sports a tiny center of specialty shops, furniture stores, and cafés that draws out many San Francisco shoppers on weekends. The ivy-covered **San Francisco Theological Seminary** off Bolinas Avenue, which dominates the town from the hill above, is worth a quick visit for the view and architecture. At serene **Robson-Harrington Park** on Crescent Avenue you can picnic among well-tended gardens, and the very green and leafy **Creek Park** follows the creek that winds through the town center, but otherwise there's not a lot to do but eat and drink – or browse through fine bookstores, such as Oliver's Books, at 645 San Anselmo Ave (☏415/454-4421).

Center Boulevard follows the tree-lined creek west for a mile to **FAIRFAX**, a much less ostentatiously hedonistic community than the harborside towns, though in many ways it still typifies Marin lifestyles, with an array of wholefood stores and bookstores geared to a thoughtfully mellow crowd. From Fairfax, the narrow Bolinas Road twists up and over the mountains to the coast at Stinson Beach, while Sir Francis Drake Boulevard winds through a pastoral landscape of ranch houses hidden away up oak-covered valleys.

Ten miles west of Fairfax along Sir Francis Drake Boulevard, **Samuel Taylor State Park** has a range of pleasant trails and alternative camping facilities; five miles more bring you to the coastal Hwy-1 and **OLEMA**, a hamlet at the entrance to the park with a decent food and lodging choices (see p.350). A couple of miles north sits the tourist town of **POINT REYES STATION**, a good place to stop off for a bite to eat or to pick up picnic supplies before heading off to enjoy the wide-open spaces of the Point Reyes National Seashore just beyond.

The Point Reyes National Seashore

From Point Reyes Station, Sir Francis Drake Boulevard heads out to the westernmost tip of Marin County at Point Reyes through the **Point Reyes National Seashore**, a near-island of wilderness surrounded on three sides by more than fifty miles of isolated coastline – pine forests and sunny meadows bordered by rocky cliffs and sandy, windswept beaches. This wing-shaped landmass, something of an aberration along the generally straight coastline north of San Francisco, is in fact a rogue piece of the earth's crust that has been drifting slowly and steadily northward along the San Andreas Fault, having started some six million years ago as a suburb of Los Angeles. When the great earthquake of 1906 shattered San Francisco, the land here – the epicenter – shifted over sixteen feet in an instant, though damage was confined to a few skewed cattle fences.

The park's **visitor center**, two miles southwest of Point Reyes Station near Olema, just off Hwy-1 on Bear Valley Road, holds engaging displays on the geology and natural history of the region. Rangers dish out excellent hiking and cycling itineraries and have up-to-date information on the weather, which can change quickly and be cold and windy along the coast even when it's hot and sunny here, three miles inland. Keep in mind that the point-to-point distances within Point Reyes are relatively vast and speed limits are slow, doubling most laymen's estimates of travel time. The rangers can help you realistically plan your itinerary and arrange for any hiking permits you'll need; they can also help with reservations at the various hike-in **campgrounds** within the park. Nearby, a replica of a native Miwok village has an authentic religious **roundhouse**, and a popular hike follows the Bear Valley Trail along Coast Creek four miles to **Arch Rock**, a large tunnel in the seaside cliffs that you can walk through at low tide.

North of the visitor center, Limantour Road heads west six miles to the *HI-Point Reyes Hostel* (see p.350), before continuing another two miles to the coast at **Limantour Beach**, one of the best swimming beaches and a good place to watch the seabirds in the adjacent estuary. Bear Valley Road rejoins Sir Francis Drake Boulevard just past Limantour Road, leading north along Tomales Bay through the village of **INVERNESS**, so named because the landscape reminded an early settler of his home in the Scottish Highlands. Eight miles west of Inverness, a turn leads down past **Drake's Bay Oyster Farm** (Tues–Sun 8am–4pm; ☎415/669-1149, ⓦwww.drakesbayfamilyfarms.com) – which sells bivalves for less than half the price you'd pay in San Francisco – to **Drake's Beach**, one likely landing spot of Sir Francis in 1579 (whose journal makes the exact location unclear). Appropriately, the coastline here resembles the southern coast of England – often cold, wet, and windy, with chalk-white cliffs rising above the wide sandy beach. The road continues southwest another four miles to the very tip of Point Reyes, where a precariously sited **lighthouse** (Thurs–Sun 10am–4.30pm; tours first and third Sat of each month; free) stands firm against the crashing surf. The bluffs here are an excellent place for watching migrating **gray whales**, from mid-March to April and late December to early February. Just over a mile back from the lighthouse a narrow road leads to **Chimney Rock**, where you can often see basking **elephant seals** or **sea lions** from the overlook.

The northern tip of the Point Reyes seashore, **Tomales Point**, is accessible via Pierce Point Road, which turns off Sir Francis Drake Boulevard two miles north of Inverness. Jutting out into Tomales Bay, it's the least-visited section of the park and a refuge for hefty **tule elk**; it's also a great place to admire the lupines, poppies, and other wildflowers that appear in the spring. The best swimming (at least the warmest water) is at **Heart's Desire Beach**, just before the end of the road. Down the bluffs from where the road comes to a dead end, there are excellent tidal pools at rocky **McClure's Beach**. North of Point Reyes Station, Hwy-1 continues along the coast past the famed oyster beds of Tomales Bay and through Bodega Bay, where Alfred Hitchcock's *The Birds* was shot, up to Mendocino and the Northern California coast.

San Rafael and around

You may pass through **SAN RAFAEL** on your way north from San Francisco, but there's little worth stopping for. The county seat and the only big city in Marin County, it has none of the woodsy qualities that make the other towns special, though you'll come across a couple of good restaurants and bars along Fourth Street, the main drag. Downtown's one attraction is

Gray whales

The most commonly spotted whale along California's coast, the **gray whale** migrates annually from its summer feeding grounds near Alaska to its winter breeding grounds off Baja California and back again. Some 23,000 whales make the 13,000-mile round-trip, swimming just a half-mile from the shoreline in small groups, with pregnant females leading the way on the southbound journey. Protected by an international treaty from hunters since 1938, the gray whale population has been increasing steadily each year, and its migration brings out thousands of humans hoping to catch a glimpse of their fellow mammals. Point Reyes is a favorite watching spot, as are the beaches along Hwy-1 south to Santa Cruz. For information on whale-watching expeditions or the latest information on the migration, contact Oceanic Society Expeditions, Building E, Fort Mason, San Francisco, CA 94123 (☎415/441-1106, ⓦwww.oceanic-society.org).

the **Mission San Rafael Arcangel** on Fifth Avenue at A Street (daily 11am–4pm; free), which is in fact a 1949 replica built near the site of the 1817 original (razed in 1861 to make way for development), and thus the least interesting of the chain to visit.

Better to head out of town to the **Marin County Civic Center** (Mon–Fri 9am–5pm; tours Wed 10.30am; $5 tour; ☎415/499-3237, ⓦwww.co.marin.ca.us), which spans the hills just east of US-101 a mile north of central San Rafael. A strange, otherworldly complex of administrative offices, it has an excellent performance space that resembles a giant viaduct capped by a bright-orange-tiled roof. These buildings were architect **Frank Lloyd Wright**'s one and only government project, and although the huge circus tents and amusement park at the core of the designer's conception were never built, it does have some interesting touches, such as the atrium lobbies that open directly to the outdoors. The tours start from the gift shop in room #233 on the second floor, where you can buy a 50¢ pamphlet to conduct a self-guided tour, if you are not there on a Wednesday morning.

From the Civic Center, North San Pedro Road loops around the headlands through **China Camp State Park** (☎415/456-0766), an expansive area of pastures and open spaces that's hard to reach without your own transportation. It takes its name from the intact but long-abandoned Chinese shrimp-fishing village at the far eastern tip of the park, the sole survivor of the many small Chinese communities that once dotted the California coast. The ramshackle buildings, small wooden pier, and old boats lying on the sand are pure John Steinbeck, though today there's a chain-link fence to protect the site from vandals. On the weekend you can get beer and sandwiches from the old shack at the foot of the pier, but the atmosphere is best during the week at sunset, when there's often no one around at all. There's a hike-in **campground** (see p.351) at the northern end of the park, about two miles from the end of the Golden Gate Transit bus #23 route.

Six miles north of San Rafael, the **Lucas Valley Road** turns off west, twisting across Marin to Point Reyes. It was not, however, named after the *Star Wars* filmmaker George Lucas, whose sprawling **Skywalker Ranch** studios are well hidden off the road. He still lives here, although much of his work now goes on down in San Francisco. Hwy-37 cuts off east, eight miles north of San Rafael, heading around the top of the Bay into the Wine Country of the Sonoma and Napa valleys (see Chapter 19).

Eating

Marin County's **restaurants** are as varied in personality as the people who inhabit the county – homely neighborhood cafés dish out nutritious portions to healthy mountain-bikers, well-appointed waterside restaurants cater to tourists, and gourmet establishments serve delicate concoctions to affluent executives.

Avatar's Punjabi Burritos 15 Madrona St, Mill Valley ☎415/381-8293. A dastardly simple cross-cultural innovation: inexpensive burritos stuffed with delicious spicy curries. Does a brisk take-out trade, as there are only two tables inside.
Broken Drum 1132 Fourth St, San Rafael ☎415/456-4677. Lively brewery/grill with pavement seating, where you can tuck into

cheapish fish tacos with mango salsa or mesquite grilled ribs, washed down with a fine amber or IPA.
Bubba's Diner 566 San Anselmo Ave, San Anselmo ☎415/459-6862. Hip, old-fashioned diner with a friendly and casual atmosphere. Try a delicious biscuit with your meal.
Caffe Trieste 1000 Bridgeway Ave, Sausalito ☎415/332-7770. This distant relative of San

Francisco's North Beach institution serves a wide menu of pastas and salads, and great *gelati* to go with excellent coffee.

Deer Park Villa 367 Bolinas Rd, Fairfax ☎415/456-8084. Moderate to expensive Italian/Californian-style cuisine, ranging from pastas to meat in adventurous sauces, is dished up indoors or in the leafy garden.

Farmhouse Grill 10005 Hwy-1, Olema ☎415/663-1264. The farm-fresh ingredients that go into the downhome cooking make this a good stop for mostly meaty lunches or dinners. Also a friendly bar.

Guaymas 5 Main St, Tiburon ☎415/435-6300. Some of the most unique, inventive Cal-Mex cuisine in the Bay Area (and priced accordingly), paired with a spectacular view of the city. The tamales are especially worth trying.

The Lark Creek Inn 234 Magnolia Ave, Larkspur ☎415/924-7766. The place to go in Marin for fine dining. The contemporary American food at this classy restored Victorian is expensive, but not without reason: delights such as pan-seared sweetbreads and gorgonzola soufflé are exquisite, the service first-rate, and the atmosphere charming.

Mikayla 801 Bridgeway Ave, Sausalito ☎415/331-5888. Mediterranean staples meet California cuisine in this expensive, but highly rated restaurant in the *Casa Madrona* hotel (see p.349). Romantic views of the harbor and excellent seafood. Huge Sunday brunch buffet offered.

Mountain Home Inn 810 Panoramic Hwy, above Mill Valley ☎415/381-9000. A place that's as good for the view as for the food, with broiled meat and fish dishes served up in a rustic lodge on the slopes of Mount Tamalpais.

Piazza D'Angelo 22 Miller Ave, Mill Valley ☎415/388-2000. Good salads, tasty pasta, and affordable pizzas, served up in a lively but comfortable room right off the downtown plaza.

Rice Table 1617 Fourth St, San Rafael ☎415/456-1808. From the shrimp chips through the crab pancakes and noodles on to the fried plantain desserts, these fragrant and spicy Indonesian dishes are excellent value and worth planning a day around. Dinners only.

Sam's Anchor Cafe 27 Main St, Tiburon ☎415/435-4527. Popular waterfront spot with Marin day-trippers and locals alike. You can have a filling meal or just sip a beverage while waiting in the sun for the ferry back to San Francisco.

Sartaj India Cafe 43 Caledonia St, Sausalito ☎415/332-7103. Great, inexpensive Indian place that does a selection of meat and veggie dishes, including *thalis*, and, oddly enough, bagels for those who can't stomach a spicy breakfast.

Station House Café 11180 Hwy-1 (Main St), Point Reyes Station ☎415/663-1515. Serving three meals daily, this friendly local favorite entices diners from miles around to sample their grilled seafood and top-notch steaks.

Stinson Beach Grill 3465 Shoreline Hwy, Stinson Beach ☎415/868-2002. Somewhat pricey, but relaxed, with outdoor dining – look out for the bright-blue building right in the heart of town. Mainly steaks and seafood but leave room for the glorious puddings.

Sweet Ginger 400 Caledonia St, Sausalito ☎415/332-1683. Moderately priced small Japanese restaurant that serves sushi, sashimi, and main courses like tempura and teriyaki.

Thai Orchid 726 San Anselmo Ave, San Anselmo ☎415/457-9470. Family restaurant dishing up spicy fare, including a fine range of curries and zesty salads.

Tommy's Wok 3001 Bridgeway, Sausalito ☎415/332-5818. This Chinese spot specializes in organic vegetables, free-range meats, and fresh seafood, cooked in Mandarin, Hunan, and Szechuan recipes.

Vladimir's Czech Restaurant 12785 Sir Francis Drake Blvd, Inverness ☎415/669-1021. This relic of rural Bohemia in the far West has been serving up tasty items like Moravian cabbage roll, roast duckling, and apple strudel since 1960.

Cafés, drinking, and nightlife

While the Marin County **nightlife** is never as charged as it gets in San Francisco, almost every town has at least a couple of **cafés** that are open long hours for a jolt of caffeine or a snack, and any number of saloon-like **bars** where you'll feel at home immediately. In addition, since most of the honchos of the Bay Area music scene and dozens of lesser-known but no less brilliant session musicians and songwriters live here, Marin's nightclubs are unsurpassed for catching big names in intimate locales.

Cafés

Bridgeway Café 633 Bridgeway, Sausalito ☎415/332-3426. A good place to relax over a coffee or grab a gourmet egg breakfast at reasonable prices by local standards.

Depot Bookstore and Café 87 Throckmorton Ave, Mill Valley ☎415/383-2665. Lively café in an old train station, sharing space with a bookstore and news-stand. Weekly readings from local and nationally recognized authors.

Dipsea Café 200 Shoreline Hwy, Mill Valley ☎415/381-0298. Hearty pancakes, omelets, sandwiches, and salads, especially good before a day out hiking on Mount Tamalpais. Breakfast and lunch only.

Fairfax Café 33 Broadway, Fairfax ☎415/459-6404. Excellent Mediterranean food and European coffee with occasional evening poetry readings.

Java Rama 546 San Anselmo Ave, San Anselmo ☎415/453-5282. Specialty coffees and pastries, along with modern rock on the stereo, attract a young crowd.

New Morning Café 1696 Tiburon Blvd, Tiburon ☎415/435-4315. Lots of healthy wholegrain sandwiches, plus salads and omelets.

Sweden House 35 Main St, Tiburon ☎415/435-9767. Great coffee and marvelous pastries on a jetty overlooking the yacht harbor, all for surprisingly reasonable prices.

Bars and live music

19 Broadway 19 Broadway, Fairfax ☎415/459-0293. Live music every night,

featuring a wide range of acts, some quite well known, others local or up-and-coming talent.

The Bar With No Name 757 Bridgeway Ave, Sausalito ☎415/332-1392. An ex-haunt of the Beats, which hosts live jazz several times a week beginning at 8pm and on Sundays 3–7pm.

Café Amsterdam 23 Broadway, Fairfax ☎415/256-8020. Live alternative folk-rock nightly with an outdoor patio, microbrews, espresso drinks, and an extensive menu.

Fourth Street Tavern 711 Fourth St, San Rafael ☎415/454-4044. Gutsy, no-frills beer bar with free, bluesy music most nights.

Marin Brewing Company 1809 Larkspur Landing, Larkspur ☎415/461-4677. Lively pub opposite the Larkspur ferry terminal, with half a dozen tasty ales – try the malty Albion Amber or the Marin Hefe Weiss – all brewed on the premises.

Pelican Inn Hwy-1, Muir Beach ☎415/383-6000. Fair selection of traditional English and Californian ales, plus fish'n'chips (and rooms to rent in case you overdo it).

Smiley's Schooner Saloon 41 Wharf Rd, Bolinas ☎415/868-1311. The bartender calls the customers by name at one of the oldest continually operating bars in the state.

Sweetwater 153 Throckmorton Ave, Mill Valley ☎415/388-3820. Due to relocate late in 2008, Marin's prime live-music venue brings in some of the biggest names in music, from jazz and blues all-stars to Jefferson Airplane survivors. A sister venue in Larkspur is also in the pipeline.

19

The Wine Country

C oming from often foggy San Francisco, a trip to the golden, arid Napa and Sonoma valleys, known jointly as the **Wine Country**, can feel like entering another country altogether. With its cool, oak tree-shaded ravines climbing up along creeks and mineral springs to chaparral-covered ridges, it would be a lovely place to visit even without the vineyards. But, as it is, the "Wine Country" tag dominates almost everything here, including many oft-overlooked points of historical and literary interest. The lusher and wilder Russian River Valley to the northwest is not generally regarded as being part of the Wine Country, but is included here as a less commercial alternative to its more famous cousins.

Between the Napa and Sonoma valleys around 30,000 acres of **vineyards**, feeding hundreds of wineries and their upscale patrons, make the area the heart of the American wine industry in reputation, if not in volume. In truth, less than five percent of California's wine comes from the region, but what it does produce is some of America's best. This is hardly surprising, considering that the region has been producing wine since the days of the Spanish missions. During Prohibition, though, most of the vines withered up, and, later on, phylloxera – insidious plant lice – all but decimated what remained, necessitating the transplant of root stock from Europe into the Californian soil. Today, the vineyards are still struggling against mother nature and increased land costs – inflated by the sudden trend among retired millionaires living out their dream of owning a little winery – but many vintners nevertheless manage to turn out premium wines that satisfy oenophiles around the world.

The region is also among America's wealthiest and most provincial, a fact that draws – and repels – a steady stream of tourists. For every grape on the vine there seems to exist a quaint bed-and-breakfast or spa; in fact, tourism is gaining on wine production as the Wine Country's leading industry, so expect clogged highways and full hotels during the lengthy peak season (May–Oct). Apart from the multiple wine experiences available – quite a few wineries have fun attractions on top of their regular **tastings** – there are numerous **activities** like ballooning or horse-riding and **historical sights** to be visited, including Spanish missions and Jack London's homestead.

Around **Napa** – accessible by Hwy-29, which takes you north through the valley – nothing is cheap, and the town itself can be quickly seen (though you can board the over-hyped **Wine Train** here; see p.368). Continuing northward, there's a string of somewhat monotonous villages until reaching a few places of greater interest further along: **St Helena** has retained much of its circa 1900 homestead character, and **Calistoga**, at the top of the valley, is famous for its hot springs, massages, and spas.

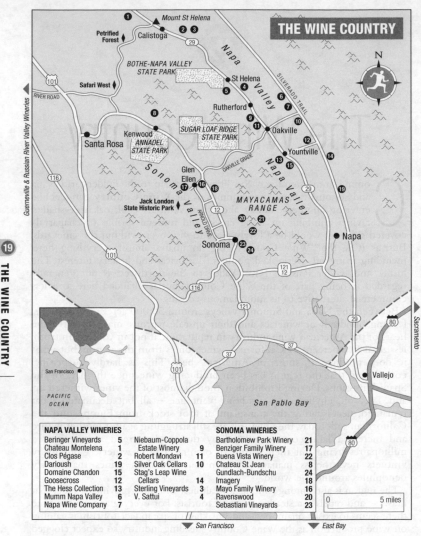

Mount St Helena

Petrified
Forest
Calistoga

29

Napa Valley

SILVERADO TRAIL

BOTHE-NAPA VALLEY
STATE PARK

St Helena

Safari West

RIVER ROAD

101

Rutherford

Oakville

Kenwood

SUGAR LOAF RIDGE
STATE PARK

ANNADEL
STATE PARK

Santa Rosa

Yountville

116

Sonoma Valley

OAKVILLE GRADE

Napa Valley

Glen
Ellen

29

19

Jack London
State Historic Park

MAYACAMAS
RANGE

ARNOLD DRIVE

12

Sonoma

Napa

121
12

116

121

San Francisco

PACIFIC
OCEAN

37

29

80

Sacramento

San Pablo Bay

Vallejo

80

Guerneville & Russian River Valley Wineries

NAPA VALLEY WINERIES

Beringer Vineyards	5
Chateau Montelena	1
Clos Pégase	2
Darioush	19
Domaine Chandon	15
Goosecross	12
The Hess Collection	13
Mumm Napa Valley	6
Napa Wine Company	7
Niebaum-Coppola	
Estate Winery	9
Robert Mondavi	11
Silver Oak Cellars	10
Stag's Leap Wine	
Cellars	14
Sterling Vineyards	3
V. Sattui	4

SONOMA WINERIES

Bartholomew Park Winery	21
Benziger Family Winery	17
Buena Vista Winery	22
Chateau St Jean	8
Gundlach-Bundschu	24
Imagery	18
Mayo Family Winery	16
Ravenswood	20
Sebastiani Vineyards	23

0 ————— 5 miles

San Francisco   East Bay

On the western side of the alluring **Mayacamas Mountains**, which separate the two valleys, the smaller back-road wineries of the **Sonoma Valley** reflect the more down-to-earth nature of the place, which is both more beautiful and less crowded than its neighbor to the east. The town of **Sonoma** itself is by far the most attractive of the Wine Country communities, retaining a number of fine Mission-era structures around its gracious central plaza. **Santa Rosa**, at the north end of the valley, is the region's sole urban center, handy for budget lodgings but otherwise unremarkable.

Still further northwest, around two hours from San Francisco, the **Russian River Valley** is a sleepy backwater community hidden in among the redwoods lining the Russian River before it spills into the sea. This is one of the most intimate places to discover California wines, along single-lane roads that twist through peaceful vineyards. The valley's seat, **Guerneville**, has the most nightlife and lodging, and is a summertime resort, especially popular with San Francisco's gay community.

Arrival and getting around

The Wine Country region spreads north from the top of the San Francisco Bay in two parallel, thirty-mile-long valleys, **Napa** and **Sonoma**. As long as you avoid the rush-hour traffic, it's about an hour's drive from San Francisco along either of the two main routes: through Marin County via the Golden Gate Bridge and US-101, or through the East Bay via the Bay Bridge and I-80. Good highways ring the region, and a loop of the two valleys is conceivable in a day or so. Consider working against the flow of traffic by taking in Sonoma, Glen Ellen, and Santa Rosa first before crossing the Mayacamas and dropping into Calistoga, St Helena, and Napa.

As the Wine Country's attractions are spread over a fairly broad area, a **car** is pretty much essential for proper touring. There are several other options, however: Golden Gate Transit (☏415/923-2000 or 707/541-2000, ⓦ www.goldengate .org) runs commuter **buses** every 30min to one hour from San Francisco via Petaluma to Santa Rosa (2hr 15min; $8.80); Greyhound (☏1-800/231-2222, ⓦ www.greyhound.com) has just one pricier daily bus to Santa Rosa (1hr 45min; $21.50); from Santa Rosa, Sonoma County Transit (☏707/576-7433, ⓦ www .sctransit.com) buses serve the entire Sonoma Valley and Russian River Valley on a comprehensive, if less than frequent, schedule. From Santa Rosa, Mendocino Transit Authority (☏1-800/696-4MTA) runs one bus daily up the Russian River Valley as far north as Fort Bragg and Mendocino.

Another option is to sign up for a Gray Line **guided bus tour** ($68; ☏415/558-9400, ⓦ www.grayline.com) from San Francisco, which leaves from the Transbay Terminal at 9.15am. The tour covers both valleys and visits

▲ Passenger aboard the Wine Train

If you don't want to drive all day, **cycling** is a great way to get around. You can bring your own bike on Greyhound (though it costs $10 and the bike must be in a box), or rent one locally for around $25–60 per day/$120–200 per week. If renting, try Napa Valley Bike Tours, 6488 Washington St, Yountville (℡707/255-3377 or 1-800/707-2453, ⊛www.napavalleybiketours.com); Getaway Bike Shop, 2228 North Point Parkway, Santa Rosa (℡707/568-3040 or 1-800/499-2453, ⊛www.getaway adventures.com); St Helena Cyclery, 1156 Main St, St Helena (℡707/963-7736, ⊛www.sthelenacyclery.com); or the Sonoma Cyclery, 20093 Broadway, Sonoma (℡707/935-3377, ⊛www.sonomavalleycyclery.com).

Both main valleys are generally flat, although the peaks in between are steep enough to challenge the hardiest of hill-climbers. If the main roads through the valleys are full of cars, as they are most summer weekends, try the smaller parallel routes: the **Silverado Trail** in Napa Valley and pretty **Arnold Drive** in Sonoma Valley. For the more athletically inclined, the **Oakville Grade** between Oakville in the Napa Valley and Glen Ellen in the Sonoma Valley has challenged the world's finest riders. The **King Ridge-Meyers Grade** – a 55-mile loop with a tough 4500-foot climb – begins at the north end of the bridge over the Russian River in Monte Rio and heads along the Cazadero Highway up into the hills, taking in the river, the redwoods, and the solitary mountains before finally descending to the coast and Hwy-1. Contact the Santa Rosa Cycling Club (℡707/544-4803, ⊛www.srcc.com), for a complete itinerary for this or any area rides. Alternatively, plot your own route with the *Bicycle Rider Directory* (see Contexts, p.408).

Most local firms organize **tours**, providing bikes, helmets, food, and sag wagons in case you get worn out. In Calistoga, Getaway Adventures offers trips of varying lengths, and Napa Valley Bike Tours sets up more leisurely tours – highlighted by gourmet lunches – all over the Napa area; see above for contact details on both. More ambitious (and quite expensive) overnight tours are run most weekends by Backroads, 801 Cedar St, Berkeley (Mon–Fri 7am–5pm, Sat 9am–3pm; ℡510/527-1555 or 1-800/462-2848, ⊛www.backroads.com).

three wineries, including favorites Sebastiani in downtown Sonoma and Sutter Home in St Helena, with a stop for lunch in pleasant Calistoga. To bypass San Francisco altogether, take the Sonoma Airporter (4 daily; 1hr 30min; $50; ℡707/938-4246 or 1-800/611-4246, ⊛www.sonomaairporter.com; reservations required) from San Francisco airport directly to Sonoma City Hall. The bus also stops at the corner of Geary Boulevard and Park Presidio in San Francisco's Richmond District.

Blue & Gold Fleet **ferries** travel from the Ferry Building (11 daily; $11.50 single; ℡415/705-8200, ⊛www.blueandgoldfleet.com) in San Francisco to Vallejo, and are met by hourly Napa Valley Transit (VINE) buses (Mon–Sat; ℡1-800/696-6443), which has a comprehensive system covering the whole valley. Blue & Gold also runs a Wine Country bus tour leaving daily from Pier 43 (daily 9.15am; $65).

The three-hour **Wine Train** ($49.50 ticket only, $89–150 with meal; ℡707/253-2111 or 1-800/427-4124, ⊛www.winetrain.com) runs two or three times daily from Napa's station at 1275 McKinstry St, east of downtown. The ten-car train of restored 1950s Pullman cars chugs up the valley to St Helena, usually with a stop at Grgich Hills or Domaine Chandon wineries (tour and tasting $24 and $39 extra respectively). The scenery en route is pleasant, but the ride is really more of a wining-and-dining experience for older travelers than a proper means of transportation.

The Wine Country by air

The most exciting way to see the region is on one of the widely touted **hot-air balloon rides**. These usually lift off at dawn and last sixty to ninety magical minutes, winding up with a Champagne brunch. The most established of the operators is Napa Valley Balloons (☎707/253-2224 or 1-800/253-2224, ⊛www.napavalley balloons.com), who fly out of Yountville. Other options in Napa include the slightly cheaper Balloons Above the Valley (☎1-800/464-6824, ⊛www.balloonrides.com) and Aerostat Adventures (☎1-800/579-0183, ⊛www.aerostat-adventures.com). The crunch comes when you realize the price – around $200 a head whichever company you use – but it really is worth every cent. Make reservations a week in advance, especially in summer, though with the increasing number of balloon companies, same-day drop-bys are a possibility.

If it's thrills you're looking for, consider taking to the air in a World War II-era propeller biplane. Vintage Aircraft Company, 23982 Arnold Drive, Sonoma (☎707/938-2444, ⊛www.vintageaircraft.com), operates one- or two-person flights that take in the Sonoma Valley between loops and rolls. The basic choice is between the twenty-minute Scenic Flight ($150) and various forty-minute Explorer Flights ($295): add $50 to either for the extra thrill of some aerobatics.

Information

Not surprisingly for such a tourist-dependent area, the Wine Country has a well-developed network of **tourist information** outlets, though the rivalry between the two main valleys makes it next to impossible to find out anything about Sonoma when you're in Napa, and vice versa. Both the **Napa Valley Visitors Bureau**, 1310 Napa Town Center off First Street in downtown Napa (daily 9am–5pm; ☎707/226-7459, ⊛www.napavalley.com), and the **Sonoma Valley Visitors Bureau**, 453 First St E at the center of the plaza in Sonoma (daily 9am–5pm, open until 6pm throughout summer; ☎707/996-1090, ⊛www.sonomavalley.com), should be able to tell you all you need to know about their respective areas – and the smaller towns usually have a tourist office, too. If you're keen on touring the wineries, both of the above places hand out basic free **maps** and sell more detailed ones ($3–5) giving the lowdown on the hundreds of producers. In the Russian River Valley, the **Chamber of Commerce & Visitor Center**, 16209 First St, Guerneville (Mon–Fri 9am–5pm; 24hr info line ☎707/869-9000 or 1-877/644-9001, ⊛www .russianriver.com), is welcoming and has good free maps of the area, plus helpful listings for accommodation, dining options, and wineries.

The Napa Valley

A thirty-mile strip of gently landscaped corridors and lush hillsides, the **NAPA VALLEY** looks more like southern France than the rest of Northern California. In spring the valley floor is covered with brilliant wildflowers which mellow into autumnal shades by grape-harvest time. Local Native Americans named the then fish-rich river flowing through the valley "Napa," meaning "plenty"; the name was adopted by Spanish missionaries in the early 1800s, but the natives themselves were soon wiped out. The few ranches the Spanish and Mexicans managed to establish were in turn taken over by Yankee traders, and by the 1850s the town of Napa had become a thriving river port, sending agricultural goods such as prunes to San Francisco and serving as a supply point for farmers and ranchers. The 1852 opening in town of White Sulphur Springs, California's first mineral springs resort, made Napa the vacation choice for San Francisco's elite. Sun-loving settlers such as Jacob Beringer came too; in 1870, Beringer realized that the valley's rocky, well-drained soil resembled that of his homeland, Mainz, a major wine region in Germany, and by 1875 he and his brother had established what has today become America's oldest continually operating winery.

Before long, Napa was bypassed by the railroads and unable to compete with other, deep-water Bay Area ports, but the area's fine climate saved it from oblivion, with plenty of visitors pouring in to enjoy the scenery, hot springs, and growing number of wineries. Today, especially in summer, the area is overrun with visitors from all over the world, making the offseason months the best time to come, though there are enough smaller wineries in the valley's lesser-traveled byways to make a day trip in even the busiest months of summer worthwhile.

Accommodation

Most people are content to visit the Napa Valley as a day trip from San Francisco, visiting a few of the wineries and maybe having a picnic or a meal before heading back to the city. But to properly absorb what the region has to offer, plan to spend at least one night in the region, pampering yourself in one of the many (generally pricey) **hotels** and **bed-and-breakfast inns** that provide the bulk of the area's accommodation options. During summer weekends, prices can rise as much as fifty percent, so call ahead. From November to March, lodging prices drop considerably, often up to half-off. At peak times, rooms of all descriptions get snapped up, so if you have a hard time finding a place, ask at the tourist office (see p.369) or make use of one of the several **accommodation services** such as Bed and Breakfast Inns of Napa Valley (☎707/944-4444, ⓦwww.bbinv.com).

Hotels and motels

Calistoga Inn 1250 Lincoln Ave, Calistoga ☎707/942-4101, ⓦwww.calistogainn.com. Relaxing, good-value rooms with one bed, most with private bath, in a landmark building with its own restaurant and micro-brewery right on the main street, creating a lively atmosphere. $89.

Discovery Inn 500 Silverado Trail, Napa ☎707/253-0892, ⓦwww.napadiscoveryinn.com. This small motel-style place has adequately furnished modern rooms and is well placed a short drive south of Napa and the Silverado Trail wineries. $85.

Dr Wilkinson's Hot Springs 1507 Lincoln Ave, Calistoga ☎707/942-4102, ⓦwww.drwilkinson .com. Legendary health spa and hotel downtown. Choose from a variety of spacious, well-lit rooms with sparse furnishings, facing the courtyard or pool patio. A/C and TV standard. $109.

El Bonita Motel 195 Main St, St Helena ☎707/963-3216 or 1-800/541-3284, ⓦwww .elbonita.com. Old roadside motel done up to hotel standard in Art Deco style, with a pool and hot tub. Surrounded by a 2.5-acre garden, the rooms here contain micro-waves, refrigerators, and coffeemakers. $140.

Harvest Inn 1 Main St, St Helena ☎707/963-9463 or 1-800/950-8466, ⓦwww.harvestinn .com. Mock-Tudor cottages at the edge of a vineyard. The place to stay if you can afford it, as the rooms are huge and loaded with perks like a down-feather bed, fireplace, and private terrace overlooking the garden or fourteen-acre vineyard. Two outdoor heated pools, whirlpool spas, and jogging/biking trails complete the package. $259.

Mount View Hotel and Spa 1457 Lincoln Ave, Calistoga ☎707/942-6877 or 1-800/816-6877, Ⓦ www.mountviewhotel.com. Lively Art Deco-style hotel with nightly jazz and an excellent Cajun restaurant, *Catahoula*, on the ground floor. Most rooms comfortable but compact. Twenty-percent AAA discount midweek. $211; cottage with patio and hot tub $357.

Vintage Inn 6541 Washington St, Yountville ☎707/944-1112 or 1-800/351-1133, Ⓦ www .vintageinn.com. Huge luxury rooms, all with fireplaces, in a modern hotel complex, plus swimming pool and free bike rental. Handy for Yountville's many fine restaurants, and great for romantic getaways but vastly overpriced with suites up to $655. $350.

Wine Country Inn 1152 Lodi Lane, St Helena ☎707/963-7077 or 1-888/465-4608, Ⓦ www .winecountryinn.com. Patios, strolling gardens, and vineyard-side swimming pool highlight this inn. The rooms are tasteful, open, and uncluttered with antiques. A fireplace comes with most rooms; there are also suites and spacious cottages for around $600. $215.

B&Bs

Adagio Inn 1417 Kearney St, St Helena ☎707/963-2238 or 1-888/823-2446, Ⓦ www .adagioinn.com. There are just three suites in this delightful Edwardian house; only two blocks from Main St but very quiet. Each suite is lavishly furnished and the largest has a whirlpool tub. $275.

Ambrose Bierce Inn 1515 Main St, St Helena ☎707/963-3003, Ⓦ www.ambrosebiercehouse .com. Luxury accommodation in the 1872 house once inhabited by Bierce himself (see p.374). Breakfast is washed down with complimentary Champagne. $199.

Candlelight Inn 1045 Easum Drive, Napa ☎707/257-3717 or 1-800/624-0395, Ⓦ www.candlelightinn.com. Spacious mock-Tudor mansion with a pool in its lovely grounds and a luxurious interior, featuring rooms of varying sizes, all beautifully decorated. Friendly and informal atmosphere with free drinks and snacks. $169.

Christopher's Inn 1010 Foothill Blvd, Calistoga ☎707/942-0680 or 1-866/876-5755, Ⓦ www .christophersinn.com. Large yet friendly B&B with over 20 comfortable rooms and two huge suites, one block north of the center of town. Set in a lovely English-style garden. $195.

Garnett Creek Inn 1139 Lincoln Ave, Calistoga ☎707/942-9797, Ⓦ www.garnettcreekinn.com. Lavishly and gaily decorated old house with a wraparound porch at the Hwy-29 end of the main street, complete with five beautifully decorated, welcoming rooms. The innkeeper is both friendly and knowledgeable. $165.

Oleander House 7433 St Helena Hwy (Hwy-29), Yountville ☎707/944-8315, Ⓦ www.oleander .com. Cosy and friendly B&B, with tastefully and simply furnished rooms, in a handy mid-valley location. Quiet enough despite being on the main road and not too far from restaurants and shops. $180.

Napa

Ironically, the rather congested town of **NAPA** lacks both excitement and charm, and is best avoided in favor of the wineries and smaller towns north along Hwy-29. It does, though, have a decent number of good restaurants (see p.376). Suburban highway sprawl gives way to the collection of chain stores that anchor the compact downtown, situated on a curve of the Napa River. Apart from the helpful Napa Valley Visitors Bureau (see p.369 for details), the **Napa County Historical Society**, across the street at 1219 First St (Tues & Thurs noon–4pm; ☎707/224-1739), has free, informative materials and photographic displays on the region's pre-wine era. It's housed in the town's proud old courthouse, which looks like a relic from another era compared to the modern, characterless buildings that comprise the rest of downtown.

The other reason to visit is the smart wine and arts center **COPIA**, built as the showcase for an organization founded by Robert Mondavi, at 500 First St (daily 10am–6pm; free; ☎707/259-1600, Ⓦ www.copia.org). The free entry grants access to a thirty-minute video, the exclusively wine-or-food-themed art galleries, including an interesting wall display of spent matches ignited by one of the Mondavi clan and some original Greek and Roman pottery, and the obligatory gift shop and restaurant. You can also sign up for classes and special events, some of which are also free. Smaller attractions include the **Napa**

Napa Valley wineries

Almost all of the Napa Valley's **wineries** offer tastings, which have become increasingly expensive in recent years; most also offer tours of some description. There are more than three hundred wineries in all, producing wines of a very high standard, so your taste should ultimately determine the ones you visit. The following selections are some long-standing favorites, plus a few lesser-known hopefuls. Keep in mind that the intention is for you to get a sense of a winery's product, and perhaps buy some, rather than get drunk on the stuff, so don't expect more than a sip or two of any one sort – though some wineries do sell wines by the glass. If you want to buy a bottle, particularly from the larger producers, you can in fact usually get it cheaper in supermarkets than at the wineries themselves, unless you buy in bulk.

Beringer Vineyards 2000 Main St, St Helena ☎707/963-7115, ⑩www.beringer.com. Napa Valley's most famous piece of architecture, the gothic "Rhine House," modeled on the ancestral Rhine Valley home of Jacob Beringer, graces the cover of many a wine magazine. Expansive lawns and a grand tasting room, heavy on dark wood, make for a regal experience. Daily 10am–5pm; tasting $5 and tours $10–35.

Chateau Montelena 1429 Tubbs Lane, two miles north of Calistoga ☎707/942-9105, ⑩www.montelena.com. Smaller but highly rated winery, nestled below Mount St Helena. The Cabernet Sauvignon, in particular, is gradually acquiring a fine reputation. Tasting daily 9.30am–4pm; $15. Estate tour and tasting 2pm; $25.

Clos Pégase 1060 Dunaweal Lane, Calistoga ☎707/942-4981, ⑩www.clospegase .com. A flamboyant upstart at the north end of the valley, this high-profile winery amalgamates fine wine and fine art, with a sculpture garden around buildings designed by postmodern architect Michael Graves. Free tours daily at 11am and 2pm. Tasting daily 10.30am–5pm; $5.

Darioush 4240 Silverado Trail, northeast of Napa ☎707/257-2345, ⑩www.darioush .com. Grandiose new winery modeled on Persepolis and constructed with stone blocks imported by the owner from his native Iran. Cabernet Sauvignon and Shiraz are the signature wines. Tasting daily 10.30am–5pm; $20. Tour 2pm; $50.

Domaine Chandon 1 California Drive, Yountville ☎707/944-2280, ⑩www.chandon .com. Sparkling wines from this progeny of France's Moët & Chandon can challenge the authentic Champagnes from France. Vast and modern, this winery and gallery is popular with connoisseurs and features a highly regarded but expensive restaurant. Tasting summer daily 10am–6pm, winter daily 11am–5pm; $10–20. Tours 11am, 1pm, 3pm & 5pm; $7.

Goosecross Cellars 1119 State Lane, east of Yountville ☎707/944-1986 or 1-800-276-9210, ⑩www.goosecross.com. It's well worth taking time to locate this friendly family-run winery, tucked away off Yountville Cross Road. Crush-time is fun and their Chardonnay especially good. Tasting daily 10am–4.30pm; $5. Estate tour Sat 2.30pm May–Oct; $20.

The Hess Collection 4411 Redwood Rd, Napa ☎707/255-1144 or 1-877/707-4377, ⑩www.hesscollection.com. This secluded winery features, in addition to its superior wines, a surprisingly good collection of modern art and a nice view of the valley. Self-guided tour. Tasting daily 10am–4pm; $10.

Mumm Napa Valley 8445 Silverado Trail, Rutherford ☎707/942-3434 or 1-800/686-6272, ⑩www.mummnapa.com. Opened in 1986 by G.H. Mumm, France's renowned

Firefighters Museum at 1201 Main St (Wed–Sun 11am–4pm; free; ☎707/259-0609), or you might want to take in some culture at the newly refurbished **Opera House** at 1030 Main St (☎707/226-7372, ⓦwww .napavalleyoperahouse.org).

Champagne house, and Seagrams, the sparkling wines from this beautifully situated winery are good but superseded by sweeping views of the surrounding valleys. The tours are particularly engaging and fun, led by witty and informative guides. Tasting daily 10am–5pm, $5–20. Free hourly tours 10am–3pm, on the hour.

Napa Wine Company 7830–40 St Helena Hwy, Oakville ☎707/944-1710 or 1-800/848-9630, ⓦwww.napawineco.com. Modeled on the cooperative wineries of France, the Napa Wine Company offers 25 small-vineyard owners access to state-of-the-art crushing and fermentation machinery, and also acts as a sales outlet for their vintages, which have received accolades from *Wine Spectator*. Their tasting room is one of the best – and certainly the broadest – in Wine Country; daily 10am–3.30pm; $10–25.

Niebaum-Coppola Estate Winery & Vineyards 1991 St Helena Hwy, Rutherford ☎707/968-1100 or 1-800/782-4266, ⓦwww.niebaum-coppola.com. In 1975, Francis Ford Coppola purchased this Inglenook estate, originally established by Gustav Niebaum in 1879. Memorabilia from Coppola's movie career are on display in the entryway to the massive wine-tasting room, featuring their signature Rubicon wine. Tasting daily 10am–5pm; $15. Ninety-minute tours and tasting at 10.30am, 12.30pm and 2.30pm; $25 inc valet parking.

Robert Mondavi 7801 St Helena Hwy, Oakville ☎707/251-4097 or 1-888/766-6328, ⓦwww.robertmondavi.com. Long the standard-bearer for Napa Valley wines ("Bob Red" and "Bob White" are house wines at many Californian restaurants), they have one of the most informative and least hard-sell tours. Tours and tasting daily 10am–4.30pm, reservations recommended. Tastings from $15, tours from $25.

Silver Oak Cellars 915 Oakville Cross Rd, Oakville ☎1-800/273-8809, ⓦwww .silveroak.com. Lovers of Cabernet Sauvignon mustn't miss a stop at Silver Oak, the crème de la crème of the heady red that costs over $100 a bottle in some San Francisco restaurants. Sadly, though, the original winery building burnt down in 2006. Tasting daily 9am–4pm; $10.

Stag's Leap Wine Cellars 5766 Silverado Trail, east of Yountville ☎707/944-2020 or 1-866/422-7523, ⓦwww.stagsleapwinecellars.com. The winery that put Napa Valley on the international map by beating a bottle of Château Lafitte-Rothschild at a Paris tasting in 1976. Still quite highly rated. Tasting daily 10am–4.30pm; $15–40. Tours by appointment; $40.

Sterling Vineyards 1111 Dunaweal Lane, Calistoga ☎707/942-3344 or 1-800/726-6136, ⓦwww.sterlingvineyards.com. Famous for the aerial tram ride that brings visitors up the 300-foot knoll to the tasting room, the view of Napa Valley from on high is gorgeous. The extravagant white mansion, modeled after a monastery on the Greek island of Mykonos, is Napa's most recognizable. Tasting its wide selection of wines on the View Terrace is a memorable experience. Aerial tram, tasting, self-guided tour 10.30am–4.30pm; Mon–Fri $15, Sat & Sun $20.

V. Sattui 1111 White Lane, St Helena ☎707/963-7774, ⓦwww.vsattui.com. Small family-owned winery right off Hwy-29 with award-winning wines – the Riesling and Gamay Rouge are particularly good. Sattui wines are only sold at the winery or through the mail. A gourmet deli next door is perfectly placed to stock up for a picnic in the popular tree-shaded grove. Voted best California winery in 2004. Tasting daily summer 9am–6pm, winter 9am–5pm; $10–25.

Yountville and Oakville

Nine miles north of Napa on Hwy-29, **YOUNTVILLE** was named in honor of George C. Yount, the valley's first settler of European descent in 1831. There's not much to grab your attention, just some antique shops, restaurants, and the stores at Vintage 1870, at 6525 Washington St (daily 10.30am–5.30pm; ☎707/944-2451, ⓦwww.vintage1870.com), a shopping and wine complex in a former winery. You may as well push on three more miles on Hwy-29 to smaller **OAKVILLE**, which holds no fewer than a dozen wineries of interest to serious aficionados including the massive Robert Mondavi Winery (see box, p.372). More down to earth is the Oakville Grocery, at 7856 St Helena Hwy, a delightfully crowded deli, spilling over with the finest local and imported foods. Nearby, at nos. 7830–40, the Napa Wine Company (see box, p.372) serves as a cooperative for more than fifty small boutique wineries, with an excellent tasting room featuring varietals that have made it into the *Wine Spectator*'s top ten.

St Helena

Some eighteen miles north from Napa, **ST HELENA** is the largest of all the antique-shop-filled villages you'll encounter heading north; it's also the town that boasts the greatest concentration of wineries and a nice complement of places to stay and eat. Hwy-29 becomes the town's Main Street here, and is lined by some of the Wine Country's finest nineteenth-century brick buildings, most of which stand in prime condition, holding inns, bakeries, and shops. The historic bakery at no. 1357 is the best place to meet local wine growers, who assemble to chat or check the community bulletin board on the wall. If driving through, at least stop off to see the quaint Craftsman-style homes that line residential **Oak Avenue**, and also to see reminders of two unlikely past residents: Robert Louis Stevenson and Ambrose Bierce, both of whom lived in St Helena back in its days as a resort. Information and orientation for the area can be had at the **Chamber of Commerce**, 1010 Main St (Mon–Fri 10am–5pm, Sat 10am–4pm, Sun 11am–3pm; ☎707/963-4456 or 1-800/799-6456, ⓦwww.sthelena.com). The **Silverado Museum** (Tues–Sun noon–4pm; free; ☎707/963-3757, ⓦwww.silveradomuseum.org), housed in St Helena's former Public Library building just off Main Street in the center of town, has a collection of some eight thousand articles relating to Robert Louis Stevenson, who spent just under a year in the area, honeymooning and recovering from an illness. It's claimed to be the second most extensive collection of Stevenson artifacts in the US, though the only thing of interest to any but the most obsessed fan is a scribbled-on manuscript of *Dr Jekyll and Mr Hyde*. The other half of the building is taken up by the **Napa Valley Wine Library** (same hours), a briefly entertaining barrage of photos and clippings relating to the development of local viticulture. On the north side of town, at 1515 Main St, Bierce's former residence has been converted into the **Ambrose Bierce House** bed-and-breakfast inn (see p.371). The inn houses a very small collection of memorabilia relating to the misanthropic ghost-story writer and author of *The Devil's Dictionary*, who lived here for some fifteen years, before mysteriously vanishing after heading off to fight for Pancho Villa in the Mexican Revolution.

Calistoga and around

Beyond St Helena, toward the far northern end of the valley, the wineries become prettier and the traffic a little thinner, though it swells again at the very tip of the valley near **CALISTOGA**, a town that takes pride in being the source of the sparkling water that adorns every Californian supermarket shelf. Sam Brannan, the young Mormon entrepreneur who made a mint out of the Gold Rush, established a resort community here in 1860. In his groundbreaking speech, as legend has it, he attempted to assert his desire to create the "Saratoga of California," but got tongue-tied, thus coining the town's name.

Calistoga's main attraction – then as now – is the opportunity to soak in the calming hot water that bubbles up here from deep in the earth. A multitude of **spas** and volcanic **mud baths**, together with a homely and health-conscious atmosphere, beckon city-dwellers and tourists alike. The extravagant might enjoy *Dr. Wilkinson's Hot Springs*, 1507 Lincoln Ave (treatments from $77; ☎707/942-4102, ⓦwww.drwilkinson.com), a renowned health spa and hotel whose heated mineral water and volcanic-ash treatments have been overseen by the same family for almost fifty years. *Mount View Spa*, 1457 Lincoln Ave (☎707/942-5789 or 1-800/772-8838, ⓦwww.mountviewspa.com), can soothe you with a variety of combined herbal therapies; it also has mud treatments for in excess of $100; it also offers shorter but cheaper hydrotherapy sessions. If swaddled luxury isn't what you're after, a number of slightly more down-to-earth establishments are spread along and off the mile-long main drag, Lincoln Avenue. *Golden Haven Hot Springs Spa and Resort*, 1713 Lake St (☎707/942-6793, ⓦwww.goldenhaven.com), for example, offers a one-hour mud bath, hot mineral Jacuzzi, and blanket wrap for $74 ($49 each for couples), and *Calistoga Spa*, 1006 Washington St (☎707/942-6269 or 1-866/822-5772, ⓦwww.calistogaspa.com), has similar rates. If that's still too expensive, ask a local resident to spray you down with their garden hose – although even that might cost a few bucks given Calistoga water's restorative reputation.

Calistoga has one standard tourist attraction, in the shape of the **Sharpsteen Museum and Sam Brannan Cottage**, 1113 Washington St (daily 11am–4pm; suggested donation $3; ☎707/942-5911, ⓦwww.sharpsteen-museum .org). Founded by long-serving Disney producer Ben Sharpsteen, the quaint little museum contains some of his personal effects, including his Oscar for the pearl-diving film *Ama Girls*, as well as a model of the original resort and lots of biographical material on Sam Brannan, plus a full-size recreation of his cottage. You can check what else is going on in town and get maps at the friendly **Chamber of Commerce**, 1458 Lincoln Ave (Mon–Fri 10am–5pm, Sat 10am–4pm, Sun 11am–3pm; ☎707/942-6333, ⓦwww.calistogachamber.com).

Calistoga's outskirts

Heading northwest out of town on Hwy-128 takes you up the ridge of the **Mayacamas**, a picturesque and steep drive that winds to the summit and spirals southwest, depositing you in Santa Rosa. More evidence of Calistoga's lively underground activity can be seen on this route at the **Old Faithful Geyser** (daily 9am–6pm; $8), two miles north of town on Tubbs Lane, which spurts boiling water sixty feet into the air at nine- to forty-minute intervals, depending on the time of year. The water source was discovered during oil-drilling here in the 1920s, when search equipment struck a force estimated to be up to a thousand pounds per square foot; the equipment was blown away and, despite heroic efforts to control it, the geyser has continued to go off like clockwork ever since. Landowners finally realized that they'd never tame it and turned it into a high-yield tourist attraction, using the same name as the famous spouter at Yellowstone National Park. Just south of the geyser, stylish Venetian artist Carlo Marchiori conducts weekly guided tours of his imaginatively decorated house **Ca'Toga** (May–Oct Sat only 11.15am; $25 per person with minimum of 25 people). The Palladian villa is full of delicate whimsy – one room is painted as if you are a bird in a cage, another is decorated with cows – and the grounds secrete mock ruined temples, a Buddhist corner, and a shell-encrusted cave. An idea of his art can be gleaned, and tours arranged, through his gallery at 1206 Cedar St, Calistoga (℡707/942-3900, ⓦwww.catoga.com).

The **Petrified Forest**, five miles west of Calistoga on the steep road over the hills to Santa Rosa (daily summer 9am–7pm, winter 9am–5pm; $6; ℡707/942-6667, ⓦwww.petrifiedforest.org), made the roster of California Historical Landmarks, though Robert Louis Stevenson dubbed it "a pure little isle of touristry among the solitary hills." Indeed, unless you're a geologist or really into hardened wood, you may not fully appreciate the importance of these fossils, some of the largest in the world, up to 150 feet long. The forest here was petrified by the action of the silica-laden volcanic ash which gradually seeped into the decomposing fibers of trees uprooted during an eruption of Mount St Helena some three million years ago.

Mount St Helena

The clearest sign of the local volcanic unrest is the massive conical mountain that marks the north end of the Napa Valley, **MOUNT ST HELENA**, about eight miles north of Calistoga. The 4343-foot summit is worth a climb for its great views – on a very clear day you can see Point Reyes and the Pacific coast to the west, San Francisco to the south, the towering Sierra Nevadas to the east, and impressive Mount Shasta to the north. It is, however, a long, steep climb (ten miles round-trip) and you need to set off early in the morning to enjoy it – take plenty of water.

The mountain and most of the surrounding land is protected and preserved as the **Robert Louis Stevenson Park** (daily 8am–sunset; free), though the connection is fairly weak: Stevenson spent his honeymoon here in 1880 in a bunkhouse with Fanny Osborne, recuperating from tuberculosis and exploring the valley. In Stevenson's novel *Silverado Squatters*, he describes the highlight of the honeymoon as the day he managed to taste eighteen of local wine baron Jacob Schram's Champagnes in one sitting. A plaque marks the spot where his bunkhouse once stood, but little else about the park's winding roads and dense shrub growth evokes its former fame.

Eating and drinking

Fine dining is a Wine Country tradition and the Napa Valley has more than its fair share of excellent restaurants, many offering top California cuisine, especially in Napa, Yountville, St Helena, and Calistoga. Humbler fare is also available, especially cheap Mexican food, served up in low-key diners frequented by migrant workers. The consistent wine consumption during the day means **nightlife** is generally subdued but a few decent bars are dotted along the valley.

Inexpensive restaurants, cafés, and take-outs

Armadillo's 1304 Main St, St Helena ℡707/963-8082. Good-value Mexican cuisine, including fine quesadillas and burritos, in a brightly painted dining room.

Bosko's Trattoria 1364 Lincoln Ave, Calistoga ℡707/942-9088. Standard Italian restaurant preparing moderately priced

fresh pasta dishes. Cheerful, and popular with families.

Café Sarafornia 1413 Lincoln Ave, Calistoga ℡707/942-0555. Famous for delicious and enormous breakfasts and lunches, with lines around the block on weekends.

The Model Bakery 1357 Main St, St Helena ℡707/963-8192. Local hangout serving the best bread in Napa Valley, as well as sandwiches and pizza.

Peking Palace 1001 Second St, Napa ☎707/257-7197. Mandarin and Szechuan cuisine served up in a spacious and snazzy space in the heart of downtown Napa.

Puerto Vallerta 1473 Lincoln Ave, Calistoga ☎707/942-6563. Heaps of tasty and genuine Mexican grub can be consumed in the shady courtyard of this establishment, tucked in beside the Cal-Mart supermarket.

Soo Yuan 1354 Lincoln Ave, Calistoga ☎707/942-9404. Good-value Mandarin and Szechuan cuisine in a small but friendly place on the main street.

Upmarket restaurants

All Seasons Bistro 1400 Lincoln Ave, Calistoga ☎707/942-9111. Exquisite main courses such as roasted monkfish with fava beans and Bohemian pheasant cost $20–30 in this upscale but relaxed bistro.

Bouchon 6534 Washington St, Yountville ☎707/944-8037. Parisian chic and haute cuisine at high prices – the *terrine de fois gras* goes for $45, but most entrees are around $25–30.

Brannan's 1374 Lincoln Ave, Calistoga ☎707/942-2233. Dishes like pecan-stuffed quail and fresh steamed oysters, plus a wonderful wooden interior, make this rather expensive, high-profile eatery worth a visit.

Celadon 1040 Main St, Napa ☎707/254-9690. Quality international nouvelle cuisine with such plates as truffle and honey-glazed pork chops or Algerian-style lamb, served in an intimate setting.

Cole's Chop House 1122 Main St, Napa ☎707/224-6328. This is the place to come for huge chunks of well-prepared red meat. Very spacious inside and top service, but the atmosphere is rather stilted.

Mustards Grill 7399 St Helena (Hwy-29), Yountville ☎707/944-2424. Credited with starting the late-1980s trend toward "grazing" food, emphasizing tapas-like tidbits rather than main meals. Reckon on spending well over $20 a head and waiting for a table if you come on a weekend.

Rutherford Grill 1180 Rutherford Rd, Rutherford ☎707/963-1920. Large portions of basic contemporary American food – the mashed potatoes should not be missed – served in a handsome dining room. In a

perhaps related twist, locals recently voted the restaurant both home of the best martini and best place to meet a member of the opposite sex.

Tra Vigne 1050 Charter Oak Ave, St Helena ☎707/963-4444. Just north of town, but it feels as if you've been transported to Tuscany. Excellent food and fine wines, served up in a lovely vine-covered courtyard or elegant dining room – but you pay for the privilege. They also have a small deli, where you can pick up picnic goodies.

Wappo Bar Bistro 1226 Washington St, Calistoga ☎707/942-4712. Creative cuisine, featuring unheard-of combinations like *chile rellenos* with walnut pomegranate sauce or roasted rabbit with potato gnocchi, makes this restaurant a culinary adventure.

Wine Spectator Greystone Restaurant 2555 Main St, St Helena ☎707/967-1010. Created by budding Culinary Institute of America chefs, the California/Mediterranean cuisine is served in an elegant ivy-walled mansion just outside of town, with a tastefully wacky Art Deco interior. Reasonably priced considering the delicious, large portions of chicken, duck, fish, and venison.

Zinsvalley Restaurant 3253 Browns Valley Rd, Napa ☎707/224-0695. In a leafy corner of Napa, this laid-back place serves a refreshing range of dishes with Mediterranean, Creole, and Asian touches, such as chicken and Anouille jambalaya, plus a fresh fish of the day special. Mains $14–25.

Zuzu 829 Main St, Napa ☎707/224-5885. Not the place to come if ravenous, as portions are modest in size for $6–14, but this popular tapas bar offers tasty fare such as *paella del dia* and a good wine list in its trendy interior.

Bars

Ana's Cantina 1205 Main St, St Helena ☎707/963-4921. Long-standing, down-to-earth saloon and Mexican restaurant with billiards and darts tournaments.

Compadres Bar and Grill 6539 Washington St, Yountville ☎707/944-2406. Outdoor patio seating and amazing martinis and margaritas, with free salsa and chips.

Downtown Joe's 902 Main St at Second, Napa ☎707/258-2337. One of Napa's most popular and lively spots for sandwiches, ribs, and pasta, with outdoor dining by the river and beer brewed on the premises. About the only place in town open until midnight, and a good spot to meet locals.

The Sonoma Valley

On looks alone the crescent-shaped Sonoma Valley beats Napa Valley hands down. This smaller, altogether more rustic stretch of greenery curves between oak-covered mountain ranges from **SONOMA** a few miles north along Hwy-12 to the hamlet of **Glen Ellen** and **Jack London State Park**, and ends at the booming bedroom community of **Santa Rosa**. The area is known as the "Valley of the Moon," a label that's mined by tour operators for its connection to long-time resident Jack London, whose book of the same name retold a Native American legend about how, as you move through the valley, the moon seems to rise several times from behind the various peaks. Long a favorite among visitors, Sonoma has been claimed, at different moments of its relatively brief recorded history, by Spain, England, Russia, and Mexico. The US took over in 1846 during the Bear Flag Revolt against Mexico (see box on p.382), which took place in Sonoma's central plaza when locals raised the flag of an independent California Republic.

Sonoma Valley's **wineries** are generally more intimate and casual than their Napa counterparts, even though Sonoma Valley established the wine industry from which Napa derives its fame. Colonel Agostin Haraszthy first started planting grapes here in the 1850s, and his Buena Vista winery in Sonoma still operates today.

▲ Wine Country vineyard

Accommodation

Though there are not quite as many **places to stay** in the Sonoma Valley as in its neighbor, there are still plenty of good, mostly upmarket options. Again prices are hiked and beds at a premium in high season, but you can receive help in getting situated from the Visitors Bureau (see p.369) or the Bed and Breakfast Association of Sonoma Valley (1-800/969-4667, ⓦwww.sonomabb.com). **Campers** can find a pitch eight miles north of Sonoma at the Sugar Loaf Ridge State Park, 2605 Adobe Canyon Rd ($20; ☎707/833-5712), or outside Santa Rosa at the Spring Lake Regional Park, Newanga Avenue (May–Sept daily; Oct–April Sat & Sun; $19; ☎707/539-8092).

Hotels and motels

Astro Motel 323 Santa Rosa Ave, Santa Rosa ☎707/545-8555, ⓦwww.sterba.com/astro. No-frills motel, but some of the cheapest Wine Country rooms available. $50.

Jack London Lodge 13740 Arnold Drive, Glen Ellen ☎707/938-8510, ⓦwww.jacklondonlodge.com. Modern motel near Jack London State Park, with a fine restaurant and pool. A good place to try if Napa and Sonoma hotels are booked, or if you want a truly rural setting and fine stargazing. $120.

Hotel La Rose 308 Wilson St, Santa Rosa ☎707/579-3200 or 1-800/527-6738, ⓦwww.hotellarose.com. Restored lodging on Railroad Square. Clean rooms with two phone jacks in each room for Internet use. $129.

🏂 **Metro Hotel** 508 Petaluma Blvd S, Petaluma ☎707/773-4900, ⓦwww.metrolodging.com. Handily placed for both the Sonoma Valley and the coast, this newly renovated hotel offers unexpected touches of European style in its decor and a French café, all at unbeatable rates for such quality. $99.

Motel 6 2760 Cleveland Ave, Santa Rosa ☎707/546-1500 or 1-800/466-8356, ⓦwww.motel6.com. A little distant from the main wine areas, but good and cheap. There's another branch down the street at 3145 Cleveland Ave. Both $62.

Swiss Hotel 18 W Spain St, Sonoma ☎707/938-2884, ⓦwww.swisshotelsonoma.com. A 90-year-old landmark building situated right on the plaza with a fine restaurant. The five cramped rooms each have a view of either the garden patio or Sonoma's plaza, and come with a four-poster queen-size bed. $150.

B&Bs

Bungalows 313 313 First St E, Sonoma ☎707/996-8091, ⓦwww.bungalows313.com. Pleasant collection of six spacious suites arranged round a shady courtyard and period house. $219.

Cottage Inn & Spa 302 First St E, Sonoma ☎707/996-0719 or 1-800/944-1490, ⓦwww.cottageinnandspa.com. A calm, downtown B&B owned by two interior designers, with hot tub and a relaxing courtyard. $205.

🏂 **Gaige House Inn** 13540 Arnold Drive, Glen Ellen ☎707/935-0237 or 1-800/935-0237, ⓦwww.gaige.com. Beautifully restored Queen Anne farmhouse in a quiet and contemporary country setting. Splendid new pine cottages out by the brook available as well. No young children. $272.

Kenwood Inn & Spa 10400 Sonoma Hwy, Kenwood ☎707/833-1293 or 1-800/353-6966, ⓦwww.kenwoodinn.com. Deluxe, beautiful, and secluded Italian-villa-style B&B with a fireplace in all suites, some of which reach $700 in season. $375.

Ramekins Bed and Breakfast Inn 450 W Spain St, Sonoma ☎707/933-0452, ⓦwww.ramekins.com. European-style lodging above a famous cooking school – so you can bank on being fed a fine breakfast and take part in cooking classes to boot. $165.

Thistle Dew Inn 171 W Spain St, Sonoma ☎707/938-2909 or 1-800/382-7895, ⓦwww.thistledew.com. Sonoma's most-raved-about B&B, near Sonoma plaza, features elegantly restored rooms, an amazing breakfast, and free bike rental, yet remains cheaper than many others. Some rooms come with a fireplace, private hot tub, and patio. $165.

Around forty-five fine **wineries** are scattered all over the Sonoma Valley, but there's a good concentration in a well-signposted group a mile east of Sonoma Plaza, down East Napa Street. Some are within walking distance, but often along quirky backroads, so take a winery map from the tourist office and follow the signs closely. Tasting charges are generally a little lower than in Napa. If you're tired of driving around, visit the handy Wine Exchange of Sonoma, 452 First St E (℡707/938-1794), a commercial tasting room where for a small fee, you can sample the best wines from all over California; should you be more in the mood for hops, they also boast a selection of 300 beers.

Bartholomew Park Winery 1000 Vineyard Lane ℡707/935-9511, ⓦwww.bartpark .com. This lavish Spanish-colonial building is surrounded by some great topiary in the gardens and extensive vineyards. The wines are relatively inexpensive vintages that appeal to the pocket and palate alike; a safe bet for buying a case. There's a good little museum, too, of regional history that also provides an introduction to local viticulture. Self-guided tours of the winery and tastings daily 11am–4.30pm; $10.

Benziger Family Winery 1883 London Ranch Rd, Glen Ellen ℡707/935-3000 or 1-888/490-2739, ⓦwww.benziger.com. Beautiful vineyard perched on the side of an extinct volcano next to Jack London State Park. $15 tram tours through the fields with emphasis on viticulture nine times daily or self-guided tour introducing trellis techniques. Tastings daily 10am–5pm; $10–15.

Buena Vista Carneros 18000 Old Winery Rd ℡707/252-7117 or 1-800/926-1266, ⓦwww.buenavistacarneros.com. Oldest and grandest of the wineries, established in 1857, whose wine is regaining a good reputation after some slim years. The tasting room, a restored state historical landmark, features a small art gallery. Tasting daily 10am–5pm; $5–10 inc glass. Various tours available, ranging from free self-guided ones to the two-hour Sonoma Wine and Cheese Experience for $50.

Chateau St Jean 8555 Sonoma Hwy, Kenwood ℡707/833-4134 or 1-800/543-7572, ⓦwww.chateaustjean.com. Attractive estate with an overwhelming aroma of wine

Sonoma

Behind a layer of somewhat touristy stores and restaurants, **SONOMA** retains a good deal of its Spanish and Mexican architecture. The town's charm emanates from the grassy plaza centering downtown, which has lots of shady spots to relax in and a peaceful duck pond. This communal space is at its liveliest every Tuesday during daylight savings months from 5pm to 9pm, when there is a weekly **farmers' market**, usually with live music.

Just off the plaza, a number of historic buildings and relics preserve history in the **Sonoma State Historic Park** ($2 combined entry to all sites; daily 10am–5pm). The restored **Mission San Francisco Solano de Sonoma** was the last and northernmost of the California missions, established by Mexican rulers fearful of expansionist Russian fur traders. Half a mile west stands the **General Vallejo Home**, the leader's ornate former residence, dominated by decorated filigree eaves and slender Gothic-revival arched windows. The chalet-style storehouse next door has been turned into a **museum** of artifacts from the general's reign.

Few come to Sonoma to visit the historic buildings, however, and relaxing coffee shops, great restaurants, rare-book stores, and a 1930s-era movie house ring the plaza, making Sonoma a wonderful place to stroll after a day spent in the vineyards.

throughout the buildings. Quirky tower to climb from where you can admire the view. Tours daily 11am & 2pm; $15. Tasting daily 10am–5pm; $5–10.

Gundlach-Bundschu 2000 Denmark St, Sonoma ☎707/938-5277, ⓦwww.gundlach -bundschu.com. Set back about a mile away from the main cluster, Gun-Bun, as it's known to locals, is highly regarded, having stealthily crept up from the lower ranks of the wine league. The plain, functional building is deceptive – this is premium stuff and definitely not to be overlooked. The winery also hosts various theatrical, cinema, and musical events throughout the summer. Tasting daily 11am–4.30pm; $5–10. Unreserved tours Sat & Sun hourly noon–3pm, weekdays by appointment; free.

Imagery 14335 Sonoma Hwy, Glen Ellen ☎707/935-4500, ⓦwww.imagerywinery .com. An offshoot of Benziger, specializing in unusual varietals like Petit Verdot. Its most striking feature is the gallery of paintings, each of which has featured on a label. Tastings Sun–Thurs 10am–4.30pm, Fri & Sat 10am–5.30pm; $10.

Mayo Family Winery 13101 Arnold Drive, Glen Ellen ☎707/938-9401, ⓦwww .mayofamilywinery.com. Relatively new winery with a cozy feel and friendly welcome, matching the small-time production of under five thousand cases annually. Complimentary tasting daily 10.30am–6.30pm; barrel tasting tours Fri–Sun 2 & 4pm. Check website for its three other

Ravenswood locations. 18701 Gehricke Rd, Sonoma ☎707/933-2332 or 1-888/669-4679, ⓦwww.ravenswood-wine.com. Noted for their "gutsy, unapologetic" Zinfandel and advertising a "no wimpy" approach to the wine business, the staff at this unpretentious winery are particularly friendly and easygoing. Well known to locals for its summer barbecues. Tastings daily 10am–4.30pm; $10, inc 10.30am tour if you're there early.

Sebastiani Vineyards & Winery 389 Fourth St E, Sonoma ☎707/938-5532 or 1-800/888-5532, ⓦwww.sebastiani.com. One of California's oldest family wineries, only four blocks from central Sonoma, it now boasts a newly renovated hospitality center, while the rest of the estate is being returned to its original appearance. There is another tasting room on the central square at 103 W Napa St (☎707/933-3291). Free tasting and tours via tram every half-hour. Daily 10am–5pm.

Glen Ellen and Jack London State Park

Continuing five miles north on Hwy-12, you'll come upon the cozy hamlet of **GLEN ELLEN** whose main street (Hwy-12, or Arnold Drive as it's also known) is a three-block-long collection of boutique shops and restaurants along the banks of Sonoma Creek. More interestingly, Glen Ellen is the home of **JACK LONDON STATE PARK** (daily 9.30am–5pm; $6 per vehicle; ☎707/938-5216, ⓦwww.jacklondonpark.com), which begins a half-mile up London Ranch Road past the Benziger Family Winery, and covers 140 acres of ranchland that the famed author of *The Call of the Wild* owned with his wife. From a small parking lot near the entrance, a one-mile walk on a groomed trail through the woods leads to the ruins of **Wolf House**, which was to be the London ancestral home. "My house will be standing, act of God permitting, for a thousand years," wrote London. In 1913, a month before they were to move in, the house burned to the ground, sparing only the boulder frame. Mounted blueprints point out the splendor it was to contain: plans included a manuscript room, stag party room, sleeping tower, gun room, and indoor reflecting pool.

Nearby is the final resting place of London – a red boulder from the house's ruins under which his wife Charmian sprinkled his ashes. Just off the parking lot, **The House of Happy Walls** (daily 10am–5pm; free) houses an interesting collection of souvenirs he and Charmian picked up traveling the globe:

The Bear Flag Revolt

Sonoma Plaza was the site of the **Bear Flag Revolt**, the 1846 action that propelled California into independence from Mexico, and then statehood. In this much-romanticized episode, American settlers in the region, who had long lived in uneasy peace under the Spanish and, later, Mexican rulers, were threatened with expulsion from California along with all other non-Mexican immigrants. In response, a band of thirty armed settlers – including the infamous John Fremont and Kit Carson – descended upon the disused and unguarded presidio at Sonoma, taking the retired and much-respected commander, Colonel Mariano Guadalupe Vallejo, as their prisoner. Ironically, Vallejo had long advocated the American annexation of California and supported the aims of his rebel captors, but he was nonetheless bundled off to Sutter's Fort in Sacramento and held there while the militant settlers declared California an independent republic. The Bear Flag, which served as the model for the current state flag, was fashioned from a "feminine undergarment and muslin petticoat" and painted with a grizzly bear and single star. Raised on Sonoma Plaza, where a small plaque marks the spot today, the Bear Flag flew over the Republic of California for a short time. Three weeks later, the US declared war on Mexico and, without firing a shot, took possession of the entire Pacific coast. While far from a frontier town now, the town once had a much wilder side and in fact gave the English language a slang word for prostitutes. Not long after the Bear Flag revolt, General Lee Hooker arrived, bringing along a group of ladies employed to cheer up the troops. The ladies soon became known as "Hooker's girls," and then simply "hookers."

manuscripts, rejection letters (more than six hundred), the couple's letter of resignation from the Socialist Party, and plenty of photographs. A nearby trail leads past a picnic ground to **London's Cottage** (Sat & Sun 10am–4pm; free), where he died. A video display gives background to his life, his wife, and the era. West of the cottage, a trail leads one mile toward the mountains and into the woods, ending at the lake London had built so he and Charmian could fish and swim. Bring a bottle of wine and soak in the sunny charm; given the hoopla of the Wine Country, the usually uncrowded museum and lovely parkgrounds feel like an oasis of tranquility.

Santa Rosa and around

Sixty miles due north of San Francisco on US-101, and about twenty miles from Sonoma on Hwy-12, **SANTA ROSA**, the largest town in Sonoma County, sits at the top end of the Sonoma Valley and is more or less the hub of this part of the Wine Country. It's a very different world from the indulgence of other Wine Country towns, however; much of it is given over to shopping centers and roadside malls. In an attempt to form a central pedestrian-only hub, **Historic Railroad Square** – a strip of redbrick-facade boutiques – has been developed, but it will never be mistaken for St Helena's Main Street or Sonoma's Plaza. With the real estate prices higher than ever in the Bay Area, Santa Rosa is exploding with growth, making it both a bedroom community for San Francisco and site of the Wine Country's cheapest lodging, with major hotel and motel chains located around town. It also has a decent selection of restaurants and bars. Full listings of what the town has to offer can be found at the **CVB & California Welcome Center**, 9 Fourth St (Mon–Sat 10am–5pm, Sun 10am–3pm; ☎707/577-8674 or 1-866/918-5685, ⓦwww.visitsantarosa .com), close to Railroad Square.

Probably the most interesting thing about Santa Rosa is that it was the hometown of Raymond Chandler's fictional private eye Philip Marlowe. Other than that, you can kill an hour or two at the **Luther Burbank Home and Gardens**, at the junction of Santa Rosa and Sonoma avenues (gardens daily 8am–dusk; free; guided tours Tues–Sun every half-hour 10am–3.30pm; $4; ℡707/524-5445, Ⓦwww.lutherburbank.org), where California's best-known horticulturist is remembered in the house where he lived and in the splendid gardens in which he created some of his most unusual hybrids. **Snoopy's Home Ice**, 1667 West Steele Lane (℡707/546-7147, Ⓦwww .snoopyshomeice), is a skating arena built by *Peanuts* creator Charles Schulz as a gift for the community. It actually comprises two buildings: the ice skating rink and Snoopy's Gallery, a museum/gift shop of all things *Peanuts* (Mon–Fri 11am–5pm, Sat & Sun 10am–5pm, closed Tues in winter; $8; ℡707/546-3385, Ⓦwww.schultzmuseum.org) and a lasting tribute to the much-loved Schulz, who died at the turn of the millennium.

One enterprise few people would expect to find tucked away in the Wine Country is a full-blown **wildlife refuge** – yet spreading over four hundred acres of the pristine hills between the two valleys, five miles northeast of Santa Rosa, is **Safari West**, 3115 Porter Creek Rd (℡707/579-2551 or 1-800/616-2695, Ⓦwww.safariwest.com). Set up in 1989 by Peter Lang, son of *Daktari* producer Otto, the refuge runs breeding programs for hundreds of rare mammal and bird species. Three-hour African-style **jeep tours** (daily 9am, 1pm, & 4pm in summer, 10am & 2pm in winter; $65) take you through vast open compounds of herd animals, and you can wander at leisure past large cages of cheetahs and primates or the leafy aviary, while expert guides supply detailed background on the furry and feathered inhabitants. Accommodation in genuine African luxury tents, hung on stilted wooden decks, is available from a princely $230 per unit, and filling buffet meals are served in the mess tent.

Eating and drinking

The Sonoma Valley has its fair share of fancy **restaurants**, particularly around the town of Sonoma and ritzy Glen Ellen. A sprinkling of simpler eateries and **bars** completes the possibilities for a night out.

Inexpensive restaurants, cafes, and takeouts

Arrigoni's Deli 701 Fourth St, Santa Rosa
℡707/545-1297. The place to go for picnic supplies, serving an array of gourmet meats, cheeses, and other indulgences.
Café Citti 9049 Sonoma Hwy, Kenwood
℡707/833-2690. Small, inexpensive trattoria with great Italian food and an intimate, yet casual, atmosphere.
Coffee Garden Café 421 W First St, Sonoma
℡707/996-6645. Fresh sandwiches are served on the back patio of this 150-year-old adobe, converted into a café with small gift shop.
Cucina Viansa 400 E First St, Sonoma
℡707/935-5656. Very reasonably priced at $9–15, considering the small but creative

and delicious selection of Italian specialities such as veal *piatto* on offer.
Gary Chu's 611 Fifth St, Santa Rosa
℡707/526-5840. Large helpings of high-quality Chinese food at very reasonable prices.
La Casa 121 E Spain St, Sonoma ℡707/996-3406. Friendly, festive, and inexpensive Mexican restaurant just across from the Sonoma Mission. Enjoy an enchilada on the sunny outdoor patio.
Rins Thai 139 E Napa St, Sonoma ℡707/938-1462. Good range of spicy curries and other Thai favourites available at this modest restaurant right on the main square.
The Schellville Grill 22900 Broadway, Sonoma ℡707/996-5151. No longer *Ford's Café* of

yore but still an institution with locals, who flock here for the ample burgers and sandwiches, some with surprisingly imaginative touches thrown in.

Upmarket restaurants
Café La Haye 140 E Napa St, Sonoma ☎707/935-5994. Only eleven tables, and always packed for its lovely, lively interior and tasty Italian food.

The General's Daughter 400 W Spain St, Sonoma ☎707/938-4004. Moderately priced California/Mediterranean hybrid dishes like wild mushroom ravioli, salmon and asparagus, and pork tenderloin in a Victorian building formally owned by General Vallejo's daughter.

The Girl & The Fig 110 W Spain St, Sonoma ☎707/938-3634. This well-known restaurant offers French dinners and weekend brunch from a menu as eclectic as its name and pricey to match; delights include grilled polenta with portobello mushrooms.

Glen Ellen Inn 13670 Arnold Drive, Glen Ellen ☎707/996-6409. Husband-and-wife team cook and serve slightly pricey Califonia-style gourmet dishes in an intimate, romantic dining room with half a dozen tables. Daily 5.30–9.30pm.

La Salette 452 First St E, Sonoma ☎707/938-1927. New restaurant serving Portuguese home-cooking with seafood a specialty; try the Mozambique prawns or *bacalhau* (baked cod).

Saffron Restaurant 13648 Arnold Drive, Glen Ellen ☎707/996-4844. The food has a Hispanic touch in this new establishment, which also stocks fine wines from Spain. The excellent lentil soup is indeed laced generously with saffron.

Bars
Amigos Grill and Cantina 19315 Sonoma Hwy, Sonoma ☎707/939-0743. Award-winning margaritas made using your choice of one of twenty tequilas and a home-made mix.

Murphy's Irish Pub 464 First St E, Sonoma ☎707/935-0660. Small bar with an eclectic interior and a few outdoor tables serving basic pub grub and European beers.

Third Street Aleworks 610 Third St, Santa Rosa ☎707/523-3060. Frequent live music and hearty American grub like burgers and pizza, washed down with microbrewed beer, are the order of the day at this lively joint.

The Russian River Valley

Starting some ten miles northwest of Santa Rosa, the remote **RUSSIAN RIVER VALLEY** contains some of the most secluded vineyards and bucolic landscapes in the state. Tree-lined Hwy-116 follows the river's course through twenty miles of what appear to be lazy, backwater resorts but in fact are major stomping grounds for partying weekenders from San Francisco. The valley's seat, **Guerneville**, has the most nightlife and lodging, augmented by its close neighbour **Monte Rio**, while **Healdsburg** serves as the gatekeeper for the **wine area**, bordering US-101 and the Dry Creek and Alexander valleys.

Today, the fortunes of the Russian River Valley have come full circle; back in the 1920s and 1930s, it was a recreational **resort** for well-to-do city folk who abandoned the area when newly constructed roads took them elsewhere. Drawn by low rents, city-saturated hippies started arriving in the late 1960s, and the Russian River took on a nonconformist flavor that lingers today. More recently, an injection of affluent Bay Area property seekers, many of them gay, has sustained the region's economy, and turned the place into a popular upcountry haven for the Castro crowd.

Accommodation

The quiet Russian River Valley has a much smaller selection of **places to stay** than its more famous cousins to the south and they are mainly mid-range hotels to luxury resorts. The Guerneville Chamber of Commerce (see p.369) has accommodation listings for the whole valley. The dearth of cheap motels (unless you head east to US-101) makes **camping** the economical answer. Of numerous options in the area, the following are among the best and all in or around Guerneville: the Austin Creek State Recreation Area, Armstrong Woods Road (☎707/865-2391; $15), is guaranteed RV-free, while *Johnson's Beach and Resort*, 16241 First St ($15 per vehicle plus one person, extra people $3 each; ☎707/869-2022, ⓦwww.johnsonsbeach.com), also has cabins and rooms available by the week. Finally, there are $3 walk-in backcountry sites in Armstrong Redwoods State Reserve (☎707/869-2015).

Applewood Inn & Restaurant 13555 Hwy-116, Guerneville ☎707/869-9093 or 1-800/555-8509, ⓦwww.applewoodinn.com. Luxury B&B with rooms spread between three attractive properties. Room/dinner packages are available as there's a gourmet restaurant on site. $195.

Best Western Dry Creek Inn 198 Dry Creek Rd, Healdsburg ☎707/433-0300 or 1-800/222-5784, ⓦwww.drycreekinn.com. Safe franchise with the standard levels of comfort on the north side of town, handy for the wineries. $99.

Creekside Inn and Resort 16180 Neely Rd, Guerneville ☎707/869-3623 or 1-800/776-6586, ⓦwww.creeksideinn.com. Comfortable and friendly B&B that makes for one of the more reasonably priced options in the valley. $98.

Highland Dell Resort 21050 River Blvd, Monte Rio ☎707/865-2300, ⓦwww.highlanddell.com. Tucked behind the river, this hotel has been completely renovated in tasteful style, with a range of room prices and a highly rated restaurant. $109.

Madrona Manor 1001 Westside Rd, Healdsburg ☎707/433-4231 or 1-800/258-4003, ⓦwww.madronamanor.com. Luxurious Victorian-style bed and breakfast mansion, crowning a hilltop, with meticulously maintained gardens and a gourmet restaurant. $250.

New Dynamic Inn 14030 Mill St, Guerneville ☎707/869-5082, ⓦwww.newdynamicinn.com. A relaxed, New Age motel where "cosmic energies unite with you" and you can soothe yourself with alternative healing therapies. $85.

Rio Villa Beach Resort 20292 Hwy-116, Monte Rio ☎707/865-1143 or 1-877/746-8455, ⓦwww.riovilla.com. Comfortable resort located right on the river, whose rooms mostly have kitchens for self-catering or at least fridges. $139.

Village Inn 20822 River Blvd, Monte Rio ☎707/865-2304, ⓦwww.villageinn-ca.com. Most of the stylishly rustic rooms have balconies nestling under a majestic stand of redwoods, with views of the river or across the tranquil garden. $125.

Guerneville

The main town of the Russian River Valley, **GUERNEVILLE**, has finally come out. No longer disguised by the tourist office as a place where "a mixture of people respect each other's lifestyles," it's quite clearly a **gay resort** and has been for the last fifteen years: a lively retreat popular with tired city-dwellers who come here to unwind. Gay men predominate during the summer, except during two **Women's Weekends** (☎707/869-9000) – in early May and late September – when many of the hotels take only women.

If you don't fancy venturing along the valley, there's plenty to keep you busy without leaving town. Weekend visitors flock here for the canoeing, swimming, and sunbathing that comprise the bulk of local activities. **Johnson's Beach** (May–Sept), on a placid reach of the river in the center of town, is the prime spot, with canoes, pedal boats, and tubes for rent at reasonable rates. But Guerneville's biggest natural asset is the magnificent **Armstrong Redwoods State Reserve** (☎707/869-2015), two miles north at the top of Armstrong Woods Road ($6 per vehicle) – seven hundred acres of massive redwood trees, hiking, and riding trails, and primitive camping sites.

The Guerneville Chamber of Commerce (see p.369) issues an excellent *Russian River Wine Road* map, which lists all the **wineries** that spread along the entire course of the Russian River. Unlike their counterparts in Napa and Sonoma, few of the wineries here either organize guided tours or charge for wine tasting. You can usually wander around at ease, guzzling as many and as much of the wines as you please. Some of the wines are of remarkably good quality, if not as well known as their Wine Country rivals. By car, you could easily travel up from the Sonoma Coast and check out a couple of Russian River wineries in a day, although the infectiously slow pace may well detain you longer.

Belvedere four miles south of Healdsburg at 4035 Westside Rd, ☏707/431-4442, ⓦwww.belvederewinery.com. Pleasantly situated winery with good views from the terraced garden. Live jazz on summer Saturday afternoons. Tastings daily 11am–5pm.

Dry Creek Vineyard 3770 Lambert Bridge Rd, four miles northwest of Healdsburg at corner of Dry Creek Road ☏707/433-1000 or 1-800/864-9463, ⓦwww.drycreekvineyard.com. This family-owned operation is well known for its consistently top-notch wines – particularly the Cabernet Sauvignon and Chardonnay. Picnic facilities. Tastings daily 10.30am–4.30pm.

Ferrari Carano 8761 Dry Creek Rd, six miles northwest of Healdsburg ☏707/433-6700 or 1-800/831-0381, ⓦwww.ferrari-carano.com. One of the smartest wineries in the region, Ferrari is housed in a Neoclassical mansion with beautiful landscaped grounds. They specialize in Italian-style wines. Tastings daily 10am–5pm; $5; tours by appointment.

Hop Kiln 6050 Westside Rd, over five miles south of Healdsburg ☏707/433-6491, ⓦwww.hopkilnwinery.com. Recently established rustic winery with a traditional atmosphere but not a snobbish attitude. Ironically a plaque marks the spot where kilns used to dry the hops when this was beer country. Tastings daily 10am–5pm.

Korbel Champagne Cellars 13250 River Rd, two miles east of Guerneville ☏707/824-7000, ⓦwww.korbel.com. The bubbly itself – America's best-selling premium Champagne – isn't anything you couldn't find in any supermarket, but the wine and brandy are sold only from the cellars, and are of such notable quality that you'd be crazy not to swing by for a glass or two. The estate where they are produced is lovely, surrounded by hillside gardens covered in blossoming violets, coral bells, and hundreds of varieties of roses – perfect for quiet picnics. A micro-brewery and upscale deli are also on the premises. Tastings daily summer 9am–5pm, winter 9am–4.30pm.

Lake Sonoma 9990 Dry Creek Rd, Geyserville ☏707/473-2999, ⓦwww.lakesonomawinery.net. In a fine elevated setting at the far end of Dry Creek Valley from Healdsburg, this has a good range of wines and a particularly fine port, as well as a microbrewery on the premises. Tastings daily 10am–5pm.

Porter Creek 8735 Westside Rd, over five miles east of Guerneville ☏707/433-6321, ⓦwww.portercreekvineyards.com. Small winery with a country feel, producing all-organic wines including their specialty, Pinot Noir. Tastings daily 10.30am–4.30pm, closed Tues & Wed in winter.

Russian River Vineyards 5700 Gravenstein Hwy, Forestville, five miles from Guerneville along Hwy-116 ☏707/887-1575 or 1-800/867-6567, ⓦwww.topolos.net. One of the Russian River Valley's most accessible wineries, specializing in Zinfandels. The popular on-site restaurant *Stella's* (☏707/887-1562) serves Greek-inspired Californian dishes – dine on the patio and feast your eyes on the wildflower gardens. Tastings daily 11am–5.30pm; tours by appointment.

The visitor center (daily 11am–3pm) can provide trail maps: take food and water and don't stray off the trails, as the densely forested central grove is quite forbidding and very easy to get lost in. One of the best ways to see it is on **horseback**; Horseback Adventures (☎707/887-2939, ⓦ www.redwood horses.com) offers guided horseback tours that range from a half-day trail ride ($70) to overnight pack trips ($250 per horse per day). A natural amphitheater provides the setting for the **Redwood Forest Theater**, once used for dramatic and musical productions during the summer but now simply a fine spot for rustic contemplations.

The busiest the town ever gets is over the first weekend after Labor Day, when the region hosts the long-established **Jazz on the River Festival**. This is something of a wild weekend around here and a good time to come: bands set up on Johnson's Beach by the river and in the woods for impromptu jamming sessions as well as regular scheduled events. The newer **Russian River Blues Festival** in late June is proving to be almost as popular. Check out ⓦ www .russianriverfestivals.com for details on both events.

Monte Rio

The small town of **MONTE RIO**, four miles west along the river from Guerneville, is definitely worth a look: a lovely, crumbling old resort town with big Victorian houses in stages of graceful dilapidation. For years it has been the entrance to the 2500-acre **Bohemian Grove**, a private park that plays host to the San Francisco-based Bohemian Club. A grown-up summer camp, its membership includes a very rich and very powerful male elite – ex-presidents, financiers, politicians, and the like. Every year in July they descend for "Bohemian Week" – noted for its hijinks and high-priced hookers, away from prying cameras in the seclusion of the woods.

The lonely, narrow **Cazadero Highway** just to the west makes a nice drive from here, curving north through the wooded valley and leading back to Fort Ross on the coast. At the north end of the bridge over the Russian River in Monte Rio, **cyclists** can begin the world-renowned King Ridge–Meyers Grade ride, a 55-mile loop (and 4500 feet of climb) that heads along the Cazadero Highway and into the hills, finally descending to the coast and Hwy-1. Contact the Santa Rosa Cycling Club (☎707/544-4803, ⓦ www.srcc .com) for a complete itinerary.

Healdsburg

The peaceful town of **HEALDSBURG**, along with its diminuitive neighbour **Geyserville**, straddles the invisible border between the Wine Country proper and the Russian River Valley, and thus in a quiet way manages to get the best of both worlds. **Veterans Memorial Beach**, a mile south of the plaza along the banks of the Russian River, is a popular spot for swimming, picnicking, and canoeing in the summertime; there are also some twenty wineries, most of them family-owned, within a few miles of the center of town. The only cultural diversion in town is **The Healdsburg Museum**, 221 Matheson St (Tues–Sun 11am–4pm; free; ⓦ www.healdsburgmuseum.org), which displays local history through a decent collection of Pomo Indian basketry, nineteenth-century tools and crafts, and eight thousand original photos. Although the town's economic well-being is almost exclusively dependent on tourism, it still manages to maintain a relaxed, back-country feel. The Healdsburg Area **Chamber of Commerce**, 217 Healdsburg Ave (Mon–Fri 9am–5pm, Sat 9am–3pm, Sun

10am–2pm; ☎707/433-6935 or 1-800/648-9922, ⓦwww.healdsburg.org),
provides winery and lodging information.

Eating and drinking

Although you certainly won't go hungry, there is not such a choice of high-class
restaurants in the Russian River Valley, but Guerneville's **nightlife** is the best
of all three valleys, with a welcoming selection of predominantly gay **bars**.

Restaurants and cafés

🏃 **Bear Republic Brewing Co** 345 Healdsburg Ave, Healdsburg ☎707/433-2337. If
you want an inexpensive pub meal, washed
down with an excellent ale in a lively atmosphere, this is the spot.

Bistro Ralph 109 Plaza St, Healdsburg
☎707/433-1380. With sparse modern decor
and well-crafted French-style dishes (around
$20 per main course), this is one of the
town's finest dining options.

Brew Moon 16248 Main St, Guerneville
☎707/869-0201. Down-to-earth café serving
tasty barbecued meats on paper plates in
addition to cheap breakfasts and good
coffee.

Burdon's Restaurant 15405 River Rd,
Guerneville ☎707/869-2615. Popular and
classy establishment with excellent gourmet
meat and pasta dishes for around $15.

Flying Goat Coffee Roastery and Café 324
Center St, Healdsburg ☎707/433-9081. Just off
the main plaza, this is a great place to
unwind with a newspaper and a good cup
of coffee or light snack.

Northwood Restaurant 19400 Hwy-116, Monte
Rio ☎707/865-2454. Tasty California cuisine
at average prices, served up in a large
roadside restaurant, with a separate bar.

Pat's Restaurant 16236 Main St,
Guerneville ☎707/869-9904. Also known
as *Chef Patrick* after the congenial proprietor, this local favorite churns out ample
portions of whole-hearted diner fare such
as pork loin with creamy mashed potatoes
at little cost.

Taqueria La Tapatia 16632 Hwy-116, Guerneville ☎707/869-1821. Excellent, authentic,
and cheap Mexican joint, just west of town.

Bars

Club Yamagata 16225 Main St, Guerneville
☎707/869-9910. Friendly new gay bar that
also serves food and later buzzes to dance
vibes and occasional live acts.

Main Street Station 16280 Main St, Guerneville
☎707/869-0501. Nightly live music, mostly
jazz, and pizza, in case you feel peckish.

🏃 **The Pink Elephant** 9895 Main St, Monte
Rio ☎707/865-0500. Well-established
local hangout with simple ambience and
cheap drinks. Features regular live music
and open-mic nights on Mon.

Rainbow Cattle Co 16220 Main St, Guerneville
☎707/869-1916. One of the most popular
gay bars that gets livelier as the night
draws on.

Contexts

Contexts

History

T hough its recorded history may not stretch back very far by European standards, in its 150-plus years of existence, San Francisco has more than made up for time. It first came to life during the California Gold Rush of 1849, the adventurous tone of which the city sustains to this day, both in its valuing of individual effort above corporate enterprise and in the often nonconformist policies that have given it perhaps the most progressive image of any US city. The following account is intended to give an overall view of the city's development; for a rundown of the figures – both past and present – who have helped to shape the city, see the "San Francisco people" glossary on p.421.

Native peoples

For thousands of years before the arrival of Europeans, the **aboriginal peoples** of the Bay Area lived healthily and apparently fairly peacefully on the naturally abundant land. Numbering around 15,000, and grouped in small, tribal villages of a few hundred people, they supported themselves mainly by hunting and fishing rather than with agriculture. Most belonged to the coastal **Miwok** tribe, who inhabited much of what is now Marin County, as well as the Sonoma and Napa valleys; the rest were **Ohlone**, who lived in smaller villages sprinkled around the Bay and down the south coast of the Peninsula.

Very few artifacts from the period survive, and most of what anthropologists have deduced is based on the observations of the early explorers, who were by and large impressed by the Indian way of life – if not their "heathen" religion: one of the first colonists characterized them as "constant in their good friendship, and gentle in their manners." Indian boats, fashioned from lengths of tule reed, were remarkably agile and seaworthy. Of the buildings, few of which were ever intended to last beyond the change of seasons, the most distinctive was the *temescal*, or sweat lodge. Kule Loklo, a replica Miwok village in the Point Reyes National Seashore, provides a good sense of what their settlements might have looked like.

Since there was no political or social organization beyond the immediate tribal level, it did not take long for the colonizing Spaniards effectively to wipe them out, if more through epidemics than through outright genocide. Nowadays no Bay Area Native Americans survive on their aboriginal homelands.

Exploration and conquest

Looking at the Golden Gate from almost any vantage point, it's hard to imagine that anyone might fail to notice such a remarkable opening to the Pacific. Nevertheless, dozens of **European explorers**, including some of the most legendary names of the New World conquest – Juan Cabrillo, Sir Francis Drake, and Sebastián Vizcaíno – managed to sail past for centuries, oblivious to the great harbor it protected. Admittedly, the passage is often obscured by fog, and even on a clear day the Bay's islands, and the East Bay hills that rise up behind, do disguise the entrance to the point of invisibility.

Sir Francis Drake came close to finding the Bay when he arrived in the *Golden Hinde* in **1579**, taking a break from plundering Spanish vessels in order to make repairs. The "white bancks and cliffes" of his supposed landing spot – now called Drake's Bay, off Point Reyes north of San Francisco – reminded him of Dover. Upon going ashore, he was met by a band of Miwok, who greeted him with food and drink and placed a feathered crown upon his head; in return, he claimed all of their lands, which he called Nova Albion (New England), for Queen Elizabeth. He was supposed to have left behind a brass plaque (since proved a fake) – even so, a copy remains on display in the Bancroft Library at the University of California in Berkeley.

Fifteen years later the Spanish galleon **San Augustín** – loaded to the gunwales with treasure from the Philippines – moored in the same spot but met with tragically different results. After the crew renamed Drake's Bay to honor their patron saint, San Francisco de Asis (Francis of Assisi), the ship was dashed against the rocks of Point Reyes and wrecked. The crew was able to salvage some of the cargo and enough of the ship to build a small lifeboat, on which they traveled south all the way to Acapulco, hugging the Pacific Coast for the entire voyage and still sailing right past the Golden Gate. Indeed, it was not until the end of 1769 that European eyes set sight on the great body of water now called San Francisco Bay.

Colonization: the mission era

The **Spanish occupation** of the West Coast, which they called "Alta California," began in earnest in the late 1760s, following the Seven Years' War. Although this was partly owing to military expediency to prevent another power from gaining a foothold, the conquest was fueled more by religious fervor: both Catholic missionary zeal to convert the heathen Indians, and Franciscan eagerness to replace the Jesuits who'd been expelled from all Spanish dominions by King Don Carlos III in 1767. Early in 1769, a company of three hundred soldiers and clergy, led by Father **Junípero Serra**, set off from Mexico in Baja California to establish an outpost at Monterey; half traveled by ship, the other half overland. A number stopped to set up the first Californian mission at San Diego, while an advance party – made up of some sixty soldiers, mule skinners, priests, and Indians, under the leadership of **Gaspàr de Portola** – continued up the coast, blazing an overland route. It was hard going, especially with their inadequate maps, and not surprisingly they overshot their mark, ending up somewhere around Half Moon Bay. Ironically, after two centuries of sea voyages designed to map the coastline, it would be this landlocked expedition that would first sight the magnificent San Francisco Bay.

Trying to regain their bearings, Portola sent out two scouting parties, one north along the coast and one east into the mountains. Both groups returned with extraordinary descriptions of the Golden Gate and the great Bay, which they thought must be the same "Bahia de San Francisco" where the *San Augustín* had come to grief almost two centuries earlier. On November 4, 1769, the entire party gathered together on the ridgetop, overwhelmed by the incredible sight: Father Crespi, their priest, wrote that the Bay "could hold not only all the armadas of our Catholic Monarch, but also all those of Europe." Portola's band barely stayed long enough to gather up supplies before turning around and heading back to Monterey; that mission was to become the capital and commercial center of Spanish California.

It took the Spanish another six years to send an expedition 85 miles north to the bay Portola had discovered. In May 1775, when he piloted the *San Carlos* through the Golden Gate, Juan Manuel de Ayala became the first European to sail into San Francisco Bay. The next year **Captain Juan Bautista de Anza** returned with some two hundred soldiers and settlers to establish the **Presidio of San Francisco** overlooking the Golden Gate. His party also set up a mission three miles to the southeast beside a lake, which they named *Laguna de los Dolores* – "The Lake of Our Lady of Sorrows" – because it was settled on the so-called Friday of Sorrows before Palm Sunday. From this came the mission's popular – and still current – name, **Mission Dolores**; the first Mass at the mission also marks the official founding of the city later known as San Francisco.

Over the coming years four other Bay Area **missions** were established along the El Camino Real, or the "Royal Road": it was built between 1769 and 1823 to link the 21 missions in the chain, running along the Californian coast from San Diego up to the final outpost in Sonoma. **Santa Clara de Asis**, forty miles south of Mission Dolores, was founded in 1777; **San José de Guadalupe**, set up in 1797 near today's Fremont, grew into the most successful of the lot. In 1817, the *asistencia*, or auxiliary mission, **San Rafael Arcangel**, was built in sunny Marin County as a convalescent hospital for priests and Indians who had been taken ill at Mission Dolores. The last, **San Francisco Solano**, built at Sonoma in 1823, was the only mission established under Mexican rule.

Each of the mission complexes was broadly similar, with a church and cloistered residence structure surrounded by irrigated fields, vineyards, and more distant ranchlands, the whole protected by a small contingent of soldiers. Indian catechumens were put to work making soap and candles, but were treated as retarded children, often beaten and never educated. Objective facts about the missionaries' treatment of the Indians are hard to come by, though mission registries record twice as many deaths as they do births, and their cemeteries are packed with Indian dead in their thousands, most of them in unmarked graves. Many of the missions suffered from Indian raids, as evidenced by the red-tiled, fire-resistant roofs that replaced earlier thatch designs.

To grow food for the missions and the forts or presidios, **towns** – called *pueblos* – were established, part of the ongoing effort to attract settlers to this distant and as yet undesirable territory. The first was laid out in 1777 at San Jose in a broad fertile valley south of the Mission Santa Clara. Though it was quite successful at growing crops, it had no more than a hundred inhabitants until well into the 1800s. Meanwhile, a small village – not sanctioned by the Spanish authorities – was beginning to emerge between Mission Dolores and the Presidio, around the one deepwater landing spot, southeast of today's Telegraph Hill. Called **Yerba Buena**, "good grass," after the sweet-smelling minty herb that grew wild over the windswept hills, it was little more than a collection of shacks and ramshackle jetties. This tiny outpost formed the basis of today's city, though it wasn't officially tagged as San Francisco until 1847, when opportunistic settlers on the East Bay, looking to capitalize on their closeness to bustling Sacramento, planned a town called Francisca, after the San Francisco Bay. In response, Yerba Buena bigwigs – anxious to flag their pre-eminent position on the coast – quickly renamed their town San Francisco to eclipse the upstarts.

The Mexican revolutions and the coming of the Americans

The emergence of an independent **Mexican state** in 1821 spelled the end of the mission era. In 1834, the new republic had secularized the missions, the excuse being that they were originally intended only as temporary places to "train" Indians in good Christian ways before letting them run their affairs. The Mexican government didn't pass the land onto native peoples – instead, in a politically savvy maneuver, it bequeathed the territory to the few powerful families of the "Californios" – mostly ex-soldiers who had settled here after completing their military service. Mexico exerted hardly any control over distant Yerba Buena, and was generally much more willing than the Spanish had been to allow foreigners to remain as they were, so long as they behaved themselves. A few trappers and adventurers had passed by in the early 1800s, and, beginning in the early 1820s, a number of British and Americans started arriving in the Bay Area, most of them sailors who jumped ship, but also including a few men of property. The most notable of these immigrants was **William Richardson**, an Englishman who arrived on a whaling ship in 1822 and stayed for the rest of his life, marrying the daughter of the Presidio commander and eventually coming to own most of southern Marin County. Here, he started a profitable shipping company and ran the sole ferry service across the tricky Bay waters. In Richardson's wake, dozens followed – almost without exception males who, like him, tended to fit in with the existing Mexican culture, often marrying into established families and converting to the Catholic faith.

As late as the mid-1840s, Monterey was still the only town of any size on the entire West Coast, and tiny Yerba Buena (population two hundred or so) made its livelihood from supplying passing ships, mainly Boston-based whaling vessels and the fur-traders of the British-owned **Hudson's Bay Company**. Though the locals lived well, the Bay Area was not obviously rich in resources, and so was not by any means a major issue in international relations. However, from the 1830s onwards, the US government decided that it wanted to buy all of Mexico's lands north of the Rio Grande, California included, fulfilling the "Manifest Destiny" of the United States to cover the continent from coast to coast. Any negotiations were rendered unnecessary when, in June 1846, the **Mexican–American War** broke out in Texas, and US naval forces quickly took over the entire West Coast, capturing San Francisco's Presidio on **July 9, 1846**.

Just before this, however, a historically insignificant revolt in the Bay Area left an unusual, lasting legacy for California. An ambitious US Army captain, John C. Fremont, had been working to encourage unhappy settlers to declare independence from Mexico and to set himself up as their leader. By assembling an unofficial force of some sixty sharpshooting ex-soldiers, and by spreading rumors that war with Mexico was imminent and unstoppable, he managed to persuade settlers to take action, leading to the **Bear Flag Revolt**. On June 14, some thirty farmers and trappers descended upon the abandoned Presidio in Sonoma and took the retired commandant captive, raising a makeshift flag over the town's plaza and declaring California independent. The flag – which featured a roughly drawn grizzly bear above the words "California Republic" – was eventually adopted as the California state flag, but this "Republic" was short-lived. Three weeks after the disgruntled settlers hoisted their flag in Sonoma, it was replaced by the Stars and Stripes, and California was thereafter **US territory**.

Ironically, just nine days before the Americans took formal control, **gold** was discovered on January 24, 1848, in the Sierra Nevada foothills a hundred miles east of the city – something that was to change the face of San Francisco forever. Gold would eventually be discovered in 54 out of California's 58 counties; ironically San Francisco – the city whose identity and future were forged in the heat of the Gold Rush – stands in one of the four barren counties.

The Gold Rush

At the time gold was discovered, the Bay Area had a total (non-native) population of around two thousand, about a quarter of whom lived in tiny

San Francisco. By the summer of 1848, rumors of the find attracted a trickle of gold seekers, and when news of their subsequent success filtered back to the coast, soldiers deserted and sailors jumped ship.

The first prospectors on the scene made fantastic fortunes – those working the richest "diggings" could extract more than an ounce every hour – but the real money was being made by merchants charging equally outrageous prices for essentials. (This is how jeans genius Levi Strauss made his fortune, and how Domenico Ghirardelli turned chocolate into gold.) Even the most basic supplies were hard to come by, and what little was available cost exorbitant amounts: a dozen eggs for $50, a shovel or pickaxe twice that. Exuberant miners willingly traded glasses of gold dust for an equal amount of whiskey – something like $1000 a shot. Though it took some time for news of the riches to travel, soon men were flooding into California from all over the globe to share the wealth. Within a year, some 100,000 men – known collectively as the **forty-niners** – had arrived in California: it was the greatest peacetime migration in modern history, and for a time, the men arrived in such numbers that San Francisco's population doubled every ten days. About half of the hopefuls came overland, after a three-month slog across the continent – they headed straight for the mines. The rest arrived by ship and landed at San Francisco, expecting to find a city where they could recuperate before continuing on the arduous journey. They must have been disappointed with what they found: hulks of abandoned

The rise and fall of Sam Brannan

Sam Brannan was one of the smartest and most ruthless of the Gold Rush's business tycoons; Levi Strauss and Domenico Ghirardelli may be more famous now, but Brannan was both more notorious and wealthier in their time. He arrived in San Francisco via New York in 1846 as the leader of a 230-strong Mormon missionary group, who fled here by boat hoping to found a new settlement free from what they considered the United States' religious intolerance (while the group was at sea, sadly, California was annexed and its plans scuppered). It's unlikely to have troubled Brannan deeply as he was an iffy Mormon at best – eventually excommunicated from the church for dipping into its cash reserves for his own treats. However, on arriving, Brannan's followers were industrious enough to put up more than two hundred buildings; while he himself used the printing press he'd hauled from the East Coast to publish the first local newspaper, *The California Star*, in 1847.

As the Gold Rush era's answer to Rupert Murdoch, he was in an ideal position to fan – and profit from – the hysteria that emerged on the discovery of the first deposits. Never one to let scruples get in the way of sheckels, Brannan effectively orchestrated the entire thing. Aside from his printing press, Brannan owned a dry-goods and supply store, and realized he could make a fortune from hordes of get-rich-quick types needing hammers, pails, and tents for prospecting. He waited until his warehouses were full of products, and then published a special issue of the *Star* in 1848 that focused on local gold mining. His strategy was flawless, and it earned him $36,000 in just nine weeks; he sold prospecting equipment at such a premium, Brannan later became California's first-ever millionaire.

He used the money for two things: first, to buy chunks of local land for a town he was planning, later named Calistoga. The official reason for the name was a combination of New York's Saratoga and California; the more likely basis is that Brannan named it during a speech he gave while drunk on whisky. After all, liquor was the second thing he spent his fortune on – so much so, in fact, that he frittered away his business, was married and divorced three times, and ended up living in Mexico, selling pencils on the streets to earn a few pennies. When he died, his body lay in a vault for a year until the money to bury him could be found.

ships formed the only solidly constructed buildings; rats overran the filthy streets; and drinking water was scarce and often contaminated.

Few of the new arrivals stayed very long in ruthless San Francisco, but, if anything, life in the mining camps proved even less hospitable. As thousands of moderately successful but worn-out miners returned to San Francisco, especially during the torrential rains of the **winter of 1849–50**, the shanty-town settlement began to grow into a proper city. It suffered six infernos in the six months following Christmas 1849, the last of which spurred the formation of the first Committee of Vigilance. Ex-miners set up foundries and sawmills to provide those starting out with the tools of their trade, and traders arrived to profit from the miners' success, selling them clothing, food, drink, and entertainment. The city where the successful miners came to blow their hard-earned cash was a place of luxury hotels and burlesque theaters, which featured the likes of Lola Montez, whose semi-clad "spider dance" enthralled legions of fans. Throughout the early 1850s immigrants continued to pour through the Golden Gate, and although the great majority hurried on to the mines, enough stayed around to bring the city's population up to around 35,000 by the end of 1853. Of these, more than half were from foreign parts – a wide-ranging mix of Mexicans, Germans, Chinese, Italians, and others.

Within five years of the discovery of gold, the easy pickings were all but gone. As the freewheeling mining camps evolved into increasingly large-scale, corporate operations, San Francisco swelled from frontier outpost into a substantial city, with a growing industrial base, a few newspapers, and even its own branch of the US Mint. When revenues from the gold fields ceased to expand in the late 1850s, the speculative base that had made so many fortunes quickly vanished. Lots that had been selling at a premium couldn't be given away, banks went bust, and San Francisco had to declare itself **bankrupt** as a result of years of corrupt dealings. The already volatile city descended into near-anarchy, with vigilante mobs roaming the streets. By the summer of 1856, the Committee of Vigilance, led by William Coleman and Sam Brannan and composed of the city's most successful businessmen, was the **de facto government** of the city, having taken over the state militia. It installed itself inside its "Fort Gunnybags" headquarters on Portsmouth Square, outside which it regularly hanged petty criminals (admittedly after giving them a trial), to the amusement of gathered throngs.

Events reached a boiling point when the future California Supreme Court Justice **David Terry** shot a committee member (Terry would go on to shoot the state's first senator a few years later), bringing the vigilantes into direct confrontation with the official government. A few of the most radically minded proposed secession from the US, but calmer heads prevailed, and the city was soon restored to more legitimate governance. Ironically, the task of defending the rabidly pro-slavery Terry fell to a failed banker and young local military commander named **William Sherman**, who would later go into the history books for razing much of the state of Georgia during the Civil War.

The boom years (1860–1900)

In the 1860s, San Francisco enjoyed a bigger boom than that of the Gold Rush, following the discovery of an even more lucrative band of precious **silver ore** in the Great Basin Mountains of western Nevada. Discovered just east of Reno in late 1859 and soon known as the **Comstock Lode**, it was one of the most fantastic deposits ever encountered. A single, solid vein of silver, mixed with gold, it ranged from ten to over a hundred feet wide and stretched a little over two miles long, most of it buried hundreds of feet underground. Mining here was in complete contrast to the freelance prospecting of the California gold fields, and required a scale of operations unimagined in the Californian mines. Many of San Francisco's great engineers, including George Hearst, Andrew Hallidie, and Adolph Sutro, put their minds to the task.

As the mines had to go increasingly deeper to get at the valuable ore, the mining companies needed larger and larger amounts of capital, which they attracted by issuing shares dealt on the burgeoning **San Francisco Stock Exchange**. Speculation was rampant, and the value of shares could rise or fall by a factor of ten, depending on the day's rumors and forecasts; Mark Twain got his literary start publicizing, for a fee, various new "discoveries" in his employers' mines. Hundreds of thousands of dollars were made and lost in a day's trading, and the cagier players, like James Flood and James Fair, made millions.

While the Comstock silver enabled many San Franciscans to enjoy an unsurpassed prosperity throughout the 1860s, few people gave much thought to the decade's other major development, the building of the **transcontinental railroad**, completed in 1869 using imported Chinese laborers. Originally set up in Sacramento to build the western link, the **Central Pacific** and later **Southern Pacific** railroad soon expanded to cover most of the West, ensnaring San Francisco in its web. Wholly owned by the so-called **Big Four** – Charles Crocker, Collis P. Huntington, Mark Hopkins, and Leland Stanford – the Southern Pacific "octopus," as it was caricatured in the popular press, exercised an essential monopoly over transportation in the Bay Area. Besides controlling the long-distance railroads, they also owned San Francisco's streetcar system, the network of ferries that crisscrossed the Bay, and even the cable-car line that lifted them up California Street to their Nob Hill palaces (see box, p.80).

Not everyone, however, reaped the good fortune of the Nob Hill elite. The coming of the railroad usurped San Francisco's primacy as the West Coast's supply point, and products from the East began flooding in at prices well under anything local industry could manage. At the same time the Comstock mines ceased to produce such enormous fortunes, and a depression began to set in. The lowering of economic confidence was compounded by a series of droughts that wiped out agricultural harvests, and by the arrival in San Francisco of thousands of now unwanted **Chinese workers**. As unemployment rose throughout the late 1870s, frustrated workers took out their aggression in racist assaults on the city's substantial Chinese population. Railroad baron **Leland Stanford** campaigned for governor on an anti-immigrant platform (though his company's employment of masses of Chinese laborers on construction gangs seriously undercut his candidacy), and at mass demonstrations all over the city, thousands rallied behind the slogan "The Chinese Must Go!"

Though San Francisco was popularly seen as powered by ignoble motives and full of self-serving money-grabbers, there were a few exceptions, even among its wealthiest elite. **Adolph Sutro**, for example, was a German-born engineer who made one fortune in the Comstock mines and another buying up land in the city – in 1890 he was said to own ten percent of San Francisco, even more than the Big Four. But Sutro was an unlikely millionaire, as compassionate and public-spirited as the Big Four were ruthlessly single-minded; in fact, when the Southern Pacific tripled fares to a quarter on the trolley line out to Golden Gate Park, Sutro built a parallel line that charged a nickel. He also built the Sutro Baths and the Cliff House and in 1894 was elected mayor of San Francisco on the Populist Party ticket. Campaigning on an anti-Southern Pacific manifesto, he promised to rid San Francisco of "this horrible monster which is devouring our substance and debauching our people, and by its devilish instincts and criminal methods is every day more firmly grasping us in its tentacles." Sutro died in 1898, with the city still firmly in the grasp of the "octopus."

The Great Earthquake and its aftermath

San Francisco experienced another period of economic expansion in the **early years of the 1900s**, owing in equal part to the Spanish–American War and the Klondike Gold Rush in Alaska. Both of these events increased ship traffic through the port, where dockworkers were beginning to organize themselves into **unions** on an unprecedented scale; the mighty longshoremen's association they formed was to become a political force to be reckoned with for years to come. The fight to win recognition and better wages was long and hard; unrest was virtually constant, and police were brought in to scare off strikers and prevent picket lines from shutting down the waterfront. But this economic instability was nothing compared to the one truly earth-shattering event of the time: the **Great Earthquake of 1906.**

The quake that hit San Francisco on the morning of April 18, 1906, was, at 8.1 on the Richter Scale, the most powerful ever to hit anywhere in the US, before or since (over ten times the force of the 1989 earthquake, see p.403). It destroyed hundreds of buildings, but by far the worst destruction was wrought by the **post-earthquake conflagration**, as ruptured gas mains exploded and chimneys toppled, starting fires that spread rapidly across the city. Temperatures often reached 2000°F, which meant that spontaneous ignition could occur at distances of up to 125ft. The fire all but leveled the entire area from the waterfront, north and south of Market Street, and west to Van Ness Avenue, whose grand mansions were dynamited in a politically daring move to form a firebreak. The statistics are staggering: 490 city blocks and 28,000 buildings were destroyed, causing $300–500m worth of damage – at the time, two-thirds of the property value of the city and one-third of the taxable property in all California. Half of San Francisco's population – some 100,000 people – were left homeless and fled the city. Many of those who stayed set up camp in the barren reaches of what's now Golden Gate Park, where soldiers from the Presidio undertook the mammoth task of establishing and maintaining a tent city for about 20,000 displaced San Franciscans. The official death toll has long been touted at only 500 people, but historians have challenged such figures and upped estimates to at least 3000 dead and likely thousands more.

During the ensuing ten years, San Francisco was rebuilt with a vengeance, although the grand plan drawn up by designer Daniel Burnham just a year before the disaster was ignored in favor of the old city layout. The city council had given its approval to this plan, which would have replaced the rigid grid of streets with an eminently more sensible system of axial main boulevards filled in with curving avenues skirting the hills and smaller, residential streets climbing their heights. However, such was the power and influence of the city's vested interests that the status quo was quickly reinstated, despite the clear opportunity afforded by the earthquake. (One contemporary rumor was that politicians were considering moving the city across the Bay to the better weather and more stable land in Marin. Landowners quickly scrambled to rebuild on their property to spoil such plans.) At least cartographers cleaned up the mishmash of street names here – in 1910, by city ordinance, duplicates (often pioneer names like Sutter) were eliminated and dozens of streets renamed for clarity.

To celebrate its recovery, and the opening of the Panama Canal – a project that had definite implications for San Francisco's trade-based economy – the city fathers set out to create the magnificent **1915 Panama–Pacific International Exhibition**. Land was reclaimed from the Bay for the exhibition, and an elaborate complex of exotic buildings was constructed on it, including Bernard Maybeck's exquisite Palace of Fine Arts and centering on the 100-yard-high, gem-encrusted Tower of Jewels (a few of its dazzling gems can be seen in the Wells Fargo History Museum; see p.56). Hundreds of thousands visited the fair, which lasted throughout the year, but when it ended all the buildings, save the Palace of Fine Arts, were torn down, and the land was sold off for housing, forming the area now known as the Marina.

The great success of the exhibition proved to the world that San Francisco had recovered from the earthquake. But the newly recovered civic pride was tested the next year when, on the eve of America's involvement in **World War I**, a pro-war parade organized by San Francisco's business community was devastated by a **bomb attack** on Steuart Street near the Ferry Building, that killed ten marchers and severely wounded another forty. In their haste to find the culprit, the San Francisco police arrested half a dozen radical union agitators. With no evidence other than perjured testimony, activist **Tom Mooney** was convicted and sentenced to death, along with his alleged co-conspirator **Warren Billings**. Neither, fortunately, was executed, but both spent most of the rest of their lives in prison; Billings wasn't pardoned until 1961, 45 years after his fraudulent conviction.

The Roaring Twenties

The war years had little effect on San Francisco, but the period thereafter, the **Roaring Twenties**, was in many ways the city's finest era. Despite Prohibition, the jazz clubs and speakeasies of the Barbary Coast district were in full swing: San Francisco was still the premier artistic and cultural center of the West Coast, although it would relinquish that role to Los Angeles by the next decade. Furthermore, its status as an international financial hub (the two major international credit-card companies – Visa and Access – had their starts here) equaled that of New York City. The strength of San Francisco as a banking power was highlighted by the rise of Bank of America – founded as the Bank of Italy in 1904 by A.P. Giannini in North Beach – into the largest bank in the world.

The buoyant 1920s gave way to the Depression of the 1930s, but, despite the sharp increases in unemployment, there was only one major battle on the industrial-relations front. On **"Bloody Thursday"** – July 5, 1934 – police protecting strike-breakers from angry picketers fired into the crowd, wounding thirty and killing two longshoremen. The Army was sent in to restore order, and in retaliation the unions called a **General Strike** that saw some 125,000 workers down tools, bringing the Bay Area economy to a halt for four days. It was one of the largest strikes in the nation's history. Otherwise there was remarkably little unrest, and some of the city's finest monuments – Coit Tower, for example, and, most importantly, the two great bridges – were built during this time under **WPA sponsorship**. Before the **Bay and Golden Gate bridges** went up, in 1936 and 1937 respectively, links between the city and the surrounding towns of the Bay Area were provided by an impressive network of **ferry boats**, some of which were among the world's largest. In 1935, the ferries' peak year, some 100,000 commuters per day crossed the Bay by boat; just five years later the last of the boats was withdrawn from service, unable to compete with the increasingly popular automobile.

World War II

The Japanese attack on Pearl Harbor and US involvement in **World War II** transformed the Bay Area into a massive war machine, its industry mobilizing quickly to provide weaponry and ships for the war effort. **Shipyards** opened all around the Bay – the largest, the Kaiser Shipyards in Richmond, was employing more than 100,000 workers on round-the-clock shifts just six months after its inception – and men and women flooded into the region from all over the country to work in the lucrative concerns. In fact, in 1943, for perhaps the first and only time in its history, the city was so crowded that civic groups discouraged conventions and tourists. Entire cities were constructed to house the workers, many of which survive – not least Hunter's Point, on the southern edge of the San Francisco waterfront, which was never intended to last beyond the end of hostilities but still houses some 15,000 of the city's poorest people. A more successful example is Marin City, a workers' housing community just north of Sausalito, which – surprisingly, considering its present-day air of leisured affluence – was one of the most successful wartime shipyards, able to crank out a ship a day.

Certainly, there was a strong male-only culture in San Francisco that dated back to the time of the forty-niners, but it was the war that inadvertently established the city as a **gay center**. Young men, barred from embarkation under suspicion of homosexuality and thus discharged before they saw combat, remained in the city rather than return home in disgrace; others, whose sexuality had come under question while overseas, were summarily discharged when they docked in San Francisco for the same reason. Both groups received distinctive blue-colored discharge papers – vital to show a new employer – marked with a large red H to denote "homosexual"; little wonder so many dismissed in that way chose to settle in the city and try to make new lives here rather than return home. In the process, those disgraced military men helped found the roots of the current community.

The 1950s... and the Beats go on

After the war, thousands of GIs returning from the South Pacific came home through San Francisco, and many decided to stay. The city spilled out into new districts, and, especially in suburbs like the Sunset, massive tracts of identical dwellings, subsidized by federal loans and grants, were thrown up to house the returning heroes – many of whom still live here. The accompanying economic prosperity continued unabated well into the 1950s, and in order to accommodate increasing numbers of cars on the roads, huge **freeways** were constructed, cutting through the city. The Embarcadero Freeway in particular formed an imposing barrier, perhaps appropriately dividing the increasingly office-oriented Financial District from the declining docks and warehouses of the waterfront, which for so long had been the heart of San Francisco's economy.

As the increasingly mobile and prosperous middle classes moved out from the inner city, new bands of literate but disenchanted middle-class youth began to move into the areas left behind, starting, in the middle part of the decade, in the bars and cafés of North Beach, which swiftly changed from a staunch Italian neighborhood into the Greenwich Village of the West Coast. The **Beat Generation**, as they became known, reacted against what they saw as the empty materialism of Fifties America by losing themselves in a bohemian orgy of jazz, drugs, and Buddhism, expressing their disillusionment with the status quo through a new, highly personal, and expressive brand of fiction and poetry. The writer **Jack Kerouac**, whose *On the Road* became widely accepted as the handbook of the Beats, both for the style of writing (fast, passionate, unpunctuated) and the lifestyle it described, was in some ways the movement's main spokesman, and is credited with coining the term "Beat" to describe the group. Later, columnist Herb Caen somewhat derisively turned "Beat" into "Beatnik," after Sputnik, since the rebellious youngsters' behavior was as "far out" as the Russian satellite. San Francisco, and particularly the **City Lights Bookstore**, at the center of North Beach, became the main meeting point and focus of this diffuse group, though whatever impetus the movement had was gone by the early 1960s. For more on the Beats, see box on p.70.

San Francisco and the Summer of Love

If the 1950s belonged to the Beats, then the 1960s were ruled by the inexperienced but enthusiastic young people who followed in their hedonistic footsteps – derisively christened junior hipsters, or **hippies**. The first hippies appeared in the early Sixties, in cafés and folk-music clubs around the fringes of Bay Area university campuses. Like the Beats they eschewed the materialism and the nine-to-five consumer world. But while the Beats were nitty-gritty, their successors were hippy-dippy, preferring an escapist fantasy of music and marijuana that morphed into a half-baked political indictment of society and where it was going wrong.

The main difference between the Beats and the early hippies, besides the five years that elapsed, was that the hippies had discovered – and regularly experimented with – a new hallucinogenic drug called LSD, better known as **acid**. Since its synthesis, LSD had been legally and readily available, mainly through psychologists who were interested in studying its possible therapeutic benefits. Other, less scientific, research was also being done by a variety of people, many of whom, from around 1965 onward, began to settle in the **Haight-Ashbury district** west of the city center, living communally in huge low-rent Victorian houses in which they could take acid and "trip" in safe, controlled circumstances. Music was an integral part of the acid experience, and a number of bands – the **Charlatans**, **Jefferson Airplane**, and the **Grateful Dead** – came together in San Francisco during the summer of 1966, playing open-ended dance music at such places as the Fillmore Auditorium and the Avalon Ballroom.

Things remained on a fairly small scale until the spring of **1967**, when a free concert in Golden Gate Park, the "Human Be-In," drew a massive crowd and, for the first time, media attention. Articles describing the hippies, most of which focused on their prolific appetites for sex and drugs, attracted a stream of newcomers to the Haight from all over the country, and within a few months the **Summer of Love** was well under way, with some 100,000 young people descending upon the district. For more on this period, see the box on p.133.

In contrast to the hippie indulgence of the Haight-Ashbury scene, across the Bay in Berkeley and Oakland **revolutionary politics**, rather than drugs, were at the top of the agenda. While many of the hippies opted out of politics, the student radicals threw themselves into political activism, beginning with the Free Speech Movement at the University of California in 1964. The FSM, originally a reaction against the university's banning of on-campus political activity, laid the groundwork for the more passionate **anti-Vietnam War** protests that rocked the entire country for the rest of the decade. The first of what turned out to be dozens of **riots** occurred in June 1968, when students marching down Telegraph Avenue in Berkeley in support of the Paris student uprising were met by a wall of police, leading to rioting that continued for the next few days. Probably the most famous event in Berkeley's radical history took place in **People's Park**, a plot of university-owned land that was taken over as a community open space by local people. Four days later an army of police, under the command of Edwin Meese – later head of the US Department of Justice during the Reagan years – tear-gassed and stormed the park, accidentally killing a bystander and seriously injuring more than one hundred others.

Probably the most extreme element of late-1960s San Francisco emerged out of the impoverished flatlands of Oakland – the **Black Panthers**, established by Bobby Seale, Huey Newton, and Eldridge Cleaver in 1966 (see box, p.296). The Panthers were a heavily armed but numerically small band of militant black activists with an announced goal of securing self-determination for America's blacks. From their Oakland base they set up a nationwide organization, but the threat they posed, and the chances they were willing to take in pursuit of their cause, were too great. Thirty of their members died in gun battles with the police, and the surviving Panthers lost track of their aims: Eldridge Cleaver later became a right-wing Republican, while Huey Newton was killed over a drug deal in West Oakland in 1989.

The gay decade

The unrest of the 1960s continued into the **early 1970s**, if not at such a fever pitch. One last headline-grabber was the kidnapping in 1974 of heiress Patty Hearst from her Berkeley apartment by the Symbionese Liberation Army, or **SLA**, a hardcore bunch of revolutionaries who used their wealthy hostage to demand free food for Oakland's poor. Hearst later helped the gang to rob a San Francisco bank, wielding a submachine gun (she was sent to jail for her crime, although later pardoned). Otherwise, the 1970s were quiet times (certainly compared to the previous decade). They saw the opening of the long-delayed **BART** high-speed transportation system, as well as the establishment of the **Golden Gate National Recreation Area** to protect and preserve 75,000 acres of open space on both sides of the Golden Gate Bridge.

Throughout the 1970s, it wasn't so much that San Francisco's rebellious thread had been broken, but rather that the battle lines were being drawn elsewhere. The most distinctive political voices were those of the city's large **gay and lesbian communities**. Inspired by the Stonewall Riots in New York City in 1969, San Francisco's homosexuals began to organize themselves politically, demanding equal status with heterosexuals. Most importantly, gays and lesbians stepped out into the open and refused to hide their sexuality behind closed doors, giving rise to the gay liberation movement that has prospered worldwide. One of the leaders of the gay community in San Francisco, **Harvey Milk**, won a seat on the Board of Supervisors, becoming the first openly gay man to take public office. When Milk was **assassinated** in City Hall, along with Mayor George Moscone, by former supervisor Dan White in 1978 – see box on p.125 – the whole city was shaken. The fact that White was found guilty of manslaughter, not murder, caused the gay community to erupt in riotous frustration, burning police cars and laying siege to City Hall.

The onslaught of AIDS and the 1989 earthquake

The **1980s** saw the city's gay community in retreat to some extent, with the advent of **AIDS** in the early part of the decade devastating the confidence of activists and decimating its population. City Hall, led by Mayor **Dianne**

▲ Harvey Milk celebrating his election to the Board of Supervisors

Feinstein (nicknamed Di-Fi), who took over after the death of Moscone, responded to the crisis more quickly and efficiently than other cities hard hit by the virus, supporting the community's Herculean efforts with well-funded urban relief and education programs. Together, they managed to stabilize new infection rates by the 1990s. Treatment and caretaking efforts for those infected by HIV, meanwhile, remained largely driven by volunteers' fundraising efforts, nearly exhausting the energies of the community, which became almost exclusively focused on the crisis.

At the same time, Feinstein oversaw the construction of millions of square feet of office towers in Downtown's Financial District, despite angry protests against the Manhattanization of the city. Although Feinstein's attempts to spend the city out of its financial slump dumped a tangled mess of financial worries into the lap of her successors, she went on to become senator in 1992 and remains one of the most prominent female politicians in America today.

But before the already tough 1980s came to an end, the city was shaken by a major **earthquake** in October 1989, 7.1 on the Richter Scale – an event watched by a hundred million people on nationwide TV, since it hit during a World Series game between the San Francisco Giants and the Oakland Athletics.

It's a wired, wired world – the 1990s

Following this rather grim decade, the **1990s** seemed sunnier, at least for some of the city's residents. A national boom in high-tech industries, initiated by companies such as Apple, Oracle, Netscape, and Yahoo! based south of the city in **Silicon Valley**, proved particularly lucrative for the Bay Area. The rush for new-technology jobs – at one peak moment, the valley was supposedly cranking out 63 new millionaires per day – created a region-wide population boom. In San Francisco, the influx of wealthy young computer professionals into an incredibly tight housing market led to the rapid **gentrification** of certain city neighborhoods (Hayes Valley and parts of the Mission, to name two), where rents skyrocketed by as much as a hundred percent per year; meanwhile, an entirely new upscale community sprung up along the South Beach waterfront, adjacent to a sparkling new (and privately financed) baseball stadium.

Merrily riding the wave of prosperity was **Willie Brown**, self-dubbed "da Mayor," who began his remarkable climb to power from being a child of African-American sharecroppers in Texas by driving a cab to fund his law degree, eventually becoming the most influential man in California's state senate and one of the most powerful black politicians in the nation. Brown noisily focused on ambitious programs to fix the city's overburdened mass-transit system and aging public housing. His detractors, however, pointed out the lack of substance behind his style, and the failure of the city's newfound wealth to solve such longstanding problems as homelessness argued in their favor. Evidence that gentrification hadn't completely killed the city's liberal spirit came during Brown's campaign for re-election in 1999, when write-in candidate Tom Ammiano, a popular gay stand-up comedian and President of the city's Board of Supervisors, nearly staged an upset with his progressive agenda. The victory may have been Brown's, but it was a pyrrhic one, as in his second term he struggled to balance the extravagant campaign promises he made to help the disenfranchised while protecting corporate interests.

Across the Bay, the successes of Oakland mayor **Jerry Brown** showed up "da Mayor's" failings all too acutely. Jerry's deft populist approach contrasted with Willie's ham-fisted tub-thumping and easily earned him a second term in office during the 2002 election. A former governor of California, Jerry's political platform centered on turning central Oakland, drained by suburban exodus and dogged by second-fiddle status to San Francisco, into a lively town crammed with amenities and residential space – a concept he called "elegant density." He made some progress before handing Oakland mayoral duties off to current city chief **Ron Dellums** in 2006, but the city's continued economic shortcomings indicate there's still plenty left to do.

San Francisco in the new millennium

The torrid **Internet industry** imploded in 2000–01, and the end of the dot-com boom left savage marks on San Francisco's cityscape, from empty warehouse offices in SoMa to the closure of new restaurants now devoid of patrons. The city stumbled on for a few years, with housing rates deflating, a marked drop in population, and a general listlessness uncharacteristic of San Francisco. By the middle of the decade, however, much of the city's energy had returned, thanks to a rebounded economy fueled in no small part by a flurry of Web 2.0 companies intent on learning from their predecessors' – or in some cases, their own – prior overindulgences.

It's a new era in San Francisco for another reason: the city's current mayor is native son **Gavin Newsom**, a suave restaurateur turned young-lion politico (the onetime city supervisor was 36 when inaugurated as mayor in early 2004). Newsom has surprised many in his mayorship: where Brown was pro-development, millionaire Newsom has focused on social issues like homelessness, not to mention his surprisingly staunch stance on gay marriage in 2004 (see box, p.241, which found him bucking state laws to wed hundreds of same-sex couples at City Hall. Despite a flurry of controversy in the early months of 2007 – the recently divorced mayor admitted to having an affair with his campaign manager's wife, then began treatment for alcohol abuse – Newsom's popularity at the polls soared: in the 2003 election, he narrowly defeated his comparatively underfunded opponent, city supervisor Matt Gonzalez; up for re-election four years later, Newsom ran virtually unopposed and won the office easily, garnering over 72 percent of all votes cast. It's been widely reported that the telegenic Newsom, now well into his second term as San Francisco mayor, is eyeing a run for the California governorship in 2010.

Books

Most of the books recommended below are currently in print, and those that aren't should be easy enough to find in secondhand bookstores. Books with the ⽊ symbol are particularly recommended.

Travel and impressions

John Miller (ed) *San Francisco Stories: Great Writers on the City*. Patchy collection of writings on the city with contributions from Lewis Lapham, Tom Wolfe, Dylan Thomas, and Hunter S. Thompson, to name a few.

Czeslaw Milosz *Visions from San Francisco Bay*. Written in Berkeley during the unrest of 1968, these dense and somewhat ponderous essays show a European mind trying to come to grips with California's nascent Aquarian Age.

Mick Sinclair *Cities of the Imagination: San Francisco*. Fact-crammed and immensely readable, but its thematic, rather than linear, history can make the narrative frustratingly circular and repetitive.

⽊ **Mark Twain** *Roughing It*. Vivid, semi-fantastical tales of frontier California, particularly evocative of life in the silver mines of the 1860s Comstock Lode, where Twain got his start as a journalist and storyteller. His descriptions of San Francisco include a moment-by-moment description of an earthquake.

Edmund White *States of Desire*. Part of a cross-country sojourn that includes a rather superficial account of the gay scene in 1970s San Francisco.

⽊ **Tom Wolfe** *The Electric Kool-Aid Acid Test*. Wolfe at his most expansive, floridly riding with the Grateful Dead and Hell's Angels on the magic bus of Ken Kesey and the Merry Pranksters as they travel through the early 1960s, turning California onto LSD.

History, politics, and society

Nan Alamilla Boyd *Wide Open Town: A History of Queer San Francisco to 1965*. This gay history is sadly rather heavy going and academic in its analysis; where it shines is in the first person oral histories, scattered throughout the book, which are interviews with everyday gays and lesbians who lived here in the early and mid-twentieth century.

Walton Bean *California: An Interpretive History*. Blow-by-blow account of the history of California, including all the shady deals and backroom politicking, presented in accessible, anecdotal form.

Mark Bittner *The Parrots of Telegraph Hill*. Homeless drifter-cum-hippie befriends the flock of parrots living on the power lines in this neighborhood, gains local notoriety, and then has his story recorded by a documentary filmmaker. A charming, low-key gem.

Gray Brechin *Imperial San Francisco*. Crisply written, tough-minded account of the questionable dealings that helped drive the city's rapid growth around the end of the nineteenth century.

Herb Caen *Baghdad by the Bay; The Best of Herb Caen*. Two collections by the city's most indefatigable promoter. Though rather light, Caen's bemused writing always portrays the city as a charming, cosmopolitan stomping ground.

Barnaby Conrad *Name Dropping: Tales from My Barbary Coast Saloon.* Author, bullfighter, and once-proud owner of the happening 1950s Bay Area bar *El Matador* spills the beans on his celebrity clientele, which included the likes of Kerouac, Sinatra, and Marilyn Monroe. Conrad has also edited a book about one of his long-time pals, *The World of Herb Caen.*

Peter Coyote *Sleeping Where I Fall.* The author, a minor actor, chronicles his hippie days giving out food as a member of the Diggers and directing radical theater with the SF Mime Troupe.

Joan Didion *Slouching Toward Bethlehem.* Selected essays from one of California's most renowned journalists, taking a critical look at the West Coast of the 1960s, including San Francisco's acid culture. In a similar style, *The White Album* traces the West Coast characters and events that shaped the 1960s and 1970s, including The Doors, Charles Manson, and the Black Panthers.

Philip L. Fradkin *The Great Earthquake and Firestorms of 1906: How San Francisco Nearly Destroyed Itself.* Stunning overview that brings fresh insight to a well-known topic; local journalist Fradkin follows not just the mistakes which led to the city's devastation (essentially, ignoring every earthquake warning) but also the political power struggles that erupted in the wake of the disaster.

Joshua Gamson *The Fabulous Sylvester: The Legend, the Music, the 70s in San Francisco.* Gamson uses an early disco diva, the flamingly gay Sylvester, as an entry point into the "Anything Goes" San Francisco of the 1970s. Sylvester's story is compelling

even for casual readers: a kid from the hood in LA becomes a falsetto-voiced, fabulous drag star in San Francisco before succumbing to AIDS in the late 1980s.

Milton Gould *A Cast of Hawks.* Juicy but overcooked account of San Francisco's early days, when the distinction between crook and statesman was at its vaguest; the book's details on the city's vigilante government are interesting.

Joyce Jansen *San Francisco's Cable Cars.* An informal history of the city's most prominent moving landmarks with some good historic photos of them.

David A. Kaplan *The Silicon Boys.* A witty, entertaining, and thorough account of the history and culture of the Silicon Valley.

Dan Kurtzman *Disaster!.* Hour-by-hour account of the Great Fire of 1906, crisply told as a gripping narrative focusing on the fate of a handful of local residents.

Pat Montandon *The Intruders.* Breathless true-life account of the supposed curse society hostess Montandon endured in the late 1960s, taking in the mysterious deaths and rattling around her Pacific Heights home. Hokey but great trashy fun.

Charles Perry *The Haight-Ashbury.* Curiously distant but detailed account of the Haight during the Flower Power years, written by an editor of *Rolling Stone.*

Rand Richards *Historic San Francisco.* Part history and part guide-book, this is a superb introduction to the city's odd narrative. The sight descriptions are rather redundant, but the intriguing, oddball historical digressions illuminate.

Randy Shilts *The Mayor of Castro Street: The Life and*

Times of Harvey Milk. Exhaustively researched epic biography of Milk that explores the assassinated supervisor's place in the struggle for gay rights. Shilts also wrote the most thorough account of the early days of the AIDS epidemic, *And the Band Played On*.

Jay Stevens *Storming Heaven: LSD and the American Dream*. An engaging account of psychedelic drugs and their effect on American society through the 1960s, with an epilogue covering "designer drugs" – Venus, Ecstasy, Vitamin K, and others – and the inner space they help some modern Californians to find.

Susan Stryker and Jim Van Buskirk *Gay by the Bay*. Pithy illustrated history of the city's gay and lesbian community. Though they touch on the city's history, the authors focus their attention on the post–World War II boom in the gay scene and the subsequent movement for artistic expression and political liberation.

Pam Tent *Midnight at The Palace: My life as a Fabulous Cockette*. Tent was one of the pan-sexual, LSD-fueled performance artists known as *The Cockettes* who scandalized and symbolized early 1970s San Francisco; she was unusual mostly for being a woman. Tent's anecdotal, affectionate recap of the troupe and era is surprisingly sweet.

Hunter S. Thompson *Hell's Angels*. The book that put the late Thompson's "gonzo" journalism on the map, as he chronicles violent parties with the notorious biker gang. *The Great Shark Hunt* is a collection of often barbed and cynical essays on 1960s American life and politics that's thought-provoking and hilarious. *Generation of Swine* is a more recent collection of caustic musings on the state of America and those who control it, assembled from his columns in the *San Francisco Examiner*.

Tom Wolfe *Radical Chic & Mau Mauing the Flak Catchers*. Wolfe's waspish account of Leonard Bernstein's fundraising party for the Black Panthers – a protracted exercise in character assassination – is coupled with an equally sharp analysis of white guilt and radical politics in City Hall, San Francisco.

Specific guides

Daniel Bacon *Walking San Francisco on the Barbary Coast Trail*. A fantastic, enthusiastic resource on the early days of San Francisco that's amusing, highly detailed, and informative. Highly recommended.

Adab Bakalinsky *Stairway Walks in San Francisco*. This guide details pretty back streets and stairways through San Francisco's hills. It's excellent for turning up lesser-known spots on a walking tour.

Bicycle Rider Directory Low-cost guide to do-it-yourself bicycle touring around the Bay Area and Napa and Sonoma valleys, with good fold-out route maps.

Jack Boulware *San Francisco Bizarro*. As its name suggests, this is a poppy, snappy survey of the offbeat and strange; some of Boulware's information is a little out of date, but his gossipy approach is appealing.

Don Herron *The Literary World of San Francisco*. A walk through the San Francisco neighborhoods associated with authors who have lived in and written about the city. Detailed and well presented, it's an essential handbook for anyone interested in San Francisco's literary heritage. If you're a hard-bitten crime hound, try *The Dashiell Hammett Tour* by the same author.

Grant Peterson *Roads to Ride*. As its subtitle says, this is a bicyclist's topographic guide to the whole Bay Area, and is particularly good on the back roads of Marin County.

Sidra Sitch *Art Sites San Francisco*. An exhaustive overview of the city's architecture, whether classic Victorians or modern skyscrapers Downtown. A little po-faced and dry, but packed with information.

🏃 **Walking the West Series:** *Walking the California Coast and*

Walking California's State Parks and others. Well-written and -produced paperbacks, each covering over a hundred excellent day walks from two to twenty miles. They're strong on practical details (maps, route descriptions, and so on), and boast inspiring prose and historical background.

Peggy Wayburn *Adventuring in the San Francisco Bay Area*. If you are planning to spend any time hiking in the Bay Area's many fine wilderness regions, pick up this fact-filled guide, which also details a number of historical walks through the city's urban areas.

Fiction and poetry

James d'Alessandro *1906: A Novel*. Rollicking page-turner using the disaster of 1906 as a backdrop. The vivid story is narrated by a feisty Italian-American reporter Annalisa Passarelli and fuses factual chunks with inventive subplots (including one starring world-famous tenor Enrico Caruso, who was indeed performing here during the disaster).

🏃 **Ambrose Bierce** *The Enlarged Devil's Dictionary*. Spiteful but hilarious compilation of definitions ("Bore: a person who talks when you wish him to listen") by this journalist working at the end of the nineteenth century. Bierce also wrote some superb chilling tales, including the stream-of-consciousness hanging in "An Occurrence at Owl Creek Bridge," collected in *Can Such Things Be* and his *Collected Works*.

Philip K. Dick *The Man in the High Castle*. Long-time Berkeley- and Marin County-based science-fiction author imagines an alternative San Francisco, following a Japanese victory in World War II. Of his dozens of other brilliant novels and short stories, *Bladerunner* and *The*

Trans-migration of Timothy Archer make good use of Bay Area locales.

John Dos Passos *USA*. Massive, groundbreaking trilogy, combining fiction, poetry, and reportage to tap the various strands of the American Experience. Much of the first part, *The 42nd Parallel*, takes place around the Sutro Baths and Golden Gate Park.

William Gibson *Virtual Light* and *All Tomorrow's Parties*. Two books showcasing the cyberpunk sci-fi author's futuristic vision of the city, complete with squatters on the Golden Gate Bridge and heroic bike messengers.

Allen Ginsberg *Howl and Other Poems*. The attempted banning of the title poem assured its fame; *Howl* itself is an angry rant that often descends into wince-inducing Beatnik jive, but a Whitmanesque voice often shines through.

Oakley Hall *Ambrose Bierce and the Queen of Spades*. Rich mystery of old-time San Francisco, in which colorful characters of the city's late-nineteenth-century cultural scene collide against a backdrop of murder, corruption, big business, and investigative journalism.

🏃 **Dashiell Hammett** *The Four Great Novels* (Random House/Picador). Seminal detective stories including *The Maltese Falcon* and starring Sam Spade, the private investigator working out of San Francisco. See also Diane Johnson's absorbing *The Life of Dashiell Hammett* (Fawcett/Picador).

🏃 **Maxine Hong Kingston** *Chinamen*. Hugely popular and affecting magical-realist depiction of one family's immigration from China to the gold coast. Kingston manages to combine both telling period details and the larger mythic quality of the passage of generations.

🏃 **Jack Kerouac** *On the Road*. The book that launched a generation with its "spontaneous bop prosody," it chronicles Beat life in a series of road adventures, featuring some of San Francisco and a lot of the rest of the US. His other books, many set in the Bay Area, include *Lonesome Traveler*, *The Dharma Bums*, and *Desolation Angels*.

David Lodge *Changing Places*. Thinly disguised autobiographical tale of an English academic who spends a year teaching at UC Berkeley (renamed in the book) and finds himself bang in the middle of the late-1960s student upheaval.

Jack London *Martin Eden*. Jack Kerouac's favorite book, a semi-autobiographical account tracking the early years of this San Francisco-born, Oakland-bred adventure writer. The lengthy opus tells of his rise from waterfront hoodlum to high-brow intellectual and of his subsequent disenchantment with the trappings of success.

Armistead Maupin *Tales of the City*; *Further Tales of the City*; *More Tales of the City*; *Babycakes*; *Significant Others*;

Sure of You. Six twisty, plot-crammed novels that wittily detail the sexual (and emotional) antics of four housemates – Michael (the gay one, Maupin's alter ego), Brian (the stud), MaryAnn (the virgin), and Mona (the flower child). The story, based on Maupin's newspaper columns, takes the characters from free-living and -loving late-1970s San Francisco to the hard realities of the late 1980s.

Ken McGoogan *Kerouac's Ghost*. Beat homage in which the author raises Kerouac from the dead and sticks him in the 1970s to write about Haight-Ashbury and play mentor to a struggling French-Canadian writer.

Seth Morgan *Homeboy*. Novel charting the sleazy San Francisco experiences of the former junkie boyfriend of Janis Joplin.

John Mulligan *Shopping Cart Soldiers*. Fictionalized memoir of a homeless vet who hangs out in Washington Square, where he meets the ghost of Robert Louis Stevenson. Offbeat and well written.

Fae Myenne Ng *Bone*. Well-crafted first novel that gives a good taste of hardscrabble life in San Francisco's Chinatown.

Frank Norris *McTeague: A Story of San Francisco*. Dramatic, extremely violent but engrossing saga of love and revenge in San Francisco at the end of the nineteenth century; later filmed by Erich von Stroheim as *Greed*. Norris's *Octopus* tells the bitter tale of the Southern Pacific Railroad's stranglehold over the Californian economy.

Thomas Pynchon *The Crying of Lot 49*. Obtuse but sharp and quite hilarious novel that follows the labyrinthine adventures of conspiracy freaks and potheads in 1960s California.

Kenneth Rexroth *An Autobiographical Novel*. Rather stiffly written account of the influential poet and translator's freewheeling life and times. A leading figure in San Francisco's postwar artistic community, Rexroth's experimental nature was an inspiration to a younger generation of Beat writers.

Douglas Rushkoff *The Ecstasy Club*. Cyberculture pundit concocts a frothy, well-paced novel ribboned with conspiracy theories and occult esoterica. Ravers, Deadheads, and other Bay Area riffraff wander in and out of the plot.

Vikram Seth *The Golden Gate*. Slick novel in verse, tracing the complex social lives of a group of San Francisco yuppies. Seth would go on to write the blockbuster *A Suitable Boy*.

Gary Snyder *Left Out in the Rain*. One of the original Beat writers, and the only one whose work ever matured, Snyder's poetry is direct and spare, yet manages to conjure up a deep animistic spirituality underlying everyday life.

Amy Tan *The Joy Luck Club*. Four Chinese-American women and their daughters gather together to look back over their lives. The mothers' lyrical tales of life in China dance with Tan's vivid and imaginative touch; the daughters' stories are soapier and less transporting.

William T. Vollman *The Rainbow Stories*. Brutal, gut-level portraits of street life: Tenderloin whores, Haight Street skinheads, beggars, junkies, and homeless Vietnam vets. Engaging stuff for those who can handle it.

San Francisco on film

San Francisco is a favorite with Californian filmmakers, the city's staggering range of settings and chameleon-like geography making an often economical choice for the director who needs sunny beaches, swirling fogs, urban decay, and pastoral elegance all at once. Thrillers, in particular, seem to get good mileage out of the city; Hitchcock loved it, while the ridiculous gradients are almost ideally suited to the car chases that Hollywood loves so much. Below is a list of the obvious and not-so-obvious films made about or in California's most beautiful city.

Ten classic San Francisco films

Barbary Coast (Howard Hawks 1935). Set in misty, fog-bound, c.1900 San Francisco, where Edward G. Robinson finds he has competition when he tries to seduce the exotic dancer played by Miriam Hopkins. A brawling adventure film that captures the spirit of a lawless San Francisco.

Bullitt (Peter Yates 1968). Though Steve McQueen is the star (his character is actually based on real-life SFPD plodder Dave Toschi who investigated the Zodiac Killer), San Francisco steals the show in the definitive high-speed, hillside car chase the film revolves around. It was filmed mostly on the steep streets of Pacific Heights and Potrero Hill.

The Conversation (Francis Ford Coppola 1974). Local boy Coppola directs this brilliant Watergate-era thriller, starring Gene Hackman as a surveillance expert slowly descending into paranoia. A foggy Union Square provides the perfect backdrop.

Days of Wine and Roses (Martin Manulis 1962). Jack Lemmon plays a likeable drunk who drags his wife into alcoholism too, only to leave her there once he's on the road to recovery. Smart satirical comedy that occasionally slips into melodrama.

Dirty Harry (Don Siegel 1971). Sleek and exciting sequel-spawning thriller casting Clint Eastwood in his definitive role as a quasi-fascist San Francisco cop. Morally debatable, but technically dynamic.

Greed (Erich von Stroheim 1924). Legendary, lengthy silent masterpiece based on Frank Norris's *McTeague* (see p.410) detailing the squalid, ultimately tragic marriage between a blunt ex-miner with a dental practice on San Francisco's Polk Street and a simple girl from nearby Oakland. Dated but nonetheless unforgettable, including the classic finale in Death Valley.

The Lady From Shanghai (Orson Welles 1948). Orson Welles' brief marriage to Rita Hayworth resulted in this twisted mystery about a double-crossing couple. The finale, shot in a hall of mirrors, is one of the most famous scenes in film history.

The Maltese Falcon (John Huston 1941). Possibly the greatest detective movie of all time, starring a hard-bitten Humphrey Bogart, as private dick Sam Spade, and Peter Lorre (stroking a remarkably suggestive cane).

Out of the Past (Jacques Torneur 1947). Real-life, lantern-jawed tough guy Robert Mitchum stars in this iconic film *noir* about one man's date with destiny.

Vertigo (Alfred Hitchcock 1958). Known during production as the

"San Francisco movie," Hitchcock's remarkable film looks at fear, obsession, and voyeurism. Jimmy Stewart gives an uncharacteristically dark performance as an ex-cop slowly becoming unhinged because of a romantic obsession. Excellent use of locations, including Nob Hill, Fort Point, Muir Woods, and Mission Dolores.

Documentaries

Berkeley in the Sixties (Mark Kitchell 1990). Well-made documentary about the heyday of political protest in Berkeley. Combination of modern-day interviews with startling clips showcasing nearly every movement that occurred back in the day.

The Cockettes (Bill Weber & David Weissman 2002). Irresistible, explicit, and sweet portrait of the way-out 1970s rock-meets-drag-meets-drugs performance troupe, combining archive footage with modern-day interviews.

Common Threads: Stories from the Quilt (Robert Epstein 1989). The maker of *The Times of Harvey Milk* (see below) documents the history of the Names Project Memorial Quilt, talking to six bereaved partners of people who died from AIDS complications.

Crumb (Terry Zwigoff 1994). Disturbing portrait of Robert Crumb, the wildly eccentric comic artist whose Mr Natural became a 1960s icon, and his even more bizarre relatives.

Fillmore (Richard T. Heffron 1972). Bad rock movie about San Francisco's famous music venue in the last week of its existence, leavened by its good footage of the Grateful Dead, Jefferson Airplane, and Boz Scaggs: sadly, Bill Graham's egomaniacal ranting between the acts soon becomes wearying.

Gimme Shelter (David & Albert Maysles/Charlotte Zwerin 1970). Legendary film about the Rolling Stones' Altamont concert (see box, p.321). Lots of shots of Mick Jagger looking bemused during and after the notorious murder.

Jimi Plays Berkeley (Peter Pilafian 1971). The historic Memorial Day Jimi Hendrix concert in Berkeley, interspersed with lots of shots of rampaging students waving their peace signs. Hendrix ignores the peripheral action and just plays.

Last Call at Maude's (Paris Poirier 1993). Sweet ode to a bygone lesbian bar – a window into over twenty years of Bay Area lesbian history.

Neighborhoods: the Hidden Cities of San Francisco (Peter L. Stein 1997). A popular four-part mini-series on the history of San Francisco, focusing on Chinatown, the Castro, the Fillmore, and the Mission.

The Times of Harvey Milk (Robert Epstein 1984). Academy Award-winning documentary chronicling Milk's career in San Francisco politics and the aftermath of his 1978 assassination.

The Wild Parrots of Telegraph Hill (Judy Irving 2005). While living in a Telegraph Hill cottage, former homeless musician Mark Bittner made friends with the flock of cherry-headed conures, also called red-masked parakeets, that populates the neighborhood. The film won Sundance and Emmy awards.

Thrillers

48 Hours (Walter Hill 1982). Eddie Murphy puts in a slick comic performance as the criminal sidekick to Nick Nolte's tough-talking cop, who has 48 hours to wrap up a homicide case. Fantastic shots of San Francisco and quick-witted dialog make this fast-paced comedy-thriller immensely entertaining.

Basic Instinct (Paul Verhoeven 1992). Sharon Stone is vampish as a pickaxe-wielding, bisexual writer pursued by bug-eyed Michael Douglas around the dramatic city landscape in this conventional murder mystery. The movie drew howls of protest from San Francisco's gay and lesbian community over alleged homophobia.

Big Trouble in Little China (John Carpenter 1986). In this cult classic, rough-and-tumble truck driver Jack Burton (Kurt Russell) helps friend Wang Chi (Dennis Dun) rescue his girlfriend from a mysterious underworld located beneath Chinatown.

Chan is Missing (Wayne Wang 1982). A friend's disappearance provides an excuse for a good-humored tour through Chinatown's back alleys in local director Wang's breakthrough indie hit.

Cherish (Finn Taylor 2002). In a lovely commentary on urban isolation, Robin Tunney plays a lonely San Francisco animator who is plagued by a stalker and is unjustly accused of murder.

Copycat (Jon Amiel 1995). An exceedingly run-of-the-mill serial-killer story, saved by the presence of actresses Holly Hunter and Sigourney Weaver; worth watching for its terrific hilltop photography, too.

Dark Passage (Delmer Davies 1947). Classic couple Humphrey Bogart and Lauren Bacall steam up foggy San Francisco as they try to clear the wrongfully accused Bogey's good name. Good locations and some exotic camerawork.

D.O.A. (Rudolph Mate 1949). A thriller with a terrific gimmick that makes excellent use of its San Francisco and LA locales: a poisoned man with only a few hours to live searches to uncover his murderer.

The Enforcer (James Fargo 1976). *Dirty Harry* Part Three finds Clint Eastwood in a typically aggressive mood, at odds with the liberal supervisors who want him to stop killing every teenage delinquent in sight. Slight relief is provided by Tyne Daly, as a female cop facing ridiculous odds.

Escape from Alcatraz (Don Siegel 1979). Clint Eastwood reteams with *Dirty Harry* director Don Seigel for this well-made retelling of a true-life escape attempt from the infamous prison.

Experiment in Terror (Blake Edwards 1962). The inspiration for David Lynch's *Twin Peaks*, this entertaining Cold War period piece has dozens of FBI agents trying to track down an obscene phone caller in San Francisco's Twin Peaks neighborhood.

Eye of the Cat (David Lowell Rich 1969). *Psycho*-esque thriller in which a man with a cat phobia goes to stay with an aunt who has an army of them.

Family Plot (Alfred Hitchcock 1976). The master's light-hearted final film is a lark about stolen jewels, kidnapping, and psychic sleuthing in and around San Francisco.

Fog over Frisco (William Dieterle 1934). A very young Bette Davis plays a wayward heiress who is kidnapped in this terse thriller.

Foul Play (Colin Higgins 1978). Goldie Hawn and Chevy Chase team up to thwart an albino and a midget from assassinating the pope in this enjoyably silly action-comedy, which highlights North Beach and the Opera House.

The Game (David Fincher 1996). Stylish but strangely pointless thriller from the director of *Seven* follows a wealthy executive who becomes involved in an all-too-real role-playing game, which results in his nearly drowning in the Bay.

High Crimes (Carl Franklin 2002). Ashley Judd plays yet another feisty woman in peril (this time, she's a lawyer) in this Marin County-set thriller – picturesque and fun, but formulaic.

Interview with the Vampire (Neil Jordan 1994). Jordan's stylish adaptation of Anne Rice's hugely popular novel is well filmed, even if the leading actors, Tom Cruise and Brad Pitt, are miscast. Pivotal scenes were shot on the Golden Gate Bridge and along Market Street.

Invasion of the Body Snatchers (Philip Kaufman 1978). Instead of indulging in Cold War paranoia, this remake of the 1960s horror classic parodies New Age culture and features a distinctly alien-looking Donald Sutherland as earth's last best hope: an uptight restaurant inspector.

It Came From Beneath the Sea (Charles Schneer 1955). A giant octopus attacks the city and tries to destroy Golden Gate Bridge in this B-grade monster flick.

The Killer Elite (Sam Peckinpah 1975). Typically violent outing from tough-guy auteur Peckinpah, with James Caan as an agent bent on revenge against his double-crossing bosses.

The Lineup (Frank Cooper 1958). Film adaptation of the TV series *San Francisco Beat*, about the SFPD capturing a junkie gunman. An unconvincing plot, but polished acting and fantastic shots of San Francisco.

Magnum Force (Ted Post 1973). The sequel to *Dirty Harry*, with more shots of Clint Eastwood looking tough and the city skyline looking beautiful.

The Organization (James Webb 1971). Sidney Poitier returns again as uptight cop Virgil Tibbs, from *In the Heat of the Night*, and ends up breaking the law to help a radical group trying to stop the flow of heroin into the inner city.

Pacific Heights (John Schlesinger 1990). Michael Keaton is the tenant from hell trying to evict his landlords from their lovingly restored Victorian. Shaky plot mechanics, though the picture delivers a few rusty thrills not to mention a thorough tour through the city's contentious rental laws.

Point Blank (John Boorman 1967). Lee Marvin plays a double-crossed gangster out for revenge on his cheating bosses. Remarkable, stylish camerawork and set design embellish a borderline-abstract plot that moves from LA to Alcatraz. Angie Dickinson plays a convincingly faithless wife.

The Presidio (Peter Hyams 1988). TV star Mark Harmon tries the big screen in this bland mystery about murder on the military base. Co-star Sean Connery seems to be wishing he was elsewhere.

The Rock (Michael Bay 1996). Embarrassingly enjoyable action adventure starring Nicholas Cage as an FBI scientist trying to save the city from biological warheads hidden on Alcatraz. Sean Connery, as the only man ever to escape from the island prison, looks on with droll amusement during the absurd proceedings. Look out for the geographically impossible car chase.

Romeo Must Die (Andrzej Bartkowiak 2000). Sparky, action-packed update of the Romeo and Juliet story, this time set against the background of organized crime in the Bay Area, both Chinese and American. Jet Li and the late singer Aaliyah star.

They Call Me Mister Tibbs! (Gordon Douglas 1970). Another benign follow-up thriller to *In the Heat of the Night*, with Sidney Poitier as Virgil Tibbs, the black San Francisco cop who sleuths his way to unraveling a murder mystery.

THX-1138 (George Lucas 1970). Shot in the then brand-new BART's tunnels, the *Star Wars* mogul's debut is a bleak look at an Orwellian future.

Thieves' Highway (Jules Dassin 1949). The brutal reality of a trucker's life bringing fruit to the market is told in this *noir* crime thriller. Nick Garcos (Richard Conte) comes home from the war to find his father has been disabled by a mob boss who runs a produce racket. Garcos joins up with the smuggling ring in order to get revenge.

Time After Time (Nicholas Meyer 1979). Courtesy of the Time Machine, Malcolm McDowell chases Jack the Ripper into twentieth-century San Francisco accompanied by a lot of cheap jokes and violence.

The Towering Inferno (John Guillermin/Irwin Allen 1974). An all-star cast – including Steve McQueen, Faye Dunaway, Fred Astaire, and Paul Newman – gets alternately burned, blown-up, smashed, or dropped from great heights in this borderline-camp disaster epic about a fire in the world's tallest building.

A View to a Kill (John Glen 1985). This glossy 1980s Roger Moore James Bond film takes place in the Bay Area, but the geography is mixed up (you can't actually leave San Francisco via drawbridge). Christopher Walken plays an evil mastermind who plans to flood the Silicon Valley. The final scene features a hand-to-hand fight on top of the Golden Gate Bridge.

Zodiac (David Fincher 2008). This thriller starring Jake Gyllenhaal and Robert Downey Jr meticulously re-creates the details of the *San Francisco Chronicle*'s relationship to and investigation into the Zodiac Killer crimes. The filmmakers made a painstaking effort to replicate the city in the 1970s.

Drama

Birdman of Alcatraz (John Frankenheimer 1962). Earnest but overlong study of real-life convicted killer Robert Stroud (Burt Lancaster) who becomes an authority on birds while kept in America's highest-security prison.

The Counsellor (Alberto De Martino 1973). Italian Mafia movie, dubbed into English and shot in San Francisco, that's little more than a takeoff of *Bullitt* and *The Godfather*.

Crackers (Louis Malle 1983). Donald Sutherland rescues what is otherwise a limp art film about struggling on the back streets of San Francisco.

Dragon – The Bruce Lee Story (Rob Cohen 1993). Odd mixture of biography and cartoonish chop-socky action, detailing the early years of the international film star, including his early hipster days working as a cook in Chinatown.

Freebie and the Bean (Richard Rush 1974). Former psychedelic auteur Rush descends into formula with this tough-but-funny dramedy about mismatched police partners.

The Frisco Kid (Samuel Bischoff 1935). James Cagney stars in this rough-and-tumble tale of a shang-haied sailor who rises to power amid the riffraff of the 1860s Barbary Coast.

Gentleman Jim (Raoul Walsh 1942). Rich evocation of 1880s San Francisco with Errol Flynn playing the charming, social-climbing boxer, Gentleman Jim Corbett.

Groove (Greg Harrison, 2000). Fast-paced but hit-and-miss (the creaking dialog constantly jars), this movie is set on a single night in the San Francisco rave scene; whatever its virtues as a film, the soundtrack is superb.

Hammett (Wim Wenders 1982). German director Wenders, never known for keeping things short and sweet, financially ruined Coppola's Zoetrope production company with this tribute to Dashiell Hammett's quest for material in the back alleys of Chinatown.

I Remember Mama (George Stevens 1948). Sentimental, nostalgic tribute to family life circa 1910 for a group of Norwegian immigrants in San Francisco. The movie's told through the memories of a now successful author, who dwells on her tough past and credits it with making her the woman she is.

Joy Luck Club (Wayne Wang 1993). Epic weepy based on the bestselling novel about first-generation Chinese women's struggle to make it in America.

Murder in the First (Marc Rocco 1995). Draining courtroom drama based on the true story of an incarcerated petty thief driven to a jailhouse murder by years of solitary confinement and torture. There are ample period trappings, including antique streetcars, plus decent turns by Gary Oldman, Christian Slater, and Kevin Bacon.

Pirates of Silicon Valley (Martyn Burke 1999). Made-for-TV docu-drama about the rivalry and rise of Microsoft's Bill Gates and Apple's Steve Jobs during the early days of Silicon Valley. Surprisingly, Gates comes off the better of the two.

The Pursuit of Happyness (Gabriele Muccino 2006). This drama tells the real-life story of Chris Gardner (Will Smith), a down-on-his-luck salesman who ends up homeless with a young son. Gardner keeps his child fed by hitting the soup kitchen at Glide Memorial Church every night while he works an unpaid internship at a brokerage firm.

Shoot the Moon (Alan Parker 1981). Albert Finney and Diane Keaton star in this strained tale of self-obsessed Marin County trauma and heartbreak that's sadly about as affecting as an episode of *Dallas*.

Star Trek IV – The Voyage Home (Leonard Nimoy 1986). In a surprising twist, this warm-hearted comic installment of the sci-fi series sends Kirk and company back in time to contemporary San Francisco in order to save some whales.

Sucker Free City (Spike Lee 2005). Shot in Chinatown, the Mission, and Hunters Point, this two-hour film, originally intended as a pilot for a Showtime series, shows the urban underside to San Francisco, rarely seen on film. A gritty, realistic look at the street gangs made up of white, Asian and African-American members.

Comedy and romance

40 Days, 40 Nights (Michael Lehmann 2002). Heart-throb vehicle for Josh Hartnett, who gives up sex in the city of the Summer of Love – days before meeting his dream girl. Passably funny, but most notable for its loving shots of San Francisco.

After the Thin Man (W.S. Van Dyke 1936). Dashiel Hammett's drunken detectives Nick and Nora Charles retire to a fabulous mansion (which, given the views, seems to be situated on top of Coit Tower) only to have their relaxation interrupted by a high-society murder.

The Bachelor (Gary Sinyor 1999). This limp remake of the Buster Keaton classic stars Chris O'Donnell as a non-committal multimillionaire desperately pursued by every woman in town. The foolishness culminates with a thousand would-be brides chasing O'Donnell through the Stockton tunnel.

Dim Sum (Wayne Wang 1985). Appealing film about a more-or-less Westernized Chinese family in San Francisco. Fittingly, given the title, it's a small, delicious treat.

The First $20m is Always The Hardest (Mick Jacksncon 2002). Ill-timed Internet satire that's disappointingly lackluster despite a script by Jon "*Swingers*" Favreau. The lame casting of Aussie Adam Garcia as a local hotshot ad exec doesn't help.

Flower Drum Song (Ross Hunter 1961). Patronizing, remorselessly cute Rodgers and Hammerstein musical about love dilemmas in San Francisco's Chinatown.

The Frisco Kid (Howard Koch Jr 1979). Implausible but amusing comedy about a rabbi who befriends an outlaw on his way to San Francisco. Silly and sentimental, it nonetheless has good comic performances from Gene Wilder and Harrison Ford.

Guess Who's Coming to Dinner (Stanley Kramer 1967). Well-meaning but slightly flat interracial comedy in which Spencer Tracy and Katharine Hepburn play the supposedly liberal but bewildered parents of a woman who brings home the black man (Sidney Poitier) she intends to marry.

Harold and Maude (Hal Ashby 1971). Black comedy about a romance between a death-obsessed teenager and the 80-year-old woman he befriends at various funerals. Intolerable for some, a cult classic for others.

High Anxiety (Mel Brooks 1977). Mel Brooks's spoof on *Vertigo*, and psychiatry in general, is one of the director's best – if you have a high tolerance for rampant silliness.

I Love You, Alice B. Toklas (Hy Averback 1968). Long before Austin Powers hit the screen, Peter Sellers' performance in this groovy film, with a script by Larry Tucker and Paul Mazursky, set the standard for Swinging Sixties farces. By today's standards, though, the film's portrayal of women seems almost as dated as the wardrobe.

Just Like Heaven (Mark Waters 2005). Reese Witherspoon plays a busy San Francisco doctor who lives in a swank wood-paneled Victorian condo in Russian Hill. After her car is hit by a truck, her apartment is rented to an architect (Mark Ruffalo) who falls in love with her ghost, which happens to be haunting the space. Dolores Park and *Caffe Trieste* are featured.

Mother (Albert Brooks 1996). Albert Brooks, the West Coast's answer to Woody Allen, gives Debbie Reynolds a memorable role as an overly attentive mother in the Sausalito area.

Mrs Doubtfire (Chris Columbus 1993). Sweet but dippy claptrap about a caddish man (Robin Williams) who pretends to be a British nanny in order to be close to his kids. A riot for Williams fans; further proof to others that his comic genius has slipped away.

Nina Takes a Lover (Alan Jacobs 1996). Small, independently produced romantic comedy about love and loneliness, well shot against the backdrop of San Francisco's street scenes.

Pal Joey (Fred Kohlmar 1957). Frank Sinatra, Rita Hayworth, and Kim Novak star in this slick musical about a rising nightclub entertainer. Begins well, but slides alarmingly into cheap sentiment.

Petulia (Richard Lester 1968). San Francisco surgeon George C. Scott takes up with unhappily married kook Julie Christie in richly detailed, deliberately fragmentary comedy-drama set in druggy, decadent society.

Play It Again, Sam (Herbert Ross 1972). Woody Allen leaves his beloved New York and enters film history as a nerdy young cinephile obsessed with Humphrey Bogart in this sweet, mildly amusing comedy.

The Princess Diaries (Garry Marshall 2001). This innocent teen romantic comedy stars Anne Hathaway as a San Francisco Catholic school student who discovers she's the unlikely heir to the throne of the fictional European country of Genovia. San Francisco, from its hills and beaches to Cliff House and cable cars, shines.

Psych-Out (Richard Rush 1968). Pumped out quickly to capitalize on the Summer of Love, this movie offers good performances from Jack Nicholson and Bruce Dern; but they can't save what is basically a compendium of every hippie cliché in the book. That didn't stop it from quickly becoming a cult movie, though.

San Francisco (W.S. Van Dyke 1936). Elaborate, entertaining hokum about a Barbary Coast love triangle circa 1906. The script is upstaged by the climactic earthquake sequence.

Serial (Bill Persky 1980). Sharply observed comedy about social neurosis and hypocrisy among wealthy ex-hippies in Marin.

Skidoo (Otto Preminger 1968). Carol Channing, Jackie Gleason, and friends drop acid on Alcatraz, under the observant eye of a stoned God, played by Groucho Marx, plus a soundtrack by Harry Nilsson.

So I Married An Axe Murderer (Thomas Schlamme 1993). Under-appreciated early Mike Myers comedy, where he's cast as a commitment-phobic San Francisco poet who finally marries what seems like the perfect woman, only to suspect she may have a darker side.

The Sweetest Thing (Roger Kumble 2002). Cameron Diaz meets the man of her dreams in a San Francisco nightclub, but doesn't get his number and sets off on a road trip with best friend Christina Applegate to hunt him down. A terrible movie, but coarse, crass, and uproarious fun.

Sweet November (Pat O'Connor 2001). Charlize Theron plays a libertine who attempts to teach advertising executive Keanu Reeves what's important in life. Her bohemian Victorian flat in Potrero Hill is contrasted to his sleek Pacific Heights penthouse.

Take the Money and Run (Woody Allen 1969). Allen's hilarious hippie spoof on the Paul Newman prison flick *Cool Hand Luke* features a crime spree through Northern California. One of Allen's most purely slapstick efforts.

Tales of the City (Alastair Reid 1993). Widely loved mini-series based on Maupin's popular books. When it was first shown on public television, there were hurricanes of controversy over its gay content which no doubt helped it go on to become the most popular program ever aired on PBS. Still, only cable would touch the sequels – *More Tales of the City* (Pierre Gang 1998) and *Further Tales of the City* (Pierre Gang 2001).

The Wedding Planner (Adam Shankman 2001). Charmingly old-fashioned romantic comedy, somewhat implausibly featuring the steely Jennifer Lopez as an ambitious wedding planner who's klutzy and love-challenged in her personal life. There's terrific footage of San Francisco's rolling urban hills.

What's Up, Doc? (Peter Bogdanovich 1972). Wildly likeable screwball comedy pastiche starring Barbra Streisand and Ryan O'Neal as a cook and a naive professor, with a famous moment shot in Alta Plaza park.

When a Man Loves a Woman (Luis Mandoki 1994). In the opening scene, Meg Ryan and Andy Garcia meet at *Buena Vista Café*. Ryan plays a mother of two who descends into alcoholism, and when she comes out of rehab, realizes her relationship with her husband (Garcia) is less than perfect.

The Woman In Red (Gene Wilder 1984). Initially sophomoric comedy about one man's obsessive lust for a beautiful stranger. Takes a pleasant twist when Wilder's character (very belatedly) realizes there's more to love than physical attraction, and more to parking on San Francisco's hills than shifting to P.

Travel
store

Africa & Middle East

Cape Town &
  the Garden Route
Dubai **D**
Egypt
Gambia
Jordan
Kenya
Marrakesh **D**
Morocco
South Africa, Lesotho
  & Swaziland
Tanzania
Tunisia
West Africa
Zanzibar

Travel Specials

First-Time Africa
First-Time Around
  the World
First-Time Asia
First-Time Europe
First-Time Latin
  America
Make the Most of
  Your Time on Earth
Travel with Babies &
  Young Children
Travel Online
Travel Survival
Ultimate Adventures
Walks in London
  & SE England
World Party

Maps

Algarve
Amsterdam
Andalucia
  & Costa del Sol
Argentina
Athens
Australia
Barcelona
Berlin
Boston & Cambridge
Brittany
Brussels
California
Chicago
Chile
Corsica
Costa Rica
  & Panama
Crete

Croatia
Cuba
Cyprus
Czech Republic
Dominican Republic
Dubai & UAE
Dublin
Egypt
Florence & Siena
Florida
France
Frankfurt
Germany
Greece
Guatemala & Belize
Iceland
India
Ireland
Italy
Kenya & Northern
  Tanzania
Lisbon
London
Los Angeles
Madrid
Malaysia
Mallorca
Marrakesh
Mexico
Miami & Key West
Morocco
New England
New York City
New Zealand
Northern Spain
Paris
Peru
Portugal
Prague
Pyrenees & Andorra
Rome
San Francisco
Sicily
South Africa
South India
Spain & Portugal
Sri Lanka
Tenerife
Thailand
Toronto
Trinidad & Tobago
Tunisia
Turkey
Tuscany

Venice
Vietnam, Laos
  & Cambodia
Washington DC
Yucatán Peninsula

Phrasebooks

Croatian
Czech
Dutch
Egyptian Arabic
French
German
Greek
Hindi & Urdu
Italian
Japanese
Latin American
  Spanish
Mandarin Chinese
Mexican Spanish
Polish
Portuguese
Russian
Spanish
Swahili
Thai
Turkish
Vietnamese

Computers

Blogging
eBay
FWD this link
iPhone
iPods, iTunes
  & music online
The Internet
Macs & OS X
MySpace
PlayStation Portable
Website Directory

Film & TV

American
  Independent Film
British Cult Comedy
Chick Flicks
Comedy Movies
Cult Movies
Film
Film Musicals
Film Noir
Gangster Movies
Horror Movies

Sci-Fi Movies
Westerns

Lifestyle

Babies
Ethical Living
Pregnancy & Birth
Running

Music Guides

The Beatles
The Best Music
  You've Never Heard
Blues
Bob Dylan
Book of Playlists
Classical Music
Elvis
Frank Sinatra
Heavy Metal
Hip-Hop
Led Zeppelin
Opera
Pink Floyd
Punk
Reggae
The Rolling Stones
Soul and R&B
Velvet Underground
World Music

Popular Culture

Classic Novels
Conspiracy Theories
Crime Fiction
Cult Fiction
The Da Vinci Code
Graphic Novels
His Dark Materials
Poker
Shakespeare
Superheroes
Tutankhamun
Unexplained
  Phenomena
Videogames

Science

The Brain
Climate Change
The Earth
Genes & Cloning
The Universe
Weather

For more information go to www.roughguides.com

Visit us online

www.roughguides.com

Information on over 25,000 destinations around the world

- **Read** Rough Guides' trusted travel info
- **Access** exclusive articles from Rough Guides authors
- **Update** yourself on new books, maps, CDs and other products
- **Enter** our competitions and win travel prizes
- **Share** ideas, journals, photos & travel advice with other users
- **Earn** points every time you contribute to the Rough Guide community and get rewards

BROADEN YOUR HORIZONS

Small print and Index

A Rough Guide to Rough Guides

Published in 1982, the first Rough Guide – to Greece – was a student scheme that became a publishing phenomenon. Mark Ellingham, a recent graduate in English from Bristol University, had been travelling in Greece the previous summer and couldn't find the right guidebook. With a small group of friends he wrote his own guide, combining a highly contemporary, journalistic style with a thoroughly practical approach to travelers' needs.

The immediate success of the book spawned a series that rapidly covered dozens of destinations. And, in addition to impecunious backpackers, Rough Guides soon acquired a much broader and older readership that relished the guides' wit and inquisitiveness as much as their enthusiastic, critical approach and value-for-money ethos.

These days, Rough Guides include recommendations from shoestring to luxury and cover more than 200 destinations around the globe, including almost every country in the Americas and Europe, more than half of Africa and most of Asia and Australasia. Our ever-growing team of authors and photographers is spread all over the world, particularly in Europe, the USA and Australia.

In the early 1990s, Rough Guides branched out of travel, with the publication of Rough Guides to World Music, Classical Music and the Internet. All three have become benchmark titles in their fields, spearheading the publication of a wide range of books under the Rough Guide name.

Including the travel series, Rough Guides now number more than 350 titles, covering: phrasebooks, waterproof maps, music guides from Opera to Heavy Metal, reference works as diverse as Conspiracy Theories and Shakespeare, and popular culture books from iPods to Poker. Rough Guides also produce a series of more than 120 World Music CDs in partnership with World Music Network.

Visit www.roughguides.com to see our latest publications.

Rough Guide travel images are available for commercial licensing at www.roughguidespictures.com

SMALL PRINT

Rough Guide credits

Text editor: Ann-Marie Shaw
Layout: Umesh Aggarwal
Cartography: Animesh Pathak
Picture editor: Sarah Cummins
Production: Rebecca Short
Proofreader: Anita Sach
Cover design: Chloë Roberts
Photographer: Greg Roden
Editorial: **London** Ruth Blackmore, Alison
Murchie, Andy Turner, Keith Drew, Edward
Aves, Alice Park, Lucy White, Jo Kirby, James
Smart, Natasha Foges, Róisín Cameron, Emma
Traynor, James Rice, Emma Gibbs, Kathryn
Lane, Christina Valhouli, Monica Woods, Mani
Ramaswamy, Joe Staines, Peter Buckley,
Matthew Milton, Tracy Hopkins, Ruth Tidball;
New York Andrew Rosenberg, Steven Horak,
AnneLise Sorensen, Ella Steim, Anna Owens,
Sean Mahoney, Paula Neudorf; **Delhi** Madhavi
Singh, Karen D'Souza
Design & Pictures: London Scott Stickland,
Dan May, Diana Jarvis, Mark Thomas, Nicole
Newman, Emily Taylor; **Delhi** Ajay Verma, Jessica
Subramanian, Ankur Guha, Pradeep Thapliyal,
Sachin Tanwar, Anita Singh, Nikhil Agarwal
Production: Vicky Baldwin

Cartography: **London** Maxine Repath, Ed
Wright, Katie Lloyd-Jones; **Delhi** Jai Prakash
Mishra, Rajesh Chhibber, Ashutosh Bharti,
Rajesh Mishra, Jasbir Sandhu, Karobi Gogoi,
Alakananda Bhattacharya, Swati Handoo,
Deshpal Dabas
Online: London George Atwell, Faye Hellon,
Jeanette Angell, Fergus Day, Justine Bright,
Clare Bryson, Áine Fearon, Adrian Low, Ezgi
Celebi, Amber Bloomfield; **Delhi** Amit Verma,
Rahul Kumar, Narender Kumar, Ravi Yadav,
Debojit Borah, Rakesh Kumar, Ganesh Sharma
Marketing & Publicity: London Liz Statham,
Niki Hanmer, Louise Maher, Jess Carter,
Vanessa Godden, Vivienne Watton, Anna
Paynton, Rachel Sprackett, Libby Jellie, Holly
Dudley; **New York** Geoff Colquitt, Nancy
Lambert, Katy Ball; **Delhi** Ragini Govind
Manager India: Punita Singh
Reference Director: Andrew Lockett
Operations Manager: Helen Phillips
PA to Publishing Director: Nicola Henderson
Publishing Director: Martin Dunford
Commercial Manager: Gino Magnotta
Managing Director: John Duhigg

SMALL PRINT

Publishing information

This eighth edition published January 2009 by
Rough Guides Ltd,
80 Strand, London WC2R 0RL
345 Hudson St, 4th Floor,
New York, NY 10014, USA
14 Local Shopping Centre, Panchsheel Park,
New Delhi 110017, India
Distributed by the Penguin Group
Penguin Books Ltd,
80 Strand, London WC2R 0RL
Penguin Group (USA)
375 Hudson Street, NY 10014, USA
Penguin Group (Australia)
250 Camberwell Road, Camberwell,
Victoria 3124, Australia
Penguin Group (Canada)
195 Harry Walker Parkway N, Newmarket, ON,
L3Y 7B3 Canada
Penguin Group (NZ)
67 Apollo Drive, Mairangi Bay, Auckland 1310,
New Zealand

Cover concept by Peter Dyer.
Typeset in Bembo and Helvetica to an original
design by Henry Iles.
Printed and bound in China
© Rough Guides, 2009
No part of this book may be reproduced in any
form without permission from the publisher except
for the quotation of brief passages in reviews.
440pp includes index
A catalogue record for this book is available from
the British Library.
ISBN: 978-1-84836-060-0

The publishers and authors have done their
best to ensure the accuracy and currency of
all the information in **The Rough Guide to San
Francisco & the Bay Area**, however, they can
accept no responsibility for any loss, injury, or
inconvenience sustained by any traveler as a result
of information or advice contained in the guide.

1 3 5 7 9 8 6 4 2

Help us update

We've gone to a lot of effort to ensure that the
eighth edition of **The Rough Guide to San
Francisco & the Bay Area** is accurate and up
to date. However, things change – places get
"discovered", opening hours are notoriously
fickle, restaurants and rooms raise prices or lower
standards. If you feel we've got it wrong or left
something out, we'd like to know, and if you can
remember the address, the price, the hours, the
phone number, so much the better.

Please send your comments with the subject
line "**Rough Guide San Francisco & the Bay
Area Update**" to ® mail@roughguides.com. We'll
credit all contributions and send a copy of the
next edition (or any other Rough Guide if you
prefer) for the very best emails.
Have your questions answered and tell others
about your trip at
® community.roughguides.com

Acknowledgements

Nick would like to thank the good people at *Mill Rose Inn*, Cetrella and Cameron's Pub, all in Half Moon Bay, as well as Peter & Nancy Lang at Safari West for a warm welcome; also to Kelly Chamberlin of HMB and Adele of Berkeley CVB for invaluable help. Hearty cheers as ever to the Berkeley Bonita committee of Clint, Laramie, Wendi and Anandamayi, and Oakland ex-pats Carol and Simon for fine hospitality. Thanks to Justin Sane for the backstage pass and great Anti Flag show at the Fillmore – the people united will never be defeated! Finally, many hugs to Maria for joining in on the western adventure this time and plunging into the even bigger transatlantic one.

Charles: Thanks to Todd Gemmer, Aaron Best, Cate Czerwinski, Jeff Raad, Parker Johnson, Brolin Winning, Nick Dedina, Brock Keeling, and Anthony Bedard for the subject-specific insight; to Kelly Chamberlin, Nancy Uber, and Lisa Bellomo for the restaurant reservations; to City Guides for the engaging walking tours; to CNET, CCA, and UCSF for all the time off!; to Gregory Dicum and Jeff Cranmer for the referral; to Andrew Rosenberg for inviting me aboard; to Nick Edwards, Lisa Hix, Ann-Marie Shaw, and Anna Owens for being great to work with; to Emily for being a pal among pals; to Sonja for all the love, affection, and laughs; and to Mom, who always enjoyed coming to San Francisco.

Lisa: Big thanks to my personal assistant Isaac Amala, without whom I could not have finished this project, and particularly for all his input on the Shopping chapter and for running around Union Square visiting hotels with me. Thanks to my research assistant Lizzy Hughes, particularly for her help on the Basics chapter. Thanks to my Mom, Joan Hix, for putting up with me when I'm stressed out. Thanks to Tanya Houseman at the San Francisco Convention and Visitors Bureau for all the tips and information. Thanks to all the hotels who graciously let us tour them, and particularly to Kelly Chamberlin of Chamberlin PR for Personality Hotels for her help. Thanks to Nyereris Britt for being ready and willing to go clubbing in the name of research, and also to all my San Francisco experts who gave me their priceless input, including Heather Cummings, Neil "Mr. Dodgy" Motteram, Matt Sussman, Gordon Winiemko, Chelsea Junget, Conan Neutron, Erika J. Bock, Erika Christensen, Josh Gowan, Tanya Feldman, Sharon Senser McKellar, Heather Lynch, and N. Moses Corrette. Thanks to my co-writing team, Charles and Nick, and to our ever-patient and kind copy editor Ann-Marie Shaw. Thank you to Gregory Dicum for recommending me for this project, and to Andrew Rosenberg, Steven Horak, and Anna Owens at the Rough Guides offices for giving me this opportunity.

Finally, the **editor** would like to thank Umesh Aggarwal for his outstanding typesetting, Sarah Cummins for creative picture editing, Animesh Pathak for great maps, Anita Sach for eagle-eyed proofreading, and Steven Horak and Anna Owens for Stateside support.

Photo credits

All photos © Rough Guides except the following:

Cover

Front picture: Golden Gate Bridge © Giovanni Simeone/4cornersimages
Back picture: Mural, Mission district © travelstock44/Alamy
Inside back picture: Cable car © Angus Oborn/ Rough Guides

Things not to miss

02 Gay Pride Parade © Terry Schmitt/Drr.net
04 Musée Méchanique © Richard Wong/Alamy
08 AT&T Park © Lee Foster/Alamy
17 Alcatraz © Nicole Newman

San Francisco Hills colour section

Cable car on Hyde Street © Walter Bibikow/ Danita Delimont agency/Drr.net
Cable car on Russian Hill © David Barnes/Drr.net

Music color section

Billie Joe Armstrong of Green Day © Neil Lupin/ Redferns
Janis Joplin on Haight Street © Peter Larsen/Rex
Tupac Shakur © Raymond Boyd/Michael Ochs Archive/Getty Images

Black and whites

p.196 Taqueria © Charles Hodgkins
p.230 Beach Blanket Babylon performers © Morton Beebe/Corbis
p.268 Windsurfer at Golden Gate Bridge © Clive Sawyer/Alamy
p.278 Cinco de Mayo festival © Visions of America/Alamy
p.320 Cyclist in Mount Diablo State Park © Gary Crabbe/Drr.net
p.403 Harvey Milk, 1977 © Robert Clay/Drr.net

Index

Map entries are in color.

N

P

O

INDEX

437

Map symbols

maps are listed in the full index using colored text

---	Chapter boundary	ⓘ	Tourist office
Interstate		★	Bus stop
US Highway		✈	Airport
Highway		🅿	Parking
Steps		🗼	Lighthouse
Tunnel		◆	Place of interest
Pedestrianized road		⚲	Church (regional maps)
River		🏛	Historic house
Ferry route		◯	Stadium
Cable car		✚	Church (town maps)
BART			Building
Mountain peak			Cemetery
Peak			Park/forest
Accommodation			Beach
Gate			

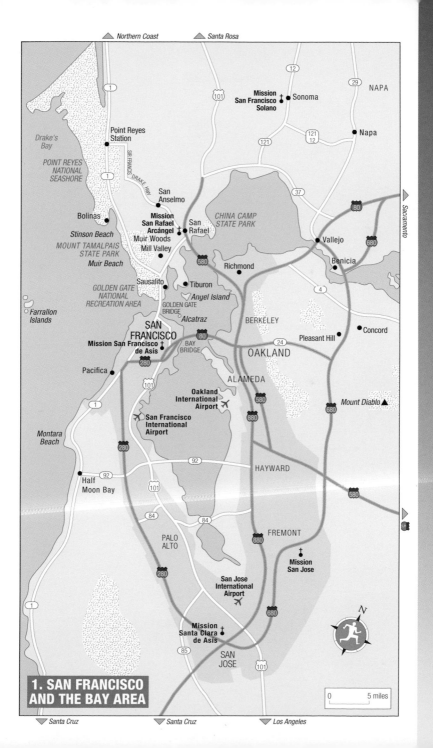

1. SAN FRANCISCO AND THE BAY AREA

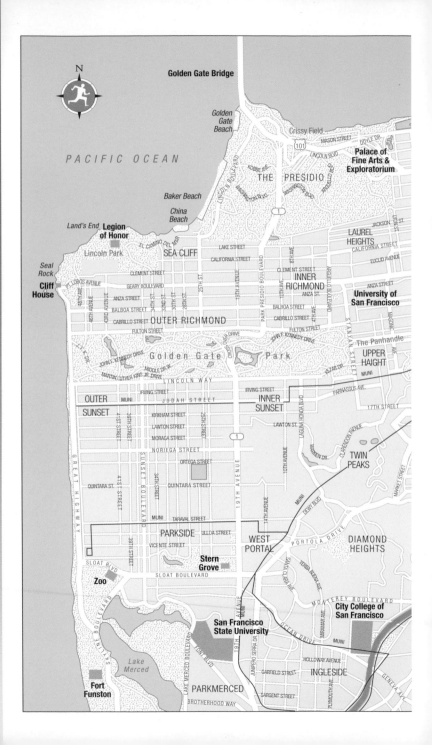

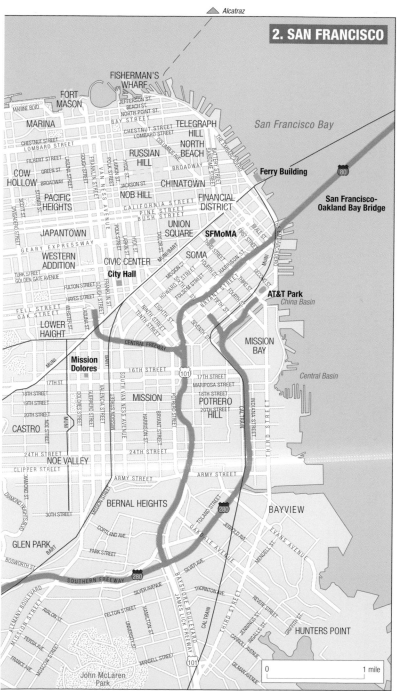

△ Alcatraz

2. SAN FRANCISCO

FISHERMAN'S
WHARF

FORT
MASON

MARINA

San Francisco Bay

JEFFERSON ST.
BEACH ST.
NORTH POINT ST.
BAY STREET

MARINE BLVD

CHESTNUT STREET
LOMBARD STREET

CHESTNUT STREET
LOMBARD STREET

FILBERT STREET

TELEGRAPH
HILL

NORTH
BEACH

RUSSIAN
HILL

COLUMBUS AVE.

BROADWAY

Ferry Building

COW
HOLLOW

GREEN ST.
BROADWAY

PACIFIC
HEIGHTS

DIVISADERO STREET

SCOTT ST.

FRANKLIN STREET

LAGUNA STREET

POLK STREET

HYDE ST.

LARKIN ST.

VAN NESS AVENUE

JACKSON ST.

CHINATOWN

NOB HILL

CALIFORNIA STREET
PINE STREET
BUSH STREET

FINANCIAL
DISTRICT

BATTERY STREET

SANSOME STREET

THE EMBARCADERO

80

**San Francisco-
Oakland Bay Bridge**

JAPANTOWN

GEARY EXPRESSWAY

WESTERN
ADDITION

TURK STREET
GOLDEN GATE AVENUE

POLK STREET

LARKIN ST.

HYDE ST.

TAYLOR ST.

MUNI/BART

UNION
SQUARE

SFMoMA

SOMA

CIVIC CENTER

City Hall

FULTON STREET

FRANKLIN ST.

GOUGH STREET

HAYES STREET

MISSION ST.

HOWARD ST.

FOLSOM ST.

SIXTH ST.

FIFTH ST.

FOURTH ST.

THIRD ST.

SECOND ST.

FIRST ST.

BEALE ST.

MAIN ST.

MUNI

AT&T Park

China Basin

FELL STREET
OAK STREET

LOWER
HAIGHT

MUNI

17TH ST.

WEBSTER STREET

LAGUNA ST.

NINTH ST.

EIGHTH ST.

TENTH STREET

CENTRAL FREEWAY

BRYANT STREET

FOURTH ST.

SEVENTH ST.

MISSION
BAY

Central Basin

**Mission
Dolores**

16TH STREET

VALENCIA STREET

SOUTH VAN NESS AVENUE

MISSION STREET

18TH STREET
19TH STREET
20TH STREET

CASTRO

NOE ST.

DOLORES STREET

GUERRERO STREET

MISSION

HARRISON ST.

BRYANT STREET

POTRERO AVENUE

101

17TH STREET
MARIPOSA STREET
18TH STREET

POTRERO
HILL

20TH STREET

CALTRAIN

INDIANA STREET

THIRD STREET

NOE VALLEY

24TH STREET

CLIPPER STREET

24TH STREET

ARMY STREET

ARMY STREET

GLEN PARK

DIAMOND STREET

DIAMOND HEIGHTS BLVD

30TH STREET

MISSION STREET

BERNAL HEIGHTS

CORTLAND AVE.

280

TOLAND ST.

OAKDALE AVENUE

JERROLD AVE.

EVANS AVENUE

BAYVIEW

MENDELL ST.

BOSWORTH ST.

BART

PARK STREET

SOUTHERN FREEWAY

280

SILVER AVENUE

BAYSHORE BOULEVARD

JAMES LICK FREEWAY

SILVER AVE.

THORNTON AVE.

CALTRAIN

THIRD STREET

REVERE STREET

GRIFFITH ST.

ALEMANY BOULEVARD

AVALON ST.

MISSION BLVD

PERSIA AVE.

MOSCOW STREET

FRANCE AVE.

FELTON STREET

HAMILTON STREET

UNIVERSITY STREET

MANSELL STREET

BAYSHORE BOULEVARD

101

JENNINGS ST.

INGALLS ST.

CARROLL AVENUE

GILMAN AVENUE

HUNTERS POINT

John McLaren
Park

0   1 mile

▽ *SF Airport (5 miles)*

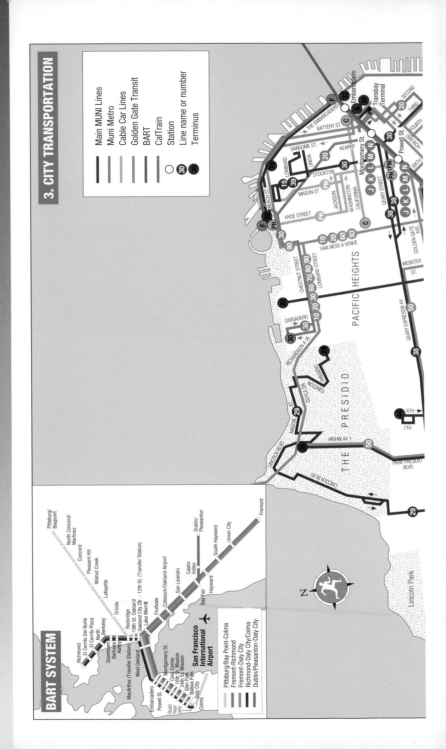

3. CITY TRANSPORTATION

BART SYSTEM

Main MUNI Lines
Muni Metro
Cable Car Lines
Golden Gate Transit
BART
CalTrain
Station
Line name or number
Terminus

Pittsburg/Bay Point-Colma
Fremont-Richmond
Fremont-Daly City
Richmond-Daly City/Colma
Dublin/Pleasanton-Daly City

Richmond
El Cerrito Del Norte
El Cerrito Plaza
North Berkeley
Downtown Berkeley
Ashby
Rockridge
Orinda
Lafayette
Walnut Creek
Pleasant Hill
Concord
North Concord/Martinez
Pittsburg/Baypoint

MacArthur (Transfer Station)
19th St. Oakland
Oakland City Ctr - 12th St. (Transfer Station)
West Oakland
Lake Merritt
Fruitvale
Coliseum/Oakland Airport
San Leandro
Bay Fair
Castro Valley
Hayward
South Hayward
Union City
Fremont

Dublin/Pleasanton

San Francisco International Airport

Embarcadero
Powell St.
Montgomery St.
Civic Center
16th St. Mission
24th St. Mission
Glen Park
Balboa Park
Daly City
Colma

Rush hour only

THE PRESIDIO

PACIFIC HEIGHTS

Lincoln Park

THE EMBARCADERO
BATTERY ST.
SANSOME ST.
KEARNY
UNION
STOCKTON
MASON ST.
JACKSON
WASHINGTON
CALIFORNIA
Montgomery St.
GEARY STREET
GOLDEN GATE AVE.
WEBSTER ST.
VAN NESS AVENUE
LOMBARD
BEACH ST.
HYDE STREET
CHESTNUT STREET
LOMBARD STREET
DIVISADERO
RICHARDSON AVE.
MASON ST.
LINCOLN BLVD.
DOYLE DR.
FUNSTON
DIVISION
HIGHWAY 1
GEARY EXPRESSWAY
PARK PRESIDIO BLVD
LINCOLN BLVD
Powell St.
Transbay Terminal
SECOND
THIRD
FOURTH
FIFTH
SIXTH
6TH
7TH
Embarcadero

N

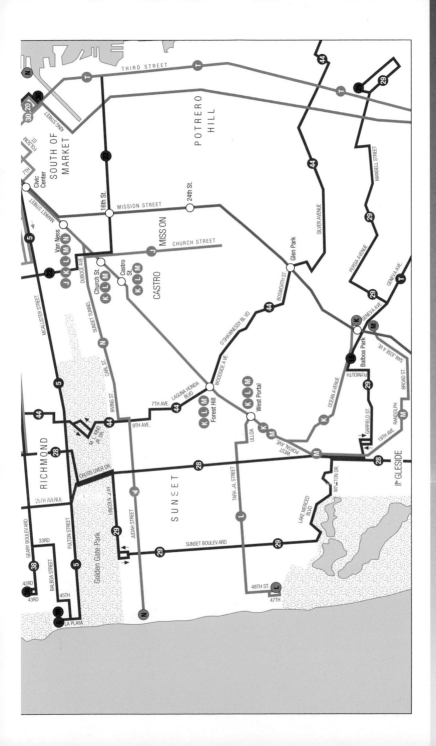

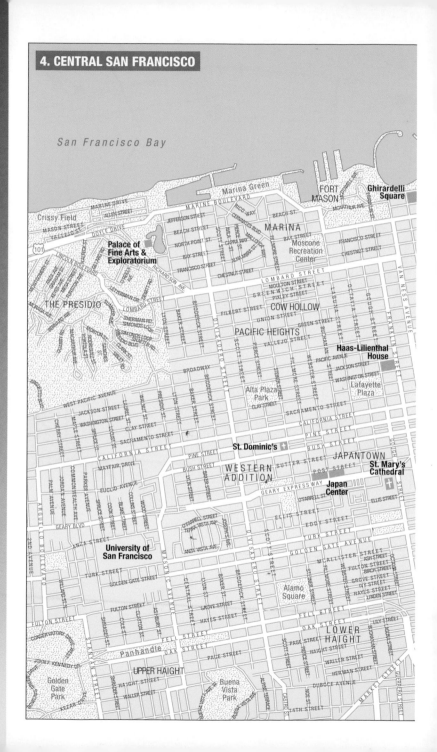

4. CENTRAL SAN FRANCISCO

San Francisco Bay

Marina Green

FORT MASON

Ghirardelli Square

Crissy Field

MARINA

MARINE DRIVE

ALLEN STREET

MASON STREET

VALLEJO ST

DOYLE DRIVE

MARINE BOULEVARD

PICO WAY

JEFFERSON STREET

BEACH STREET

BEACH STREET

NORTH POINT ST

BAY STREET

CERVANTES BLVD

BAY STREET

CAPRA WAY

Moscone Recreation Center

FRANCISCO STREET

CHESTNUT STREET

Palace of Fine Arts & Exploratorium

RICHARDSON AVE

FRANCISCO STREET

CHESTNUT STREET

LOMBARD STREET

MOULTON STREET

GREENWICH STREET

PIXLEY STREET

VAN NESS AVENUE

THE PRESIDIO

LOMBARD STREET

SHERMAN RD

SIMONDS LOOP

FILBERT STREET

UNION STREET

COW HOLLOW

GREEN STREET

PACIFIC HEIGHTS

VALLEJO STREET

Haas-Lilienthal House

FRANKLIN STREET

JACKSON STREET

WASHINGTON STREET

Lafayette Plaza

WEST PACIFIC AVENUE

BROADWAY

PACIFIC AVENUE

JACKSON STREET

Alta Plaza Park

CLAY STREET

WASHINGTON STREET

CLAY STREET

SACRAMENTO STREET

SACRAMENTO STREET

CALIFORNIA STREET

CALIFORNIA STREET

PINE STREET

CHERRY STREET

MAYFAIR DRIVE

PINE STREET

St. Dominic's

BUSH STREET

JAPANTOWN

St. Mary's Cathedral

EUCLID AVENUE

BUSH STREET

WESTERN ADDITION

SUTTER STREET

POST STREET

COMMONWEALTH AVE

PARKER AVENUE

JORDAN AVENUE

PALM AVENUE

SPRUCE STREET

COOK STREET

BLAKE STREET

WOOD STREET

GEARY EXPRESSWAY

Japan Center

GEARY BLVD

O'FARRELL ST

ELLIS STREET

ANZA STREET

O'FARRELL STREET

TERRA VISTA AVE

JOSEPHA AVE

ELLIS STREET

EDDY STREET

2ND AVENUE

ARGUELLO BOULEVARD

University of San Francisco

ANZA VISTA AVE

TURK STREET

GOLDEN GATE AVENUE

MCALLISTER STREET

ASH STREET

FULTON STREET

BIRCH STREET

TURK STREET

GOLDEN GATE STREET

MASON STREET

CENTRAL AVE

LYON STREET

GROVE STREET

IVY STREET

HAYES STREET

LINDEN STREET

Alamo Square

FULTON STREET

CLIFTON STREET

ASHBURY STREET

FELL STREET

LILY STREET

CONSERVATORY DRIVE

SHRADER ST

FELL STREET

HAYES STREET

OAK STREET

LOWER HAIGHT

JOHN F KENNEDY DR

STANYAN STREET

Panhandle

OAK STREET

PAGE STREET

HAIGHT STREET

WALLER STREET

Golden Gate Park

UPPER HAIGHT

HAIGHT STREET

WALLER STREET

Buena Vista Park

HERMAN STREET

DUBOCE AVENUE

MARKET STREET

GUERRERO STREET

KEZAR DRIVE

14TH STREET

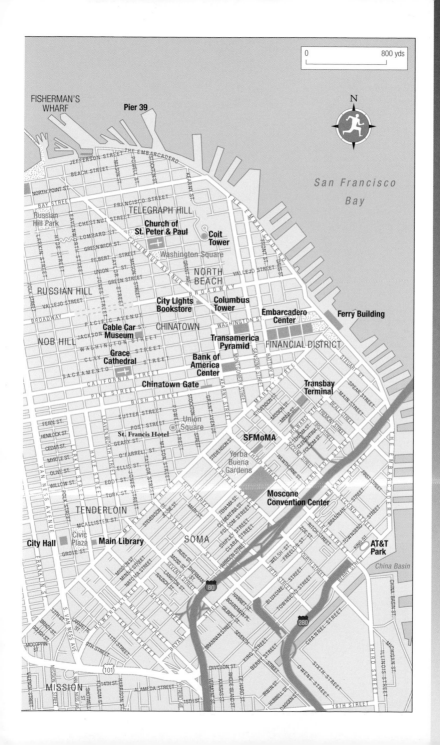

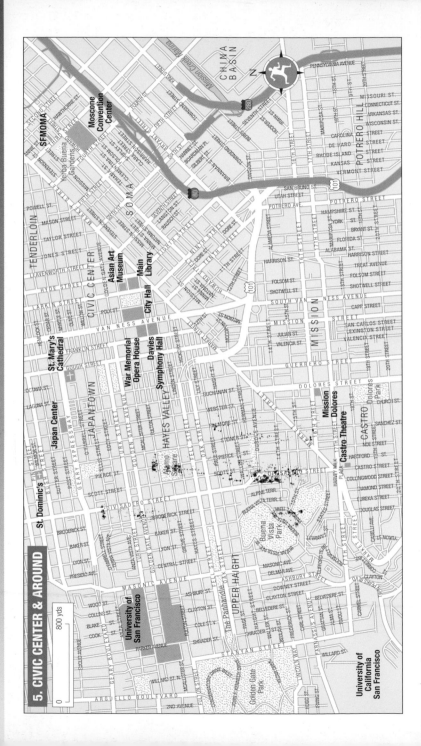